ANNUAL REVIEW OF
INFORMATION SCIENCE AND TECHNOLOGY

VOLUME **28** 1 9 9 3

ISBN: 0-938734-75-X
ISSN: 0066-4200
CODEN:ARISBC
LC No. 66-25096

ANNUAL REVIEW OF

INFORMATION SCIENCE AND TECHNOLOGY

Volume 28, 1993

Edited by

Martha E. Williams
University of Illinois
Urbana, Illinois, USA

asis

Published on behalf of the
American Society for Information Science
by Learned Information, Inc.

1993

 **Learned Information, Inc.
Medford, New Jersey**

ISBN: 0-938734-75-X
ISSN: 0066-4200
CODEN: ARISBC
LC No. 66-25096

Published and distributed by:
Learned Information, Inc.,
143 Old Marlton Pike
Medford, NJ 08055-8750
for the
American Society for Information Science
8720 Georgia Avenue, Suite 501
Silver Spring, MD 20910-3602, U.S. A.

Distributed outside North America by:
Learned Information Ltd.
Woodside, Hinksey Hill
Oxford OX1 5AU
England

ARIST Production staff, for ASIS:
Charles & Linda Holder, Graphic Compositors
Cover design by Sandy Skalkowski
Printed in the U.S.A.

Contents

281212

Preface

PUBLISHING HISTORY

This is the 28th volume of the *Annual Review of Information Science and Technology* (*ARIST*). It was produced for the American Society for Information Science (ASIS) and published by Learned Information, Inc. ASIS initiated the series in 1966 with the publication of Volume 1 under the editorship of Carlos A. Cuadra, who continued as Editor through Volume 10. Martha E. Williams has served as Editor starting with Volume 11. ASIS is the owner of *ARIST*, maintains the editorial control, and has the sole rights to the series in all forms.

Through the years several organizations have been responsible for publishing and marketing *ARIST*. Volumes 1 and 2 were published by Interscience Publishers, a division of John Wiley & Sons. Volumes 3 through 6 were published by Encyclopaedia Britannica, Inc. Volumes 7 through 11 were published by ASIS itself. Volumes 12 through 21 were published by Knowledge Industry Publications, Inc. Volumes 22 through 25 were published by Elsevier Science Publishers B.V., Amsterdam, The Netherlands. With Volume 26 Learned Information, Inc., assumed the role of publisher of *ARIST* for ASIS.

POLICY

ARIST is an annual publication that reviews numerous topics within the broad field of information science and technology. The contents vary from year to year; no single topic is treated on an annual basis. Inasmuch as the field is dynamic, the contents (chapters) of the various *ARIST* volumes must change to reflect this dynamism. *ARIST* chapters are scholarly reviews of specific topics as substantiated by the published literature. Some material may be included, even though not backed up by literature, if it is needed to provide a balanced and complete picture of the state of the art for the subject of the chapter. The time period covered varies from chapter to chapter, depending on whether the topic has been treated previously by *ARIST* and, if so, on the length of the interval from the last treatment to the current one. Thus, reviews may cover a one-year or a multiyear period. The reviews aim to be critical in that they provide the author's expert opinion regarding developments and activities within the chapter's subject area. The review guides the reader to or from specific publications. Chapters aim to be scholarly, thorough within the scope defined by the chapter author, up to date, well written, and readable by an audience that goes beyond the author's immediate peer group to researchers and practitioners in information science and technology, in general, and ASIS members, in particular.

PURPOSE

The purpose of *ARIST* is to describe and to appraise activities and trends in the field of information science and technology. Material presented should be substantiated by references to the literature. *ARIST* provides an annual review of topics in the field. One volume is produced each year. A master plan for the series encompasses the entire field in all its aspects, and topics for each volume are selected from the plan on the basis of timeliness and an assessment of reader interest.

REFERENCES CITED IN TEXT AND BIBLIOGRAPHY

The format for referring to bibliographic citations within the text involves use of the cited author's name instead of reference numbers. The cited author's surname is printed in upper case letters. The reader, wishing to find the bibliographic references, can readily locate the appropriate reference in the bibliography (alphabetically arranged by first author's last name). A single author appears as SMITH; coauthors as SMITH & JONES; and multiple authors as SMITH ET AL. If multiple papers by the same author are cited, the distinction is made by indicating the year of publication after the last name (e.g., SMITH, 1986), and if a further distinction is required for multiple papers within the same year, a lower case alpha character follows the year (e.g., SMITH, 1986a). Except for the fact that all authors in multi-authored papers are included in bibliographic references, the same basic conventions are used in the chapter bibliographies. Thus, the reader can easily locate in the bibliography any references discussed in the text.

Because of the emphasis placed on the requirement for chapter authors to discuss the key papers and significant developments reported in the literature, and because *ARIST* readers have expressed their liking for comprehensive bibliographies associated with the chapters, more references may be listed in the bibliographies than are discussed and/or cited in the text.

The format used for references in the bibliographies is based on the *American National Standard for Bibliographic References*, ANS Z39.29. We have followed the ANSI guidelines with respect to the sequence of bibliographic data elements and the punctuation used to separate the elements. Adoption of this convention should facilitate conversion of the references to machine-readable form as need arises. Journal article references follow the ANSI guide as closely as possible. Conference papers and microform publications follow an *ARIST* adaptation of the format.

STRUCTURE OF THE VOLUME

In accordance with the *ARIST* master plan, this volume's nine chapters fit within a basic framework: I. Planning Information Systems and Services; II. Basic Techniques and Technologies; III. Applications; and IV. The Profession. Chapter titles are provided in the Table of Contents, and an Introduction to each section highlights the events, trends, and evaluations given by the chapter authors. An Index to the entire volume is provided to help the user locate material relevant to the subject content, authors, and organizations cited in the book. An explanation of the guidelines employed in the Index is provided in the Introduction to the Index. A Keyword and Author Index to this and all prior volumes follows the Index.

DATABASES AND ABSTRACTING AND INDEXING SERVICES COVERING *ARIST*

ARIST as a whole and/or individual chapters are included in a number of abstracting and indexing (A&I) journals both within the United States and internationally. Databases that both cover *ARIST* and are available through major online services in the United States are:

> INSPEC (Computer and Control Abstracts)
> Social SciSearch (Social Sciences Citation Index)
> LISA (Library and Information Science Abstracts)
> Information Science Abstracts
> BIOSIS (Biological Abstracts)
> Library Literature
> Current Contents
> CompuMath Citation Index

Publishers of other A&I journals and databases who would like to include *ARIST* in their coverage are encouraged to contact the publisher for a review copy and notify the editor who will add the database name(s) to this list when appropriate.

Appreciation

Appreciation is expressed to many individuals and organizations for their roles in creating this volume. First and foremost are the authors of the individual chapters who have generously contributed their time and efforts in searching, reviewing, and evaluating the large body of literature on which their chapters are based. The *ARIST* Advisory Committee Members and *ARIST* Reviewers provided valuable feedback and constructive criticism of the content. DIALOG Information Services generously provided the authors with online access to databases. Appreciation is expressed to all of the members of the editorial staff and *ARIST* technical support staff who are listed on the Acknowledgments page.

Martha E. Williams

Acknowledgments

The American Society for Information Science and the Editor wish to acknowledge the contributions of the three principals on the editorial staff and the technical support staff.

Mary W. Rakow, Copy Editor

Debora Shaw, Index Editor

Linda C. Smith, Bibliographic Editor

Technical Support Staff

El-Siddig At-Taras, Technical Advisor

Laurence Lannom, Technical Advisor

Scott E. Preece, Technical Advisor

Linda C. Smith, Technical Advisor

Sheila Carnder, Word Processing

Yingjiu Fann, Word Processing

Linda Holder, Compositor

Advisory Committee for *ARIST*

Tamas Doszkocs

Raya Fidel

Paul B. Kantor

Michael Koenig

Jessica L. Milstead

John Regazzi

Linda C. Smith

Fran Spigai

Carol Tenopir

Contributors

Ethel Auster
University of Toronto
Faculty of Library and Information
   Science
140 St. George St.
Toronto, Ontario M5S 1A1
Canada

J. Michael Brittain
School of Communication and
   Information Studies
University of South Australia
Adelaide SA 5000, Australia

Shan-Ju Chang
Rutgers University
Department of Communication
School of Communication,
   Information and Library Studies
P.O. Box 5067
New Brunswick, NJ 98903

Chun Wei Choo
University of Toronto
Faculty of Library and Information
   Science
140 St. George St.
Toronto, Ontario M5S 1A1, Canada

Blaise Cronin
Indiana University
School of Library and Information
   Science
Bloomington, IN 47405

Elisabeth Davenport
Indiana University
School of Library and Information
   Science
Bloomington, IN 47405

Peter Hernon
Simmons College
Graduate School of Library and
   Information Science
300 The Fenway
Boston, MA 02115

Margaret Kinnell
Loughborough University
Loughborough, Leicestershire
LE11 3TU, England

Holley R. Lange
Colorado State University Libraries
Fort Collins, CO 80523

Maurice B. Line
Information & Library Consultant
10 Blackthorn Lane
Burn Bridge, Harrogate
North Yorkshire, HG3 1NZ
England

Jennifer MacDougall
Dublin City University Library
Dublin 9, Ireland

Charles R. McClure
Syracuse University
School of Information Studies
Syracuse, NY 13244

Cheryl Metoyer-Duran
University of California at Los
   Angeles
Graduate School of Library and
   Information Science
300 Circle Drive North
Los Angeles, CA 90024-1520

Gregory B. Newby
University of Illinois at Urbana-
   Champaign
Graduate School of Library and
   Information Science
410 David Kinley Hall
Urbana, IL 61801

Ronald E. Rice
Rutgers University
Department of Communication
School of Communication,
   Information and Library Studies
P.O. Box 5067
New Brunswick, NJ 98903

Chapter Reviewers

Marcia Bates

David Becker

Nicholas J. Belkin

Wesley T. Brandhorst

Walter M. Carlson

Pauline Cochrane

Raya Fidel

Margaret Fischer

Glynn Harmon

Lee A. Hollaar

Mary Ellen Jacob

Paul Kantor

Jessica L. Milstead

John Regazzi

Elliot Siegel

Linda C. Smith

Fran Spigai

Tom Surprenant

Carol Tenopir

Herbert White

I

Planning Information Systems and Services

Section I includes three chapters. Blaise Cronin and Elisabeth Davenport of Indiana University explore the concept of "Social Intelligence" in the first *ARIST* chapter on the topic. Peter Hernon of Simmons College and Charles R. McClure of Syracuse University discuss "Electronic U.S. Government Information: Policy Issues and Directions," and Cheryl Metoyer-Duran of the University of California at Los Angeles reviews "Information Gatekeepers."

Blaise Cronin and Elisabeth Davenport open their review appropriately by defining social intelligence. They refer to William S. Learned who used the term "intelligence service" more than 50 years ago to describe the role of the library in educating and empowering individual citizens to produce an intelligent community. Then they explain that more recently the term "social intelligence" has been used to denote a similar function in a wider range of contexts: cognitive psychology, development economics, corporate management, and technology for group work, where the concept is extended from the individual to the group or nation state. The authors review a range of sources from relevant literatures (psychology, economics, information management, development studies, computer-supported cooperative work (CSCW), and ethnomethodology) to demonstrate the evolution and current stability of a construct that some claim as a new paradigm for information science. Social intelligence has been defined as the ability to source, analyze, synthesize, and apply information that is transmitted through a range of channels in a variety of formats. The authors chart the extension of library and information science to embrace integrated resource management, cooperative work, and the role of information in improved performance. In addition, they review a number of case studies from the development and management literature. They conclude with a discussion of the legitimacy of social intelligence as a field of

1

study and discuss how it may be incorporated into mainstream information science curricula.

Peter Hernon and Charles R. McClure cover the timely and pervasive topic of electronic government information policy. They present an overview of policy issues related to U.S. government policy for electronic information. In general, there is no government-wide policy for electronic information. Rather, there is a collection of laws, guidelines, and agency regulations that form an ambiguous and often contentious framework in which electronic government information is managed and disseminated.

The Hernon and McClure chapter provides background information related to the context in which federal electronic information policy is developed. The primary stakeholders interested in the development of electronic information policy are identified and described. Selected key issues related to electronic information policy are discussed. The chapter identifies two key policy areas—revision of the Office of Management and Budget's Circular A-130 and the government's use of the Internet—as areas that are likely to see significant debate and contentiousness during the next few years.

They conclude by noting that the Clinton administration's commitment to building a national information infrastructure will require a range of major changes and initiatives in electronic information policy, and they suggest that the most important change will be moving the focus of electronic information policy from concern for information management and dissemination to concern for the provision of electronic information services.

Cheryl Metoyer-Duran reviews the literature of various disciplines and professions and shows that gatekeepers—i.e., professionals who either facilitate or hinder the flow of information within a formal or informal structure—exist in a variety of contexts. The gatekeeper literature as a whole, however, does not address the cultural dimensions of information-seeking behavior. Metoyer-Duran focuses on those writings that portray the cultural dimensions and on the role of gatekeepers in culturally diverse communities, especially ethnolinguistic ones, in which the population may not speak, read, or write English or may treat English as a second language. In this context, gatekeepers connect or link their communities with the information resources that people require to solve problems. Metoyer-Duran identifies a gatekeeper model of information and six profiles of gatekeepers represented by that model. The model is user centered and provides a framework for research into the information needs and information seeking behavior of a growing segment of American and other societies. She observes that it is important for libraries and other information providers to understand the role of gatekeeping to the information services, programs, and resources intended to serve these communities.

1 Social Intelligence

**BLAISE CRONIN and
ELISABETH DAVENPORT
Indiana University, Bloomington**

INTRODUCTION

The term "social intelligence" (SI) will not be found in introductions to, or encyclopedias of, information science and technology, nor has it featured as an index term in any previous *ARIST* volume. However, a number of recent developments, within and at the periphery of the information science field, suggest that this situation may be set to change (CRONIN & DAVENPORT, 1991; CRONIN & TUDOR-ŠILOVIĆ, 1992). This chapter aims to explicate the concept, to trace its pedigree, and to suggest likely future intersections with issues of more immediate concern to the information science community.

The chapter has five parts. The first looks at the history of the concept and considers contexts in which it may be valid; part two assesses social intelligence from the perspectives of information management, information policy, and information economics; part three reviews the tools and techniques associated with social intelligence activities, while part four attempts to solidify the construct through a selective review of cases and contexts. The concluding section looks to the future and asks can social intelligence be incorporated into the established information science canon and institutionalized within the curriculum, or is the concept too porous to be attached to one field of study?

We are extremely grateful to Joseph T. Ross for his help in compiling the bibliography.

Annual Review of Information Science and Technology (ARIST), Volume 28, 1993
Martha E. Williams, Editor
Published for the American Society for Information Science (ASIS)
By Learned Information, Inc., Medford, N.J.

HISTORY AND CONTEXT

Social intelligence is a chameleon concept. Despite, or perhaps because of, its portability, a standard or consensus definition is impossible to find. Usage remains doggedly context dependent. The term does, however, feature as a LIBRARY OF CONGRESS Subject Heading (LCSH), reserved for works dealing with the ability to understand and adjust to social relations, although not with materials that deal with social skills. Although the notion of social intelligence has taken root in a number of domains, it has been most notably operationalized in the research literatures of education and psychology, wherein it denotes the ability to effectively handle social relations—an amalgam of inter- and intrapersonal skills—and changing social situations.

In education, it is clear from even a cursory review of the literature that social intelligence has a respectable academic lineage; for example, the 1928 article by HUNT, "The Measurement of Social Intelligence," is one of several that makes explicit use of the term. The idea that social intelligence is a measurable skill, like motor coordination or abstract reasoning, but somehow distinct from other categories of intelligence, has a long history in the research literature of psychology. In the early part of this century, THORNDYKE posited three kinds of intelligence: (1) mechanical, (2) social, and (3) abstract. By the 1980s, GARDNER (1983) had formalized his theory of multiple intelligences—linguistic, musical, logical-mathematical, spatial, bodily-kinesthetic, and personal intelligence. In a subsequent development of this model social intelligence is a major category that covers four discrete categories: (1) leadership, (2) caretaking, (3) mediation of conflicts, and (4) social analysis (GARDNER, 1993).

The term has also been used to denote the skills that characterize social interaction in higher primates (JOLLY). Within the research literature of ethology and primatology, the terms social intelligence and Machiavellian intelligence are used interchangeably and are often contrasted with object or technical intelligence (WHITEN & BYRNE, 1988a). For example, HUMPHREY (p. 16) treats Machiavellian intelligence as a synonym for social intelligence, arguing that in complex societies there are benefits to be gained by each member both in preserving the overall structure of the group while simultaneously outmaneuvering others within it. Social primates are required by the nature of the system they create and maintain to be "able to calculate the consequences of their own behavior, to calculate the likely behavior of others, to calculate the balance of advantage and loss" in a chesslike game of social plot and counterplot. The core skill involved in Machiavellian intelligence is the ability to make and keep alliances with the right individuals (HARCOURT). Such a skill is, of course, a sine qua non of survival in the worlds of politics and business at both the local and global level.

Social intelligence encompasses more than the behavior of individual social actors. In the writings of John Dewey, social intelligence seems to imply collective action and responsibilities—a democratic process designed to "bring human beings voluntarily into greater accord" (GOUINLOCK, p. 57). This view finds a contemporary echo in PIGANIOL (p. 23), who sees social intelligence expressed in various needs and behaviors, ranging from the desire of citizens to participate fully in a democracy to the individual's search for a better quality of life based on informed decision-making and unfettered access to information. Similar ideas infuse Doctor's recent *ARIST* chapter in which he reviews information democracy and citizen empowerment issues in the North American context (DOCTOR).

On this basis, social intelligence implies taking responsibility for one's actions. It might also describe initiatives by governments and technocrats to promote transparency and accountability. Alternatively, as CRONIN (1992c, p. 4) suggests, the skills involved can empower grassroots activists: "as democratic pluralism takes root, community groups, activists, lobbyists and concerned citizens will increasingly become adept at gathering and marshalling intelligence to support their social and environmental objectives." This orientation to action is also stressed by Ventura who maintains that a social intelligence system is "dynamic and focused on results," whereas the typical information system "revolves mainly around access and the user." In a social intelligence system, information is "fuel for action" (VENTURA, 1988, p. 164).

Given this background, the volatility of the coupling of the term social with intelligence is perfectly understandable. The word "intelligence" alone has a particularly rich and complex semantic history, reflecting both extensive scholarly and lay use in the English language from the 14th century on (DURANT). Part of the problem stems from the fact that intelligence can refer to a thing (e.g., military intelligence) or to a mental attribute (e.g., Rommel showed great intelligence in regrouping his forces). Further difficulties arise when the term is translated (BAUMARD). Many languages do not capture the sometimes subtle distinction between intelligence and information as understood in English, and in some cases the term carries loaded, if not exactly pejorative, connotations. A spirited review of definitions and assumptions has been provided recently by TROY.

In the Anglo-Saxon world, the word intelligence in one context triggers a fairly predictable set of associations: undercover agents, cryptologists, counterespionage plots, ideological sabotage, and cloak-and-dagger activities; but the intelligence function in contemporary society extends far beyond such popular notions. KENT (p. vii), in his classic text, *Strategic Intelligence for American World Policy*, begins by saying that:

> Intelligence is a simple and self-evident thing. As an activity it is the pursuit of a certain kind of knowledge; as a phenomenon it is the resultant knowledge. In a small way it is what we all do every day. When a housewife decides to increase her inventory, when a doctor diagnoses an ailment—when almost anyone decides upon a course of action—he usually does some preliminary intelligence work. Sometimes the work is so informal and distinctive that he does not recognize it as intelligence—like finding the right garage man in the classified section of a telephone book.

As HERMAN points out, intelligence uses rather formal military language and concepts but actually has the untidiness of any living activity. In many countries, the intelligence community embraces an extended family of agencies and activities, from military intelligence through internal security intelligence to trade intelligence networks. As the multiplicity of intelligence functions and types (e.g., human intelligence, signals intelligence, radar intelligence) has expanded and as the associated technologies for analyzing intelligence data have become more expensive and sophisticated, the tendency to centralize has grown commensurately; the classical embodiment of this practice is, of course, the U.S. Central Intelligence Agency (CIA). The untidiness to which Herman alludes is a feature, semantically and operationally, of social intelligence.

Given all this, why should *ARIST* devote a chapter to such an untidy construct? First, the connections between information science and social intelligence are not difficult to articulate. Second, *ARIST* has previously addressed issues of information access and grassroots democracy (DOCTOR). More generally, in an age of communitarianism and self-help, social intelligence may rapidly acquire legitimacy (HARRIS; HENDERSON, 1989). Indeed some of this was strikingly anticipated almost 70 years ago by LEARNED, who, in his book *The American Public Library and the Diffusion of Knowledge*, reconceptualized the traditional public library as "the central intelligence service of the town" to be staffed by an appropriately trained and motivated intelligence personnel, and not by "mere grubbers in books according to professional tradition" (p. 17). For others the connection between information science and social intelligence lies in the fact that information science has as its "fundamental social objective" the mobilization of information stored in documents in order to further individual learning and social well being (RAYWARD, p. 50). The global vision for world intelligence articulated by OTLET has been explored in detail by RAYWARD, who places him in a millenialist tradition.

Third, the social intelligence/information science interface has already been acknowledged explicitly or implicitly. For example, CAWKELL (p. 29) recently described how the *Science Citation Index* can be used for intelligence gathering: "This process opens up a means of gathering intelligence for such purposes as estimating the impact of work done by an individual or an organization, or noting the growth, diminution, or change in the activities of a science-based company, educational or research establishment, or even an entire country." Elsewhere TELL (1988) recounts how the Venezuelan Ministry of Energy and Mines developed a coordinated intelligence system by combining traditional library, archival, and documentation functions with computer and communications. The resultant information system was designed to satisfy the diverse information requirements of the ministry, which included trade pact negotiations, foreign aid negotiations, license purchasing, major systems purchases, hiring of consultants and their utilization, national equity negotiations, catastrophe and disaster alleviation agreements, state and privately owned enterprises, foreign and domestic technology transfer, joint ventures, and cooperative endeavors. The expanded role reflects the conspectus of concerns associated with social intelligence.

Perspectives on Social Intelligence

It should be clear already that many perspectives can be brought to bear on social intelligence. For psychometricians, social intelligence is something that can be measured; for primatologists it also implies social expertise/social competence (WHITEN & BYRNE, 1988b) or social gamesmanship (HUMPHREY); for social scientists and philosophers it is an instrument or process of citizen empowerment and democratization. For still others, social intelligence is neither prowess nor process, but raw material (intelligence data) that can be manipulated and applied at the individual, organizational, or nation state level. Interestingly, many of the concepts touched on so far were anticipated by HENDERSON (1973a) in a comprehensive review of what she calls "ecological-economic" studies.

Interest in intelligence issues has grown in recent years. The short handbook, *Real-World Intelligence* (MEYER), discusses similarities between the operations of state/government intelligence agencies and those of civilian/commercial enterprises under the label "the new intelligence" (MEYER, p. 13). Institutionalized examples of social intelligence gathering on a gargantuan scale include the East German Stasi or Romanian Securitate, whereby the state intelligence apparatus was augmented by legions of part-time civilian informers (RADY), while a recent analysis of the highly secretive corporations that dominate the world grain trade provides a powerful insight into commercial intelligence management strategies (BLANC).

However, the term is not used exclusively in academe. In fact, it has surprisingly wide currency. BUCKLEY and BRUCE, writing in the popular press, assume no specialist knowledge on the part of readers. Others are more particular. ANTONOPOULOS defines social intelligence as intimate knowledge of the rules, procedures, histories, possibilities, and desires that operate at any given time and place as well as the feints and tricks used by ordinary individuals in organizational settings. An essentially similar interpretation is offered by BREWER (p. 189), who, in a discussion of street culture, uses the term to describe "those informants who hold the most cultural knowledge relative to their peers in order to get the most reliable and valid representations of cultural patterns."

Despite, or because of, the fragmentation, there have been calls to develop a unified theory of intelligence. In the late 1970s and early 1980s, the case for an integrated and holistic approach to intelligence studies was consistently made by Dedijer (VENTURA, 1988). The content of Dedijer's first interdisciplinary course on social intelligence at Lund University in Sweden was revealingly eclectic. It included: the history of intelligence; intelligence problems of less-developed countries; industrial intelligence; social insight and control; secrecy and privacy; nature, benefits, and costs of the intelligence function; computers and intelligence; journalism and intelligence; national intelligence organizations; and a future-oriented theory of social intelligence. DEDIJER draws on research and methods from a wide variety of academic disciplines and application areas (DEDIJER & JÉQUIER), and he speaks confidently in terms of an intelligence revolution and the emergence of an intelligence science that will integrate the research of all aspects of intelligence, from biological and individual to machine and governing intelligence (DEDIJER). Two English-language festschriften (ANNERSTEDT & JAMISON; SIGURDSON & TÅGERUD) offer useful summaries and evaluations of Dedijer's work.

The convergence of ideas and individuals interested in social intelligence was facilitated in the late 1980s by a series of international conferences held in Dubrovnik (CRONIN & TUDOR-ŠILOVIĆ, 1990; 1992). One outcome was the journal *SOCIAL INTELLIGENCE*, subsequently renamed the *JOURNAL OF ECONOMIC AND SOCIAL INTELLIGENCE*. In the introductory issue, the editors (CRONIN & DAVENPORT, 1991) define social intelligence as the process by which a society, organization, or individual scans the environment, interprets what is there, and constructs versions of events that may afford competitive advantage. The distinguishing feature of this approach is that the total environment is explored: what is visible and what is masked, what is stated and what is understood, and what is overt and what is covert. The raw material is "text" in the widest possible sense: it may be a sound bite, technical report, scholarly paper, body language, map, movie, or word of mouth. It is the emphasis on interpretation, the hermeneutic dimension, that distinguishes this approach from information science's traditional information search-and-retrieval paradigm.

An alternative label to social intelligence might be cultural sociology, as defined by WUTHNOW (p. 6): "A branch of the human sciences concerned with observations. . .essentially a study of texts: texts of all kinds, including the printed word, graphic images, spoken utterances, and even the messages 'given off' in social settings by such behaviors as bodily movements and positions. . .gestures, facial expressions, or the public 'face' of organizations and institutions." Elsewhere, CRONIN (1991) presents social intelligence as a multifaceted concept that embraces activities (e.g., multisourcing, linking, pattern matching, analysis and synthesis, and social exchange), content (e.g., weak signals, public domain data, and tacit knowledge), and capabilities (e.g., ability to access intellectual capital, network conductivity, and metacognition).

Whether the journal can achieve its goals will depend in part on whether it can focus on "specific areas of overlap between different sources of and means for acquiring information" sufficient to establish "a common set of objectives, methodologies and standards of explanation" (DURANT, p. 177-178). It will also depend on whether or not it can identify a niche and differentiate itself sufficiently from other, often more focused journals with an interest in social intelligence-related issues. Journals or newsletters belonging to this group might include *COMPETITIVE INTELLIGENCE REVIEW* (published by the Society of Competitive Intelligence Professionals in the United States), *INTELLIGENCE AND NATIONAL SECURITY, INTERNATIONAL JOURNAL OF INTELLIGENCE AND COUNTERINTELLIGENCE, KNOWLEDGE AND POLICY, SOCIAL EPISTEMOLOGY,* and *THE INTELLIGENT ENTERPRISE* (first published in 1991 by the Association for Information Management in London, but now discontinued).

DEDIJER predicts a shift in emphasis from intelligence for national security to intelligence for national growth and development, maintaining that an organization, like an individual, should have its own intelligence capability to learn about its environment and about itself. Certainly in the post-cold war era, the privatization-of-intelligence theme has been picked up with gusto by the general and business press and has resulted in a proliferation of articles with titles such as: "Multinationals vs. the Snoops" (DEBES), "Corporate Spies Snoop to Conquer" (DUMAINE), "Corporate Cops at the Keyhole" (H. KAY), "Should the CIA Start Spying for Corporate America?" (GALEN), "The New Race for Intelligence" (TEITELBAUM), and "Still Spying after All These

Years" (ZAGORIN). This kind of thinking was powerfully reinforced by the publication of *Powershift* (TOFFLER), which includes the chapter, "A Market for Spies." In a similar vein, CUBILLO discusses the migration of the function from military to civilian life and has proposed the term "techno-economic intelligence" to underscore the differences between military and civilian intelligence issues and approaches, while HULNICK suggests that "intelligence resources might be used on an international basis to monitor environmental hazards and damage to fragile land and water areas, monitor crop growth to prevent potential famine, or track population movements to enable governments to shift resources to care for their people" (p. 458). Paul Kantor[1] notes that these uses for intelligence reduce the marginal cost of developing national missile defense systems.

MULTIPLE PERSPECTIVES

Although the term social intelligence has not previously been the subject of a chapter in *ARIST*, several related concepts and techniques have been described in the contexts of information management, information economics and policy, and information systems. In the late 1960s, PAISLEY published heavily cited material that stressed the importance of the environment as a factor in the communication of scientific information and in information retrieval. The environments described may be constructs or conceptual frameworks (i.e., "within his own head" (PAISLEY, p. 6)) or may refer to the current political climate or to one of a number of loci between these two extremes. The term "environment," for these authors, acts as a portmanteau for the broad range of psychological, organizational, and political variables, which are reflected in current use of the term social intelligence.

Information Management

Why, then, was this focus on environmental analysis, which is a central aspect of social intelligence, not sustained? There are several possible reasons. First, the requisite technology for capturing and analyzing the broad range of data that might allow a researcher to understand different contextual levels was not available in the 1960s. TAYLOR (1968), for example, in his discussion of the prospects for information retrieval, references Engelbart, whom he does not recognize as potentially useful. Today, however, thanks to Engelbart's early work, hypertext and other tools for cooperation are one of the technical platforms for the management of social intelligence (DAVENPORT, 1991;

---

[1]Personal communication, 1993.

DAVENPORT & CRONIN, 1991; DREXLER, 1991; TELL, 1990; WHYTE).
Second, in the mid-1960s, methodologies for analyzing the environment and the social conditions under which science is produced were
only just emerging (GARVEY & GRIFFITH). Much of the work on social
studies of science and techniques for ethnomethodological inquiry, for
instance, appeared in the late 1960s (GARFINKEL; GLASER &
STRAUSS). Moreover, the eponymous journal, *SOCIAL STUDIES OF
SCIENCE*, first appeared in 1970, to be followed by a substantial literature of highly detailed case studies over the next two decades (e.g.,
KNORR-CETINA; KNORR-CETINA & MULKAY; LATOUR &
WOOLGAR). In other words, many of the technical tools and investigative techniques that underpin the praxis of social intelligence had either
not been developed or had been inadequately incorporated into professional thinking.

The route to recognizing intelligence gathering, environmental scanning, and issue management as mainstream information science activities was tortuous. Taylor's work subsequent to his 1968 paper may
serve as a guiding thread, as he moved away from modeling the document and the individual user to modeling the environment (TAYLOR,
1986a) and analyzing the signals that emerge from it (TAYLOR, 1986b).
Likewise, Marchand and Horton's work is part of an expanding body of
empirical research and theory addressing intelligence capability at the
institutional level under the rubric of information resources manage-
ment/strategic information management (BROADBENT & KOENIG;
DAVENPORT & CRONIN, 1988; MARCHAND & HORTON; PORTER
& MILLAR; PRUSAK & MATARAZZO).

However, there has been a perceptible shift in recent years, and
intelligence is now a widely discussed issue in, for example, the context
of business and international trade. Indeed, the message behind the
word "intelligence" in the business literature of the past decade is no
longer simply, "beat the competition" (JAMES; SYNNOTT); in the 1990s,
it has become "competitive cooperation" (STANAT), and a further
message is, "know thyself," which permeates the literature on the
learning organization (PEDLER ET AL., 1991).

Organizational Learning and Intelligence

If, as suggested, the concept of social intelligence is latent in the
works discussed above, has any theorist explicitly constructed an organizational paradigm premised on such a concept? Beer, author of such
titles as *Brain of the Firm* and *The Heart of the Enterprise*, specifically uses
intelligence, as explained by the neurological model of the day, as a
blueprint for organizing information input, processing, and output at
any level of aggregation within the firm (BEER, 1979; 1981; 1985). He

addresses several fundamental questions. For example, how can an institution organize itself to ensure that the activities of intelligence gathering, filtering, amplification, and adaptation—the identifying components of applied social intelligence—are clearly visible and understood? A comparable systems approach is provided by WESTRUM in a discussion of what constitutes science. He maintains that science, like every other system of vision, has its blind spots and that anomalies and implausibilities, such as the battered child syndrome or unidentified flying objects (UFOs), remain hidden because of failures in the social intelligence mechanisms (he uses the actual term) that are used to report and evaluate such events. The parallels between a social intelligence system and a military intelligence system are explicitly acknowledged in his analysis.

Beer is confident that his Viable Systems Model (VSM) can be applied to groups within groups and is relevant to the management of intelligence at the level of the department, enterprise, or nation state (BEER, 1985). Intelligence and viability are thus linked. This principle of scaling up from the individual to the complex organization is evident in the use of the IQ (intelligence quotient) metaphor, transposed from the measurement of individual intellect to the ranking of organizations and nations as highbrow, middlebrow, or lowbrow (TOFFLER). There are other examples of the transfer to corporate analysis of constructs from psychology designed to categorize individuals. Notable among these is the model of individual intelligence as self-government (STERNBERG), which is paralleled in recent managerial theory on decentralization, team building, and local autonomy where tasks are negotiated and regulated at the level of distributed groups (BOLAND; CIBORRA; MUMFORD). The "smart" firm is the one in which distributed groups retain sufficient connectivity to be recognized collectively as an organization while making decisions individually.

An understanding of such groups, including the social rules and protocols that make sense at this organizational level, is the basis of a series of case studies and grounded theories that take two main approaches: (1) understanding the norms that emerge from observing tasks and dialogs (SUCHMAN; TRIGG ET AL.); or (2) imposing norms or filters that seek to direct the flow of conversation and information exchanges in groups (MALONE & FRY; WINOGRAD & FLORES). A further question is raised at the level of the small group; if, as Gardner suggests (WINN), social intelligence is the art of making the most of colleagues, how should group participants present themselves to others, especially in the context of an electronic environment in which some of the social cues that inform social interaction may not apply (SPROULL & KIESLER)?

Information Economics

The link between information and viability, which characterizes social intelligence, is at the heart of information economics. Here the driving concern is to determine the tradeoffs between investment in information and the personal or organizational advantage to be gained. Does information make a difference? What are the payoffs from investment in information systems and resources? *ARIST* has a long tradition of addressing information economics issues at both the micro and macro level (KOENIG; LAMBERTON, 1984, 1990; REPO, 1987). Early attempts to understand the economic significance of information focused on inputs and outputs at the level of national accounts (COOPER; MACHLUP; PORAT). Other studies attempted to assess inputs and outputs at the sectoral level (BRAUNSTEIN; HAYES & ERICKSON; MÄKINEN). Still others have suggested that it is more effective to compare intrasectoral information investments and yields at the level of the firm (BUZZELL; KEEN; STRASSMANN, 1985, 1990).

Much recent analysis focuses on value assessments of specific information units, activities, or services (KING & GRIFFITHS), while PARKER ET AL. discuss enterprise-wide information management in terms of projects—i.e., information system investments at the level of the line of business or strategic business unit. An extreme version of microeconomics is based on the work of DAWKINS, a geneticist who describes the behavior of genes in terms of an information economy at a level not normally considered by information scientists. His work has, however, influenced the thinking of some economists who are seeking to describe distributed information at the quantum level (DREXLER, 1986).

This heritage is relevant to social intelligence in cases where the methodologies or approaches described can be applied to the measurement and development of national capability (IRVINE & MARTIN). Perhaps the most obvious context is scientometrics. Science policy makers can compare scientific performances to evaluate their country's global position and market share in a particular field or subfield and then attenuate or amplify national capability accordingly by reallocating resources. According to the U.S. NATIONAL SCIENCE BOARD (p. xiii): "Governments have increasingly come to see science and technology policy as a key ingredient in their strategies for development and economic competitiveness." A similar assessment in the civilian context is advocated by PORTER (1990) in *The Competitive Advantage of Nations*, an influential treatise that functions as a *vade mecum* for senior corporate executives and industrial policy makers. His book explores the interaction of factors that turn some clusters of industries in a particular sector into dominant global players. Among the critical factors he identifies are skilled labor, supplier networks, infrastructure, domestic competition, local demand, firm strategy, structure, and rivalry. A nation, says Porter, does not inherit but creates the most important factors of production, such as skilled human resources or a scientific base.

What is the connection with social intelligence? In both these examples—science and industry—self-awareness and self-analysis will allow for a realistic assessment of the tradeoffs. In almost every definition of social intelligence, the development of indigenous capabilities is a primary condition for the creation and exploitation of SI, and this, in turn, is predicated on knowledge of one's self, of one's relative strengths and weaknesses. This applies to the nation state as much as to the individual. In this context, the following constructs—all of which relate to self-awareness at the national level—have been reviewed by ONYANGO (1990): (1) indigenous technological capability (ITC), (2) indigenous technology learning capacity (ITLC), (3) independent world technology reconnaissance capacity (IWTRC), (4) indigenous technology-creating capacity (ITCC), and (5) aid-negotiating capability (ANC).

STERNBERG goes so far as to maintain that there are clear parallels between human intelligence and the functions, level, scope, political color, and efficacy of government. This perspective conditions much of the discussion of the development gap between first and third world countries, which may be seen as a cognitive rather than purely technological issue (CRONIN & DAVENPORT, 1990b; VENTURA, 1987) if, for example, technology transfer failures are reconceptualized as failures in intelligence management (ONYANGO, 1991). In the opinion of STURGES ET AL. (p. 27), based on their review of development initiatives in Africa, a social intelligence model could offer a viable alternative to traditional development strategies by placing "self-reliance at the centre" and by involving the continent in "taking control of its own indigenous knowledge base." Strong support for this thinking comes from PÁEZ-URDANETA, MENOU, and MCHOMBU, who point to the suboptimal utilization of knowledge stocks in most developing nations, and from GEORGE, who, in her analysis of the third world debt crisis, introduces some concrete proposals for harnessing indigenous resources and capabilities (e.g., the collection and recording of traditional agricultural, medical, nutritional, and pharmaceutical knowledge).

This theme is echoed widely by others. For example, the report of the SOUTH COMMISSION (p. 278) notes: "Unless the South learns to harness the forces of modern science and technology, it has no chance of fulfilling its developmental aspirations or its yearning for an effective voice in the management of global interdependence. All its societies must therefore mount a determined effort to absorb, adapt, and assimilate new technological advances." In a similar vein, HENDERSON (1973b, p. 32) observed that "conservation technology" was one way to avoid the tragedy of the commons, a point also made by OSTROM and P.M. ALLEN.

The connection between development strategies and social intelligence was acknowledged by HENDERSON (1989), who has sought to broaden the base of variables required for effective development economics. She points out that all nations are developing and that general indicators can be applied to both North-South and East-West. "An expanded theoretical framework is needed, based on broader interdisciplinary concepts, such as those of general systems theory, information and decision theory, thermodynamics, physics, engineering, ecology and the life sciences, as well as advanced approaches to human motivation, psychology and anthropology" (HENDERSON, 1989, p. 573). Development economics for Henderson must emerge from a "general debate between different countries, cultures and academic disciplines" which will "accelerate social learning in all countries" (HENDERSON, 1989, p. 572). In her analysis of the breakup of the macroeconomic order in North America, she highlights the importance of alternative local economies, where currency may involve the exchange of skills or other "new forms of computer-assisted barter" (p. 572). This parallels the mechanisms described by DE SOTO in his landmark analysis of the informal, or "black," economy in Peru.

The new paradigm in development economics is based on self-analysis, self-reliance, and self-renewal, which would seem to necessitate a "development orientated intelligence policy" (JÉQUIER & DEDIJER). In many cases, this may mean abandoning those established institutions and protocols that have become self-legitimizing and thus hinder rather than enhance the political process. The terms "terrain opacity" and "terrain transparency" have been used in this context to characterize open and closed systems (ONYANGO, 1990, p. 10, 14). Wherever the level of terrain opacity is high, alternative economic structures and responses will emerge (DAVENPORT, 1992a; DE SOTO).

The need for alternative ways of seeing extends to conceptions of intelligence. It is important that intelligence not be defined too narrowly or equated with formally recorded information because folklore, informal sources, and traditional skills may be a distinctive component of comparative advantage. Social intelligence thus calls for a wide-angled vision and a willingness to tolerate ambiguity. As PORTER (1990, p. 48) says: "Information plays a large role in the process of innovation—information that is not sought or available to competitors, or information available to others that is interpreted in new ways. . . simply looking in the right place, unencumbered by or unconcerned with conventional wisdom."

Information Policy

If social intelligence is the ability to gather, analyze, and apply information to ensure viability or success in a particular environment, what policies might governments adopt to create the conditions for building national advantage? The following cases confirm that it is not clear if there is a single, best policy. In France, centralized and subsidized provision of access to basic directory information via Minitel (the national videotex system) blossomed in unforeseen ways, as subscribers identified opportunities for exchange and service that had not been anticipated: "New services to benefit those with special needs are being created daily by the special interest groups. The government also uses Minitel to provide these special groups with better services" (HOUSEL & DAVIDSON, p. 43). The net effect has been compared with putting a stethoscope to the soul of France (RAMBALI).

The French experience of grassroots growth contrasts sharply with the history of Prestel in the United Kingdom. Minitel is a manifestation of a conscious strategy to transform French society through "télématique" (telematics), first outlined by Nora and Minc in a publicly released, far-sighted report to the president of France. To quote: "The computer is not the only technological innovation of recent years, but it does constitute the common factor that speeds the development of all the others. Above all. . .it will alter the entire nervous system of social organization . . . blending pictures, sounds, and memories and transforming the pattern of our culture" (NORA & MINC p. 3, 4). In contrast, Prestel did not take off: it was overengineered in design terms, failed to attract any kind of sustained government subsidy, and was mismarketed. The hoped-for "multi-billion pound market" (ALDRICH, p. 4) did not materialize.

Different still is the situation in the United States. Here grassroots exchange has to some extent emerged in the vacuum arising from the lack of direct government intervention and investment in the information marketplace. The Free-Net phenomenon allows community-level exchange, or "cultural chatting" (GRIMES, p. B1), similar to that carried by Minitel via bulletin boards, conferences, directories, and e-mail, all of which can trap traditional word-of-mouth exchanges. In theory at least, the nets allow these exchanges to be conserved and exploited as community intelligence.

LEHNER describes an initiative by the Countryside Computer Alliance in Upstate New York to provide even the smallest rural communities with low-cost, state-of-the-art computer training and access to intelligent services, and ROGERS ET AL. (p. 303) show how public electronic networks are being "utilized for political action processes, such as for gender equality, for the issue of homeless men, and for local environmental action." In the United States, Prodigy and CompuServe currently dominate the domestic electronic information market, with Prodigy's members sending 65,000 e-mail transmissions and posting 80,000 bulletin board messages per day (SCHWARTZ & LEWYN). Even in the former Soviet Union, computer networking is developing rapidly, a phenomenon graphically illustrated by TRAVICA & HOGAN in their analysis of the social impact of networking during the failed 1991 coup. More generally, bulletin boards across the globe are described as a matrix and have been reviewed by QUARTERMAN. It is clear that the infrastructure and conditions for community-wide social intelligence are gradually being put in place, as the guide to the Internet by KROL makes abundantly clear. In fact, if the telephone is taken into account, the necessary infrastructure has been in place a considerable time. A study of women and the telephone in Australia demonstrates the existence of "psychological neighbourhoods" and "telephone neighbourhoods" and the importance of these virtual groups in the everyday lives of Australian women (MOYAL, p. 92).

In the wake of infrastructure building, however, comes a host of complex public policy issues. At the federal level, debate currently focuses on how much government intervention is required to fund and manage a national education and research network, the NREN. As BROMLEY observed in his 1989 position statement on the Federal High Performance Computing Program: "A future national high-speed network could have the kind of catalytic effect on our society, industries, and universities that the telephone system has had during the twentieth century." MCCLURE ET AL. included relevant federal documentation in their 1991 review of NREN-related issues. Governance and access have become highly controversial issues in the context of the Internet. GRUNDNER, of the National Public Telecomputing Network, and founder of the Cleveland Free-Net, comments on the "balkanization of the information age" and laments the absence of "a common framework with enough 'conceptual bandwidth' to include everyone" (p. 7). Controversy also surrounds issues of control and surveillance, areas in which the Electronic Frontier Foundation acts as a watchdog (KAPOR). These and related topics have been reviewed in a special issue of *SCIENTIFIC AMERICAN*.

TOOLS AND TECHNIQUES

An integrated technology base is one of the conditions that allows individuals or groups to harvest and process intelligence. In the military environment different intelligence sources—e.g., signals intelligence, human intelligence, radar intelligence—are combined to provide a framework for analysis and synthesis (HERMAN). We would argue that the equivalent civilian capability is social intelligence on the basis of the following characteristics. First is the ability to communicate and exchange information via telecommunications networks. The basic version of this is, of course, the telephone, but telephone exchange can only count as intelligence when it has a framework. Second, the ability to exchange must be supplemented with the ability to trap such exchanges and the ability to analyze what is trapped (HINDUS & SCHMANDT). Analysis, however, can only take place in context. The significance of a message may not be manifest until it is placed in a frame or assessed against a background of other messages. So, a further requirement of the technical base is the ability to broadcatch (BRAND) or gather information from multiple channels in multiple formats. The one-sided version of events results in tunnel vision; a message in one format must be matched with others to gain a truly composite picture. Positive redundancy is thus a requirement of effective intelligence gathering (CRONIN, 1992b).

Networks

Many of the key functions of social intelligence (communication, broadcatching, linking, pattern matching) are embodied in tools that can be examined through different literature sets. The networking, or communication, literature includes the development of standards, whose scope extends from global network interconnection to tagging bibliographic records; broadcatching and linking are covered in the literature of hypertext; connectionism in the literatures of computer science and cognition; human communication, as distinct from telecommunication, is explored in the literatures of computer-supported cooperative work (CSCW) and computer-mediated communications (CMC).

The history of networking is reviewed by QUARTERMAN & HOSKINS, MCCLURE ET AL., DEMPSEY, and, negatively, by SIMONS, who claims that a functionally integrated global network would lend itself to abuse by authoritarian control, but, he adds, lack of standardization makes such a scenario unlikely. His complacency may be unwarranted; in the six years since his text appeared, standards for connectivity at the local and global levels have become a major preoccupation of vendors, buyers, and policy makers. Both DEMPSEY and SPRING review the protocols for both connectivity and text transmission, while standards for linking across media are reviewed by FISH & KRAUT.

Hypermedia

Developments in the integration of material delivered in multiple formats—so important in the context of intelligence gathering and analysis—can be explored in the hypermedia/hypertext literature, which has developed rapidly in the past five years (NIELSEN). DAVENPORT & BAIRD have attempted to identify emergent classics in the field by bibliometrically analyzing conference proceedings. The pioneering work of ENGELBART & ENGLISH, ENGELBART ET AL., ENGELBART & HOOPER, and NELSON, with its emphasis on general human augmentation, has been followed recently by work on more specific implementations. Much of this material covers document management, but those elements that deal with community information (BAIRD & PERCIVAL) and integrated e-mail (BORENSTEIN) are particularly relevant to social intelligence.

The role of hypertext in training and orientation—one of the memex applications envisaged by BUSH—has been described by DAVENPORT & CRONIN (1991); its use in a library context has been discussed by BORGMAN, and its role as a working implementation in a corporate accounting firm has been described by GREGORY. Hypertext in the context of business intelligence, analysis, and planning is discussed by BAIRD ET AL. and by DAVENPORT (1991), and in the conduct of science by DAVENPORT & CRONIN (1990), who argue that hypertext could facilitate the tracking and sharing of information that has eluded capture by traditional recording protocols. Part of the attraction of hypermedia systems is their ability to combine the formal and informal, an important feature that has been underscored in different ways by CAPURRO, DAVENPORT (1992a), and RADOŠEVIĆ (1992); each of these authors recognizes the paradox of excessive formulation, or overdependence, on information technology in the context of intelligence management systems. Clearly Polanyi's observation—if "tacit knowledge forms an indispensable part of all knowledge, then the ideal of eliminating all personal elements of knowledge would, in effect, aim at the destruction of all knowledge"(POLANYI, p. 20)—holds true in the context of networked organizations and collaboratories (DAVENPORT, 1992b).

Connectionism

If hypertext can allow material from many sources in many formats to be harvested and stored, can it help with the analysis of intelligence? Skeptics who doubt the capacity of human processors to find and to exploit connections in hyperspace (SHNEIDERMAN) propose that machine-bred agents—"knowbots"—will be required (DAVISS); one step toward this may be the development of self-documenting metadatabases, as described by GRIFFITHS. RADA, another advocate of machine-aided composition, has coined the term "expertext" to describe the synthetic document (finished intelligence) that such agents might produce. Early work on computer-bred agents is discussed by BRAND,

A.C. KAY, and LAUREL. Of particular interest, however, is the work of HILLIS, designer of the Connection Machine, and also that of GELERNTER (1989; 1992). Hillis envisages not just agents but parallel teams of agents whose processing capability can be compared to the neural networks that drive human intelligence. A further technical development that contributes to social intelligence is the suite of tools supporting CSCW. These were first reviewed by GREIF and have been covered in subsequent Association for Computing Machinery (ACM) publications. The work of WINOGRAD & FLORES, STEFIK ET AL., and MALONE & FRY has resulted in commercial products that embody some of the principles of social intelligence (MCNURLIN & SPRAGUE).

Techniques, both qualitative and quantitative, for analyzing social interaction are an important complement to, and in some cases the basis of design for, the computer tools that facilitate the practice of social intelligence. HERMAN describes the use of such tools in the context of military intelligence; MYERS explores the application of a battery of statistical measures to assess the potential of real estate. In the world of market research, the established tools of life style analysis, value group analysis, demographic profiling, and psychographics are geared to generating and exploiting social intelligence, even if the term is not used explicitly (KOTLER). Sociometric approaches expose underlying communication patterns and behaviors in organizations and can be used to assess the frequency and intensity of interaction between identified individuals or groups (T.J. ALLEN; KRACKHARDT). At a more general level, the understanding of motives, values, beliefs, and sense making afforded by ethnomethodological investigation is highly relevant to social intelligence. Specific mapping techniques for understanding local strategy are reviewed in the book edited by HUFF, while at the level of understanding organizations, a range of published methodologies is available (CHECKLAND & SCHOLES; GEERTZ; GUBA & LINCOLN). Software for capturing and analyzing such observations—"rich pictures" and "thick descriptions"—has been reviewed by FIELDING & LEE.

CONTEXTS AND CASES

How can the idea of social intelligence be made operational? Here we provide examples of intelligence management at the national and enterprise/community levels. RADOŠEVIC (1991) maintains that underdevelopment can be analyzed in terms of three main gaps: (1) the information sector gap, (2) the information technology gap, and (3) the intelligence gap. Using the former Yugoslavia as a case study, RADOŠEVIC & DEDIJER attempt to show that paying more "attention to the intelligence capability of governments and enterprises could greatly improve the management of information resources in developing countries" (p. 31). Their views are echoed in the mainstream literature of competitive strategy. Porter's seminal analysis of the factors that shape industrial and commercial competitiveness in global markets explicitly acknowledges the importance of information: "The amount and quality of information available in a nation is of growing importance in modern international competition. Information is a means to overcome inertia. . .is integral to the upgrading of competitive advantage in established industries" (PORTER, 1985; 1990, p. 639).

National Level

Perhaps the most frequently cited example of the networked nation of tomorrow is Singapore, often referred to by its citizens as an "intelligent island." Singapore is atypical—an extremely small land mass (less than 250 square miles) with fewer than three million inhabitants. It lacks virtually all natural comparative resource advantages, yet it is a recognized leader in leveraging and sustaining its competitive edge through far-sighted investments in information and communication technologies. However, as civil libertarians and others have repeatedly noted, there has been a price to pay: the drive to "create an information-enabled, networked society has a built-in irony: there is an inherent conflict between the democratization of information creation and access and the government's long-standing determination to control closely the information its citizens receive" (SISODIA, p. 48). Social intelligence in Singapore is centralized rather than diffused. The tradeoff is a lessening of personal freedom for a higher disposable income. Lacking the traditional sources of natural comparative advantage, Singapore has sought to combine strategic location and investment in networked, knowledge-based industries. In that sense, the way in which it has achieved success constitutes a plausible blueprint for other newly industrialized or developing nations.

For a developing nation, as much as for a Fortune 500 corporation, the right choices and the allocation of scarce resources for optimum effect are partly a function of national intelligence capability. Porter's remarks on the importance of information analysis in the context of strategic planning have a special piquancy for developing nations; all too often information/intelligence management shortcomings result in governments' investing in structurally unattractive industries, thus squandering critical resources (PALVIA ET AL.; PORTER, 1990, p. 36). Along with the rapid globalization and liberalization of economic markets comes an additional set of pressures for third world countries. Currently more than three-quarters of the world's population lives in developing nations, most of which are weakly integrated with the global economy; their combined share of global trade is less than 17% (WORLD BANK). If that situation is to change, major infrastructural investment in information systems and services, as well as technical training, is required. At the most basic level, entry into the global economy requires high-grade techno-economic and market intelligence on, inter alia, standards, regulations, consumer preferences, competitor strategies, business styles, and strategies.

International trade can be viewed as a game (CRONIN, 1992b) with rules (e.g., manufacturing standards, negotiating styles, accounting procedures, and intellectual property legislation), referees (e.g., regulatory agencies, auditors, and trade conventions), and risks (e.g., financial, political, and entry/exit barriers). Increasingly, trade performance will be influenced by knowledge of the existing rules, referees, and risks, which in turn will depend on the quality of a country's coordinated intelligence capability. Whether a country is targeting specific industrial sectors for investment, rescheduling debts with creditor nations, negotiating with donor agencies or potential foreign direct investors, the cost of ignorance—intelligence blind spots (CRONIN, 1990)—can be crippling. For VENTURA (1988, p. 170) social intelligence in international relations is necessary to "discern the changing face of friends and disclose the interests of adversaries."

A critique by ONYANGO (1990) of Kenya's recent industrialization and technology transfer leads him to conclude that the country's already disadvantaged position is exacerbated by the lack of coordination and synthesis of government information, coupled with a persistent failure to capitalize on indigenous technological capability. However, the intelligence imperative is bidirectional because the donor agencies can fail to "'decode' the cultural DNA of a recipient country" (HENDERSON, 1989, p. 575), with the result that inappropriate projects are sponsored or appropriate projects are mismanaged; weak social intelligence capability leads to lost opportunity. Commenting on the situation in Latin America, SALINAS laments that economic liberalism has been imported without consideration of the great information demands that market economies pose and without a recognition that information is at the "centre of the international division of labour, with all its unequal terms and related crises" (p. 154). She illustrates her general observations on the underdevelopment of Latin American information systems and services with a detailed comparative analysis of the debt crisis of the early 1980s from an information management perspective.

According to Salinas, the contrast between the attitudes and expenditures of the creditor banks and the banking systems of the debtor nations was stark. In 1979 the Bank of America was spending $18.5

million on telecommunications and information services, while in 1984 four Latin American central banks spent a combined total of $2.6 million (SALINAS, p. 156). While their Latin American counterparts debated and discussed the options for greater information sharing, the major creditor banks established a cooperative venture in Washington, the Institute for International Finance (IIF), specifically to centralize the collection and exchange of relevant financial information. Unlike their counterparts in Latin America, the first world's bankers clearly grasped the leverage effect of fiscal, monetary, and economic intelligence in the context of international bargaining. As VENTURA (1988, p. 168) notes: "Equitable negotiations are largely determined by equitable knowledge."

However, asymmetries in information advantage—or "creative advantage," to use the language of HENDERSON (1989, p. 583)—are not restricted to the intercountry or interregional level; they can be seen operating within major industralized nations. To illustrate the point, HENDERSON (1989) describes the difficulties facing local officials in their attempts to lure major corporations to locate/relocate in their regions; the U.S. government alone has 25,000 agencies offering incentives of one kind or another. "Local officials can never win at such games in the global financial fast lane, since their responsibilities involve real people who must be trained or retrained and real facilities that must be built, whereas the corporate players and investors are operating at the speed of global electronic funds transfer, with no allegiance to any locality" (HENDERSON, 1989, p. 576).

Enterprise/Community Level

What applies at the aggregate level also applies at the enterprise/ community level. One of the first to articulate the relationship between strategic planning and the corporate intelligence function was Porter. In his classic work, *Competitive Strategy: Techniques for Analyzing Industries and Competitors* (PORTER, 1980), he identified the generic drivers of competition in an industry and proposed a suite of appropriate response strategies. His model includes a clear conceptual framework for competitor analysis along with guidelines for establishing an in-company competitor intelligence system under the direction of a competitor intelligence coordinator. Porter's ideas, directly or indirectly, have stimulated numerous reviews of current practice (e.g., LESTER & WATERS) and practical, step-by-step guides to competitor intelligence gathering and analysis (e.g., FULD; HERRING).

With the intensification of competitive pressures on manufacturing and service industries of all kinds, companies are taking competitor intelligence (CI) seriously. The CI function begins with broadcatching, the "process of collecting various kinds of data thought to be relevant—anything from trade rumors and financial statistics to product specifications and news of plant construction—and then selecting, interpreting, and presenting the data as information to be used in decision making. What generally separates competitive intelligence from basic market-share and product-tracking information is that in its highest form it has strategic import" (SUTTON, p. vii). The formation of the Society of Competitor Intelligence Professionals is one indicator of the gradual institutionalization of the function in the business sector. Another is the growth of articles in the general business, strategic planning, and business information literatures. Much current literature has been reviewed by COMBS & MOORHEAD. In addition, two notable overviews of current practice are *Competitive Information Programmes—A Research Report* (BRENNER) commissioned by EUSIDIC (European Association of Information Services) and, from the United States, the Conference Board's *Competitive Intelligence* (SUTTON), which includes a series of mini case studies of intelligence units in such companies as AT&T, Kraft, Motorola, Coors, and Pfizer.

Awareness of CI has percolated to special librarians in the corporate sector, who seem to have recognized the growing bandwidth of their functions. Certainly, GINMAN, CRONIN (1988), HÄMÄLÄINEN, and LAUNO clearly understand how changes in the conditions under which business is conducted will affect information strategies and functions within companies. One consequence of this trend is that traditional information taxonomies (e.g., internal vs. external, textual vs. numerical) simply do not capture the complexities of the real world.

In an information audit of the marketing and sales division of a major corporation, CRONIN & DAVENPORT (1990a; 1990c) suggested a threefold knowledge classification: (1) street, (2) terrain, and (3) horizon. Each category was characterized in terms of its primary source, time frame (i.e., useful life cycle), diffusion channel, and sales perspective (i.e., is the focus a specific deal with a named customer or a long-term sectoral analysis of possibilities?). Street knowledge is derived principally from the sales force and industry insiders and is often disseminated orally (rapid decay is a feature). Terrain knowledge is the consolidated knowhow of the sectoral/division managers, bolstered by rolling trend analyses and results from commissioned market research studies. Horizon knowledge is the stuff of strategic planning, in which the focus is long term and necessarily speculative. In short: "street knowledge comes from looking down at your feet, terrain knowledge from over your shoulder and horizon knowledge from looking ahead" (CRONIN & DAVENPORT, 1990c, p. 29). Contrary to the assumptions of many information professionals, street knowledge often has much greater value-in-use than either of the other categories, an observation reinforced by the evidence from Africa where pavement radio (*radio trottoir*) is preferred over official news media (ELLIS).

EDUCATION AND TRAINING

Can social intelligence be taught formally and included in academic programs? Intelligence skills, by their nature, present a paradox for educators because in many cases intelligence must be exclusive to be useful—i.e., it must be contained at the intradepartmental or intraenterprise level. There are two ways in which intelligence can be exclusive: (1) because of its source, or (2) because the analytic skills of those who process the raw intelligence furnish a particular perspective or interpretation. Although exclusivity is a local property, the factors that contribute to and confer exclusivity are neither exclusive nor local. Of course, an understanding of sources, access to sources, and analytic skills can all be taught.

Given the emphasis in social intelligence on informal communication, intuition, and reading between the lines (CRONIN & DAVENPORT, 1991) and given the covert nature of much intelligence work, how best can the area be incorporated into established curricula? In which schools or academic disciplines would it most comfortably find a niche, and where should the focus lie—on improving the social intelligence capability of the individual, of the organization, of the nation state, or of the trading bloc? As far as locus is concerned, plausible options are business, anthropology, cognitive science, social psychology, international relations, and information science programs. Each can stake a claim, and each can bring a particular dimension to the analysis and practice of intelligence management. PRESCOTT (p. 1), for example, does not see competitor intelligence as being the preserve of business schools. He believes that schools of library and information science are natural candidates for curricular innovation in CI because they have "an established tradition in this area." JONES discusses appropriate locations for the academic study of intelligence. He suggests that the methods of historians are close to those of intelligence officers and the methods of operations research can help with assessing the effectiveness of systems. He also believes that monitoring developments in information technology is important and that business studies, politics, international relations, and geography can provide useful information on surveillance and methods. Our own perception is that social intelligence draws on different subject areas and specialists skills and is thus likely to fit best in academic disciplines that are natural boundary spanners, like communications or library and information science. As a component of a course on Strategic Information and Intelligence Management currently taught in the School of Library and

Information Science at Indiana University, social intelligence is presented as a broad-based envelope for the more narrowly focused and structured approach of information management. Students are alerted to a wider range of sources and techniques than would be implied in a traditional information management or librarianship course. These include discourse and network analysis, rumor validation, transcultural negotiation, and content analysis of informal communications, all of which are deployed in project work.

Whether the focus should be at the individual or collective level depends very much on local conditions and requirements, which, in turn, will influence the literature base that is used. Much of the work on augmenting the social intelligence of the individual appears in the literature of child psychology and deviance; for example, the work of GARDNER (1983; 1993) is the basis of programs for socialization (WINN) that encourage the reading of cues and mutually beneficial interaction. On a larger scale, Venezuela initiated a major national program to improve the intelligence of school children in the 1980s. Such skills are the basis of adult programs and practices designed to mitigate cultural shock (HALL). For instance, a salient literature set exists on how to do business with the Japanese (MCLEOD).

At the level of the firm, many of these skills can be found in the marketing, public relations, and advertising departments of large corporations, KOTLER being one of the first to demonstrate the benefits of megamarketing and strategic philanthropy. One traditional path for acquiring such skills is through military education; in the post-cold war era, the scope for privatization of the intelligence function is considerable; the DEFENSE INTELLIGENCE COLLEGE actually offers an accredited M.S. degree in strategic intelligence. At present the military does not make its courses commercially available, but it has never been difficult to obtain the services of their graduates.

CONVERGENCE OF THEORIES

We have tried to show that social intelligence has a diverse history and that current use of the term can be traced across a range of disciplines and publications. By examining the subject here, we wish to address more than the porosity of the information science field, an issue explored by one of the authors elsewhere (CRONIN & PEARSON). The literature of social intelligence reflects a manifest convergence of contemporary organizational philosophies, economic models, policy initiatives, and electronic platforms. To date, rhetorical response has been mixed: some have hailed such convergence as a cusp in the evolution of human intelligence and societal development (DEDIJER; DREXLER, 1991), a tradition that can be traced back as far as Bush (BUSH; SMITH);

others have condemned it as nothing less than a faustian mix (DREYFUS & DREYFUS; ROSZAK; SCHILLER; SIMONS). The primary focus of this chapter is not, however, the macrorhetoric but what has been observed in, or proposed for, working environments.

Have we simply selected, reshuffled, and relabeled topics previously covered by *ARIST*, or have we identified a new paradigm? At first sight, it may seem more appropriate to treat social intelligence as a lens rather than as a field with its own proprietary literature like information management or information science. The use of the term allows the reader to adjust the resolution of certain literatures and perceive significance and make connections previously undetected. Another approach is to present social intelligence as an extension of information science: core skills, such as sourcing, validating, collating, analyzing, and synthesizing, applied in any environment and at any level of aggregation, not simply formally recorded information.

However, why should a new lens or an extension of traditional thinking be required in the late 20th century? First, globalization implies heightened mobility, international competition, and greater environmental uncertainty. Survivors must acquire the skills and flexibility associated with social intelligence. For less-developed countries, techno-economic intelligence is a particularly important factor in national strategic planning (CRONIN, 1992a). Second, networks now impinge on all areas of social interaction, from joint exploration of soap operas on Prodigy to Internet-mediated collaboration in highly specialized scientific fields. Such networks are much more than message channels; participants must understand the social norms and codes ("netiquette") that characterize special interest groups. Third, social intelligence can empower those who may be threatened or oppressed by faceless and bureaucratic control systems; an understanding of local terrain and conditions and of status within that space is, after all, the basis of active citizenship. Such "self-management and information-sharing networks" have been described by YAMAGUCHI (p. 1033) as "the most essential features of the information age." He posits "infonomics" as a new science to address these issues. Recent legislation for the library literacy program uses "literacy" in a similar fashion: "an individual's ability to read, write, and speak in English, compute and solve problems at levels of proficiency necessary to function on the job and in society; to achieve one's goals; and to develop one's knowledge and potential" (*FEDERAL REGISTER*, p. 49265). This mission statement, in defining the library as a social intelligence agency, reiterates the 1924 vision of LEARNED.

With its emphasis on action and multisourcing, social intelligence appears to meet the criteria put forward by WERSIG (p. 201) in his presentation of information science as a "new/postmodern" science. He claims that this "strategy-driven science. . .will not become a discipline but has to find another organizational scheme." Social intelligence as presented in this chapter, and as implied by Dedijer's phrase, "an intelligence science," is an instance of what Wersig calls "inter-concepts," that is, concepts that "constitute something like magnets or attractors, sucking the focus-oriented materials out of the disciplines and restructuring them within the information scientific framework" (WERSIG, p. 215).

In this chapter, concepts and techniques have been drawn from a range of disciplines in an effort to instantiate an inter-concept. To summarize, social intelligence is both a multidimensional and a multifaceted construct: process, product, and potential are combined. It implies skills in gathering, decoding, analyzing, and applying intelligence for effective action and in using techniques and technologies that come from various fields and contexts, some of which can be learned only from experience. Social intelligence also entails knowledge of the environment, proprietary knowhow, and the ability to access stocks of raw and processed intelligence. Finally, social intelligence is synonymous with a high level of social interaction skills, an ability to negotiate the rules of the game, and a high level of self-awareness. It is not, however, a concept that succumbs to ready definition; if it were, its usefulness as a synthesizing agent would be virtually nil.

BIBLIOGRAPHY

ALDRICH, MICHAEL. 1982. Videotex: Key to the Wired City. London, England: Quiller Press; 1982. 115p. ISBN: 0-907621-12-0.

ALLEN, PETER M. 1988. Evolution, Innovation and Economics. In: Dosi, Giovanni, ed. Technical Change and Economic Theory. Dover, NH: Frances Pinter Publishers; 1988. 95-119. ISBN: 0-86187-949-X.

ALLEN, THOMAS J. 1971. Communication Networks in R&D Laboratories. R&D Management. 1971; 1(1): 14-21. ISSN: 0033-6807.

ANNERSTEDT, JAN; JAMISON, ANDREW, eds. 1988. From Research Policy to Social Intelligence: Essays for Stevan Dedijer. Basingstoke, England: Macmillan; 1988. 181p. ISBN: 0-333-45275-5.

ANTONOPOULOS, ANNA. 1992. The Guiles of Corporate Culture, Part II: Learning the Art of Action. The Intelligent Enterprise. 1992; 1(11/12): 20-23. OCLC: 23858657.

BAIRD, PATRICIA M.; CRONIN, BLAISE; DAVENPORT, ELISABETH. 1991. Hypertext and Added Value. In: Brown, Heather, ed. Hypermedia/Hypertext and Object-oriented Databases. London, England: Chapman & Hall; 1991. 71-90. (UNICOM Applied Information Technology, v. 8). ISBN: 0-412-39970-9.

BAIRD, PATRICIA M.; PERCIVAL, MARK. 1989. Glasgow On-line: Database Development Using Apple's HyperCard. In: McAleese, Ray, ed. Hypertext: Theory and Practice. Norwood, NJ: Ablex Publishing Corp.; 1989. 75-92. ISBN: 0-89391-575-0.

BAUMARD, PHILIPPE. 1991. Toward Less Deceptive Intelligence. Social Intelligence. 1991; 1(3): 179-190. ISSN: 0961-2882.

BEER, STAFFORD. 1979. The Heart of the Enterprise. New York, NY: John Wiley & Sons; 1979. 582p. ISBN: 0-471-27599-9.

BEER, STAFFORD. 1981. Brain of the Firm. 2nd edition. New York, NY: John Wiley & Sons; 1981. 417p. ISBN: 0-471-27687-1.

BEER, STAFFORD. 1985. Diagnosing the System for Organizations. New York, NY: John Wiley & Sons; 1985. 152p. ISBN: 0-471-90675-1.

BLANC, GÉRARD. 1987. The Grain Traders: Masters of the Intelligence Game. In: Dedijer, Stevan; Jéquier, Nicolas, eds. Intelligence for Economic Development: An Inquiry into the Role of the Knowledge Industry. Oxford, England: Berg; 1987. 139-157. ISBN: 0-85496-520-3.

BOLAND, RICHARD J. 1987. The In-formation of Information Systems. In: Boland, Richard J.; Hirschheim, R.A., eds. Critical Issues in Information Systems Research. New York, NY: John Wiley & Sons; 1987. 363-379. ISBN: 0-471-91281-6.

BORENSTEIN, NATHANIEL S. 1992. Computational Mail as Network Infrastructure for Computer-Supported Cooperative Work. In: Turner, Jon; Kraut, Robert, eds. CSCW '92: Sharing Perspectives: Proceedings of the Conference on Computer-Supported Cooperative Work; 1992 October 31-November 4; Toronto, Canada. New York, NY: Association for Computing Machinery; 1992. 67-73. ISBN: 0-89791-542-9.

BORGMAN, CHRISTINE L., ed. 1990. Scholarly Communication and Bibliometrics. Newbury Park, CA: Sage Publications; 1990. 363p. ISBN: 0-8039-3879-9.

BRAND, STEWART. 1988. The Media Lab: Inventing the Future at MIT. New York, NY: Penguin Books; 1988. 285p. ISBN: 0-14-009701-5.

BRAUNSTEIN, YALE M. 1985. Information as a Factor of Production: Substitutability and Productivity. Information Society. 1985; 3(3): 261-273. ISSN: 0197-2243.

BRENNER, EVERETT H. 1991. Competitive Information Programmes—A Research Report: EUSIDIC (European Association of Information Services) Research Report 1990-91. Calne, Wiltshire, England: EUSIDIC; 1991.

BREWER, DEVON D. 1992. Hip Hop Graffiti Writers' Evaluation of Strategies to Control Illegal Graffiti. Human Organization. 1992; 51(2): 188-196. ISSN: 0018-7259.

BROADBENT, MARIANNE; KOENIG, MICHAEL E.D. 1988. Information and Information Technology Management. In: Williams, Martha E., ed. Annual Review of Information Science and Technology: Volume 23. Amsterdam, The Netherlands: Elsevier Science Publishers for the American Society for Information Science; 1988. 237-270. ISSN: 0066-4200; ISBN: 0-444-70543-0.

BROMLEY, D. ALAN. 1989. Position Statement. In: The Federal High Performance Computing Program. Washington, DC: Executive Office of the President, Office of Science and Technology Policy; 1989 September 8. (unnumbered opening page). SUDOCS: PrEx 23.2:C73/1x.

BRUCE, PETER. 1985. Body to Be Exhumed in Brazil May Be Mengele. Financial Times. 1985 June 7; 2. ISSN: 0307-1766.

BUCKLEY, WILLIAM F. 1984. Introduction. In: Hart, Benjamin. Poisoned Ivy. New York, NY: Stein and Day; 1984. 7-10. ISBN: 0-8128-2990-5.

BUSH, VANNEVAR. 1945. As We May Think. Atlantic Monthly. 1945; 176(1): 101-108. ISSN: 0004-6795.

BUZZELL, ROBERT D. 1987. The PIMS Principles: Linking Strategy to Performance. New York, NY: Free Press; 1987. 322p. ISBN: 0-02-904430-8.

CAPURRO, RAFAEL. 1992. What Is Information Science For? A Philosophical Reflection. In: Vakkari, Pertti; Cronin, Blaise, eds. Conceptions of Library and Information Science: Historical, Empirical and Theoretical Perspectives. London, England: Taylor Graham; 1992. 82-96. ISBN: 0-947568-52-2.

CAWKELL, TONY. 1991. Using the Science Citation Index for Intelligence-Gathering. The Intelligent Enterprise. 1991 November/December; 1(9/10): 28-32. LC: 91-640728; OCLC: 23858657.

CHECKLAND, PETER; SCHOLES, JIM. 1990. Soft Systems Methodology in Action. New York, NY: John Wiley & Sons; 1990. 329p. ISBN: 0-471-92768-6.

CIBORRA, CLAUDIO U. 1987. Research Agenda for a Transaction Costs Approach to Information Systems. In: Boland, Richard J.; Hirschheim, R.A., eds. Critical Issues in Information Systems Research. New York, NY: John Wiley & Sons; 1987. 253-274. ISBN: 0-471-91281-6.

COMBS, RICHARD E.; MOORHEAD, JOHN D. 1992. The Competitive Intelligence Handbook. Metuchen, NJ: Scarecrow Press; 1992. 187p. ISBN: 0-8108-2606-2.

COMPETITIVE INTELLIGENCE REVIEW. 1990-. Hohhoff, Bonnie, ed. Washington, DC: Society of Competitive Intelligence Professionals. ISSN: 1058-0247.

COOPER, M.D. 1983. The Structure and Future of the Information Economy. Information Processing & Management. 1983; 19(1): 9-26. ISSN: 0306-4573.

CRONIN, BLAISE. 1988. New Horizons for the Information Profession: Strategic Intelligence and Competitive Advantage. In: Dyer, H.; Tseng, G., eds. New Horizons for the Information Profession: Meeting the Challenge of Change. London, England: Taylor Graham; 1988. 3-22. ISBN: 0-947568-32-8.

CRONIN, BLAISE. 1990. Blind Spots and Opaque Terrains. See reference: CRONIN, BLAISE; TUDOR-ŠILOVIĆ, NEVA, eds. 1990. 1-3.

CRONIN, BLAISE. 1991. What Is Social about Social Intelligence? Social Intelligence. 1991; 1(2): 137-145. ISSN: 0961-2882.

CRONIN, BLAISE. 1992a. Information and Market Integration in Latin America. Journal of Economic and Social Intelligence. 1992; 2(3): 233-243. ISSN: 0961-2882.

CRONIN, BLAISE. 1992b. Intelligence Management Systems for Intelligent Corporations. In: Sigurdson, Jon; Tågerud, Yael, eds. The Intelligent Corporation: The Privatisation of Intelligence. London, England: Taylor Graham; 1992. 143-159. ISBN: 0-947568-55-7.

CRONIN, BLAISE. 1992c. Playing the Intellectual Capital Markets: The Conditions of Flight and Formation. In: Cronin, Blaise; Tudor-Šilović,

Neva, eds. From Information Management to Social Intelligence: The Key to Open Markets. London, England: Aslib; 1992. 1-12. ISBN: 0-85142-284-5.

CRONIN, BLAISE; DAVENPORT, ELISABETH. 1990a. Laptops and the Marketing Information Chain: The Benefits of Salesforce Automation. International Journal of Information Management. 1990; 10(4): 278-287. ISSN: 0268-4012.

CRONIN, BLAISE; DAVENPORT, ELISABETH. 1990b. Social Intelligence as a Means of Bridging the Development Gap: A Conference Report. Bulletin of the American Society for Information Science. 1990; 17(1): 10-12. ISSN: 0095-4403.

CRONIN, BLAISE; DAVENPORT, ELISABETH. 1990c. Strategic Information Management. In: Cronin, Blaise; Klein, Stefan, eds. Informationsmanagement und Forschung [Information Management in Science and Research]. Braunschweig, Germany: Friedrich Vieweg & Sohn; 1990. 25-39. ISBN: 3-528-05114-0.

CRONIN, BLAISE; DAVENPORT, ELISABETH. 1991. The Compound Eye/I: An Introduction to Social Intelligence. Social Intelligence. 1991; 1(1): 1-6. ISSN: 0961-2882.

CRONIN, BLAISE; PEARSON, STEPHEN. 1990. The Export of Ideas from Information Science. Journal of Information Science. 1990; 16(6): 381-391. ISSN: 0165-5515.

CRONIN, BLAISE; TUDOR-ŠILOVIĆ, NEVA, eds. 1990. The Knowledge Industries: Levers of Economic and Social Development in the 1990s: Proceedings of an International Conference Held at the Inter-University Centre for Postgraduate Studies; 1989 May 29-June 3; Dubrovnik, Yugoslavia. London, England: Aslib; 1990. 332p. ISBN: 0-85142-266-7.

CRONIN, BLAISE; TUDOR-ŠILOVIĆ, NEVA, eds. 1992. From Information Management to Social Intelligence: The Key to Open Markets. London, England: Aslib; 1992. 110p. ISBN: 0-85142-284-5.

CUBILLO, JULIO. 1992. Techno-Economic Intelligence (INTELL): What's in It for Developing Countries? Journal of Economic and Social Intelligence. 1992; 2(2): 123-148. ISSN: 0961-2882.

DAVENPORT, ELISABETH. 1991. The World in a Grain of Sand. In: Advanced Information Systems: The New Technologies in Today's Business Environment: Proceedings of the 6th International Expert Systems Conference; 1991 March 19-21; London, England. Oxford, England: Learned Information; 1991. 111-118. ISBN: 0-904933-78-4.

DAVENPORT, ELISABETH. 1992a. Preparing the Ground for Business: The Development and Management of Frames of Reference. In: Cronin, Blaise; Tudor-Šilović, Neva, eds. From Information Management to Social Intelligence: The Key to Open Markets. London, England: Aslib; 1992. 43-52. ISBN: 0-85142-284-5.

DAVENPORT, ELISABETH. 1992b. What Do We Look at When We Do Information Science? In: Vakkari, Pertti; Cronin, Blaise, eds. Conceptions of Library and Information Science: Historical, Empirical and Theoretical Perspectives. London, England: Taylor Graham; 1992. 286-298. ISBN: 0-947568-52-2.

DAVENPORT, ELISABETH; BAIRD, PATRICIA M. 1992. Hypertext '91: A Bibliometric Briefing. Hypermedia. 1992; 2(4): 123-134. ISSN: 0955-8543.

DAVENPORT, ELISABETH; CRONIN, BLAISE. 1988. Strategic Information Management: Forging the Value Chain. International Journal of Information Management. 1988; 8(1): 25-34. ISSN: 0268-4012.

DAVENPORT, ELISABETH; CRONIN, BLAISE. 1990. Hypertext and the Conduct of Science. Journal of Documentation. 1990 September; 46(3): 175-192. ISSN: 0022-0418.

DAVENPORT, ELISABETH; CRONIN, BLAISE. 1991. The Virtual Apprentice. Journal of Information Science. 1991; 17(1): 65-70. ISSN: 0165-5515.

DAVISS, BENNETT. 1991. Knowbots. Discover. 1991 April; 12(4): 21-23. ISSN: 0274-7529.

DAWKINS, RICHARD. 1986. The Power and the Archives. In: Dawkins, Richard. The Blind Watchmaker. New York, NY: Norton; 1986. 111-137. ISBN: 0-393-02216-1.

DE SOTO, HERNANDO. 1989. The Other Path: The Invisible Revolution in the Third World. New York, NY: Harper & Row; 1989. 271p. ISBN: 0-06-016020-9.

DEBES, CHERYL. 1986. Multinationals vs. the Snoops. Business Week. 1986 June 23; 30-33. ISSN: 0007-7135.

DEDIJER, STEVAN. 1991. Does IBM Know What Business It Is In? Social Intelligence. 1991; 1(2): 121-136. ISSN: 0961-2882.

DEDIJER, STEVAN; JÉQUIER, NICOLAS, eds. 1987. Intelligence for Economic Development: An Inquiry into the Role of the Knowledge Industry. Oxford, England: Berg; 1987. 264p. ISBN: 0-85496-520-3.

DEFENSE INTELLIGENCE COLLEGE. 1991. Defense Intelligence College Catalog: Academic Year 1991-92. Washington, DC: Defense Intelligence College; 1991. 77p. SUDOCS: D 5.210:991-92.

DEMPSEY, LORCAN. 1992. Libraries, Networks, and OSI: A Review, with a Report on North American Developments. Westport, CT: Meckler; 1992. 232p. ISBN: 0-88736-818-2.

DOCTOR, RONALD D. 1992. Social Equity and Information Technologies: Moving toward Information Democracy. In: Williams, Martha E., ed. Annual Review of Information Science and Technology: Volume 27. Medford, NJ: Learned Information for the American Society for Information Science; 1992. 43-96. ISSN: 0066-4200; ISBN: 0-938734-66-0.

DREXLER, K. ERIC. 1986. Engines of Creation. Garden City, NY: Anchor Press/Doubleday; 1986. 298p. ISBN: 0-385-19972-2.

DREXLER, K. ERIC. 1991. Hypertext Publishing and the Evolution of Knowledge. Social Intelligence. 1991; 1(2): 87-120. ISSN: 0961-2882.

DREYFUS, HUBERT L.; DREYFUS, STUART E. 1988. Making a Mind versus Modeling the Brain: Artificial Intelligence Back at a Branchpoint. In: Graubard, Stephen R., ed. The Artificial Intelligence Debate: False Starts, Real Foundations. Cambridge, MA: The MIT Press; 1988. 15-43. ISBN: 0-262-57074-2.

DUMAINE, BRIAN. 1988. Corporate Spies Snoop to Conquer. Fortune. 1988 November 7; 118(11): 66-68, 70. ISSN: 0015-8259.

DURANT, ALAN. 1991. "Intelligence": Issues in a Word or in a Field? Social Intelligence. 1991; 1(3): 171-178. ISSN: 0961-2882.

ELLIS, STEPHEN. 1989. Tuning in to Pavement Radio. African Affairs. 1989 July; 88(352): 321-330. ISSN: 0001-9909.

ENGELBART, DOUGLAS C.; ENGLISH, WILLIAM K. 1968. A Research Center for Augmenting Human Intellect. In: Proceedings of the American Federation of Information Processing Societies (AFIPS) Fall Joint Computer Conference: Volume 33; 1968 December 9-11; San Francisco, CA. Washington, DC: Thompson Book Company: 1968. 295-410. LC: 55-44701.

ENGELBART, DOUGLAS C.; HOOPER, KRISTINA. 1988. The Augmentation System Framework. In: Ambron, Sueann; Hooper, Kristina, eds. Interactive Multimedia. Redmond, WA: Microsoft Press; 1988. 15-31. ISBN: 1-55615-124-1.

ENGELBART, DOUGLAS C.; WATSON, RICHARD W.; NORTON, JAMES C. 1973. The Augmented Knowledge Workshop. In: Proceedings of the American Federation of Information Processing Societies (AFIPS) National Computer Conference and Exposition: Volume 42; 1973 June 4-8; New York, NY. Montvale, NJ: AFIPS Press; 1973. 9-21. ISSN: 0095-6880.

FEDERAL REGISTER. 1992. Department of Education: Library Literacy Program. Federal Register. 1992 October 30; 57 (211): 49263-49270. ISSN: 0097-6326.

FIELDING, NIGEL G.; LEE, RAYMOND M., eds. 1991. Using Computers in Qualitative Research. Newbury Park, CA: Sage Publications; 1991. 216p. ISBN: 0-8039-8424-3.

FISH, ROBERT; KRAUT, ROBERT. 1992. Audio/Video Networks for Collaboration: Tutorial Notes: CSCW '92: Association for Computing Machinery 1992 Conference on Computer-Supported Cooperative Work; 1992 October 31-November 4; Toronto, Canada. 50p. Available from: Association for Computing Machinery, 1515 Broadway, New York, NY 10036.

FULD, LEONARD M. 1988. Monitoring the Competition: Find Out What's Really Going on Over There. New York, NY: John Wiley & Sons; 1988. 204p. ISBN: 0-471-85261-9.

GALEN, MICHELE. 1991. Should the CIA Start Spying for Corporate America? Business Week. 1991 October 14; 96-97. ISSN: 0007-7135.

GARDNER, HOWARD. 1983. Frames of Mind: The Theory of Multiple Intelligences. New York, NY: Basic Books; 1983. 440p. ISBN: 0-465-02508-0.

GARDNER, HOWARD. 1993. Multiple Intelligences: The Theory in Practice. New York, NY: Basic Books; 1993. 304p. ISBN: 0-465-01821-1.

GARFINKEL, HAROLD. 1967. Studies in Ethnomethodology. Englewood Cliffs, NJ: Prentice-Hall; 1967. 288p. LC: 67-22565.

GARVEY, WILLIAM D.; GRIFFITH, BELVER C. 1966. Studies of Social Innovations in Scientific Communities in Psychology. American Psychologist. 1966 November; 21: 1019-1036. ISSN: 0003-066X.

GEERTZ, CLIFFORD. 1973. Thick Description: Toward an Interpretive Theory of Culture. In: Geertz, Clifford. The Interpretation of Cultures. New York, NY: Basic Books; 1973. 3-30. ISBN: 0-465-03425-X.

GELERNTER, DAVID. 1989. The Metamorphosis of Information Management. Scientific American. 1989 August; 261(2): 54-61. ISSN: 0036-8733.

GELERNTER, DAVID. 1992. Mirror Worlds or the Day Software Puts the Universe in a Shoebox: How It Will Happen and What It Will Mean. New York, NY: Oxford University Press; 1992. 237p. ISBN: 0-19-506812-2.

GEORGE, SUSAN. 1988. A Fate Worse Than Debt. New York, NY: Grove Press; 1988. 292p. ISBN: 0-8021-1015-0.

GINMAN, MIRIAM. 1988. Information Culture and Business Performance. IATUL Quarterly. 1988; 2(2): 93-106. ISSN: 0950-4117.

GLASER, BARNEY G.; STRAUSS, ANSELM L. 1967. The Discovery of Grounded Theory: Strategies for Qualitative Research. New York, NY: Aldine de Gruyter; 1967. 271p. ISBN: 0-202-30028-5.

GOUINLOCK, JAMES. 1986. Excellence in Public Discourse: John Stuart Mill, John Dewey, and Social Intelligence. New York, NY: Teachers College Press; 1986. 173p. ISBN: 0-8077-2825-X.

GREGORY, DIK. 1991. Corporate Hypertext: A Grand Design. In: Advanced Information Systems: The New Technologies in Today's Business Environment: Proceedings of the 6th International Expert Systems Conference; 1991 March 19-21; London, England. Oxford, England: Learned Information; 1991. 119-124. ISBN: 0-904933-78-4.

GREIF, IRENE, ed. 1988. Computer-Supported Cooperative Work: A Book of Readings. San Mateo, CA: Morgan Kaufmann; 1988. 783p. ISBN: 0-934613-57-5.

GRIFFITHS, JOSÉ-MARIE. 1992. Self-Documenting Systems: A Role for Machine-Aided Indexing. In: Raitt, David I., ed. Online Information 92: Proceedings of the 16th International Online Information Meeting; 1992 December 8-10; London, England. Medford, NJ: Learned Information; 1992. 291-296. ISBN: 0-904933-83-0.

GRIMES, WILLIAM. 1992. Computer Networks Foster Cultural Chatting for Modem Times. New York Times. 1992 December 1; B1, B4. ISSN: 0362-4331.

GRUNDNER, TOM. 1992. Whose Internet Is It Anyway?—A Challenge. Online. 1992 July; 16(4): 6-10. ISSN: 0146-5422.

GUBA, EGON G.; LINCOLN, YVONNA S. 1989. Fourth Generation Evaluation. Newbury Park, CA: Sage Publications; 1989. 294p. ISSN: 0-8039-3235-9.

HALL, EDWARD T. 1976. Beyond Culture. Garden City, NY: Anchor Press; 1976. 256p. ISBN: 0-385-08747-0.

HÄMÄLÄINEN, PATRICIA. 1990. Niche Products for the Manager. In: Wormell, Irene, ed. Information Quality: Definition and Dimensions. London, England: Taylor Graham; 1990. 34-41. ISBN: 0-947568-43-3.

HARCOURT, ALEXANDER H. 1988. Alliances in Contests and Social Intelligence. In: Byrne, Richard W.; Whiten, Andrew, eds. Machiavellian Intelligence: Social Expertise and the Evolution of Intelligence in Monkeys, Apes, and Humans. New York, NY: Oxford University Press; 1988. 132-152. ISBN: 0-19-852179-0.

HARRIS, KEVIN. 1991. Information and Social Change in the 1990s. International Journal of Information & Library Research. 1991; 3(1): 75-85. ISSN: 0953-556X.

HAYES, ROBERT M.; ERICKSON, TIMOTHY. 1982. Added Value as a Function of Purchases of Information Services. Information Society. 1982; 1(4): 307-338. ISSN: 0197-2243.

HENDERSON, HAZEL. 1973a. Ecologists versus Economists. Harvard Business Review. 1973 July-August; 51(4): 28-36, 152-157. ISSN: 0017-8012.

HENDERSON, HAZEL. 1973b. The Limits of Traditional Economics: New Models for Managing a "Steady State Economy." Financial Analysts Journal. 1973 May-June; 29: 28-32, 79-87. ISSN: 0015-198X.

HENDERSON, HAZEL. 1989. Mutual Development: Towards New Criteria and Indicators. Futures. 1989 December; 21(6): 571-584. ISSN: 0016-3287.

HERMAN, MICHAEL. 1992. Governmental Intelligence: Its Evolution and Role. Journal of Economic and Social Intelligence. 1992; 2(2): 91-113. ISSN: 0961-2882.

HERRING, JAN P. 1992. The Unique Role of the Future in Intelligence. In: Sigurdson, Jon; Tågerud, Yael, eds. The Intelligent Corporation: The Privatisation of Intelligence. London, England: Taylor Graham; 1992. 161-181. ISBN: 0-947568-55-7.

HILLIS, W. DANIEL. 1985. The Connection Machine. Cambridge, MA: MIT Press; 1985. 190p. ISBN: 0-262-08157-1.

HINDUS, DEBBY; SCHMANDT, CHRIS. 1992. Ubiquitous Audio: Capturing Spontaneous Collaboration. In: Turner, Jon; Kraut, Robert, eds. CSCW '92: Sharing Perspectives: Proceedings of the Conference on Computer-Supported Cooperative Work; 1992 October 31-November 4; Toronto, Canada. New York, NY: Association for Computing Machinery; 1992. 210-217. ISBN: 0-89791-542-9.

HOUSEL, THOMAS J.; DAVIDSON, WILLIAM H. 1991. The Development of Information Services in France: The Case of Public Videotex. International Journal of Information Management. 1991 March; 11(1): 35-54. ISSN: 0268-4012.

HUFF, ANNE SIGISMUND, ed. 1990. Mapping Strategic Thought. New York, NY: John Wiley & Sons; 1990. 426p. ISBN: 0-471-92632-9.

HULNICK, ARTHUR S. 1991/92. Intelligence Cooperation in the Post-Cold War Era: A New Game Plan? International Journal of Intelligence and Counterintelligence. 1991/92 Winter; 5(4): 455-465. ISSN: 0885-0607.

HUMPHREY, NICHOLAS K. 1988. The Social Function of Intellect. In: Byrne, Richard W.; Whiten, Andrew, eds. Machiavellian Intelligence: Social Expertise and the Evolution of Intelligence in Monkeys, Apes, and Humans. New York, NY: Oxford University Press; 1988. 13-26. ISBN: 0-19-852179-0.

HUNT, THELMA. 1928. The Measurement of Social Intelligence. Journal of Applied Psychology. 1928; 12(3): 317-334. ISSN: 0021-9010.

INTELLIGENCE AND NATIONAL SECURITY. 1986-. Brown, F. Reese, ed. London, England: Frank Cass & Co. ISSN: 0268-4527.

THE INTELLIGENT ENTERPRISE. 1991-1992. Wyllie, Jan, ed. London, England: Aslib. LC: 91-640728; OCLC: 23858657.

INTERNATIONAL JOURNAL OF INTELLIGENCE AND COUNTERINTEL-LIGENCE. 1986-. Brown, F. Reese, ed. Stroudsburg, PA: Intel Publishing Group. ISSN: 0885-0607.

IRVINE, JOHN; MARTIN, BEN R.   1984.   Foresight in Science: Picking the Winners. Dover, NH: Frances Pinter; 1984. 166p. ISBN: 0-86187-496-X.

JAMES, BARRIE G.   1984.   Business Wargames.   New York, NY: Viking Penguin; 1984. 234p. ISBN: 0-14-008104-6.

JÉQUIER, NICOLAS; DEDIJER, STEVAN.   1987. Information, Knowledge and Intelligence: A General Overview.   In: Dedijer, Stevan; Jéquier, Nicolas, eds.   Intelligence for Economic Development: An Inquiry into the Role of the Knowledge Industry.   Oxford, England: Berg; 1987.   1-23.   ISBN: 0-85496-520-3.

JOLLY, ALISON.   1966.   Lemur Social Behavior and Primate Intelligence. Science. 1966; 153: 501-506. ISSN: 0036-8075.

JONES, REGINALD V.   1992.   Intelligence as an Academic Discipline.   In: Sigurdson, Jon; Tågerud, Yael, eds.   The Intelligent Corporation: The Privatisation of Intelligence. London, England: Taylor Graham; 1992. 71-80. ISBN: 0-947568-55-7.

JOURNAL OF ECONOMIC AND SOCIAL INTELLIGENCE. 1992-. Cronin, Blaise, ed. London, England: Taylor Graham. ISSN: 0961-2882.

KAPOR, MITCHELL.   1991.   Civil Liberties in Cyberspace: When Does Hacking Turn from an Exercise of Civil Liberties into Crime?   Scientific American. 1991 September; 265(3): 158-164. ISSN: 0036-8733.

KAY, ALAN C. 1990. User Interface: A Personal View. In: Laurel, Brenda, ed. The Art of Human-Computer Interface Design. Reading, MA: Addison-Wesley Publishing; 1990. 191-207. ISBN: 0-201-51797-3.

KAY, HELEN. 1990. Corporate Cops at the Keyhole: Minder or Management? Management Today. 1990 June; 90-93. ISSN: 0025-1925.

KEEN, PETER G.W.   1991.   Shaping the Future: Business Design through Information Technology. Cambridge, MA: Harvard Business School Press; 1991. 264p. ISBN: 0-87584-237-2.

KENT, SHERMAN.   1949.   Strategic Intelligence for American World Policy. Princeton, NJ: Princeton University Press; 1949. 226p. LC: 49-8503.

KING, DONALD; GRIFFITHS, JOSÉ-MARIE.   1991.   Indicators of the Use, Usefulness and Value of Scientific and Technical Information.   In: Raitt, David I., ed. Online Information 91: Proceedings of the 15th International Online Information Meeting; 1991 December 10-12; London, England. Medford, NJ: Learned Information; 1991. 361-377. ISBN: 0-904933-79-2.

KNORR-CETINA, KARIN D. 1981. The Manufacture of Knowledge. Elmsford, NY: Pergamon Press; 1981. 189p. ISBN: 0-08-025777-1.

KNORR-CETINA, KARIN D.; MULKAY, MICHAEL, eds.   1983.   Science Observed: Perspectives on the Social Study of Science. Beverly Hills, CA: Sage Publications; 1983. 272p. ISBN: 0-8039-9782-5.

KNOWLEDGE AND POLICY. 1988-. Dunn, William N., ed. New Brunswick, NJ: Transaction Publishers. ISSN: 0897-1986.

KOENIG, MICHAEL E.D.   1990.   Information Services and Downstream Productivity. In: Williams, Martha E., ed. Annual Review of Information Science and Technology: Volume 25.   Amsterdam, The Netherlands: Elsevier Science Publishers for the American Society for Information Science; 1990. 55-86. ISSN: 0066-4200; ISBN: 0-444-88531-5.

KOTLER, PHILIP. 1986. Megamarketing, or Breaking into Blocked Markets. Harvard Business Review. 1986 March-April; 64: 117-124. ISSN: 0017-8012.

KRACKHARDT, DAVID. 1989. Graph Theoretical Dimensions of Informal Organizations. Paper presented at: National Meeting of the Academy of Management; 1989 August; Washington, DC. 43p. Available from: the author, Graduate School of Business Administration, Harvard Business School, Soldiers Field, Boston, MA 02163.

KROL, ED. 1992. The Whole Internet: User's Guide & Catalog. Sebastopol, CA: O'Reilly & Associates; 1992. 376p. ISBN: 1-56592-025-2.

LAMBERTON, DONALD M. 1984. The Economics of Information and Organization. In: Williams, Martha E., ed. Annual Review of Information Science and Technology: Volume 19. White Plains, NY: Knowledge Industry Publications for the American Society for Information Science; 1984. 3-30. ISSN: 0066-4200; ISBN: 0-86729-093-5.

LAMBERTON, DONALD M. 1990. Information Economics: "Threatened Wreckage" Or New Paradigm? 1990. 12p. (CIRCIT (Centre for International Research on Communication and Information Technologies) Working Paper 1990/1). Available from: CIRCIT Ltd., 1st floor, Riverside Quay, 4 Byrne Street, South Melbourne, Australia. ISSN: 1035-5537.

LATOUR, BRUNO; WOOLGAR, STEVE. 1979. Laboratory Life: The Social Construction of Scientific Facts. Beverly Hills, CA: Sage Publications; 1979. 294p. (Sage Library of Social Research). ISBN: 0-8039-0993-4.

LAUNO, RITVA. 1992. Changes in Industry and World Economy: From IRM Organisation into Knowledge Creating Company. In: Adler, Karin; Helmer, Erik; Holm, Hans I., eds. Teknologi och Kompetens: Proceedings from the 8th Nordic Conference on Information and Documentation; 1992 May 19-21; Helsingborg, Sweden. Stockholm, Sweden: Tekniska Litteratursällskapet; 1992. 27-31. ISBN: 91-7390-026-5.

LAUREL, BRENDA. 1991. Computers as Theatre. Reading, MA: Addison-Wesley; 1991. 211p. ISBN: 0-201-51048-0.

LEARNED, WILLIAM S. 1924. The American Public Library and the Diffusion of Knowledge. New York, NY: Harcourt, Brace; 1924. 89p. LC: 24-22066.

LEHNER, J. CHRIS. 1990. Toward Rural Revival: The Telco-Community Partnership. Rural Telecommunications. 1990 Summer; 9(3): 10-15. ISSN: 0744-2548.

LESTER, RAY; WATERS, JUDITH. 1989. Environmental Scanning and Business Strategy. Boston Spa, England: British Library Board; 1989. 148p. (Library and Information Research Report 75). ISBN: 0-7123-3203-0.

LIBRARY OF CONGRESS. 1992. Library of Congress. Subject Headings. 15th edition. Washington, DC: Cataloging Distribution Service, Library of Congress; 1992. 4 volumes. ISSN: 1048-9711.

MACHLUP, FRITZ. 1962. The Production and Distribution of Knowledge in the United States. Princeton, NJ: Princeton University Press; 1962. 416p. LC: 63-7072.

MÄKINEN, HELENA. 1990. Information Industries in the Economy. See reference: CRONIN, BLAISE; TUDOR-ŠILOVIĆ, NEVA, eds. 1990. 79-84.

MALONE, THOMAS W.; FRY, CHRISTOPHER. 1992. Experiments with Oval: A Radically Tailorable Tool for Cooperative Work. In: Turner, Jon; Kraut, Robert, eds. CSCW '92: Sharing Perspectives: Proceedings of the Conference on Computer-Supported Cooperative Work; 1992 October 31-November 4; Toronto, Canada. New York, NY: Association for Computing Machinery; 1992. 289-297. ISBN: 0-89791-542-9.

MARCHAND, DONALD A.; HORTON, FOREST WOODY, JR. 1986. Infotrends: Profiting from Your Information Resources. New York, NY: John Wiley & Sons; 1986. 324p. ISBN: 0-471-81680-9.

MCCLURE, CHARLES R.; BISHOP, ANN P.; DOTY, PHILIP; ROSENBAUM, HOWARD. 1991. The National Research and Education Network (NREN): Research and Policy Perspectives. Norwood, NJ: Ablex Publishing Corp.; 1991. 744p. ISBN: 0-89391-813-X.

MCHOMBU, KINGO. 1992. Information Management in Africa: An Uncharted Terrain. FID News Bulletin. 1992 September; 42(9): 186-189. ISSN: 0014-5874.

MCLEOD, METTA. 1992. Doing Business with the Japanese. Journal of Economic and Social Intelligence. 1992; 2(1): 49-77. ISSN: 0961-2882.

MCNURLIN, BARBARA C.; SPRAGUE, RALPH H., eds. 1989. Information Systems Management in Practice. Englewood Cliffs, NJ: Prentice-Hall; 1989. 570p. ISBN: 0-13-464919-2.

MENOU, MICHEL. 1990. Information Management: A New Paradigm for Information Development in the Less Developed Countries (LDCs). In: Information Management: Practice and Education: International Seminar Proceedings: Volume 2; 1990 April 24-27; Budapest, Hungary. Budapest, Hungary: Országos Műszaki Információs Központ és Könyvtár; 1990. 504-528. Available from: Országos Műszaki Információs Központ és Könyvtár, 1428 Budapest, POB 12, Muzeum ú. 17, Hungary.

MEYER, HERBERT E. 1987. Real-World Intelligence: Organized Information for Executives. New York, NY: Weidenfeld & Nicolson; 1987. 102p. ISBN: 1-55584-147-3.

MOYAL, ANN. 1989. Women and the Telephone in Australia: A Study Prepared for Telecom Australia. 1989 April. 110p. (CIRCIT (Centre for International Research on Communication and Information Technologies) Working Paper). Available from: CIRCIT, Ltd., 1st floor, Riverside Quay, 4 Byrne Street, South Melbourne, Australia.

MUMFORD, ENID. 1985. From Bank Teller to Office Worker: The Pursuit of Systems Designed for People in Practice and Research. In: Gallegos, Lynn; Welke, Richard; Wetherbe, James, eds. Proceedings of the 6th International Conference on Information Systems; 1985 December 16-18; Indianapolis, IN. Baltimore, MD: Association for Computing Machinery; 1985. 249-258. OCLC: 13306119.

MYERS, JOHN M. 1991. Social Intelligence in Real Estate Planning. Social Intelligence. 1991; 1(1): 7-24. ISSN: 0961-2882.

NELSON, THEODOR HOLM. 1987. Literary Machines: The Report on, and of, Project Xanadu Concerning Word Processing, Electronic Publishing,

Hypertext, Thinkertoys, Tomorrow's Intellectual Revolution and Certain Other Topics, Including Knowledge, Education and Freedom. Edition 87.1. San Antonio, TX: Theodor Holm Nelson; 1987. 1 volume (discontinuous paging). Also available from: the Distributors, 702 South Michigan, South Bend, IN 46618. ISBN: 0-89347-056-2.

NIELSEN, JAKOB. 1990. Hypertext and Hypermedia. Boston, MA: Academic Press; 1990. 263p. ISBN: 0-12-518410-7.

NORA, SIMON; MINC, ALAIN. 1981. The Computerization of Society. Cambridge, MA: The MIT Press; 1981. 186p. ISBN: 0-262-14031-4.

ONYANGO, RICHARD A.O. 1990. The Knowledge Industries: Aids to Technological and Industrial Development in Africa. See reference: CRONIN, BLAISE; TUDOR-SILOVIĆ, NEVA, eds. 1990. 5-29.

ONYANGO, RICHARD A.O. 1991. Indigenous Technological Capacity: Can Social Intelligence Help? A Kenyan Case Study. Social Intelligence. 1991; 1(1): 25-42. ISSN: 0961-2882.

OSTROM, ELINOR. 1990. Governing the Commons: The Evolution of Institutions for Collective Action. New York, NY: Cambridge University Press; 1990. 280p. ISBN: 0-521-37101-5.

OTLET, PAUL. 1989. Traité de documentation: le livre sur le livre, théorie et pratique. Liège, Belgium: Centre de lecture publique de la communauté française de Belgique; 1989. 432p. (Reprint of the 1934 ed.). ISBN: 2-87130-015-1.

PÁEZ-URDANETA, IRASET. 1989. Information in the Third World. International Library Review. 1989; 21: 177-191. ISSN: 0020-7837.

PAISLEY, WILLIAM J. 1968. Information Needs and Uses. In: Cuadra, Carlos A., ed. Annual Review of Information Science and Technology: Volume 3. Chicago, IL: Encyclopaedia Britannica for the American Society for Information Science; 1968. 1-30. ISSN: 0066-4200.

PALVIA, PRASHANT; PALVIA, SHIAILENDRA; ZIGLI, RONALD M. 1990. The Theory and Practical Use of Executive Information Systems. International Journal of Information Management. 1990 June; 10(2): 117-126. ISSN: 0268-4012.

PARKER, MARILYN M.; BENSON, ROBERT J.; TRAINOR, H. EDWARD. 1988. Information Economics: Linking Business Performance to Information Technology. Englewood Cliffs, NJ: Prentice-Hall International; 1988. 287p. ISBN: 0-13-465014-X.

PEDLER, MIKE; BURGOYNE, JOHN; BOYDELL, TOM. 1991. The Learning Company: A Strategy for Sustainable Development. New York, NY: McGraw-Hill Book Company; 1991. 213p. ISBN: 0-07-707479-3.

PIGANIOL, PIERRE. 1992. The Emergence of Corporate Intelligence. In: Sigurdson, Jon; Tågerud, Yael, eds. The Intelligent Corporation: The Privatisation of Intelligence. London, England: Taylor Graham; 1992. 23-27. ISBN: 0-947568-55-7.

POLANYI, MICHAEL. 1966. The Tacit Dimension. Garden City, NY: Doubleday; 1966. 108p. LC: 66-21015.

PORAT, MARC URI. 1977. The Information Economy: Definition and Measurement. Washington, DC: U.S. Department of Commerce; 1977 May. 250p. (Office of Telecommunications Special Publication 77-12(1)). GPO: 003-000-00512-7.

PORTER, MICHAEL E. 1980. Competitive Strategy: Techniques for Analyzing Industries and Competitors. New York, NY: The Free Press; 1980. 396p. ISBN: 0-02-925360-8.
PORTER, MICHAEL E. 1985. Competitive Advantage: Creating and Sustaining Superior Performance. New York, NY: The Free Press; 1985. 557p. ISBN: 0-02-925090-0.
PORTER, MICHAEL E. 1990. The Competitive Advantage of Nations. New York, NY: The Free Press; 1990. 855p. ISBN: 0-02-925361-6.
PORTER, MICHAEL E.; MILLAR, VICTOR E. 1985. How Information Gives You Competitive Advantage. Harvard Business Review. 1985 July-August; 63(4): 149-160. ISSN: 0017-8012.
PRESCOTT, JOHN. 1991. A Competitive Assessment of SCIP. Competitive Intelligence Review. 1991 Spring; 2(1): 1-2. ISSN: 1058-0247.
PRUSAK, LAURENCE; MATARAZZO, JAMES. 1992. Information Management and Japanese Success. Washington, DC: Special Libraries Association; 1992. 15p. (Center for Information Technology and Strategy Special Report). ISBN: 0-87111-383-X.
QUARTERMAN, JOHN S. 1990. The Matrix: Computer Networks and Conferencing Systems Worldwide. Burlington, MA: Digital Press; 1990. 719p. ISBN: 1-55558-033-5.
QUARTERMAN, JOHN S.; HOSKINS, JOSIAH C. 1986. Notable Computer Networks. Communications of the ACM (Association for Computing Machinery). 1986 October; 29(10): 932-971. ISSN: 0001-0782.
RADA, ROY. 1991. Hypertext: From Text to Expertext. New York, NY: McGraw-Hill Book Company; 1991. 237p. ISBN: 0-07-707401-7.
RADOŠEVIĆ, SLAVO. 1991. Techno-Economic Intelligence in the 1990s: A Development Policy Perspective. Social Intelligence. 1991; 1(1): 55-71. ISSN: 0961-2882.
RADOŠEVIĆ, SLAVO. 1992. Techno-Economic Networks and Social Intelligence as Useful Concepts in Technology Policy-Making. In: Cronin, Blaise; Tudor-Silović, Neva, eds. From Information Management to Social Intelligence: The Key to Open Markets. London, England: Aslib; 1992. 29-42. ISBN: 0-85142-284-5.
RADOŠEVIĆ, SLAVO; DEDIJER, STEVAN. 1990. Knowledge Industries, Information Technologies and Intelligence: The Case of Yugoslavia. See reference: CRONIN, BLAISE; TUDOR-SILOVIĆ, NEVA, eds. 1990. 31-44.
RADY, MARTIN. 1991. The Management of Secret Police Files in Eastern Europe. Records Management Journal. 1991; 3(3): 70-77. ISSN: 0956-5698.
RAMBALI, PAUL. 1989. French Blues: A Not-so-sentimental Journey through Lives and Memories in Modern France. London, England: W. Heinemann; 1989. 225p. ISBN: 0-434-62012-2.
RAYWARD, W. BOYD. 1992. Restructuring and Mobilising Information in Documents: A Historical Perspective. In: Vakkari, Pertti; Cronin, Blaise, eds. Conceptions of Library and Information Science: Historical, Empirical and Theoretical Perspectives. London, England: Taylor Graham; 1992. 50-68. ISBN: 0-947568-52-2.
REPO, AATTO J. 1987. Economics of Information. In: Williams, Martha E., ed. Annual Review of Information Science and Technology: Volume 22.

Amsterdam, The Netherlands: Elsevier Science Publishers for the American Society for Information Science; 1987. 3-35. ISSN: 0066-4200; ISBN: 0-444-70302-0.

ROGERS, EVERETT; COLLINS-JARVIS, LORI; SCHMITZ, JOSEPH. 1992. The PEN Project in Santa Monica: Interactive Communication and Political Action. In: Shaw, Debora, ed. ASIS '92: Proceedings of the American Society for Information Science (ASIS) 55th Annual Meeting: Volume 29; 1992 October 26-29; Pittsburgh, PA. Medford, NJ: Learned Information for ASIS; 1992. 303. ISSN: 0044-7870; ISBN: 0-938734-69-5.

ROSZAK, THEODORE. 1986. The Cult of Information: The Folklore of Computers and the True Art of Thinking. New York, NY: Pantheon; 1986. 238p. ISBN: 0-394-54622-9.

SALINAS, RAQUEL. 1986. Forget the NWICO...And Start All Over Again. Information Development. 1986; 2(3): 154-158. ISSN: 0266-6669.

SCHILLER, HERBERT I. 1981. Who Knows: Information in the Age of the Fortune 500. Norwood, NJ: Ablex Publishing Corp.; 1981. 187p. ISBN: 0-89391-069-4.

SCHWARTZ, EVAN I.; LEWYN, MARK. 1992. Prodigy Installs a New Program. Business Week. 1992 September 14; 96, 100. ISSN: 0007-7135.

SCIENTIFIC AMERICAN. 1991. Communications, Computers and Networks: How to Work, Play and Thrive in Cyberspace. Scientific American. 1991 September; 265(3): 190p. ISSN: 0036-8733.

SHNEIDERMAN, BEN. 1989. Reflections on Authoring, Editing, and Managing Hypertext. In: Barrett, Edward, ed. The Society of Text: Hypertext, Hypermedia, and the Social Construction of Information. Cambridge, MA: MIT Press; 1989. 115-131. ISBN: 0-262-02291-5.

SIGURDSON, JON; TÅGERUD, YAEL, eds. 1992. The Intelligent Corporation: The Privatisation of Intelligence. London, England: Taylor Graham; 1992. 199p. ISBN: 0-947568-55-7.

SIMONS, GEOFF. 1987. Eco-Computer: The Impact of Global Intelligence. New York, NY: John Wiley & Sons; 1987. 206p. ISBN: 0-471-91340-5.

SISODIA, RAJENDRA S. 1992. Singapore Invests in the Nation-Corporation. Harvard Business Review. 1992 May-June; 70: 40-50. ISSN: 0017-8012.

SMITH, LINDA C. 1991. Memex as an Image of Potentiality Revisited. In: Nyce, James M.; Kahn, Paul, eds. From Memex to Hypertext: Vannevar Bush and the Mind's Machine. Boston, MA: Academic Press; 1991. 261-286. ISBN: 0-12-523270-5.

SOCIAL EPISTEMOLOGY. 1987-. Fuller, Steve, ed. New York, NY: Taylor & Francis. ISSN: 0269-1728.

SOCIAL INTELLIGENCE. 1991. Cronin, Blaise, ed. London, England: Taylor Graham. (Title changed with v. 2 (1992) to Journal of Economic and Social Intelligence). ISSN: 0961-2882.

SOCIAL STUDIES OF SCIENCE. 1971-. Edge, David, ed. London, England: Sage Publications. ISSN: 0306-3127.

SOUTH COMMISSION. 1990. The Challenge to the South: The Report of the South Commission. New York, NY: Oxford University Press; 1990. 325p. ISBN: 0-19-877311-0.

SPRING, MICHAEL B. 1991. Information Technology Standards. In: Williams, Martha E., ed. Annual Review of Information Science and

Technology: Volume 26. Medford, NJ: Learned Information for the American Society for Information Science; 1991. 81-111. ISSN: 0066-4200; ISBN: 0-938734-55-5.

SPROULL, LEE; KIESLER, SARA. 1991. Connections: New Ways of Working in the Networked Organization. Cambridge, MA: MIT Press; 1991. 212p. ISBN: 0-262-19306-X.

STANAT, RUTH. 1990. The Intelligent Corporation: Creating a Shared Network for Information and Profit. New York, NY: American Management Association; 1990. 270p. ISBN: 0-8144-5957-9.

STEFIK, MARK; FOSTER, GREGG; BOBROW, DANIEL G.; KAHN, KENNETH; LANNING, STAN; SUCHMAN, LUCY. 1987. Beyond the Chalkboard: Computer Support for Collaboration and Problem Solving in Meetings. Communications of the ACM (Association for Computing Machinery). 1987 January; 30(1): 32-47. ISSN: 0001-0782.

STERNBERG, ROBERT J. 1990. Metaphors of Mind: Conceptions of the Nature of Intelligence. New York, NY: Cambridge University Press; 1990. 344p. ISBN: 0-521-35579-6.

STRASSMANN, PAUL A. 1985. Information Payoff: The Transformation of Work in the Electronic Age. New York, NY: The Free Press; 1985. 298p. ISBN: 0-02-931720-7.

STRASSMANN, PAUL A. 1990. The Business Value of Computers: An Executive's Guide. New Canaan, CT: The Information Economics Press; 1990. 530p. ISBN: 0-9620413-2-7.

STURGES, PAUL; MCHOMBU, KINGO; NEILL, RICHARD. 1992. The Indigenous Knowledge Base in African Development. Journal of Economic and Social Intelligence. 1992; 2(1): 5-29. ISSN: 0961-2882.

SUCHMAN, LUCY A. 1987. Plans and Situated Actions: The Problem of Human-Machine Communication. New York, NY: Cambridge University Press; 1987. 203p. ISBN: 0-521-33137-4.

SUTTON, HOWARD. 1988. Competitive Intelligence. New York, NY: Conference Board; 1988. 39p. (Research Report no. 913). ISBN: 0-8237-0357-6.

SYNNOTT, WILLIAM. 1987. Information Weapon: Winning Customers and Markets with Technology. New York, NY: John Wiley & Sons; 1987. 334p. ISBN: 0-471-84557-4.

TAYLOR, ROBERT S. 1968. Question-Negotiation and Information Seeking in Libraries. College and Research Libraries. 1968 May; 29(3): 178-194. ISSN: 0010-0870.

TAYLOR, ROBERT S. 1986a. On the Study of Information Use Environments. In: Hurd, Julie M.; Davis, Charles H., eds. ASIS '86: Proceedings of the American Society for Information Science (ASIS) 49th Annual Meeting: Volume 23; 1986 September 28-October 2; Chicago, IL. Medford, NJ: Learned Information for ASIS; 1986. 331-334. ISSN: 0044-7870; ISBN: 0-938734-14-8.

TAYLOR, ROBERT S. 1986b. Value-Added Processes in Information Systems. Norwood, NJ: Ablex Publishing Corp.; 1986. 257p. ISBN: 0-89391-273-5.

TEITELBAUM, RICHARD S. 1992. The New Race for Intelligence. Fortune. 1992 November 2; 126(10): 104-107. ISSN: 0015-8259.

TELL, BJÖRN. 1988. Libraries and Social Intelligence: Experiences from the Third World. In: Annerstedt, Jan; Jamison, Andrew, eds. From Research Policy to Social Intelligence: Essays for Stevan Dedijer. Basingstoke, England: Macmillan Press; 1988. 153-162. ISBN: 0-333-45275-5.

TELL, BJÖRN. 1990. Information Analysis Systems and Social Intelligence: An Overview of the Development of Specialised Information Centres as Part of Government Policies. See reference: CRONIN, BLAISE; TUDOR-SILOVIĆ, NEVA, eds. 1990. 147-159.

THORNDYKE, EDWARD L. 1920. Intelligence and Its Uses. Harper's Magazine. 1920 January; 140: 227-235. ISSN: 0017-789X.

TOFFLER, ALVIN. 1990. Powershift: Knowledge, Wealth, and Violence at the Edge of the 21st Century. New York, NY: Bantam Books; 1990. 585p. ISBN: 0-553-05776-6.

TRAVICA, BOB; HOGAN, MATTHEW. 1992. Computer Networks in the X-USSR: Technology, Uses and Social Effects. In: Shaw, Debora, ed. ASIS '92: Proceedings of the American Society for Information Science (ASIS) 55th Annual Meeting: Volume 29; 1992 October 26-29; Pittsburgh, PA. Medford, NJ: Learned Information, Inc. for ASIS; 1992. 120-135. ISSN: 0044-7870; ISBN: 0-938734-69-5.

TRIGG, RANDY; SUCHMAN, LUCY; HALASZ, FRANK. 1986. Supporting Collaboration in NoteCards. In: CSCW '86: Proceedings of the Conference on Computer-Supported Cooperative Work; 1986 December 3-5; Austin, TX. Austin, TX: Conference Committee for Computer-Supported Cooperative Work; 1986. 153-162. OCLC: 15913327.

TROY, THOMAS F. 1991/92. The "Correct" Definition of Intelligence. International Journal of Intelligence and Counterintelligence. 1991/92 Winter; 5(4): 433-454. ISSN: 0885-0607.

U.S. NATIONAL SCIENCE BOARD. 1991. Science & Engineering Indicators—1991. 10th edition. Washington, DC: U.S. Government Printing Office; 1991. 487p. ISSN: 1048-6313.

VENTURA, ARNOLDO. 1987. Jamaica's Bauxite Battle. In: Dedijer, Stevan; Jéquier, Nicolas, eds. Intelligence for Economic Development: An Inquiry into the Role of the Knowledge Industry. Oxford, England: Berg; 1987. 111-127. ISBN: 0-85496-502-3.

VENTURA, ARNOLDO. 1988. Social Intelligence: Prerequisite for the Management of Science and Technology. In: Annerstedt, Jan; Jamison, Andrew, eds. From Research Policy to Social Intelligence: Essays for Stevan Dedijer. Basingstoke, England: Macmillan; 1988. 163-172. ISBN: 0-333-45275-5.

WERSIG, GERNOT. 1992. Information Science and Theory: A Weaver Bird's Perspective. In: Vakkari, Pertti; Cronin, Blaise, eds. Conceptions of Library and Information Science: Historical, Empirical and Theoretical Perspectives. London, England: Taylor Graham; 1992. 201-217. ISBN: 0-947568-52-2.

WESTRUM, RON. 1989. Social Intelligence about Hidden Events. In: Chubin, Daryl E.; Chu, Ellen W., eds. Science off the Pedestal: Social Perspectives on Science and Technology. Belmont, CA: Wadsworth; 1989. 19-30. ISBN: 0-534-09858-4.

WHITEN, ANDREW; BYRNE, RICHARD W.   1988a.   The Machiavellian Intelligence Hypotheses.   In: Byrne, Richard W.; Whiten, Andrew, eds. Machiavellian Intelligence: Social Expertise and the Evolution of Intelligence in Monkeys, Apes, and Humans. New York, NY: Oxford University Press; 1988. 1-11. ISBN: 0-19-852179-0.

WHITEN, ANDREW; BYRNE, RICHARD W.   1988b. Taking (Machiavellian) Intelligence Apart. In: Byrne, Richard W.; Whiten, Andrew, eds. Machiavellian Intelligence: Social Expertise and the Evolution of Intelligence in Monkeys, Apes, and Humans. New York, NY: Oxford University Press; 1988. 50-65. ISBN: 0-19-852179-0.

WHYTE, ANGUS.   1991.   Evolution and Social Intelligence.   Social Intelligence. 1991; 1(3): 191-212. ISSN: 0961-2882.

WINN, M.   1990.   New Views of Human Intelligence.   New York Times Magazine, Part 2. 1990 April 29; 16, 17, 28, 30. ISSN: 0362-4331.

WINOGRAD, TERRY; FLORES, FERNANDO. 1986. Understanding Computers and Cognition: A New Foundation for Design. Norwood, NJ: Ablex Publishing Corp.; 1986. 207p. ISBN: 0-89391-050-3.

WORLD BANK.   1991.   The Challenge of Development: World Development Report 1991. New York, NY: Oxford University Press; 1991. 290p. ISBN: 0-19-520869-2.

WUTHNOW, ROBERT, ed.   1992.   Vocabularies of Public Life: Empirical Essays in Symbolic Structure.   New York, NY: Routledge; 1992.   270p. ISBN: 0-415-07636-6.

YAMAGUCHI, KAORU.   1990.   Fundamentals of a New Economic Paradigm in the Information Age.   Futures.   1990 December; 22(10): 1023-1076. ISSN: 0016-3287.

ZAGORIN, ADAM. 1992. Still Spying after All These Years. Time. 1992 June 29; 139(26): 58-59. ISSN: 0040-781X.

2 Electronic U.S. Government Information: Policy Issues and Directions

PETER HERNON
Simmons College

CHARLES R. MCCLURE
Syracuse University

INTRODUCTION

The federal government allocated $25.4 billion in fiscal year 1991 to develop a technological infrastructure (U.S. OFFICE OF MANAGEMENT AND BUDGET, 1992a). One result has been the increased production and availability of electronic information. A person can now access more government information from home or business via modem, telephone, cable television, and computer networks than was previously possible.

The increasing amounts of government electronic information available, however, have raised policy issues that often defy simple and straightforward solutions. Indeed, many of the issues affect the very fabric of how this society operates and challenge assumptions about the role of the government in the management of information resources. Government policy related to the management of and access to electronic information has a pervasive impact on virtually ail other policy areas.

This section provides an overview of U.S. federal information policy and its treatment of electronic information resources. The issues raised here are more fully covered in later sections of the chapter. Because

We thank Linda Watkins, library science librarian at Simmons College, for her assistance with the bibliography, William E. Moen, doctoral student at Syracuse University, for providing information for the section on standards, and Wally Babcock of Syracuse University for locating bibliographic information for some of the congressional material cited.

Annual Review of Information Science and Technology (ARIST), Volume 28, 1993
Martha E. Williams, Editor
Published for the American Society for Information Science (ASIS)
By Learned Information, Inc., Medford, N.J.

electronic information policy comprises a subset of general information policy, the discussion must naturally cover both.

Information Policy: An Overview

Information policy encompasses information science, public policy, political science, economics, and other disciplines. Much of the discussion of information policy in the various literatures focuses on federal and state governmental policies, their development, revision, strengths and weaknesses, implications, interpretation, impacts, and use. Despite the reference to information policy, "there is no single all encompassing policy. Rather, information policies tend to address specific issues and, at times, to be fragmented, overlapping, and contradictory" (HERNON & RELYEA, 1991, p. 176).

U.S. federal information policy is a set of interrelated principles, laws, guidelines, rules and regulations, directives, procedures, judicial interpretations, and practices that guide the oversight and management of the information life cycle, which consists of: (1) creation or collection; (2) production; (3) protection (where necessary); (4) distribution/dissemination; (5) retrieval; and (6) retirement of information. Information policy also embraces access to and the use of information. Collectively these policies become an integral part of information resources management (IRM), privacy, security, economic competitiveness, and other issues.

The purpose of federal information policy is to provide: (1) broad generalized guidelines to all agencies for managing the life cycle of information and information technologies; (2) specific guidance either for or within a particular agency; and (3) guidance for managing the life cycle of information and information technologies for a particular subject or topical area.

A number of existing policy instruments were developed before electronic information became so pervasive. Between 1977 and 1990, CHARTRAND (1991) identified more than 300 public laws related to information policy and technology. This number does not reflect the policies emanating from the appropriations process and agency administration of public laws. Many of these laws, together with a number of administrative regulations and legislation prior to 1977, gave inadequate attention to issues associated with the emerging electronic information environment.

The Literature

The literature on government information policy is both cross-disciplinary and interdisciplinary. Moreover, it cannot keep up with rapid change, such as that associated with the life cycle of electronic government information resources. Newspapers, newsletters, and indexes to government source material as well as conference proceedings and personal contacts with policy makers provide important means for monitoring current and planned developments.

The congressional Office of Technology Assessment (OTA) produces relevant reports that are accessible through the Government Printing Office's (GPO) sales program, the National Technical Information Service (NTIS), or OTA itself. Another congressional agency, the General Accounting Office (GAO), investigates issues and conducts surveys at the request of a congressional agency or member of Congress. GAO publishes reports pertaining to electronic information. Congressional committees might use these reports to introduce legislation or to compel an agency to change its practices. Another source of policy analyses is the Congressional Research Service (CRS) at the Library of Congress (LC), which produces Committee Prints and other information useful for committee deliberations and for keeping members of Congress informed. Finally, agencies produce studies and reports on various information policies, as do the private sector, academia, public interest groups, professional associations, and others. Source material on various information policies might be listed in indexes such as those presented in Table 1; other material can be obtained through personal contact with agency officials or membership in organizations such as OMB Watch and the Information Industry Association (IIA).

Three government publications (U.S. CONGRESS. HOUSE. COMMITTEE ON GOVERNMENT OPERATIONS, 1986a, 1986b; U.S. CONGRESS. OFFICE OF TECHNOLOGY ASSESSMENT, 1988), although somewhat dated, provide an excellent introduction to the policy issues related to the collection and dissemination of electronic government information. Along with the article by ENGLISH, the first publication (U.S. CONGRESS. HOUSE. COMMITTEE ON GOVERNMENT OPERATIONS, 1986a), which is a transcript of a congressional hearing, provides background information for the preparation of the subsequent report issued to guide legislative and executive branch policy related to the planning, implementation, and use of electronic data systems. The report (U.S. CONGRESS. HOUSE. COMMITTEE ON GOVERNMENT OPERATIONS, 1986b, p. 9) stresses that government information, whether in electronic or nonelectronic form, should remain "freely accessible and easily reproducible." In addition, agencies should consult with each other and learn from past mistakes and successes, and they should not exercise a "monopoly or near-monopoly over information" (p. 5).

Commenting on the third publication (U.S. CONGRESS. OFFICE OF TECHNOLOGY ASSESSMENT, 1988), WOOD (p. 83) emphasizes that

Table 1
Selected Sources for Current Awareness of
Information Policy Topics and Issues

INDEXES

CIS Index (1970-)
Government Reports Announcements & Index (1975-); its predecessors date
  back to 1946. (NTIS has database version).
Library Literature (1921-)
Monthly Catalog of United States Government Publications (1895-)
Resources in Education (ERIC) (1966-)
Social Sciences Index (1974-)

NEWSPAPERS and PERIODICALS

Federal Computer Week (1986-)
Government Computer News (1981-)
Government Information Insider (1990-)
Government Information Quarterly (1984-)
The *New York Times* (1851-)
The *Washington Post* (1877-)

NEWSLETTERS

Access Reports (Freedom of Information) (1975-)
American Library Association Washington Office Newsletter (1949-)
Electronic Public Information Newsletter (1991-)
Information Hotline (1969-)
Information Industry Association Friday Memo (1978?-)
The *OMB Watcher* (1982-)
Privacy Journal (1974-)
Privacy Times (1981-)

ELECTRONIC SOURCES

American Association of Law Librarians Government Line (1991-)
  [accessible via the Internet]
American Library Association Washington Office Newsline (1992-)
  [accessible via the Internet]
GovDoc-L Discussion List (1989-) [accessible via the Internet]
Government Printing Office Bulletin Board (1991-)

information technology "could revolutionize the public information functions of the Federal government." The OTA report summarized the extent to which agencies disseminated electronic products and libraries could absorb these products in their collections and services. OTA also encouraged the reorganization of NTIS, GPO, and GPO's depository library program to cope better with information technology and information dissemination.

HERNON & MCCLURE (1987, p. 262, 264) offer a typology of general information policy issues. They also identify and summarize other typologies (see Appendix H and p. 260–261, 263). HERNON & MCCLURE (1991b, p. 5–7, 40–42), who revised and updated their earlier typology, identified 70 issues. Clearly the range of issues related to government information and electronic information policy is broad.

Thus, this chapter is selective in the issues discussed and the literature referenced. For example, it does not focus per se on federal telecommunications policy (see, e.g., U.S. CONGRESS. HOUSE. COMMITTEE ON ENERGY AND COMMERCE) or federal statistical policies (see SY & ROBBIN). In addition, the discussion complements chapters in previous editions of *ARIST* (i.e., CHARTRAND, 1986; HERNON & RELYEA, 1988; LYNCH & PRESTON; LYTLE; SPRING). In general, the literature cited covers the mid-1980s to spring 1993. However, with the exception of legislation for a locator system within the GPO, the discussion does not present legislative initiatives of the 103rd Congress or the Clinton administration.

What Comprises a Government Publication?

HERNON & RELYEA (1988), who discussed the U.S. government as a publisher, note that "librarians and others for years have used one particular definition of what constitutes a government publication. That definition [44 *UNITED STATES CODE (U.S.C.)* 1901] was created when printing/publication was equated with a paper copy or microform" (p. 3). Section 1901 defines a publication as "informational matter which is published as an individual document at government expense, or as required by law"; that section also notes that this definition applies only to GPO's distribution of publications through its depository library program. Neither Title 44 nor its legislative history defines "informational matter," "published," or "as an individual document." A key question is to what extent this definition applies to electronic information resources. The term "informational matter" could apply to these resources, but the terms "published" and "as an individual document" are more restrictive.

MOREHEAD & FETZER (p. 24) write:

> Of critical importance for the future will be the amount of information furnished to GPO that is prepared in electronic format and will no longer be printed on paper for dissemination, but will be disseminated in electronic formats only. Such information need no longer be sent to GPO but instead will remain under the control of the agency, which will decide the method of dissemination.

The amount of paper copy printing and distribution may indeed decline. However, the number of paper and microfiche titles produced per year and distributed to depository libraries remains sizable (HERNON, 1992b).

The most recent set of general terms and definitions relating to government information policy appeared in the Office of Management and Budget, Office of Information and Regulatory Affair's (OMB-OIRA) proposed revision of OMB Circular A-130 (U.S. OFFICE OF MANAGEMENT AND BUDGET, 1992b, p. 18298–18299). While that discussion is useful, Congress and the executive branch are still debating about what exactly comprises "electronic government information and publication." An implication of this debate is that according to the interpretation of Section 1901 and other sources, agencies may decide not to provide GPO with some electronic information for distribution through the depository library program.

Amount, Types, and Examples of
Electronic Government Information

The federal government is the largest publisher/printer and producer of information in the United States and probably in the world. Every four months it generates "a stack of records equal to all those produced in the 124 years between George Washington and Woodrow Wilson" (RITCHIE, p. A44). The number of presidential records is especially large for recent administrations. For example, it took 19 tractor trailers to move former President Carter's White House material to Atlanta, Ga., and five military cargo airplanes to transport former President Reagan's records to California (HERNON & MCCLURE, 1992, p. 68).

Electronic records and information resources take the form of electronic mail (e-mail), CD-ROM, magnetic tapes of machine-readable files, desktop or word-processed publications, dial-up services, geographic information systems (GISs), spreadsheet and relational database files, floppy disks, bulletin boards, and so forth. When government officials respond to e-mail messages, they might convey or declare official policy. In 1991 the government provided half of the English-language CD-ROM titles issued worldwide (HERNON & MCCLURE, 1992, p. 68). A conservative estimate is that government agencies could easily release more than 1,500 CD-ROM titles per year. These products include reference (bibliographic) databases and source (numeric, textual-numeric, visual or image, and full-text) databases (HERNON & MCCLURE, 1992, p. 69).

One congressional committee identifies "creative ways" in which government agencies disseminate information, including electronic methods (U.S. CONGRESS. HOUSE. COMMITTEE ON GOVERNMENT OPERATIONS, 1992). For instance, in 1990 the U.S. Geological Survey (USGS), the National Aeronautics and Space Administration (NASA), and the National Oceanic and Atmospheric Administration (NOAA) began JEdi, a joint initiative "to develop a set of educational materials to enhance and promote the teaching of earth science at the pre-college level" (p. 7). JEdi has produced a set of three CD-ROM discs and a workbook. "The unique aspect of this project lies in the fact that these teaching materials incorporate many of the actual databases used by earth scientists and environmental researchers in the various agencies" (p. 7).

The U.S. GENERAL ACCOUNTING OFFICE (1992c) offers examples of government-produced and -disseminated CD-ROMs, bulletin boards, voice messaging and facsimile, and floppy disks. "Once data are on the disk, they can be manipulated using a word processing, spreadsheet, or data base software package" (p. 11). GAO has also experimented with making selected reports available over the Internet. MCCLURE ET AL. (1992c, p. 47-52) list and describe a range of government electronic services, formats, and delivery mechanisms currently in use.

Each year since 1985, GPO has distributed between 30,000 and 55,000 different titles to depository libraries (HERNON, 1992b, p. 101). As GPO shifts its budgetary priorities and experiences shortfalls, the number of titles distributed per year in paper copy and microfiche to depository libraries will decline. These developments will increase the backlog of titles awaiting distribution, will result in the release of fewer paper copy titles and in more microfiche titles, will lead to smaller print runs, and will limit the distribution of some hardcover titles to regional depositories only (KELLEY).

Nonetheless, through five pilot projects, GPO and the congressional Joint Committee on Printing (JCP) have introduced electronic media (CD-ROM and bulletin boards) to depository distribution (ALDRICH & JOBE). Also the Patent and Trademark Office has supplied its depository libraries with CD-ROM access to patents. In addition, more and more databases, CD-ROMs, bulletin boards, and other electronically supplied information are available directly from individual agencies. At the same time, both GPO and NTIS have implemented gateways to connect computer users electronically to different agency files, databases, and programs.

Electronic information and data, as these pilot projects have shown, appear in various forms, including visual. Such information and data might be included, for example, as part of a GIS. USGS and the U.S. Bureau of the Census are two agencies that maintain such systems. As to the data in these systems, some important issues are:

- What infrastructure (hardware/software) is needed to collect, archive, refine, disseminate, and use the data?
- How can users interface with the datasets?
- What, if any, restrictions can be placed on use? and
- Will costs exclude some individuals from access to the data?

A GIS, such as the TIGER, which is comprised of files of the Bureau of the Census, is expensive for libraries to load, manage, and make available. These files require special expertise, dedicated microcomputers with sufficient memory, access to laser printers and plotters, and a highly trained staff.

As libraries and others place government information in locator systems and online catalogs, the use of this information will spread. That use, however, will increasingly be remotely based and will provide direct access to data sources in government agencies. Thus, tallies of those who visit depository libraries (MCCLURE & HERNON, 1989b) or other organizations that provide access to government information may underrepresent the number of users and the types of uses of electronic government information products and services. At the same time, more users will create their own information, thereby demonstrating that life-cycle management does not necessarily proceed automatically from collection to demise; rather, use may revert to the steps for production or protection.

STAKEHOLDERS

MCINTOSH (1990, p. 2) discusses the "competing interests" of various stakeholders: OMB, the information industry, and "the 'access community' of libraries, public interest groups, and other major users of government information." Using OMB Circular A-130 and reauthorization of the Paperwork Reduction Act (PRA) (Public Law (P.L.) 96-511; Public Law 99-500) (U.S. CONGRESS. 96TH CONGRESS; U.S. CONGRESS. 99TH CONGRESS) as examples, he shows how some stakeholders have willingly compromised, while others have not. This section identifies and briefly describes the role of selected key stakeholders in policy development related to electronic government information. The document *Information Policies* (COALITION FOR NETWORKED INFORMATION) is a compilation of principles and positions of different stakeholders on various topics, not all of which pertain to electronic government information.

Office of Management and Budget

With the inauguration of Ronald Reagan as president and implementation of PRA, OMB has increasingly served as a central source for information policy planning and development. During the eight years of the Reagan administration, OMB consistently expanded its role and direct involvement in information resources management, information policy development, and information infrastructure deployment (MCCLURE ET AL., 1989; see also MCCLURE ET AL., 1991a). REEDER, then head of OMB-OIRA, outlined basic principles of information policy that guided his agency's activities as it tried to meet its responsibilities under PRA for information policy development.

OMB, however, involves itself in many other activities. For example, OIRA provided the staff for the Quayle Council on Competitiveness, which eased the impact of federal regulations on industry, often to the dismay of executive agencies and Congress. In accordance with PRA, OIRA attempted to reduce the paperwork burden on business and industry and blocked politically unpopular regulations (see TRIANO & BASS). "In the process, OIRA micromanaged the government's paperwork through the OMB clearance process and became deeply involved in the regulatory strategies of key agencies" (SPREHE, 1992a, p. 18).

If the Clinton administration and the 103rd Congress can agree on PRA's reauthorization, which lapsed in 1989, and reauthorize OIRA, that office could "shift its emphasis toward information resources management," "develop a program to certify agencies for delegation of the clearance powers," and "de-emphasize approving and disapproving individual paperwork transactions" (SPREHE, 1992a, p. 18, 20).

National Technical Information Service

NTIS acquires and sells reports, data files, bibliographic products, and software from source agencies. It also provides bibliographic control, document distribution, patent licensing, accounts receivable management services to other agencies, and so forth. MCCLURE criticizes the structure of NTIS, its inability to better identify and meet user information needs, its limited use of innovative information technology, and its pricing policies.

During most of the Reagan administration, OMB and, to some extent, the Department of Commerce considered NTIS as a prime candidate for privatization (see HERNON, 1989; STEWART). Once Congress blocked this effort, NTIS began to refocus on improving and modernizing its information products and services for the next century (U.S. DEPARTMENT OF COMMERCE. NATIONAL TECHNICAL INFORMATION SERVICE, 1989).

As discussed in its modernization and automation plan (U.S. DEPARTMENT OF COMMERCE. NATIONAL TECHNICAL INFORMATION SERVICE, 1992b, p. 1), "NTIS is in a difficult business position. It depends heavily on the sale of printed technical reports for its livelihood, and as the movement toward electronic information distribution grows, that segment of the information market has been declining for several years." Moreover (p. 1), "NTIS's long term success will require development of new products and services to augment and eventually replace the income from printed reports."

To move in new directions, NTIS, under the National Technical Information Act of 1988 (15 *U.S.C.* 3704b) (U.S. CONGRESS. 100TH CONGRESS, 2ND SESSION, 1988b), is exploring its role as "a player" in the "networked marketplace" and is pursuing joint venture "business opportunities" through the Internet and "commercial private networks" (U.S. DEPARTMENT OF COMMERCE. NATIONAL TECHNICAL INFORMATION SERVICE, 1992b, p. 11). "Although revenue streams will result from these and related network activities, online dissemination of information will not produce a significant impact on the NTIS financial bottom line" in the next five years (U.S. DEPARTMENT OF COMMERCE. NATIONAL TECHNICAL INFORMATION SERVICE, 1992b, p. 11).

The American Technology Preeminence Act (P. L. 102-245) (U.S. CONGRESS. 102ND CONGRESS, 2ND SESSION, 1992b) authorizes NTIS to disseminate electronic information and to use revenue generated from information distribution to fund its operating costs. The act also mandates that the secretary of commerce explore the feasibility of having NTIS establish and operate a federal online information product catalog, called FEDLINE, and that NTIS implement a government-wide information locator system.

The Electronic Media Production Services (EMPS) program, begun in 1990, provides electronic media production services to federal agencies (e.g., CD-ROM mastering and duplication). The program "accounts for 12 percent of the total production and brokerage services revenue" of NTIS, and NTIS has discovered that agency demands for EMPS have grown "faster than the NTIS infrastructure could cope with." More agencies realize "that attractive savings could result from the use of CD-ROM as a storage and dissemination medium" (U.S. DEPART-

MENT OF COMMERCE. NATIONAL TECHNICAL INFORMATION SERVICE, 1992a, p. 77).

NTIS will rely more on CD-ROM as a distribution or sales mechanism. However, it will be at least a decade before its major contributors, the Department of Defense, the Department of Energy, and NASA,

> fully capture their data electronically. . . .Although NTIS has started to incorporate the new electronic and optical technologies, it will continue with a dual microfiche and electronic (optical) storage system until a transition is complete. Over the next several years, electronic storage will be emphasized and microfiche will be deemphasized as a medium for storage and distribution. (U.S. DEPARTMENT OF COMMERCE. NATIONAL TECHNICAL INFORMATION SERVICE, 1992a, p. 8)

Currently NTIS is undergoing a major reorganization, is attempting to modernize, and is experimenting with new information services such as FedWorld, its dial-up bulletin board gateway to a number of federal databases (HERMAN).

Government Printing Office

In preparing to assume a larger role in the life cycle of electronic information resources, GPO developed a long-range strategic planning document (U.S. CONGRESS. GOVERNMENT PRINTING OFFICE, 1991; 1993). However, realization of that vision may require revision of parts of Title 44, *U.S.C.*, and "the development of new information partnerships" between GPO and agencies (U.S. CONGRESS. GOVERNMENT PRINTING OFFICE, 1991, p. ii).

Recalling past problems in dealing with GPO, many agencies may be unwilling to forge new partnerships. At the same time, the vision may place GPO in competition with the National Archives and Records Administration as a data archives for providing electronic files so that libraries can "purge their on-line electronic systems regularly" (U.S. CONGRESS. GOVERNMENT PRINTING OFFICE, 1991, p. 37).

Forging partnerships is essential if GPO is to be efficient in its operations. For example, the U.S. GENERAL ACCOUNTING OFFICE (1992a) notes that agencies prepare most of their submissions to the Office of the Federal Register on paper for inclusion in the *Federal Register* on paper. This means that GPO must retype them. GAO maintains that if agencies submitted one-third of the documents in electronic form with the inclusion of the appropriate typesetting codes, agencies would save $2 million annually. GPO would also save millions of dollars in typesetting costs.

The GPO Wide Information Network for Data Online Act of 1991 (House Resolution 2772) (U.S. CONGRESS. 102ND CONGRESS, 1ST SESSION, 1991g) and the GPO Gateway to Government Act (Senate Bill 2813) (U.S. CONGRESS. 102ND CONGRESS, 2ND SESSION, 1992a)—both known as the WINDO legislation—proposed GPO as a point of online access to a diversity of federal databases containing electronically stored public information. Many of the proposed databases were unavailable online from the government. The legislation ignored the separation of powers among government branches by proposing that GPO scrutinize the fees agencies charge for making their databases publicly available. It also mandated that depository libraries receive free access to the databases, while others, including nondepository libraries, would pay "reasonable fees." Two basic questions are:

- How cost-effective and timely is it for agencies to publish or disseminate through GPO as opposed to other channels?
- To what extent can GPO meet the needs of agencies and users?

Critics of the legislation, such as the Information Industry Association, maintained that GPO needed to establish a track record before it engaged in broad dissemination of electronic information through a gateway. In addition, they wanted Congress to specify the criteria for deciding which databases to distribute and to maintain effective oversight to ensure that public access is indeed improved.

The Government Printing Office Electronic Information Access Enhancement Act of 1992 (House Resolution 5983) replaced the two previously mentioned WINDO bills. This legislation also failed to pass Congress and become public law. However, it would have required GPO to conduct a feasibility study into "enhancing public access to Federal electronic information" (CONGRESSIONAL RECORD, 1992, p. E2738). That study would have considered the provision of such information through the Internet and the National Research and Education Network (NREN) and would have addressed issues of cost savings.

In 1993 Senate Bill 564 and House Resolution 1328 (Government Printing Office Electronic Information Access Enhancement Act of 1993 (CONGRESSIONAL RECORD, 1993)) were introduced into Congress. These bills, which represent a scaled-down version of the WINDO legislation, call for GPO to offer distribution services for improved public access to federal government electronic information and for low-cost online access to the Federal Register and the Congressional Record. GPO, according to the bills, is also to provide a storage facility and archive federal information, especially congressional information.

Agency participation in the system would be voluntary. In addition, neither bill specifies funding for the provision of an electronic directory to online government information, programs, and services.

As both bills proceed through Congress, it is evident that the legislation is intended to preserve a role for GPO in the electronic information age. However, the nature and scope of that role remain to be seen. For example, other agencies want to provide electronic information locator services, and the National Archives and Records Administration traditionally functions as the main repository of archival material.

Competing views from stakeholders do not provide GPO with clear guidance in trying to move more extensively into an electronic environment. The Government Documents Round Table (GODORT) (AMERICAN LIBRARY ASSOCIATION) has identified "priorities for disseminating electronic products and services from the U.S. Government Printing Office," but other groups are unlikely to endorse all of these recommendations.

Congressional Committees

Congressional committees may introduce policy initiatives, conduct oversight hearings on agency management of information resources, and request studies related to a range of topics. A number of committees, such as those listed below, are important stakeholders in the development and application of federal information policies:

- Joint Committee on Printing;
- Senate Committee on Judiciary, Subcommittee on Technology and the Law;
- House Committee on Government Operations, Government Information, Justice, and Agriculture Subcommittee;
- Senate Committee on Governmental Affairs, Subcommittee on Government Information and Regulation;
- House Committee on House Administration, Subcommittee on Procurement and Printing;
- House Committee on Science, Space, and Technology, Subcommittee on Science, Research, and Technology; and
- Senate Committee on Commerce, Science, and Transportation.

While many concerns related to electronic information policy come before these committees, other committees, such as those dealing with appropriations, may play central roles.

In general, however, Congress rarely gives information policy issues high visibility. Thus, individual staff members frequently serve to focus attention on such issues. Nonetheless, as WEISS points outs, many factors affect congressional decision making and the extent to which committees determine their involvement in a particular policy issue.

The Public Access Community

The term "public access community" includes assorted stakeholders that generally monitor government activities and lobby for broader public access to government information. Members of this community include professional associations, such as the American Library Association (ALA), American Association of Law Librarians (AALL), and the American Society for Information Science (ASIS), all of which have some type of government relations committee.

Also included are such groups as OMB Watch, the Electronic Frontier Foundation, The Reporter's Committee for Freedom of the Press, and the Coalition for Networked Information. These groups regularly issue position statements on electronic government information and often serve as watchdogs on how the government manages and distributes information.

Information Industry Association

Founded in 1968, IIA is the trade association of numerous companies that create and distribute information products and services. In general, IIA "wants government to avoid being a competitor, particularly in the 'value-added' area of taking raw government data and making it more accessible through marketing or good software" (MCINTOSH, 1989, p. C1).

As an example, IIA recently released a policy statement on information infrastructure issues that is based on the following principles (INFORMATION INDUSTRY ASSOCIATION):

- A thriving information marketplace and a well-informed citizenry depend upon the encouragement of a range of diverse sources of information stimulated by competitive market forces. Government should set technological and administrative ground rules that promote competition and diversity and discourage monopolistic control over information by any entity, public or private;
- Clear protection for copyright and other proprietary rights is vital to the development of innovative and valuable information products and services;

- A consistent and predictable policy environment is essential; the prospect of a patchwork of inconsistent state regulations casts a cloud over the bright horizons of the information age; and
- Legitimate consumer interests such as a realistic expectation of privacy must be acknowledged and balanced with the need for a free flow of information throughout America's future telecommunications networks.

Accordingly, IIA has developed numerous policy positions intended to promote and enhance the private sector.

As RUSSELL (p. 251) notes:

the Federal government has enormous power to influence the development and diffusion of new information technologies. Through the use of electronic information systems, it also has the opportunity to make more government information readily available to more public users. Defining the appropriate uses of, and controls on, this power are of critical importance in determining whether the government will be a positive or a negative force, particularly with respect to the private sector.

IIA has been active and articulate in making its positions known on a range of electronic information policy issues.

KEY ISSUES

The following policy issues were identified as requiring further study and perhaps congressional action (U.S. CONGRESS. OFFICE OF TECHNOLOGY ASSESSMENT, 1986b, p. 147-158):

- Cost effectiveness of electronic information options;
- Equity of access to electronic government information;
- Private-sector role in federal electronic information activities;
- Public information index or clearinghouse;
- Mechanism for exchange of learning and innovation;
- Freedom of Information Act implementation;
- Electronic record keeping and archiving;
- Scientific and technical information; and
- Other issues (transborder information flow, depository library program, federal statistical system, and copyright protection).

Clearly there are many policy issues related to electronic government information. Since 1985 the literature dealing with various aspects of these issues has increased dramatically. This section identifies major issues and incorporates recent writings. The criteria used to select the issues include:

- Pervasiveness—degree to which the issue affects a range of stakeholder groups in a variety of settings;
- Access—degree to which the issue affects effective access to government information; and
- Impacts—degree to which the issue may have significant societal impacts, costs, and other consequences.

Public's Right to Know

The Freedom of Information Act (FOIA), first enacted in 1966 (5 *U.S.C.* 552) (U.S. CONGRESS. 89TH CONGRESS), and the 1974 Privacy Act (5 *U.S.C.* 552a) (U.S. CONGRESS. 93RD CONGRESS, 2ND SESSION, 1974a) prominently stand for the people's right to know about the business of government. There are other statutes in the same tradition (e.g., the Federal Advisory Committee Act (5 *U.S.C.* Appendix) (U.S. CONGRESS. 92ND CONGRESS), Family Educational Rights and Privacy Act (20 *U.S.C.* 1232g) (U.S. CONGRESS. 93RD CONGRESS, 2ND SESSION, 1974b) and Government in the Sunshine Act (44 *U.S.C.* 2201-2207) (U.S. CONGRESS. 94TH CONGRESS)). Together these laws "sustain our form of government and help the citizenry to keep it" (HERNON & MCCLURE, 1987, p. 78). They ensure access to *public* information, "that which is collected and/or developed at government expense or as required by public law, and not considered to be classified, personal, [proprietary,] or otherwise subject to exemption" (HERNON & MCCLURE, 1987, p. 6).

In contrast, private information is intended exclusively for use within the government and "is held in confidence out of respect for a privacy right or a statutory obligation" (HERNON & MCCLURE, 1987, p. 7). HERNON & MCCLURE (1987, p. 7–8) identify six types of public information. Examples include information in the possession of private individuals and information subject to ownership.

BERMAN (p. 39) notes that the:

> transformation of public information and public decision making into computerized data processes has occurred without serious public policy attention being paid to how it may affect the public's right to know. Moreover, there has been no public policy debate or concerted effort initiated to re-

solve electronic information policy issues with citizen access rights as a core concern.

Instead, during the 1980s, agencies developed their own automated systems—e.g., the patent office's automated trademark system and the Securities and Exchange Commission's (SEC) Electronic Data Gathering, Analysis, and Retrieval System (EDGAR). (For a discussion of the development of these systems see U.S. CONGRESS. HOUSE. COMMITTEE ON GOVERNMENT OPERATIONS, 1986a, 1986b.) In some instances, the public has had to demand access rights to databases, while the policy-related discussion revolved, in part, around the role of the private sector in the management and provision of electronic government information.

BERMAN (p. 66) maintains that FOIA must be revised to include "a right of access to electronic records." MCINTOSH (1990, p. 3) notes that there is "substantial variation in agency practices concerning access to electronic records." Further, "the law remains unclear on whether requesters should be able to have records searched electronically to answer a specific request. . . . Requesters have no defined right to obtain computer tapes or diskettes instead of a paper printout. Critics argue that such problems limit access."

Two bills were introduced in the 102nd Congress to clarify and extend the degree to which FOIA pertained to electronic records: The Freedom of Information Improvement Act of 1991 (Senate Bill 1939) (U.S. CONGRESS. 102ND CONGRESS, 1ST SESSION, 1991a) and the Electronic Freedom of Information Improvement Act of 1991 (Senate Bill 1940) (U.S. CONGRESS. 102ND CONGRESS, 1ST SESSION, 1991c). Neither bill became public law.

Despite this failure, GOLDMAN believes that FOIA does guarantee public access to electronic information. ALLEN (p. 69), however, maintains that a "critical problem is that the principles underlying FOIA— which were developed in response to traditional paper medium—may not be transferable to an electronic age." Further, he argues (p. 69) that:

> the structure of an electronic database may not include discrete items of data equivalent to records as defined in a paper environment. Similarly, FOIA provides that citizens may have access to information that already exists—but does not require government agencies to "create" new records in order to respond to a public request. Electronic information can be "queried" in many different ways. However, a strict interpretation of FOIA would suggest that citizens can only obtain information gathered in response to a previously performed inquiry by a government employee.

GOLDMAN (p. 389), who would disagree, maintains that "it is inherently risky for Congress to legislate" enhanced access rights: "There is no guarantee that Congress can provide a better structure than the one that is already in place." Instead, she advocates that Congress oversee agency practices more strictly.

The U.S. WHITE HOUSE CONFERENCE ON LIBRARY AND INFORMATION SERVICES issued 96 recommendations and petitions. Some particularly vague recommendations advancing the public's right to know include:

- Amendment of FOIA "to ensure access to all nonexempt information" (p. 35);
- Increased "support for the depository library program to ensure improved access to information in electronic form" (p. 35);
- Creation of "an 'ERIC-like' information clearinghouse for scientific research" (p. 35);
- Reduction of the scope of national security (p. 36), presumably as an exemption to compliance with FOIA; and
- "Open, timely, free and uninhibited access to public information. . .regardless of format, except where restricted by law" (p. 38).

An assessment of these and other recommendations appears in a special symposium issue of *Government Information Quarterly* and in the introduction (CURTIS & O'HARE).

As laudable as these recommendations might be, the public's right to know regarding electronic information is unclear. Based on a May 1989 survey by the Department of Justice, executive agencies vary widely in their perceptions of FOIA obligations for electronic data (BURR & BLANTON). Until new policy instruments are established, litigation will likely be the major determinant of the degree to which the public's right to know regarding electronic information will be interpreted.

Public Access and Use

MEENAN & WYMAN, FOWLIE, and GRIFFITH present an overview of the information systems within Congress. PERRITT discusses the "most prominent" electronic acquisition systems and release programs. He also highlights other electronic release initiatives (see also LOVE).

SPREHE (1992b) asks, "Under what conditions should the public have online access to Federal computers—querying databases and downloading government information or data?" The answer depends on such factors as the agency's mission and position on information dissemination, existing statutes and past practices, "the nature of the database itself and the nature of the public's interest" (p. 200), and "perceptions of the security threat" (p. 201). "The real question Federal agencies will be facing in the next few years is how to organize and administer online public access to yield the least disruption to agency programs and the greatest benefit to information users in the public" (p. 202).

The EDGAR system automates the filing, analysis, and dissemination of information filed with the SEC by entities seeking to raise money from the public and whose securities are publicly traded (see GELLMAN; MC GRANE). "The SEC is still struggling today with requirements for a system that was conceived over 10 years ago" (U.S. GENERAL ACCOUNTING OFFICE, 1992e, p. 9). As developers of the system try to meet the dramatic increase in the number of "user requirements. . . significant cost overruns and schedule delays" result (p. 3). The "SEC is. . .faced with the task of obtaining and prioritizing user needs and system requirements, establishing problem tracking and resolution methods, and setting realistic project milestones" (p. 2). Such problems impede public access and use.

The U.S. Department of Agriculture's (USDA) Computerized Information Delivery Service (CIDS) enables agencies within the department to disseminate electronically perishable and time-sensitive data—data with a "limited useful life"—"to news and information services for distribution to their subscribers or to others interested in large amounts of USDA information" (U.S. GENERAL ACCOUNTING OFFICE, 1992b, p. 8). CIDS, operated by Martin Marietta Data Systems since 1985, "augment[s] rather than replace[s] the published reports of USDA agencies" (p. 8).

USDA claims that "the use of a contractor allows information to be available from a single source, avoids security risks associated while allowing the public to access the Department's computer, and provides more responsive service to the public" (p. 8). The contractor's charges for use of the

> CIDS vary depending on the type of user. The contract between USDA and Martin Marietta specifies that federal agencies (including USDA), and cooperators are charged the same unit price for services; all other users pay a rate established by the contractor based on standard commercial rates. The prices for federal agencies and cooperators are subject to volume discounts, and cover services such as computer utilization, hourly connect time, file loading and storing, peripheral device utilization, software surcharges, and microfiche.

> In addition, the contract provides for a rebate to USDA
> based on overall CIDS usage. (p. 11)

GAO examined the electronic dissemination policies and practices of the CIDS and the Toxic Release Inventory (TRI) at the Environmental Protection Agency (EPA). The review found no evidence that the former impeded public access (DESANTI, 1991) and made only a cursory examination of the latter because a separate review of the EPA's database, mandated by statute, was in progress (MCINTOSH, 1990, p. 48; U.S. GENERAL ACCOUNTING OFFICE, 1990).

Apparently CIDS was reviewed in response to charges raised by KRANICH and others. SHILL, who reviewed the arguments of both sides and GAO's methodology, supported Kranich's position. However, he noted the complexity of the phrase "information public" and the need to marry marketing research with information needs and information dissemination programs and services.

One congressional committee advises agencies to consider the needs of users when they plan and implement automated systems (U.S. CONGRESS. HOUSE. COMMITTEE ON GOVERNMENT OPERATIONS, 1986b). The revision of OMB's Circular A-130, proposed in 1992, also requires agencies to conduct user needs assessments as a normal part of information systems design and operation (U.S. OFFICE OF MANAGEMENT AND BUDGET, 1992b).

MARSHALL addresses a neglected topic, the use of electronic government information by the blind and others who cannot read print. "Information," he notes, "must be presented in certain ways in order for it to be read by a speech synthesizer or translated into hardcopy braille output" (p. 15). "Agencies such as the Department of Defense have...adopted a version of the SGML [Standard Generalized Markup Language] document definition system," thereby allowing individuals to reformat information to accommodate their personal preferences. Furthermore, refinement of that standard will better meet the access requirements of "print disabled persons":

> This special document type definition for the blind will
> either be incorporated directly into the AAP [Association of
> American Publishers] SGML and other public SGML defini-
> tions, or will be made available as a utility program which a
> blind person could use to convert an SGML document into a
> form which can easily be read with synthetic speech or
> translated into braille. (MARSHALL, p. 15)

For the disabled, limited access to electronic government information does not relate to issues of hardware, software, and standards. Rather, certain products, such as the *Federal Register,* are too expensive for purchase by many private-sector companies and thus are inaccessible to certain user populations. Unless this issue is resolved, "blind citizens of this nation" might become more of "an information underclass" (MARSHALL, p. 16).

Information Resources Management (IRM)

The Paperwork Reduction Act (PRA) as amended in 1986 (P. L. 99-500) (U.S. CONGRESS. 99TH CONGRESS) provides the basis for federal information resources management (IRM) and charges OMB with responsibility for implementing it. A number of policy instruments from OMB provide guidelines to agencies regarding IRM, one of the most important being OMB Circular A-130 (U.S. OFFICE OF MANAGEMENT AND BUDGET, 1985).

Given PRA's history and the failure to gain its reauthorization, Congress clearly does not understand the implications of legislation that seeks to improve IRM (PHILLIPS & CARROLL). Through PRA, Congress has focused more on paperwork reduction than it has on IRM.

A number of writers have commented on problems with federal IRM and its inability, both conceptually and practically, to manage government information successfully in the electronic environment (BISHOP ET AL.; CAUDLE & LEVITAN; U.S. GENERAL ACCOUNTING OFFICE, 1992d). Some problems particular to managing electronic information include:

- Lack of government-wide standards for information systems design and interoperability;
- Too much emphasis on information technology procurement and management;
- Limited interest in life-cycle management of electronic information, especially aspects related to public access and dissemination;
- Lack of a service perspective in managing electronic information both within the agency and for the public;
- Need for long-range planning and development for information infrastructure deployment; and
- Lack of coordinated government planning and enforcement of IRM policies and procedures.

These are a few of the problems and issues yet to be resolved regarding federal IRM.

In the 102nd Congress, HORTON introduced legislation (House Resolution 5851) to create the Commission on Information Technology and Paperwork Reduction. This commission would promote "the use of advancements in information technology" and minimize federal paperwork (p. 15). SPREHE (1992c) countered that it is more important to emphasize IRM over paperwork reduction and the scrutinizing of information collection. (This bill did not become law.)

The most recent *Information Resources Management Plan of the Federal Government*, however, states (U.S. OFFICE OF MANAGEMENT AND BUDGET, 1992c, p. III-10):

> Finally, the IRM community should work to build a Federal *service delivery* infrastructure—using information technology better to perform its missions. At root this requires new partnerships within and across agencies. Specifically, these partnerships could support: improving interagency coordination in service delivery; testing new citizen-service technologies such as kiosks; increasing the active dissemination of government information; reducing administrative burden and paperwork through the use of information technologies; and creating policies and incentive structures that encourage innovation.

This vision, however, is in stark contrast to the existing realities of federal IRM and its inability to cope effectively with the electronic environment (U.S. GENERAL ACCOUNTING OFFICE, 1992d).

Preservation and Deposit

The Committee on the Records of Government was a joint product of the American Council of Learned Societies, the Council on Library Resources (CLR), and the Social Science Research Council. The Mellon, Rockefeller, and Sloan foundations, together with CLR, provided funding. The report of the COMMITTEE ON THE RECORDS OF GOVERNMENT (p. 9; see also NELSON) observed that "the United States is in danger of losing its memory." The availability and use of computer technology have added to, not reversed, this trend. Government officials and employees may be unaware that "potentially precious documents disappear as word processors erase old texts and substitute new ones with no human saying 'Stop'" (p. 9).

The report identified two examples to dramatize the need to preserve America's heritage and programs. First, "by the mid-1970s, when computer tapes for the 1960 census came to the attention of archivists, there remained only two machines capable of reading them. One was already in the Smithsonian. The other was in Japan!" (p. 9). Second, "Because of erasures of electronic records, future historians may know less about the Reagan Administration's 1985 arms control initiatives than about those of 1972 which led to SALT I or, for that matter, those of 1921 which led to the Washington naval treaties" (p. 9). Calling for immediate resolution of these problems, the introduction of proper records management and IRM practices, and a more proactive role by the National Archives and Records Administration, the report emphasized that "although the condition of federal executive branch records is, with rare exceptions, deplorable, those of states, counties, cities, and towns are even worse" (p. 9). The report also reminded federal officials that they should recopy or recode "existing files or bodies of data" so that these files and bodies would remain "usable" and cost-beneficial (p. 44).

A U.S. House report (U.S. CONGRESS. HOUSE. COMMITTEE ON GOVERNMENT OPERATIONS, 1990, p. 2) notes that "a record remains useful only as long as the medium on which its information is stored can be read and understood." The National Archives needs to develop a forward-looking position in the preservation of government records, especially since "federal records of enduring value are increasingly being created and managed in electronic formats" (p. 7). "The National Archives must adjust its policies and its mission not just to today's technology but to the fact that changes in technology will occur constantly and rapidly in the future" (p. 24).

This report is a reminder that the "transfer of data in electronic form...may no longer be a simple task of cleaning up and copying sequential flat files and transferring them with their documentation to the National Archives" (p. 13). There is need for compatibility between computer hardware and software, "documentation about the organization, coding, and contents of electronic records" (p. 16), and standards. "Unless archival considerations are taken into account at the earliest possible stage, many computer files may disappear without ever being reviewed for historical value" (p. 26).

The report also notes that e-mail serves "as a means of written interoffice communication on both administrative and policy matters" and "as a repository of information crucial not only for historians but for current policy, oversight, and investigatory purposes." The Tower Commission and the congressional committees investigating the Iran-Contra affair used information captured in a White House computer system, known as the PROFS system. This system contains information that constantly changes and whose archival preservation presents a challenge; no "final" product can be transferred to the National Archives until the White House no longer needs the records or other information contained in the system.

Twice a federal judge issued a restraining order prohibiting the Reagan and Bush administrations from destroying backup computer tapes to the PROFS system containing e-mail messages (QUINDLEN). Printouts of the material in the electronic records are insufficient for public accountability because they do not contain all the "notations in the electronic messages—for example, which messages had gone to whom—that could be vital in helping scholars and others reconstruct the development of policy decisions and other events" (MILLER, p. A44).

Two important issues are: (1) to what extent do these messages constitute public or private records and merit archival retention, and (2) which sources are federal records and which are presidential records? (There is no judicial review of the latter type of record.) Complicating the answer to both questions, in regards to the PROFS system, is that on January 20, 1993, the Archivist of the United States granted President Bush or his *designee* the right to review all material on White House computer tapes held within the National Archives before allowing anyone else access to it. This controversial agreement could lead to endless review of the content and extensive litigation. Further, the archivist entered into the agreement and immediately accepted the position of executive director of the George Bush Center at Texas A&M University. His action, at the very least, creates an appearance of wrongdoing. Another problem is that the agreement overrides the Presidential Records Act of 1978 (44 *U.S.C.* 2204) (U.S. CONGRESS. 95TH CONGRESS, 2ND SESSION, 1978b) and the Federal Records Act (P. L. 92-915) (U.S. CONGRESS. 81ST CONGRESS; see also U.S. CONGRESS. 95TH CONGRESS, 2ND SESSION, 1978a) governing access to White House records.

The U.S. NATIONAL ARCHIVES AND RECORDS ADMINISTRATION, through its instructional guide series, offers agencies detailed guidance on managing electronic records as part of their records management program. Appendices highlight the disposition of electronic records under General Records Schedules 20, "Electronic Records," and 23, "Records Common to Most Offices with Agencies." Other appendices reprint "electronic records management," from section 1234 of Title 36 of the *Code of Federal Regulations* (*CFR*), and the "transfer of machine readable records to the National Archives," from section 1228.188 of Title 36 of *CFR*.

At the request of the National Archives, the National Academy of Public Administration prepared a report to "identify the major electronic databases in the agencies, particularly those 'Fortune 500' or so that have significant historical and research value" and to develop criteria by which the National Archives can "appraise databases to determine which ones to transfer to the National Archives" (NATIONAL ACADEMY OF PUBLIC ADMINISTRATION, p. iii). OMB and the

General Services Administration (GSA) also have a "responsibility for ensuring that history is not lost" (NATIONAL ACADEMY OF PUBLIC ADMINISTRATION, p. iii).

The report noted that agencies have often failed to extend the life cycle of electronic databases of historical value to the final stage, retirement at the National Archives. Agencies may not even associate retirement with placement in the collections of the National Archives. The NATIONAL HISTORICAL PUBLICATIONS AND RECORDS COMMISSION summarizes the issues and research problems yet to be addressed in preserving electronic government records; the list is daunting, to say the least.

With over a decade of reports that have pointed to the urgency of developing and instituting a plan for dealing with the preservation of electronic records, some still believe that the National Archives has failed to implement such a plan (WINKLER). Some even maintain that it will take a new archivist to deal with these issues as well as "a pretty weak management structure" within the agency (MCALISTER; U.S. CONGRESS. SENATE).

Treatment of CD-ROM

EBERSOLE mentions that since 1846 the Library of Congress (LC) has used the Copyright law (17 *U.S.C.*) and its stipulation that copies of books published in the United States be deposited there (whether or not copyright registration is sought) to develop its collection. In 1991, LC issued regulations denoting CD-ROM as a type of publication and, therefore, one requiring deposit at LC. Publishers have "balked. . .because of concern about possible misuse of their products and because the deposit mechanism could conflict with their obligations to content providers [those responsible for the content of the product]" (EBERSOLE, p. 15). They regard CD-ROM as "different from printed works" because the technology can be networked, and because "the CD-ROM publisher is a licensee of both the contents and the search and retrieval software," it must "abide by all the restrictions that inhere in these licenses" (p. 15). "The publisher retains the title and leases the CD-ROM to the purchaser. The latter has possession but does not own the CD-ROM" (p. 15).

The problem of deposit may not affect many CD-ROMs produced by the government unless commercial software is required to use them. However, CD-ROMs generated by the private sector using government information would be a different matter. Currently a task force consisting of the members from the Copyright Office, LC, the library community, and IIA are trying to resolve the problem without having to request an amendment to the Copyright Act.

Standards

Information technology standards involve compatibility between systems and networks, the costs of software development and maintenance, security, data preservation, resource sharing, and other issues. As RADACK (p. 39) states, "Standards are a means to achieve common solutions to common problems such as improving staff productivity, overcoming incompatibilities between systems and networks, and reducing the costs of software development and maintenance." Various public and administrative laws, including the Brooks Act (P. L. 100-503) (U.S. CONGRESS. 100TH CONGRESS, 2ND SESSION, 1988a), the Computer Security Act of 1987 (P. L. 100-235) (U.S. CONGRESS. 100TH CONGRESS, 1ST SESSION), PRA and its 1986 reauthorization (U.S. CONGRESS. 96TH CONGRESS; U.S. CONGRESS, 99TH CONGRESS), and OMB's Circular A-119, *Federal Participation in the Development and Use of Voluntary Standards* (U.S. OFFICE OF MANAGEMENT AND BUDGET, 1982) outline standards responsibilities. In addition, guidelines, such as Federal Information Processing Standards (FIPS), direct agencies in managing and processing electronic information.

In general, the National Institute for Standards and Technology (NIST) is responsible for developing and coordinating standards in the government. However, the existence of many different policy instruments has produced a situation in which there is no clear authority for enforcing the adoption and use of standards, even those promulgated as part of the FIPS programs. The U.S. GENERAL ACCOUNTING OFFICE (1978) identified many problems related to coordination and enforcement. It is unclear if the situation has greatly improved (see U.S. CONGRESS. OFFICE OF TECHNOLOGY ASSESSMENT, 1992).

MCCLURE ET AL. (1992c) conclude that standards development for electronic government information has lagged far behind the emergence and use of the technology. IRM managers and policy makers should be concerned about the selection of specific information technology standards, the development and coordination of standards policy, and the enforcement of existing standards. They can develop or choose standards that will serve larger information policy goals, such as improved public access to government information, but the goals must guide the planning of federal standards.

Neither Circular No. A-119 (U.S. OFFICE OF MANAGEMENT AND BUDGET, 1982), nor its proposed replacement (U.S. OFFICE OF MANAGEMENT AND BUDGET, 1992d) deals exclusively with information technology standards. Furthermore, neither the Interagency Committee on Standards Policy (ICSP) specified in the circular nor the Standards Executive detailed in the revised circular can provide the needed coordination or enforcement. One congresssional report (U.S. CON-

GRESS. OFFICE OF TECHNOLOGY ASSESSMENT, 1992) is critical of ICSP's effectiveness in coordinating standards policy.

In the increasingly internetworked environment of information processing and technology, hardware and software based on proprietary systems and their protocols limit the potential for sharing information and delivery services across a wide variety of platforms. Recognizing this problem, NIST has promulgated a number of FIPS to support its Applications Portability Profile (APP), the government's program to establish an Open Systems Environment (OSE) for information technology. Operating since 1989, APP relies on a foundation of specific standards such as the Portable Operating Systems Interface and the Government Open Systems Interconnection Profile.

Open systems enable users to achieve the following (U.S. OFFICE OF MANAGEMENT AND BUDGET. OFFICE OF INFORMATION AND REGULATORY AFFAIRS, p. 23-24):

- Portability (the ability to use or migrate systems or applications software, and data across different computing platforms from multiple vendors);
- Interoperability (the ability to have applications and computers from different vendors work together on a network);
- Scalability (the ability to use the same applications and systems software on all classes of computers from desktop workstations to supercomputers);
- Common program interfaces (the ability to develop applications based on a set of standard programming tools that can be easily transferred across platforms); and
- Common user interfaces (the ability to create applications with a similar "look and feel" so that users can easily learn new applications after gaining an understanding of the first).

An advantage of an open systems environment, especially for NIST, is that it offers a framework for choosing what standards are needed. For example, FIPS 146-1, *Government Open Systems Interconnection Profile (GOSIP)*, FIPS 151-1, *POSIX: Portable Operating System* Interface for Computer Environments, and FIPS 158, The User Interface Component of the Applications Portability Profile, contribute to the development of an open systems environment. It is likely that application-level standards for open systems interconnection, such as file transfer, access and management (FTAM) and message-handling systems (MHS), will be adopted as components of GOSIP. While standards developed under the Open Systems Interconnection Reference Model look to the future, the current network environment of the Internet is based on a separate suite of protocols (TCP/IP) (Transmission Control Protocol/Internet Protocol). In this regard, it is important to ask what this will mean for agency systems that are compliant with FIPS but are not interoperable in the Internet environment.

NIST has adopted other important information processing standards in recent years. Standards such as FIPS 152, Standard Generalized Markup Language (SGML), and FIPS 161, Electronic Data Interchange (EDI), provide agencies with opportunities for handling text for publication and data transmission. Yet, on what basis are standards chosen for adoption or development? For example, SGML is one of several document-handling standards. SGML is not an open systems interconnection (OSI) application-level standard, whereas Office Document Architecture (ODA) and Interchange Format (ODA/ODIF) are. It is possible that there will be two conflicting or redundant standards.

Important policy issues focus on different information technology standards, the development and coordination of standards policy, and the enforcement of standards implementation. Within this context, it is important to develop or select standards that will guide and serve information policy goals such as those relating to public and client access to electronic government information.

Depository Library Program

In May 1983, JCP appointed the Ad Hoc Committee on Depository Library Access to Federal Automated Data Bases "to evaluate the feasibility and desirability of providing access to Federal government information in electronic formats to depository libraries" (U.S. CONGRESS. JOINT COMMITTEE ON PRINTING, 1984, p. iii). JCP also supported the finding of the ad hoc committee that GPO implement a pilot program for introducing electronic sources to the depository library program (U.S. CONGRESS. JOINT COMMITTEE ON PRINTING, 1985).

In preparing its report, *Informing the Nation* (U.S. CONGRESS. OFFICE OF TECHNOLOGY ASSESSMENT, 1988), OTA asked GAO to conduct two surveys, one of "agency needs and practices" and the services that GPO might provide, and the other of the "current and future technology needs of libraries." Two Fact Sheets from the U.S. GENERAL ACCOUNTING OFFICE (1988a; 1988b) tabulate survey findings without offering an interpretation. The first survey showed that agencies held electronic sources of public interest. The "survey results provide a remarkable picture of agency operational use of electronic information technologies for information dissemination" (U.S. CONGRESS. OFFICE OF TECHNOLOGY ASSESSMENT, 1988, p. 33). The library survey is more difficult to interpret given the assortment of library types examined and the inability to generalize the findings to a particular population. It would seem, however, that responding libraries made some use of government information and were interested in access through electronic services. Clearly the commitment of depository libraries to the use of information-handling technologies and the provision of increased service to electronic government information was on the rise.

Between 1989 and 1991, GPO initiated five pilot projects to assess the viability of depository distribution of federal publications or products in electronic format (see ALDRICH & JOBE; DUGAN & CHEVERIE). ALDRICH & JOBE analyzed the projects and concluded that the lessons learned should assist GPO and agencies in their efforts to develop and distribute future products: "The primary implication of the pilot projects is that input from depository libraries is essential from the ground level in future planning efforts if electronic products are to succeed in depository libraries" (p. 75). They maintain that:

> One apparent outcome of this dialogue should be a list of criteria suggesting how electronic products might be configured to be considered user friendly in the library setting. The pilot projects also suggest that two criteria for software targeted for depository libraries is (sic) that the software be both powerful and easy to use. (p.75)

The final evaluation for the pilot project that disseminated the *Congressional Record* on CD-ROM concluded that (U.S. CONGRESS. GOVERNMENT PRINTING OFFICE, 1992, p. iv):

> The *Congressional Record* CD-ROM Pilot Project demonstrated the feasibility of disseminating the publication in electronic format. . . .The pilot project less clearly demonstrated the practicality of such dissemination. Although the CD-ROM format was more economical than a comparable quantity in paper, the total cost to the Government for dissemination of the 1985 [*Congressional*] *Record* [on] CD-ROM was greater than the estimated cost for disseminating the microfiche format. Additionally, the librarians reported problems that diminished the. . .CD-ROM's usefulness.

Thus, a range of tradeoffs has to be considered in the dissemination of government information in one electronic format vs. another or vs. print or nonprint (e.g., microfiche and microfilm).

Some librarians support the position that "when a library accepts depository status, it accepts the responsibility of supporting the dissemination of government information regardless of the format" (RYAN, p. 278). They believe that libraries in the depository program must provide access to information rather than just publications, as mentioned in 44 *U.S.C.* 1901. Further, all depositories, they suggest, must collect and service electronic and nonelectronic information.

The introduction of new technologies into smaller depository libraries may present serious challenges: "increased pressure on staff and resources during a time of fiscal constraint; shift of activity from end-user to staff; need for new instructional programs; and difficulties involved in using new CD-ROM products" (BERK, p. 203; see also CHAPMAN).

There is increased recognition that the depository program, founded in 1814 and grounded in outdated legislation, is similar to a "vacuum cleaner" operating "on an outdated 'electrical' system" (HERNON, 1992b, p. 99). According to CORNWELL ET AL. (p. 123):

> this analogy does raise the ultimate question of whether the DLP [Depository Library Program] can be overhauled and patched? Should it be replaced with an alternative model? What other models of depository programs exist, and would they complement each other? How would the different models handle more than paper publications?. . .How do information safety nets fit together and provide the public with access to government publications, products, and services? It is time to examine how the various parts of the access puzzle fit together.

In response, the Depository Library Council to the Public Printer now calls for a restructuring of the program. It encourages a review of the types of models depicted in several publications (ASSOCIATION OF RESEARCH LIBRARIES; CORNWELL ET AL.; HERNON & MCCLURE, 1988 (p. 365-390), 1991a; LEIGHTON; SPREHE, 1993; U.S. CONGRESS. OFFICE OF TECHNOLOGY ASSESSMENT, 1988; see also U.S. DEPARTMENT OF COMMERCE. BUREAU OF THE CENSUS).

Any replacement of the present depository program with a new model will require congressional and presidential assent through legislation. If such an approach is not feasible, GPO and the depository library program will continue to operate within the gray area of existing law and press agencies to release more resources through the program. However, budget cuts and program priorities within GPO (see ZAGAMI), together with congressional efforts at deficit reduction, general pressure to control the cost of all government programs, and the desire of more agencies to maintain control over the dissemination of their electronic products and services may prevent the depository program from being the type of safety net and dissemination program that many librarians favor.

Locator Systems

The development of a government-wide information inventory locator system (GIILS) has received increased attention in the past five years. PRA requires that "each agency shall systematically inventory its major information systems and periodically review its information resources management activities" (44 *U.S.C.* 3586). The development of such a locator system has support from a number of sources (NATIONAL HISTORICAL PUBLICATIONS AND RECORDS COMMISSION (p. 13); Senate Bill 1044, reauthorization of PRA (U.S. CONGRESS. 102ND CONGRESS, 1ST SESSION, 1991e); U.S. CONGRESS. OFFICE OF TECHNOLOGY ASSESSMENT, 1988)).

MCCLURE ET AL. (1990) noted that a GIILS was both essential for effective access to electronic government information and feasible to develop. They considered a GIILS to be a machine-readable database that could identify different information resources (e.g., databases, libraries, clearinghouses, print publications, bulletin boards, and guides), and they described the information available in these resources. Usually the locator does not provide the actual information but points the user to the proper sources.

BASS & PLOCHER believe that a GIILS should be modeled after the originally mandated Federal Information Locator System (FILS), a system, they maintain, that was never successfully implemented by OMB. The American Technology Preeminence Act of 1991 (P. L. 102-245) (U.S. CONGRESS. 102ND CONGRESS, 2ND SESSION, 1992b) required NTIS to conduct a feasibility study by November 1992 for implementing some type of a government information locator system.

MCCLURE ET AL. (1992a) conducted a follow-up study on the development of a GIILS. They identified more than 50 locators in operation as well as a process to create an Internet-based locator system. That system would use a client-server architecture and be based on the American National Standard Z39.50, Information Retrieval Service Definitions and Protocol Specification for Library Appplications (NATIONAL INFORMATION STANDARDS ORGANIZATION). As part of their report, they included diskettes that described each locator (MCCLURE ET AL., 1992b).

A government committee (U.S. INTERAGENCY PUBLIC ACCESS WORKING GROUP) is responding to the recommendations of MCCLURE ET AL. (1992a) and intends to develop a CD-ROM product containing the locators identified. The group also plans for Internet access to government locators using wide area information servers (WAIS) technology.

Pricing Policy and User Fees

Different stakeholders "view information dissemination and pricing issues based on their primary values" (PHILLIPS & CARROLL; see also KENT):

- Librarians want maximum access at no charge;
- Budgeteers want to minimize the deficit by raising revenue;
- Economists want to maximize economic efficiency by marginal cost pricing;
- Lawyers are concerned with precedents and consistency with other laws such as FOIA and the Privacy Act;
- Political scientists want a fair process for setting prices;
- Politicians see information dissemination as a secondary issue that affects other issues;
- Researchers/scientists want to know what data are available and whether they are available in a format that is easily researchable; they are not much interested in prices;
- Statisticians/demographers want to maintain the integrity and accuracy of the data in their presentation;
- Business entrepreneurs want to encourage and reward risk taking;
- Accountants and auditors (such as those in GAO) want a stated policy and an audit trail showing compliance with that policy;
- Mainframe computer specialists want allocation mechanisms to ensure efficient use of limited computer resources by price or other controls;
- Personal computer specialists want user friendliness and flexibility; and
- IRM managers want consistent practice; they recognize a need for a policy statement on guidelines (or a framework).

Also IIA does not want the government to charge high prices and to inhibit product development.

Although "economic analysis is a tool to be used in developing public policy," there are many "voices...to be heard" (KENT, p. 130) concerning the determination of the price of government information, who should pay and how much, and the definition of marginal cost.

A senior policy analyst for OMB summarized the "pros and cons in the argument about whether agencies should be permitted to keep funds received for information products and services" (PHILLIPS & CARROLL):

The ability to keep the money would encourage agencies to be more active in their dissemination programs; at the same time, since there is no formula for setting prices, agencies might set prices too high and discourage use. Not being able to keep the money encourages agencies to price on the low side, but it may limit dissemination based on the availability of funds. . . . Costs that people are willing to pay may determine the value of a product or service. Agencies must address how much they can afford to take from appropriations, when information budgets are tight and information dissemination is not required. People are willing to pay, but barriers to dissemination are constructed when the money received cannot be used to provide the service, offset dissemination costs, or set up new systems.

To guide pricing policies of the agencies, the following are available (see LASKA):

- OMB Circulars A-25 and A-130;
- 31 *U.S.C.* 9701, which covers "fees and charges for government services and things of value";
- 31 *U.S.C.* 3302, which addresses "custodians of money";
- 5 *U.S.C.* 552, which provides for the charging of fees when authorized by statute for records given in response to a request;
- 44 *U.S.C.* 1701-1702, 1708-1709, which covers GPO's user charges;
- 15 *U.S.C.* 1151-1157, 1525-1526, which oversees NTIS's user charges;
- FOIA; and
- Selected court cases and legislation specific to individual agencies.

There are significant variations in pricing policies among agencies and branches of government (LOVE), and in some cases there is "direct conflict" among the policy instruments (LASKA, p. 113).

The information-dissemination business plan for the U.S. Patent and Trademark Office (PTO), as one example, maintains that "the program should recover no more than its marginal costs." Specifically, it must (PHILLIPS & CARROLL):

- Identify costs and revenues;
- Show "long-term" balance;
- Show "benefits" to justify fixed resources, external revenue, and so forth;

- Be explicit on subsidies, and upper management must know what these are;
- Identify products/services set;
- Estimate direct costs and indirect costs: data gathering, processing, market research, product development, advertising, distribution, fee collection, and user support (after-market);
- Attribute costs to individual products and services;
- Determine revenue sources;
- Estimate sales; and
- Set prices.

Furthermore, the "PTO has considered differential pricing for all products; legislation requires fewer fees for small applicants for patents and trademarks. PTO is currently using fees from some users to subsidize others" (PHILLIPS & CARROLL).

EISENBEIS summarizes the development of pricing policies related to the Landsat system. She notes that since 1985 these policies have undergone numerous changes. However, in general, prices are excessive and limit the likelihood that academic libraries will collect such information, forcing more individuals either to not use the information or to incur significant costs.

An emerging trend is for government to consider electronic information as a possible source of revenue. For example, in 1992 Congress passed legislation requiring the Federal Maritime Commission to charge for disseminating information products and services to offset lost income from other taxes (House Resolution 2152; see U.S. CONGRESS. 102ND CONGRESS, 1ST SESSION, 1991f) (P. L. 102-582). The ERIC clearinghouse had intended to implement user charges and allow its contractor to copyright the ERIC database to generate new income (STONEHILL). Also in 1992 and 1993, LC requested legislation to provide a range of fee-based information services and products (Senate Bill 345) (U.S. CONGRESS. 103RD CONGRESS). Although Congress has not passed the legislation as part of its efforts at cost reduction and more effective use of information-handling technologies, it has shown an inclination to collect fees for information access to replace declining sources of revenue.

Copyright

GOLDSTEIN discusses copyright and intellectual property rights and observes that "copyright law...is complex and burdened by layers of history and nuance" (p. 99). Although the government is prohibited from asserting copyright over the information it collects and creates, agencies, such as NTIS and the National Library of Medicine (NLM), have asserted copyright-like privileges over their information.

ALLEN (p. 72) identifies "two dangerous principles" associated with government copyright:

> First, government assertion of copyright suggests that government has a right of "ownership" over information. Second, exercising this right of ownership would permit government agencies to selectively decide who can have access to information. Moreover, in order to enforce this authority, agencies have to ask requesters who they are and why they want the information.

Government copyright of electronic information may also limit public access to that information.

In 1991 legislation was introduced to allow the government to copyright software (Senate Bill 1581) (see U.S. CONGRESS. 102ND CONGRESS, 1ST SESSION, 1991d). This legislation highlighted a key controversy. On the one hand, copyright of government information might facilitate technology transfer and improve international competitiveness. On the other hand, public access to this software could be severely restricted (MORELLA). The legislation did not pass, but controversy over copyright and ownership of government electronic information is likely to continue.

Privacy Rights

There are serious threats to individual privacy as a result of the government's move to embrace electronic information. FLAHERTY provides an excellent overview of the key issues. The 1974 Privacy Act (U.S. CONGRESS. 93RD CONGRESS, 2ND SESSION, 1974a) still serves as the basic law regarding the government's access to and use of an individual's electronic records.

Although it is dated, an OTA report (U.S. CONGRESS. OFFICE OF TECHNOLOGY ASSESSMENT, 1986a) provides an excellent introduction to privacy issues. It shows that "Federal agency use of electronic technologies in processing personal information has eroded the protection of the Privacy Act" (p. 99). The study encouraged the establishment of a privacy or data protection board.

To that end, legislation was introduced in the 101st Congress to establish a Data Protection Board to review existing privacy law and guidelines and make recommendations for improving those guidelines (House Resolution 3669) (U.S. CONGRESS. 101ST CONGRESS). In the

next Congress, House Resolution 2443 (U.S. CONGRESS. 102ND CON-
GRESS, 1ST SESSION, 1991b) was introduced to amend portions of the
Privacy Act to clarify laws related to disclosure of records maintained
on individuals.

Despite the strong justification for updating privacy law in an electronic environment as articulated by WISE, neither bill became law.
BERMAN & WEITZNER have noted the erosion of privacy rights for
government information used in a networked environment. Privacy
issues related to electronic government information, like copyright issues, will continue to be contentious.

Electronic Information Dissemination Policy

The Department of Commerce in 1988 became the first department to
propose policies that it and other federal departments could use for the
electronic dissemination of information products and services. That
policy conformed to OMB Circular A-130 and stated that "an expressed
public 'need' for information" was an insufficient rationale for dissemination (U.S. DEPARTMENT OF COMMERCE, p. 91). The policy, however, did not explain the conditions under which agencies met expressed public needs and could be interpreted as a rationale for restricting access to public information.

Three interagency conferences on public access and dissemination
held at Solomons Island, Md., in 1991 and 1992 have afforded agency
representatives an opportunity to share experiences and to work toward an integrated approach to public access to and the dissemination
of government information (OKAY & WILLIAMS; PESACHOWITZ;
PHILLIPS & CARROLL). The first conference advocated "the need for
consistency in pricing policies, concerns over vendor resale, determining cost recovery, and how to deal with cost versus free decisions"
(OKAY & WILLIAMS, p. 237).

The second conference focused on the need for a formal policy to
guide agencies in providing electronic information while at the same
time protecting the integrity, security, and privacy of the systems and
their data. Despite the tradeoffs, public access should be a priority in
the design and implementation of computer systems and should be
part of life-cycle planning.

Of importance, the second conference produced a working draft,
"Public Access to Government Electronic Information: A Policy Framework." That framework contains a purpose statement, a guiding principle, and policy considerations (guidelines covering type of program,
program rationale, technology approach, costing flexibility, security
controls, and private-sector, state, and local government roles). The
appendix indicates the considerations and conditions that go into for-

mulating a policy on public access to electronic government information (KADEC; OKAY & WILLIAMS).

DESANTI (1993) suggests that a policy framework for public access must address issues related to dissemination, some of which might be ethical (e.g., accuracy, security, fraud, and abuse). Computer matching, for example, allows the manipulation of information/data for purposes originally unintended. "Technology also makes it easy to modify information in electronic records, disseminate information that has not been verified or qualified as to source or validity, and access sensitive or restricted information" (p. 253).

DeSanti also reminds agencies that information dissemination is part of IRM and life-cycle management. As such, agencies need to establish electronic records management programs to accomplish five managerial objectives: (1) ensure system effectiveness and meet use requirements; (2) promote system economy and efficiency; (3) protect data integrity; (4) safeguard information resources; and (5) comply with laws and regulations. It is essential that plans for information dissemination be built into the design, development, implementation, and modification of a system's evolutionary life cycle (DESANTI, 1993).

The third conference focused on the draft framework and implementation of a policy on the dissemination of government information. "The goals should be to make as much information as possible available to the public in the best way possible" (PHILLIPS & CARROLL). PHILLIPS & CARROLL complement DeSanti's analysis by expressing a number of concerns about the draft framework; they also recommend changes to it. Nonetheless, the draft and its analysis influenced OMB and agencies in their approach to government-wide policy and to the dissemination practices of agencies. The Department of Agriculture, for example, has tried to develop a departmental dissemination and public access policy that adheres to the draft framework. Policy is often set at the departmental level, with agencies developing complementary procedures. Despite such efforts, there is still a need to collect policies, case studies, and documents that further address issues of concern to the agencies in developing specific programs (PHILLIPS & CARROLL).

Although the dialog involved agencies, their representatives and contractors, the conferences provided a foundation on which agencies could build. In conjunction with the stipulation in the 1992 proposed revision of OMB Circular A-130, agencies should better understand the information needs and information-gathering behavior of those individuals and groups they are mandated to serve. Further, they should use that compiled information to ensure public access. Agencies must also ascertain if large volumes of use affect the performance of computer systems. The agencies need to involve congressional oversight and appropriations committees and develop the necessary infrastructure (OKAY & WILLIAMS).

Admissibility of Electronic Records

One aspect of public access concerns the admissibility of electronic records in court. Because no law has addressed this issue, "it takes a technologically educated attorney, functioning as an agency's general counsel to understand the issues and render the judgment" (SPREHE, 1992d, p. 154). To guide the general counsels, the Department of Justice issued *Admissibility of Electronically Filed Federal Records as Evidence* (U.S. DEPARTMENT OF JUSTICE), which states that federal rules of evidence apply to records regardless of format. "In large part because of its source, the Justice Department paper constitutes a major step in removing a bureaucratic barrier to the introduction of new technology for the management of Federal. . .records" (SPREHE, 1992d, p. 154).

Scientific and Technical Information (STI)

BALLARD, MCCLURE & HERNON (1989a), and GRIFFITHS ET AL. provide useful overviews on the development and current status of STI policy. STI is being issued increasingly in electronic format only, and huge amounts of information and data must be managed, maintained, disseminated, and retired. Large-scale government research initiatives, such as the Global Climate Change project, result in interagency working groups' creating standards and procedures for gaining access to and using electronic information on a case-by-case basis (U.S. COMMITTEE ON EARTH AND ENVIRONMENTAL SCIENCES).

"The future of STI dissemination will be dominated by electronic formats" (U.S. CONGRESS. OFFICE OF TECHNOLOGY ASSESSMENT, 1989, p. 57). Thus, there is need for "an overall strategy on dissemination of STI" (p. 1). That strategy must address issues related to IRM, "timely, cost-effective storage and dissemination" and the need to balance "the free flow of Federal STI...against concerns about protection of national security and international competitiveness" (p. 1). The strategy will require leadership and commitment from the executive branch, in particular OMB and the Office of Science and Technology Policy (OSTP).

The policy research related to STI is sparse and often occurs absent a broader framework. Such a framework developed for the North Atlantic Treaty Organization (NATO) aerospace community merits careful consideration (HERNON, 1992a, pp. 29-31). That matrix contains three themes: (1) information management, (2) provision of information, and (3) access to information. Except for the first theme, there are subthemes. Each theme or subtheme has four possible aspects: (1) human resources, (2) quality assurance, (3) cost, and (4) technology. With some modification, the matrix can accommodate life-cycle management, information use, and information-gathering behavior.

The electronic provision of STI is accelerating more rapidly than that for government information in general. Many of the issues, however, are being confronted and resolved on an ad-hoc agency basis rather than under a coordinated government-wide policy.

CURRENT POLICY CONCERNS

The movement toward the development of government electronic information and information services has raised policy concerns related to the effective management of electronic information. Some of these policy initiatives are associated with ongoing information policy issues, whereas others are the result of new concerns and problems. This section highlights two key areas in which there is need for policy initiatives to manage electronic government information better.

Revision of OMB Circular A-130

OMB-OIRA issued OMB Circular A-130 on December 24, 1985 (U.S. OFFICE OF MANAGEMENT AND BUDGET, 1985) under the responsibilities assigned to that office under PRA. The circular links government information resources to IRM and the treatment of these resources as a commodity with both economic and social benefits (for background information see SPREHE, 1984, 1988). However, it was not until the proposed amendment of Circular A-130 in January 1989 that OMB began to address electronic dissemination (MCINTOSH, 1990, p. 19).

Proposed revision.   On April 29, 1992, OMB-OIRA issued a draft circular to replace the original Circular A-130 (see U.S. OFFICE OF MANAGEMENT AND BUDGET, 1992b). The draft document incorporates Circular No. 3, *Government Publications,* and Circular No. A-114, *Management of Federal Audiovisual Activities.* Among its other features, the new document emphasizes the connection between IRM and the information life cycle, records management and the need to manage electronic records, and the electronic collection of government information as a cost-reduction measure and as a means to provide better service to the public.

HERNON & MCCLURE (1993) analyzed the draft circular and called for its reissuance once major flaws are corrected. Suffice to say, OMB-OIRA has amended its definition of the information life cycle but offers contradictory coverage of the protection stage. The discussion treats the life cycle as a step-by-step process from collection to demise; the use of electronic information can result in the creation of new products, some of which merit protection.

The draft circular acknowledges but misquotes the definition of a government publication contained in 44 *U.S.C.* 1901. The proposed

revision defines an information product as (U.S. OFFICE OF MAN-
AGEMENT AND BUDGET, 1992b, p. 18298): "any book, paper, map,
machine-readable material, audiovisual production, other documentary material, regardless of physical form or characteristic disseminated
by an agency to the public." Thus, the difference between a government
publication and an information product is unclear. Adding to the confusion, the circular later refers to an electronic information product.
How does a publication differ from a product?

Issues of terminology.   In the past several years, policy makers and
analysts have distinguished between information products and information services and have suggested that depository libraries may have
access to the former but not the latter, primarily because of cost considerations. Appendix IV of the draft circular states that the term "information product" encompasses both products and services (p. 18301)
but advises agencies that they can provide electronic information products "within budgetary limitations."

Section 8a(3), which discusses the collection of electronic information, advises agencies to use "such techniques [to] reduce burden on the
public, increase efficiency of government programs, reduce costs to the
government and the public, and/or provide better service to the public." The section also lists five conditions under which agencies can
consider electronic collection.

Section 8a(7)(b) specifies that agencies must: "consider whether an
information product available from other Federal or nonfederal sources
is equivalent to an agency information product and reasonably achieves
the dissemination objectives of the agency." The extent to which agencies can meet this expectation relates to Section 8a(7)(c), which requires
agencies to "maintain inventories of all agency information products."
Clearly, the circular needs to clarify how any agency should develop an
information inventory/locator system.

As clarification of Circular A-25, *User Charges,* OMB instructs agencies to: "set user charges for information products at a level sufficient to
recover the cost of dissemination but no higher. They shall exclude
from calculation of the charges costs associated with original collection
and processing of information" (8a(8c)). The section notes three exceptions to this policy, and the appendix adds further clarification.

Other issues.   The circular should provide more guidance in cost
recovery. However, what are acceptable principles as well as specific
practices? Circular A-130 should define what is (and is not) a dissemination cost, clarify the distinction between cost and price, and explain
how to calculate that difference. Agencies do not want to have OMB
second guessing them as they determine user fees.

Circular A-130 should also address how agencies phase out old
information technologies as they acquire new ones. At the same time,

agencies should not lose their ability to gain access to information that is accessible only through outdated technologies.

There is a need to address: (1) the agency's role in information dissemination through the Internet/NREN; (2) who pays for the placement of resources in and use of the Internet/NREN; and (3) the extent to which the archival requirements for agencies are similar to or different from dissemination requirements. Strangely, the draft revision made no mention of how OMB-OIRA expects agencies to disseminate information through the Internet/NREN and to better define their roles and responsibilities in a networked environment.

As of spring 1993, the replacement for Circular A-130 had not appeared, and it is not clear when (or if) a final version will be issued or if there will be an opportunity for additional public comment on a second revision. Finally, the Clinton administration may wish to link the revision of Circular A-130 with PRA's reauthorization. Regardless of the scenario, issues related to a revised Circular A-130 and PRA's reauthorization will be critical policy issues for the foreseeable future.

The Internet/NREN

KAHIN (p. 455) observes that development of an infrastructure of computer networks based on the present Internet is creating a versatile new environment for disseminating public information. MCCLURE ET AL. (1992b) maintain that the development of the Internet and the establishment of the National Research and Education Network (NREN) through the High-Performance Computing Act of 1991 (P.L. 102-194) (U.S. CONGRESS. 102ND CONGRESS, 1ST SESSION, 1991h) offers government agencies unparalleled opportunities to design and to implement a host of information-dissemination activities and other services to better meet the needs of the public.

The Internet evolved from work done by the Defense Advanced Research Projects Agency (DARPA), and it primarily supports scientific research and communication (LYNCH & PRESTON). As a result of NREN's authorization, however, the Internet is evolving into a broader-based telecommunications system, one used by educators, librarians, government officials, and the public (MCCLURE ET AL., 1991b). As of July 1992, 6,500 networks were connected to the Internet, with 992,000 host sites, and perhaps as many as 10 million users (LOTTOR).

These numbers change daily, but exponential growth, improved interconnectivity, ubiquity, higher network speeds with greater bandwidth, and easier access to the Internet/NREN are current trends. This growth along with the trend toward a broader-based, multipurpose national network and its commercialization will continue through the decade (WEIS).

The development of the Internet/NREN, new client-server network-ing software, and high-speed computing make widespread access to and dissemination of electronic government information a realistic goal. The issue is not whether agencies will use the Internet/NREN, but when, how, and with what applications. As the U.S. NATIONAL ACAD-EMY OF SCIENCES (p. 53) notes, "crucial to setting up and running a national network infrastructure is participation by users." Government agencies are only beginning to obtain user input in the development of Internet-based services.

Agency use of the Internet/NREN. There is no comprehensive picture of either the number of agencies using the Internet/NREN or, for those agencies using it, the types of information dissemination and other services they provide. In a recent analysis, LOTTOR identified 62,000 hosts with a domain of *.gov*, indicating that 62,000 governmental units had been allocated an address domain for accessing the Internet.

Knowledgeable Internet spokespersons suggest that there are, on average, between six and ten addresses per host. Assuming that the multiplier is six, that 10% of the *.gov* hosts are state and local govern-mental units, and that the same 10% is offset by nongovernmental host sites providing access to government officials through a domain other than *.gov*, the number of federal addressees on the Internet can be estimated as 6 x 62,000, or 372,000 accounts.

This figure may be conservative. For example, at LC, the number of accounts on the host is well into the hundreds. The estimate of accounts accessible through the Internet depends on the multiplier. The total number of government accounts available through the various govern-ment hosts may well approach one million.

Despite the numerous governmental accounts that provide access to the Internet, the number of government information products or ser-vices these agencies provide via the Internet is exceedingly small, al-though growing. Overall, most agencies are only now becoming aware of the Internet and its potential uses for information services delivery.

Remote access to information services. Government bulletin boards, such as the Department of Commerce's Economic Bulletin Board, in-creasingly provide the public with a broad range of services and infor-mation (SANDLER, p. 42). Most of these are still dial-up, but there appears to be interest in and a trend toward making bulletin boards accessible over the Internet.

Some agencies are already offering access to information services on the Internet. An agency makes its computer an Internet/NREN host, allowing users at remote locations to log onto the agency computer (using Telnet, for example) and search its database for information. NASA's Master Directory is an example of this approach. Another is the

EPA's Online Library System (OLS). OLS includes EPA's *National Catalog*, which contains citations and summaries of the contents of all 28 EPA libraries, EPA documents distributed through NTIS, and EPA's Hazardous Waste Collection. NIST and the Department of Commerce have made the Computer Security Bulletin Board System available on the Internet/NREN to encourage sharing of information that will help protect data resources. The service provides reference materials, bibliographies, seminars, and conference dates, software reviews, and NIST publications (MCCLURE ET AL., 1992a, p. B-5).

FEDIX (Federal Information Exchange), an online information system operated by the private sector and accessible through the Internet/NREN, provides a broad range of electronic government information. It links the federal government, academia, and other research organizations to facilitate research, education, and other services. Currently FEDIX covers ten federal agencies (FEDERAL INFORMATION EXCHANGE, INCORPORATED).

In contrast to bulletin boards, another type of network-based access to agency information is anonymous file transfer protocol (FTP). The agency stores full-text files on an Internet host that functions as a file server. Individuals at remote locations can then log onto the agency's computer via the Internet, anonymously using a universal guest password, and download copies of these files across the network to their own local hosts. During the summer of 1992, LC used its Internet node [seq1.loc.gov] to make selected materials from its exhibit "Revelations from the Russian Archives" available via anonymous FTP.

A newer network access tool that is rapidly gaining widespread use is the Wide Area Information Server (WAIS), a standards-based method for network information retrieval. WAIS and WAIS-like software are comprised of a number of programs based on a client-server architecture and designed specifically for network information retrieval. ANSI standard Z39.50 allows connections among databases built on different computing platforms. The USGS operates a WAIS available over the Internet to enable network users to locate and access USGS databases from remote locations (CHRISTIAN & GAUSLIN).

In June 1990, the U.S. Supreme Court announced Project Hermes, a two-year pilot test, to release its opinions in electronic format, simultaneously with the release of the paper format to 12 sites, including the GPO electronic bulletin board and the Cleveland Free-Net, the latter accessible over the Internet. For the first time, a Supreme Court decision was widely available within hours of the judgment. The alternative to this system is LEXIS, a commercial fee-based online database service. The pilot project, now completed, has been successful. Project Hermes will be expanded and enhanced in 1993.

Technology-related barriers to agency use of the Internet/NREN.   There are a number of barriers to agency use of the Internet/NREN (MCCLURE ET AL., 1992c, p. 29):

- Some agencies believe that access to the Internet/NREN is not pervasive enough in society and/or will not serve as an effective communication link with that agency's particular clientele groups;
- There is limited awareness of what the Internet/NREN is and how it might be used to disseminate information or provide other services; there is wide discrepancy among the various agencies in terms of their knowledge and use of the Internet;
- Many agencies lack specific Internet/NREN operating knowledge; some agencies have a technical literacy problem; they do not understand the uses of networks telecommunications for the dissemination of information and services; and
- It is difficult for some agencies to establish connections to the Internet/NREN; they need technical instructions and guidelines.

Despite these difficulties, there is little doubt that government agencies must move their services into the Internet/NREN.

Position papers and research on how agencies might best use the Internet/NREN are needed. RUHLIN ET AL. offer a starting point for discussions about the role of the Internet/NREN in GPO's depository library program. Additional planning for the successful management of and access to electronic information via the Internet/NREN is needed.

Possible Internet/NREN services and applications.   Little published literature has discussed possible government Internet/NREN applications and services although the topic is frequently mentioned in the GovDoc-L Discussion List (see Table 1). Nonetheless, the following service types are likely to evolve, and policy guidance will be needed (MCCLURE ET AL., 1992c, p. 30):

- Providing access to agency information. For example, the Internal Revenue Service (IRS) could mount all of its booklets for completing tax forms on a file server, making them available for anonymous FTP. Individuals could then download this information as needed. If this service accounted for only 15% of the distribution of such forms, it could still save the IRS considerable money;
- Disseminating information to the public or to specific

target audiences. For example, individual agencies could develop electronic lists of information and services that are automatically distributed over the Internet to "subscribers" among the public; and

- Engaging in a range of value-added services. These services either rely on or use information resources already mounted on and available over the Internet, or they are "stand-alone" services; they do not depend on other information resources. The ELECTRONIC FRONTIER FOUNDATION discusses examples of such value-added services.

There is no lack of ideas for types of services that might be provided electronically over the Internet. What is yet unclear is the willingness of agencies to engage in Internet-based services, the extent to which additional policy is needed to promote such services, and the nature of actual public benefits for access to such electronic services.

The High-Performance Computing Act of 1991 (U.S. CONGRESS. 102ND CONGRESS, 1ST SESSION, 1991h) states that (Section 101a) "The President shall implement a National High Performance Computing Program, which shall: . . .provide for improved dissemination of Federal agency data and electronic information." Section 101(c) gives OMB oversight on agency budget requests for high-performance computing programs and initiatives. Should OMB so choose, it can use a number of techniques to "encourage" agencies to make government information available over the Internet. As agencies move into the Internet/NREN environment to provide public access to government information, numerous policy issues will have to be resolved (see *POLICY MATTERS*).

LOOKING TOWARD THE CLINTON ADMINISTRATION
AND THE 103RD CONGRESS

To a large extent, the existing federal electronic information policy system inhibits agencies from developing electronic services. There is considerable confusion about existing policies that guide the development of such services—e.g., pricing of electronic services or understanding which standards are to be followed in what situations. Such confusion and ambiguity can inhibit agency experimentation and risk taking as well as agency compliance with existing policy.

Numerous key issues require attention—e.g., the role of GPO as a government-wide printer and distributor of electronic products and services, OMB's policy expectations, and the uses that agencies make of the Internet, NREN, and other electronic networks.

For GPO and its depository library program to undertake significant change, the White House and Congress must alter Chapter 19 of the *United States Code* (U.S. CONGRESS. HOUSE. COMMITTEE ON HOUSE ADMINISTRATION). The potential for further decentralization of the information life cycle, and thus access to information, underscores the urgency of implementing locator systems, of marketing existing ones better, and of expanding agency use of the Internet. These actions will offset the disadvantages of increased decentralization and will improve public access to government information resources and services.

MCCLURE ET AL. (1992c) maintain that government electronic information policy must evolve into a service-oriented perspective. That perspective suggests that provision of electronic *information*, while laudable, must be replaced with goals related to the government's provision of electronic *services*, all of which depend on electronic information. Table 2 summarizes electronic information policy questions that must be addressed if the government is to move effectively to provide electronic services.

President Clinton campaigned on the slogan of "putting people first" and promoting the use of information technologies to solve a host of societal problems (BROAD). The existing federal electronic information policy needs extensive work if it is to support such goals. Government officials must be willing to assume a leadership stance in forging agreements among key stakeholders to shape electronic information policy. Many citizens believe they have a right to have access to electronic information and services and that it is a reasonable expectation to transact business with and obtain services electronically from the government.

The new administration and Congress will have to make a commitment to establish national electronic information infrastructures and policies if the government is to be connected to the public. Apparently the administration and some members of Congress are willing to make that commitment to ensure long-term economic growth, enhance U.S. access to foreign science, technology, and markets, and to ensure that government is more productive and responsive to the information needs of the American public (CLINTON & GORE). They recognize that "efficient access to information is becoming critical for all parts of the American economy" and that there is a need to use "new computer and networking technology to make. . .information more available to the taxpayers who paid for it" (CLINTON & GORE, p. 16). Until this commitment results in fully developed, effective, and efficient programs and services, efforts to provide government information and services electronically are likely to be costly, duplicative, disjointed, effective for only select target audiences, and of limited vision.

Table 2
Evolving Issues Related to the Delivery of
Electronic Information and Services

MODERNIZING THE GOVERNMENT'S INFORMATION INFRASTRUCTURE

What constitutes a "modern" and "effective" government-wide information infrastructure?

Should the government provide a basic level of information infrastructure
that other agencies can draw on, or should agencies develop their own?
What level of compatibility should exist across agency infrastructures?

Is OMB-OIRA responsible for ensuring the development of a government-
wide information infrastructure; otherwise which agency is responsible?
How successful has OMB-OIRA been in this area, and to what degree are
additional policy guidelines required?

How can adequate funds be obtained, authorized, and effectively managed
to support the development of a modern and effective government
information infrastructure?

LINKING CITIZENS TO THE GOVERNMENT ELECTRONICALLY

What type of technology functioning under what type of administrative
structure is most appropriate as a national electronic network?

How can existing federal networks be interconnected and linked to the
Internet or other electronic networks?

Can NREN serve as the national electronic network for linking government
with the citizenry?

What is the role of libraries in supporting the national electronic network,
and how might they best serve as intermediaries in linking the public to
the government electronically?

Can a single, easy-to-use interface be devised to provide effective access to
a range of electronic government services and products?

INCENTIVES FOR EFFECTIVE INFORMATION TECHNOLOGY
MANAGEMENT/SERVICES PROVISION

What policy initiatives could be developed to remove the disincentives for
agencies to provide services electronically?

Can specific cost savings or other benefits be demonstrated by agencies
that provide services electronically?

Table 2
Continued

REDEFINING IRM FOR ELECTRONIC SERVICES PROVISION

What measures can be taken such that agencies develop an overall IRM framework with a deliberate service orientation?

How can funds be made available within each agency for employees to participate in IRM training and education? How might additional attention in these programs be given to security and privacy issues?

How can mechanisms be created that encourage external partnerships (with other levels of government, as well as with the nonprofit and private sectors) in reaching citizens electronically?

How can agency heads be mandated to provide electronic services where feasible and appropriate via a federal government information infrastructure?

How can a deliberate effort be created to entice agencies to join government-wide and other national information infrastructure configurations?

What are IRM managers' responsibilities to safeguard the privacy and security of government information—for both the government and the individual—in a networked environment?

COORDINATION AND AGENCY ROLE (RE)DEFINITION

How can a concentrated and directed commitment to IRM be instilled in agency heads?

What mechanisms and incentives can be offered to reorient agency heads and IRM and telecommunications managers to think and operate in terms of services and joint, cooperative, and government-wide strategic efforts?

What organizational and government/cultural changes might be needed to bring about flexible, dynamic, and networked IRM?

PRODUCTIVITY IN INFORMATION TECHNOLOGY (IT) MANAGEMENT IN ELECTRONIC SERVICES PROVISION

How can policy makers create an innovative IRM operating environment within the federal government that encourages directed and limited risk taking so that appropriate IT applications can be explored for productivity gains?

How can policy makers ensure that certain features of newer IT (e.g., ubiquity and portability) be exploited creatively and appropriately within agencies' missions to provide electronic services?

Table 2
Continued

What mechanisms can policy makers develop to provide motivation and incentives for IRM organizations to implement applications with high-potential productivity gains in providing electronic services?

PARTNERING

How can government agencies recognize needs and opportunities to engage in IT and electronic services partnerships, especially in the evolving national information infrastructure environment?

Which policy initiatives could be developed to encourage partnering with other agencies, levels of government, and the private sector in order to maximize electronic service delivery to citizens?

What policy initiatives can be devised to create a strategic vision, incentives, and direction for agencies to engage in partnering since this effort might be a new and possibly only means, to reach citizens electronically?

EDUCATION AND TRAINING

Should Congress provide funds/legislation to support agency education and training activities related to that legislation, or should such initiatives be a government-wide effort?

SERVICE ATTITUDE IN GOVERNMENT

Should government-wide guidelines define and stress the importance of a "customer-orientation" to information services and suggest strategies for making agencies more responsive to the public's service needs?

To what degree does enabling legislation recognize the role of agencies as "providing services" to the public?

Do agency guidelines and policies define and promote a customer-oriented service perspective within the agency?

What assessments are done to determine the degree to which agencies identify and meet clientele service needs?

COORDINATING THE PACE OF POLICY DEVELOPMENT

What mechanisms can be established to involve the public, the agencies, and the nonprofit and private sectors more fully in developing information policies?

What is the role of federal IRM in developing and coordinating information policy?

CONCLUSION

The range of topics and policy issues related to electronic U.S. government information is extensive and continues to have significant impact on such areas as economic development, health care, education, and science and technology. The topics and policy issues are complex, interrelated, and eschew easy categorization as, for example, an "economic" or a "privacy" issue. They frequently defy easy analysis and are embedded in a political context that requires careful study to identify underlying causes and impacts.

Yet much of the writing on information policies, including electronic government information policies, is anecdotal, editorial, or nonempirically based. The few research studies that have been done tend to use traditional social science techniques. Experimentation with multimethod techniques and qualitative, anthropological, sociological, public policy, and evaluation approaches may help researchers study information policy issues better.

An incredible range of policy initiatives and proposals confronts the Clinton administration and the 103rd Congress. One of the most important is the future development of the National Information Infrastructure (NII). How the existing Internet, the program for NREN, and the public and private sectors (especially the computer, cable TV, telecommunications, and regional telephone companies) will work together to establish this NII is unclear and extremely contentious.

Nonetheless, there is an excitement about deploying new information technologies throughout society, of reconnecting individuals within society electronically, and of exploiting these information technologies for improving the quality of life and the public's satisfaction with the services that they receive. The development of these technologies, however, outpaces society's ability to deal with the social, behavioral, and policy issues that electronic government information raises.

BIBLIOGRAPHY

ALDRICH, DUNCAN M.; JOBE, JANITA. 1993. GPO Pilot Projects. In: Swanbeck, Jan; Hernon, Peter, eds. Depository Library Use of Technology. Norwood, NJ: Ablex; 1993. 59-76. ISBN: 0-89391-908-X; LC: 92-40351; OCLC: 27149893.

ALLEN, KENNETH B. 1992. Access to Government Information. Government Information Quarterly. 1992; 9(1): 67-80. ISSN: 0740-624X.

AMERICAN LIBRARY ASSOCIATION. GOVERNMENT DOCUMENTS ROUND TABLE. FEDERAL DOCUMENTS TASK FORCE. 1992. Priorities for Disseminating Electronic Products and Services from the U.S. Government Printing Office. Documents to the People. 1992; 20(2): 78-79. ISSN: 0091-2085.

ASSOCIATION OF RESEARCH LIBRARIES. 1987. Technology & U.S. Government Information Policies: Catalysts for New Partnerships. Washington, DC: Association of Research Libraries; 1987. 29p. LC: 88-156281; OCLC: 18628716.

BALLARD, STEVE. 1987. Federal Science and Technology Information Policies: An Overview. In: McClure, Charles R.; Hernon, Peter, eds. Federal Information Policies in the 1980s. Norwood, NJ: Ablex; 1987. 195-225. ISBN: 0-89391-382-0; LC: 86-22292; OCLC: 14243217.

BASS, GARY D.; PLOCHER, DAVID. 1991. Finding Government Information: The Federal Information Locator System (FILS). Government Information Quarterly. 1991; 8(1): 11-32. ISSN: 0740-624X.

BERK, LAWRENCE S. 1993. Florida Keys Community College. In: Swanbeck, Jan; Hernon, Peter, eds. Depository Library Use of Technology. Norwood, NJ: Ablex; 1993. 203-209. ISBN: 0-89391-908-X; LC: 92-40351; OCLC: 27149893.

BERMAN, JERRY J. 1989. The Right to Know: Public Access to Electronic Information. In: Newberg, Paula R., ed. New Directions in Telecommunications Policy: Volume 2. Durham, NC: Duke University Press; 1989. 39-69. ISBN: 0-8223-0948-3; LC: 89-1446; OCLC: 19514978.

BERMAN, JERRY J.; WEITZNER, DANIEL J. 1992. Keys to Privacy in the Digital Information Age. Electronic Networking: Research, Applications, and Policy. 1992; 2(4): 2-5. ISSN: 1051-4805.

BISHOP, ANN; DOTY, PHILIP; MCCLURE, CHARLES R. 1989. Federal Information Resources Management (IRM): A Policy Review and Assessment. In: Katzer, Jeffrey; Newby, Gregory B., eds. ASIS '89: Proceedings of the American Society for Information Science (ASIS) 52nd Annual Meeting: Volume 26; 1989 October 30-November 2; Washington, DC. Medford, NJ: Learned Information, Inc. for ASIS; 1989. 40-47. ISSN: 0044-7870; ISBN: 0-938734-40-7; OCLC: 3601238.

BROAD, WILLIAM J. 1992. Clinton to Promote High Technology, with Gore in Charge. New York Times. 1992 November 10; 142 (49,146): C1. ISSN: 0362-4331.

BURR, B.; BLANTON, T. 1989. Federal Agency Responses to Electronic Records Requests under the Freedom of Information Act: A Preliminary Assessment. Paper presented at: Electronic Public Information and Public's Right to Know: Symposium Sponsored by the Benton Foundation and the Bauman Family Foundation; 1989 October 21; Washington, DC. Available from: Bauman Foundation, 1731 Connecticut Ave. NW, 4th Floor, Washington, DC 20009-1146.

CAUDLE, SHARON L.; LEVITAN, KAREN B. 1989. Improving the Role of Information Resources Management in Federal Information. In: McClure, Charles R.; Hernon, Peter; Relyea, Harold C., eds. U.S. Government Information Policies. Norwood, NJ: Ablex; 1989. 296-314. ISBN: 0-89391-563-7; LC: 89-35081; OCLC: 18984027.

CHAPMAN, BERT. 1992. Willing to Provide But Unable to Support: The Dilemma of Smaller Depositories in an Electronic Era. Government Information Quarterly. 1992; 9(1): 81-87. ISSN: 0740-624X.

CHARTRAND, ROBERT LEE. 1986. Information Technology in the Legislative Process: 1976-1985. In: Williams, Martha E., ed. Annual Review of Information Science and Technology: Volume 21. White Plains, NY: Knowledge Industry Publications, Inc. for the American Society for Information Science; 1986. 203-239. ISSN: 0066-4200; ISBN: 0-86729-209-1; LC: 66-25096; OCLC: 17320444.

CHARTRAND, ROBERT LEE. 1991. Information Policy and Technology Issues: Public Laws of the 95th through 101st Congresses. Washington, DC: Library of Congress, Congressional Research Service; 1991. 47p.

CHRISTIAN, ELIOT J.; GAUSLIN, TIMOTHY L. 1992. Wide Area Information Servers: Information Systems Development. Reston, VA: U.S. Geological Survey; 1992. 92-96.

CLINTON, WILLIAM J.; GORE, ALBERT, JR. 1993. Technology for America's Economic Growth: A New Direction to Build Economic Strength. 1993. 36p. Available from: the Executive Office of the President, Office of Science and Technology Policy.

COALITION FOR NETWORKED INFORMATION. 1991. Information Policies: A Compilation of Position Statements, Principles, Statutes, and Other Pertinent Statements. Washington, DC: Coalition for Networked Information; 1991. 196p. ISBN: 0-918006-21-X.

COMMITTEE ON THE RECORDS OF GOVERNMENT. 1985. Report. Washington, DC: Council on Library Resources; 1985. 191p. ERIC: ED 269018; OCLC: 18156324.

CONGRESSIONAL RECORD. 1992. Government Printing Office Electronic Information Access Enhancement Act of 1992. Congressional Record. 1992 September 22; 138(130): E2737-E2738. ISSN: 0363-7239; OCLC: 02437919.

CONGRESSIONAL RECORD. 1993. Government Printing Office Electronic Information Access Enhancement Act of 1993. Congressional Record. 1993 March 11; 139(30): H1231, S2781-S2782. ISSN: 0363-7239; OCLC: 02437919.

CORNWELL, GARY; KESSLER, RIDLEY R., JR.; ALDRICH, DUNCAN; ANDERSEN, THOMAS K.; HAYES, STEPHEN M.; SULZER, JACK; TULLIS, SUSAN. 1993. Problems and Issues Affecting the U.S. Depository Library Program and the GPO: The Librarians' MANIFESTO. Government Publications Review. 1993; 20(1): 121-140. ISSN: 0277-9390.

CURTIS, JEAN M.; O'HARE, MARGARET F. 1992. Introduction to Symposium on the Summary Report of the White House Conference on Library and Information Services: Information 2000—Library and Information Services for the 21st Century. Government Information Quarterly. 1992; 9(2): 325-364. ISSN: 0740-624X.

DESANTI, VINCENT. 1991. On Public Access to Electronic Information: Will the "Public" Step Forward, Please? Government Information Quarterly. 1991; 8(1): 101-104. ISSN: 0740-624X.

DESANTI, VINCENT. 1993. A Policy Framework on the Dissemination of Government Electronic Information: Some Remarks. Government Information Quarterly. 1993; 10(2): 253-258. ISSN: 0740-624X.

DUGAN, ROBERT E.; CHEVERIE, JOAN. 1992. Electronic Government Information and the Depository Library Program: Paradise Found? Government Information Quarterly. 1992; 9(3): 269-289. ISSN: 0740-624X.

EBERSOLE, JOSEPH L. 1992. CD-ROMs Pose Depository Problem for the Library of Congress. Federal Computer Week. 1992 December 7; 6(36): 15. ISSN: 0893-052X.

EISENBEIS, KATHLEEN. 1992. Buying U.S. Satellite Remote Sensing Data since the Commercialization of the Landsat System. Documents to the People. 1992; 20(4): 233-235. ISSN: 0091-2085.

ELECTRONIC FRONTIER FOUNDATION. 1992. Applications Paper [Draft]. Washington, DC: Electronic Frontier Foundation; 1992. 27p. (Mimeograph). Available from: Electronic Frontier Foundation, 666 Pennsylvania Ave., SW, Suite 303, Washington, DC 20003.

ENGLISH, GLENN. 1985. Electronic Filing of Documents with the Government: New Technology Presents New Problems. Government Information Quarterly. 1985; 2(2): 183-186. ISSN: 0740-624X.

FEDERAL INFORMATION EXCHANGE, INCORPORATED. 1992. FEDIX User's Guide. Gaithersburg, MD: Federal Information Exchange, Inc.; 1992. 57p.

FLAHERTY, DAVID H. 1989. Protecting Privacy in Surveillance Societies. Chapel Hill, NC: University of North Carolina Press; 1989. 483p. ISBN: 0-8078-1871-2; LC: 89-4762; OCLC: 19353605.

FOWLIE, LEA. 1991. House Information Systems Online Services: Today and Tomorrow. Government Information Quarterly. 1991; 8(3): 285-291. ISSN: 0740-624X.

GELLMAN, ROBERT M. 1988. Authorizing EDGAR: Information Policy in Theory and Practice. Government Information Quarterly. 1988; 5(3): 199-211. ISSN: 0740-624X.

GOLDMAN, PATTI A. 1990. The Freedom of Information Act Needs No Amendment to Ensure Access to Electronic Records. Government Information Quarterly. 1990; 7(4): 389-402. ISSN: 0740-624X.

GOLDSTEIN, PAUL. 1989. Copyright Law and Policy. In: Newberg, Paula R., ed. New Directions in Telecommunications Policy: Volume 2. Durham, NC: Duke University Press; 1989. 70-100. ISBN: 0-8223-0948-3; LC: 89-1446; OCLC: 19514978.

GRIFFITH, JEFFREY C. 1991. The Development of Information Technology in the Congressional Research Service of the Library of Congress. Government Information Quarterly. 1991; 8(3): 293-307. ISSN: 0740-624X.

GRIFFITHS, JOSÉ-MARIE; CARROLL, BONNIE; KING, DONALD W.; WILLIAMS, MARTHA E.; SHEETZ, CHRISTINE. 1991. Description of Scientific and Technical Information in the United States. Knoxville, TN: University of Tennessee, Center for Information Studies; 1991. 2 volumes. 269p. (volume 1); 134p. (volume 2).

HERMAN, EDITH. 1993. NTIS Opens Gateway to Fed Databases. Federal Computer Week. 1993 January 4; 7(1): 4. ISSN: 0893-052X.

HERNON, PETER. 1989. Government Publications and Publishing during the Reagan Years. Government Information Quarterly. 1989; 6(4): 395-410. ISSN: 0740-624X.

HERNON, PETER. 1992a. Information Access; A Research Agenda. In: A Research Agenda for Scientific and Technical Information. Neuilly-sur-Seine, France: Advisory Group for Aerospace Research and Development (AGARD); 1992. 14-31. (AGARD-AR-316). ISBN: 92-835-0691-X.

HERNON, PETER. 1992b. Superintendent of Documents Operates an Outdated Vacuum Cleaner. Government Information Quarterly. 1992; 9(2):
99-105. ISSN: 0740-624X.

HERNON, PETER; MCCLURE, CHARLES R. 1987. Federal Information Policies in the 1980's: Conflicts and Issues. Norwood, NJ: Ablex; 1987. 467p.
ISBN: 0-89391-382-0; LC: 86-22292; OCLC: 14243217.

HERNON, PETER; MCCLURE, CHARLES R. 1988. Public Access to Government Information: Issues, Trends, and Strategies. Norwood, NJ: Ablex;
1988. 524p. ISBN: 0-89391-522-X; LC: 88-19249; OCLC: 18106331.

HERNON, PETER; MCCLURE, CHARLES R. 1991a. Electronic Census Products and the Depository Library Program: Future Issues and Trends. Government Information Quarterly. 1991; 8(1): 59-76. ISSN: 0740-624X.

HERNON, PETER; MCCLURE, CHARLES R. 1991b. United States Information Policies. In: Schipper, Wendy; Cunningham, Ann Marie, eds. National and International Information Policies. Philadelphia, PA: The National Federation of Abstracting and Information Services; 1991. 3-48.
ISBN: 0-942308-31-X; LC: 91-195192; OCLC: 24474679.

HERNON, PETER; MCCLURE, CHARLES R. 1992. Dissemination of U.S.
Government Information in CD-ROM and Other Forms. CD-ROM Professional. 1992 March; 5(2): 67-71. ISSN: 1049-0833.

HERNON, PETER; MCCLURE, CHARLES R. 1993. U.S. Government Information Policy: The Coming of a New Administration. CD-ROM Professional. 1993 March; 6(2): 14, 16, 20-22, 24-25. ISSN: 1049-0833.

HERNON, PETER; RELYEA, HAROLD C. 1988. The U.S. Government as a
Publisher. In: Williams, Martha E., ed. Annual Review of Information
Science and Technology: Volume 23. Amsterdam, The Netherlands: Elsevier
Science Publishers for the American Society for Information Science; 1988.
3-33. ISSN: 0066-4200; ISBN: 0-444-70543-0; LC: 66-25096; OCLC: 20029322.

HERNON, PETER; RELYEA, HAROLD C. 1991. Information Policy. In: Kent,
Allen, ed. Encyclopedia of Library and Information Science: Volume 48,
Supplement 11. New York, NY: Dekker; 1991. 176-204. ISBN: 0-8247-2048-
2; LC: 68-31232; OCLC: 4380549.

HORTON, FRANK. 1992. Paperwork Reduction Commission Is Needed Now
More Than Ever. Federal Computer Week. 1992 October 12; 6(31): 15, 30.
ISSN: 0893-052X.

INFORMATION INDUSTRY ASSOCIATION. 1992. Statement of the Information Industry Association on Key Telecommunications Infrastructure Issues Facing the Clinton-Gore Administration. Washington, DC: Information Industry Association; 1992 November 30. 6p. Available from: Information Industry Association, 555 New Jersey Ave., N.W., Suite 800, Washington, DC 20001.

KADEC, SARAH. 1992. Public Access to Government Electronic Information.
Bulletin of the American Society for Information Science. 1992 October/
November; 19(1): 22-24. ISSN: 0095-4403.

KAHIN, BRIAN. 1991. Information Policy and the Internet: Toward a Public
Information Infrastructure in the United States. Government Publications
Review. 1991 September/October; 18(5): 451-472. ISSN: 0277-9390.

KELLEY, WAYNE P. 1992. Letter [to Depository Librarians]. Administrative Notes. 1992 November 30; 13(23): 5-10. SUDOCS: GP3.16/3-2: 13; OCLC: 1233354494.

KENT, CALVIN A. 1989. The Privatization of Government Information: Economic Considerations. Government Publications Review. 1989 March/April; 16(2): 113-132. ISSN: 0277-9390.

KRANICH, NANCY C. 1989. Information Drought: Next Crisis for the American Farmer. Library Journal. 1989 June 15; 114 (11): 22-27. ISSN: 0363-0277.

LASKA, RICHARD. 1989. Initiation of a User Fee Program by Federal Agencies. Government Information Quarterly. 1989; 6(2): 113-126. ISSN: 0740-624X.

LEIGHTON, H. VERNON. 1992. Electronic Availability Lists for U.S. Federal Document Depository Libraries: Opportunities and Realities. Government Publications Review. 1992 May/June; 19(3): 279-287. ISSN: 0277-9390.

LOTTOR, MARK. 1992. Internet Domain Survey. Menlo Park, CA: SRI International; 1992. Available from: the author, SRI International, Network Information Systems Center, 333 Ravenswood Ave., Menlo Park, CA 94025.

LOVE, JAMES P. 1992. The Marketplace and Electronic Government Information. Government Publications Review. 1992 July/August; 19(4): 397-412. ISSN: 0277-9390.

LYNCH, CLIFFORD A.; PRESTON, CECILIA. 1990. Internet Access to Information Resources. In: Williams, Martha E., ed. Annual Review of Information Science and Technology: Volume 25. Amsterdam, The Netherlands: Elsevier Science Publishers for the American Society for Information Science; 1990. 263-312. ISSN: 0066-4200; ISBN: 0-444-88531-5; LC: 66-25096; OCLC: 23208190.

LYTLE, RICHARD H. 1986. Information Resource Management: 1981-1986. In: Williams, Martha E., ed. Annual Review of Information Science and Technology: Volume 21. White Plains, NY: Knowledge Industry Publications, Inc. for the American Society for Information Science; 1986. 309-336. ISSN: 0066-4200; ISBN: 0-86729-209-1; LC: 66-25096; OCLC: 17320444.

MARSHALL, SCOTT. 1992. The Key to Access. Government Information Insider. 1992; 2(4): 14-16. Available from: OMB Watch, 1731 Connecticut Ave., NW, Washington, DC 20009-1146.

MC GRANE, JAMES. 1991. The EDGAR CHALLENGE: Automating the U.S. Security [sic] and Exchange Commission's Internal Review Process, Filing, and Information Dissemination Systems. Government Publications Review. 1991 March/April; 18(2): 163-169. ISSN: 0277-9390.

MCALISTER, BILL. 1992. Archivist Reshuffles Staff, Pledges to Improve Agency: Moves Win Tentative Approval of Hill, Private Critics. The Washington Post. 1992 November 24; 115(355): A19. ISSN: 0190-8286.

MCCLURE, CHARLES R. 1990. The Future of the National Technical Information Service: Issues & Options. Syracuse, NY: Syracuse University, School of Information Studies; 1990. 45p. ERIC: ED 326248.

MCCLURE, CHARLES R.; BISHOP, ANN; DOTY, PHILIP. 1989. Federal Information Policy Development: The Role of the Office of Management and Budget. In: McClure, Charles R.; Hernon, Peter; Relyea, Harold C., eds. United States Government Information Policies: Views and Perspectives. Norwood, NJ: Ablex; 1989. 51-76. ISBN: 0-89391-563-7; LC: 88-35081; OCLC: 18984027.

MCCLURE, CHARLES R.; BISHOP, ANN; DOTY, PHILIP; BERGERON, PIERETTE. 1990. Federal Information Inventory/Locator Systems: From Burden to Benefit, Final Report. Syracuse, NY: Syracuse University, School of Information Studies; 1990. 100p. ERIC: ED 326427.

MCCLURE, CHARLES R.; BISHOP, ANN; DOTY, PHILIP; BERGERON, PIERETTE. 1991a. OMB and the Development of a Government-wide Information Inventory/Locator System. Government Information Quarterly. 1991; 8(1): 33-57. ISSN: 0740-624X.

MCCLURE, CHARLES R.; BISHOP, ANN; DOTY, PHILIP; ROSENBAUM, HOWARD. 1991b. The National Research and Education Network: Research and Policy Perspectives. Norwood, NJ: Ablex; 1991. 744p. ISBN: 0-89391-813-X; LC: 91-14028; OCLC: 23693371.

MCCLURE, CHARLES R.; HERNON, PETER, eds. 1989a. United States Scientific and Technical Information Policies. Norwood, NJ: Ablex; 1989. 417p. ISBN: 0-89391-571-8; LC: 89-278; OCLC: 19325043.

MCCLURE, CHARLES R.; HERNON, PETER. 1989b. Users of Academic and Public GPO Depository Libraries. Washington, DC: Government Printing Office; 1989. 81p. SUDOCS: GP3.2:Us2; OCLC: 19866610.

MCCLURE, CHARLES R.; RYAN, JOE; MOEN, WILLIAM E. 1992a. Identifying and Describing Federal Information Inventory/Locator Systems: Design for Networked-Based Locators. Bethesda, MD: U.S. National Audiovisual Center; 1992. 2 volumes. 143p. (volume 1); 395p. (volume 2). ERIC: ED 349031.

MCCLURE, CHARLES R.; RYAN, JOE; MOEN, WILLIAM E. 1992b. Design for an Internet-based Government-wide Information Locator System. Electronic Networking: Research, Applications, and Policy. 1992; 2(4): 6-37. ISSN: 1051-4805.

MCCLURE, CHARLES R.; WIGAND, ROLF T.; BERTOT, JOHN C.; MCKENNA, MARY; MOEN, WILLIAM E.; RYAN, JOE; VEEDER, STACY B. 1992c. Federal Information Policies and Management for Electronic Services Delivery. Syracuse, NY: Syracuse University, School of Information Studies; 1992. 150p. ERIC: ED 349031.

MCINTOSH, TOBY J. 1989. Electronic Access to Federal Information Prompts Debate. Daily Report for Executives [The Bureau of National Affairs]. 1989 August 11; 154: C1-C17. ISSN: 0148-8155.

MCINTOSH, TOBY J. 1990. Federal Information in the Electronic Age: Policy Issues for the 1990s. Washington, DC: The Bureau of National Affairs; 1990. 492p. ISBN: 1-55871-170-8; LC: 90-2404; OCLC: 22005240.

MEENAN, THOMAS G.; WYMAN, CHARLES R. 1991. Information Systems in the United States Senate: An Overview of Current and Projected Applications. Government Information Quarterly. 1991; 8(3): 273-283. ISSN: 0740-624X.

MILLER, PAGE P. 1993. Insuring the Preservation of Electronic Records. The Chronicle of Higher Education. 1993 February 3; 39(22): A44. ISSN: 0009-5982.

MOREHEAD, JOE; FETZER, MARY. 1992. Introduction to United States Government Information Sources. 4th edition. Englewood, CO: Libraries Unlimited; 1992. 474p. ISBN: 1-56308-066-4; ISBN: 0-87287-909-7; LC: 92-13251; OCLC: 25630932.

MORELLA, CONSTANCE A. 1992. Federal Software Needs Protection. Federal Computer Week. 1992; 6(11): 17, 53. ISSN: 0893-052X.

NATIONAL ACADEMY OF PUBLIC ADMINISTRATION. 1991. The Archives of the Future: Archival Strategies for the Treatment of Electronic Databases. A Report for the National Archives and Records Administration. Washington, DC: National Academy of Public Administration; 1991. 1 volume. OCLC: 25619077.

NATIONAL HISTORICAL PUBLICATIONS AND RECORDS COMMISSION. 1991. Research Issues in Electronic Records. Washington, DC: National Historical Publications and Records Commission; 1991. 37p. OCLC: 24624469.

NATIONAL INFORMATION STANDARDS ORGANIZATION. 1992. American National Standard Z39.50, Information Retrieval Service Definition and Protocol Specification for Library Applications. New Brunswick, NJ: Transaction Publishers; 1992. 48p. ISBN: 0-88738-934-1; OCLC: 27382354.

NELSON, ANNA KASTEN. 1987. The 1985 Report of the Committee on the Records of Government: An Assessment. Government Information Quarterly. 1987; 4(2): 143-150. ISSN: 0740-624X.

OKAY, JOHN; WILLIAMS, ROXANNE. 1993. Interagency Workshop on Public Access. Government Information Quarterly. 1993; 10(2): 235-251. ISSN: 0740-624X.

PERRITT, HENRY H., JR. 1990. Determining the Content and Identifying Suppliers of Public Information in Electronic Form. Government Publications Review. 1990 July/August; 17(4): 325-332. ISSN: 0277-9390.

PESACHOWITZ, ALVIN. 1992. Interagency Conference on Public Access. Government Information Quarterly. 1992; 9(2): 187-198. ISSN: 0740-624X.

PHILLIPS, REED; CARROLL, THERESA. 1993. Interagency Public Access Conference: Summary Report. Government Information Quarterly. 1993; 10(4). (in press). ISSN: 0740-624X.

POLICY MATTERS. 1993. Toward a National Research and Education Network—Who's in Charge? Policy Matters [Newsletter of the Information Industry Association, Public Policy and Government Relations Council]. 1993 March; 4.

QUINDLEN, TERRY HATCHER. 1993. Judge to Decide If Presidential E-mail Is Federal Record. Government Computer News. 1993; 12(1): 58. ISSN: 0738-4300.

RADACK, SHIRLEY M. 1990. More Effective Federal Computer Systems: The Role of NIST and Standards. Government Information Quarterly. 1990; 7(1): 37-49. ISSN: 0740-624X.

REEDER, FRANKLIN S. 1986. Federal Information Resources Management. Bulletin of the American Society for Information Science. 1986; 12(5): 11-12. ISSN: 0095-4403.

RITCHIE, DONALD A. 1988. Oral Histories May Help Scholars Plow through the Rapidly Accumulating Mass of Federal Paper. Chronicle of Higher Education. 1988 November 2; 35(10): A44. ISSN: 0009-5982.

RUHLIN, MICHELE; SOMERS, HERB; ROWE, JUDITH. 1991. National Research and Education Network and the Federal Depository Library Program. Documents to the People. 1991; 19(2): 106-109. ISSN: 0091-2085.

RUSSELL, JUDITH COFFEY. 1988. Trends in Information Technology and Private Sector Activities. Government Information Quarterly. 1988; 5(3): 251-266. ISSN: 0740-624X.

RYAN, SUSAN M. 1992. CD-ROMs in the Smaller U.S. Depository Library: Public Service Issues. Government Publications Review. 1992 May/June; 19(3): 269-278. ISSN: 0277-9390.

SANDLER, GREGORY. 1992. Economic Bulletin Board Expands Services. Information Today. 1992 May; 9(5): 42. ISSN: 8755-6286.

SHILL, HAROLD B. 1992. Information "Publics" and Equitable Access to Electronic Government Information: The Case of Agriculture. Government Information Quarterly. 1992; 9(3): 305-322. ISSN: 0740-624X.

SPREHE, J. TIMOTHY. 1984. Developing a Federal Policy on Electronic Collection and Dissemination of Information. Government Publications Review. 1984; 11(5): 353-362. ISSN: 0277-9390.

SPREHE, J. TIMOTHY. 1988. Policy Perspectives on Electronic Collection and Dissemination of Information. Government Information Quarterly. 1988; 5(3): 213-221. ISSN: 0740-624X.

SPREHE, J. TIMOTHY. 1992a. Clinton Admin. Could Refocus OIRA's Role. Federal Computer Week. 1992 November 30; 6(35): 18, 20. ISSN: 0893-052X.

SPREHE, J. TIMOTHY. 1992b. Online Public Access to Federal Agency Computers. Government Information Quarterly. 1992; 9(2): 199-203. ISSN: 0740-624X.

SPREHE, J. TIMOTHY. 1992c. Paperwork Commission Must Focus on Management, Not Collection, of Information. Federal Computer Week. 1992 October 12; 6(32): 15, 30. ISSN: 0893-052X.

SPREHE, J. TIMOTHY. 1992d. The Significance of "Admissibility of Electronically Filed Federal Records as Evidence." Government Information Quarterly. 1992; 9(2): 153-154. ISSN: 0740-624X.

SPREHE, J. TIMOTHY. 1993. The U.S. Depository Library Program and the Separation of Powers. Government Publications Review. 1993; 20(1): 141-144. ISSN: 0277-9390.

SPRING, MICHAEL B. 1991. Information Technology Standards. In: Williams, Martha E., ed. Annual Review of Information Science and Technology: Volume 26. Medford, NJ: Learned Information, Inc. for the American Society for Information Science; 1991. 79-111. ISSN: 0066-4200; ISBN: 0-938734-55-5; LC: 66-25096; OCLC: 20029322.

STEWART, ROBERT K. 1990. Access and Efficiency in Reagan-Era Information Policy: A Case Study of the Attempt to Privatize the National Technical Information Service. Seattle, WA: University of Washington; 1990. 300p. (Ph.D. dissertation). Available from: University Microfilms International, Ann Arbor, MI. (UMI order no. 9104302).

STONEHILL, ROBERT M. 1992. Letter to ERIC Users. Washington, DC: U.S. Department of Education, Office of the Assistant Secretary for Educational Research and Improvement; 1992 November 3. 3p.

SY, KAREN J.; ROBBIN, ALICE. 1990. Federal Statistical Policies and Programs: How Good Are the Numbers? In: Williams, Martha E., ed. Annual Review of Information Science and Technology: Volume 25. Amsterdam, The Netherlands: Elsevier Science Publishers for the American Society for Information Science; 1990. 3-54. ISSN: 0066-4200; ISBN: 0-444-88531-5; LC: 66-25096; OCLC: 23208190.

TRIANO, CHRISTINE; BASS, GARY D. 1992. The New Game in Town: Regulation, Secrecy, and the Quayle Council on Competitiveness. Government Information Quarterly. 1992; 9(2): 107-120. ISSN: 0740-624X.

UNITED STATES CODE. 1989. 1988 edition. Washington, DC: Government Printing Office; 1989. SUDOCS: Y1.2/5:988; OCLC: 20082554.

U.S. COMMITTEE ON EARTH AND ENVIRONMENTAL SCIENCES. 1992. The U.S. Global Change Data and Information Management Program Plan. Washington, DC: National Science Foundation; 1992. 94p. OCLC: 26812412.

U.S. CONGRESS. 81ST CONGRESS, 2ND SESSION. 1950. To Amend the Federal Property and Administrative Services Act of 1949, and for Other Purposes: Public Law 754 (Chapter 849), 81st Congress, 2nd Session. United States Statutes at Large. 1950; 64: 583-591. Washington, DC: Government Printing Office; 1952. (Federal Records Act of 1950).

U.S. CONGRESS. 89TH CONGRESS, 2ND SESSION. 1966. To Amend Section 3 of the Administrative Procedure Act, Chapter 324, of the Act of June 11, 1946 (60 Stat. 238), to Clarify and Protect the Right of the Public to Information, and for Other Purposes: Public Law 89-487, 89th Congress, 2nd Session. United States Statutes at Large. 1966; 80: 250-251. Washington, DC: Government Printing Office; 1967.

U.S. CONGRESS. 92ND CONGRESS, 2ND SESSION. 1972. To Authorize the Establishment of a System Governing the Creation and Operation of Advisory Committees in the Executive Branch of the Federal Government, and for Other Purposes: Public Law 92-463, 92nd Congress, 2nd Session. United States Statutes at Large. 1972; 86: 770-776. Washington, DC: Government Printing Office; 1973. (Federal Advisory Committee Act).

U.S. CONGRESS. 93RD CONGRESS, 2ND SESSION. 1974a. To Amend Title 5, United States Code, by Adding a Section 552a to Safeguard Individual Privacy from the Misuse of Federal Records, to Provide That Individuals Be Granted Access to Records Covering Them Which Are Maintained by Federal Agencies, to Establish a Privacy Protection Study Commission, and for Other Purposes: Public Law 93-579, 93rd Congress, 2nd Session. United States Statutes at Large. 1974; 88: 1896-1910. Washington, DC: Government Printing Office; 1976. (Privacy Act of 1974).

U.S. CONGRESS. 93RD CONGRESS, 2ND SESSION. 1974b. To Extend and Amend the Elementary and Secondary Education Act of 1965, and for Other Purposes: Public Law 93-380, 93rd Congress, 2nd Session. United States Statutes at Large. 1974; 88: 571-574. Washington, DC: Government Printing Office; 1976. (Family Educational Rights and Privacy Act of 1974).

U.S. CONGRESS. 94TH CONGRESS, 2ND SESSION. 1976. To Provide That
Meetings of Government Agencies Shall Be Open to the Public, and for
Other Purposes: Public Law 94-409, 94th Congress, 2nd Session. United
States Statutes at Large. 1976; 90: 1241-1248. Washington, DC: Govern-
ment Printing Office; 1978. (Government in the Sunshine Act).

U.S. CONGRESS. 95TH CONGRESS, 2ND SESSION. 1978a. To Amend
Chapter 21 of Title 44, United States Code, to Include New Provisions
Relating to the Acceptance and Use of Records Transferred to the Custody
of the Administrator of General Services: Public Law 95-416, 95th Con-
gress, 2nd Session. United States Statutes at Large. 1978; 92: 915-916.
Washington, DC: Government Printing Office; 1980.

U.S. CONGRESS. 95TH CONGRESS, 2ND SESSION. 1978b. To Amend Title
44 to Insure the Preservation of and Public Access to the Official Records of
the President, and for Other Purposes: Public Law 95-591, 95th Congress,
2nd Session. United States Statutes at Large. 1978; 92: 2523-2528. Washington, DC: Government Printing Office; 1980. (Presidential Records Act
of 1978).

U.S. CONGRESS. 96TH CONGRESS, 2ND SESSION. 1980. To Reduce
Paperwork and Enhance the Economy and Efficiency of the Government
and the Private Sector by Improving Federal Information Policymaking,
and for Other Purposes: Public Law 96-511, 96th Congress, 2nd Session.
United States Statutes at Large. 1980; 94: 2812-2826. Washington, DC:
Government Printing Office; 1981. (Paperwork Reduction Act of 1980).

U.S. CONGRESS. 99TH CONGRESS, 2ND SESSION. 1986. Making Continu-
ing Appropriations for the Fiscal Year 1987, and for Other Purposes:
Public Law 99-500, 99th Congress, 2nd Session. United States Statutes at
Large. 1986; 100: 1783-335 to 1783-340. Washington, DC: Government
Printing Office; 1989. (Paperwork Reduction Reauthorization Act).

U.S. CONGRESS. 100TH CONGRESS, 1ST SESSION. 1988. To Provide for a
Computer Standards Program within the National Bureau of Standards, to
Provide for Government-wide Computer Security, and to Provide for the
Training in Security Matters of Persons Who Are Involved in the Manage-
ment, Operation, and Use of Federal Computer Systems, and for Other
Purposes: Public Law 100-235, 100th Congress, 1st Session. United States
Statutes at Large. 1988; 101: 1724-1730. Washington, DC: Government
Printing Office; 1989. (Computer Security Act of 1987).

U.S. CONGRESS. 100TH CONGRESS, 2ND SESSION. 1988a. To Amend Title
5 of the United States Code, to Ensure Privacy, Integrity, and Verification
of Data Disclosed for Computer Matching, to Establish Data Integrity
Boards within Federal Agencies, and for Other Purposes: Public Law 100-
503, 100th Congress, 2nd Session. United States Statutes at Large. 1988;
102: 2507-2514. Washington, DC: Government Printing Office; 1990. (Computer Matching and Privacy Act of 1988).

U.S. CONGRESS. 100TH CONGRESS, 2ND SESSION. 1988b. To Authorize
Appropriations to the Secretary of Commerce for the Programs of the
National Bureau of Standards for Fiscal Year 1989, and for Other Purposes:
Public Law 100-519, 100th Congress, 2nd Session. United States Statutes at

Large. 1988; 102: 2594-2596. Washington, DC: Government Printing Office; 1990. (National Technical Information Act of 1988).

U.S. CONGRESS. 101ST CONGRESS, 1ST SESSION. 1989. A Bill to Establish a Data Protection Board. H.R. 3669. 101st Congress, 1st Session. Washington, DC: Government Printing Office; 1989 November 15. 13p.

U.S. CONGRESS. 102ND CONGRESS, 1ST SESSION. 1991a. A Bill to Amend Title 5, United States Code, to Amend the Freedom of Information Act. S. Bill 1939. 102nd Congress, 1st Session. Washington, DC: Government Printing Office; 1991 November 7. 9p.

U.S. CONGRESS. 102ND CONGRESS, 1ST SESSION. 1991b. A Bill to Amend Title 5, United States Code, to Clarify the Laws Relating to the Disclosure of Records Maintained on Individuals. H.R. 2443. 102nd Congress, 1st session Washington, DC: Government Printing Office; 1991 May 22. 8p.

U.S. CONGRESS. 102ND CONGRESS, 1ST SESSION. 1991c. A Bill to Amend Title 5, United States Code, to Provide for Public Access to Information in Electronic Format and to Amend the Freedom of Information Act. S. Bill 1940. 102nd Congress, 1st Session Washington, DC: Government Printing Office; 1991 November 7. 8p.

U.S. CONGRESS. 102ND CONGRESS, 1ST SESSION. 1991d. A Bill to Amend the Stevenson-Wydler Technology Innovation Act of 1980 to Enhance Technology Transfer for Works Prepared under Certain Cooperative Research and Development. S. Bill 1581. 102nd Congress, 1st Session. Washington, DC: Government Printing Office; 1991 July 29. 4p.

U.S. CONGRESS. 102ND CONGRESS, 1ST SESSION. 1991e. A Bill to Enact the Federal Information Resources Management Act. S. Bill 1044. 102nd Congress, 1st Session. Washington, DC: Government Printing Office; 1991 May 14. 69p.

U.S. CONGRESS. 102ND CONGRESS, 1ST SESSION. 1991f. A Bill to Enhance the Effectiveness of the United Nations International Driftnet Fishery Conservation Program. H.R. 2152. 102nd Congress, 1st Session. Washington, DC: Government Printing Office; 1991 April 30. 14p.

U.S. CONGRESS. 102ND CONGRESS, 1ST SESSION. 1991g. A Bill to Establish in the Government Printing Office a Single Point of Online Public Access to a Wide Range of Federal Databases Containing Public Information Stored Electronically. H.R. 2772. 102nd Congress, 1st Session. Washington, DC: Government Printing Office; 1991 June 26. 5p.

U.S. CONGRESS. 102ND CONGRESS, 1ST SESSION. 1991h. To Provide for a Coordinated Federal Program to Ensure Continued United States Leadership in High-Performance Computing: Public Law 102-194, 102nd Congress, 1st Session. United States Statutes at Large. 1991; 105: 1594-1604. Washington, DC: Government Printing Office; 1992. (High-Performance Computing Act of 1991).

U.S. CONGRESS. 102ND CONGRESS, 2ND SESSION. 1992a. A Bill to Establish in the Government Printing Office an Electronic Gateway to Provide Public Access to a Wide Range of Federal Databases Containing Public Information Stored Electronically. S. Bill 2813. 102nd Congress, 2nd Session Washington, DC: Government Printing Office; 1992 June 4. 7p.

U.S. CONGRESS. 102ND CONGRESS, 2ND SESSION. 1992b. To Authorize
Appropriations for the National Institute of Standards and Technology
and the Technology Administration of the Department of Commerce, and
for Other Purposes: Public Law 102-245, 102nd Congress, 2nd Session.
United States Statutes at Large. 1992; 106: 7-30. Washington, DC: Government Printing Office; n.d. (American Technology Preeminence Act of
1991).

U.S. CONGRESS. 103RD CONGRESS, 1ST SESSION. 1993. A Bill to Establish
the Library of Congress Fund Act of 1993. S. Bill 345. 103rd Congress, 1st
Session. Washington, DC: Government Printing Office; 1993 February 4. 9p.

U.S. CONGRESS. GOVERNMENT PRINTING OFFICE. 1991. GPO/2001:
Vision for a New Millennium. Washington, DC: Government Printing
Office; 1991. 43p. SUDOCS: GP1.2:V82; OCLC: 25248984.

U.S. CONGRESS. GOVERNMENT PRINTING OFFICE. 1992. Reading the
Congressional Record on CD-ROM. Washington, DC: Government Printing Office; 1992. 123p. SUDOCS: GP3.2:C76/2; OCLC: 27719449.

U.S. CONGRESS. GOVERNMENT PRINTING OFFICE. 1993. GPO Moving
Forward in the Electronic Age: A Strategic Outlook. Washington, DC:
Government Printing Office; 1993. 45p. Available from: Public Printer,
GPO, Washington, DC 20401.

U.S. CONGRESS. HOUSE. COMMITTEE ON ENERGY AND COMMERCE.
101ST CONGRESS, 2ND SESSION. 1990. Review of National Telecommunications Policy: A Staff Report. Washington, DC: Government Printing Office; 1990. 983p. (Committee Print 101-0). SUDOCS: Y4.En2/3:101-
0; OCLC: 21273737.

U.S. CONGRESS. HOUSE. COMMITTEE ON GOVERNMENT OPERA-
TIONS. 99TH CONGRESS, 1ST SESSION. 1986a. Hearings on Electronic
Collection and Dissemination of Information by Federal Agencies before
the Committee on Government Operations, 99th Congress, 1st Session.
Washington, DC: Government Printing Office; 1986. 592p. SUDOCS:
Y4.G74/7:El2/5; OCLC: 13143692.

U.S. CONGRESS. HOUSE. COMMITTEE ON GOVERNMENT OPERA-
TIONS. 99TH CONGRESS, 2ND SESSION. 1986b. Electronic Collection
and Dissemination of Information by Federal Agencies: A Policy Over-
view. House Report no. 560. 99th Congress, 2nd Session. Washington,
DC: Government Printing Office; 1986. 70p. SUDOCS: Y1.1/8:99-560;
OCLC: 13578254.

U.S. CONGRESS. HOUSE. COMMITTEE ON GOVERNMENT OPERA-
TIONS. 101ST CONGRESS, 2ND SESSION. 1990. Taking a Byte Out of
History: The Archival Preservation of Federal Computer Records. House
Report no. 978. 101st Congress, 2nd Session. Washington, DC: Govern-
ment Printing Office; 1990. 30p. SUDOCS: Y1.1/8:101-978; OCLC: 22876907.

U.S. CONGRESS. HOUSE. COMMITTEE ON GOVERNMENT OPERA-
TIONS. 102ND CONGRESS, 1ST AND 2ND SESSIONS. 1992. Hearings
on Creative Ways of Using and Disseminating Federal Information before
the Committee on Government Operations, 102nd Congress, 1st and 2nd
Sessions. Washington, DC: Government Printing Office; 1992. 452p.
ISBN: 0-16-039242-X; SUDOCS: Y4.G74/7:In3/24; OCLC: 26790778.

U.S. CONGRESS. HOUSE. COMMITTEE ON HOUSE ADMINISTRATION. SUBCOMMITTEE ON PROCUREMENT AND PRINTING. 1989. Title 44 U.S.C.—Review. Hearings. Washington, DC: Government Printing Office; 1989. 224p. SUDOCS: Y4.H81/3:T53; OCLC: 21543730.

U.S. CONGRESS. JOINT COMMITTEE ON PRINTING. 98TH CONGRESS, 2ND SESSION. 1984. Provision of Federal Government Publications in Electronic Format to Depository Libraries: Report of the Ad Hoc Committee on Depository Library Access to Federal Automated Data Bases. 98th Congress, 2nd Session. Washington, DC: Government Printing Office; 1984. 126p. SUDOCS: Y4.P93/1:P96/2; OCLC: 11569801.

U.S. CONGRESS. JOINT COMMITTEE ON PRINTING. 99TH CONGRESS, 1ST SESSION. 1985. An Open Forum on the Provision of Electronic Federal Information to Depository Libraries: Committee Print of the Joint Committee on Printing, 99th Congress, 1st Session. Washington, DC: Government Printing Office; 1985. 170p. SUDOCS: Y4.P93/1:El2/4; OCLC: 12704735.

U.S. CONGRESS. OFFICE OF TECHNOLOGY ASSESSMENT. 1986a. Federal Government Information Technology: Electronic Record Systems and Individual Privacy. Washington, DC: Government Printing Office; 1986. 153p. (OTA-CIT-296). SUDOCS: Y3.T22/2:2/El2/6; OCLC: 14921769.

U.S. CONGRESS. OFFICE OF TECHNOLOGY ASSESSMENT. 1986b. Federal Government Information Technology: Management, Security, and Congressional Oversight. Washington, DC: Government Printing Office; 1986. 190p. (OTA-CIT-297). SUDOCS: Y3.T22/2:2F31/2; OCLC: 13290529.

U.S. CONGRESS. OFFICE OF TECHNOLOGY ASSESSMENT. 1988. Informing the Nation. Washington, DC: Government Printing Office; 1988. 333p. (OTA-CIT-396). SUDOCS: Y3.T22/2:2In3/9; OCLC: 18595428.

U.S. CONGRESS. OFFICE OF TECHNOLOGY ASSESSMENT. 1989. Federal Scientific and Technical Information in an Electronic Age: Opportunities and Challenges. Washington, DC: Office of Technology Assessment; 1989. 36p. (OTA Staff Paper). OCLC: 20748365.

U.S. CONGRESS. OFFICE OF TECHNOLOGY ASSESSMENT. 1990. Helping America Compete: The Role of Federal Scientific & Technical Information. Washington, DC: Office of Technology Assessment; 1990. 68p. (OTA-CIT-454). SUDOCS: Y3.T22/2:2Am3/2; OCLC: 22091573.

U.S. CONGRESS. OFFICE OF TECHNOLOGY ASSESSMENT. 1992. Global Standards: Building Blocks for the Future. Washington, DC: Government Printing Office; 1992. 114p. ISBN: 0-16-036163-X; SUDOCS: Y3.T22/2:2G51/3; OCLC: 25621281.

U.S. CONGRESS. SENATE. COMMITTEE ON GOVERNMENTAL AFFAIRS. 102ND CONGRESS, 2ND SESSION. 1992. Serious Management Problems at the National Archives and Records Administration. Report by the Committee on Governmental Affairs, 102nd Congress, 2nd Session. Washington, DC: Government Printing Office; 1992. 102p. SUDOCS: Y4.G74/9:S.PRT.102-108; OCLC: 27345044.

U.S. DEPARTMENT OF COMMERCE. 1989. Draft Policy of the U.S. Department of Commerce on the Dissemination of Information in Electronic

Format. Government Information Quarterly. 1989; 6(1): 89-96. ISSN: 0740-624X.

U.S. DEPARTMENT OF COMMERCE. BUREAU OF THE CENSUS. 1990. Use of Census Bureau Data in GPO Depository Libraries: Future Issues and Trends. Washington, DC: Bureau of the Census; 1990. 142p. SUDOCS: C3.2:D26/9; OCLC: 23111992.

U.S. DEPARTMENT OF COMMERCE. NATIONAL TECHNICAL INFORMATION SERVICE. 1989. NTIS 2000. Springfield, VA: National Technical Information Service; 1989. 25p.

U.S. DEPARTMENT OF COMMERCE. NATIONAL TECHNICAL INFORMATION SERVICE. 1992a. Business Plan. Springfield, VA: National Technical Information Service; 1992. 78p.

U.S. DEPARTMENT OF COMMERCE. NATIONAL TECHNICAL INFORMATION SERVICE. 1992b. Modernization Plan. Springfield, VA: National Technical Information Service; 1992. 15p.

U.S. DEPARTMENT OF JUSTICE. SYSTEMS POLICY STAFF. JUSTICE MANAGEMENT DIVISION. 1992. Admissibility of Electronically Filed Federal Records as Evidence. Government Information Quarterly. 1992; 9(2): 155-167. ISSN: 0740-624X.

U.S. GENERAL ACCOUNTING OFFICE. 1978. The Federal Information Processing Standards Program. Washington, DC: General Accounting Office; 1978. 57p. (FGMSD-78-23). OCLC: 3930355.

U.S. GENERAL ACCOUNTING OFFICE. 1988a. Federal Information: Agency Needs and Practices. Fact Sheet for the Chairman, Joint Committee on Printing. Washington, DC: General Accounting Office; 1988. 71p. (GAO/GGD-88-115FS). SUDOCS: GA1.13:GGD-88-115FS; OCLC: 18851860.

U.S. GENERAL ACCOUNTING OFFICE. 1988b. Federal Information: Users' Current and Future Technology Needs. Fact Sheet for the Chairman, Joint Committee on Printing. Washington, DC: General Accounting Office; 1988. 97p. (GAO/GGD-89-20FS). SUDOCS: GA1.13: GAO/GGD-89-20FS. OCLC: 19038852.

U.S. GENERAL ACCOUNTING OFFICE. 1990. Public Access: Two Case Studies of Federal Electronic Dissemination. Report to the Chairman, House Subcommittee on Government Information, Justice, and Agriculture, Committee on Government Operations. Washington, DC: General Accounting Office; 1990. 12p. (GAO/IMTEC-90-44BR). OCLC: 21915205.

U.S. GENERAL ACCOUNTING OFFICE. 1992a. Federal Register: Better Electronic Technology Planning Could Improve Production and Dissemination. Report to House Committee on Government Operations. Washington, DC: General Accounting Office; 1992. 45p. (GAO/GGD-93-5). SUDOCS: GA1.13: GGD-93-5; OCLC: 27163912.

U.S. GENERAL ACCOUNTING OFFICE. 1992b. Information Dissemination: Case Studies on Electronic Dissemination at Four Agencies. Fact Sheet for the Chairman, Senate Committee on Governmental Affairs. Washington, DC: General Accounting Office; 1992. 47p. (GAO/IMTEC-92-6FS). SUDOCS: GA1.13: IMTEC-92-6FS; OCLC: 26379505.

U.S. GENERAL ACCOUNTING OFFICE. 1992c. Information Dissemination: Innovative Ways Agencies Are Using Technology. Testimony before the

Subcommittee on Government Information, Justice, and Agriculture, Committee on Government Operations. Washington, DC: General Accounting Office; 1992. 12p. (GAO/IMTEC-92-6). OCLC: 25782443.

U.S. GENERAL ACCOUNTING OFFICE. 1992d. Information Resources Summary of Federal Agencies' Information Resources Management Problems. Washington, DC: Government Printing Office; 1992. 35p. SUDOCS: GA1.13:IMTEC-92-13FS; OCLC: 25695541.

U.S. GENERAL ACCOUNTING OFFICE. 1992e. Securities and Exchange Commission: Effective Development of the EDGAR System Requires Top Management Attention. Report to Chairman, House Subcommittee on Oversight and Investigation, Committee on Energy and Commerce. Washington, DC: General Accounting Office; 1992. 12p. (GAO/IMTEC-92-85). SUDOCS: GA 1.13:IMTEC-92-85; OCLC: 26868939.

U.S. INTERAGENCY PUBLIC ACCESS WORKING GROUP. SUBGROUP ON LOCATOR AND STANDARDS. 1993. January 12, 1993 Agenda. Reston, VA: U.S. Geological Survey; 1993. 3p. (Mimeograph). Available from: Tim Gauslin, United States Geological Survey, National Center, Reston, VA 22092.

U.S. NATIONAL ACADEMY OF SCIENCES. NATIONAL ACADEMY OF ENGINEERING. INSTITUTE OF MEDICINE. COMMITTEE ON SCIENCE, ENGINEERING, AND PUBLIC POLICY. 1989. Information Technology and the Conduct of Research: The User's View. Report of the Panel on Information Technology and the Conduct of Research. Washington, DC: National Academy Press; 1989. 72p. ISBN: 0-309-03888-X; LC: 88-28903; OCLC: 18520680.

U.S. NATIONAL ARCHIVES AND RECORDS ADMINISTRATION. OFFICE OF RECORDS ADMINISTRATION. 1990. Managing Electronic Records. Washington, DC: National Archives and Records Administration; 1990. 82p. (Instructional Guide Series). SUDOCS: AE1.108:M31/3; OCLC: 22202851.

U.S. OFFICE OF MANAGEMENT AND BUDGET. 1982. Circular No. A-119, Federal Participation in the Development and Use of Voluntary Standards. Washington, DC: Office of Management and Budget; 1982. 10p. OCLC: 14061565.

U.S. OFFICE OF MANAGEMENT AND BUDGET. 1985. The Management of Federal Information Resources. Federal Register. 1985 December 24; 50 (247): 52730-52751. (OMB Circular A-130). ISSN: 0364-1406; SUDOCS: AE2.106:50/247; OCLC: 02505035.

U.S. OFFICE OF MANAGEMENT AND BUDGET. 1992a. Current Information Technology Resource Requirements of the Federal Government: Fiscal Year 1993. Washington, DC: Government Printing Office; 1992. 466p. OCLC: 27164838.

U.S. OFFICE OF MANAGEMENT AND BUDGET. 1992b. Management of Federal Information Resources: Proposed Revision of OMB Circular No. A-130. Federal Register. 1992 April 29; 57(83): 18296-18306. ISSN: 0364-1406; SUDOCS: AE2.106:57/83; OCLC: 02505035.

U.S. OFFICE OF MANAGEMENT AND BUDGET. 1992c. Information Resources Management Plan of the Federal Government. Washington, DC:

Government Printing Office; 1992. 251p. SUDOCS: PrEx2.2:In3/2; OCLC: 25290969.

U.S. OFFICE OF MANAGEMENT AND BUDGET. 1992d. Revision of the Office of Management and Budget (OMB) Circular No. A-119, Request for Public Comment. Federal Register. 1992 March 20; 57(55): 9749-9751. ISSN: 0364-1406; SUDOCS: AE2.106:57/55; OCLC: 02505035.

U.S. OFFICE OF MANAGEMENT AND BUDGET. OFFICE OF INFORMA-TION AND REGULATORY AFFAIRS. 1992. Budget Examining Tech-niques for Evaluating Information Technology Investments. Washington, DC: Office of Management and Budget; 1992. 27p. OCLC: 26827101.

U.S. WHITE HOUSE CONFERENCE ON LIBRARY AND INFORMATION SERVICES. 1991. Information 2000: Library and Information Services for the 21st Century. Summary Report of the 1991 White House Conference on Library and Information Services. Washington, DC: Government Print-ing Office; 1991. 78p. SUDOCS: Y3.W58/20:2In3/sum; OCLC: 24879367.

WEIS, ALAN H. 1992. Commercialization of the Internet. Electronic Network-ing: Research, Applications, and Policy. 1992; 2(3): 7-16. ISSN: 1051-4805.

WEISS, CAROL H. 1991. Policy Research as Advocacy: Pro and Con. Knowl-edge and Policy. 1991; 4(1-2): 37-55. ISSN: 0897-1986.

WINKLER, KAREN. 1993. Scholarly Groups Press for Reform of National Archives, Charging Mismanagement and Politicization. The Chronicle of Higher Education. 1993 January 13; 39(20): A22-A23. ISSN: 0009-5982.

WISE, BOB. 1991. Statement [upon Introduction of the Privacy Act Amend-ments of 1991 (H.R. 2443)]. Congressional Record. 1991 May 22; 137(78): H3449-H3453. ISSN: 0363-7239; OCLC: 02437919.

WOOD, FRED B. 1987. Technology, Public Policy, and the Changing Nature of Federal Information Dissemination: Overview of a New Office of Technol-ogy Assessment Study. Government Information Quarterly. 1987; 4(1): 83-96. ISSN: 0740-624X.

ZAGAMI, ANTHONY J. 1991. Memorandum: "Cost Sharing" for the Dissemi-nation of Government Information in Electronic Formats. Government Information Quarterly. 1991; 8(4): 387-391. ISSN: 0740-624X.

3 Information Gatekeepers

CHERYL METOYER-DURAN
University of California, Los Angeles

INTRODUCTION

The literature on information gatekeepers can be divided into four categories. The first overviews the human gatekeeping concept as developed and applied within different disciplines and fields. The next examines gatekeeping within the context of information-seeking behavior and considers information-use models, especially taxonomic models in communication and education research. A third and smaller body of literature concerns the cultural dimensions of information-seeking behavior. The final category considers the information-seeking behavior of gatekeepers in ethnolinguistic communities and includes the gatekeeper model. Although this chapter discusses the four categories, the final one is the focus.

The chapter examines human gatekeepers, such as those serving culturally diverse populations and does not equate these gatekeepers with electronic gateways to information management, delivery, and use. Conceivably as the National Research and Education Network (NREN) emerges and extends throughout the educational system, human gatekeepers and the populations they serve may draw on gateways and the so-called electronic gatekeepers that serve as information filters to a community of users. However, the research and other literature have not made the necessary connections to the populations discussed in this chapter. Anyone who wants to make such connections in the future should recognize and address the assorted variables identified throughout this chapter.

Annual Review of Information Science and Technology (ARIST), Volume 28, 1993
Martha E. Williams, Editor
Published for the American Society for Information Science (ASIS)
By Learned Information, Inc., Medford, N.J.

Research into gatekeeping in culturally diverse communities has started to receive more attention and to be linked to research in the other three categories. At the same time, some of the research into culturally diverse communities has examined the information roles of gatekeepers in ethnolinguistic communities—i.e., those communities in which English may be treated as a second language. Gatekeepers control the flow of information to many people within their communities and become links between the community and the larger society. As such, they represent an important aspect of information seeking that is often missing from models depicting the information-seeking behavior of the general public.

TRENDS IN GATEKEEPER RESEARCH

LEWIN (1943; 1947a; 1947b), one of the first researchers to use the term "gatekeeper," identified housewives as gatekeepers who influenced the eating habits of their families. Lewin found that some household members were more important than others in deciding what is eaten. He concluded that social change could occur by working through those individuals who had the most control over food selection.

A review of appropriate databases (i.e., ERIC, Sociofile, PsycLit, Public Affairs Information Service Bulletin (PAIS), National Technical Information Service (NTIS), America: History and Life, Dissertation Abstracts Online, LISA, and Information Science Abstracts in December 1992 provided 803 citations to writings on gatekeepers since 1977. Researchers in linguistics, social anthropology, urban planning, information science, and, more recently, health care, business, education, and communications have used gatekeepers to describe individuals who influence opinions, disseminate information, or facilitate cultural adaptation in many different settings.

This section highlights representative studies that most frequently referenced gatekeeping research in the health sciences, education, science and technology, communication studies, journalism, and library and information science. Although science and technology provide less gatekeeping research, that literature is included because it studies the gatekeeping concept within the broader context of information-seeking behavior, and it incorporates discussions of formal and informal gatekeepers and the important linking function of gatekeeping.

Health Sciences

The gatekeeping model has been frequently studied and applied to research concerning the development and implementation of community-based health services, especially alcohol, drug abuse, and mental health programs for the elderly. This type of research includes the work of Beckman and Mays (BECKMAN & MAYS; MAYS & BECKMAN), who examined the role of gatekeepers in alcohol abuse programs and who designed strategies to increase the awareness of and participation in these programs. They view gatekeepers as community-based individuals who can assist health care professionals in providing information to people at risk in the community.

Gatekeepers are also individuals with fixed social roles who can provide either direct service or referrals to the mental health system. EMLET & HALL and RASCHKO, for example, report on the use of nontraditional or informal community-based gatekeepers who act as referral agents to identify the elderly at risk. SCOTT ET AL. compared 175 gatekeepers to 436 nongatekeeper community residents on the basis of their awareness of a community mental health center. The gatekeepers (e.g., clergy, physicians, school counselors, and police) were more aware of the center and its services than were members of the general community. RUMBERGER & ROGERS and V. BROWN addressed the importance of the gatekeepers' referral function in mental health programs. These researchers also equated gatekeeping with the activities of persons with fixed community roles (e.g., clergy, bartenders, police, teachers, and hairdressers).

In a report on medication profiles, ANSELLO & LAMY built on studies of rural pharmacists who act as gatekeepers when they encourage the adoption of new practices or procedures in their communities. ROGERS & SHOEMAKER, in their analysis of the innovation and diffusion process, described how gatekeepers may act as the change agents.

A smaller body of health sciences literature uses the term gatekeepers to describe the cost-controlling role of health care professionals, such as primary care physicians (CLANCY & HILNER; DOUGLASS; S.H. MOORE ET AL.; SOMERS).

Education

The literature on higher, secondary, and adult education contains a number of interpretations and applications of the gatekeeping concept. Most often, gatekeeping denotes the process of controlling access to information or admission into a specific facet of the educational system. For example, KAREN used the gatekeeping analogy to describe how political and organizational factors affected admissions practices at Harvard University. Similarly, SCOLLON, who applied the gatekeeping model to study retention patterns of Alaska natives at the University of Alaska, equated gatekeeping with institutional barriers that affect student retention and faculty retention and promotion.

The gatekeeper metaphor has been applied to the role and influence of academic advisors or counselors who act as decision makers (ERICKSON; FARKAS ET AL.). Erickson used the term to describe counseling practices that affect ethnic groups. Farkas and his co-authors applied the gatekeeping model to test the informal academic standards by which students were judged in 22 urban middle schools. According to Farkas et al., the gatekeeping model accounted for grade differences in gender, ethnicity, and poverty groups.

Other applications of the model in education include the work of COOK & FONOW, who examined controlling factors in feminist scholarship. They saw gatekeeping as an arbitrary function and used it to characterize the controlling process. MERRIAM, who studied adult education, views gatekeeping in a positive light, which is akin to the change agent as examined by ROGERS & SHOEMAKER. According to Merriam, gatekeeping is the process by which an informal system of networkers and advisors help educators put research findings into practice.

Finally, the work of THOMPSON parallels the use of the adopter categories and change agents explored by Rogers and Shoemaker. In her analysis of textbook adoption practices, Thompson identified three levels of gatekeeping that affect innovation (i.e., textbook design and adoption): (1) primary gatekeepers (i.e., publishers); (2) secondary gatekeepers (e.g., editors, authors, writers, consultants, and salespeople); and (3) tertiary gatekeepers (e.g., educators, general public, and textbook researchers). She concluded that change in textbook quality depends on a more careful analysis of the role of tertiary gatekeepers.

Science and Technology

ALLEN ET AL. (1971a; 1971b) developed the concept of the "technological gatekeeper" and provided the framework for subsequent studies of gatekeeping, such as those conducted by ALLEN (1977a; 1977b), ALLEN & COONEY, KATZ & TUSHMAN, KAULA, L.A. MYERS, and SUBRAMANYAM. In their study of communication channels, Thomas Allen and his co-authors found that both the international and domestic transfer of information is a two-step process in which technological gatekeepers function as intermediaries. The effectiveness of technological gatekeepers is related to their links with external information networks (i.e., foreign information sources) as well as internal or domestic networks of information users.

In a subsequent study of communication networks, ALLEN (1977b) discussed the limits of the gatekeeper concept when applied to science as opposed to technology. He contrasted the gatekeeper's role to that of opinion leader as defined by E. KATZ, ROGERS, and ROGERS & SHOEMAKER. According to ALLEN (1977b), most of these studies have considered individuals (e.g., farmers, physicians, and consumers) who function as opinion leaders independently of a bureaucratic or hierarchical structure. In contrast, gatekeepers have a boundary-spanning role because they operate within an organizational hierarchy and disseminate information by linking internal and external networks. While Allen's research focuses on technological gatekeepers, the distinction between an opinion leader and a gatekeeper parallels that of METOYER-DURAN (1991a; 1991b; 1993b; 1993c) in her research on ethnolinguistic gatekeepers.

In their examination of the roles and career paths of gatekeepers functioning in research and development (R&D) environments, KATZ & TUSHMAN apply the gatekeeper definition of ALLEN & COHEN. Katz and Tushman consider gatekeepers as technologists who are linked to both internal and external networks: "Gatekeepers act to reduce the communications boundary separating their projects from outside areas" (p. 104).

L.A. MYERS, who applied multivariate techniques to refine the technological gatekeeper model of Allen and Cohen, found various types of gatekeepers in R&D laboratories for different types of information. Myers identified the attributes associated with gatekeeping; these focus on interpersonal communication, organizational hierarchy, and demographic characteristics. These attributes help differentiate specialist from global gatekeepers. Global gatekeepers have access to and use all categories of information. Specialized gatekeepers handle specific categories of information; there are "specialized gatekeepers for different categories of information" (L.A. MYERS, p. 200).

Myers concluded that the specialist gatekeeper may account for the conflicting results in other studies that equated technological gatekeepers with global information gatekeepers. Myers's model, which distinguished between types of gatekeepers based on their attributes, complements the taxonomic approach used by METOYER-DURAN (1991b; 1993b) to develop gatekeeper profiles.

Like Myers, COGAN, in a recent doctoral dissertation, differentiates between "key actors" in the process of introducing technology (i.e., computer implementation). Cogan's "actors" include gatekeepers who introduce the technology, sponsors who provide resources, and champions who elicit commitment or support for the project.

The study by KOENIG of the information environment of major pharmaceutical companies in the United States addressed gatekeeping in a limited context. Although he did not focus on gatekeepers within the companies, as did ALLEN (1970; 1977a; 1977b), he did probe management's perceptions of gatekeeping. Koenig found that gatekeeping is part of standard terminology and that the concept appears to be understood and accepted within the pharmaceutical R&D community.

KAULA, who considered gatekeeping within the context of technological information handling and practice, views technological
gatekeeping as one aspect of an information-retrieval and -dissemina-
tion system.

KELLY, who studied the design of scientific and technical information systems in R&D laboratories, argued that if a system is to be widely
used, the organization must design it by addressing the information
needs of gatekeepers and other informal groups. Gatekeepers represent
a small number of individuals who effectively gain access to formal
information systems. Hence, any systems analysis must recognize the
information needs of both formal and informal user groups.

In their study of the control of scientific research by government
agencies and private foundations, BROADHEAD & RIST presented a
different view of gatekeeping. They defined gatekeeping as a controlling function that limits the objectivity of scientific study. That function
determines the type and scope of research that is conducted and where
that research is published.

Communication Studies

Gatekeepers often act as agents of acculturation when they disseminate information within ethnic communities. In some circumstances,
gatekeepers serve as opinion leaders who regulate the flow of information between western nations and developing nations. ROGERS &
SHOEMAKER, HARIK, and LIN & BURT applied this gatekeeper model
of communication behavior to rural areas and developing nations. They
analyzed a two-step model of the communication process in which key
individuals disseminate information, exert influence within their indigenous communities, and facilitate the adoption of innovations. BECKER,
LANCASTER & WHITE , and TURNBULL & MEENAGHAN applied
the model to European and American settings to study the adoption of
innovations in agriculture, industry, and technology.

PAISLEY developed the conceptual framework for much of the subsequent information-seeking behavior research. His work was refined
by ALLEN (1966; 1969; 1970; 1977a; 1977b), DERVIN (1973; 1976; 1977;
1980; 1983) and others who sought more unity and consistency in
communications research. That framework portrayed the user as an
information processor who progressed through a series of concentric
information systems. It is possible to view the user's information-seeking behavior in the context of available information systems; these
include an individual's research group, organization, professional society, "invisible college," and formal information system (ALLEN, 1969).

DURAN, DURAN & MONROE, WELCH ET AL., and WILLIAMS
ET AL. tested the hypothesis that gatekeepers share information and

maintain links beyond their immediate sphere of influence by interacting within their reference group and with clusters of other gatekeepers. These researchers found that individuals with formal and informal ties to local and nonlocal institutions, organizations, or associations have higher rates of information use than do those who lack such affiliations.

Journalism

SHOEMAKER defines gatekeeping as the process in which the number of possible messages is decreased to reach a particular person in a specific setting and time. She traces the history of the gatekeeping concept by examining the research of LEWIN (1947a; 1947b; 1951) and of WHITE, who applied Lewin's gatekeeping theory to journalism. She also analyzes the work of other researchers who sought to apply and refine Lewin's gatekeeping model (BASS; DONOHUE ET AL., 1972; GIEBER; WESTLEY & MACLEAN).

Contrary to O'SULLIVAN ET AL., Shoemaker suggests that the gatekeeper metaphor has value in communications studies, especially for examining the role and use of interpersonal channels. She notes that gatekeepers serve as information filters, ensuring that society deal only with manageable amounts of information. Further, she proposes a gatekeeper model that shows three levels of communication behavior, the most important of which focuses on "intraindividual-level" life experience.

As Shoemaker demonstrates, much of the literature on gatekeeping in journalism equates the concept to the role of editors in controlling the flow of information. They determine what information is disseminated to their readership (R.M. BROWN; JANOWITZ; LARSON; OLIEN ET AL.).

Larson presents the sender–receiver model of communication and refers to the editor as a gatekeeper who decides whether the message will appear. Similarly, R.M. Brown examines the early research of LEWIN (1943) and of WHITE, who applied Lewin's research to the mass media. Brown, who assesses White's methodologies, concludes that Lewin's concept of gatekeeping, as applied by White, aids in understanding the dissemination process in news magazine coverage. Janowitz, who defines gatekeeping as weighing evidence and arriving at an objective conclusion, juxtaposes gatekeepers and advocates and treats both as models of journalistic behavior.

Library and Information Science

Most of the literature concerning gatekeeping in library and information science is appropriately discussed as part of information needs and use studies. However, some studies attribute an editorial dimension to gatekeeping. GLOGOFF equates the refereeing process in scholarly library journals to that of gatekeeping. JOYCE uses gatekeeping to describe the relationship between African-American culture and African-American book publishing. CHAMBERLAIN employs the term to identify the librarian's role in the acquisitions process. SHEARER uses gatekeepers to analyze and describe problems and approaches in library selection.

Summary

The literature shows that the term gatekeeper is often defined in one of two ways. The first definition designates gatekeepers as individuals who either limit access to information or restrict the scope of information, thereby decreasing opportunities within an organizational structure. Essentially, gatekeepers are individuals who control resources within either a formal or informal organizational structure and who hinder rather than help in the provision of information. LEMAY, who provides an illustration of gatekeeping as a metaphor for controlling access, equates gatekeeping with the immigration policies of countries, such as the United States, that inhibit the entry of immigrants.

The other application of the gatekeeping metaphor denotes an innovator, change agent, communication channel, link, intermediary, helper, adapter, opinion leader, broker, and facilitator who positively affects the transfer or use of information within an organization. The common element in both applications of the metaphor is that gatekeepers participate in an informal network of information transfer in an organizational setting. The difference in the application of the concept concerns whether the gatekeeping function is an asset or a liability within the organization.

Gatekeepers in a Cultural Context

Much of the literature on gatekeepers, especially that in the health sciences, education, science and technology, and library and information science, equates them with professionals (e.g., health care providers, teachers, counselors, engineers, scientists, and librarians). This research tends not to focus on gatekeepers who may not be professionals such as those in culturally diverse communities.

As noted in the discussion of the science and technology literature, some of the research that concerns gatekeeping in cultural or ethnic groups has focused on technological gatekeeping in international settings, especially in developing nations (ALLEN & COONEY; ALLEN

ET AL., 1971a, 1971b; BARQUIN; G. MYERS; SUBRAMANYAM). In the international arena, the intent of technological gatekeeping appears to be to encourage or facilitate research and the adoption of technological innovations between and among gatekeepers.

The research concerning gatekeeping among ethnic or cultural groups in the United States considers it as a social phenomenon, whereby individuals actively participate in the information-retrieval and -dissemination process in their communities. For example, some researchers have applied the gatekeeper model to the urban assimilation and acculturation patterns of immigrant groups, particularly the Spanish speaking. In one of the first studies of acculturation agents, KURTZ defined gatekeepers as individuals who move between two cultures to provide information that links people with alternatives or solutions. Kurtz identified clusters of individuals in Denver, Colo., who function as gatekeepers and facilitate the socialization of Mexican immigrants into their new social environment.

MATTHIASSON, J. MOORE, and SHANNON & SHANNON, who further refined the gatekeeper model within the urban setting, monitored the exchange of information between clusters of information providers in urban centers with growing Latino communities. They found that gatekeepers who, by definition, interpret community information needs and broker information to their constituencies had significant status within the community.

BOOTH & OWEN applied the case-study method to examine the network of human service agencies in primarily African-American and white communities in Maryland. They showed the role and importance of community gatekeepers who serve as active agents in community development. Gatekeepers serve as links between formal networks (e.g., schools, churches, businesses, government agencies, and labor unions) and informal networks (e.g., families, neighbors, and nonstructured community groups), which are essential to the success of community development. Booth and Owen indicate how residents use formal and informal networks, how the networks connect, and how to maximize gatekeeping (informal) channels.

BOROWIEC examined cultural groups within the gatekeeping context and analyzed the leadership roles of 83 Polish-American leaders in Buffalo, N.Y. These leaders often act as mediators between public agencies and ethnic citizens. In their gatekeeping role, they may provide information and personal assistance to alleviate communications breakdown between the community and service agencies. These leaders perceive their gatekeeping activities to be important, and they do not consider their gatekeeping status to be affected by their official role as either appointed or elected officials. This finding parallels that of METOYER-DURAN (1993b) that gatekeepers can have either a formal or an informal status within the community and need not be designated as formal leaders (i.e., given an official title).

A narrower interpretation of gatekeeping within a cultural context views gatekeepers as those who guard and protect their local constituencies from outside influences. Some of the research suggests that gatekeepers often perceive their primary mission as preserving cultural integrity and "guarding" their ethnic enclaves from the incursions of the external culture (KURTZ; MERTON; SNYDER; TAKAKI). METOYER-DURAN (1991b; 1993b) designated this type of gatekeeping activity as that of the impeder who withholds information from the community.

To study communication behavior within the Latino population, MATTHIASSON, J. MOORE, and SHANNON & SHANNON developed data-collection methods that were language and culture sensitive. A few researchers in library and information science used the gatekeeper concept to examine the information role that influential members of language or cultural groups have played in their communities (DURAN; DURAN & MONROE; HSIA; SNYDER). These investigators explain how certain individuals use information to influence or moderate change within their cultural communities and between their cultural communities and the dominant or other ethnic communities. This limited research suggests that gatekeepers have greater awareness of and use more information resources than do other community members, notwithstanding educational level, employment status, income, and longevity in the community (DERVIN ET AL.; DURAN; DURAN & MONROE; HSIA).

Cross-cultural studies. The research discussed above concerned primarily the gatekeeping process within a single ethnic or cultural group. SNYDER, who studied gatekeepers in Los Angeles, conducted one of the few cross-cultural studies of information-seeking behavior. Commissioned by the National Institute of Mental Health (NIMH), the study identified neighborhood gatekeepers in the American Indian, Chicano, African American, Arab, and white communities. It described their information-dispersing activities, which range from direct provision of information to an individual, to a referral point, and to an institutional contact.

Snyder developed a set of information-seeking profiles that could be applied to the five groups. The profiles considered the gatekeepers' use of language, kinship networks, and organizational attitudes. Among his recommendations Synder called for health service institutions to create ties with neighborhood gatekeepers in order to disseminate health information more effectively. As noted above, the health sciences literature proposes use of community gatekeepers for providing health care information and instruction to the elderly and for drug education and alcohol rehabilitation programs (BECKMAN & MAYS; EMLET & HALL; MAYS & BECKMAN; RASCHKO).

The term opinion leader is often used to describe individuals who provide information because they listen, are listened to, and influence their communities (CHILDERS & POST; DURRANCE, 1980; KIDD; WARNER ET AL.). CHATMAN (1985; 1987; 1990) investigated the information-seeking activity of the urban poor, including African-Americans and Latinos. Collectively, these studies document the existence of opinion leaders who share new ideas with the community and who encounter social barriers that limit their access to information.

Some cross-cultural studies do not focus on information dissemination per se, but they examine other aspects of gatekeeping (given below). MURRAY, who studied interpersonal communication behavior, found a relationship between gatekeeping and effective work performance. He analyzed conversational breakdowns and misinterpretations among English-speaking ethnic groups and noted that communication problems excluded some ethnic minorities from participating in informal gatekeeping. TRICARICO studied acculturation patterns between the Italians and Irish in Greenwich Village, N.Y., and showed that the Irish were the gatekeepers who controlled entry into political, social, and religious activities.

FIKSDAL viewed academic advisors as gatekeepers who interact with foreign students, some of whom may speak English as a second language. She portrayed the communication between the two groups as a new model of conversation that considers verbal, nonverbal, and other expressions of communication.

CARLSON ET AL. assessed the information needs of Asians, African Americans, Hispanics, and Native Americans in California. They also examined differences between categories of end users and information providers (e.g., librarians and minority leaders) in their perceptions of the information needs of these ethnic groups. Although they did not identify gatekeepers as such, they did consider differences between community members and their leaders.

INFORMATION NEEDS AND USE MODELS

A vast amount of research concerns information needs, users, and uses. Since 1966, *ARIST* has provided 11 comprehensive reviews of the literature on information needs and use studies.

In the most recent review, HEWINS updates the review of DERVIN & NILAN, which covered the period 1978–1986. While the reviews include many types of information needs and user/use studies, there is little emphasis on gatekeeping models in culturally diverse communities. Yet information needs and use studies have been the primary

means by which libraries have planned and evaluated services to culturally diverse communities (CARLSON ET AL.; CHEN & HERNON;
CHILDERS & POST; DERVIN, 1973, 1976; DERVIN ET AL.; WARNER
ET AL.). These studies have not distinguished between the information
needs of the community and those who act as intermediaries (i.e.,
gatekeepers) in providing and disseminating information in culturally
diverse communities.

This section considers only the literature that relates to the gatekeeping
model of information-seeking behavior. Moreover, it highlights those
early conceptual models that are relevant to the gatekeeper model and,
where appropriate, cites and references the *ARIST* reviews of DERVIN
& NILAN and HEWINS.

User-Centered Approaches

The traditional paradigm of information seeking and use focused on
the retrieval systems and information processing. The critical-incident
method used by ALLEN (1966) and the situational analysis techniques
adopted by Dervin (DERVIN, 1976; DERVIN ET AL.) were two early
methodological departures from this paradigm. DERVIN & NILAN (p.
16) asked: "How do people define needs in different situations, how do
they present these needs to systems, and how do they make use of what
systems offer them?" CHEN & HERNON (p. 9) discussed the relevance
of situational analysis techniques and noted that "an information need
cannot be separated from the situation which created it and the individual who perceived it." As noted by MARCHIONINI ET AL. (p. 38),
"recognition of an information problem may be characterized as a gap
(DERVIN & NILAN), a visceral need (TAYLOR, 1962), an anomaly
(BELKIN, 1980) or a defect in a mental model (MARCHIONINI)."

MARCHIONINI ET AL. address both how individuals search for
information and the implications of their information-seeking strategies for the design of information systems. They examined the effects of
electronic access on the information-seeking behavior of subject (i.e.,
"domain") experts and search experts.

DERVIN & NILAN trace the paradigmatic shift in information
needs and use studies. They identify three alternative needs-assess-
ment approaches, each containing a set of related assumptions, theses,
and techniques for analyzing and interpreting data from information
studies considering different user groups. TAYLOR (1968) defined a
progressive question-negotiation technique for matching the inquirer's
real information need to available and appropriate resources. KRIKELAS
had also proposed an information-seeking behavior model based on a
hierarchy of preferences. In contrast to CHEN & HERNON, these and
other hierarchical approaches equate information needs to unarticulated

questions shaped by an individual's background and the external environment.

In a more recent study, TAYLOR (1991) provides a useful typology of classes (i.e., professionals, entrepreneurs, special interest groups, and special socioeconomic groups) and types of information needs. Taylor developed "information use environments" (IUE) to illustrate types of information needs. Although he includes minorities as a "special socioeconomic group," there seems to be no evidence that this typology has been applied to culturally diverse professionals or nonprofessionals (TAYLOR, 1991, p. 222).

DOSA ET AL. apply the gatekeeping model to information professionals. They reintroduce the concept of the information gatekeeper, as defined in the communications literature, and they propose that organizations provide information counselors to function as professional gatekeepers. The tasks of these counselors parallel those of informal gatekeepers and include networking, advising, filtering, transmitting, and repackaging information to provide added value to user-oriented systems.

Some researchers, seeking to better understand user behavior, have applied theories from cognitive learning and organizational psychology. This approach shifts attention from system performance measures (such as recall and precision) to other measures that describe the impact of information on changing user attitudes and resolving problems. In addition to JAKOBOVITS & NAHL-JAKOBOVITS, KUHLTHAU and KUHLTHAU ET AL. also considered the cognitive and affective dimensions of behavior. They found that at least some types of library users increase their acquisition and use of information by enhancing their knowledge of and affective orientations toward the library.

DERVIN (1973, 1976; DERVIN ET AL.) focused on the needs of the "average citizen" and formulated and applied the sense-making approach to the process. She provides a set of conceptual premises and related methodologies for assessing how people make sense out of their worlds and how they use resources to solve problems. This approach led to the development of a taxonomy of information needs based on the situational analysis of the needs of everyday citizens. Dervin's conceptual framework and taxonomy have since been used in a number of community studies, including those on the urban poor (DURAN; DURAN & MONROE; METOYER-DURAN, 1991b, 1993b; WARNER ET AL.).

In their discussion of the needs of the average citizen, DERVIN (1973, 1976; DERVIN ET AL.) and others have included some culturally diverse groups. Except for the research of the NATIONAL EDUCATION RESOURCES INSTITUTE, DURAN, and DURAN & MONROE, no published study in library and information science has differentiated between the information needs of citizens and noncitizens, which may include documented (legal) and undocumented (illegal) residents.

Belkin (BELKIN, 1978; BELKIN ET AL.) also focuses on the situational approach and analyzes situations in which the user experiences anomalous states of knowledge (ASK) and finds it difficult to articulate or recognize what is wrong. Belkin examines the problematic situation and looks for ways to make "best matches" between the ASK situation and the information retrieval systems.

As previously noted, DERVIN & NILAN postulated that a new paradigm for user studies is emerging that questions the traditional assumptions about user interactions with information-provision systems. Hewins's review of information needs and use studies commented that "past assumptions place the user in the passive position of having to adapt to the information-provision mechanism rather than the mechanism's adapting to the user's particular characteristics" (HEWINS, p. 146). The literature indicates that these approaches emphasize users and their ability to process information actively and deemphasize the information system itself.

According to METOYER-DURAN (1991b, p. 323), "A common thread in the new paradigm is the effort to understand the real nature of the information request and relate the request to the user's value system and social environment." Application of the approaches discussed by Dervin and Nilan and Hewins to culturally diverse communities have been limited to a few studies (CHANG & HAR-NICOLESCU; CHILDERS & POST; COCHRANE & ATHERTON; DERVIN, 1976, 1980; DERVIN ET AL.; DURAN; DURAN & MONROE; GOMEZ; HSIA; LOUIE; WARNER ET AL.).

More recently, METOYER-DURAN (1991a; 1991b; 1993b) has built on these user-centered models and proposed a new model, the gatekeeper model, to understand the information-seeking behavior of these groups. Within culturally diverse communities, unequal access to information is often a barrier that affects the gatekeeper's role as an information provider within the community. In some instances, community members seek the assistance of a gatekeeper because they are unable to get the information they require to solve problems.

Information Inequity

The public and equal access. Despite the increase in the amount of information available to society in general, there is evidence that information inequity exists in culturally diverse communities (CARLSON ET AL.; CHILDERS & POST; COCHRANE & ATHERTON; DERVIN, 1980; METOYER-DURAN, 1993a; VALENTINE; WARNER ET AL.). The public library's determination of who constitutes its public is central to the library's duty to meet its mission in serving culturally diverse communities. According to HERNON & METOYER-DURAN, the "public" means all the people in a specific area, be they citizens or noncitizens of a community, state, or nation. This definition includes documented (legal) and undocumented (illegal) residents.

The *1990 Census Profile: Race and Hispanic Origin* (U.S. BUREAU OF THE CENSUS) indicates that the white population increased only 6% between 1980 and 1990, while other groups showed significant increases: Asian/Pacific Islanders (108%), Latinos (53%), and African-Americans (13.2%). Demographers project that in some states (e.g., California) the culturally diverse minority may well become the majority. The provision of information services to these "new publics" becomes an issue of necessity and public policy.

In their analysis of social equality in the United States, VERBA & NIE postulate that less well-informed individuals, especially members of culturally diverse groups, would exhibit less political participation and representation than would the general population. A segment of their research documented the role of culturally diverse individuals who acted as opinion leaders. Other researchers have focused on the influence of language loyalty (non-English language preference) in the socialization rates of culturally diverse groups (ANTUNES & GAITZ; AXELROD; EDELSTEIN ET AL.; FISHMAN; WELCH ET AL.). They dispute the traditional model of social participation, which maintains that language loyalty inhibits assimilation into another culture. In their view, the preference and use of a non-English or a second language may encourage opportunities for social participation. It is possible that the use of the non-English language facilitates communication among those who share it and builds confidence in their ability to interact with the majority society.

Information and Referral Models

In the 1970s, public libraries sought to determine and to eradicate the barriers preventing culturally diverse groups from gaining fuller access to information. One approach was the development of services designed to meet local information needs. Some researchers argued that traditional reference services did not meet the information needs of nonusers, including culturally diverse communities, and that new delivery systems were required (CHILDERS & POST; KOCHEN; WARNER ET AL.). Borrowing a term and a concept from the social service delivery system, many public libraries used the information and referral (I&R) model as the most appropriate response (see METOYER-DURAN, 1993c).

In their analysis of I&R services, some writers, including CHILDERS (1979; 1984), BUNGE, and DURRANCE (1984), distinguished between traditional reference services and I&R services. Their discussions reveal that many public libraries purporting to have I&R services lacked a component that linked the information need to the utility of the information and that these libraries were still providing traditional reference services. The core of the I&R model is the implementation of a community information needs assessment that incorporates cultural factors. With a few notable exceptions (DERVIN & GREENBERG; DURAN; DURAN & MONROE; HSIA; NATIONAL EDUCATION RESOURCES INSTITUTE), there is little evidence that I&R research accounts for language or cultural differences. Studies in other fields consider language factors in the provision of programs and services. For example, MALGADY ET AL. found that ethnocultural and linguistic bias operates among non-Spanish speaking case workers who evaluate mental health problems in the Latino community. They concluded that monolingual Spanish speakers were significantly more disadvantaged when they interacted with English monolingual case workers.

To investigate the I&R process in culturally diverse communities, METOYER-DURAN (1993c) applied the model of HERNON & MCCLURE and the information-seeking situation categories of DERVIN ET AL. to the findings of an earlier study on gatekeeping (METOYER-DURAN, 1991a; 1993b). The Hernon and McClure model explains I&R in the context of the library's ability to serve the user. METOYER-DURAN (1993c) found that gatekeepers function as I&R agents in the American Indian, Chinese, Japanese, Korean, and Latino communities. In this capacity, gatekeepers link their communities with information resources by using a range of information sources, electronic and non-electronic, and incorporating referral activity whenever appropriate.

Taxonomic Models

In addition to the I&R model for addressing the information needs of culturally diverse communities, other models have focused on classifying or studying the behavior of information seekers. The taxonomic approach to classifying information-seeking behavior has been applied in many fields, including communication, education, computer science, and library and information science. In his study of the adoption of new agricultural and technological practices, ROGERS developed one of the earliest taxonomic approaches to a user's or client's orientation to information. He classified individuals as innovators, early adopters, early majority, late majority, or laggards in their readiness to accept change. Innovators and early adopters use more information sources in responding to changing social and economic environments than do other types of individuals (CHERRY; LIN & BURT; MERTON).

BLOOM and KRATHWOHL ET AL. constructed a set of taxonomies that classified educational behavior and performance according to a scheme that maps intended outcomes for the cognitive and affective domains. According to Bloom, educational institutions focus primarily on the cognitive domain, stressing learning objectives associated with recall and knowledge application. He argued that the schools tested students and developed curricula on the basis of their cognitive growth and neglected the equally important affective, or emotional, growth of the individual. The affective domain is concerned with the emotional state or feelings of students as characterized by their interests, attitudes, values, and emotional sets or biases associated with learning. METOYER-DURAN (1991b; 1993b) adapted and applied the taxonomic framework of Bloom and Krathwohl et al. to ethnolinguistic gatekeepers. JAKOBOVITS & NAHL-JAKOBOVITS, who use the taxonomy of Bloom and Krathwohl et al., demonstrate the utility of the taxonomic approach in their study of the library-based information-seeking behavior of students. They tracked student library patrons who moved from simple to complex activities in the affective and cognitive domains.

FRAND and FRAND & DANUTAK applied the educational taxonomy of BLOOM and KRATHWOHL ET AL. to the information orientation of office professionals. Frand developed a set of computer literacy profiles for office professionals based on the relationship between the workers' cognitive and affective attributes. His taxonomic approach to developing these profiles was important in the analysis of gatekeeper information-seeking behavior by METOYER-DURAN (1991b; 1993b).

INFORMATION AND CULTURE

Information-seeking behavior describes how individuals go about fulfilling a need to know. Information-seeking behavior should be viewed within the context of the individual's cultural experience. This is especially important for ethnic groups that may communicate in non-English languages. As previously discussed, the relationship between ethnic groups and the information-seeking behavior of their members has received only limited attention in the literature (CHATMAN, 1985, 1987, 1990; DURAN; DURAN & MONROE; METOYER-DURAN, 1991a, 1991b, 1993a, 1993b, 1993c).

MENOU and MACHLUP & MANSFIELD examined the role of information in society and concluded that it is culture specific. According to these authors, data are collected, organized, and communicated within a cultural context and with cultural tools. In his description of the cultural dimension of information, MENOU (p. 121) stated that "information and culture could hardly be separated" since culture consists of all transmitted social knowledge. These and other writers

(COCHRANE & ATHERTON; EDELSTEIN ET AL.; KAPLAN) contend that in a dynamic society more information is generated when many cultural influences intersect and that there is a need for segments of society to cooperate.

In the past two decades, the culture-sensitive attributes of information began to receive more attention. CHERRY and EDELSTEIN ET AL. consider language and culture as barriers to learning or assimilation. COCHRANE & ATHERTON investigated the cultural dimension of information and identified deficiencies in the existing models. They suggest that the proper unit of analysis for considering information services in a culturally diverse society would be the "cultural community." This community is composed of individuals who may have distinct values, beliefs, and attitudes toward external information services.

Menou also articulated the culturally intrinsic dimension of information and wrote that "information is culture specific and, consequently, is largely uncommunicable unless it has been 'acculturated'" (MENOU, p. 121). When gatekeepers disseminate information in their ethnic communities, they often act as agents of acculturation.

PRITCHARD and others agree with Menou and Cochrane and Atherton that the proper unit of study is the cultural community. Pritchard, who reviewed the literature on information networks in developing nations, urges Unesco (the United Nations Educational, Scientific and Cultural Organization) to focus on users rather than systems in providing more effective networks. Pritchard also overviews information networks that might be useful to developing nations and offers recommendations concerning their adoption. Similarly, AINA suggests that the network of libraries in Africa should identify gatekeepers within the farming communities and use gatekeepers as intermediaries in addressing the information needs of farmers. Aina explains that potential gatekeepers are literate farmers who may be more effective than librarians in communicating with illiterate farmers. Both Pritchard and Aina view gatekeepers as cultural and technical links who could assist and guide their communities in the use of information.

An essential element in studying the relationships between information and cultural groups and the role of gatekeepers in culturally diverse communities is the use of appropriate (i.e., culture sensitive) methodologies and procedures.

Methodological Considerations of Cross-Cultural Research

There is limited research on the relationship between cultural factors and the information-seeking behavior of culturally diverse groups. Correspondingly, there is a paucity of research on the methodological issues related to cross-cultural research.

Library and information science research. Duran's study of the communication patterns of Mexican, Cuban, and Puerto Rican residents of
Chicago was one of the first in library and information science to
consider the methodological issues involved in cross-cultural research
(DURAN). He developed training procedures to guide bilingual, bicultural interviewers who administered English- and Spanish-language
interviews. A comprehensive report of the procedures is found in
DURAN & MONROE.

LOUIE and HURH & KIM discuss the methodological problems of
conducting research in Asian immigrant communities. Louie's study of
the information-seeking behavior of Chinese immigrants in Los Angeles noted that these problems included unfamiliarity with public in-
quiries, privacy issues, and language barriers. Louie addressed these
problems by translating the data-gathering instrument into Chinese,
administering the questionnaire in group settings, using bilingual proc-
tors, and carefully sequencing sensitive questions.

In their examination of Korean immigrants in Chicago and Los Angeles, HURH & KIM analyzed methodological difficulties, which include translation between western and non-western languages, communication problems between the interviewer and the respondent, and
sampling problems.

CARLSON ET AL. interviewed and mailed questionnaires to librarians and minority leaders in California's Asian, African-American,
Latino, and American Indian communities. Although they did not
emphasize the complexity of the methodological issues involved, they
did refer to these issues in their application of Dervin's six methods for
analyzing library use and information needs (DERVIN & CLARK, 1987).
METOYER-DURAN (1993a) examined the methodological considerations related to the conduct of research in culturally diverse communities. Her study considers cultural factors, demographics and data-gathering and analysis techniques (including translation of data-gathering
instruments), and the dissemination of findings in these communities.
She provides strategies for dealing with sampling problems and other
issues, with the focus on implementing community analysis studies for
public libraries. An important element in the discussion are the sampling
issues involved in properly defining culturally diverse communities:

> A critical and complex problem when conducting research
> about ethnic groups is the proper identification of individu-
> als and communities who belong to the cultural or ethnic
> group. While cultural variations among people in the United
> States have been a historical reality, it is increasingly difficult
> to identify and sample ethnic populations. The reason is that
> people do not necessarily fit within conventional classifica-

tions; they may perceive themselves as members of more than one ethnic group. (METOYER-DURAN, 1993a, p. 21)

Social and behavioral science research.. Much of the discussion concerning cross-cultural research methods comes from anthropology, psychology, sociology, communication studies, and education. Although a comprehensive review of the literature is not possible here, some research merits discussion because of its relevance to the information-seeking behavior of gatekeepers in ethnolinguistic communities.

LONNER & BERRY present guidelines for the effective conduct of field research in cross-cultural settings. While psychology is the focus, the principles, guidelines, and strategies are applicable to other fields. For example, they discuss the drawing of inferences from data, sampling issues, research instruments, and observational methods. Of particular note is their observation that there are no universal formulas to ensure adequate representation in every cross-cultural setting.

GREEN proposes the concept of "ethnic competence" as a means of guiding research and practice in culturally diverse communities. "To be ethnically competent means to be able to conduct one's professional work in a way that is congruent with the behavior and expectations that members of a distinct culture recognize as appropriate among themselves" (GREEN, p. 52). Based on the concept of "ethnic competence," Green proposes a transactional model to understand ethnicity. The model requires an examination of the values, signs, and behavioral styles through which individuals convey their identity in cross-cultural encounters. GUYETTE and WAX focus on special considerations for conducting research in American Indian communities. Guyette presents community-based research as a device for community development and stresses the communications problems often encountered in research endeavors among this community. Wax examines the ethical dimensions of conducting research among American Indians, with an emphasis on Indian reservations. For example, he discusses confidentiality, procedures for consent, and protocols for disseminating findings, all of which may have political implications in tribal communities.

While MARIN & MARIN focus on the issues involved in conducting research in Hispanic communities, the principles they identify can be applied to other nonnative English-speaking groups. For example, they distinguish between universal (etic) and group-specific (emic) concepts and warn, along with LONNER & BERRY, that cross-cultural research should not assume the universality of a concept or construct.

ETHNOLINGUISTIC GATEKEEPERS

The gatekeeping approach was indirectly tested in studies of the information needs of urban residents. A few studies concluded that some people function as opinion leaders and information resources (CHILDERS & POST; DURRANCE, 1980; KIDD; VERBA & NIE; WARNER ET AL.). For the most part, these studies did not recognize that gatekeeping has a special role and meaning in ethnic communities. DURAN, DURAN & MONROE, and METOYER-DURAN (1991b; 1993b; 1993c) suggest that gatekeepers act as community links and filters in information gathering and dissemination.

METOYER-DURAN (1991a; 1991b) defines an ethnolinguistic gatekeeper as

> an individual who typically operates in two or more speech communities (one English), and who links these communities by providing information. Ethnolinguistic gatekeepers can include monolingual individuals who operate within the context of two cultures. (METOYER-DURAN, 1991b, p. 321)

There is need for a new conceptual model for understanding ethnolinguistic gatekeepers because most previous researchers, except for DURAN, DURAN & MONROE, DERVIN & GREENBERG, HSIA, and NATIONAL EDUCATION RESOURCES INSTITUTE did not consider language and cultural differences in their model development. In addition, few studies incorporated bilingual data-gathering techniques in cross-cultural information-seeking behavior (DURAN; DURAN & MONROE; GOMEZ; HSIA). METOYER-DURAN (1993a) maintained that while the user-centered model is the appropriate approach for studying the information-seeking behavior of ethnolinguistic gatekeepers, the design and conduct of such studies must include cultural and linguistic factors to ensure accuracy.

The Gatekeeper Study

METOYER-DURAN (1991a; 1993b) investigated the information-seeking behavior of ethnolinguistic gatekeepers in the American Indian, Chinese, Japanese, Korean, and Latino communities in the Los Angeles, Orange, and San Diego counties of California. The study identified 129 formal (institutionally based) and informal (not included in agency directories or files) gatekeepers from the five ethnic communities.

She explored how gatekeepers receive and disseminate information in their communities, where they get their information, and the types of information they need for themselves and their communities. She also compared the information-seeking behavior of gatekeepers across the five ethnic groups, examined and compared the role of language in the information-seeking behavior of gatekeepers, and provided strategies for the exchange of information between gatekeepers and information providers.

Among the findings of her study that concern information dissemination were that gatekeepers use interpersonal networks, rely heavily on the telephone for receiving and responding to information requests, and use information technologies, such as computers, fax machines, and answering machines. METOYER-DURAN (1991a; 1993b) found that gatekeepers receive their information from interpersonal networks and mass media, especially non-English mass media. They most often seek information related to public affairs, education, and finance for their personal information needs. Subjects involving information needs resulting from community requests tend to concern finance, housing, and public affairs. She also found that language:

> is a determining factor in defining the gatekeepers' use of all information sources including the interpersonal and mass media; and the use and facility of multiple languages more than any other factor seems (sic) to affect the gatekeepers' recognition and status as an information provider in the community. (METOYER-DURAN, 1993b, p. 87)

METOYER-DURAN (1991a; 1993b) addressed culture- and language-specific issues by using bilingual, bicultural interviewers, allowing respondents their language and site preference for interviews, and translating the interview instrument into the appropriate language (Chinese, Japanese, Korean, and Spanish). She provides all four language translations (METOYER-DURAN, 1991a) and the English and Spanish versions of the interview instrument (METOYER-DURAN, 1993b).

The Gatekeeper Model: A Taxonomy

METOYER-DURAN (1991b) developed the gatekeeper model of information-seeking behavior in ethnolinguistic communities. That model is a user-centered framework that is sensitive to both language and culture. It builds on the taxonomic framework of BLOOM and KRATHWOHL ET AL. and the research of KURTZ, DERVIN (1976), DERVIN ET AL., SNYDER, FRAND, FRAND & DANUTAK, DURAN, and DURAN & MONROE.

The conceptual model emphasizes the user's view of information wherein information is defined as the content of a message that is conveyed and assimilated by the person who receives that message. Information in this context usually results in a decision, action, behavioral change, or addition to one's knowledge.

In the METOYER-DURAN (1991b; 1993b) model, the gatekeeper's information environment is characterized by three axes: the cognitive domain, which is divided into two dimensions or axes of information management skills: (1) the concept-usage dimension and (2) the data-usage dimension. The third axis portrays the value set or affective domain of the gatekeeper's information-seeking environment.

A set of six profiles derived from the model interprets the cognitive and affective attributes of the gatekeeper's information-seeking behavior. The profiles (i.e., impeder, affiliated, unaffiliated, broker, information professional, and leader/executive) represent a graduated progression from gatekeepers who inhibit the flow of information (impeder) to those who act intentionally as change agents (leader/executive).

Gatekeeper Profiles

The taxonomy evaluates the ethnolinguistic gatekeeper's information orientation and skills within the cognitive and affective domains. METOYER-DURAN (1991a; 1993b) found that generalizations and/or similarities that evolved from previous information needs and use studies did not match the patterns found among formal and informal ethnolinguistic gatekeepers. In contrast, the gatekeeper study indicated that in culturally diverse communities, there is not one type of gatekeeper but several possible types of gatekeeping activity. METOYER-DURAN (1991b; 1993b) provides a detailed discussion of the profiles derived from the model.

Each profile describes anticipated or probable levels of information-seeking behavior for the different types of gatekeepers who fall along three axes: concept usage, data usage, and affective domain. DOSA ET AL. noted the complexity of studying informal information-seeking behavior:

> Informal information resource sharing is a complicated social process because its effectiveness depends on behavioral and psychological variables. Not only the continuous processes of information seeking/finding and information providing/accepting, but also the nature and quality of the information content depend on individual cognitive styles, personal circumstances, and time-bound events. (DOSA ET AL., p. 9-10)

To measure the cognitive and affective domains, METOYER-DURAN (1993b) developed a set of indexes (affective domain index, concept usage index, data usage index, library index, and literacy index). These indexes plotted the gatekeepers' placement along the three axes of the taxonomy.

As discussed in the sections on research in communications studies and journalism, researchers often equate gatekeepers with impeders (R.M. BROWN; JANOWITZ; LARSON). In ethnolinguistic communities, gatekeeping has a special meaning and impeders are not synonymous with gatekeepers. Rather, impeders represent only one type of gatekeeper. A range of gatekeeper types is reflected in the six profiles.

One example of a gatekeeper profile is the leader/executive. This profile includes elected officials, highly visible mass media commentators, and business executives who maintain their cultural ties and identification. The leaders and executives have extensive interpersonal networks both within and outside their organizations and communities. Their time is spent largely in negotiating, planning, and allocating many types of resources, especially those with information components (METOYER-DURAN, 1993b).

The leader/executive facilitates change and develops strategy, especially in the area of information resources and utilization. One responsibility is to allocate resources and ensure that information becomes a strategic asset rather than an operational expense. The few ethnolinguistic gatekeepers who fit this profile may serve as role models for other gatekeepers.

RESEARCH IMPLICATIONS

Cross-cultural studies become increasingly essential for examining a culturally diverse society. In previous eras, most notably during the 1960s, many social programs, including library outreach programs, were implemented with little grounding in theory and evaluation. The 1990s may result in the creation of a sustained research base that links the information professions with social and other changes within culturally diverse communities. As this section discusses, some possible areas for research are model development, national and international population groups, community analysis and development, and technology.

Model Development

Few existing models of information needs and information-seeking behavior adequately address cultural diversity and gatekeeping. It is important that further research:

- Develop additional gatekeeper profiles derived from the gatekeeper model and examine these in other ethnic settings. These settings might include culturally diverse monolingual (English-speaking) communities such as African-Americans residing in urban and rural settings; and

- Refine those gatekeeper profiles that are most representative of gatekeeper information-seeking behavior. For example, it might be possible to distinguish among gatekeepers who fit the broker profile. These distinctions would necessitate revision and enhancement of the indices discussed in the section on gatekeeper profiles.

National and International Population Groups

Using different models and profiles, research could:

- Compare differences among monolingual and bilingual or multilingual gatekeepers;
- Compare differences among ethnolinguistic groups that share the same language family (e.g., information needs and information-seeking behavior of gatekeepers from Spanish-speaking groups, such as Central and South Americans, Cubans, Mexicans, and Puerto Ricans); and
- Apply the models and profiles to culturally diverse groups in other countries.

Community Analysis and Community Development

It is possible to:

- Use gatekeeper profiles to differentiate and analyze the behavior of individuals involved in community development. For example, the gatekeeper taxonomy (METOYER-DURAN, 1993b) suggests that some profiles (e.g., leader/executive) place a strategic value on using information to develop the community, while others (e.g., the impeder) may not. Research is needed to determine how best to provide information to gate-keepers whose profiles suggest a community development orientation;
- Develop and test hypotheses that compare gatekeepers' and nongatekeepers' use of institutionally based information resources (e.g., libraries); and
- Study the roles and information-seeking behavior of ethnolinguistic gatekeepers in order to design systems

and to provide services that meet the information needs of an increasingly pluralistic and interdependent global society.

Technology

Because gatekeepers, including those serving culturally diverse communities, use and want increased access to electronic information and technology itself, additional research might:

- Explore the implications of culturally diverse communities' gaining greater access to electronic information and new technologies from the public, private, and not-for-profit sectors. Such public policy research includes studies of the diffusion and acceptance of new technologies, equity of public access, privacy issues, and reconciling literacy with the new technologies; and
- Investigate the gatekeepers' knowledge and use of databases, and barriers to access and use, including language format, thesaurus construction, and ability to pay. Such studies might consider the utility and value of applying non-English formats to database and thesaurus construction.

CONCLUSION

The literature on information gatekeepers is dispersed among a number of disciplines, professions, and fields. It lacks cohesion and precision in the definition and use of the term. Gatekeeper once meant a conduit who simply passed on information or limited access to information. Some literature (e.g., education and journalism) has used the term pejoratively to denote someone who withholds information in either a formal or informal organizational setting.

The move within library and information science literature to user-centered frameworks is an important step in understanding the information-seeking process in any context, including that of gatekeeping. The taxonomic models that incorporate the cognitive and affective dimensions of behavior provide a strong basis for focusing on a three-dimensional or integrated view of information-seeking behavior.

Information users increasingly reflect various cultures, ethnic backgrounds, social structures, behaviors, and language proficiencies. However, the literature has paid little attention to cultural factors that affect an individual's information-seeking behavior. Even less research has considered the activity of gatekeepers who link ethnolinguistic communities and the information resources needed to solve their problems.

In culturally diverse communities, especially ethnolinguistic ones, gatekeeping focuses on the receipt and dissemination of information. Because gatekeepers are proactive information providers, a one-dimensional characterization of gatekeeping does not account for the ethnolinguistic gatekeeper's role in actively seeking and disseminating information within formal and informal settings.

As the U.S. workforce becomes increasingly diverse, as people need more information in work and nonwork situations, and as people change careers with greater frequency, it is important to ensure and enhance information access to culturally different groups. This means that libraries and other information providers who serve these groups must understand the role that gatekeepers play. It is also essential to learn how gatekeepers and their communities receive, value, use, disseminate, and diffuse information and to apply that knowledge to information programs, services, and resources.

BIBLIOGRAPHY

AINA, L.O. 1991. Information for Successful Agriculture. Third World Libraries. 1991 Fall; 2(1): 49-53. ISSN: 1052-3049.

ALLEN, THOMAS J. 1966. Managing the Flow of Scientific and Technological Information. Cambridge, MA: Massachusetts Institute of Technology, Alfred P. Sloan School of Management; 1966. 1 volume (discontinuous paging). (Ph.D. dissertation). NTIS: PB 174440.

ALLEN, THOMAS J. 1969. Information Needs and Uses. In: Cuadra, Carlos A.; Luke, Ann W., eds. Annual Review of Information Science and Technology: Volume 4. Chicago, IL: Encyclopaedia Britannica for the American Society for Information Science; 1969. 3-29. ISSN: 0066-4200; ISBN: 0-85229-147-7; LC: 66-25096.

ALLEN, THOMAS J. 1970. Roles in Technical Communications Networks. In: Nelson, Carnot E.; Pollock, Donald K., eds. Communications among Scientists and Engineers. Lexington, MA: Heath Lexington Books; 1970. 191-208. LC: 71-129156.

ALLEN, THOMAS J. 1977a. Managing the Flow of Technology: Technology Transfer and the Dissemination of Technological Information within the R&D Organization. Cambridge, MA: MIT Press; 1977. 320p. ISBN: 0-262-01048-8; LC: 76-57670.

ALLEN, THOMAS J. 1977b. The Role of Person to Person Communication Networks in the Dissemination of Industrial Technology. Cambridge, MA: Massachusetts Institute of Technology, Alfred P. Sloan School of Management; 1977 March. 29p. ERIC: ED 181875.

ALLEN, THOMAS J.; COHEN, S.I. 1969. Information Flow in Two R&D Laboratories. Administrative Science Quarterly. 1969 March; 4(1): 12-19. ISSN: 0001-8392.

ALLEN, THOMAS J.; COONEY, SEAN. 1973. Institutional Roles in Technology Transfer: A Diagnosis of the Situation in One Small Country. R & D Management. 1973; 4(1): 41-51. ISSN: 0033-6807.

ALLEN, THOMAS J.; PIEPMEIER, J.M.; COONEY, S. 1971a. The International Technological Gatekeeper. Technology Review. 1971 March; 73(5): 36-43. ISSN: 0040-1692.

ALLEN, THOMAS J.; PIEPMEIER, J.M.; COONEY, S. 1971b. Technology Transfer to Developing Countries: An International Technological Gatekeeper. Cambridge, MA: Massachusetts Institute of Technology, Alfred P. Sloan School of Management; 1971 February. 29p. ERIC: ED 052796.

ANSELLO, EDWARD F.; LAMY, PETER P. 1989. Regional Differences in Medication Profiles: Responding with Geropharmacy Curricula. Paper presented at: Gerontological Society of America 42nd Annual Meeting; 1989 November 17-21; Minneapolis, MN. 18p. ERIC: ED 313623.

ANTUNES, GEORGE; GAITZ, CHARLES M. 1975. Ethnicity and Participation: A Study of Mexican-Americans, Blacks, and Whites. American Journal of Sociology. 1975 March; 80(5): 1192-1211. ISSN: 0002-9602.

ATWOOD, RITA; DERVIN, BRENDA. 1981. Challenge to Socio-cultural Predictors of Information Seeking: A Test of Race vs. Situation Movement State. In: Burgoon, M., ed. Communication Yearbook 5. New Brunswick, NJ: Transaction Books for the International Communication Association; 1981. 549-569. ISSN: 0147-4642; ISBN: 0-87855-477-5.

AXELROD, MORRIS. 1956. Urban Structure and Social Participation. American Sociological Review. 1956 February; 21(1): 13-18. ISSN: 0003-1224.

BARQUIN, R.C. 1982. Transferring Informatics Technology to Developing Countries: Report of Some Findings. In: Foster, F.G., ed. Informatics and Industrial Development: Proceedings of the International Conference on Policies for Information Processing for Developing Countries; 1981 March 9-13; Dublin, Ireland. Dublin, Ireland: Tycooly International; 1982. 84-93. (Information Technology and Development Series v. 2). ISBN: 0-907567-28-2; ISBN: 0-907567-29-0 (pbk); NTIS: AD-P001 460/5.

BASS, A.Z. 1969. Refining the "Gatekeeper" Concept: A UN Radio Case Study. Journalism Quarterly. 1969 Spring; 46(1): 69-72. ISSN: 0196-3031.

BECKER, MARSHALL H. 1970. Sociometric Location and Innovativeness: Reformulation and Extension of the Diffusion Model. American Sociological Review. 1970 April; 35(2): 267-282. ISSN: 0003-1224.

BECKMAN, LINDA J.; MAYS, VICKIE M. 1985. Educating Community Gatekeepers about Alcohol Abuse in Women: Changing Attitudes, Knowledge and Referral Practices. Journal of Drug Education. 1985; 15(4): 289-309. ISSN: 0047-2379.

BELKIN, NICHOLAS J. 1978. Information Concepts for Information Science. Journal of Documentation. 1978 March; 34(1): 55-85. ISSN: 0022-0418.

BELKIN, NICHOLAS J. 1980. Anomalous States of Knowledge as a Basis for Information Retrieval. Canadian Journal of Information Science. 1980 May; 5: 133-143. ISSN: 0380-9218.

BELKIN, NICHOLAS J.; ODDY, R.N.; BROOKS, H.M. 1982. ASK for Information Retrieval. Part I: Background and Theory. Journal of Documentation. 1982 June; 38(2): 61-71. Part II: Results of Design Study. Journal of Documentation. 1982 September; 38(3): 145-164. ISSN: 0022-0418.

BISSONETTE, RAYMOND. 1977. The Mental Health Gatekeeper Role: A Paradigm for Conceptual Pretest. International Journal of Social Psychiatry. 1977 Spring; 23(1): 31-34. ISSN: 0020-7640.

BLOOM, BENJAMIN S., ed. 1956. Taxonomy of Educational Objectives: The Classification of Educational Goals. Handbook I: Cognitive Domain. New York, NY: David McKay Co., Inc.; 1956. 207p. LC: 64-012369; OCLC: 25478139.

BOOTH, NAN; OWEN, EUGENE. 1985. The Relevance of Formal and Informal Networks for Community Development: Lessons Learned from Three Cases. In: Fear, Frank A.; Schwarzweller, Harry K., eds. Focus on Community. Greenwich, CT: JAI Press; 1985. 159-172. (Research in Rural Sociology and Development v. 2). ISBN: 0-89232-558-5.

BOROWIEC, WALTER A. 1975. Persistence and Change in the Gatekeeper Role of Ethnic Leaders: The Case of the Polish-American. Political Anthropology. 1975 March; 1(1): 21-40. OCLC: 1730250.

BROADHEAD, ROBERT S.; RIST, RAY C. 1976. Gatekeepers and the Social Control of Social Research. Social Problems. 1976 February; 23(3): 325-336. ISSN: 0037-7791.

BROWN, RICHARD M. 1979. The Gatekeeper Reassessed: A Return to Lewin. Journalism Quarterly. 1979 Autumn; 56(3): 595-601, 679. ISSN: 0196-3031.

BROWN, VALERIE. 1983. Mental Health Gatekeeping in Community Development: An Open and Shut Case? Community Development Journal. 1983 October; 18(3): 214-221. ISSN: 0010-3802.

BUNGE, CHARLES. 1980. Reference Services. In: Wedgeworth, R., ed. ALA World Encyclopedia of Library and Information Services. Chicago, IL: American Library Association; 1980. 468-474. ISBN: 0-8389-0305-3.

CARLSON, DAVID B.; MARTINEZ, ARABELLA; CURTIS, SARA A.; COLES, JANET; VALENZUELA, NICHOLAS A. 1990. Adrift in a Sea of Change: California's Public Libraries Struggle to Meet the Information Needs of Multicultural Communities. Oakland, CA: Center for Policy Development; 1990. 125p. Available from: California State Library, 1001 Sixth Street, Suite 300, Sacramento, CA 95814-3324.

CHAMBERLAIN, C. 1991. The Gatekeeper and Information. Library Acquisitions: Practice and Theory. 1991; 15(3): 265-269. ISSN: 0364-6408.

CHANG, HENRY C.; HAR-NICOLESCU, SUZINE. 1983. Needs Assessment Study of Library Service for Asian American Community Members in the United States. In: U.S. Task Force on Library and Information Services to Cultural Minorities. Report. Washington, DC: National Commission on Libraries and Information Science; 1983. 79-99. LC: 83-017407; OCLC: 9895270.

CHATMAN, ELFREDA A. 1985. Information, Mass Media Use and the Working Poor. Library and Information Science Research. 1985 April-June; 7(2): 97-113. ISSN: 0740-8188.

CHATMAN, ELFREDA A. 1987. Opinion Leadership, Poverty, and Information Sharing. RQ. 1987 Spring; 26: 341-353. ISSN: 0033-7072.

CHATMAN, ELFREDA A. 1990. Alienation Theory: Application of a Conceptual Framework to a Study of Information among Janitors. RQ. 1990 Spring; 29: 355-368. ISSN: 0033-7072.

CHEN, CHING-CHIH; HERNON, PETER. 1982. Information Seeking: Assessing and Anticipating User Needs. New York, NY: Neal-Schuman; 1982. 205p. ISBN: 0-918212-50-2(pbk); LC: 82-006320.

CHERRY, COLIN. 1978. World Communication: Threat or Promise? Chichester, England: Wiley; 1978. 229p. ISBN: 0-471-99616-5; LC: 78-003761.
CHILDERS, THOMAS. 1979. Trends in Public Library I&R Services. Library Journal. 1979 October 1; 104(17): 2035-2039. ISSN: 0363-0277.
CHILDERS, THOMAS. 1984. Information and Referral: Public Libraries. Norwood, NJ: Ablex; 1984. 307p. ISBN: 0-89391-147-X; LC: 83-021492.
CHILDERS, THOMAS; POST, JOYCE A. 1975. The Information Poor in America. Metuchen, NJ: Scarecrow Press; 1975. 182p. ISBN: 0-8108-0775-0.
CLANCY, C.M.; HILNER, B.E. 1989. Physicians as Gatekeepers: The Impact of Financial Incentives. Archives of Internal Medicine. 1989; 149(4): 917-920. ISSN: 0003-9926.
COCHRANE, GLYNN; ATHERTON, PAULINE. 1980. The Cultural Appraisal of Efforts to Alleviate Information Inequity. Journal of the American Society for Information Science. 1980; 31(4): 283-292. ISSN: 0002-8231.
COGAN, RICHARD BRIAN. 1990. Large-Scale Computer Implementations and Systematic Organizational Change. Cleveland, OH: Case Western Reserve University; 1990. (Ph.D. dissertation). 464p. Available from: University Microfilms International, Ann Arbor, MI. (UMI order no. 90-35276).
COOK, JUDITH A.; FONOW, MARY MARGARET. 1984. Am I My Sister's Gatekeeper? Cautionary Tales from the Academic Hierarchy. Humanity and Society. 1984 November; 8(4): 442-452. ISSN: 0160-5976.
DERVIN, BRENDA. 1973. Information Needs of Urban Residents: A Conceptual Context. In: Warner, Edward S.; Murray, Ann D.; Palmour, Vernon S., eds. Information Needs of Urban Residents: Final Report. Baltimore, MD: Regional Planning Council; 1973. 8-42. ERIC: ED 088464.
DERVIN, BRENDA. 1976. The Everyday Information Needs of the Average Citizen: A Taxonomy for Analysis. In: Kochen, Manfred; Donohue, Joseph C., eds. Information for the Community. Chicago, IL: American Library Association; 1976. 19-38. ISBN: 0-8389-0208-1.
DERVIN, BRENDA. 1977. Useful Theory for Librarianship: Communication, Not Information. Drexel Library Quarterly. 1977 July; 13(3): 16-32. ISSN: 0012-6160.
DERVIN, BRENDA. 1980. Communication Gaps and Inequities: Moving toward a Reconceptualization. In: Dervin, Brenda; Voigt, Melvin, eds. Progress in Communication Sciences: Volume 2. Norwood, NJ: Ablex; 1980. 73-112. ISSN: 0163-5689; ISBN: 0-89391-060-0.
DERVIN, BRENDA. 1982. Citizen Access as an Information Equity Issue. In: Schement, Jorge Reina; Gutierrez, Felix; Sirbu, Marvin A., eds. Telecommunications Policy Handbook. New York, NY: Praeger; 1982. 290-302. ISBN: 0-03-059169-4.
DERVIN, BRENDA. 1983. An Overview of Sense-Making: Concepts, Methods, and Results to Date. Paper presented at: International Communication Association Annual Meeting; 1983 May 26-30; Dallas, TX. 73p. Available from: the author, Department of Communication, Ohio State University, Columbus, OH 43210.
DERVIN, BRENDA. 1989. Users as Research Inventions: How Research Categories Perpetuate Myths. Journal of Communication. 1989 Summer; 39(3): 216-232. ISSN: 0021-9916.

DERVIN, BRENDA. 1992. From the Mind's Eye of the User: The Sense-Making Qualitative-Quantitative Methodology. In: Glazier, Jack D.; Powell, Ronald R., eds. Qualitative Research in Information Management. Englewood, CO: Libraries Unlimited; 1992. 61-84. ISBN: 0-89287-806-6.

DERVIN, BRENDA; CLARK, KATHLEEN D. 1987. ASQ: Asking Significant Questions, Alternative Tools for Information Needs and Accountability Assessments of Libraries. Sacramento, CA: California State Library; 1987 July. 48p. Available from: Brenda Dervin, Department of Communication, Ohio State University, Columbus, OH 43210.

DERVIN, BRENDA; CLARK, KATHLEEN D. 1989. Communication as Cultural Identity: The Invention Mandate. Media Development. 1989; 34(2): 5-8. ISSN: 0092-7821.

DERVIN, BRENDA; CLARK, KATHLEEN D. 1992. Communications and Democracy: A Mandate for Procedural Invention. In: Splichal, Slavko; Wasko, Janet, eds. Communication and Democracy. Norwood, NJ: Ablex; 1992. 103-140. ISBN: 0-89391-725-7.

DERVIN, BRENDA; GREENBERG, BRADLEY S. 1972. The Communication Environment of the Urban Poor. In: Kline, F. Gerald; Tichenor, Phillip J., eds. Current Perspectives in Mass Communication Research. Beverly Hills, CA: Sage Publications; 1972. 195-234. ISBN: 0-8039-0171-2; LC: 72-84051.

DERVIN, BRENDA; NILAN, MICHAEL. 1986. Information Needs and Uses. In: Williams, Martha E., ed. Annual Review of Information Science and Technology: Volume 21. White Plains, NY: Knowledge Industry Publications, Inc. for the American Society for Information Science; 1986. 3-33. ISSN: 0066-4200; ISBN: 0-86729-209-1; LC: 66-25096.

DERVIN, BRENDA; ZWEIZIG, DOUGLAS; BANISTER, MICHAEL; GABRIEL, MICHAEL; HALL, EDWARD P.; KWAN, COLLEEN. 1976. The Development of Strategies for Dealing with the Information Needs of Urban Residents: Phase I: The Citizen Study. Seattle, WA: University of Washington, School of Communications; 1976. 968p. (Final report on project number L0035JA to the U.S. Office of Education). ERIC: ED 125640.

DONOHUE, GEORGE A.; OLIEN, CLARICE N.; TICHENOR, PHILLIP J. 1989. Structure and Constraints on Community Newspaper Gatekeepers. Journalism Quarterly. 1989 Winter; 66(4): 807-811, 845. ISSN: 0196-3031.

DONOHUE, GEORGE A.; TICHENOR, PHILLIP J.; OLIEN, CLARICE N. 1972. Gatekeeping: Mass Media Systems and Information Control. In: Kline, F. Gerald; Tichenor, Phillip J., eds. Current Perspectives in Mass Communication Research. Beverly Hills, CA: Sage; 1972. 41-70. ISBN: 0-8039-0171-2; LC: 72-084051.

DOSA, MARTA; FARID, MONA; VASARHELYI, PAL. 1988. From Informal Gatekeeper to Information Counselor: Emergence of a New Professional Role. Syracuse, NY: Syracuse University School of Information Studies; 1988. 87p. ERIC: ED 322908.

DOUGLASS, RICHARD L. 1987. Gatekeepers: Changing Roles and Responsibilities for Primary Care Physicians with Aging Family Systems. In: Altman, Harvey J., ed. Alzheimer's Disease: Problems and Prospects, and Perspectives. New York, NY: Plenum Press; 1987. 191-195. ISBN: 0-306-42662-5.

DURAN, DANIEL FLORES. 1977. Latino Communication Patterns: An Investigation of Media Use and Organizational Activity among Mexican, Cuban, and Puerto Rican Residents of Chicago. Madison, WI: University of Wisconsin-Madison; 1977. 526p. (Ph.D. dissertation). Available from: University Microfilms International, Ann Arbor, MI. (UMI order no. 78-00011).

DURAN, DANIEL FLORES; MONROE, MARGARET E. 1977. Latino Communications Project: An Investigation of Communication Patterns and Organizational Activity among Mexican, Cuban and Puerto Rican Residents of Chicago: Final Report. Madison, WI: University of Wisconsin, Library School; 1977. 555p. ERIC: ED 157535.

DURRANCE, JOAN COACHMAN. 1980. Citizen Groups and the Transfer of Public Policy Information in a Community. Ann Arbor, MI: University of Michigan; 1980. 238p. (Ph.D. dissertation). Available from: University Microfilms International, Ann Arbor, MI. (UMI order no. 81-06131).

DURRANCE, JOAN COACHMAN. 1984. Community Information Services: An Innovation at the Beginning of Its Second Decade. In: Simonton, Wesley, ed. Advances in Librarianship: Volume 13. Orlando, FL: Academic Press; 1984. 99-128. ISBN: 0-12-024613-9; LC: 79-88675.

EDELSTEIN, ALEX S.; BOWES, JOHN E.; HARSEL, SHELDON M., eds. 1978. Information Societies: Comparing the Japanese and American Experiences. Seattle, WA: University of Washington, School of Communications, International Communications Center; 1978. 297p. ISBN: 0-933236-00-X; LC: 78-071366.

EMLET, CHARLES; HALL, ANN MARIE. 1991. Integrating the Community into Geriatric Case Management: Public Health Interventions. Gerontologist. 1991 August; 31(4): 556-560. ISSN: 0016-9013.

ERICKSON, FREDERICK. 1975. Gatekeeping and the Melting Pot. Harvard Educational Review. 1975 February; 45(1): 44-70. ISSN: 0017-8055.

FARKAS, GEORGE; GROBE, ROBERT P.; SHEEHAN, DANIEL; SHUAN, YUAN. 1990. Cultural Resources and School Success: Gender, Ethnicity, and Poverty within an Urban School District. American Sociological Review. 1990 February; 55(1): 127-142. ISSN: 0003-1224.

FIKSDAL, SUSAN. 1990. The Right Time and Pace: A Microanalysis of Cross-cultural Gatekeeping Interviews. Norwood, NJ: Ablex; 1990. 180p. ISBN: 0-89391-556-4; ISBN: 0-89391-557-2 (pbk).

FISHMAN, JOSHUA A. 1966. Language Loyalty in the United States: The Maintenance and Perpetuation of Non-English Mother Tongues by American Ethnic and Religious Groups. The Hague, The Netherlands: Mouton; 1966. 478p. LC: 66-005055.

FRAND, JASON. 1983. Computer Literacy for General Management. Los Angeles, CA: University of California, John E. Anderson Graduate School of Management; 1983. 18p. (Working paper 10-83). Available from: the author, John E. Anderson Graduate School of Management, University of California, Los Angeles, CA 90024.

FRAND, JASON; DANUTAK, CHARWAT. 1986. Computer Literacy Profile for Office Professionals: An Organizational Approach. Personnel Management. 1986 October; 18: 101-110. ISSN: 0031-5761.

GARVEY, WILLIAM D.; TOMITA, KAZUO; WOOLF, PATRICIA. 1979. The Dynamic Scientific-Information User. In: Garvey, William D. Communication: The Essence of Science. Elmsford, NY: Pergamon Press; 1979. 256-279. ISBN: 0-08-022254-4.

GEERTZ, CLIFFORD. 1960. The Javanese Kijaji: The Changing Role of a Culture Broker. Comparative Studies in Society and History. 1960 January; 2: 228-249. ISSN: 0010-4175.

GIEBER, W. 1960. How the "Gatekeepers" View Local Civil Liberties News. Journalism Quarterly. 1960 Spring; 37(2): 199-205. ISSN: 0196-3031.

GLOGOFF, STUART. 1988. Reviewing the Gatekeepers: A Survey of Referees of Library Journals. Journal of the American Society for Information Science. 1988 November; 39(6): 400-407. ISSN: 0002-8231.

GOMEZ, MARTIN. 1987. A Study of Reference and Referral Service for Spanish Language Library Users in Northern California: Final Report. Oakland, CA: Bay Area Library and Information System; 1987. 30p. Available from: Bay Area Library and Information System, 520 Third Street, Suite 202, Oakland, CA 94607-3520.

GREEN, JAMES W. 1982. Cultural Awareness in the Human Services. Englewood Cliffs, NJ: Prentice-Hall; 1982. 257p. ISBN: 0-13-195362-1; LC: 81-015869.

GUYETTE, SUSAN. 1983. Community-based Research: A Handbook for Native Americans. Los Angeles, CA: University of California, American Indian Studies Center; c1983. 375p. ISBN: 0-935626-10-7 (pbk); LC: 83-070627.

HALL, HOMER J. 1981. Patterns in the Use of Information: The Right to Be Different. Journal of the American Society for Information Science. 1981 March; 32(2): 103-112. ISSN: 0002-8231.

HARIK, ILIYA. 1971. Opinion Leaders and the Mass Media in Rural Egypt: A Reconsideration of the Two-Step Flow of Communication Hypothesis. American Political Science Review. 1971; 65: 731-740. ISSN: 0003-0554.

HERNON, PETER; MCCLURE, CHARLES. 1982. Referral Services in U.S. Academic Depository Libraries: Findings, Implications, and Research Needs. RQ. 1982 Winter; 22(2): 152-163. ISSN: 0033-7072.

HERNON, PETER; METOYER-DURAN, CHERYL. 1992. The Public. Government Information Quarterly. 1992; 9(1): 1-10. ISSN: 0740-624X.

HEWINS, ELIZABETH T. 1990. Information Need and Use Studies. In: Williams, Martha E., ed. Annual Review of Information Science and Technology: Volume 25. Amsterdam, The Netherlands: Elsevier Science Publishers for the American Society for Information Science; 1990. 145-172. ISSN: 0066-4200; ISBN: 0-444-88531-5.

HIRSCH, P.M. 1978. Occupational, Organizational and Institutional Models in Mass Media Research: Toward an Integrated Framework. In: Hirsch, P.M.; Miller, P.V.; Kline, F.G., eds. Strategies for Communication Research. Beverly Hills, CA: Sage; 1978. 187-200. ISBN: 0-8039-0892-X.

HSIA, H.J. 1973. A Preliminary Report on Motivation and Communication Patterns of the Black, Chicano, White, and Affluent White in a Typical Southwest U.S. City. Paper presented at: Association for Education in Journalism Annual Meeting; 1973 August 19-23; Fort Collins, CO. 110p. ERIC: ED 081009.

HURH, WON MOO; KIM, KWANG CHUNG. 1981. Methodological Problems in Cross Cultural Research: A Korean Immigrant Study in the United States. California Sociologist. 1981 Winter; 4(1): 17-32. ISSN: 0162-8712.

JAKOBOVITS, LEON A.; NAHL-JAKOBOVITS, DIANE. 1987. Learning the Library: Taxonomy of Skills and Errors. College and Research Libraries. 1987 May; 48(3): 203-214. ISSN: 0010-0870.

JANOWITZ, MORRIS. 1975. Professional Models in Journalism: The Gatekeeper and the Advocate. Journalism Quarterly. 1975 Winter; 52(4): 618-626, 662. ISSN: 0196-3031.

JOYCE, DONALD FRANKLIN. 1983. Gatekeepers of Black Culture: Black-owned Book Publishing in the United States, 1817-1981. Westport, CT: Greenwood Press; 1983. 249p. (Contributions in Afro-American and African Studies v. 70). ISBN: 0-313-23332-2; LC: 82-009227.

KAPLAN, ROBERT B. 1966. Cultural Thought Patterns in Inter-cultural Education. Language Learning. 1966; 16(1): 1-20. ISSN: 0023-8333.

KAREN, DAVID. 1990. Toward a Political-Organizational Model of Gatekeeping: The Case of Elite Colleges. Sociology of Education. 1990 October; 63(4): 227-240. ISSN: 0038-0407.

KATZ, ELIHU. 1957. The Two-Step Flow of Communication: An Up-to-Date Report as an Hypothesis. Public Opinion Quarterly. 1957 Spring; 21(1): 61-78. ISSN: 0033-362X.

KATZ, RALPH, ed. 1988. Managing Professionals in Innovative Organizations: A Collection of Readings. Cambridge, MA: Ballinger; 1988. 593p. ISBN: 0-88730-351-X (pbk).

KATZ, RALPH; TUSHMAN, MICHAEL L. 1981. An Investigation into the Managerial Roles and Career Paths of Gatekeepers and Project Supervisors in a Major R&D Facility. R & D Management. 1981 July; 11(3): 103-110. ISSN: 0033-6807.

KAULA, P.N. 1991. Trends in Information Handling Systems: Gatekeeper Technology. International Forum on Information and Documentation. 1991; 16(4): 9-14. ISSN: 0304-9701.

KELLY, PATRICK. 1976. Overcoming the Non-User Nonsense and Other Fallacies: A Basis for the Design of Formal STI Subsystems. Paper presented at: National Information Retrieval Colloquium; 1976 May 4-6; Philadelphia, PA. 31p. ERIC: ED 122797.

KIDD, JERRY S. 1976. Determining Information Needs in Civic Organizations and Voluntary Groups. In: Kochen, Manfred; Donohue, Joseph C., eds. Information for the Community. Chicago, IL: American Library Association; 1976. 39-54. ISBN: 0-8389-0208-1.

KOCHEN, MANFRED. 1972. Directory Design for Networks of Information and Referral Centers. Library Quarterly. 1972 January; 42(1): 59-73. ISSN: 0024-2519.

KOENIG, MICHAEL E.D. 1992. The Information Environment and the Productivity of Research. In: Collier, H., ed. Recent Advances in Chemical Information. Cambridge, England: Royal Society of Chemistry, Information Services; c1992. 133-143. ISBN: 0-85186-496-1.

KRATHWOHL, DAVID R.; BLOOM, BENJAMIN S.; MASIA, BERTRAM B. 1964. Taxonomy of Educational Objectives: The Classification of Educa-

tional Goals: Handbook II: Affective Domain. New York, NY: David McKay Co., Inc.; 1964. 196p. LC: 64-012369; OCLC: 25478151.
KRIKELAS, JAMES. 1983. Information-Seeking Behavior: Patterns and Concepts. Drexel Library Quarterly. 1983 Spring; 19(2): 5-20. ISSN: 0012-6160.
KUHLTHAU, CAROL COLLIER. 1988. Developing a Model of the Library Search Process: Cognitive and Affective Aspects. RQ. 1988 Winter; 28(2): 232-242. ISSN: 0033-7072.
KUHLTHAU, CAROL C.; TUROCK, BETTY J.; GEORGE, MARY W.; BELVIN, ROBERT J. 1990. Validating a Model of the Search Process: A Comparison of Academic, Public and School Library Users. Library and Information Science Research. 1990 January-March; 12(1): 5-31. ISSN: 0740-8188.
KURTZ, NORMAN. 1968. Gate-Keepers: Agents in Acculturation. Rural Sociology. 1968 March; 33(1): 64-70. ISSN: 0036-0112.
LANCASTER, GEOFFREY A.; WHITE, M. 1976. Industrial Diffusion Adoption and Communication. European Journal of Marketing. 1976; 10(5): 280-298. ISSN: 0309-0566.
LARSON, MARK A. 1988. The Sender-Receiver Model and the Targeting Process. Paper presented at: Association for Education in Journalism and Mass Communication 71st Annual Meeting; 1988 July 2-5; Portland, OR. 21p. ERIC: ED 296403.
LEMAY, MICHAEL C. 1989. The Gatekeepers: Comparative Immigration Policy. New York, NY: Praeger; 1989. 208p. ISBN: 0-275-93079-3.
LEWIN, KURT. 1943. Forces behind Food Habits and Methods of Change. In: National Research Council, Committee on Food Habits. The Problem of Changing Food Habits: Report. Washington, DC: National Research Council, National Academy of Sciences; 1943. 35-65. LC: 44-002196.
LEWIN, KURT. 1947a. Frontiers in Group Dynamics. Part I: Concept, Method and Reality in Science, Social Equilibria and Social Change. Human Relations. 1947; 1: 5-41. Part II: Channels of Group Life, Social Planning and Action Research. Human Relations. 1947; 1: 143-153. ISSN: 0018-7267.
LEWIN, KURT. 1947b. Group Decision and Social Change. In: Society for the Psychological Study of Social Issues. Readings in Social Psychology. New York, NY: Holt; 1947. 197-211. LC: 47-006255.
LEWIN, KURT. 1951. Field Theory in Social Science: Selected Theoretical Papers. New York, NY: Harper; 1951. 346p. LC: 51-009715.
LIN, NAN; BURT, RONALD S. 1975. Differential Effects of Information Channels in the Process of Innovation Diffusion. Social Forces. 1975; 54: 256-274. ISSN: 0037-7732.
LIPETZ, BEN-AMI. 1970. Information Needs and Uses. In: Cuadra, Carlos A.; Luke, Ann W., eds. Annual Review of Information Science and Technology: Volume 5. Chicago, IL: Encyclopaedia Britannica for the American Society for Information Science; 1970. 1-32. ISBN: 0-85229-156-6.
LONNER, WALTER J.; BERRY, JOHN W., eds. 1986. Field Methods in Cross-cultural Research. Newbury Park, CA: Sage Publications; 1986. 368p. ISBN: 0-8039-2549-2.
LOUIE, RUBY LING. 1976. A Community Profile Approach toward Expanding Public Library Services: Communication Survey Procedures Reaching Chinese Americans in the Los Angeles Chinatown Community and Ob-

taining Their Information Seeking-Patterns. Los Angeles, CA: University
of Southern California; 1976. 247p. (Ph.D. dissertation). OCLC: 4089213.
MACHLUP, FRITZ; MANSFIELD, UNA, eds. 1983. The Study of Information:
Interdisciplinary Messages. New York, NY: Wiley; 1983. 743p. ISBN: 0-
471-88717-X.
MACMULLIN, SUSAN E.; TAYLOR, ROBERT S. 1984. Problem Dimensions
and Information Traits. The Information Society. 1984; 3(1): 91-111. ISSN:
0197-2243.
MALGADY, ROBERT G.; ROGLER, LLOYD H.; CONSTANTINO, GIUSEPPE.
1987. Ethnocultural and Linguistic Bias in Mental Health Evaluation of
Hispanics. American Psychologist. 1987 March; 42(3): 228-234. ISSN:
0003-066X.
MARCHIONINI, GARY. 1989. Making the Transition from Print to Electronic
Encyclopedias: Adaptation of Mental Models. International Journal of
Man-Machine Studies. 1989; 30: 591-618. ISSN: 0020-7373.
MARCHIONINI, GARY; DWIGGINS, SANDRA; KATZ, ANDREW; LIN, XIA.
1993. Information Seeking in Full-Text End-User-Oriented Search Sys-
tems: The Roles of Domain and Search Expertise. Library and Information
Science Research. 1993 Winter; 15(1): 35-69. ISSN: 0740-8188.
MARIN, GERARDO; MARIN, BARBARA VANOSS. 1991. Research with
Hispanic Populations. Newbury Park, CA: Sage Publications; 1991. 130p.
ISBN: 0-8039-3720-2; LC: 90-026197.
MATTHIASSON, CAROLYN J. 1974. Coping in a New Environment: Mexi-
can-Americans in Milwaukee, Wisconsin. Urban Anthropology. 1974;
3(2): 262-277. ISSN: 0894-6019.
MAYS, VICKIE M.; BECKMAN, LINDA J. 1989. Importance of the Character-
istics of Gatekeepers in the Design of Effective Alcohol Education Pro-
grams. Journal of Drug Education. 1989; 19(1): 29-41. ISSN: 0047-2379.
MENOU, MICHEL J. 1983. Cultural Barriers to the International Transfer of
Information. Information Processing and Management. 1983; 19(3): 121-
129. ISSN: 0306-4573.
MERRIAM, SHARAN B. 1986. The Research to Practice Dilemma. Columbus,
OH: Ohio State University, National Center for Research in Vocational
Education; 1986. 17p. (Occasional paper no. 123). ERIC: ED 278801.
MERTON, ROBERT K. 1968. Social Theory and Social Structure. New York,
NY: Free Press; 1968. 702p. LC: 68-28789.
METOYER-DURAN, CHERYL. 1991a. Information Gatekeepers in California's
Ethnic Communities. Los Angeles, CA: University of California, Graduate
School of Library and Information Science; 1991. 91p. ERIC: ED 333877.
METOYER-DURAN, CHERYL. 1991b. Information Seeking Behavior of
Gatekeepers in Ethnolinguistic Communities: Overview of a Taxonomy.
Library and Information Science Research. 1991 October-December; 13:
319-346. ISSN: 0740-8188.
METOYER-DURAN, CHERYL. 1993a. Cross-cultural Research in
Ethnolinguistic Communities: Methodological Considerations. Public Li-
braries. 1993 January-February; 32(1): 18-25. ISSN: 0163-5506.
METOYER-DURAN, CHERYL. 1993b. Gatekeepers in Ethnolinguistic Com-
munities. Norwood, NJ: Ablex Publishing Corp.; 1993. 211p. ISBN: 0-
89391-891-1; LC: 92-33265.

METOYER-DURAN, CHERYL. 1993c. The Information and Referral Process in Culturally Diverse Communities. RQ. 1993 Spring; 32(3): 359-371. ISSN: 0033-7072.

MOORE, JOAN. 1971. Mexican Americans and Cities: A Study in Migration and Use of Formal Resources. International Migration Review. 1971; 5(3): 292-306. ISSN: 0197-9183.

MOORE, S.H.; MARTIN, D.P.; RICHARDSON, W.C. 1983. Does the Primary-Care Gatekeeper Control the Costs of Health-Care? Lessons from the SAFECO Experience. New England Journal of Medicine. 1983; 309(22): 1400-1404. ISSN: 0028-4793.

MURRAY, STEPHEN O. 1991. Ethnic Differences in Interpretive Conventions and the Reproduction of Inequality in Everyday Life. Symbolic Interaction. 1991 Summer; 14(2): 187-204. ISSN: 0195-6086.

MYERS, GLENDA. 1990. Use of the Gatekeeper as an Adjunct to CAI in the Training of Database End Users in a Dichotomous Information Society. In: Raitt, David, ed. Online Information 90: Proceedings of the 14th International Online Information Meeting; 1990 December 11-14; London, England. Oxford, England: Learned Information; 1990. 83-90. ISBN: 0-90493-375-X.

MYERS, L.A. 1983. Information Systems in Research and Development: The Technological Gatekeeper Reconsidered. R & D Management. 1983; 13(4): 199-206. ISSN: 0033-6807.

NATIONAL EDUCATION RESOURCES INSTITUTE. 1972. A Systems Analysis of Southwestern Spanish Speaking Users and Nonusers of Library and Information Services: Developing Criteria to Design an Optimal Model Concept. Washington, DC: National Education Resources Institute; 1972. 463p. ERIC: ED 066173.

NOCHUR, K.S.; ALLEN, THOMAS J. 1992. Do Nominated Boundary Spanners Become Effective Technological Gatekeepers? IEEE Transactions on Engineering Management. 1992; 39(3): 265-269. ISSN: 0018-9391.

O'SULLIVAN, T.; HARTLEY, J.; SAUNDERS, D.; FISKE, J., eds. 1983. Key Concepts in Communication. New York, NY: Methuen; 1983. 270p. ISBN: 0-416-34250-7; ISBN: 0-416-34260-4 (pbk); LC: 83-13180.

OLIEN, CLARICE N.; TICHENOR, PHILLIP J.; DONOHUE, GEORGE A.; SANDSTROM, K.L.; MCLEOD, D.M. 1990. Community Structure and Editor Opinions about Planning. Journalism Quarterly. 1990; 67(1): 119-127. ISSN: 0196-3031.

PAISLEY, WILLIAM J. 1968. Information Needs and Uses. In: Cuadra, Carlos A., ed. Annual Review of Information Science and Technology: Volume 3. Chicago, IL: Encyclopaedia Britannica for the American Society for Information Science; 1968. 1-30. ISSN: 0066-4200; LC: 66-25096.

PONTIUS, STEVEN K. 1983. The Communication Process of Adoption: Agriculture in Thailand. The Journal of Developing Areas. 1983 October; 18(1): 93-118. ISSN: 0022-037X.

PORAT, MARC URI. 1977. The Information Economy: Volume 1. Definition and Measurement. Washington, DC: U.S. Department of Commerce, Office of Telecommunications; 1977. 249p. (OT Special Publication 77-12). LC: 77-603585; OCLC: 5184933.

PRESS, IRWIN. 1969. Ambiguity and Innovation: Implications for the Genesis of the Culture Broker. American Anthropologist. 1969 April; 71(2): 205-217. ISSN: 0002-7294.

PRITCHARD, ROGER. 1977. Information Networks and Education: An Analytic Bibliography. Paper presented at: Unesco Symposium on Future Programmes of Information and Communication in Educational Policy and Planning; 1977 November 21-25; Paris, France. 96p. ERIC: ED 182247.

RASCHKO, RAYMOND. 1985. Systems Integration at the Program Level: Aging and Mental Health. Gerontologist. 1985 October; 25(5): 460-463. ISSN: 0016-9013.

ROGERS, EVERETT M. 1962. Diffusion of Innovations. New York, NY: Free Press of Glencoe; 1962. 367p. LC: 62-015348.

ROGERS, EVERETT M.; SHOEMAKER, F. FLOYD. 1971. Communication of Innovations. New York, NY: Free Press; 1971. 476p. LC: 78-122276.

ROLLWAGEN, JACK. 1974. Mediation and Rural-Urban Migration in Mexico: A Proposal and a Case Study. Latin American Urban Research. 1974; 4: 47-63. ISSN: 0075-8167.

RUMBERGER, DANIEL J.; ROGERS, MARTHA L. 1982. Pastoral Openness to Interaction with a Private Christian Counseling Service. Journal of Psychology and Theology. 1982 Winter; 10(4): 337-345. ISSN: 0091-6471.

SCOLLON, RON. 1981. Gatekeeping: Access or Retention? Paper presented at: American Anthropology Association Annual Meeting; 1981 December; Los Angeles, CA. 21p. ERIC: ED 215652.

SCOTT, REDA R.; BALCH, PHILIP; FLYNN, TODD C. 1984. Assessing a CMHC's Impact: Resident and Gatekeeper Awareness of Center Services. Journal of Community Psychology. 1984 January; 12(1): 61-66. ISSN: 0090-4392.

SHANNON, LYLE; SHANNON, MAGDALINE. 1973. Minority Migrants in the Urban Community: Mexican-American and Negro Adjustment to Industrial Society. Beverly Hills, CA: Sage Publications; 1973. 352p. ISBN: 0-8039-0158-5.

SHEARER, KENNETH D. 1983. Applying New Theories to Library Selection. Drexel Library Quarterly. 1983 Spring; 19(2): 73-90. ISSN: 0012-6160.

SHIELDS, PETER; DERVIN, BRENDA; RICHTER, CHRISTOPHER; SOLLER, RICHARD E.; CREATURA, LISA. 1992. Who Needs "Pots-Plus" Services? A Comparison of Residential User Needs along the Rural-Urban Continuum. Paper presented at: International Association for Mass Communication Research Meeting; 1992 August 16-23; Guaruja, Brazil. 35p. Available from: Brenda Dervin, Department of Communication, Ohio State University, Columbus, Ohio 43210.

SHOEMAKER, PAMELA J. 1991. Gatekeeping. Newbury Park, CA: Sage Publications; 1991. 88p. (Communications Concepts 3). ISSN: 1057-7440; ISBN: 0-8039-4436-5; ISBN: 0-8039-4437-3 (pbk).

SNIDER, P.B. 1967. "Mr. Gates" Revisited: A 1966 Version of the 1949 Case Study. Journalism Quarterly. 1967 Autumn; 44(3): 419-427. ISSN: 0196-3031.

SNYDER, PETER. 1976. Neighborhood Gate-Keepers in the Process of Urban Adaptation: Cross Ethnic Commonalities. Urban Anthropology. 1976; 5: 35-52. ISSN: 0894-6019.

SOMERS, ANNE R. 1983. And Who Shall Be Gatekeeper? The Role of the Primary Physician in the Health Care Delivery System. Inquiry. 1983 Winter; 20: 301-313. ISSN: 0046-9580.

SUBRAMANYAM, K. 1977. A Didactic Model for Science Communication. Indian Librarian. 1977; 31(4): 157-167. ISSN: 0019-5774.

TAKAKI, RONALD. 1989. Strangers from a Different Shore: A History of Asian Americans. Boston, MA: Little, Brown & Co.; 1989. 570p. ISBN: 0-316-83109-3.

TAYLOR, ROBERT S. 1962. The Process of Asking Questions. American Documentation. 1962; 13: 391-397. ISSN: 0002-8231.

TAYLOR, ROBERT S. 1968. Question-Negotiation and Information Seeking in Libraries. College and Research Libraries. 1968 May; 29(3): 178-194. ISSN: 0010-0870.

TAYLOR, ROBERT S. 1991. Information Use Environments. In: Dervin, Brenda; Voigt, Melvin, eds. Progress in Communication Sciences: Volume 10. Norwood, NJ: Ablex; 1991. 217-255. ISSN: 0163-5689; ISBN: 0-89391-645-5.

THOMPSON, PATRICIA J. 1984. The Gatekeepers: Monitors of Textbook Innovation. Paper presented at: American Educational Research Association 68th Annual Meeting; 1984 April 23-27; New Orleans, LA. 27p. ERIC: ED 246402.

TRICARICO, DONALD. 1986. Influence of the Irish on Italian Communal Adaptation in Greenwich Village. Journal of Ethnic Studies. 1986; 13(4): 127-137. ISSN: 0091-3219.

TURNBULL, PETER W.; MEENAGHAN, A. 1980. Diffusion of Innovation and Opinion Leadership. European Journal of Marketing. 1980; 14(1): 3-33. ISSN: 0309-0566.

TUSHMAN, MICHAEL L.; KATZ, RALPH. 1980. External Communication and Project Performance: An Investigation into the Role of Gatekeepers. Management Science. 1980 November; 26(11): 1071-1085. ISSN: 0025-1909.

U.S. BUREAU OF THE CENSUS. 1991. 1990 Census Profile: Race and Hispanic Origin. Washington, DC: Government Printing Office; 1991 June. 4-5. (Series no. 2). Available from: Customer Services, U.S. Bureau of the Census, Washington, DC 20233.

VALENTINE, CHARLES A. 1968. Culture and Poverty: Critique and Counter-Proposals. Chicago, IL: University of Chicago Press; 1968. 216p. LC: 68-016718.

VAN HOUSE, NANCY A. 1989. Output Measures in Libraries. Library Trends. 1989 Fall; 38(2): 268-279. ISSN: 0024-2594.

VERBA, SIDNEY; NIE, NORMAN. 1972. Participation in America: Political Democracy and Social Equity. New York, NY: Harper and Row; 1972. 451p. ISBN: 0-06-046823-8.

WARNER, EDWARD S.; MURRAY, ANN D.; PALMOUR, VERNON S., eds. 1973. Information Needs of Urban Residents: Final Report. Baltimore, MD: Regional Planning Council; 1973. 293p. ERIC: ED 088464.

WAX, MURRAY L. 1991. The Ethics of Research in American Indian Communities. The American Indian Quarterly. 1991 Fall; 15: 431-456. ISSN: 0095-182X.

WELCH, SUSAN; COMER, JOHN; STEINMAN, MICHAEL. 1975. Ethnic Differences in Social and Political Participation: A Comparison of Some Anglo and Mexican Americans. Pacific Sociological Review. 1975 July; 18(3): 361-382. ISSN: 0030-8919.

WESTLEY, B.H.; MACLEAN, M.S., JR. 1957. A Conceptual Model for Communications Research. Journalism Quarterly. 1957 Winter; 34(1): 31-38. ISSN: 0196-3031.

WHITE, DAVID M. 1950. The "Gate Keeper": A Case Study in the Selection of News. Journalism Quarterly. 1950 Fall; 27(4): 383-390. ISSN: 0196-3031.

WILLIAMS, J. ALLEN; BABCHUK, NICHOLAS; JOHNSON, DAVID R. 1973. Voluntary Associations and Minority Status: A Comparative Analysis of Anglo, Black, and Mexican-Americans. American Sociological Review. 1973 October; 38(5): 637-646. ISBN: 0003-1224.

WOLF, ERIC. 1956. Aspects of Group Relations in a Complex Society: Mexico. American Anthropologist. 1956 December; 58(6): 1005-1078. ISSN: 0002-7294.

ZWEIZIG, DOUGLAS; DERVIN, BRENDA. 1977. Public Library Use, Users, Uses: Advances in Knowledge and Characteristics and Needs of the Adult Clientele of American Public Libraries. In: Voigt, Melvin; Harris, Michael, eds. Advances in Librarianship: Volume 7. New York, NY: Academic Press; 1977. 231-255. ISBN: 0-12-785007-4; LC: 79-88675.

ZWEIZIG, DOUGLAS; RODGER, ELEANOR J. 1982. Output Measures for Public Libraries: A Manual of Standardized Procedures. Chicago, IL: American Library Association; 1982. 100p. ISBN: 0-8389-3272-X (pbk).

II

Basic Techniques and Technologies

Section II includes three chapters. Holley R. Lange of Colorado State University has written the first *ARIST* chapter devoted to speech synthesis and recognition in the chapter entitled "Speech Synthesis and Speech Recognition: Tomorrow's Human–Computer Interfaces?" She notes the obvious fact that speech has the potential to serve as the most natural of all human–computer interfaces and that by communicating to and from a computer via the spoken word the user is freed from the keyboard, mouse, printer, and screen. Although bounded by language, speech does not depend on the ability to read or write; thus, the world of information is opened to non- or preliterate individuals. Popular computer journals mention available speech systems with increasing frequency, and librarians are now installing speech systems to give disabled library users access to the many library and information computer systems. Perhaps with this increased exposure through more widely available products we will become familiar with the advantages and disadvantages of speech systems and be able to apply them to additional uses in the future. Lange's chapter examines current research, implementation, and potential for two of the speech technologies: (1) speech synthesis, or speech output from a computer, and (2) speech recognition, or speech input to a computer. Through a selection of the available literature, this chapter: (1) provides an introduction to the subject; (2) discusses speech synthesis and speech recognition: history, current work, human factors, and applications; (3) examines library applications; and (4) looks to future use and development for these technologies.

Gregory B. Newby of the University of Illinois at Urbana-Champaign has written the first *ARIST* chapter on "Virtual Reality." VR refers to simulation of environments and activities. The simulations are highly interactive and may give the user a feeling of being elsewhere or doing something else. Most VR environments are computer generated. After introducing the concept of VR, Newby provides a logical progression through the foundations of VR, current VR technologies, and application areas (medicine, education, art and entertainment, scientific analysis, business, and telerobotics). He discusses VR as it is related to information science and the information professions and follows this with speculation about the future of VR. In concluding, Newby notes that "good work has been done to investigate the ways in which virtual worlds might supplement human existence in the 'real' world," but he speculates about the future of VR as a single area of study vs. its fading into the background as specific applications go their own way and VR technologies become more common.

Shan-Ju Chang and Ronald E. Rice of Rutgers University provide the first *ARIST* review devoted solely to browsing in the chapter entitled "Browsing: A Multidimensional Framework." Browsing has been discussed as a part of many other topics in past *ARIST* chapters. It has been observed and investigated in the context of information seeking in the library in general and has increasingly assumed greater importance in human–machine interaction in particular. However, because the concept and nature of browsing have not been systematically studied, browsing is not well understood.

Chang and Rice view browsing from many different disciplinary contexts, integrating the diverse literatures on browsing: library and information science (e.g., library information seeking); end-user IR and system design (e.g., online database searching); consumer behavior (e.g., store shopping); mass media audiences (e.g., TV channel switching); organizational communication (e.g., organizational scanning); and wayfinding and environmental design. Within each of these contexts the authors ask: what is browsing, what influences browsing, and what are the consequences of browsing? The chapter attempts to identify the underlying common dimensions of browsing. These considerations then lead to a multidimensional framework for better understanding the nature, influences, and consequences of browsing in a wide variety of human activities.

4

Speech Synthesis and Speech Recognition: Tomorrow's Human–Computer Interfaces?

HOLLEY R. LANGE
Colorado State University

INTRODUCTION

Speech has the potential to serve as the most natural of all human–computer interfaces. Communication with a computer via the spoken word can free a person from a keyboard, mouse, printer, or screen. Although bounded by language, speech does not depend on an ability to read or write and thus can open the computer world to non- or preliterate individuals. Imagine if we needed neither keyboard nor screen to seek and gain information from computer systems, if we could speak and information would be recorded, listen and hear a response, or if we no longer were restricted by location or vocabulary. If such systems were available, would we seek them out and be able to use them with ease? Computer-based speech systems are more prevalent than ever, and the current focus on multimedia with audio/speech components will make them even more familiar.

Whoever develops a system for human–computer interaction with unrestricted natural-language input and responsive, understandable, human-sounding output will have achieved the near impossible, for as Doddington notes: "Speech is inextricably intertwined with intelligence itself" (LANGE ET AL., p. 96). In the meantime, we will seek to develop systems incorporating speech technologies that can make our work more efficient and more appealing, that can save money, or that provide computer access for those unable to use traditional computer interfaces.

Current research into speech technologies results in constant gains, but to date only science fiction can boast natural human–computer

Annual Review of Information Science and Technology (ARIST), Volume 28, 1993
Martha E. Williams, Editor
Published for the American Society for Information Science (ASIS)
By Learned Information, Inc., Medford, N.J.

speech interaction. HAL, in *2001: A Space Odyssey*, is undoubtedly one of the best-known speech interactive computers (CLARKE). Will technological developments allow us to achieve HAL's degree of natural speech-based interaction by the year 2001? Researchers are beginning to investigate the use of neural networks to create systems that learn speech much as humans do; although the systems are in the very preliminary stages and will depend on enormous increases in computer power for implementation, we are moving in the direction of a HAL-like system. Popular computer journals mention available speech systems with increasing frequency. Librarians are currently installing such systems, particularly screen readers that use speech synthesis, to provide access for disabled library users to the many library/information computer systems. Perhaps with this increased exposure through more widely available products we will become familiar with the advantages and disadvantages of speech systems and be able to apply them appropriately.

This chapter examines current research on the implementation of and the potential for two speech technologies: (1) speech synthesis or response (speech output from a computer), and (2) speech recognition (speech input to a computer). This is the first *ARIST* chapter dedicated to the speech technologies, but the inaugural *ARIST* volume in 1966 did mention speech as an input/output interface, albeit briefly (ANNUAL REVIEW STAFF), and similar treatments have appeared over the years. Literally hundreds of articles, papers, and books are published each year on the speech technologies, covering a vast array of literature in many languages. They range from highly technical reports of research in progress to general pieces outlining applications in a certain job or task. Only a sample of the literature from English-language publications is included here to introduce the reader to the technology and its potential. It is presented from the view of the provider and user of information. Most works cited were published between 1989 and 1992. Through the literature, this chapter: (1) introduces the subject; (2) discusses speech synthesis and speech recognition—history, current work, human factors, and applications; (3) examines library applications; and (4) looks to the future of these technologies.

AN OVERVIEW OF SPEECH SYNTHESIS AND RECOGNITION

Speech synthesis and speech recognition are known as hands-busy–eyes-busy technologies since they substitute speech for traditional computer input and output methods, such as a keyboard, mouse, printed page, or computer screen. They are most useful when computer devices are awkward or impossible to use, for example, when the hands or eyes are involved in inspection activities or are disabled, or when the work must be carried out in an extreme or perhaps very dusty environment. In speech-synthesis systems, computers analyze digitized text to identify the speech units and then create a synthetic voice based on that information; speech-recognition systems convert the spoken word into a digital form so it can be compared with an existing database of words or sound units, recognized, and responded to or output in textual form. While we can imagine fluent systems using speech as an input and output method, present systems are neither as efficient nor as effective as we might hope.

Because speech comes easily to most of us, we do not consider the physical and mental effort required to make or understand a sound. Speech technologies are based on these intricacies. Words alone are often not enough to convey meaning. Prosody, the stress, rhythm, and intonation of our words, our body language and facial expression, the syntax or pattern of our speech, and the semantics (meaning) of our language all affect how speech is interpreted. When reading aloud we gather clues from context and punctuation about pronunciation or intonation, and we also know how to interpret an abbreviation or identify a foreign word. To produce truly natural speech, synthesizers must also be able to incorporate these nuances. Speech-recognition systems may have difficulty in understanding different patterns of speech, different accents, the speech of a tired or stressed person, words spoken in a noisy environment, or words that are run together. In comparing speech synthesis and recognition, O'MALLEY (p. 20) notes: "Generally speaking, text-to-speech systems are limited by our current knowledge of linguistics. Speech recognition systems are more limited by computing resources and by our ability to apply the linguistic knowledge available."

To understand the problems involved in computer speech processing we must first understand the complexities of human speech. O'SHAUGHNESSY provides this foundation to the speech technologies in his discussion of human speech and hearing. He places speech recognition and synthesis in the broader context of speech processing as he discusses human and computer production and recognition of speech. TETSCHNER also examines the range of speech technologies but focuses on telephone-based services. He includes information on the technologies as well as on specific products and applications.

In a more recent work, FURUI & SONDHI present a broad range of speech-related papers from experts in the field. The first section of their book covers speech analysis and speech coding and is followed by chapters on speech enhancement—how to improve a speech signal that is obscured by noise or echos, for example, and quality assessment—how to judge a speech coder or a text-to-speech synthesizer. A lengthy section deals with speech recognition and verification and includes such topics as dynamic programming (adjusting to time variations in speech), hidden Markov models (statistical techniques to recognize speech), and neural networks. The last and briefest section deals with text-to-speech synthesis.

Numerous authors in various journals present concise introductions to the speech technologies (e.g., CAUDILL; DAS & NADAS; LAZZARO, 1992). FLANAGAN (1992), FLANAGAN & DEL RIESGO, and WILPON ET AL. look to the past, present, and future of the speech technologies. HELMS describes these systems in the accounting literature, while FREEMAN ET AL. speculate on their use in the securities industry. Other articles suggest the use of speech systems for retailers, on the assembly line, with machine tools, and in fabrication (*CHAIN STORE AGE EXECUTIVE*; KUELZOW; J. MARTIN). BERGERON & LOCKE describe speech systems for medical applications, and WETZEL (1991a) does this for education. These introductory articles will give readers a basic knowledge of the technologies before they consider actual systems use.

FROM VODER AND RADIO REX TO NEURAL NETS

We cannot date the earliest occurrence of human speech, but we assume that the acquisition of speech was gradual and incremental. We can document more precisely the beginnings of machine-based speech, but its development has also been gradual and incremental.

Speech Synthesis

Of the two technologies, speech synthesis is more familiar and more widely used than speech recognition. It allows a computer to communicate through speech rather than through a visual display. If the eyes are busy, speech provides another way to present instructions, and for those who must work away from a computer monitor, speech provides feedback on work in progress. Speech synthesis permits those with visual disabilities to "hear" text, and it enables others to "speak."

Speech output may come from stored speech in which the individual records the message to be "spoken." The speech is natural, a reproduction of the original, but this method requires extensive computer memory and is limited to what has been recorded. Speech output that is pulled together piece by piece, or concatenated, from digitized chunks is somewhat more flexible. Speech output may also be synthesized from text using rules for pronunciation and intonation. Synthesized speech may sound machine-like and unnatural, with mispronounced words, but it uses less computer storage and can be generated from any input text.

FLANAGAN & RABINER capture the early years of research in speech synthesis through a collection of articles from the 1950s to the

1970s that demonstrates how interest in speech and hearing led to simulation of the vocal system. The background in these articles adds perspective to current state-of-the-art reports on applications, ongoing research, and unresolved problems.

FLANAGAN (1973) introduces his brief history of speech synthesis with a quote from an 1871 *Scientific American*:

> Machines which, with more or less success, imitate human speech are the most difficult to construct, so many are the agencies engaged in uttering even a single word—lungs, larynx, tongue, palate, teeth, lips—so many are the inflections and variations of tone and articulation, that the mechanician finds his ingenuity taxed to the utmost to imitate them.

Researchers continue to be "taxed to the utmost" in their quest for a system that will emulate human–human interactive speech. Flanagan's work summarizes early efforts to imitate speech, from Greek and Roman times to 1779, when Kratzenstein constructed a set of acoustic resonators that could imitate the five vowels, to 1791, when von Kempelen invented a machine that could generate "connected utterances," later replicated by Alexander Graham Bell.

While current systems are far from perfect, they have come a long way since "Voder," a synthetic speaker described by DUDLEY ET AL. Developed by Bell Laboratories, Voder was first demonstrated in 1939 at the Franklin Institute and later at the New York World's Fair. It was designed to show the physical nature of speech and was constructed from telephone apparatus. This electrical device synthesized speech sound when operators manipulated levers with their hands, feet, and fingers. The operators at the World's Fair trained for six half-hour periods a day, and after six months could carry out simple conversations; after a year they developed "good technique." The article provides a clear but brief assessment of speech synthesis in the 1930s.

Speech synthesis has been widely and usefully applied in the more than 50 years since Voder's appearance. BAILLY ET AL. provide an overview of recent developments through papers on text-to-speech synthesis presented at a 1990 European Speech Communication Association workshop. Authored by experts, the papers cover a range of topics related to speech synthesis and demonstrate the direction of current research: linguistic processing, prosody, system design, the assessment of synthetic speech, and the newer area of synthetic visual speech.

O'MALLEY also presents a clear and up-to-date introduction to speech synthesis, covering human speech, the vocal tract, and acoustical modeling. He notes that in order to produce speech, a system must:

(1) process the input text; (2) normalize it (e.g., convert abbreviations to words); (3) check an exception dictionary; (4) convert letters to phonemes; (5) create intonation in the text using prosody rules; (6) improve pronunciation through phonetic rules; (7) generate the voice; and (8) output the speech. BREEN focuses on translating letters to phonemes, the smallest distinguishable sound; he also describes human speech and notes the stages necessary to transfer text to speech.

COLLIER ET AL. emphasize their own work on speech synthesis. They focus on the prosodic aspects of speech and describe their approach, which is based on diphone synthesis. Here bits taken from digitized human speech are joined by concatenation; these bits (diphones) contain the difficult transitions between consonants and vowels. More frequently, speech synthesis is phoneme- or allophone-based, where the system identifies these sound units, and rules must then produce the transitions between them. The authors propose that researchers reconsider current approaches and turn to the diphone as the basis for speech synthesis. O'MALLEY, however, counters that use of the diphone does not solve any significant problems in synthetic-speech production.

Digital stored speech and text-to-speech synthesis differ and should be used according to the needs of the particular task. HIRSCHBERG ET AL. suggest many uses for stored speech, particularly in situations in which the speech output will be limited, predictable, and structured. Call routing, order tracking and entry, college class registration, and telephone banking all use stored speech. Synthesis is more frequently used when flexibility is important and when the system must be able to "speak" any sentence the user may generate, as in talking terminals, in devices to assist the disabled, or in speech-based training products. Synthesis requires less computer storage and is easier to maintain in a database because only the text needs to be updated. COWLEY & JONES conclude that recorded digital speech is useful if a good reader can create the message quickly, if it does not need editing, and if it must sound natural. Text-to-speech synthesis is better when computer memory is limited, when precise transcription is necessary, and when a printed version might also be needed.

Speech Recognition

Researchers must address many problems in developing speech-recognition systems. A fluent system must identify an almost infinite number of words entered continuously, must function despite environmental or background noise, and must deal with all kinds of speakers, including those with poor articulation, pronunciation, and accents. At present, no system can do this. Most systems recognize only isolated words spoken by a person who has "trained" the computer. The systems allow limited vocabularies, recognizing perhaps only the digits zero to nine and the alphabet or a few words or phrases. Some systems look for specific words in context (word spotting) and others limit the tasks or language involved. More sophisticated systems can identify several thousand words, and new ones claim up to 40,000.

GRANT explains that in the most basic speech-recognition method, a template is created in a training session; in more complex systems, a statistical model represents the word. Most isolated word- and speaker-dependent systems must be trained by the person who will use them, creating templates for the words they will enter. It takes time and forethought to use those systems. Users must speak clearly and distinctly, carefully isolating each word because the systems work by matching sounds to the stored templates. Speaker-independent systems also operate by matching sounds but do not require the creation of user-specific templates. However, these systems are generally less accurate unless the vocabulary is extremely restricted; accented or poorly pronounced words also reduce accuracy. As LEONARD points out, even in these systems, where a 95% recognition rate might appear high, potential users should know that an error rate of only 5% will cause a system to dial a ten-digit telephone number incorrectly nearly half the time.

Many systems that are still experimental have more complex foundations. Systems are now under development that recognize speaker-independent continuous speech as well as very large or virtually unlimited vocabularies. These are based on the acoustic features of language and use statistical modeling techniques (e.g., hidden Markov modeling) and learning algorithms that allow them to adapt to a variety of speakers and to recognize large vocabularies (RABINER; WAIBEL & LEE). All systems are tied to some sort of input device, such as a microphone or telephone.

Just as FLANAGAN & RABINER collected key writings on speech synthesis, LEA (1980b) gathered papers that examine the development of speech recognition. His collection assesses the technology, past and present, and includes chapters on system design, the impact of ARPA funding (Advanced Research Projects Agency of the Department of Defense) to develop continuous speech recognizers and some of the resulting systems, contemporary developments, and predictions for the future.

In one chapter, LEA (1980a) reports that the earliest speech recognizer was built as part of a toy dog, Radio Rex, which was designed to jump from its house when its name was spoken. In reality, Rex responded to almost any word that sounded even remotely like "Rex." Lea does not provide a date for the event, but he reports that by 1952 the first complete speech recognizer was developed, a speaker-dependent digit recognizer based on template matching. By 1972 the first commercial products appeared, and research for the 1970s focused on continuous speech recognition. LEA (1980a, p. 67) cites John Pierce of Bell Laboratories, who in 1969 objected to work in speech recognition and questioned if a continuous speech recognizer would be possible unless something approaching human intelligence and linguistic competence could become part of a machine. Today researchers seem to be working toward that goal as they apply neural networks that simulate the workings of the brain to automated speech systems.

The development of speech-recognition systems has been truly revolutionary, advancing from simple template matching to complex matching algorithms. WAIBEL & LEE trace this development in their collection of significant papers published between the 1970s and the 1990s. One section addresses template-based approaches to speech recognition, wherein whole words are spoken and then matched with templates, often with the assistance of dynamic programming or dynamic time warping that allows words to be matched even when the speaking rate varies. Knowledge-based approaches add linguistic and phonetic information on human-speech processing to the matching process. Stochastic approaches are even more advanced, and the papers document several methods. One of them is hidden Markov modeling (HMM), where "probabilistic models. . .deal with uncertain or incomplete information" (WAIBEL & LEE, p. 263). In this way an unknown spoken utterance can be compared against stored models to determine the most likely match. Generally the match is based on phonemes or phoneme-like symbols or units. If linguistic knowledge is incorporated in the matching algorithm, the system performance improves further.

The most recent development is the connectionist or neural network approach, in which systems "learn" to recognize speech. Waibel and Lee note: "The computing units are simple in nature, and knowledge is not programmed into any individual unit's function; rather, it lies in the connections and interactions between linked processing elements. . . [This method] bears some resemblance to the style of computation in the nervous system," so the systems are sometimes called neural networks (p. 371). Still in the very preliminary stages, this approach may be feasible with increased computer processing power and speed. The book contains sections on speech analysis (how to encode the speech signal) and language processing (the addition of language modeling to speech recognition). The editors also include articles that describe some of the "seminal" speech-recognition systems: Hearsay, Harpy, Tangora, Byblos, and Sphinx, among others. Although the articles are quite technical, this collection traces the history, development, and current research in the field through works written by experts and represents a fine one-volume examination of speech recognition.

LAFACE & DE MORI include papers that address current developments in speech recognition and research in progress. They begin with the advanced approaches to speech recognition, including recent work with hidden Markov models, continuous speech-recognition systems, and innovative connectionist models of speech. This collection also covers systems for speech understanding and speech coding.

While Waibel and Lee and LaFace and De Mori cover speech recognition fairly completely, SPANIAS & WU provide a clear but much briefer explanation and include an extensive bibliography. PEACOCKE & GRAF also discuss developments in this area and give a list of products illustrating the range of available systems. Some recognize as few as 13 words, others as many as 40,000; some claim 90% accuracy, others 99%; and some products cost a few hundred dollars while others run to tens of thousands of dollars.

Computing resources have increased greatly in recent years with digital signal processing, which improves the quality and complexity of available speech-recognition systems. As an example of a complex system, and one that uses HMM, K.-F. LEE describes Sphinx, a speaker-independent continuous recognition system with a relatively large vocabulary of about 1,000 words. Lee discusses HMM, the addition of "human knowledge" to recognition models, the computer's ability to learn and adapt to a speaker's voice, and the proposal of a new unit of speech for his model (Sphinx), the "function-word-dependent phone model" (K.-F. LEE, p. 12). K.-F. LEE ET AL. update progress on Sphinx, noting that their goal is an unlimited vocabulary speaker-independent continuous-speech recognizer, with a vocabulary of 20,000 words. This ambitious and future system could improve its own performance as the user speaks into it. As a more realistic goal, Lee and colleagues plan to design a 5,000-word speaker-independent continuous-speech recognition system, with 95% accuracy achieved through appropriate training data, a learning paradigm, and knowledge-based modeling techniques.

HOUSE provides a survey of the speech-recognition literature, including journal articles, conference papers, dissertations and theses, books, and book chapters. He lists more than 4,000 unannotated citations from the 1950s through 1986; most are in English, but there are some references to works in other languages.

Interest in speech understanding, artificial intelligence (AI), and neural networks has prompted new approaches to speech synthesis and recognition. If the ultimate goal is to develop a computer that can truly understand and respond to human speech, then this ability must be a key component in system development. For example, a recent paper by FALLSIDE discusses how machines might acquire speech. He calls this ASM, "the acquisition of speech by machines," whereby human speech is learned by the computer. Through the application of neural networks, systems could be trained in both recognition and synthesis from speech data. Although this work is in the preliminary stages, it represents new avenues of research. WU ET AL. examine another recent research focus that incorporates neural networks. The system combines speech features and image features to determine if the recognition rate might improve by using both. The authors conclude: "When the effective features. . .are extracted, we can expect an increment in the recognition rate and a reduction in the training time for the neural network" (WU ET AL., p. 106). WAIBEL & LEE, LAFACE & DE MORI, FURUI & SONDHI, and BAILLY ET AL. all include sections on research into neural networks for speech synthesis and/or recognition.

HUMAN FACTORS RESEARCH

Speech recognition and synthesis depend not only on the availability of systems that meet technical requirements but also on human acceptance of these systems. Researchers must test existing systems to determine how they can be used to advantage, and must point the way so that systems will be designed and developed with the user in mind. People become tired when listening to synthetic speech for long periods and find it difficult to retain certain types of spoken information—e.g., lists of numbers and complex ideas. Speech input is fatiguing and requires microphones or other devices; existing systems can frustrate users, causing their voices to change. People frequently do not respond to speech systems in anticipated ways, and if a defined response is required, training or interface design issues must be addressed with this in mind. Each person who uses a speech system responds according to his or her physical requirements, personality, or inclination. People are simply not accustomed to listening to and talking with computers.

The human factors involved in using speech technologies are of key importance. TUCKER & JONES provide a coherent overview of pertinent work in both speech synthesis and recognition. They list factors important in system use, reminding us that speech is public, that it is a poor vehicle for describing spatial information and that it induces anthropomorphism. They present guidelines for use of speech vs. visual output or combinations of the two. They also provide guidelines for using speech recognition, noting problems of accuracy, the need to coordinate text and task, and the need for user training. Systems should be designed to accommodate the user whose voice changes with stress and time, and because of the propensity for error, system designers must consider feedback issues.

Sometimes human factors research results in unexpected correlations. Work by DEHAEMER & WALLACE associated the acceptance of speech systems with personality type. When these researchers added computer speech output to a microcomputer workstation, they found a relationship between decision style (as determined by the Myers-Briggs personality test) and response time. Those with a heuristic decision style performed less well when spoken computer instructions were presented simultaneously with the displayed screen instructions than they did when there was no speech option. Because of the impact of personality type on performance when speech output was present, Dehaemer and Wallace concluded that systems designers should offer a flexible interface with a choice of mode.

Turning to speech recognition, JONES ET AL. (1992) summarized human factors research that reported on systems used in vehicles, at the office, in industry, and by disabled individuals. They looked at vocabulary, syntax, feedback, and error-correction capabilities and examined both user training and system training. They also considered physical and psychological issues: stress, mental workload, mental and physical fatigue, the ability to switch input mode, and such practical issues as microphone location. Few large-scale applications of speech recognition systems exist, but inspection activities and materials handling were the most common. Jones et al. proposed that the future role of the human factors expert will be to examine current practices to determine where speech might be applicable and to advise in making the proposed system efficient and acceptable to users.

In another article, JONES ET AL. (1989) present several design guidelines for using speech-recognition systems. Speech-input systems should be selectively and consistently applied but should not be used for spatial description. Speech input can be combined with nonverbal tasks but not with other verbal ones and should be designed to use a specialized vocabulary with a carefully designed command syntax. Speech systems should provide feedback to verify recognition, but the user should have control over the mode and timing of the feedback. Users will need training to create templates. Finally, any system application should provide a method to assess the ergonomics, accuracy, task structure, user response, and training requirements.

While Jones et al. (1989; 1992) studied human factors research for speech systems in general, most research focuses on specific aspects. A natural-seeming speech input may be based on a limited vocabulary, and ZOLTAN-FORD tested the feasibility of reducing input vocabulary through modeling, stating that if a system used a consistent output vocabulary, users would follow it. Error messages should use the required vocabulary to help users know what words to choose. BABER ET AL. stress the importance of user training in learning to operate a speech-recognition system. Users can most easily understand proper system use by watching a demonstration given by someone who is familiar with it.

Our voices change with time and are affected by stress and anger, which in turn affect recognition accuracy. FRANKISH ET AL. investigated these short-term changes in speech patterns that impact recognition accuracy. During system use, the voice drifts and no longer matches the training templates. Speech-input systems must be able to adjust to voice drift, perhaps through speech variations during template training, through retraining, or through adaptive training. Since even small changes, like voice drift, can cause system errors, appropriate error-correction strategies are vital. AINSWORTH & PRATT studied car telephone dialing by voice and looked at two error-correction methods: (1) repetition with elimination, and (2) elimination without repetition; they preferred the former. The user should be allowed to repeat the misrecognized word rather than have the system guess the correct word according to pattern matching.

G. L. MARTIN examined claims that speech is faster than typed input and increases user productivity by providing an additional communication channel through a review of the studies completed to date and his own research. The studies did not uniformly support the claim that speech was more efficient than typing, particularly in applied evaluations, although psychological and simulation studies supported this claim. The research did show that speech input enhanced user performance by adding an additional information channel for multiple tasks and short interactions. Users could do more tasks when speech was available but had to decide which input method was appropriate for each task.

Simulation studies are important, particularly in evaluating the potential applications for speech recognition since no available system can attain the level of recognition hoped for in the future. Even so, these future systems must be planned with the user in mind. FRASER & GILBERT report on the "Wizard of Oz" simulation technique, in which a human plays the role of the computer in the human–computer interaction. The authors include a summary of investigations using this approach.

APPLICATIONS: SPEECH SYSTEMS IN USE

Only when systems have been researched, created, and designed can we use them in either actual or test situations. Numerous articles, books, and conference papers report on such applications. Those cited here, while certainly not all-inclusive, provide examples of current use on the job or in the laboratory. Many systems are still quite limited, but uses are wide ranging. Systems may join speech input and output in one application or use only one or the other. To date speech systems are most commonly used in education, industrial, medical, and military settings, in products that assist disabled individuals, and in personal computers.

Disabled individuals use speech synthesis and recognition in various ways. Speech synthesizers can read computer screens to the blind and visually impaired and can speak for those who are unable to talk, perhaps providing them their primary or only means of communication. Speech-recognition devices also allow disabled persons to control appliances or operate a word processor. In his book, A.D.N. EDWARDS (1991) focuses on speech synthesis and its potential to assist disabled individuals. Although specific applications are an important subject for this volume, including details for their operation as well as lists of products and manufacturers, Edwards also explains the basics of human and synthesized speech. He discusses speech synthesizers, such as DEC talk, speech communicators, and screen readers. He also considers the general human factors involved and addresses the specific needs of the disabled. Edwards explains his subject clearly while defining problems and detailing systems.

Try to imagine the difficulty a blind or visually impaired person might experience in operating a computer, particularly a computer system that uses a window environment and GUIs (graphical user interfaces) that depend on vision-oriented icons, pull-down menus, and a mouse. A number of products can read a traditionally displayed computer screen, and several are mentioned by LAZZARO (1990), but a windowed screen that uses GUIs presents a complex problem. A.D.N. EDWARDS (1989) reports on an interface designed to describe the location of a cursor through sound and speech. Edwards turned a highly visual environment requiring hand–eye coordination into one requiring hand–ear coordination. The screen is divided into a grid of auditory windows that produce different sounds as the cursor crosses the lines, with synthetic speech reporting the cursor's exact location. Edwards noted that it was difficult for individuals who tested the system to remember the complex layout within the windows, even though they could remember the general layout of the screen. SCHWERDTFEGER reports on similar packages that can read a GUI through a speech synthesis-based screen reader and points out the utility of such products to both the blind and the learning disabled.

Just as disabled individuals now benefit from speech synthesis and recognition, nonreaders are another possible user group. CRON introduces speech technologies to educators and lists available hardware and software. She also stresses the potential for speech synthesis in education, particularly to help young students through available products that use speech output, such as talking word processors that read a student's typed composition aloud. BALAJTHY mentions how similar speech-synthesis packages help students who are learning English as a second language as well as beginning readers.

WETZEL (1991b) imagines how these technologies will be used in the future. A first grader speaks into a microphone, telling a story; as she speaks, the words appear on her computer screen. She can print out her story and then follow along as the computer reads it back to her, highlighting the words as it goes. Wetzel envisions speech technologies as supporting reading teachers, assisting students in transcribing writing assignments, and aiding the disabled. He reminds us that if these technologies are to be adopted, we must rethink our approach and methods: "We must determine the thinking strategies students need when a keyboard is no longer the only or the optimal method of text entry . . . .We need to explore the new organizing and memory skills required to make efficient use of the new technology" (WETZEL, 1991b, p. 21).

Speech is also growing as an alternative input/output method for personal computers. Speech input can substitute for a function key or a macro, and software products can generate speech from a screen display or add voice to other applications. These are relatively minor uses today, but they are important because: (1) they permit users to become more familiar with speech as a human–computer communication device, and (2) they allow computer and software designers to gain further experience in how best to integrate these into day-to-day operations. PAUL reports on the use of speech systems with Lotus 1-2-3. Articulate Systems' Voice Navigator works with the Macintosh, adding a speech-recognition feature that can be used to activate macros (TESSLER). Experiments into such products are ongoing as well. SCHMANDT ET AL. report on XSpeak, an experimental speech interface for X Windows, a graphics workstation in a window environment. Using a speaker-dependent system, some mouse functions can be carried out through speech, allowing individuals to use windows without removing their hands from the keyboard.

One of the most attractive future speech products is a "talking typewriter," which allows a person to speak or dictate text directly to the computer. Among available systems is DragonDictate, an "automatic transcription system" that recognizes a large vocabulary in a natural-language discrete-utterance system (BAKER). The system begins with a 16,000-word recognition of common words, with a capacity to recognize up to 30,000 words. Although it is slower than a good typist, the system is quicker to use than manual writing or slow typing. DragonDictate is being used in medicine, law, business, word processing, and by the disabled. Dragon Systems has also joined with IBM to produce the IBM VoiceType, a 7,000-word speech recognizer.

As noted by JONES ET AL. (1992), inspection activities are particularly well suited to speech systems because they require the eyes and/

or hands to be occupied in an evaluation, which is usually done away from a computer terminal. Through speech input a worker can speak the results of the inspection into the microphone while continuing to focus on the item being examined. Speech input is often confirmed through speech output. Employees at Motorola Corp. used a speech system while inspecting integrated circuits (GAVASKAR & WELDY; GAVASKAR ET AL.). The system helped them reduce errors because they could keep their eyes on the microscope while entering the information into the computer. Ford Motor Co. used a speech-based system in final car inspections, thus permitting untrained workers to function in a computer environment (J. MARTIN). In another example, meat inspectors entered information about carcasses through a speech-based meat grading system (CHEN & ROBINSON).

Medical inspection activities also are enhanced through speech. For example, COHEN describes a system that records pap smear results through speech; previously workers had to look at a slide and then look away to record results. The author cautions that care must be taken so that these speech uses are applied correctly and that required levels of quality and accuracy are maintained. SHIFFMAN ET AL. developed a speech interface for a medical diagnostic system in a clinical setting that physicians would accept and find easy to use. The authors considered the requirements of such a system, the type of medical terminology needed, and the system's limitations. They suggest that speech enhanced with graphics might be one way to limit, guide, and control input vocabulary and to increase system accuracy and ease of use.

Advanced speech-driven systems could provide tactical advantages for the military. Weapons could be voice directed at a distance, perhaps allowing personnel to tend to multiple tasks through different modalities or to gather information from a database without a computer. During the 1970s the military heavily supported research and development of speech systems. WEINSTEIN cites and summarizes past research and notes work in progress. Speech systems are under investigation for use in fighter aircraft, helicopters, battle management, and training air-traffic controllers, with further work planned to develop interactive speech-enhanced workstations, a voice-controlled system for pilots, more advanced air-traffic controller training, and battle management command and control. Finally, Weinstein summarizes areas that are critical for future research, including problems of noisy or severe environments and increasing vocabulary size and natural-language capabilities. Weinstein's bibliography is particularly useful. The article by BEEK ET AL. covers the early years of military interest in the speech technologies.

Ongoing military research may focus on speech systems for pilots, such as that described by BYBLOW, which compares speech vs. pictorial displays in the cockpit. SALISBURY ET AL. examined the test use of speech input and output in the Airborne Warning and Control System (AWACS) as a way to help operators cope with increased demands in their jobs. If military vehicles could be remotely controlled, the number of people needed in an operation might be reduced. PHILIPS reports on one such experiment involving stereographic equipment to support military applications where vehicles were remotely controlled through speech commands.

Since telephones are voice-based systems, it is only natural that they be the focus for applications of speech synthesis and recognition. AT&T has an automated operator in service, which is a speaker-independent system with a highly regulated input vocabulary (ECONOMIST). The system recognizes five phrases: (1) collect, (2) calling card, (3) person-to-person, (4) third-party billing, and (5) operator; through "social engineering" it is designed to make the user say the proper phrase. LENNIG describes a similar system, Northern Telecom's automated alternate billing service, which also operates with "dialog design" to guide the user. In both cases the computer can spot the anticipated word within a sentence or phrase, and both systems feature easy error recovery, which moves the caller to a human operator if the system cannot understand the input speech.

BERKLEY & FLANAGAN report on a project at AT&T Bell Laboratories to integrate speech technologies in an experimental computer/voice controlled network, HuMaNet. The user can control the facility, the database, or ISDN (Integrated Services Digital Network) and thus dim the lights, call up images or information from a database, and place telephone calls through speech, with an additional built-in voice security system. This conference room environment utilizes a microphone array to enhance sound pickup, lessen the problems of background noise, and free the user from having to wear or speak into a particular microphone.

A great deal of work in China and Japan focuses on the development of a practical speech-recognition system to allow speech input of text into a computer. Because the Chinese and Japanese written languages confound most computer input, there is considerable interest in speech-recognition systems that could circumvent a keyboard. There are 15,000 frequently used Chinese characters, an impossible number for any keyboard, but only 1,300 Mandarin syllables. As examples of this work, L.-S. LEE ET AL. describe a system using these syllables as the basis for experiments with a Mandarin speech-recognition system. Although it is still being tested, the authors see the results as promising. As an extension of the work being carried out in speech recognition and speech synthesis some researchers are investigating automatic speech-to-speech translation. KUREMATSU ET AL. report on a very preliminary effort to combine speech recognition, speech translation, and speech synthesis systems to form an "automatic telephone interpretation system" that translates from Japanese to English.

SPEECH TECHNOLOGIES IN INFORMATION ACCESS

Information scientists have been interested in talking and listening computers for many years. In the library-related literature, reports on speech technologies have been steady but sparse over the past ten years. Today the broad focus of speech-based or enhanced systems in libraries lies in providing computer access for disabled individuals. One of the first notices of actual use of speech systems in libraries was a 1983 report by Columbia Law School about a speech synthesizer that supported access to WESTLAW (*ONLINE REVIEW*) for the visually impaired.

A 1984 report by GERALD on voice response systems summarized the technology and examined the then current applications. Gerald predicted that these systems would eventually permit round-the-clock access to catalogs and databases without the need for mediation. She also addressed the benefits of such systems to the "disenfranchised," the poor, visually impaired, disabled, and confined through a Touch Tone phone. Her call was for an open view of such speech-based enhancements in the library environment, noting the need for vision and commitment as well as resources.

Other authors, writing in information/library science journals, also reported on these technologies, usually in general terms. LANGE (1989; 1990a; 1990b; 1991) has produced bibliographies and articles on speech technologies that focused partly on the speech potential in the library setting. Researchers at OCLC, Inc. (Online Computer Library Center, Inc.) have done some preliminary work in this area (*OCLC NEWSLETTER*), but George Philip, from the Queen's University, Belfast, and his colleagues have conducted the primary practical experiments on speech as a computer interface in information retrieval (PETERS ET AL.; PHILIP; PHILIP ET AL., 1988, 1990, 1991; PHILIP & YOUNG). These articles detail their investigation of speech as an input and output device for an online computer catalog.

In 1987 PHILIP & YOUNG provided a state-of-the-art review of speech technologies, including a brief discussion of their features, potential problems, and selected library and nonlibrary applications. The authors note that motivation is the key to human use and acceptance of speech systems. Users must cope with a headset or microphone, synthetic speech may be difficult to understand, and humans do not always respond predictably. The authors address potential problems with the traditional "quiet" library setting and speculate on library applications in acquisitions for ordering and receipt of material, in circulation, and in authorizing staff work in an online catalog. Primarily, they see these technologies as potential interfaces in online searching, noting that: "Spoken messages offering help, information or prompting the user would be more quickly understood than material displayed on the VDU or printed. This would also avoid breaking up the elements of the search already visible, or filling the screen so that they disappear" (PHILIP & YOUNG, p. 22).

PHILIP ET AL. (1988) investigated speech input and output in an online information retrieval system. Their goal was to use speech to parallel and complement visual output, thus circumventing or lessening problems presented by speech recognition, and to compare this with traditional keyboard access. They assumed that the system would be speaker dependent and require isolated word input. Previously they had worked with a more limited system to retrieve office documents. Here they would use five input options: (1) keyboard; (2) voice for search-term input; (3) voice only, spelled with the pilot's or International Civil Aviation alphabet (e.g., alpha, bravo, charlie); (4) voice only, spelled using letters; and (5) speaking the search term. Output options would be computer screen, speech and computer screen, and speech only. The research was updated in an interim report (PETERS ET AL.). Based on their previous experience with the office document retrieval system, they sought a speech-enhanced online computer system to: (1) take advantage of the syntax limitations in the search vocabulary; (2) give the user control over the interface mode; (3) give speech input precedence over output; and (4) make error recovery easy and efficient. The first factor was based on the need to use an isolated word recognizer; the remaining factors were designed to lessen user frustration.

The final project summary appears in article and report form (PHILIP ET AL., 1990; PHILIP ET AL., 1991). The authors review their goals to use speech as a means to ease the search process, to augment avenues of communication, to investigate its role as a training tool in online systems, and to serve as the basis for remote-system access. The pilot's alphabet, although considered necessary to ensure accuracy when entering search terms, caused problems, but their work showed that: "single-user isolated word speech recognisers can be successfully utilised in voice interfaces even for complex database systems" (PHILIP ET AL., 1991, p. 34). While speech input was faster than typing in the preliminary system, it was slower in the more complex one, although still used. The authors concluded that speech recognizers are not yet practical for accessing databases and will not be until vocabulary sizes increase and they become more widely and economically available. Short voice prompts were more useful than was speech output for complex data.

Screen and keyboard were faster in accessing databases, but speech as an input/output device could provide an enhanced interface.

A 1991 "print forum" (LANGE ET AL.) gathered input from library and computer/technology experts on the potential for speech technologies in a library setting. Their projections for future library use of speech systems are addressed in the next section of this chapter, as is Koenig's discussion of the stages of information systems development, the fourth stage being defined by the attainment of continuous-speech recognition systems (KOENIG, 1987; 1992).

For a number of years, Kurzweil reading machines have been used in libraries by blind and visually impaired individuals. Today some libraries also provide speech-based systems to enhance computer or computer catalog access. S. EDWARDS (1989a; 1989b) reports on technologies available for disabled library patrons: screen enlargers, speech synthesizers that read computer screens, and other devices that speak. A speech synthesizer and software to read a computer screen allow the disabled to access resources on CD-ROM (journal articles, textbooks, newspapers, encyclopedias, and bibliographic indexes) (CARTER & JACKSON; GOLD). MATES describes a CD-ROM-based reference service provided to blind, visually, and physically disabled patrons. In response to an information request, library staff can output pertinent CD-ROM files in various ways—voice, large-type print, and braille. ROSEN ET AL. report on how some of these enabling devices are implemented at the American Foundation for the Blind Library. Finally, Ball State University provides access for blind and visually impaired students to the library's online catalog as well as to university and city information (HSU & LEE).

THE FUTURE

Researchers and authors continue to debate the future for speech systems. Some are wildly enthusiastic about their potential, others are cautiously hopeful, and still others are extremely doubtful. In 1980, Doddington commented that while technology forecasting in general tends to be conservative, speech systems are a "tantalizing mirage. . . . Knowledgeable people have continued to forecast speech recognition capabilities which have either never materialized or have fallen far short of expectations" (DODDINGTON, p. 556). Today most authors agree that there will be no fluent human–computer speech-based systems in the near term, but they also allow that existing systems will provide new and improved ways of carrying out old tasks. Successful applications will take advantage of system strengths, acknowledge and accommodate their weaknesses, and result in improvements to past routines. In discussing the past, DODDINGTON (p. 558) notes: "Fuzzy thinking tends to dominate the application of speech recognition," but he reminds us that speech is nothing more than another interface option, which should be selected only after examining cost, productivity, potential error rates, and human factors.

Comments on the future potential of speech technologies are frequently incorporated in reports. FLANAGAN & DEL RIESGO provide an optimistic summary of that potential. They argue that speech is the preferred human–machine communication method and that future systems will provide easy access to computer and information sources. Personal multimedia information systems will be common, and users will demand easy, hands-free communication methods. Digital signal processors will develop and expand, making advanced speech systems more possible. Future speech-recognition systems—accurate, connected speech, speaker-independent—will be used for task-specific applications. Vocabulary size will increase, language models will improve, and users who can apply these systems despite limitations will find them useful. In the future, synthesized speech will approach more natural levels in both quality and intelligibility. Present problems in synthesis and recognition may be solved in a joint approach through a mimic algorithm, which would require much more computing power than is currently available. FLANAGAN (1992) reports that technologies to build speech-interactive machines exist and that: "Single-chip computers with power in excess of 1 gigaFLOPS should be deployed before the year 2000, and, the year 2001 may actually see a HAL-like conversational machine!" (p. 89).

WILPON ET AL. see "significant applications" of speech technologies in the coming years. They warn, however, that speech recognition will not be completely reliable for some time, so the best applications will be: (1) simple, natural, perhaps menu-driven with limited vocabularies; (2) extensions of current systems; and (3) error prone, but the problems caused by the errors will be reduced as much as possible. In examining text-to-speech technologies, O'MALLEY also expresses cautious optimism, warning not to expect too much too quickly, predicting that the "same slow, steady pace" that has produced gradual progress in accuracy and intelligibility will continue. He believes that other, more sweeping predictions for rapid advancement have not considered the complexities of speech.

Computer and human-factors specialists will need to cooperate if future speech systems are to be applied appropriately and accepted by users. If speech is to be an alternative method for computer input/output, JONES ET AL. (1992) remind us that the applications must offer improvements over present methods or they will not be accepted and used, and human-factors considerations will be vital in determining if new systems are an improvement. TUCKER & JONES note that speech should not be applied universally; its strengths and weaknesses must be tailored to users and tasks.

Authors writing for the current popular computer literature are also outspoken about speech interfaces. VAN NAME & CATCHINGS say that users are ready for computers to add speech options: "We believe that until we can tell our computer what to do, we're not working naturally" (p. 72). However, others firmly believe that the keyboard will not disappear soon. According to LEVY many consider speech recognition to be a technology that is always "just around the corner," but Levy stresses there is no evidence for this assumption and predicts that in another ten years he will still be using his keyboard for computer entry. He admits, however, that some limited speech technologies will supplement the keyboard and run particular applications. OWEN looks at the practical and human aspects of talking to a computer. He provides the example of doing some writing while waiting for a band concert to begin, accomplishing quite a bit using traditional keyboard input on his computer. He questions if he could or would have done this if data had to entered by voice. DVORAK also argues that the keyboard is still more convenient than speech input. Speech recognition will be a "niche" product but, he predicts, it will not replace the keyboard.

Speech technologies are already arriving in libraries as niche products. Introduced through speech systems that make library computer systems available to all, other uses may well follow as information users and providers gain increased exposure to them. Experts, responding to questions about speech applications in a library setting, viewed these technologies in various ways. Generally they agreed that while fluent human–computer interfaces will not be available in the near term, speech systems might be useful in a library setting (LANGE ET AL.). George Philip (LANGE ET AL.) views speech as a complementary method of input/output alongside the keyboard and screen, with potential applications in library technical processing, circulation, and accessing remote databases. He stresses the importance of considering human factors in a library setting, and he predicts that by the year 2000 speech input and output systems will be as common as the keyboard and screen are today.

Bradley Watson (LANGE ET AL.), who has investigated speech technologies in a library setting, discusses the problems of "human inclination," pondering what types of questions a library user would ask a human vs. a machine. Although he emphasizes that computers are far from understanding speech, today's speech systems could be an asset to disabled or illiterate individuals. John Kountz (LANGE ET AL.) categorizes speech systems as primitive solution-based technologies and predicts that we will not reach a HAL-level of human–computer interaction anytime soon. Although Samuel Waters (LANGE ET AL.) considers dramatic progress in natural-language understanding unlikely, he believes that even the limited systems now available can have a "considerable beneficial impact on our lives." Doddington sees that even vast increases in computer power will not greatly affect speech recognition: "But I do share the feeling that we're close to having major economic impact. I do share the feeling that speaker verification and recognition performance are becoming good enough to support economic applications of tremendous impact in the telecommunications field" (LANGE ET AL., p. 96).

KOENIG (1987; 1992) discusses the stages of information-systems development, the fourth stage beginning with the arrival of continuous-speech recognition. This stage is derived from Mooers' law that: "an information system will be used only when it is more trouble not to use it than it is to use it" (KOENIG, 1987, p. 590). Information access will be speech driven and "natural." Privacy will be a concern when documents are created through speech, perhaps encouraging telecommuting; he sees this stage as bringing the illiterate back into the workforce. Most importantly, Koenig cautions that we must realize that this stage is coming and try to understand and plan for it rather than simply reacting to it when it arrives.

CONCLUSIONS

The current reality for speech-recognition systems is not a conversational HAL but a system like AT&T's automated operator that allows any caller to use it but restricts the input to only five phrases. The reality is also Articulate Systems' Voice Navigator that allows the user to substitute a spoken sound for a mouse click, or the DragonDictate, a transcription system that recognizes a large vocabulary but uses a discrete word recognizer. For speech output, the reality today is a synthesizer that "reads" printed text or the computer screen, generally in a machine-like voice. Even though speech systems are freed from traditional input and output mechanisms, they are tied to a microphone or speaker. These realities represent a less than fully natural human–computer interface, but they demonstrate potentially useful applications for speech systems that could enhance access to computers and information. Applied appropriately speech interfaces could be of increasing benefit.

In some situations, speech might not be the input/output interface of choice, but speech technologies could be useful if we want to access a database from a remote site, if we have to work in an environment in which computers could not survive, if we could not use a keyboard or read a computer screen, or if we want to enhance a manuscript with spoken comments. We may want to retrieve e-mail or a fax through a telephone-based voice connection, and we will want to dial a cellular phone by voice. The Americans with Disabilities Act will demand further development of these speech-based technologies to enhance access to information, computers, and the work environment for disabled persons.

As speech input/output devices become more familiar and as current work with neural networks advances, speech systems may eventually become interactive speech systems, enhanced with visual images, and ultimately conversational computers. Until then we must look ahead, for we will need new strategies, new skills, and new ways of approaching computers, information, and communication to deal with such systems. In the meantime we must continue to question, and learn. We must know enough about speech as a computer–human interface to see where it might be useful and understand it well enough so it can be applied wisely.

Future uses for the speech technologies in libraries will follow trends elsewhere. Information seekers and providers will become more familiar with them through implementation for disabled individuals and through increased exposure in their own personal computers. Because speech systems promise enhanced access to information, particularly from remote sites, they may emerge as an important tool in the information arena. As Doddington suggested, we must consider costs, productivity, error rates, and human factors when considering speech for any application. Until systems are more fluent, users must be able to control when and if they want to use a speech interface. People are not used to talking to or listening to computers, and libraries have traditionally been "quiet" places. We will have to overcome some of our natural resistance to talking to a machine and possibly to making our requests public before we accept speech as an interface device. However, these scenarios and concerns are built on a world that resembles today's. If truly fluent human–computer interfaces are developed, these traditional interactions will change drastically.

BIBLIOGRAPHY

AINSWORTH, WILLIAM A. 1988. Speech Recognition by Machine. London, England: Peter Peregrinus; 1988. 206p. (IEE Computing Series, no. 12). ISBN: 0-86341-115-0.

AINSWORTH, WILLIAM A.; PRATT, S.R. 1992. Feedback Strategies for Error Correction in Speech Recognition Systems. International Journal of Man-Machine Studies. 1992 June; 36(6): 833-842. ISSN: 0020-7373.

ANNUAL REVIEW STAFF. 1966. New Hardware Developments. In: Cuadra, Carlos A., ed. Annual Review of Information Science and Technology:

Volume 1. New York, NY: Interscience Publishers for the American Documentation Institute; 1966. 191-220. LC: 66-25096.

BABER, C.; STAMMERS, R.B.; USHER, D.M. 1990. Instructions and Demonstration as Media for Training New Users of Automatic Speech Recognition Devices. Behaviour & Information Technology (UK). 1990 October; 9(5): 371-379. ISSN: 0144-929X.

BAILLY, G.; BENOIT, C., eds.; SAWALLIS, T.R., assistant ed. 1992. Talking Machines: Theories, Models, and Designs. Amsterdam: New York: North-Holland; 1992. 523p. ISBN: 0-444-89115-3.

BAKER, JANET M. 1989. DragonDictate-30K: Natural Language Speech Recognition with 30,000 Words. In: Tubach, J.P.; Mariani, J.J., eds. Eurospeech 89: European Conference on Speech Communication and Technology: Volume 2; 1989 September 26-28; Paris, France. Edinburgh, Scotland: CEP Consultants; 1989. 161-163. ISBN: 0-905941-36-5.

BALAJTHY, ERNEST. 1988. Voice Synthesis for Emergent Literacy. The Reading Teacher. 1988 October; 42(1): 72. ISSN: 0034-0561.

BEEK, BRUNO; NEUBERG, EDWARD P.; HODGE, DAVID C. 1977. An Assessment of the Technology of Automatic Speech Recognition for Military Applications. IEEE Transactions on Acoustics, Speech, and Signal Processing. 1977 August; 25(4): 310-322. ISSN: 0096-3518.

BENNETT, RAYMOND W.; GREENSPAN, STEVEN L.; SYRDAL, ANN K.; TSCHIRGI, JUDITH E.; WISOWATY, JOHN J. 1989. Speaking to, from, and through Computers: Speech Technologies and User-Interface Design. AT&T Technical Journal. 1989 September/October; 68(5): 17-30. ISSN: 8756-2324.

BERGERON, BRYAN; LOCKE, STEVEN. 1990. Speech Recognition as a User Interface. M.D. Computing. 1990 September/October; 7(5): 329-330, 332-334. ISSN: 0724-6811.

BERKLEY, DAVID A.; FLANAGAN, JAMES L. 1990. HuMaNet: An Experimental Human-Machine Communications Network Based on ISDN Wideband Audio. AT&T Technical Journal. 1990 September/October; 69(5): 87-97. ISSN: 8756-2324.

BIERMANN, ALAN W.; FINEMAN, LINDA; HEIDLAGE, J. FRANCIS. 1992. A Voice- and Touch-Driven Natural Language Editor and Its Performance. International Journal of Man-Machine Studies. 1992 July; 37(1): 1-21. ISSN: 0020-7373.

BREEN, A. 1992. Speech Synthesis Models: A Review. Electronics and Communication Engineering Journal (UK). 1992 February; 4(1): 19-31. ISSN: 0954-0695.

BYBLOW, W.D. 1990. Effects of Redundancy in the Comparison of Speech and Pictorial Displays in the Cockpit Environment. Applied Ergonomics. 1990 June; 21(2): 121-128. ISSN: 0003-6870.

CARTER, ROBERT; JACKSON, KATHY. 1992. Speech Synthesizer and Screen Reading Software Make CD-ROM Databases Accessible to Visually Impaired Library Users. CD-ROM Professional. 1992 January; 5(1): 129-131. ISSN: 1049-0833.

CASALI, SHERRY PERDUE; WILLIGES, BEVERLY H.; DRYDEN, ROBERT D. 1990. Effects of Recognition Accuracy and Vocabulary Size of a Speech

Recognition System on Task Performance and User Acceptance. Human Factors. 1990 April; 32(2): 183-196. ISSN: 0018-7208.

CAUDILL, MAUREEN. 1992. Kinder, Gentler Computing. Byte. 1992 April; 17(4): 135-140, 142, 144, 146, 150. ISSN: 0360-5280.

CHAIN STORE AGE EXECUTIVE. 1991. Uses for Computers That Listen, Respond: Firm Envisions Voice I/O Solutions for Retailers. Chain Store Age Executive. 1991 December; 67(12, pt. 1): 75. ISSN: 0193-1199.

CHEN, Y.R.; ROBINSON, S.A. 1990. Integrating a Knowledge-Based Meat-Grading System with a Voice-Input Device. Computers and Electronics in Agriculture (Netherlands). 1990 March; 4(4): 303-313. ISSN: 0168-1699.

CLARKE, ARTHUR C. 1968. 2001: A Space Odyssey. New York, NY: New American Library; 1968. 221p. OCLC: 449499.

COHEN, PETER. 1990. Voice Entry in the Lab. Computers in Healthcare. 1990 March; 11(3): 33-35. ISSN: 0745-1075.

COLLIER, R.; VAN LEEUWEN, H.C.; WILLEMS, L.F. 1992. Speech Synthesis Today and Tomorrow. Philips Journal of Research (UK). 1992; 47(1): 15-34. ISSN: 0165-5817.

COWLEY, CHRISTOPHER K.; JONES, DYLAN M. 1992. Synthesized or Digitized? A Guide to the Use of Computer Speech. Applied Ergonomics. 1992 June; 23(3): 172-176. ISSN: 0003-6870.

CROCHIERE, RONALD E.; FLANAGAN, JAMES L. 1986. Speech Processing: An Evolving Technology. AT&T Technical Journal. 1986 September/October; 65(5): 2-11. ISSN: 8756-2324.

CRON, MARY. 1992. Sound: The Next Frontier. Technology & Learning. 1992 February; 12(5): 14-18, 35-36, 38-40, 42. ISSN: 1053-6728.

DAS, SUBRATA; NADAS, ARTHUR. 1992. The Power of Speech. Byte. 1992 April; 17(4): 151-152, 154, 156, 158, 160. ISSN: 0360-5280.

DEHAEMER, MICHAEL J.; WALLACE, WILLIAM A. 1992. The Effects on Decision Task Performance of Computer Synthetic Voice Output. International Journal of Man-Machine Studies. 1992 January; 36(1): 65-80. ISSN: 0020-7373.

DODDINGTON, GEORGE R. 1980. Whither Speech Recognition? In: Lea, Wayne A., ed. Trends in Speech Recognition. Englewood Cliffs, NJ: Prentice-Hall; 1980. 556-561. ISBN: 0-13-930768-0; LC: 79-23614.

DODDINGTON, GEORGE R.; SCHALK, THOMAS B. 1981. Speech Recognition: Turning Theory to Practice. IEEE Spectrum. 1981 September; 18(9): 26-32. ISSN: 0018-9235.

DUDLEY, HOMER; RIESZ, R.R.; WATKINS, S.S.A. 1980. A Synthetic Speaker. In: Lea, Wayne A., ed. Trends in Speech Recognition. Englewood Cliffs, NJ: Prentice-Hall; 1980. 190-215. (Reprinted from the Journal of the Franklin Institute. 1939; 227: 739-764). ISBN: 0-13-930768-0; LC: 79-23614.

DVORAK, JOHN C. 1993. Computer Commonplaces: Let's Debunk Their Misguided Logic. PC Computing. 1993 January; 6(1): 100. ISSN: 0899-1847.

ECONOMIST. 1992. Answer Me. The Economist. 1992 July 25; 324(7769): 79-80. ISSN: 0013-0613.

EDWARDS, ALISTAIR D.N. 1989. Modelling Blind Users' Interactions with an Auditory Computer Interface. International Journal of Man-Machine Studies. 1989; 30(5): 575-589. ISSN: 0020-7373.

EDWARDS, ALISTAIR D.N. 1991. Speech Synthesis: Technology for Disabled People. London, England: Paul Chapman Publishing; 1991. 157p. ISBN: 1-85396-066-7.

EDWARDS, SANDRA. 1989a. Computer Technology and the Physically Disabled. OCLC Micro. 1989 October; 5(5): 22-23, 25-26. ISSN: 8756-5196.

EDWARDS, SANDRA. 1989b. Microcomputers and the Visually Impaired (Low-Vision to No-Vision). OCLC Micro. 1989 December; 5(6): 20-21, 25-26, 28. ISSN: 8756-5196.

FALLSIDE, FRANK. 1992. On the Acquisition of Speech by Machines, ASM. Speech Communication. 1992 June; 11(2-3): 247-260. ISSN: 0167-6393.

FALLSIDE, FRANK; WOODS, WILLIAM A., eds. 1985. Computer Speech Processing. Englewood Cliffs, NJ: Prentice-Hall International; 1985. 506p. ISBN: 0-13-163841-6.

FISHER, KENNETH W. 1982. Voice Recognition: The Ultimate Computer Interface. In: Petrarca, Anthony E.; Taylor, Celianna I.; Kohn, Robert S., eds. Information Interaction: Proceedings of the American Society for Information Science (ASIS) 45th Annual Meeting: Volume 19; 1982 October 17-21; Columbus, OH. White Plains, NY: Knowledge Industry Publications, Inc. for ASIS; 1982. 84-86. ISBN: 0-86729-038-2.

FLANAGAN, JAMES L. 1973. Voices of Men and Machines. In: Flanagan, James L.; Rabiner, Lawrence R., eds. Speech Synthesis. Stroudsburg, PA: Dowden Hutchinson & Ross; 1973. 9-21. (Reprinted from the Journal of the Acoustical Society of America. 1972; 51: 1375-1387). ISBN: 0-87933-044-9; LC: 73-9728.

FLANAGAN, JAMES L. 1992. Speech Technology and Computing: A Unique Partnership. IEEE Communications Magazine. 1992 May; 30(5): 84-89. ISSN: 0163-6804.

FLANAGAN, JAMES L.; DEL RIESGO, CHARLES J. 1990. Speech Processing: A Perspective on the Science and Its Applications. AT&T Technical Journal. 1990 September/October; 69(5): 2-13. ISSN: 8756-2324.

FLANAGAN, JAMES L.; RABINER, LAWRENCE R., eds. 1973. Speech Synthesis. Stroudsburg, PA: Dowden Hutchinson & Ross; 1973. 511p. (Benchmark Papers in Acoustics). ISBN: 0-87933-044-9; LC: 73-9728.

FOURCIN, A.; HARLAND, G.; BARRY, W.; HAZAN, V., eds. 1989. Speech Input and Output Assessment: Multilingual Methods and Standards. Chichester, England: New York, NY: Ellis Horwood; Halsted Press; 1989. 290p. ISBN: 0-7458-0651-1.

FRANKISH, CLIVE R.; JONES, DYLAN M.; HAPESHI, KEVIN. 1992. Decline in Accuracy of Automatic Speech Recognition as a Function of Time on Task: Fatigue or Voice Drift? International Journal of Man-Machine Studies. 1992; 36(6): 797-816. ISSN: 0020-7373.

FRASER, NORMAN M.; GILBERT, G. NIGEL. 1991. Simulating Speech Systems. Computer Speech and Language (UK). 1991 January; 5(1): 81-99. ISSN: 0885-2308.

FREEMAN, JAMES M.; PADALA, ADITHYA M.R.; WOLFF, STEVEN B. 1991. Voice Recognition as Applied to the Securities Industry. Speech Technology. 1991 February/March; 5(3): 73-79. ISSN: 0744-1355.

FURUI, SADAOKI; SONDHI, M. MOHAN, eds. 1992. Advances in Speech Signal Processing. New York, NY: Marcel Dekker; 1992. 871p. ISBN: 0-8247-8540-1.

GAVASKAR, PRASAD; MAASS, ERIC; WELDY, LAURA; NGUYEN, HAI. 1990. Integrating Voice Recognition Technology with Inspection of Integrated Circuits. In: IEEE/SEMI International Semiconductor Manufacturing Science Symposium; 1990 May 21-23; Burlingame, CA. New York, NY: Institute of Electrical and Electronics Engineers; 1990. 123-130. Available from: IEEE Service Center, 445 Hoes Lane, Piscataway, NJ 08854.

GAVASKAR, PRASAD; WELDY, LAURA. 1991. Vocal Computing. DG Review. 1991 January; 11(7): 36-41. ISSN: 1050-9127.

GERALD, JEANETTE. 1984. Voice Response Systems Technology. Library Hi Tech. 1984 (Issue 8); 2(4): 33-38. ISSN: 0737-8831.

GOLD, PETER S. 1990. CD-ROM for the Development of Low Vision Technology. CD-ROM EndUser. 1990 May; 2(1): 36-37. ISSN: 1042-8623.

GORIN, A.L.; LEVINSON, S.E.; GERTNER, A.N.; GOLDMAN, E. 1991. Adaptive Acquisition of Language. Computer Speech and Language (UK). 1991 April; 5(2): 101-132. ISSN: 0885-2308.

GOVERN, M.P.; VYSOTSKY, G.J.; HIRTH, J.S.; GRAY, G.M. 1992. Voice Dialling: An Integration of Speech Recognition into the Telephone Network. Telecommunication Journal. 1992 July/August; 59(7-8): 367-375. ISSN: 0497-137X.

GRANT, P.M. 1991. Speech Recognition Techniques. Electronics & Communication Engineering Journal (UK). 1991 February; 3(1): 37-48. ISSN: 0954-0695.

HELMS, GLENN L. 1990. Say Hello to Voice Processing Systems. Financial & Accounting Systems. 1990 Fall; 6(3): 4-9. ISSN: 1053-2579.

HINER, L.E., III. 1987/1988. Speed of Speech Recognition versus Keyboarding as Computer Input Devices for the Severely Disabled. Journal of Educational Technology Systems. 1987/1988; 16(3): 283-293. ISSN: 0047-2395.

HIRSCHBERG, JULIA B.; RIEDERER, STEPHEN A.; ROWLEY, JAMES E.; SYRDAL, ANN K. 1990. Voice Response Systems: Technologies and Applications. AT&T Technical Journal. 1990 September/October; 69(5): 42-51. ISSN: 8756-2324.

HJELMQUIST, E.; JANSSON, B.; TORELL, G. 1990. Computer-Oriented Technology for Blind Readers. Journal of Visual Impairment & Blindness. 1990 May; 84(5): 210-215. ISSN: 0145-482X.

HOLLINGUM, JACK; CASSFORD, GRAHAM. 1988. Speech Technology at Work. Berlin: New York: Springer-Verlag; IFS Publications; 1988. 158p. ISBN: 0-387-16356-5; ISBN: 0-948507-89-6.

HOUSE, ARTHUR S. 1988. The Recognition of Speech by Machine—A Bibliography. London: San Diego: Academic Press; 1988. 498p. ISBN: 0-12-356785-8.

HSU, LEON; LEE, GARY D. 1991/1992. Providing Access for Students Who Are Visually Impaired. The Computing Teacher. 1991/1992 December/January; 19(4): 8-9. ISSN: 0278-9175.

JACOBSON, BOB. 1992. The Ultimate User Interface. Byte. 1992 April; 17(4): 175-176, 178, 180, 182. ISSN: 0360-5280.

JOHNSTONE, BOB. 1991. Look Who's Talking. Far Eastern Economic Review (Hong Kong). 1991 April 25; 151(17): 70. ISSN: 0014-7591.

JONES, DYLAN M.; FRANKISH, CLIVE R.; HAPESHI, KEVIN. 1992. Automatic Speech Recognition in Practice. Behaviour and Information Technology. 1992 March/April; 11(2): 109-122. ISSN: 0144-929X.

JONES, DYLAN M.; HAPESHI, KEVIN; FRANKISH, CLIVE R. 1989. Design Guidelines for Speech Recognition Interfaces. Applied Ergonomics. 1989 March; 20(1): 47-52. ISSN: 0003-6870.

KOENIG, MICHAEL E.D. 1987. The Convergence of Moore's/Mooers' Laws. Information Processing & Management. 1987; 23(6): 583-592. ISSN: 0306-4573.

KOENIG, MICHAEL E.D. 1992. Entering Stage III: The Convergence of the Stage Hypotheses. Journal of the American Society for Information Science. 1992 April; 43(3): 204-209. ISSN: 0002-8231.

KOHONEN, TEUVO. 1988. The "Neural" Phonetic Typewriter. Computer. 1988 March; 21(3): 11-22. ISSN: 0018-9162.

KUELZOW, CHRISTOPHER. 1992. Speech Recognition: A Good Choice for Real-Time Control. I&CS (Instrumentation & Control Systems). 1992 April; 65(4): 59-60. ISSN: 0746-2395.

KUREMATSU, AKIRA; IIDA, HITOSHI; MORIMOTO, TUYOSHI; SHIKANO, KIYOHIRO. 1991. Language Processing in Connection with Speech Translation at ATR Interpreting Telephony Research Laboratories. Speech Communication. 1991 February; 10(1): 1-9. ISSN: 0167-6393.

LAFACE, PEITRO; DE MORI, RENATO, eds. 1992. Speech Recognition and Understanding: Recent Advances, Trends and Applications: Proceedings of the NATO Advanced Study Institute on Speech Recognition and Understanding; 1990 July 1-13; Cetraro, Italy. Berlin: New York: Springer-Verlag; published in cooperation with NATO Scientific Affairs Division; 1992. 559p. (NATO ASI Series. Series F: Computer and Systems Sciences, vol. 75). ISBN: 0-387-54032-6.

LANGE, HOLLEY R. 1989. Voice Response Systems: Giving Computers a Voice. In: Wall, C. Edward, ed. Library Hi Tech Bibliography: Volume 4. Ann Arbor, MI: Pierian Press; 1989. 161-169. ISBN: 0-87650-257-5.

LANGE, HOLLEY R. 1990a. Voice Recognition and Voice Response: A Report on Tomorrow's Technologies. In: Williams, Martha E., ed. Proceedings of the 11th National Online Meeting; 1990 May 1-3; New York, NY. Medford, NJ: Learned Information, Inc.; 1990. 233-240. ISBN: 0-938734-44-X.

LANGE, HOLLEY R. 1990b. Voice Recognition Systems: Your Computer Is Listening. In: Wall, C. Edward, ed. Library Hi Tech Bibliography: Volume 5. Ann Arbor, MI: Pierian Press; 1990. 171-183. ISBN: 0-87650-262-1.

LANGE, HOLLEY R. 1991. The Voice as Computer Interface: A Look at Tomorrow's Technologies. The Electronic Library. 1991 February; 9(1): 7-11. ISSN: 0264-0473.

LANGE, HOLLEY R., ed.; PHILIP, GEORGE; WATSON, BRADLEY C.; KOUNTZ, JOHN, contributors; WATERS, SAMUEL T.; DODDINGTON, GEORGE, postscripts. 1991. Voice Technologies in Libraries: A Look into the Future. Library Hi Tech. 1991 (Issue 35); 9(3): 87-96. ISSN: 0737-8831.

LAZZARO, JOSEPH J. 1990. Opening Doors for the Disabled. Byte. 1990 August; 15(8): 258-260, 262-264, 266, 268. ISSN: 0360-5280.

LAZZARO, JOSEPH J. 1992. Even As We Speak. Byte. 1992 April; 17(4): 165-168, 170, 172. ISSN: 0360-5280.

LEA, WAYNE A. 1980a. Speech Recognition: Past, Present, and Future. In: Lea, Wayne A., ed. Trends in Speech Recognition. Englewood Cliffs, NJ: Prentice-Hall; 1980. 39-98. ISBN: 0-13-930768-0; LC: 79-23614.

LEA, WAYNE A., ed. 1980b. Trends in Speech Recognition. Englewood Cliffs, NJ: Prentice-Hall; 1980. 580p. ISBN: 0-13-930768-0; LC: 79-23614.

LEE, KAI-FU. 1989. Automatic Speech Recognition: The Development of the SPHINX System. Boston, MA: Kluwer Academic Publishers; 1989. 207p. (The Kluwer International Series in Engineering and Computer Science; VLSI, Computer Architecture, and Digital Signal Processing). ISBN: 0-89838-296-3; LC: 88-25930.

LEE, KAI-FU; HON, HSIAO-WUEN; HWANG, MEI-YUH; MAHAJAN, SANJOY. 1990. Recent Progress and Future Outlook of the SPHINX Speech Recognition System. Computer Speech and Language (UK). 1990 January; 4(1): 57-69. ISSN: 0885-2308.

LEE, LIN-SHAN; TSENG, CHIU-YU; LIN, YUEH HONG; LEE, YUMIN; TU, S.L.; GU, H.Y.; LIU, F.H.; CHANG, C.H.; HSIEH, S.H.; CHEN, C.H.; HUANG, K.R. 1991. A Fully Parallel Mandarin Speech Recognition System with Very Large Vocabulary and Almost Unlimited Texts. In: IEEE International Symposium on Circuits and Systems; 1991 June 11-14; Singapore. New York, NY: Institute of Electrical and Electronics Engineers; 1991. 578-581. ISBN: 0-7803-0050-5.

LEE, RICHARD. 1990. Speech Recognition. Information Display. 1990; 6(4): 12-14. ISSN: 0020-0042.

LEISER, R.G. 1989. Improving Natural Language and Speech Interfaces by the Use of Metalinguistic Phenomena. Applied Ergonomics. 1989 September; 20(3): 168-173. ISSN: 0003-6870.

LENNIG, MATTHEW. 1990. Putting Speech Recognition to Work in the Telephone Network. Computer. 1990 August; 23(8): 35-41. ISSN: 0018-9162.

LEONARD, MILT. 1991. Speech Poised to Join Man-Machine Interface. Electronic Design. 1991 September 26; 39(18): 43-48. ISSN: 0013-4872.

LEVY, STEVEN. 1992. Talkin' Macintosh Blues. MacWorld. 1992 September; 9(9): 75-76, 78. ISSN: 0741-8647.

LUNIN, LOIS F. 1992. On Speaking Terms with the Computer. Information Today. 1992 February; 9(2): 19-20. ISSN: 8755-6286.

MARTIN, GALE L. 1989. The Utility of Speech Input in User-Computer Interfaces. International Journal of Man-Machine Studies. 1989 April; 30(4): 355-375. ISSN: 0020-7373.

MARTIN, JOHN. 1989. Speak Up for Quality. Manufacturing Engineering. 1989 October; 103(4): 67-68. ISSN: 0361-0853.

MATES, BARBARA T. 1990. CD-ROM: A New Light for the Blind and Visually Impaired. Computers in Libraries. 1990 March; 10(3): 17-20. ISSN: 1041-7915.

NAKATSU, RYOHEI. 1990. Anser: An Application of Speech Technology to the Japanese Banking Industry. Computer. 1990 August; 21(9): 43-48. ISSN: 0018-9162.

NASH, RITA. 1986. Voice Processing: A Present or Future Technology? LASIE (Australia). 1986 September/October; 17(3): 60-75. ISSN: 0047-3774.

NEWELL, A.F.; ARNOTT, J.L.; CARTER, K.; CRUICKSHANK, G. 1990. Listening Typewriter Simulation Studies. International Journal of Man-Machine Studies. 1990 July; 33(1): 1-19. ISSN: 0020-7373.

NEWELL, A.F.; ARNOTT, J.L.; DYE, R.; CAIRNS, A.Y. 1991. A Full-Speed Listening Typewriter Simulation. International Journal of Man-Machine Studies. 1991 August; 35(2): 119-131. ISSN: 0020-7373.

NOYES, J.M.; HAIGH, R.; STARR, A.F. 1989. Automatic Speech Recognition for Disabled People. Applied Ergonomics. 1989 December; 20(4): 293-298. ISSN: 0003-6870.

O'KANE, M.J.; KENNE, P.E. 1992. Sidebar 1: Automatic Speech Recognition: One of the Hard Problems of Artificial Intelligence. Library Hi Tech. 1992 (Issue 37-38); 10(1-2): 42-43. ISSN: 0737-8831.

O'MALLEY, MICHAEL H. 1990. Text-to-Speech Conversion Technology. Computer. 1990 August; 23(8): 17-23. ISSN: 0018-9162.

O'SHAUGHNESSY, DOUGLAS. 1987. Speech Communication: Human and Machine. Reading, MA: Addison-Wesley Publishing Co.; 1987. 568p. ISBN: 0-201-16520-1.

OCLC NEWSLETTER. 1989. Responding to His Master's Voice. OCLC Newsletter. 1989 May/June; (179): 16. ISSN: 0163-898X.

OLIVE, J.P.; ROE, D.B.; TSCHIRGI, J.E. 1991. Speech Processing Systems That Listen, Too. AT&T Technology. 1991; 6(4): 26-31. ISSN: 0889-8979.

ONLINE REVIEW. 1983. Talking Terminal for WESTLAW. Online Review. 1983; 7(2): 81. ISSN: 0309-314X.

OWEN, RICK. 1992. Dick Tracy Talked to His Wristwatch—Will You Talk to Your Computer? Infoworld. 1992 October 19; 14(42): 49. ISSN: 0199-6649.

PAUL, FREDRIC. 1991. Talk Is Cheap. LOTUS. 1991 April; 7(4): 32-35. ISSN: 8756-7334.

PEACOCKE, RICHARD D.; GRAF, DARYL H. 1990. An Introduction to Speech and Speaker Recognition. Computer. 1990 August; 23(8): 26-33. ISSN: 0018-9162.

PETERS, B.F.; PHILIP, GEORGE; SMITH, F.J.; CROOKES, D. 1989. Online Searching Using Speech as a Man/Machine Interface. Information Processing & Management. 1989; 25(4): 391-406. ISSN: 0306-4573.

PHILIP, GEORGE. 1992. Speech Technology Developments in Europe. Journal of the American Society for Information Science. 1992 January; 43(1): 92-95. ISSN: 0002-8231.

PHILIP, GEORGE; PETERS, B.F.; SMITH, F.J.; CROOKES, D.; RAFFERTY, T. 1991. Design and Evaluation of a Speech Interface for Remote Database Searching. Journal of Information Science. 1991; 17(1): 21-36. ISSN: 0165-5515.

PHILIP, GEORGE; SMITH, F.J.; CROOKES, D. 1988. Voice Input/Output Interface for Online Searching: Some Design and Human Factor Considerations. Journal of Information Science. 1988 March/April; 14(2): 93-98. ISSN: 0165-5515.

PHILIP, GEORGE; SMITH, F.J.; CROOKES, D. 1990. An Investigation of the Use of a Voice Input/Output Interface for Online Searching. London, England: British Library Research and Development Department; 1990. 81p. (British Library Research Paper no. 90). ISBN: 0-7123-3243-X.

PHILIP, GEORGE; YOUNG, ELIZABETH S. 1987. Man-Machine Interaction by Voice: Developments in Speech Technology. Part I: The State-of-the-Art; Part II: General Applications, and Potential Applications in Libraries and Information Services. Journal of Information Science. 1987; 13: 3-14, 15-23. ISSN: 0165-5515.

PHILIPS, MICHAEL L. 1990. Voice Control of Remote Stereoscopic Systems. In: SOUTHEASTCON '90 Proceedings: Technologies Today and Tomorrow; 1990 April 1-4; New Orleans, LA., New York, NY: Institute of Electrical and Electronics Engineers; 1990. 594-598. ISSN: 0734-7502.

RABINER, LAWRENCE R. 1989. A Tutorial on Hidden Markov Models and Selected Applications in Speech Recognition. Proceedings of the IEEE. 1989 February; 77(2): 257-286. ISSN: 0018-9219.

RALSTON, JAMES V.; PISONI, DAVID B.; LIVELY, SCOTT E.; GREENE, BETH G.; MULLENNIX, JOHN W. 1991. Comprehension of Synthetic Speech Produced by Rule: Word Monitoring and Sentence-by-Sentence Listening Times. Human Factors. 1991 August; 33(4): 471-491. ISSN: 0018-7208.

ROSEN, LESLIE; JAEGGIN, ROBERT B.; HO, PEGGY W. 1991. Enabling Blind and Visually Impaired Library Users: INMAGIC and Adaptive Technologies. Library Hi Tech. 1991 (Issue 35); 9(3): 45-61. ISSN: 0737-8831.

ROSS, ROBERT D. 1987. Overview of the Voice Information Services Market. In: ONLINE '87 Conference Proceedings; 1987 October 20-22; Anaheim, CA. Weston, CT: Online, Inc.; 1987. 187-198. Available from: Online, Inc., 462 Danbury Road, Wilton, CT 06897-2126.

RUDNICKY, ALEXANDER I.; HAUPTMANN, ALEXANDER G. 1989. Conversational Interaction with Speech Systems. Pittsburgh, PA: Carnegie-Mellon University, School of Computer Science; 1989. 18p. (CMU-CS-89-203). Available from: Department of Computer Science, Carnegie-Mellon University.

RUEHL, H.W.; DOBLER, S.; WEITH, J.; MEYER, P.; NOLL, A.; HAMER, H.H.; PIOTROWSKI, H. 1991. Speech Recognition in the Noisy Car Environment. Speech Communication. 1991 February; 10(1): 11-22. ISSN: 0167-6393.

SALISBURY, MARK W.; HENDRICKSON, JOSEPH H.; LAMMERS, TERENCE L.; FU, CAROLINE; MOODY, SCOTT A. 1990. Talk and Draw: Bundling Speech and Graphics. Computer. 1990 August; 23(8): 59-65. ISSN: 0018-9162.

SCHMANDT, CHRIS; ACKERMAN, MARK S.; HINDUS, DEBBY. 1990. Augmenting a Window System with Speech Input. Computer. 1990 August; 23(8): 50-56. ISSN: 0018-9162.

SCHWERDTFEGER, RICHARD S. 1991. Making the GUI Talk. Byte. 1991 December; 16(13): 118-120, 122, 124, 126-128. ISSN: 0360-5280.

SHIFFMAN, SMADAR; WU, ALICE W.; POON, ALEX D.; LANE, CHRISTOPHER D.; MIDDLETON, BLACKFORD; MILLER, RANDOLPH A.; MASARIE, FRED E., JR.; COOPER, GREGORY F.; SHORTLIFFE, ED-

WARD H.; FAGAN, LAWRENCE M. 1991. Building a Speech Interface to a Medical Diagnostic System. IEEE Expert. 1991 February; 6(1): 41-50. ISSN: 0885-9000.

SPANIAS, ANDREAS S.; WU, FRANK H. 1991. Speech Coding and Speech Recognition Technologies: A Review. In: IEEE International Symposium on Circuits and Systems; 1991 June 11-14; Singapore. New York, NY: Institute of Electrical and Electronics Engineers; 1991. 572-577. ISBN: 0-7803-0050-5.

STUSSER, DANIEL I. 1992. Systems Become Interactive and Integrated. Networking Management. 1992 March; 10: 49-52, 54-56. ISSN: 0746-6072.

TESSLER, FRANKLIN N. 1993. Voice Navigator SW 2.3. MacWorld. 1993 January; 10(1): 220. ISSN: 0741-8647.

TETSCHNER, WALT. 1991. Voice Processing. Boston, MA: Artech House; 1991. 280p. (Artech House Telecommunications Library). ISBN: 0-89006-468-7; LC: 90-14459.

TOM, M. DANIEL; TENORIO, M. FERNANDO. 1991. Short Utterance Recognition Using a Network with Minimum Training. Neural Networks. 1991; 4(6): 711-722. ISSN: 0893-6080.

TSURUFUJI, S.; OHNISHI, H.; IIDA, M.; SUZUKI, R.; SUMI, Y. 1991. A Voice Activated Car Audio System. IEEE Transactions on Consumer Electronics. 1991 August; 37(3): 592-597. ISSN: 0098-3063.

TUCKER, PHILIP; JONES, DYLAN M. 1991. Voice as Interface: An Overview. International Journal of Human–computer Interaction. 1991; 3(2): 145-170. ISSN: 1044-7318.

VAN BEZOOIJEN, RENEE; POLS, LOUIS C.W. 1990. Evaluating Text-to-Speech Systems: Some Methodological Aspects. Speech Communication. 1990 August; 9(4): 263-270. ISSN: 0167-6393.

VAN NAME, MARK L.; CATCHINGS, BILL. 1992. Computer, Do What I Say, Not What I Type! PC Week. 1992 May 11; 9(19): 72. ISSN: 0740-1604.

VARNEY, SARAH E. 1991. Speech Recognition: Easier Said Than Done. Digital Review. 1991 April 22; 8(16): 7-8. ISSN: 0739-4314.

VEITH, RICHARD H. 1990. Information Retrieval via Telephone Keypad and Voice: Experiences with Telephone Directories. In: Williams, Martha E., ed. Proceedings of the National Online Meeting; 1990 May 1-3; New York, NY. Medford, NJ: Learned Information, Inc.; 1990. 443-451. ISBN: 0-938734-44-X.

WAIBEL, ALEX. 1988. Prosody and Speech Recognition. London, England: San Mateo, CA: Pitman; Morgan Kaufmann Publishers; 1988. 212p. ISBN: 0-273-08787-8; ISBN: 0-934613-70-2.

WAIBEL, ALEX; LEE, KAI-FU. 1990. Readings in Speech Recognition. San Mateo, CA: Morgan Kaufmann Publishers; 1990. 629p. ISBN: 1-55860-124-4.

WATERWORTH, JOHN A., ed.; CAMPBELL, JOHN, special consultant ed. 1987. Speech and Language-based Interaction with Machines: Towards the Conversational Computer. Chichester, England: New York, NY: Ellis Horwood; Halsted Press; 1987. 167p. ISBN: 0-7458-0146-3; LC: 87-27558.

WEINSTEIN, CLIFFORD J. 1991. Opportunities for Advanced Speech Processing in Military Computer-based Systems. Proceedings of the IEEE. 1991 November; 79(11): 1626-1641. ISSN: 0018-9219.

WETZEL, KEITH. 1991a. Speaking to Read and Write: A Report on the Status of Speech Recognition. The Computing Teacher. 1991 August/September; 19(1): 6-10, 12. ISSN: 0278-9175.

WETZEL, KEITH. 1991b. Speech Technology II: Future Software and Hardware Predictions. The Computing Teacher. 1991 October; 19(2): 19-21. ISSN: 0278-9175.

WHEATLEY, BARBARA; PICONE, JOSEPH. 1991. Voice across America: Toward Robust Speaker-independent Speech Recognition for Telecommunications Applications. Digital Signal Processing. 1991 April; 1: 45-63. ISSN: 1051-2004.

WILPON, JAY G.; MIKKILINENI, RAJENDRA P.; ROE, DAVID B.; GOKCEN, SEDAT. 1990. Speech Recognition: From the Laboratory to the Real World. AT&T Technical Journal. 1990 September/October; 69(5): 14-24. ISSN: 8756-2324.

WU, JIAN-TONG; TAMURA, SHINICHI; MITSUMOTO, HIROSHI; KAWAI, HIDEO; KUROSU, KENJI; OKAZAKI, KOZO. 1991. Speaker-independent Vowel Recognition Combining Voice Features and Mouth Shape Image with Neural Network. Systems and Computers in Japan (Japan). 1991; 22(4): 100-107. ISSN: 0882-1666.

YOUNG, S.J.; PROCTOR, C.E. 1989. The Design and Implementation of Dialogue Control in Voice Operated Database Inquiry Systems. Computer Speech and Language (UK). 1989; 3(4): 329-353. ISSN: 0885-2308.

YOUNG, S.J.; RUSSELL, N.H.; THORNTON, J.H.S. 1991. The Use of Syntax and Multiple Alternatives in the VODIS Voice Operated Database Inquiry System. Computer Speech and Language (UK). 1991; 5(1): 65-80. ISSN: 0885-2308.

ZOLTAN-FORD, ELIZABETH. 1991. How to Get People to Say and Type What Computers Can Understand. International Journal of Man-Machine Studies. 1991 April; 34(4): 527-547. ISSN: 0020-7373.

ZUE, VICTOR; SENEFF, STEPHANIE; GLASS, JAMES. 1990. Speech Database Development at MIT: TIMIT and Beyond. Speech Communication. 1990 August; 9(4): 351-356. ISSN: 0167-6393.

5   Virtual Reality

GREGORY B. NEWBY
University of Illinois, Urbana-Champaign

INTRODUCTION

The topic of virtual reality (VR) has captured the imagination and interest of scholars and the public alike. The sudden interest in VR and the surprising attention it has received in the popular media are both late in coming and terribly premature. The roots of VR and precursors of its technology are found in literature from the 1960s and 1970s, yet the surge in popular interest and rapid proliferation of scholarly conferences and discussion on VR did not occur until the middle and late 1980s. Current research, development, and applications of VR, however, barely exceed what was envisioned in the 1960s. The technical advances since then are staggering, and many dreams have been realized, yet the imaginative environments that are the focus of today's speculation—viz., direct neural input, virtual displays that truly fool the user, fully tactile feedback systems, and so forth—are not immediately forthcoming.

Overview

This chapter is directed toward scholars and practitioners in information science and related fields who want to understand the current state of the art in VR and the foundations on which it is built. There is a considerable discrepancy between the portrayals of and speculation on VR in the popular media (and in scholarly literature that does not focus on R&D) and the work actually being done. This chapter aims to lay

Annual Review of Information Science and Technology (ARIST), Volume 28, 1993
Martha E. Williams, Editor
Published for the American Society for Information Science (ASIS)
By Learned Information, Inc., Medford, N.J.

bare the reality behind virtual reality through a tour of the past and present. One section examines possible VR futures and their near-term likelihood.

The amount of "scholarly literature" on VR (including conference proceedings, refereed journals, and books aimed at researchers and practitioners) is still fairly small. I have sought to obtain a complete collection of scholarly writings from the 1980s to the present and have also consulted the works claimed as intellectual ancestors to modern VR. This chapter begins with older works and then examines the present and future of VR.

Scope

As the first *ARIST* chapter on virtual reality, almost all aspects of VR since the mid-1960s are covered in some detail. Fortunately, the body of literature is not yet unwieldy and did not even start to become coherent as "virtual reality" until the 1980s. As a new topic for *ARIST*, this chapter provides a basic background, including terminology, history, applications, taxonomies, and areas of related work.

Readers are expected only to have an interest in VR and perhaps some familiarity with the basic concepts as found in literature most familiar to information professionals. There are few workers in VR who also claim to be information professionals, but the number is growing. As this chapter shows there are strong indications of a role for VR in information-related areas. This chapter draws links between past (and present) work in information retrieval, information representation, and information seeking and use to the display and interaction capabilities of VR. It is hoped that it will provide insight into the nature and future of VR, offer a framework for distinguishing hyperbole from reality, and clarify ideas about applications for VR, especially as they pertain to information science and related areas.

First the discussion introduces the concept of VR and then gives a history and description of the current technology associated with it. Next come sections on various application areas that show promise. Here an attempt is made to distinguish between what *could* be, what *might* be, and what is talked about but almost certainly will *not* exist for some time. A section on those aspects of VR of particular interest to information professionals follows. It includes a description of current and past work in graphical presentation of bibliographic materials, some information on the changing natures of the library and the book, and a definition and consideration of cyberspace. The next section discusses work being done to give us a deeper understanding of VR and the role it might play in human society. The last section looks at the future of VR.

Introduction to VR

VR is concerned with the simulation of environments. The term is loosely applicable to any set of stimuli that creates the feeling that one is elsewhere. A distinguishing feature of all virtual realities is that they are highly interactive, responding to the user's input in ways that are designed to give him or her a feeling of control over the environment. Users are provided with a point of view, which enhances feelings of control and of being in the environment. Contrast this with a typical computer application, such as word processing, in which the user cannot change point of view, in which responses to input might not be immediate, and in which the interaction is to give a command rather than manipulate the environment. A definition of VR is elusive; currently VR efforts are most easily identified by their input and output devices (see the section on Current Technologies). Virtual worlds have a high level of interactivity in common but little else.

Most VR environments are computer generated, and many attempt to provide a feeling of total "immersion" in the virtual environment. However, reliance on a computer is not necessary, and there might be interaction with objects that are not virtual but are part of the "real" world. High-technology equipment, such as special head gear, has grabbed the public eye, yet there is a body of VR that does not require the user to wear special electronic clothing or spend a fortune on input and output devices. Feelings of immersion are also optional. Many current applications of VR techniques, such as three-dimensional design tools and information systems, do not attempt to fool the user into thinking he or she is really elsewhere but simply provide a window into elsewhere.

Ultimate visions of VR focus on a set of input and output devices that sense body movements or thought patterns and respond immediately, providing the user with a complete feeling of immersion. This scenario is not yet possible, although some steps have been taken toward it. Time lags and limitations of computer graphic techniques make most VRs of the early 1990s look more like cartoons or old movies: objects do not appear to be real, and their motion may be jerky or unconvincing. Input devices are largely limited to those that sense hand gestures or head movements. These go beyond a simple mouse or joystick but do not provide the computer with full details on body position. Output is visual and (sometimes) aural, with visual apparatus that does not provide sufficient resolution to approximate the "real" world. Tactile feedback is seldom provided, and gustatory or olfactory output is practically nonexistent.

Related *ARIST* Literature

Although several chapters in previous *ARIST* volumes are related to VR, this is the first that actually uses the term or makes specific reference to VR applications or technologies. Prior chapters describe some of the foundations of what VR has become. Most recently, SHAW covered human–computer interaction (HCI) for information retrieval. Although she did not focus on the future and made no reference to VR, any future chapter on HCI will very likely include a review of VR literature. In 1986 VIGIL mentioned three-dimensional computer graphics as an advance in the software interface. He was writing at the very start of VR's rebirth in the 1980s. Historically, *ARIST* Volumes 1 (DAVIS) and 3 (LICKLIDER) contained descriptions of the work of VR pioneers Sutherland and English (discussed later). At that time, there was speculation about how interactive computer systems could be used to aid in bibliographic retrieval or other information-related tasks. The authors' prognoses for graphical techniques in HCI were on target, but what was envisioned did not come to pass until microcomputer systems replaced mainframes for the most widely used computer applications. In a later chapter, TURTLE ET AL. accurately predicted that high-resolution graphics terminals would be in widespread use by the 1980s.

Selection of the Literature

A large body of popular literature is related to VR. Some works, such as that by RHEINGOLD, are authoritative and complete with references to appropriate publications of scholars working in VR. Many others are simply riding the tide of popularity and offer little new insight into VR's origins and destiny. This chapter occasionally draws on popular literature when a discussion on an area of application is in order, but there is little published in more scholarly forums. The review is limited to English-language materials. However, there is a fair body of literature published by Japanese workers in English, and there is some work in Germany that is indexed in English databases.

Unlike most *ARIST* chapters, attention here is given to works in progress, works not yet published in refereed journals, and works "published" or discussed in electronic forums where VR scholars and practitioners communicate. In 1992 there was a proliferation of conferences on VR and the addition of several books and journals on the topic. This chapter attempts to cover the literature of 1992 fairly, but because many materials (e.g., conference proceedings) were not available in time for full consideration and incorporation, some work may not be represented. Future chapters related to VR should give further attention to the literature on VR from 1992.

FOUNDATIONS OF VIRTUAL REALITY

This section presents the most important events that underlie current VR efforts. Importance is judged by hindsight, according to those persons and writings that are commonly cited by current authors. It is evident from a reading of the VR literature that there was no concentrated effort or core of researchers on VR until the mid-1980s.

The history of VR may be divided in several ways. First is the distinction between events that are central to VR and those that are now part of other disciplines. Another distinction is between the distant and more recent past. A final contrast, which seems less important intellectually but which played a crucial role in advancing interest in VR, is between the work of academic or military research laboratories and products and the popular literature. This section first looks at founding works across the years and then mentions some key popular events.

The most detailed historical perspective on VR is given by RHEINGOLD. Although his book was written for a lay audience, he did extensive field research and supported his observations with quotes from interviews with current and past leaders in the field. He also included citations to many scholarly works. Although not intended as a scholarly reference, the work will serve at least until a more traditional textbook is written.

Four events of the early 1960s are viewed as precursors to today's VR. First is the effort of HEILIG. He obtained patents in 1960 and 1962 relating to Sensorama, a device that simulated an environment through touch, sight, sound, and smell. A version was placed in a New York City arcade but did not stand up to daily use. Through Sensorama people could "ride" in motorcycles, helicopters, and automobiles. Film and other noncomputerized methods produced the feeling of immersion. There is little published literature on this work; it is mentioned here to point to an innovation implemented in the early 1960s, but, so far as can be ascertained, nothing like it can be found in any establishment currently involved in R&D on VR. Visual and tactile feedback are fairly commonplace today, but the incorporation of real physical phenomena, such as gasoline engines, is seldom seen. Smell is absent from all published works relating to VR implementations that were identified. Today the focus is on environments that are almost entirely computer generated.

In the same period, two advances in HCI were introduced. In 1963, SUTHERLAND (1980) wrote a computer program called Sketchpad. He used a light pen to manipulate graphical objects on a CRT (cathode ray tube). Graphical communication between humans and computers was far from the norm of the time, and such interaction did not become commonplace until the introduction of the Macintosh computer 20 years later. Another advance, which also was not a common part of computer systems then, is the "mouse" (ENGLISH ET AL.). The Lincoln Wand (ROBERTS) was an input device that used ultrasonic sensors to give the computer coordinates at which the user was holding a wand-like device. These three advances in HCI demonstrate nicely the somewhat artificial distinction between what is and is not part of VR. The mouse and graphical communication with computers are now common on all major computer platforms (e.g., Windows and the Macintosh desktop). The Lincoln Wand is not part of such common systems, though, and instead evolved into various position trackers based on ultrasonics and magnetics, which are at the core of VR (discussed in more detail later). In both the mouse and the wand we see the same crucial component of VR in its birth: the ability to interact with a computer using human gestures.

Sensorama, Sketchpad, the mouse, and the Lincoln Wand are four precursors of today's VR. Components of each may be found in HCI today. Two personalities worked in the late 1960s and early 1970s on projects that are more identifiable with mainstream VR today: SUTHERLAND (1965; 1968) and KRUEGER. Sutherland's interests in graphical computer systems led to the development of the first head-mounted display (HMD). This device allows the user to see simple graphic images, such as cubes, projected in space. Although not an immersive system, Sutherland's HMD was adapted by various researchers until the HMD that is common in VR research today emerged.

KRUEGER took a different approach to VR (he calls it "artificial reality"). Rather than compel the user to don special clothing and headware and use them in a one-on-one interaction with a computer, Krueger put individuals in a special room, sometimes with other people. He used rear-projection screens, video cameras, and a combination of computer- and human-generated graphics to provide experiences. One artificial reality he created was called CRITTER, in which an individual would see a projected shadow view of himself or herself with a small creature imposed on the shadow. The critter would engage the participant, playing various games and causing mischief. Krueger's work was unknown or ignored by other VR researchers until at least the mid-1980s (as demonstrated by the lack of citations in published works). Today he is still producing artificial experiences, and this artistic approach to VR has been adopted by other researchers (discussed further in the Applications section below).

The mid- and late 1970s were quiet times for VR. Sutherland became involved in his own computer company, and Krueger continued his various artificial reality creations. At the University of North Carolina at Chapel Hill, Henry Fuchs and Frederick Brooks (FUCHS ET AL.) led efforts to develop various input and output devices, at the same time pushing the limits of interactive computer graphics through the development of new techniques and hardware. In the U.S. Air Force, Thomas Furness and others worked to create the Supercockpit and other computer-maintained virtual environments for training fighter plane pilots (*AVIATION WEEK & SPACE TECHNOLOGY*; ELSON; FURNESS). None of these resulted in publications directly related to VR at that time. Advances in computer processing power and the rise of the microprocessor and special-purpose graphics computers laid the groundwork for the VR events of the 1980s.

The mid-1980s saw the emergence of what is now central to most VR research, the head-mounted display. NASA scientists developed a stereoscopic HMD (FISHER) (Sutherland's display was not stereographic; it presented the same image to both eyes), and NASA launched a programmed research effort in telerobotics and remote sensing. Declassified research by the U.S. Air Force and Navy was published in the open literature (*AVIATION WEEK & SPACE TECHNOLOGY*; ELSON; FURNESS), describing computer graphic simulations of flight, three-dimensional sound location, and the overlay of computer graphics on the "real" world through transparent HMDs. The University of North Carolina at Chapel Hill developed the world's fastest graphics supercomputer and built various new input and output devices. This activity alone was enough to grab the attention of financial donors, writers of popular literature, and the public, but a boost was given by two additional events: the start of the VPL company and the publication of *Neuromancer* (GIBSON).

VPL developed a gesture-oriented input device called the DataGlove (ZIMMERMAN ET AL.) and the HMD called the EyePhone (see ROBINETT & ROLLAND). These were the first products marketed for VR, at a combined price of about $60,000 (1990 U.S. dollars), not including the graphics computer. Other products, such as magnetic tracking devices, had been available previously but had not been marketed initially for VR applications. The work of NASA, the Air Force, Myron Krueger, and researchers at Chapel Hill served as at least partial inspiration for VPL but did not result in products brought to market.

Despite my reluctance to cite science fiction in this chapter, *Neuromancer* by GIBSON must be recognized. This book is cited throughout the VR literature. It has served as an imaginative jumping-off point for many students, scholars, and researchers. Its focus on direct neural input and total immersion in information space is perhaps closest to the vision of ultimate VR as shared by current enthusiasts. The link between science fiction and VR research is further demonstrated by the number of science fiction writers who have written on VR or given keynote speeches at scholarly conferences. However, the vision of a possible future is far from the reality of the work currently under way (discussed below).

The late 1980s and early 1990s saw a quantum change in VR development. In May 1990 the First Conference on Cyberspace was held at the UNIVERSITY OF TEXAS AT AUSTIN. At the University of Washington in Seattle, the Human Interface Technology Laboratory was formed under the leadership of Tom Furness, and it gathered substantial funding and support from over one dozen leading corporations in technology and manufacturing (C. MILLER). This was a substantive cross-industry collaboration on VR. A Usenet newsgroup for discussing VR topics, SCI.VIRTUAL-WORLDS, came online. Various academic and corporate VR laboratories were started, and other conferences soon followed. A slew of popular articles on VR also followed in forums as different as the *Wall Street Journal* and *Forbes,* and *Mother Earth News* and the *Village Voice.*

Many other personalities played a role in innovation for VR, and entire areas that are now required for most VR work (such as computer graphics) developed over the same time period. This view of the history of VR is supported in the works most commonly referenced by the current VR literature.

The one overwhelming conclusion of the literature review on the history of VR is that there was no clear focus on what VR was about until the early or mid-1980s. Currently there is a focus, but it is driven more by a combination of available equipment, popular perceptions, and science fiction than by a consistent model of what VR *should* be. Perhaps this is appropriate, and perhaps VR, like the microcomputer, will have such general applicability that it will be more of a tool for human endeavors in general rather than the central point of some particular type of activity.

CURRENT VR TECHNOLOGIES

This section describes the technologies currently used for VR. Few published articles are directed solely at summarizing available technology, but a reading of the literature quickly familiarizes the reader with the most common devices. Sales literature and conference exhibits are not included here, but several good resource lists point to vendors of VR-related products (e.g., *BYTE;* RUCKER ET AL.). This brief section examines some of the principal components of VR.

Visual aspects of VR are currently the most advanced. VR has benefited from advances in computer graphics and uses the same sort of techniques used in computer animation, visual data analysis, and related areas (for an overview of computer graphics techniques see FOLEY & VAN DAM). Two types of technologies are commonly used to produce a three-dimensional stereographic effect. Shutter glasses use a liquid crystal display (LCD) to enable each eye alternately to view a scene while the computer shifts the scene slightly so that the brain combines the right- and left-eye views into the sort of three-dimensional world usually perceived. Applications that do not require fooling the user employ this technique, which is relatively inexpensive (up to $2,000 in 1993 U.S. dollars). Scientific data analysis (discussed further below) is one such application. The second technology, which is more closely associated with VR, is the fully immersive display. Most products are HMDs, but at least one product is mounted on a moveable boom. By using sophisticated optics and computational techniques (ROBINETT & ROLLAND), the field of view (i.e., how much of the visual field is covered by the graphical image) can be expanded to over 100° horizontal, which produces a feeling of immersion.

Current HMD technology is limited by two factors. First is the low resolution of the display, as low as 360 x 240 pixels (comparable with a low-resolution monitor on a personal computer but spread across a much larger portion of the visual field). At this resolution, plain text, which we could read while doing word processing, is not legible in the HMD display, and the realism of graphical objects is limited. The second factor is common to all computer graphics applications: drawing speed (NIELSON). Graphical images are constructed of polygons, points, and lines plus lighting or material models. Since at least ten frames per second are needed to achieve a sense of continuity, the graphical image must be redrawn in its new position (e.g., after the user's point of view is moved) quite frequently. The result is that most VRs appear to be cartoon worlds, with simple polygons, limited shading, and few colors. A fast graphics supercomputer is available at the University of North Carolina at Chapel Hill and can provide some interactive lighting. The barrier of graphics computing speed is gradually being overcome. Affordable high-resolution HMDs, however, do not seem immediately forthcoming from vendors, but it is difficult to predict the future. The performance curve for computer graphics speed is relatively smooth, but a sudden leap in HMD technology would not be surprising (production cost, not engineering, is the main restraining factor).

Input devices for VRs do not approach the direct neural input described in Gibson's book, although some researchers have used brain-wave patterns for controlling simple application environments, such as moving a cursor around a screen (LUSTED & KNAPP). The mouse and keyboard, ubiquitous in office and home computing environments, are also used in virtual worlds. Eye-gaze devices, such as those used by some disabled people (LEXCEN), are also sometimes used in VR. The standard input devices associated with VR are position trackers and glove devices. MEYER ET AL. offer a survey of position-tracking devices. Most use electromagnets to ascertain three-dimensional coordinate and orientation data, although ultrasonic (PAUSCH) and mechanical (DAS ET AL.) devices are also found. The position trackers can be mounted on the head and/or hand to determine the position and orientation of the user. A typical application will present the appropriate view for wherever the user is looking (as indicated by head orientation) and display a floating image of the user's hand or other icon.

Glove devices are used to ascertain finger position. They may be used in conjunction with position trackers. Gloves might provide minimal data on overall finger bend, such as the PowerGlove accessory for home video games, or they might use a large number of sensors to determine the bend of every joint, spread between fingers, and shape of the palm. The famous VPL DataGlove is a middle-of-the-road device, providing very accurate finger-bend values but not measuring the rest of the hand (although optional sensors can be added).

Haptics is an umbrella term that describes our physical interaction with the world. It includes our sense of touch but also more subtle aspects, such as balance, muscular position, and resistance to movement. Some glove devices incorporate tactile feedback so that virtual objects when "touched" will produce a feeling in the fingers. This feedback can occur through the inflation of small bladders near the fingertips or by mechanical devices (BURDEA ET AL., 1992b). The University of North Carolina at Chapel Hill has developed mechanical devices that provide actual physical events to accompany virtual events—e.g., treadmills and bicycles that users operate while viewing a graphical environment (see BRICKEN).

Future work in haptics will go in two directions: (1) more sophisticated devices to provide haptic feedback, and (2) the incorporation of physical reality with VR. The second has been ongoing in the work of Krueger for years. A related method of adding real movement to interaction with a virtual world may be found in the CAVE project at the University of Illinois at Chicago (CRUZ-NEIRA ET AL.). In CAVE, computer graphics are displayed on several rear-projection screens that surround the user. He or she may move around a small space unencumbered by a HMD yet be able to interact with items in the virtual world via joystick or glove.

Sound is found in many virtual worlds and is sometimes present without a visual display. The three-dimensional location of sound can provide realism in a virtual world by having the user associate a sound with a particular location in his perceptual space. WENZEL provides an excellent overview of the literature in this area as well as a description of sound localization work at NASA. The use of taste and smell in virtual worlds is limited at best. Sensorama seems to be the best example of a full-sensory VR application (HEILIG).

Voice is used as input in some virtual environments. Typically, voice is used to convey simple commands via microphone to a voice-recognition module, which transmits recognized terms to the VR program. The use of voice fits naturally in virtual worlds because the ability to see and use a standard keyboard is limited and it is difficult to convey complex commands with hand gestures (a limitation of the number of gestures a person can remember and reliably replicate and also a limitation of the precision of glove and position-tracking devices). BIERMANN ET AL. experimented with a voice and touch-screen interface to a text editor. They found that people could effectively edit a document using spoken commands and the touch screen. They likened their system to Put-That-There (BOLT), which uses a set of heuristics to determine where the user wants to move objects in a graphical display. Input was done by voice and motion sensors. Both systems are limited by the small vocabularies of their voice-recognition systems and the need for a brief silence between spoken words. They demonstrate the usefulness of voice as input and also point toward the easy match between pointing and speaking to manipulate graphical environments.

Mixes of other technologies are found in VR laboratories. Large front- and rear-projection screens provide larger fields of view than standard computer monitors. Miniature head-mounted projection displays produce images that appear to float in front of the user (PAUSCH). Variations on position trackers, such as the University of North Carolina's cueball device, are used in applications that do not require the amount of finger-position data available from a glove. The essence of VR technology comes from two sources. First are the individuals and laboratories that develop new input and output devices as they are needed for particular applications. Several exist at both academic and government institutions. The second source is the available products from vendors. Fewer than 20 vendors claim to sell VR-related products because of high startup costs and patents on fundamental technology. Further, most products are expensive, and all require considerable expertise for application development.

A small-scale VR laboratory might cost as little as $100 plus a computer for graphics generation. It would use a PowerGlove as a gesture-oriented input device and LCD shutter glasses from a home video system (marketed by SEGA USA). A microcomputer, such as an Amiga, Macintosh, or PC, would process the incoming glove data, trigger the shutter glasses, and generate the graphics. The difficulty in such a system is that a considerable amount of engineering knowledge is required to attach the glove and glasses to the microcomputer; this is not a task for the average home hobbyist. The virtual world could contain only one- to- two dozen fairly simple objects, and the precision of input and quality of output would be limited by the relatively imprecise glove data.

Much larger VR laboratories can cost hundreds of thousands of dollars. HMDs range from $50,000 to $1 million (FISHER mentions a company that produces the million-dollar version, but I do not know if they are marketing such a product; this HMD was reputed to have very high resolution, based on fiber-optic technology). Glove devices and the tracking devices cost from several thousands to tens of thousands of dollars each. Three-dimensional sound generators are often in the $50,000 range. Computers designed to produce high-quality interactive graphics range from several thousands to hundreds of thousands of dollars (Silicon Graphics (SGI) in Mountain View, Calif., is a favorite graphics computer manufacturer). A fully equipped VR laboratory in 1993 would include a HMD, glove, tracking devices, and mid-range SGI computer at a cost of over $100,000. It would enable one person at a time to experience the virtual world. Many academic and research laboratories add to this configuration such items as wide projection screens, multi-user capabilities, and special software for interactive graphics. Laboratories so equipped might cost upward of $500,000.

The distinction between VR technology and the "standard" technologies of everyday computing is usually easy to make. Gloves, position sensors, three-dimensional sound, and head-mounted displays are clearly for VR, while mice, keyboards, and computer monitors are not. Immersion in a virtual world through technology is not a necessary component, but some incorporation of a point of view and direct response to user input is. Some applications or technologies bridge the gap, such as the use of shutter glasses for three-dimensional computer-aided design (CAD). For the future, expect a decrease in the price of VR technology and a slow increase in the diversity of products available. Advances in computer graphics and graphics software will start to soften the distinction between "just computer graphics" and "VR." Eventually, the high-technology tools of the VR trade will become common components of the home or office computer system (PRUITT & BARRETT), but this is still at least several years away.

APPLICATION AREAS

VR has found some real-world applications. A fair amount of prototype and proof-of-concept work has been done, but few efforts have resulted in publications or products other then those that are not technology driven. The following sections examine medicine, education, art and entertainment, scientific analysis, business (including training and manufacturing), and telerobotics. Throughout, the focus is on applications that are being developed. One notable area that is not covered is flight simulation. Flight simulation goes back to at least 1929 (see NUGENT) and incorporates a simulated airplane cockpit and some level of simulated interaction with an outside world. The U.S. Air Force work mentioned above reduced a largely physical training environment to a virtual training environment (see the section on the history of VR for a review of that work). As discussed above, the focus of VR as it is used now is on nonphysical surroundings or at least surroundings that do not have analogs in the "real" world. Flight simulation involves the use of genuine cockpits with genuine airplane controls, often mounted on large moveable supports to provide real movement. Most VR researchers today are trying to provide a fully "real" experience without using so many "real" props. The future may see a movement back toward the incorporation of real-world objects in virtual worlds. Currently, however, there is little overlap between the literature on flight simulation and training and VR.

Medicine

The medical fields are likely to be the stronghold of working VR applications for at least two or three years. Medicine has a head start, thanks to early VR work at University of North Carolina at Chapel Hill (cf. FUCHS ET AL.) and elsewhere. More importantly there is sufficient funding for continued R&D as well as the manufacture and sales of some VR systems. In 1992 two first-time conferences in this area were held: Medicine Meets Virtual Reality (PLASTIC SURGERY RESEARCH FOUNDATION) and Persons with Disabilities (MURPHY). An important difference between these conferences and other conferences on VR is that in medicine there is a clear path from traditional methods and techniques toward their augmentation through VR.

In most of the VR literature, however, there is only speculation about forthcoming applications. URDANG & STUART propose a scenario in which blind persons wear small audio sets to guide their movements through a city. This project probably would generate insight into navigation through virtual spaces. The major problem, of course, is funding. GREENLEAF writes about DataGloves and DataSuits[1] as input devices

---

[1]The DataSuit is largely nonexistent. VPL sold one and built another to prove the concept. The idea was that a body suit that had sensors all over could provide much more complete data about body position. However, the suit was difficult to calibrate and very expensive (more than $100,000 in 1990). Current applications do not yet have much need for such technology, but the DataSuit is precisely the sort of device that caused great excitement and speculation in the literature. (Information on the VPL DataSuit obtained by personal communication with an unnamed VPL employee, 1993).

for disabled persons who might have difficulty with spoken or keyboard commands. Again we face the problem of price, yet the ability to use VR to accommodate anyone's disability has appeal and is within the grasp of current technology and computational methods. VAMPLEW & ADAMS describe a computer program that can be trained to recognize the gestures of a person wearing a DataGlove. CAMPLANI completed similar research using Italian sign language and a neural network for gesture recognition. Randy Pausch (PAUSCH & WILLIAMS; PAUSCH ET AL.) is engaged in research on VR to aid the disabled. His user studies of body-movement driven speech synthesizers and the use of movement by those with limited mobility show great promise. The work of RUBINE with computer mouse gestures demonstrates algorithms that should transfer well to three-dimensional gestures. In each of these examples, gesture input devices show the potential to help people to communicate in ways that were previously blocked to them. They also point towards new methods of human–computer interaction for all people.

VR also offers the possibility of tailoring rehabilitation programs to the individual while removing some of the heavy involvement of a rehabilitation therapist. BURDEA ET AL. (1992b) propose a system that uses a glove device with force feedback to rehabilitate a damaged human hand or to diagnose possible hand ailments.

The VR area that seems likely to find widespread medical use is surgery. Applications include simulation and practice and also visualization and remote control of surgical instruments. Some applications are immersive; others simply provide the surgeon with a better understanding of the problem and better methods for deciding or acting on it. JOLESZ & SHTERN describe an "operating room of the future," in which advanced computer graphics, visualization of data, imaging of patients, and VR combine to give medical doctors something that looks like "direct manipulation" capability for use on their patients. In their model, various computerized tools would augment the physician's own brain and hands from the diagnosis/decision process to treatment. SHEROUSE ET AL. and SHEROUSE & CHANEY focus on the role of simulation for training and practice for physicians. The idea is to provide an environment similar to the real operating room and a real patient so that any mistakes may be made before encountering live patients. These authors also advocate the increased use for simulation of high-risk techniques using virtual models (e.g., the alignment of radiation sources to treat cancerous tumors) in order to view the possible effects on their patient in advance. CHEN ET AL. propose a similar scenario.

Areas concerning telerobotics (see below) focus on the manipulation of remote surgical devices during microsurgery. CHARLES ET AL.

describe work in progress to use multisensory feedback and gesture input to increase the physician's dexterity during microsurgery. TENDICK ET AL. support the necessity of the work by Charles et al. by demonstrating the extent to which hand dexterity is lost while using endoscopic devices.

The use of technology in medicine and computer graphics techniques is a far larger field than these specific applications would indicate. Continued development of high-technology methods for medicine will involve VR methods and equipment with increasing frequency. Medicine will likely be the first area in which the distinction between "VR applications" and those "applications that are part of the everyday job" will begin to disappear.

Education

Education is perhaps the VR area with some of the greatest potential for improvement. The lack of funds for placing VR systems (or, in many cases, more modest educational technology) in public elementary and secondary schools is the major impediment. There are almost no articles in the literature describing research and potential applications in progress that fall clearly in the elementary, secondary, or college environments. A later section, on Business applications, covers some aspects of training that might apply to education, and the section on medicine noted simulation programs for physicians.

Education applications might someday include the ability to attend simulations of historical events or to visit otherwise inaccessible places. In addition, vocational training might be provided through virtual worlds (this is currently possible for some fields with existing technology).

One VR prototype under development will enable physics students to perform basic experiments in Newtonian mechanics (SCIENTIFIC AMERICAN). This setup should prove less dangerous and more versatile than the typical high school physics lab, but there needs to be more realism in the display before it will be as convincing as the real thing. The potential to create massive chemical reactions or high-mass collisions among multiple objects will give students wider boundaries for their experiments. The Human Interface Technology Laboratory (HITL) at the University of Washington in Seattle has done some programs in which chemical reactions can be simulated as well as a program that educated about HIV/AIDS using VR techniques.[2] Both drew on the attractiveness of the VR medium for communicating messages that otherwise might go unheeded. Another application area that is mentioned frequently in nonresearch articles is virtual worlds from the past

---

[2]Personal communication with HITL laboratory worker, 1993.

or to inaccessible places, such as other planets. There are almost no descriptions in the literature of the development of such environments in VR, although there is a plethora of multimedia applications for similar purposes. One problem is that very detailed virtual worlds have seldom been constructed; another is that the existing corpus of multimedia information, films especially, does not incorporate well into computer-based virtual worlds.

VR for education, even if developed and proven successful, must await further funds before it will see widespread use. This situation is common to all countries where VR research is being undertaken. One possible exception is Japan, which has followed through on an initiative to provide technological infrastructure to students. VR is no more present in the classrooms of Japan than it is in the United States, the United Kingdom, or Germany in 1993, but it might get there first.

Art and Entertainment

From the explosion of review and introductory articles on VR to practically every audience available has emerged a handful of applications that are available to the public, either at home or in an arcade. It is not clear whether romantic views of VR potential are shared by a large segment of the public, but they are certainly shared by most mass media publishers.

The best example of art that uses VR is the work of KRUEGER. Aside from benefiting from a 20-year head start in VR, Krueger does not appear to be limited by a need to translate the "real" into the "virtually real." Krueger's exhibits engage people in experiences that are out of the ordinary, such as ARTWHEELS, in which two participants engage each other in a rear-projection shadow world. Participants can be different sizes or have powers over each other. This is more similar to a Fluxus exhibit than a typical scientific, educational, or simply "fly through" virtual world. (Fluxus exhibits, which consist of unusual art objects that are often interactive, might soon exist in VR. Current efforts to computerize popular works would be very well suited to VR (see PARTRIDGE & HUNTLEY).) Art museums might someday exist virtually, too. A recent demonstration videotape by Sense8 (Sausalito, Calif.), a manufacturer of VR software for microcomputers, gave a virtual tour through a three-dimensional computerized art gallery. Another work in progress is at Carnegie-Mellon University. Its "Telecommunications and VR" project will provide for the interactive creation of virtual environments for artists and their audience, combining networking and VR.

The entertainment industry can boast several small-scale success stories and one large one. The largest success is Mattel Co.'s PowerGlove, a low-cost approximation of the DataGlove. (DITLEA provides a perspective on VR product development taken from interviews with developers of these devices.) The PowerGlove is linked to a home game system and allows the user to interact with the game via glove instead of joystick or keypad. Some researchers use the glove in VR research (e.g., PAUSCH), but the limited precision of the PowerGlove does not make it suitable for VR applications that require the measurement of precise hand movements. The designer of the PowerGlove, AGE Inc. (New York City), plans to release a low-end HMD. By the end of 1992 Mattel had sold millions of PowerGloves for use in home entertainment systems.

Small-scale popular applications can be found in some shopping malls. Virtuality and Battletech are immersive VR video games (CARROLL). In Virtuality, players wear a lightweight HMD similar in resolution and field of view to the VPL EyePhone. They use a magnetically tracked joystick or sit at a control panel (depending on the game) and seek and destroy various electronic objects. Battletech places multiple players in the same virtual world at the same time. They sit in a simulated cockpit for an advanced robot and view the "outside" on a large television viewport. Using various weapons they try to blow up objects in the virtual environment. These objects are other players in their virtual robots.

Several themes emerge from an examination of current or pending applications in the arts and entertainment. First is the unfortunate fact that popular applications are thus far perpetuating violent and confrontational forms of entertainment. Another is that there is an inconsistency between the tools for VR used in research labs and those available to the public; the former are more expensive and more fragile but offer somewhat better performance. There are signs that this gap will gradually close. One potential direction for VR is access to fragile or inaccessible works of art through simulation. Much higher-resolution input and output devices will be necessary before serious work of this sort will be able to replace the real thing, and the technologies to faithfully store representations of three-dimensional art objects are still under development. A final theme is that VR offers new opportunities for artists. Interactive art experiences are not new, but VR seems to offer some different approaches to art. To add to Krueger's pioneering work, we can anticipate additional innovative artistic experiences, such as environments with no physical analog, art "objects" made out of materials with unstable properties, or network-based exhibits. Indications of advances in this area are readily available at the local video arcade.

Scientific Analysis

Visualization has been called the second computer revolution (FRIEDHOFF & BENZON). Visualization of data enables scientists and researchers to spot patterns and communicate findings to their colleagues. VR offers new interface options for scientific data analysis and an opportunity for true immersion in one's work. Unlike most other application areas, the transition from flat-screen visualization techniques to VR immersion techniques for data analysis is fairly straightforward. Three-dimensional techniques for data analysis are already being embraced by scientists from many fields (NIELSON). Three- or higher-dimensioned data can be viewed from any angle, moved about, colored, or processed with many existing data analysis tools. VR offers the ability to perceive data in three dimensions in the full field of view as well as the potential for engaging senses other than sight in data analysis. Gesture-input devices for data manipulation offer possible benefits not available with a keyboard or mouse.

Visualization might involve data from physical environments, such as the data found in geographic information systems (GISs) (SHAFFER), or it might involve nonphysical data such as might be gathered from a simulation of turbulence over an airplane wing. As for information visualization, however, the selection of a "good" data representation is not necessarily easy (ROBERTSON). The development of VR tools for data visualization can rapidly follow developments that do not use VR. Time-series data or data that can be viewed in many different ways are especially good candidates for VR.

Business

After medicine, various business applications appear to be the closest to widespread use of VR. Training, manufacturing, design, prototyping, and market testing are areas in which businesses might see a payoff from investment in VR technology (NEWBY, 1992a).

BUSINESS WEEK shared several articles on VR with its readers. Aside from a mention of the use of VR in the courtroom, the coverage did not mention any applications that would be of much use to managers during their regular work day; instead readers were offered the speculation typically found in other popular articles. One scenario that could change the way some people work is proposed by PRUITT & BARRETT (mentioned earlier). Their "corporate virtual workspace" is a futuristic extension of telecommuting but perhaps would allow virtual commuters to communicate directly with their cohorts. Workers would sit at a virtual desk, go to virtual meetings, and perhaps even take virtual coffee breaks.

A classic example of a business-related application is described by BROOKS ET AL. At the University of North Carolina, Chapel Hill, a simulation system was built to visualize a building during its design. With this system, the architects and clients could examine the layout and recommend changes before the foundation was even laid. HOLSINGER describes a virtual travel kiosk system that enables customers to use a joystick-driven interface connected to a movie that shows a tour of a town. Here the user can select that part of the town he or she wants to visit by changing direction as the movie point-of-view proceeds down a street. The speed of this virtual tour can also be controlled.

The sections on Telerobotics and Medicine touch on training in virtual worlds. Telerobotics also offers methods to train computers for automated manufacturing or for people to perform remote quality control. BOMAN ET AL. identified training costs for maintenance workers and found a favorable cost/benefit ratio for training in virtual environments vs. traditional methods. Design and manufacturing are the most immediate targets for VR applications, but these will be extensions of existing two-dimensional applications and robotics. Prototyping and market testing are some of the most expensive and time-consuming phases in getting a product to market. Here VR can offer a faster and cheaper way to go through several iterations of product design in response to customer preferences. BRYSON & LEVIT describe work at NASA to simulate wind turbulence over a wing. In the virtual wind tunnel, users track the trajectory of streams of air as they pass over the wing. The economy of this method will increase when virtual design is part of the process. However, it will be a number of years before VR makes it possible for managers or team leaders to "meet" in a virtual world and perceive each other as though they were in the same physical location, but perhaps this vision will inspire management to invest in VR development for other business purposes.

Telerobotics

Telerobotics is closely related to VR, but it is also a field in its own right. The interactive remote control of robots presents problems of feedback, perception of remote events, data transmission, and data representation in addition to the standard difficulties of robotics—e.g., dexterity, reliability, and "sensing" of the environment.

One of the main difficulties cited by BEJCZY in a 1980 article is that of enabling the teleoperator to use his or her "body skills." This is a problem awaiting a VR solution. Rather than needing to translate what is seen via remote sensors, a teleoperator in a virtual environment could use his or her existing skills to gather information about and interact in

the world. DURLACH describes work to use localized sound to provide position and orientation data in a teleoperation environment. As
he notes, people can locate sound in space very precisely. FISHER
describes work at NASA and elsewhere on telerobotic systems; some of
these systems involve multiple persons working together. GIBBONS
describes NASA's efforts to provide for remote surgery on orbiting
astronauts by earth-based physicians. The problems are daunting: a
low-gravity environment, delicate situations requiring great dexterity,
the possibility of temporary signal interference, and time lag.

In telerobotics the distinction between VR and not-VR is not always
clear because telerobotics involves the virtual presence—at least mentally—of a teleoperator at some remote place. What VR can offer is an
interface, a more convincing feeling of being elsewhere. Studies in the
human factors of telerobotics should provide insight into some of the
user aspects of involvement in virtual worlds.

Application Summary

The sections above introduce some of the application areas for VR
that have prototypes, systems in use, or research in progress. A recent
participant in the SCI.VIRTUAL-WORLDS forum asked, "Where are
the applications?" This question seems appropriate in light of the ratio
of potential or imagined areas for development to actual working products or prototypes. This trend will continue as long as the costs of
purchasing, developing, and maintaining VR applications remain high.
Some VR applications will be more readily available soon, such as those
in medicine and science (see JACOBSON). Some business applications,
especially those that might decrease product development time, will be
used by the manufacturing sector. Limited art and entertainment applications exist already and will continue to be reasonable in cost and
accessibility to the public for several more years. An area with perhaps
the most potential for widespread use of VR is education, and a few
small-scale research projects are under way. However, schools that can
barely afford a basic microcomputer cannot be expected to indulge in
VR. Financial constraints severely limit the area with perhaps the greatest potential benefit to society.

VR FOR INFORMATION SCIENCE
AND THE INFORMATION PROFESSIONS

Information professionals and librarians look at VR as a possible
way to interact with bibliographic data and other information through
a graphical display. In another way, VR could have a role in the chang-

ing nature of the library and alternative methods for creating and accessing books. A third area related to VR is the linking of communities and resource sharing via computer networks. Each of these is examined below. Here VR techniques do not lie at the heart of the work to advance information access, yet the technologies, ideas, and promise of VR offer new insights into the problems faced by information professionals.

Graphical Display of Bibliographical Data

ARIST has published several chapters on document description and representation (ARTANDI; BATTEN; HARRIS; RICHMOND; VICKERY). Other chapters have focused on particular aspects of information retrieval (IR), such as interfaces, programming, and storage. In general, the IR systems of today fall into two gross categories: (1) those that use some combination of key terms and fields as primary access points, and (2) those that use something else, as discussed below. It is perhaps not surprising that no chapter on document description and representation has appeared in *ARIST* since 1974 because commercially available IR systems of all types, including database software, online public access catalogs (OPACs), CD-ROM bibliographic databases, and all forms of print indexes, use term fields for primary access. Whether author-title-subject queries are used or free-text searching of abstracts, the document representations against which query terms are matched consist of sets of words associated with the documents, usually divided into fields.

There have been many calls in the literature for alternative representation methods, and there have been many experiments using other methods. BELKIN & CROFT review information storage and retrieval methods. This section does not attempt a cross-sectional summary of this part of the information science literature but examines the literature that points most clearly to VR applications—viz., work dealing with the spatial representation and retrieval of information. The discussion is also limited to those works in which the spatial aspects are particularly well suited to visualization. In particular, vector spaces discussed by Salton and others (e.g., SALTON & MCGILL) are not easily visualizable due to their highly multidimensional nature. Salton's work on IR is frequently cited, however, and has clearly inspired many researchers. (For criticism of Salton's vector space model see RAGHAVAN & WONG.)

Most IR work using spatial representation or retrieval methods began with the same fielded or free-text documents (or document surrogates) found in typical bibliographic databases. Computers are used to process the data into a form appropriate for a spatial system. A less frequent method is to base the spatial representation scheme for the contents in a database on the cognitive or psychological characteristics of a user or user group. The remainder of this section examines some work in each area.

Calls for spatial or visual approaches to IR go back at least to the 1960s. G. A. MILLER expressed his view passionately, writing that spatial navigation, organization, memory, and representation are so much a part of being human that effective information systems require that some spatial component be present. He cited examples in which people create some sort of spatial representation even when one is not present. The provision of visual access to a computer-based world is a part of VR that can help realize Miller's hope for IR. BROOKES proposed that IR systems display items in a database using perspective— e.g., objects perceived to be close (or more familiar, or more relevant) to the user would appear to be more prominent, and less important items would shrink toward the horizon. His approach could be used with or without visualization (e.g., a nonvisual system would use this criterion to decide whether a document that matched a query would be perceived as important enough to present). Of course, to model a database in this way we would need to know more about the user and his or her needs (and be able to usefully represent this information) than is currently feasible.

ROLLING mapped concept relations from a thesaurus using "arrowgraphs"—i.e., maps of terms, each with several arrows pointing to related terms. He proposed this graphical approach for its usefulness in selecting terms during IR and for watching changing relations among terms as new documents or terms were added to the thesaurus or database to which it was applied. Rolling performed his analysis by hand, taking relations of hierarchy, synonymity, and co-occurrence into account. The drawings and pictures included in this work strongly resemble the outcomes of computerized methods used by researchers years later.

Another early work that deserves mention for its ability to link intellectually the types of graphical presentations based on conceptual relatedness with physical methods for interaction found in many virtual worlds is that of RICHMOND & WILLIAMSON. They built actual physical models from wires and foam balls where the balls represented words and the wires represented relationships among the words. They drew on the work of Rolling and others to provide several representation methods for the contents of classification schemes. Another type of model they built was a paper mobile. These representations of bibliographic items could be easily translated into objects in virtual worlds, where they could be viewed from any angle or manipulated as desired.

Rolling and Richmond and Williamson took a tack that is now less favored among information scientists by generating maps from their perceptions of relations among terms. The majority of work since then has focused on computational methods to count words or measure relations to generate the same sort of outcome. This is an artifact of pragmatics, not necessarily intellectual preference, due to the large number of items in bibliographic databases (Rolling claimed to have mapped over 600 terms, but current thesauri include many thousands of terms). An alternative to computational methods is to use psychometric instruments to elicit from respondents the perceived relations among various bibliographic items.

In a recent *ARIST* chapter, RORVIG reviewed psychological methods and their applicability to IR. Many such methods are better suited for evaluating systems than creating system databases. They result in accurate measurements of how concepts are perceived by people, but the measurements often involve elaborate survey instruments or long interviews. As for Rolling's method, psychometric measurement is time consuming and unsuited to most real-world databases. MCDONALD & SCHVANEVELDT provided a useful overview of their method for eliciting user perceptions of relations among concepts, in which several psychometric methods may play a role. Their method, called Pathfinder, is not directed specifically at IR but is instead aimed at making interfaces more intuitive and easier to learn.

Because it is difficult to gather enough data from users to build a full-sized IR system based on perceived concept relations, it is often desirable to use automatic computer-based methods. One common method is co-occurrence analysis, in which the tendency of terms to occur together in documents (or document surrogates) is measured. Statistical techniques place terms with high co-occurrence scores close to each other in a multidimensional space, and terms that tend not to co-occur are placed further apart. LAW & WHITTAKER create graphical representations of important terms in a database based on term co-occurrence (which they call the "co-word method"). This method was used to assess the quality of indexing (by looking for visual patterns that would indicate indexer bias), to ascertain whether concepts that were thought to be important were found in appropriate quantity and prominence in the database, and to determine whether conceptually related concepts would be grouped together by co-occurrence analysis. All three applications affirmed the usefulness of their method.

CRAVEN (1991; 1992) built and analyzed a prototype system for displaying concepts visually. He also used co-occurrence as a measure of similarity. The microcomputer-based system enabled the user to move through space and examine relationships from different perspectives. Craven proposed this three-dimensional display as an advance over two-dimensional or nongraphical displays. The ability to change the point of view interactively brings his work closer to VR applications than most other work on spatial representation.

NEWBY (1992b) used a co-occurrence method to build an "information space" and provided a visual interface that allowed users to move around, seeking appropriate terms or document surrogates. Users could view the three-dimensional space on a large computer monitor and manipulate either a mouse or PowerGlove to navigate through the space. Research subjects who evaluated the prototype system were ambivalent about the appropriateness of the term and document locations in the space but expressed interest in the visual and virtual aspects of the interface.

CAPLINGER developed an interactive three-dimensional interface similar to that used by Newby. Documents (but not terms) were located according to their scores on chosen "dimensions" of the data. This method is similar to one proposed by MEINCKE & ATHERTON, in which the most important or desired qualities of documents in a database are chosen as axes through the space. Caplinger's system allowed users to navigate through the space and seek out appealing documents (documents appeared as points in the space, but an "instrument panel" and landmarks enabled document selection). However, the space is limited by the dimensions chosen. Topic (according to a library classification number), level of knowledge required, refinement (e.g., with multiple editions of a textbook), currency, length, and comprehensibility were proposed as possible dimensions, only three of which could be viewed at a time. The ERIC database, for example, would allow automatic placement according to all these items (at least for some documents indexed), but most databases would not. Caplinger's and Newby's works are the only examples of intentional linkage between IR and VR techniques that were identified in the literature.

One approach to IR that does not use statistical measures of association is the neural network. ROSE & BELEW (1991a; 1991b) describe systems called SCALIR and AIR, which use a combination of methods derived from connectionist and artificial intelligence (AI) work to generate graphical representations of documents. A relevance feedback model drives interaction with the system: the computer monitor represents various parts of the literature based on user response to the last display. The system focuses on "direct manipulation" (SHNEIDERMAN), the ability of the user to act on some aspect of the system with minimal mediation or interference by the system. Direct manipulation is an important quality that most virtual worlds possess but that is far less frequently found in traditional computer applications. A mouse or other pointing device enables direct manipulation in an increasing number of applications.

A semantic network with similar appearance to the systems of NEWBY (1992b) and CAPLINGER is described by FAIRCHILD ET AL., whose focus was on creating an exploratory environment for large databases. Different views of the important terms and their connections to other terms could be created. Various methods for moving through the database were available, including relative incremental movement or jumping to a particular location in the space. A difficulty with this approach, as with that of Rose and Belew's approach, is that the links among items do not translate directly into a particular "location" in a three- or higher-dimensional space, so items are placed somewhat arbitrarily.

LELU combined a neural network with principal-components analysis to produce a graphical display of database contents. This display was used to map the contents of a database so that a human user could ascertain the nature of the contents. Thus, it was not a traditional query-answer IR system, but it served a related purpose. Lelu was not as concerned with building practical systems as with creating methods for communicating the nature of a database or database subset with information seekers or indexers.

Bibliometrics (WHITE & MCCAIN) includes a long tradition of visual analysis of co-citation and other data, an application well-suited to VR methods. MCCAIN provides a nice overview of bibliographic methods, including various ways to generate visual representations of co-citation data. SPRING examines some of the possible values of VR as an interface to information—namely, for presenting relations among data elements, volumetric models of data representation, and spatial interaction with information. He considers bibliographic as well as other kinds of data (e.g., multimedia documents).

This section has examined only a few articles concerned with representing, interacting with, or navigating through bibliographic data without typing and revising keyword-based queries. They are generally well suited to VR applications. Methods for placing terms and documents in an "information space" in order to understand and/or retrieve information from a database is one approach to IR that results in an interface that allows people to interact with the system using spatial skills. There is not sufficient empirical work in the literature to claim that these approaches are superior to traditional methods; in fact, it seems that although such systems facilitate browsing behavior, they do not perform as well for retrieving known items. The deployment of these types of systems to libraries and information centers is certainly not in the near future, yet such systems, if they prove to be practical, seem close to some ideal notions of what IR systems could look like. HALBERT postulates an information retrieval system of the future in which information seekers "fly" over a virtual landscape on which qualities of the literature are represented as physical entities. In his example, the IR systems of the future found in libraries everywhere are a cross between microcomputer-based flight simulators and video games. Such systems sound as if they are fun to use, but empirical data are needed to determine the extent to which they are useful for solving real-world information needs.

The Library and the Book

One area of interest to information professionals concerns "virtual libraries," in which information resources are distributed via networks. Librarians are enthusiastic about the potential for information sharing on the Internet and the National Research and Education Network (NREN) (U.S. CONGRESS), and virtual reality is seen as one possible enhancement to library services offered over the network (BERRY). Such enhancements would go beyond finding information and would include interaction with other people or new types of books or reference works. A recent *ARIST* chapter (LYNCH & PRESTON) focuses on network services, so this chapter bypasses such literature. The relation of work on virtual libraries and hypertext to VR is briefly discussed.

Virtual libraries. The "virtual library" is a recent concept in the literature that partly overlaps VR. Like cyberspace (see the following section), it is not yet clear what a virtual library is or could be. BARKER presents a vision of the changes indicated by present trends. He discusses the changing nature of the book, from something that is a limited medium to something that can incorporate multiple media, from something that is difficult to produce, share, and transport to something whose electronic form enables ready processing in many ways. Barker also introduces the concept of a VR book, in which readers can immerse themselves to experience some story, history, or other experience created by an "author." He considers in fair detail the issues involved in creating such books and how such books might be accessed. Finally, Barker reviews some existing products that point to the future—e.g., hypermedia books, CD-ROM-based books, and talking books.

BAILEY outlines a progression of four types of high-technology systems for information access in networked library environments: (1) hypermedia, (2) multimedia databases, (3) multimedia message systems, and (4) virtual reality. This may be the progression that will eventually bring VR to the public through the library. (The next section suggests the additional notion that hypermedia research can play a strong role for the development and understanding of VR.)

BURTON (1988a; 1988b) describes the falling of barriers among library resources as virtual links are formed between institutions and databases. In doing her bibliometric research she was able to access multiple information resources transparently, ignoring both cost (through free resource sharing) and distance (through the use of the Internet). Sharing resources and developing new methods for producing and distributing books are necessary steps before ideal notions of VR can be realized.

POULTER provides a down-to-earth description of the use of VR technology for library access. He models the virtual world on the regular library, with shelves, books, and various methods of accessing them (keyword, browsing, or following a thesaurus). The VR component adds to the regular library scenario by providing information on links among items or by configuring the books according to a particular user or information need. Further, every book in this library is always available. Users can access the book in electronic form in the virtual world or charge it out in traditional paper form.

Those who approach VR from a computational or human factors standpoint have only a limited understanding of the problems of information access in real-world environments. It is the library and (previously) traditional publishers and database producers who are leading the way toward VR systems and (perhaps without planning it) filling in some of the largest gaps in VR research and applications. One issue familiar to information professionals is that of equal access. Equal access is central to library services, yet VR, at least for the near future, lies largely in the domain of the technological and information elite. This factor is seldom mentioned. Even if decreases in the price of VR hardware and software and increases in the availability and utility of applications follow the same curve as that of the personal computer, there is a long way to go before the complete VR systems of today, which cost at least several tens of thousands of dollars, will be found in large numbers in the bibliographic searching areas of public libraries.

Hypertext. A few works on hypertext are closely related to spatial representation schemes or present possible ways to use VR techniques. (For simplicity, I use the term hypertext in this section because the literature I discuss relates to text processors, readers, or retrievers. It is clear, however, that *hypermedia* is the more appropriate term for whatever sort of hypertext might exist in a virtual world.) The conceptual link between hypertext and VR is strengthened by citations to hypertext researchers in the VR literature and the presence of such personalities as Ted Nelson, the modern progenitor of hypertext, in published interviews on VR (NELSON).

To generate spatial representations of document collections for virtual interaction, there are few methods for making associations that get beyond the simple word level. CHURCHER examines the role of psychology, AI, education, information science, and hypertext in creating representations of knowledge. For her, concepts and the relations among them are fundamental components of human experience. She reviews some methods for getting at the perceived relations among terms or concepts to create useful representations, including graphics that approximate those discussed previously. MICCO discusses a pilot study to represent the links among subject headings in a library card catalog using a hypertext model. Although there was no explicit pointer to VR applications in either of Churcher's or Micco's works, their discussions indicate possible solutions to the difficulties of creating cognitively based representation schemes for information system applications of VR.

BEARD & WALKER describe their system, which has some of the qualities of the information spaces described above but which appears more like a hypertext system. The prototype is a simple dictionary, using similarity links based solely on proximity in the alphabetical word list. The importance of this work is not in the data used but in the focus on navigation skills needed to successfully move through the data. The authors mention a possible application of their work to larger and higher-dimensional spaces. Similar to ROSE & BELEW (1991a; 1991b), Beard and Walker focus on the direct manipulation of graphical objects as a base for their system design. They tested the use of zooming and roaming functions, where zooming is used to get more or less detail and roaming is used to move through the representation. Their results support the direct manipulation method and the utility of both roaming and zooming for navigating a set of data.

The many researchers and developers working with hypertext and hypermedia and the accessibility of hardware and software for hypertext are important to the advance of VR. We still lack an adequate understanding of the issues involved in navigating through virtual worlds, a problem that scholars working with hypertext are dealing with. Hypertext and hypermedia research will help us gain a better understanding of the issues, both conceptual and methodological, of VR.

Cyberspace

Current literature, especially popular literature, tends to obfuscate the distinction between VR technologies and networking technologies. This confusion appears to be a byproduct of the influence (sometimes indirect) of science fiction on popular perceptions of VR. If people can enter a virtual world, the reasoning goes, they should be able to meet other people there. Information access in this virtual world would be as easy as, say, Memex (BUSH) or exosomatic memory (BROOKES), in which finding information is much like remembering it but with the augmentation of a suprahuman IR system.

Cyberspace is an elusive concept. In one sense, it already exists as the collection of predominantly text-based communication forums that are used by millions of people who read computer mailing lists and bulletin boards or access remote computing resources and databases. In another sense cyberspace awaits the addition of such communication forums and information resources to futuristic interfaces, perhaps incorporating computer graphics, AI, and very high-bandwidth networks with visual, auditory, and even neural input and output devices.

This chapter does not review the literature on information networking. It retains the difference that is apparent in most actual VR research between VR and human communication via computer network. In the future, it may be impossible to talk about computer networking without VR, in which case future review chapters on this topic might be called "Cyberspace." However, the literature available for this review makes it easy to maintain the distinction.

Various aspects of human communication via computer networks have been covered in *ARIST* (GROSSER; LYNCH & PRESTON). The earliest review of computer networking was done by BUNCH & ALSBERG. Lynch and Preston focused on the role of the Internet for access to information resources, not only for human communication. The short article by ROMKEY offers a timely and appropriate view of the unclear relationships among VR, cyberspace, and science fiction. As is typical in such review articles, the terms "cyberspace" and "VR" are often used synonymously. My literature review included searching for written works on VR in hundreds of electronic bibliographic databases and collecting scores of articles that offered similar reviews to the readerships of scholarly, professional, and popular journals and magazines. The importance of the lack of clear distinction between the terms for information professionals is the assumption that advanced interfaces will suddenly make information retrieval of all types work much better, an assumption the readers will surely question.

In sum, graphical techniques for IR are far from perfect. We do not know when cyberspace information systems will exist; even the nature of the work that needs to be done is largely undetermined. Efforts are further limited by the extent to which the standard tools and practices of computer graphics are accessible by information professionals, let alone VR technologies. The amount of access that typical academic and (especially) public libraries have to the Internet is still quite limited (WESTIN & FINGER). The recently passed NREN legislation (U.S. CONGRESS) should help to provide connectivity, but work still needs to be done before the melding of VR and computer networks takes on both the appearance and functionality of cyberspace. (For an entertaining description of one notion of what a cyberspace interface for futuristic information retrieval might look like, see HALBERT.)

TOWARD AN UNDERSTANDING OF VR

Previous sections have focused on the history, technology, application areas, and technological development of VR. Is there a "big picture" that can emerge from this discussion? An excellent review and prognosis for all aspects of VR is offered by BISHOP ET AL. They provide some taxonomies with which to consider VR. The focus of the taxonomies is the shared-world model and the methods by which that model was maintained and accessed by participants. In everyday life, we share a world model maintained by physical objects and overlapping views about the nature of the objects and the relations among them. We might be able to access the world through a recording or transmission (e.g., a television broadcast). Another type of world model is a simulation, in which the model with which the participants interact is not accessible to everyone but only to those who are engaged in the simulation. This is the stuff of VR. The model might be something from familiar human experience, or it might involve a suspension of many aspects of the world we usually live in. A final type of model is a representation of "real" physical objects. This is telerobotics, in which remote sensors transmit information about the world and that information is represented in some useful way for the human user to interact with. The representation might be closely related to what the human could experience on his or her own, or it might be completely outside ordinary experience—e.g., the representation of temperature by force and of distance by sound. Sensations in virtual worlds may be experienced by individuals or several people (who may not experience exactly the same sort of reality).

NEWBY (1992b) and NILAN provide some framework for the building of virtual worlds. They argue for a need to design a virtual world that considers the psychological perspective of a user or user group. The focus of this type of design effort is "cognitive space." Cognitive space may be defined simply as the collection of concepts and relations among them that are perceived by individuals. For most VR applications (art being a possible exception) one goal is that the virtual world be navigable; the user should be able to get from one place to another or choose appropriate views or representations. The extent to which a virtual world is consonant with the cognitive space will determine how easily the user can learn to use that world and how readily he or she will be able to navigate through it. Navigation in this context does not apply simply to virtual realities that deal with simulations of physical phenomena, such as a system that allows one to "fly through" a city or landscape. Navigation also applies to the types of activities involved in, say, using a bibliographic IR system; if the concepts (e.g., key terms) and relations among them are what the user expects, there will be a diminished need to translate an expression of information need into something that matches the system's "view" of the world. SHUM discusses how cognitive spaces could be used to generate virtual spaces for hypertext navigation. LIU & WICKENS performed experiments that confirmed the benefit of cognitive relatedness for facilitating spatial-recognition tasks.

BIOCCA examined VR from a human communication perspective. He proposed VR as a shared place in which researchers could work. VR from this perspective is a new medium for communication, one that exceeds the capabilities of the telephone or written word and can supplement face-to-face interaction.

These examples demonstrate a beginning toward an understanding of how VR might help us further understand social phenomena, and they offer at least some promise that VR could be a base from which to seek new understanding of human communication or navigation behavior. There does seem to be something that separates VR from the everyday world and from other forms of human–computer interaction. Individually, the technologies that enable virtual realities to be built provide quantitative advances over current technologies: more field of view in visual displays, increased feedback from remote sensors, higher interactivity with a computer-supplied environment or other people, and so forth. These quantitative increases synergistically combine to provide what may be a truly different medium for interaction, not just an extension of current media.

THE FUTURE OF VR

A commitment of business, government, and academic research funds will provide for further VR work for at least several years. There are very few formal programs of study at universities or corporate or government positions that focus on VR. Momentum is gathering, however, from research, market forces, and (perhaps unfortunately) popular visions of VR as an agent of social change. The utopian view that VR might somehow transform society by bringing together people and an increasing understanding among social groups is certainly overstated and is reminiscent of the introduction of other technologies, such as television or the computer (LANIER & BIOCCA).

Computer graphics technology will continue to advance, as will the capabilities and availability of computer networks. As computing becomes ubiquitous (WEISNER), the infrastructure necessary to support VR applications will become more commonplace. ARNOLD predicts that VR and other advanced technologies will soon be necessary to interact with the massive collections of all types of data that we require to function at work or at home. VR technologies designed for easier use, at a lower price, and for mass marketing are forthcoming in the 1990s.

The possible ethical dilemmas involved have been considered from several angles. SHAPIRO & MCDONALD ask whether people who are trained using virtual realities might believe that their skills are generalizable to the "real" world only to find that the augmentation provided by the virtual interface leaves them unable to achieve what they thought possible. *THE LANCET* and *U.S. News and World Report* (LEO) both ask questions about whether VR will someday be more appealing than being in the "real" world. Given the high level of use (or abuse) of television and video games by youngsters, this question is reasonable even before VR can completely fool the user into thinking he or she is elsewhere.

GRAY & DRISCOLL critically examine VR and find it wanting. For them, VR is "the latest of a long line of technoscientific fantasmic constructions that are often more interesting for what they claim than what they do" (p. 40). This perspective is justified considering the inflated views of what VR *can* do today and is further justified by widely circulated speculations on what it *could* be. VR might follow the path of computers, which were first hailed as giant brains that would behave as intelligently as humans. Computers still do not have humanlike intelligence, yet they can perform tasks which were at the outer reaches of imagination in the 1940s and 1950s. Gray and Driscoll do not allow for this optimism (or at least openness); they portray VR as a way to perpetuate the status quo through government funding and the desire of those in power to stay there.

To keep informed of events in VR, one should avoid the popular press and articles with titles such as "Cyberpunk: A User's Guide to Virtual Sex." In writing this chapter I have tried to focus on what does exist or what is likely to exist, citing the science fiction literature only when necessary to point out long-term goals. The emotional and intellectual attractiveness of the imagined promise of VR is perpetuating the demand for a mixture of a few facts and lots of fiction in descriptions of VR, and these are just as likely to be found in refereed journals and conference proceedings as on prime-time television. There are many excellent articles in journals, and conferences are starting to focus on the "real" world of VR, not things that might be. Many articles in the popular media, too, are realistic and well researched. As mentioned previously, computer-mediated discussions such as those on Usenet's SCI.VIRTUAL-WORLDS and conferences on CompuServe and The Well (two network services) are excellent ways to keep informed. In that medium the distinction between fact and fiction is usually much easier to see. As books, conferences, and the popular media ride the tide of VR's popularity, the consumer needs to beware the strange proximity of descriptions of real products and people with futuristic fantasies.

CONCLUSION

The description of virtual reality offered at the start of this chapter did not necessarily require computers, did not rely on immersion, and engaged senses other than vision and (occasionally) hearing. The literature reveals much speculation with a focus on multisensory involvement and interaction, either with physical objects or other humans. In fact, however, existing technology has limited most endeavors to head-mounted displays, glove-input devices, position trackers, and computer graphics.

It is unclear whether VR will remain the focus of research and development or whether it will fade into the background as specific applications go their own ways and VR technologies become more common. In any case, the ideas and technologies associated with VR now will continue to evolve and will stay central to human–computer interaction through the 1990s.

VR has attracted a highly multidisciplinary group of researchers, scientists, and thinkers. THOMPSON lists over 200 organizations around the world engaged in VR projects. Good work has been done to investigate the ways in which virtual worlds might supplement human existence in the "real" world, and good work will continue to be done.

BIBLIOGRAPHY

ARNOLD, STEPHEN E. 1990. The Large Data Construct: A New Frontier in Database Design. Microcomputers for Information Management. 1990 September; 7(3): 185-203. ISSN: 0742-2343.

ARTANDI, SUSAN. 1970. Document Description and Representation. In: Cuadra, Carlos A., ed. Annual Review of Information Science and Technology: Volume 5. Chicago, IL: Encyclopaedia Britannica for the American Society for Information Science; 1970. 143-168. ISBN: 0-85229-156-6.

AVIATION WEEK & SPACE TECHNOLOGY. 1985. Virtual Cockpit's Panoramic Displays Afford Advanced Mission Capabilities. 1985 January 14; 122(2): 143-152. ISSN: 0005-2175.

BAILEY, CHARLES W., JR. 1990. Intelligent Multimedia Computer Systems: Emerging Information Resources in the Network Environment. Library Hi Tech. 1990; 8(1): 29-41. ISSN: 0737-8831.

BARKER, PHILIP. 1992. Electronic Books and Libraries of the Future. The Electronic Library. 1992 June; 10(3): 130-149. ISSN: 0264-0473.

BATTEN, WILLIAM E. 1973. Document Description and Representation. In: Cuadra, Carlos A., ed. Annual Review of Information Science and Tech-

nology: Volume 8. Washington, DC: American Society for Information
Science; 1973. 43-68. ISSN: 0066-4200; ISBN: 0-87715-208-X.

BEARD, DAVID V.; WALKER, JOHN Q., II. 1990. Navigational Techniques to
Improve the Display of Large Two-Dimensional Spaces. Behaviour &
Information Technology. 1990; 9(6): 451-466. ISSN: 0144-929X.

BEJCZY, ANTAL K. 1980. Sensors, Controls, and Man-Machine Interface for
Advanced Teleoperation. Science. 1980; 208(4450): 1327-1335. ISSN: 0036-
8075.

BELKIN, NICHOLAS J.; CROFT, W. BRUCE. 1987. Retrieval Techniques. In:
Williams, Martha E., ed. Annual Review of Information Science and
Technology: Volume 22. Amsterdam, The Netherlands: Elsevier Science
Publishers for the American Society for Information Science; 1987. 109-
145. ISSN: 0066-4200; ISBN: 0-444-70302-0.

BERRY, JOHN. 1992. Virtual Reality, Internet Capture LITA's Denver Debate.
Library Journal. 1992 October 15; 117(7): 17-18. ISSN: 0363-0277.

BIERMANN, ALAN W.; FINEMAN, LINDA; HEIDLAGE, J. FRANCIS. 1992.
A Voice- and Touch-Driven Natural Language Editor and Its Performance.
International Journal of Man-Machine Studies. 1992 July; 37(1): 1-21.
ISSN: 0020-7373.

BIOCCA, FRANK. 1992. Communication within Virtual Reality: Creating a
Space for Research. Journal of Communication. 1992 Autumn; 42(4): 5-22.
ISSN: 0021-9916.

BISHOP, GARY; BRICKEN, WILLIAM; BROOKS, FREDERICK, JR.; BROWN,
MARCUS; BURBECK, CHRIS; DURLACH, NAT; ELLIS, STEVE; FUCHS,
HENRY; GREEN, MARK; LACKNER, JAMES; MCNEILL, MICHAEL;
MOSHELL, MICHAEL; PAUSCH, RANDY; ROBINETT, WARREN;
SRINIVASAN, MANDAYAM; SUTHERLAND, IVAN; URBAN, DICK;
WENZEL, ELIZABETH. 1992. Research Directions in Virtual Environ-
ments: Report of an NSF Invitational Workshop; 1992 March 23-24; Uni-
versity of North Carolina at Chapel Hill. Available: Send electronic mail
to netlib@cs.unc.edu with the text "get 92-027.ps from techreports". 35p.

BOLT, R.A. 1980. "Put-That-There:" Voice and Gesture at the Graphics
Interface. Computer Graphics and Image Processing. 1980 March; 14(2):
262-270. ISSN: 0146-664X.

BOMAN, SCHLAGER D.; GILLE, J.; PIANTANIDA, T. 1992. The Readiness of
Virtual Environment Technology for Use in Maintenance Training. In:
Proceedings of the 14th Interservice/Industry Training Systems Confer-
ence; 1992 November 2-4; San Antonio, TX. Washington, DC: National
Security Industrial Association; 1992. 883-891. OCLC: 27021751.

BRICKEN, WILLIAM. 1992. Tomorrow's Realities at SIGGRAPH '91. Presence. 1992 Winter; 1(1): 154-156. (Conference review). ISSN: 1054-7460.

BROOKES, BERTRAM C. 1980. The Foundations of Information Science, Part
III. Quantitative Aspects: Objective Maps and Subjective Landscapes.
Journal of Information Science. 1980 December; 2(6): 269-275. ISSN: 0165-
5515.

BROOKS, FREDERICK, JR.; AIREY, JOHN; ALSPAUGH, JOHN; BELL, AN-
DREW; BROWN, RANDOLPH; HILL, CURTIS; NIMSCHECK, UWE;
RHEINGANS, PENNY; ROHLF, JOHN; SMITH, DANA; TURNER,

DOUGLASS; VARSHNEY, AMITABH; WANG, YULAN; WEBER, HANS; YUAN, XIALIN. 1992. Six Generations of Building Walkthrough: Final Technical Report to the National Science Foundation. University of North Carolina at Chapel Hill. Available: Send electronic mail to netlib@cs.unc.edu with the text "get 92-026.ps from techreports". 29p.

BRYSON, STEVE; LEVIT, CREON. 1992. The Virtual Wind Tunnel. IEEE Computer Graphics and Applications. 1992 July; 12(1): 25-34. ISSN: 0272-1716.

BUNCH, STEVE R.; ALSBERG, PETER A. 1977. Computer Communication Networks. In: Williams, Martha E., ed. Annual Review of Information Science and Technology: Volume 12. New York, NY: Knowledge Industry Publications Inc. for the American Society for Information Science; 1977. 183-216. ISSN: 0066-4200; ISBN: 0-914236-11-3.

BURDEA, GRIGORE; LANGRANA, NOSHIR; SILVER, DEBORAH; STONE, ROBERT; DIPAOLO, DENECA M. 1992a. Diagnostic/Rehabilitation System Using Force Measuring and Force Feedback Dextrous Masters. See reference: PLASTIC SURGERY RESEARCH FOUNDATION. 3p. (unpaged).

BURDEA, GRIGORE; ZHUANG, JIACHEN; ROSKOS, EDWARD; SILVER, DEBORAH; LANGRANA, NOSHIR. 1992b. A Portable Dextrous Master with Force Feedback. Presence. 1992 Winter; 1(1): 18-28. ISSN: 1054-7460.

BURTON, HILARY D. 1988a. Use of a Virtual Information System for Bibliometric Analysis. Information Processing & Management. 1988; 24(1): 39-44. ISSN: 0306-4573.

BURTON, HILARY D. 1988b. Virtual Information Systems: Unlimited Resources for Information Retrieval. In: Kinder, Robin; Katz, Bill, eds. Information Brokers and Reference Services. New York, NY: Haworth Press; 1988. 125-131. ISBN: 0-86656-730-5.

BUSH, VANNEVAR. 1945. As We May Think. Atlantic Monthly. 1945 July; 176(1): 101-108. ISSN: 0004-6795.

BUSINESS WEEK. 1992. Business Week. 1992 October 5; (3286): 150p. ISSN: 0007-7135.

BYTE. 1990. Computing without Keyboards. 1990 July; 15(7): 202-252. (Special issue). ISSN: 0360-5280.

CAMPLANI, FABIO. 1993. Dynamic Pattern Recognition: A Recognizer for the Italian Sign Language. (Unpublished Master's thesis). Abstract posted to Usenet newsgroup SCI.VIRTUAL-WORLDS. 1993 February 3. Available (abstract): Anonymous FTP to FTP.WASHINGTON.EDU File: /pub/user-supported/virtual-worlds/postings/1993/Feb_93.tar.Z.

CAPLINGER, MICHAEL. 1986. Graphical Database Browsing. SIGOIS Bulletin. 1986; 7(2/3): 113-121. ISBN: 0-89791-210-1.

CARROLL, PAUL B. 1992. Let the Games Begin. The Wall Street Journal. 1992 April 6; R: 10; col. 1.

CHARLES, STEVE; WILLIAMS, ROY E.; HUNTER, IAN W. 1992. Dexterity Enhancement in Microsurgery Using Telemicrorobotics. See reference: PLASTIC SURGERY RESEARCH FOUNDATION. 1p. (unpaged).

CHEN, DAVID T.; ROSEN, JOSEPH; ZELTZER, DAVID. 1992. Surgical Simulation Models: From Body Parts to Artificial Person. See reference: PLASTIC SURGERY RESEARCH FOUNDATION. 10p. (unpaged).

CHURCHER, P.R. 1989. A Common Notation for Knowledge Representation, Cognitive Models, Learning and Hypertext. Hypermedia. 1989; 1(3): 235-254. ISSN: 0955-8543.

CRAVEN, TIMOTHY C. 1991. Graphic Display of Larger Sentence Dependency Structures. Journal of the American Society for Information Science. 1991; 42(5): 323-331. ISSN: 0002-8231.

CRAVEN, TIMOTHY C. 1992. Three-Dimensional Displays of Concept Relation Structures. Library Science. 1992 March; 29(1): 1-14. ISSN: 0254-2553.

CRUZ-NEIRA, CAROLINA; SANDIN, DANIEL J.; DEFANTI, THOMAS A.; KENYON, ROBERT V.; HART, JOHN C. 1992. The CAVE: Audio Visual Experience Automatic Virtual Environment. Communications of the ACM. 1992 June; 35(6): 64-72. ISSN: 0001-0782.

DAS, H.; ZAK, H.; KIM, W.S.; BEJCZY, ANTAL K.; SCHENKER, P.S. 1992. Operator Performance with Alternative Manual Control Modes in Teleoperation. Presence. 1992 Spring; 1(2): 201-218. ISSN: 1054-7460.

DAVIS, RUTH M. 1966. Man-Machine Communication. In: Cuadra, Carlos A., ed. Annual Review of Information Science and Technology: Volume 1. New York, NY: Interscience Publishers for the American Documentation Institute; 1966. 221-254. LC: 66-25096.

DITLEA, STEVE. 1990. Grand Illusion: Coming Soon to Your Home...Artificial Reality. New York. 1990 August 6; 23(30): 27-34. ISSN: 0028-7369.

DURLACH, NAT. 1991. Auditory Localization in Teleoperator and Virtual Environment Systems: Ideas, Issues, and Problems. Perception. 1991; 20(4): 543-554. ISSN: 0301-0066.

ELSON, BENJAMIN M. 1985. Planners Optimize Pilot/Cockpit Interface in High-Performance Aircraft. Aviation Week & Space Technology. 1985 March 18; 122(11): 257-267. ISSN: 0005-2175.

ENGLISH, WILLIAM K.; ENGELBART, DOUGLAS C.; BERMAN, MELVYN L. 1967. Display Selection Techniques for Text Manipulation. IEEE Transactions on Human Factors in Electronics. 1967 March; HFE-8(1): 5-15. ISSN: 0096-2496.

FAIRCHILD, KIM M.; POLTROCK, STEVEN E.; FURNAS, GEORGE W. 1988. SemNet: Three-Dimensional Graphic Representation of Large Knowledge Bases. In: Guindon, Raymonde, ed. Cognitive Science and Its Applications for Human-Computer Interaction. Hillsdale, NJ: Lawrence Erlbaum; 1988. 202-233. ISBN: 0-89859-884-2.

FISHER, SCOTT S. 1990. Virtual Interface Environments. In: Laurel, Brenda, ed. The Art of Human-Computer Interface Design. Reading, MA: Addison-Wesley Publishing Co., Inc.; 1990. 423-438. ISBN: 0-201-51797-3.

FOLEY, JAMES D.; VAN DAM, ANDRIES. 1990. Computer Graphics: Principles and Practice. Reading, MA: Addison-Wesley Publishing Co., Inc.; 1990. 1174p. ISBN: 0-201-12110-7.

FRIEDHOFF, RICHARD; BENZON, WILLIAM. 1989. Visualization: The Second Computer Revolution. New York, NY: Abrams; 1989. 215p. ISBN: 0-8109-1709-2.

FUCHS, HENRY; LEVOY, MARC; PIZER, STEPHEN M. 1989. Interactive Visualization of Three-Dimensional Medical Data. Computer. 1989 August; 22(8): 46-51. ISSN: 0018-9162.

FURNESS, THOMAS A. 1986. Fantastic Voyage. Popular Mechanics. 1986 December; 163(12): 63-65. ISSN: 0032-4558.

GIBBONS, ANN. 1989. Surgery in Space. Technology Review. 1989 April; 92(3): 9-10. ISSN: 0040-1692.

GIBSON, WILLIAM. 1984. Neuromancer. New York, NY: Ace Books; 1984. 217p. ISBN: 0-441-56958-7.

GRAY, CHRIS HABLES; DRISCOLL, MARK. 1992. What's Real about Virtual Reality? Anthropology of, and in, Cyberspace. Visual Anthropology Review. 1992 Fall; 8(2): 39-49. ISSN: 1053-7147.

GREENLEAF, WALTER J. 1992. DataGlove, DataSuit and VR: Advanced Technology for People with Disabilities. See reference: MURPHY, HARRY J., ed. 21-30.

GROSSER, KERRY. 1991. Human Networks in Organizational Information Processing. In: Williams, Martha E., ed. Annual Review of Information Science and Technology: Volume 26. Medford, NJ: Learned Information, Inc. for the American Society for Information Science; 1991. 349-402. ISSN: 0066-4200; ISBN: 0-938734-55-5.

HALBERT, MARTIN. 1992. Knowbot Explorations in Similarity Space. In: Miller, R. Bruce; Wolf, Milton T., eds. Thinking Robots, an Aware Internet, and Cyberpunk Librarians: The 1992 LITA (Library and Information Technology Association) President's Program. Chicago, IL: American Library Association; 1992. 143-156. ISBN: 0-8389-7625-5.

HARRIS, JESSICA L. 1974. Document Description and Representation. In: Cuadra, Carlos A., ed. Annual Review of Information Science and Technology: Volume 9. Washington, DC: American Society for Information Science; 1974. 81-118. ISBN: 0-87715-209-8.

HEILIG, MORTON. 1992. El Cine del Futuro: The Cinema of the Future. Presence. 1992 Summer; 1(3): 279-294. [Originally appeared as: El Cine del Futuro. Espacios. 1955 January; 23/24: pages unknown. (In Spanish).]

HOLSINGER, ERIC. 1992. Virtual Travel Takes Kiosks to New Dimension. MacWeek. 1992 June 22; 6(25): 36-38.

JACOBSON, LINDA. 1991. Virtual Reality: A Status Report. AI Expert. 1991 August; 6(6): 26-34. ISSN: 0888-3785.

JOLESZ, FERENCA A.; SHTERN, FAINA. 1992. The Operating Room of the Future: Report of the National Cancer Institute Workshop, "Imaging-Guided Stereotactic Tumor Diagnosis and Treatment." Investigative Radiology. 1992 April; 27(4): 326-328. ISSN: 0020-9996.

KRUEGER, MYRON W. 1991. Artificial Reality II. Reading, MA: Addison-Wesley Publishing Co., Inc.; 1991. 286p. ISBN: 0-201-52260-8.

LANCET, THE. 1991. Being and Believing: Ethics of Virtual Reality. The Lancet. 1991 August 3; 338: 283-284. (Editorial). ISSN: 0023-7507.

LANIER, JARON; BIOCCA, FRANK. 1992. An Insider's View of the Future of Virtual Reality. Journal of Communication. 1992 Autumn; 42(4): 150-172. ISSN: 0021-9916.

LAW, J.; WHITTAKER, J. 1992. Mapping Acidification Research: A Test of the Co-Word Method. Scientometrics. 1992 March/April; 23(3): 417-461. ISSN: 0138-9130.

224   GREGORY B. NEWBY

LELU, ALAIN. 1991. From Data Analysis to Neural Networks: New Prospects for Efficient Browsing through Databases. Journal of Information Science. 1991; 17(1): 1-12. ISSN: 0165-5515.

LEO, JOHN. 1991. Gadgetry's Power and Peril. U.S. News & World Report. 1991 April 15; 110(14): 20. ISSN: 0041-5537.

LEXCEN, FRAN. 1992. Updating the Eyegaze Language Board with Software Design. See reference: MURPHY, HARRY J., ed. 305-308.

LICKLIDER, J.C.R. 1968. Man-Computer Communication. In: Cuadra, Carlos A., ed. Annual Review of Information Science and Technology: Volume 3. Chicago, IL: Encyclopaedia Britannica for the American Society for Information Science; 1968. 201-240. LC: 66-24096.

LIU, YILI; WICKENS, CHRISTOPHER D. 1992. Use of Computer Graphics and Cluster Analysis in Aiding Relational Judgment. Human Factors. 1992; 34(2): 165-178. ISSN: 0018-7208.

LUSTED, HUGH S.; KNAPP, R. BENJAMIN. 1992. Biocontrollers: A Direct Link from the Nervous System to Computer. See reference: PLASTIC SURGERY RESEARCH FOUNDATION. 2p. (unpaged).

LYNCH, CLIFFORD A.; PRESTON, CECILIA M. 1990. Internet Access to Information Resources. In: Williams, Martha E., ed. Annual Review of Information Science and Technology: Volume 25. Amsterdam, The Netherlands: Elsevier Science Publishers; 1990. 263-312. ISSN: 0066-4200; ISBN: 0-444-88531-5.

MCCAIN, KATHERINE W. 1990. Mapping Authors in Intellectual Space: A Technical Overview. Journal of the American Society for Information Science. 1990; 41(6): 433-443. ISSN: 0002-8231.

MCDONALD, JAMES E.; SCHVANEVELDT, ROGER W. 1988. The Application of User Knowledge to Interface Design. In: Guindon, Raymonde, ed. Cognitive Science and Its Applications for Human-Computer Interaction. Hillsdale, NJ: Lawrence Erlbaum; 1988. 289-339. ISBN: 0-89859-884-2.

MEINCKE, P.P.M.; ATHERTON, P. 1976. Knowledge Space: A Conceptual Basis for the Organization of Knowledge. Journal of the American Society for Information Science. 1976 January; 27(1): 18-24. ISSN: 0002-8231.

MEYER, KENNETH; APPLEWHITE, HUGH L.; BIOCCA, FRANK A. 1992. A Survey of Position Trackers. Presence. 1992 Spring; 1(2): 173-200. ISSN: 1054-7460.

MICCO, MARY. 1991. The Next Generation of Online Public Access Catalogs: A New Look at Subject Access Using Hypermedia. Cataloging & Classification Quarterly. 1991; 13(3/4): 109-132. ISSN: 0163-9374.

MILLER, CARMEN. 1992. Online Interviews: Dr. Thomas A. Furness III, Virtual Reality Pioneer. Online. 1992 November; 16(6): 14-27. ISSN: 0146-5422.

MILLER, GEORGE A. 1968. Psychology and Information. American Documentation. 1968 July; 19(3): 286-289.

MURPHY, HARRY J., ed. 1992. Persons with Disabilities: Proceedings of the 7th Annual Conference; 1992 March 18-20; Los Angeles, CA. Northridge, CA: California State University; 1992. 657p. Available from: Office of Disabled Student Services, California State University, Northridge, 18111 Nordhoff Street - DVSS, Northridge, CA 91330.

NELSON, TED. 1980. Interactive Systems and the Design of Virtuality: The Design of Interactive Systems, Tomorrow's Crucial Art Form, Rests on New Philosophical Principles. Creative Computing. 1980 November/December; 6(11/12): 56-62, 94-106. ISSN: 0097-8140.

NEWBY, GREGORY B. 1992a. Information Technology as the Paradigm High-Speed Management Support Tool: The Uses of Computer Mediated Communication, Virtual Realism, and Telepresence. Paper presented at: the Annual Conference of the Speech Communication Association; 1992 October 29-31: Chicago, IL. 13p. Available from: the author, University of Illinois, 410 David Kinley Hall, 1407 W. Gregory, Urbana, IL 61801.

NEWBY, GREGORY B. 1992b. An Investigation of the Role of Navigation for Information Retrieval. In: Shaw, Debora, ed. Proceedings of the American Society for Information Science (ASIS) 55th Annual Meeting: Volume 29; 1992 October 26-29; Pittsburgh, PA. Medford, NJ: Learned Information, Inc.; 1992. 20-25. ISSN: 0044-7870; ISBN: 0-938734-69-5.

NIELSON, GREGORY M. 1991. Visualization in Scientific and Engineering Computing. Computer. 1991 September; 24(9): 58-66. ISSN: 0018-9162.

NILAN, MICHAEL S. 1992. Cognitive Space: Using Virtual Reality for Large Information Resource Management Problems. Journal of Communication. 1992 Autumn; 42(4): 115-135. ISSN: 0021-9916.

NUGENT, WILLIAM R. 1991. Virtual Reality: Advanced Imaging Special Effects Let You Roam in Cyberspace. Journal of the American Society for Information Science. 1991 September; 42(8): 609-617. ISSN: 0002-8231.

PARTRIDGE, MICHAEL; HUNTLEY, JOAN. 1992. FluxBase: An Interactive Art Exhibition. Visible Language. 1992; 26(1/2): 221-227. ISSN: 0022-2224.

PAUSCH, RANDY. 1991. Virtual Reality on Five Dollars a Day. Robertson, S.P.; Olson, G.M.; Olson, J.S., eds. Human Factors in Computing Systems: Reaching through Technology: CHI '91 Conference Proceedings; 1991 April 27-May 2; New Orleans, LA. New York, NY: Association for Computing Machinery; 1991. 265-270. ISBN: 0-89791-383-3.

PAUSCH, RANDY; VOGTLE, LAURA; CONWAY, MATTHEW. 1992. One Dimensional Motion Tailoring for the Disabled: A User Study. In: Baversfeld, Penny; Bennett, John; Lynch, Gene, eds. Human Factors in Computing Systems: CHI '92 Conference Proceedings; 1992 May 3-7; Monterey, CA. New York, NY: Association for Computing Machinery; 1992. 405-412. ISBN: 0-89791-513-5 (pbk); ISBN: 0-89791-514-3 (hbk).

PAUSCH, RANDY; WILLIAMS, RONALD D. 1992. Giving CANDY to Children: User-Tailored Gesture Input Driving an Articulator-Based Speech Synthesizer. Communications of the ACM. 1992; 35(5): 58-66. ISSN: 0001-0782.

PLASTIC SURGERY RESEARCH FOUNDATION. 1992. Medicine Meets Virtual Reality: Discovering Applications for 3-D Multi-Media Interactive Technology in the Health Sciences: A Symposium Sponsored by the Plastic Surgery Research Foundation and the University of California, San Diego, Office of Continuing Medical Education; 1992 June 4-7; San Diego, CA. 1 volume (unpaged). Available from: Aligned Management Associates, P.O. Box 23220, San Diego, CA 92193.

POULTER, ALAN. 1993. Towards a Virtual Reality Library. Aslib Proceedings. 1993; 45(1): 11-17. ISSN: 0001-253X.

PRUITT, STEVE; BARRETT, TOM. 1992. Corporate Virtual Workspaces. In:
Benedikt, Michael, ed. Cyberspace: First Steps. Cambridge, MA: MIT
Press; 1992. 383-409. ISBN: 0-262-52177-6 (pbk); ISBN: 0-262-02327-X
(hbk).

RAGHAVAN, VIJAY V.; WONG, S.K.M. 1986. A Critical Analysis of Vector
Space Model [sic] for Information Retrieval. Journal of the American
Society for Information Science. 1986; 37(5): 279-287. ISSN: 0002-8231.

RHEINGOLD, HOWARD. 1991. Virtual Reality. New York, NY: Summit
Books; 1991. 416p. ISBN: 0-671-69363-8.

RICHMOND, PHYLLIS A. 1972. Document Description and Representation.
In: Cuadra, Carlos A., ed. Annual Review of Information Science and
Technology: Volume 7. Washington, DC: American Society for Informa-
tion Science; 1972. 73-102. ISSN: 0066-4200; ISBN: 0-87715-206-3.

RICHMOND, PHYLLIS A.; WILLIAMSON, NANCY J. 1979. Three-Dimensional Physical Models in Classification. In: Neelameghan, A., ed. Ordering Systems for Global Information Networks: Proceedings of the 3rd
International Study Conference on Classification Research; 1975 January 6-
11; Bombay, India. Bangalore, India: FID/CR; Sarada Ranganathan En-
dowment for Library Science; 1979. 188-203. LC: 80-482597.

ROBERTS, LAWRENCE G. 1966. The Lincoln Wand. AFIPS Conference
Proceedings Fall Joint Computer Conference: Volume 29; 1966 November
7-10; San Francisco, CA. Washington, DC: Spartan Books; 1966 Fall. 223-
227. LC: 55-44701.

ROBERTSON, PHILIP K. 1991. A Methodology for Choosing Data Representations. IEEE Computer Graphics & Applications. 1991 May; 11(3): 56-67.
ISSN: 0272-1716.

ROBINETT, WARREN; ROLLAND, JANNICK P. 1992. A Computational
Model for the Stereoscopic Optics of a Head-Mounted Display. Presence.
1992 Winter; 1(1): 45-62. ISSN: 1054-7460.

ROLLING, L. 1965. The Role of Graphic Display of Concept Relationships in
Indexing and Retrieval Vocabularies. In: Atherton, Pauline, ed. Classification Research: Proceedings of the 2nd International Study Conference;
1964 September 14-18; Elsinore, Denmark. Copenhagen, Denmark:
Munksgaard; 1965. 295-321. LC: 65-24483.

ROMKEY, JOHN. 1991. Whither Cyberspace? Journal of the American Society
for Information Science. 1991 September; 42(8): 618-620. ISSN: 0002-8231.

RORVIG, MARK E. 1988. Psychometric Measurement and Information Retrieval. In: Williams, Martha E., ed. Annual Review of Information Science
and Technology: Volume 23. Amsterdam, The Netherlands: Elsevier Science Publishers for the American Society for Information Science; 1988.
157-189. ISSN: 0066-4200; ISBN: 0-444-70543-0.

ROSE, DANIEL E.; BELEW, RICHARD K. 1991a. A Connection and Symbolic
Hybrid for Improving Legal Research. International Journal of Man-
Machine Studies. 1991 July; 35(1): 1-33. ISSN: 0020-7373.

ROSE, DANIEL E.; BELEW, RICHARD K. 1991b. Toward a Direct-Manipulation Interface for Conceptual Information Retrieval Systems. In: Dillon,
Martin, ed. Interfaces for Information Retrieval and Online Systems: The

State of the Art. New York, NY: Greenwood Press; 1991. 39-54. ISBN: 0-313-27494-0; LC: 91-8240.

RUBINE, DEAN. 1991. The Automatic Recognition of Gestures. Pittsburgh, PA: Carnegie-Mellon University; 1991. 286p. (Ph.D. dissertation). Available from: University Microfilms International, Ann Arbor, MI. (UMI order no. AAD92-16029).

RUCKER, RUDY; MU, QUEEN; SIRIUS, R.U. 1992. Mondo 2000: A User's Guide to the New Edge. New York, NY: HarperCollins; 1992. 317p. ISBN: 0-06-096928-8.

SALTON, GERARD; MCGILL, MICHAEL J. 1983. Introduction to Modern Information Retrieval. New York, NY: McGraw-Hill; 1983. 448p. ISBN: 0-07-054484-0.

SCI.VIRTUAL-WORLDS. 1990-. (Usenet newsgroup). Available (archives): Anonymous FTP to FTP.WASHINGTON.EDU. Directory: /pub/virtual-worlds/postings.

SCIENTIFIC AMERICAN. 1993. Surreal Science: Virtual Reality Finds a Place in the Classroom. Scientific American. 1993 February; 268(2): 103. ISSN: 0036-8733.

SHAFFER, CLIFFORD A. 1992. Data Representation for Geographic Information Systems. In: Williams, Martha E., ed. Annual Review of Information Science and Technology: Volume 27. Medford, NJ: Learned Information, Inc. for the American Society for Information Science; 1992. 135-172. ISSN: 0066-4200; ISBN: 0-938734-55-5.

SHAPIRO, MICHAEL A.; MCDONALD, DANIEL G. 1992. I'm Not a Real Doctor But I Play One in Virtual Reality: Implications of Virtual Reality for Judgments about Reality. Journal of Communication. 1992 Autumn; 42(4): 94-114. ISSN: 0021-9916.

SHAW, DEBORA. 1991. The Human-Computer Interface for Information Retrieval. In: Williams, Martha E., ed. Annual Review of Information Science and Technology: Volume 26. Medford, NJ: Learned Information, Inc. for the American Society for Information Science; 1991. 155-195. ISSN: 0066-4200; ISBN: 0-938734-55-5.

SHEROUSE, GEORGE W.; BOURLAND, DANIEL; REYNOLDS, KEVIN; MCMURRY, HARRIS L.; MITCHELL, THOMAS P.; CHANEY, EDWARD L. 1990. Virtual Simulation in the Clinical Setting: Some Practical Considerations. International Journal of Radiation: Oncology, Biology, Physics. 1990 October; 19(4): 1059-1065. ISSN: 0360-3016.

SHEROUSE, GEORGE W.; CHANEY, EDWARD L. 1991. The Portable Virtual Simulator. International Journal of Radiation: Oncology, Biology, Physics. 1991; 21(2): 475-482. ISSN: 0360-3016.

SHNEIDERMAN, BEN. 1983. Direct Manipulation: A Step beyond Programming Languages. Computer. 1983 August; 16(8): 57-69. ISSN: 0018-9162.

SHUM, SIMON. 1990. Real and Virtual Spaces: Mapping from Spatial Cognition to Hypertext. Hypermedia. 1990; 2(2): 133-158. ISSN: 0955-8543.

SPRING, MICHAEL B. 1992. Informating with Virtual Reality. In: Helsel, Sandra K.; Roth, Judith Paris, eds. Virtual Reality: Theory, Practice, and Promise. Westport, CT: Meckler; 1992. 3-19. ISBN: 0-88736-728-3.

SUTHERLAND, IVAN E. 1965. The Ultimate Display. In: Kalenich, Wayne A., ed. Information Processing 1965: Proceedings of the IFIP Congress: Volume 2; 1965 May 24-29; New York, NY. Washington, DC: Spartan Books; 1965. 506-508. LC: 65-24118.

SUTHERLAND, IVAN E. 1968. A Head-Mounted Three Dimensional Display. AFIPS Conference Proceedings Fall Joint Computer Conference: Volume 33; 1968 December 9-11; San Francisco, CA. Washington, DC: Thompson Book Co.; 1968 Fall. 757-764. LC: 55-44701.

SUTHERLAND, IVAN E. 1980. Sketchpad: A Man-Machine Graphical Communication System. New York, NY: Garland Publishers; 1980. 176p. (Originally published as the author's thesis, Massachusetts Institute of Technology, 1963). ISBN: 0-8240-4411-8.

TENDICK, FRANK; JENNINGS, RUSSELL; THARP, GREGORY; STARK, LAWRENCE. 1992. Experimental Analysis of Problems in Perception and Manipulation in Endoscopic Surgery. See reference: PLASTIC SURGERY RESEARCH FOUNDATION. 3p. (unpaged).

THOMPSON, JEREMY. 1993. Virtual Reality R&D: A Directory of Research Projects. Westport, CT: Meckler; 1993 (in press). ISBN: 0-88736-862-X.

TURTLE, HOWARD; PENNIMAN, DAVID W.; HICKEY, THOMAS B. 1981. Data Entry/Display Devices for Interactive Information Retrieval. In: Williams, Martha E., ed. Annual Review of Information Science and Technology: Volume 16. White Plains, NY: Knowledge Industry Publications Inc. for the American Society for Information Science; 1981. 55-83. ISSN: 0066-4200; ISBN: 0-914236-90-3.

U.S. CONGRESS. 102ND CONGRESS, 1ST SESSION. 1991. To Provide for a Coordinated Federal Program to Ensure Continued United States Leadership in High-Performance Computing: Public Law 102-194, 102nd Congress, 1st Session. United States Statutes at Large. 1991; 105: 1594-1604. Washington, DC: Government Printing Office; 1992. (High-Performance Computing Act of 1991).

UNIVERSITY OF TEXAS AT AUSTIN. 1990. Collected Abstracts from the 1st Conference on Cyberspace; 1990 May 4-5; Austin, TX. Austin, TX: The University of Texas at Austin; 1990. 111p. Available from: School of Architecture, The University of Texas at Austin, Austin, TX 78712.

URDANG, ERIK G.; STUART, RORY. 1992. Orientation Enhancement through Integrated Virtual Reality and Geographic Information Systems. See reference: MURPHY, HARRY J., ed. 55-61.

VAMPLEW, PETER; ADAMS, ANTHONY. 1992. The SLARTI System: Applying Artificial Neural Networks to Sign Language Recognition. See reference: MURPHY, HARRY J., ed. 71-80.

VICKERY, BRIAN C. 1971. Document Description and Representation. In: Cuadra, Carlos A., ed. Annual Review of Information Science and Technology: Volume 6. Chicago, IL: Encyclopaedia Britannica Inc. for the American Society for Information Science; 1971. 113-140. ISSN: 0066-4200.

VIGIL, PETER J. 1986. The Software Interface. In: Williams, Martha E., ed. Annual Review of Information Science and Technology: Volume 21. White Plains, NY: Knowledge Industry Publications, Inc. for the American Society for Information Science; 1986. 63-86. ISSN: 0066-4200; ISBN: 0-86729-209-1.

WEISNER, MARK. 1991. The Computer for the 21st Century. Scientific American. 1991 September; 265(3): 94-104. ISSN: 0036-8733.

WENZEL, ELIZABETH M. 1992. Localization in Virtual Acoustic Displays. Presence. 1992 Winter; 1(1): 80-107. ISSN: 1054-7460.

WESTIN, ALAN F.; FINGER, ANNE L. 1991. Using the Public Library in the Computer Age: Present Patterns, Future Possibilities. Chicago, IL: American Library Association; 1991. 70p. ISBN: 0-8389-0565-X.

WHITE, HOWARD D.; MCCAIN, KATHERINE W. 1989. Bibliometrics. In: Williams, Martha E., ed. Annual Review of Information Science and Technology: Volume 24. Amsterdam, The Netherlands: Elsevier Science Publishers for the American Society for Information Science; 1989. 119-186. ISSN: 0066-4200; ISBN: 0-444-87418-6.

ZIMMERMAN, THOMAS G.; LANIER, JARON; BLANCHARD, CHUCK; BRYSON, STEVE; HARVILL, YOUNG. 1987. A Hand Gesture Interface Device. In: Carroll, John M.; Tanner, Peter P., eds. Human Factors in Computing Systems and Graphics Interface: CHI + GI Conference Proceedings; 1987 April 5-9; Toronto, Canada. New York, NY: Association for Computing Machinery; 1987. 189-192. ISBN: 0-89791-213-6.

6 Browsing: A Multidimensional Framework

SHAN-JU CHANG and RONALD E. RICE
Rutgers University

INTRODUCTION

The ultimate goal of information systems and services has been to serve human needs for information and to facilitate the processes of information seeking, retrieval, and use. To this end, much recent research has addressed the concern for better understanding of human information behavior from the user's point of view (DERVIN & NILAN; HEWINS; KUHLTHAU).

A commonly observed form of human information behavior is browsing. According to *Webster's Third New International Dictionary* (MERRIAM-WEBSTER, INCORPORATED, p. 285), to browse is:

1. To look over casually (as a book): SKIM / he lazily browsed the headlines;
2. To skim through a book reading at random passages that catch the eye;
3. To look over books (as in a store or library) especially in order to decide what one wants to buy, borrow, or read;
4. To casually inspect goods offered for sale usually without prior or serious intention of buying;

We thank Nick Belkin for his support of this work; Marcia Bates, Gary Marchionini, and Barbara Kwasnik for their challenging discussion with us on browsing; and the *ARIST* reviewers for their useful suggestions.

Annual Review of Information Science and Technology (ARIST), Volume 28, 1993
Martha E. Williams, Editor
Published for the American Society for Information Science (ASIS)
By Learned Information, Inc., Medford, N.J.

5. To make an examination without real knowledge or purpose;
6. Browsing room: a room or section in a library designed to
   allow patrons an opportunity to freely examine and browse
   in a collection of books.

Although browsing has been observed and investigated in the general context of information seeking in the library (AYRIS; HYMAN,
1972) and has increasingly assumed an important and integral part in
human and machine interaction (ODDY & BALAKRISHNAN; TH-
OMPSON & CROFT), the concept and nature of browsing have not
been systematically studied and thus are not well understood.

In an attempt to make explicit and synthesize different concepts of
browsing, this chapter first notes several outstanding problems concerning browsing. Then it summarizes various notions of browsing and
relevant research from six disciplines, which are then integrated into a
multidimensional concept of browsing. The tentative model suggests
that several contextual factors affect other influences on browsing, the
process of browsing, and the consequences of browsing. Further, aspects of the resource and of the browser's motivation and cognition all
can influence the process of browsing. The browsing process itself can
be characterized by behavioral, motivational, and cognitive dimensions. Browsing can have various consequences. Finally, both process
and consequences can affect subsequent contexts, influences, and processes, establishing the iterative nature of browsing.

With respect to the style of this chapter, in many cases we provide
only a few of all the examples associated with a particular author's
points or suggestions (i.e., we might list only two or four of the six
categories described by the author). Further, the several authors listed
after a general statement are typically useful sources for discussions on
the topic, whether as advocates or critics of the general claim.

PROBLEMS AND ISSUES IN BROWSING

Browsing is common but not well understood. We all browse in
various contexts to make sense of the world around us, such as when
we read newspapers, scan television channels, go window shopping, or
seek information in libraries. Various forms of browsing are considered
in a wide variety of literatures, although they often focus on a specific
resource or context. However, there is little systematic, multidisciplinary,
conceptually explicit study of the concept and nature of browsing.

Browsing and searching are often treated as discrete activities, one
purposeful and the other casual or "random." However, HERNER
states that "much of what we call 'searching' is, upon dissection, prima-

rily browsing" (p. 414), and BATES (1989) argues that browsing is integrated into many forms of searching. Yet we do not have a good vocabulary to describe and discuss various forms or degrees of browsing. Indeed, when authors do attempt to compare browsing and searching, they tend to distinguish browsing in four general ways: (1) as integrated with but not identical to searching (BATES, 1989); (2) as equivalent to searching (see the section on end-user information retrieval); (3) as a subset of searching but distinct from "nonbrowsing" (BATLEY); and (4) as the extremes of multiple overlapping and continuous dimensions of information behavior (CHANG).

Historically, library and information science as well as information systems literatures exhibit biases toward specific, direct searching as opposed to exploratory, iterative browsing (for critiques of this bias, see AYRIS, BATES (1986a; 1989), HILDRETH (1989), HYMAN (1972), and TUORI). This bias is partly due to some unrealistic assumptions about users and the nature of information seeking—e.g., that users have unbounded rationality, have static and well-defined information needs, know what they want, and are output oriented (KATZER; ROBERTS). However, users are often in an anomalous state of knowledge as they initiate a search (BELKIN ET AL., 1982), do not have predefined search criteria, and may alter their interests during a search (BATES, 1989; HILDRETH, 1982).

Computer technologies, multimedia databases, and the growth of end-user searching raise new challenges for understanding and supporting browsing. It is well recognized that a system-oriented approach and the "exact-match" principle in information retrieval are problematic (BATES, 1986a; 1990). Many end-user systems are difficult to use because they require training, knowledge of mechanical and conceptual aspects of searching, and a high cognitive load from end users (BORGMAN, 1986; MARCHIONINI); all of these may be somewhat overcome through browsing (BORGMAN ET AL., 1993; TUORI). BATLEY argues that some types of information, such as pictures, are apt to be browsed because the wide interpretability of their meaning makes searching by specification more difficult. New interactive systems will need to support various search strategies, including browsing (e.g., BATES, 1990; ELLIS). As such, new criteria may be needed to account for a system's "browsability," an emerging issue in system evaluation (THOMPSON & CROFT).

All the above issues call for a multidisciplinary approach for a better understanding of the concept of browsing, the contexts in which browsing occurs, influences on browsing, the functions that browsing serves, and the consequences of browsing.

It is our belief that an understanding of general human processes, such as browsing, requires insights and perspectives from a variety of disciplines. Limiting the study of browsing to just those concepts, literature, and results from library and information science research, for example, will reinforce the limited and ambiguous focus on browsing noted above. On the one hand, issues or concepts that reappear across disciplines encourage confidence that these are relevant for understanding browsing; on the other, unique or contradictory results may cause us to reevaluate and challenge our own disciplinary presumptions. For that reason, we consider how six different disciplines treat browsing (or related concepts): (1) library and information science, (2) end-user information retrieval and system design, (3) consumer behavior, (4) mass media audiences, (5) organizational communication, and (6) wayfinding and environmental design. Other disciplinary approaches, such as cognitive psychology, acoustics, or graphic design may also provide useful insights and relevant questions.

DISCIPLINARY APPROACHES

The next sections summarize how the literatures of six disciplines relate to three generic research questions about browsing: (1) what browsing is; (2) what the factors are that influence the extent to which people engage in browsing; and (3) what the consequences of browsing are (for a more comprehensive review, see CHANG).

Library and Information Science

While linguistic origins of the word "browse" stem from French or Middle-High German, and refer to animals' nibbling on grass or shoots, one of the earliest references to browsing in relation to reading appeared in the 1823 *Oxford English Dictionary* (see HYMAN, 1972). The notion of browsing in the library community was involved in the discussion of collection-management policy (closed vs. open stacks) in the 1930s, referred to as "a patron's random examination of library materials as arranged for use" (HYMAN, 1972, p. 11).

Browsing as a specific subject for research in the library literature was emphasized in Project Intrex in the mid-1960s, when experiments on browsing were suggested to find out how a university library system might support browsing to foster unplanned discovery through planned facilities (OVERHAGE & HARMAN). Since then, browsing has been related to direct access to shelves in the library (HYMAN, 1972), collection and space management (BOLL; LAWRENCE & OJA), serendipitous findings or creativity (BANKAPUR; BAWDEN; CELORIA; DAVIES; O'CONNOR, 1988; SWANSON, 1987, 1989), search strategies (BATES, 1981, 1989; ELLIS), and exposure by researchers to identify and monitor information resources (BAWDEN; ELLIS; LARSEN;

MENZEL; O'CONNOR, 1993). It has also been related to improving the organization and provision of information via shelf classification (BAKER, 1988), display arrangement (BAKER, 1986a; 1986b), and online public access catalogs (OPACs) (AKEROYD; HANCOCK-BEAULIEU; HILDRETH, 1982).

Two major prior reviews on browsing in libraries (primarily shelf browsing) are by HYMAN (1972) and AYRIS. According to Ayris, the literature before 1972 shows great uncertainty concerning all aspects of browsing, including its definition, importance, practice, and intellectual value. Ayris's review indicates that research has progressed from 1972 to 1985 in recognizing the importance of browsing in both academic and public libraries, although the literature is still often divided on these issues, a division that stems from an inconsistency in the conceptions of browsing.

What is browsing? Browsing has been defined in many ways (APTED; BANKAPUR; BUCKLAND; HERNER; LARSEN; O'CONNOR, 1988; OVERHAGE & HARMAN, p. 119). Many descriptions portray it as an activity that is not task oriented. Terms such as "informal," "unsystematic," "unprogrammed," "casual," and "without design" refer to the unplanned nature of browsing and the lack of a specific plan of action for conducting an information search or reaching a goal, if, indeed, one is present. Elsewhere, however, the terms "formal" and "systematic" in the library literature imply a planned, task-oriented course or a form of subject access (often involving bibliographic tools) for a search (ELLIS; HILDRETH, 1982; O'CONNOR, 1988; OVERHAGE & HARMAN, p. 119). Browsing can thus be both goal directed and nongoal directed and "unplanned" rather than simply aimless.

Browsing has been loosely described as a kind of searching, in which the initial search criteria or goals are only partly defined or known in advance. Three degrees of goal orientation in browsing have been suggested (COVE & WALSH, 1987; see also APTED, HERNER, HILDRETH (1982), and LEVINE for similar categories): (1) search browsing (directed browsing, or specific, goal-oriented browsing): a closely directed and structured activity in which the desired goal is known; (2) general-purpose browsing (semidirected, predictive browsing, or purposive browsing): an activity of consulting specified sources regularly because they probably contain items of interest; and (3) serendipity browsing (undirected, not goal-oriented browsing): a purely random, unstructured, and undirected activity. One can move from one type of browsing to another in a single information-seeking episode (BELKIN ET AL., 1993), or one can engage in multiple types of browsing at the same time. These categories are mainly content oriented, "directed" in terms of knowing what to look for. However, it is conceivable that one knows what to look for but does not know how to look for it. Browsing in this situation may appear to be undirected but is not.

Thus, the searcher's knowledge of paths leading to the item can also be an important factor in distinguishing one type of browsing from another (MICHEL). Considering browsing as moving from where to what as opposed to moving from what to where as in searching, ZOELLICK describes four different browsing methods with this distinction in mind: (1) sequential browsing (moving to the next or previous document in a collection), (2) structural browsing (moving between parts of a document according to the structure of that document, such as by book chapter), (3) keyed-access browsing (using some type of access key to move between documents, such as a keyword index), and (4) linked browsing (following explicit links within or between documents, such as citation trails).

BATES (1989) argues that browsing and searching, although separate activities, occur in an integrated fashion. She describes six widely used search strategies that are associated with browsing: (1) journal run, (2) area scanning, (3) subject searches in bibliographies and abstracting and indexing, (4) author searching, (5) citation searching, and (6) footnote chasing. Both of these discussions, however, imply that browsing may involve either the content and/or the search path of the information resource and that particular conceptualizations of browsing are not yet explicit or dominant enough to guide general research.

Based on the assumption that browsing may be specific to a medium, types of browsing have also been grouped according to resource type— e.g., shelf browsing, catalog browsing, vocabulary browsing, full-text browsing, and computer browsing (AYRIS; OVERHAGE & HARMAN). However, it may not be the medium per se but the context's display and structure (or, more generally, the interface) that affects the type of browsing done (RICE).

O'Connor (1993) proposes that various strategies for browsing can each be identified with one of the sorts of internal representations of an anomalous state of knowledge that a scholar might bring to a collection. He describes four sorts of browsing activity: (1) expansion, (2) vague awareness, (3) monitoring the information environment, and (4) creativity; he discusses these in terms of the point in the collection at which browsing starts, sampling size, which attributes of the document are considered, which attributes of the scholar are engaged, and the sort of comparison made between the document attributes and the scholar attributes.

Although methodologies and definitions used may vary, empirical studies show that browsing occurs frequently in academic libraries (GREENE), that one-third of the books obtained from the shelves are not specifically sought, and that browsers do not see themselves as having a well-articulated need for the material (LAWRENCE & OJA).

Browsing is an important way of selecting fiction and nonfiction books by public library patrons in several studies (AYRIS), and only about one-fifth of shelf browsing progresses in a linear forward fashion (HANCOCK-BEAULIEU). Further, browsing may serve three functions: (1) identification, (2) familiarization, and (3) differentiation (ELLIS).

Four prominent dimensions of browsing seem to emerge from this literature: (1) scanning, (2) intention, (3) goal, and (4) knowledge. Browsing involves scanning, which has been variously described as looking, examining, or sampling, during which the person's body or eyes move smoothly at will (MORSE, 1973; O'CONNOR, 1993). Although BATES (1989) contends that browsing is usually associated with a sense of random visual movement, it could be either directed or undirected according to the different forms of browsing; thus, while movement is an essential characteristic of browsing, randomness is not. In seeking information, browsing acquires the meaning of a purposeful act characterized by the presence of an intention, regardless of how vague it is, which suggests that browsing cannot be adequately described by behavioral characteristics alone. Browsing varies according to the specificity of search criteria or goal, if any, imposed on the object sought: specific, ill defined, and undefined. The browser's prior knowledge about and experience with the resource (concerning both search paths and content) are important aspects of browsing.

What influences browsing? MARCHIONINI and others suggest four factors that influence different types of browsing techniques. The first factor concerns the object sought, which may be well or ill defined. Further, objects may be distinguished as the item itself (such as a material good or a book) or representations (surrogates, such as indexes). Note, however, that browsing does not have to be visual (consider aural browsing of radio channels) (LEVINE). By implication, electronic representations should probably include multimedia information to compensate for the decreased accessibility of representations compared with objects (O'CONNOR, 1985). The second factor relates to individual searcher characteristics. These include experience and knowledge about objects sought, motivation, purpose, learning patterns, and cognitive style (ALLINSON & HAMMOND; BORGMAN, 1989; BORGMAN ET AL., 1991). The third factor is the purpose of the search, which may include pleasure, fact retrieval, concept formation, interpretation, evaluation of ideas, and keeping abreast of developments in a field (MARCHIONINI). The final factor is the context for conducting the search. Some contextual factors that can influence the extent and type of browsing include collection size, subject divisions, subject discipline, work activity, type of medium, nature of text, display, interfiling of different media or size, vocabulary control and organizational scheme (cataloging, classification and subject arrangement) (AYRIS).

What are the consequences of browsing?   Past debates on the value of browsing in the library community often centered around judgments about the "intellectual purposefulness" or educational value of such a "random" activity (HYMAN, 1972). Potential consequences of browsing include serendipity (an accidental fortuitous discovery) (AYRIS; BAWDEN; ELLIS), modification of information requirements (HILDRETH, 1982; LANCASTER, 1968; MARCHIONINI ET AL.; ODDY), valuable learning experiences (HYMAN, 1971; 1972), and unreliable or inefficient use of resources (BOLL; GREENE).

Although there are controversies on the value of browsing, some library researchers in the past decade argue strongly that browsing is an important part of information seeking, which is exploratory and is better characterized as an incremental process, and browsing may be one way to cope with the constraints of formal bibliographic systems (BATES, 1986a, 1989; ELLIS; HILDRETH, 1982, 1989; LARSEN; O'CONNOR, 1988, 1993; SWANSON, 1987, 1989). On the other hand, although earlier literature expressed serious doubts about the feasibility of browsing in computer systems, partly due to hardware and software constraints, research on browsing has focused on and contributed to improving the "browsability" of OPACs, a point discussed below.

End-User Information Retrieval and System Design

In the information retrieval (IR) community, the notion of browsing originated as a task-oriented, problem-solving technique to cope with IR problems arising from the traditional query-based, command-driven computer interface. Browsing has been proposed as an alternative approach to IR that does not use Boolean operations or require specific search queries (ODDY; THOMPSON & CROFT). For instance, a distinction has been made between the analytic search and the browse search (LIEBSCHER & MARCHIONINI), between preplanned (e.g., consulting thesauri before search) or systematically iterated queries involving Boolean operators, and "an exploratory, information seeking strategy that depends on serendipity" (MARCHIONINI & SHNEIDERMAN, p. 71).

Browsing has become an important heuristic search strategy to be used in situations such as when the user does not look for anything specific or is unable to specify initial search requirements or is unfamiliar with the terminology of a domain of interest, or when he or she wishes to discover the general information content of the database (CUTTING ET AL.; PEJTERSEN; THOMPSON & CROFT). As a response to the difficulty in query formulation and terminological issues, earlier browsing capabilities in IR systems, especially the OPAC systems, generally fall into two categories (HILDRETH, 1982). One category is related to term selection (e.g., displaying a list of thesaurus or index terms for exploration) or vocabulary browsing (MARKEY & ATHERTON; WALKER); the other is related to result manipulation and display (e.g., showing a set of references or documents according to the user's specifications). In this human–computer interaction context, the concept of browsing is closely related to subject searching and relevance judgment. Some techniques have been proposed to facilitate browsing, including improving display structure of subject headings and classification schemes (DRABENSTOTT ET AL.; HUESTIS; MARKEY) and facilitating relevance judgment of the results via various feedback processes and clustering techniques (CUTTING ET AL.; ODDY; THOMPSON & CROFT).

Studies of browsing in computer-based systems have centered on identification of search techniques used in IR and hypertext systems (AKEROYD; BATES, 1986a, 1990; BELKIN ET AL., 1993; CANTER ET AL.; CARMEL ET AL.; ZOELLICK), disorientation in electronic environments (FOSS; MCALEESE; SODERSTON), and issues of information overload in electronic messaging systems (HILTZ & TUROFF; MALONE ET AL.). Differences between the use of printed materials and their electronic counterparts have been investigated to increase the "browsability" of a system and to devise better techniques for representing and organizing information (EGAN ET AL., 1991; MARCHIONINI & LIEBSCHER). The ultimate goal of this line of research is to facilitate effective, successful communication and information retrieval by supporting various search strategies and task requirements.

What is browsing? In the end-user IR systems literature, browsing typically means scanning a resource, and it is characterized by the presence of a goal but no well-planned search strategy, with ill-defined search criteria at the beginning of the interaction with the resource, which depend somewhat on the user's knowledge of the content and search path of the resource (ALLINSON & HAMMOND; BELKIN ET AL., 1993; COVE & WALSH, 1988; GECSEI & MARTIN; TUORI). Contents can be representations (e.g., catalogs), real objects (books, neckties), or multimedia objects.

Browsing has been associated with visual recognition and spatial reasoning as opposed to linguistic specification and logical reasoning (HULLEY; ODDY & BALAKRISHNAN; TUORI). It is an interactive, exploratory process that has a strong learning component (CARMEL ET AL.; SHNEIDERMAN ET AL.). GECSEI & MARTIN suggest that when people browse, they learn the structure and content of a database. COVE & WALSH (1988) contend that browsing is the art of not knowing what one wants until one finds it, implying that recognition is an important aspect of browsing. Similarly, in an attack on the traditional output-oriented IR paradigm, HILDRETH (1989) calls for an emphasis on a process-oriented paradigm that manifests such a learning effect.

With the development and applications of hypertext technology, browsing capabilities have been recognized as one of the central features of hypertext systems, which allow nonlinear organization of text (increasingly also multimedia files) through machine-supported links within and between documents in the database (CONKLIN). Conklin describes how a hypertext database can be explored by following links and opening windows successively to examine their contents, by searching the network (or part of it) for some string, keyword, or attribute value, and by navigating around the hyperdocument using a browser that displays the network graphically (CONKLIN & BEGEMAN). Note that no distinction is made between browsing and searching strategies in this context because browsing is usually the only way to find information in hypertext systems (THOMPSON & CROFT).

Two approaches to classifying browsing can be identified in the hypertext literature: (1) path- vs. content-based browsing; (2) facility- or function-based browsing.

CANTER ET AL. derive a taxonomy of browsing strategies based on the path and/or content focus used by hypermedia users. These strategies include: (1) scanning (covering a large area superficially), (2) browsing (following a path until a goal is achieved), (3) searching (striving to find an explicit goal), (4) exploring (determining the extent of the information given), and (5) wandering (purposeless and unstructured globetrotting). "Exploring," for example, is high in content focus but low in path focus.

In a different approach, CARMEL ET AL. identify a three-level browsing typology; the associated functions of each level are based on the characteristics of users' cognitive processes in performing both closed and open tasks in a hypertext system. The three levels are: (1) search-oriented browse, (2) review-browse, and (3) scan-browse. The first two categories correspond to Canter et al.'s searching and browsing, while the last category refers to exploring and scanning. However, Carmel et al. found that most users adopted review-browse, which is characterized by "scanning and reviewing interesting information in presence of transient browse goals that represent changing tasks," with an emphasis on the evaluation and integration components in such a browsing process (p. 865).

The notion of browsing in the sense of recognition-based, direct exposure to information resources has led to a concern with designing effective browsing capabilities. In a study of a hypertext-learning support system, ALLINSON & HAMMOND found that four major navigation tools were used differently for various types of users' tasks: (1) the tour (users select and then are guided around a sequence of frames until the tour ends or is stopped) was mostly used for studying unfamiliar material; (2) the map (to see where a user is in relation to other display frames) was used mostly for browsing and studying somewhat familiar material; (3) hypertext links were used mostly for studying familiar material; and (4) the index (directed access to keyword-coded frames or tours) was used mostly for information searching and for seeking references. Thus, system features, users' knowledge about the resource material, and tasks and purposes all influence the way people browse (CANTER ET AL.).

Feedback during browsing is an important feature in human–computer interaction (MARCHIONINI; THOMPSON & CROFT). Of course, feedback is crucial in information systems because the resource object is not otherwise available for assessment. In comparison with traditional IR feedback for query refinement, THOMPSON & CROFT emphasize that browsing as a feedback process is incremental and under the user's control in that the user examines only one item at a time and it is the user who determines which items will be examined, not the system. Further, the types or levels of feedback can vary significantly, according to both displays of organizational schemes (e.g., overviews of semantic structure, links among subject terms) or representations of content (e.g., lists of references, MARC (machine-readable cataloging) records, citations with abstracts, full text).

What influences browsing? MARCHIONINI & SHNEIDERMAN propose five general factors that influence success in seeking information: (1) setting, (2) search system, (3) task domain, (4) user, and (5) outcomes. The setting here includes physical environments as well as the user's contextual environment such as access cost. MARCHIONINI suggests three primary reasons why people browse in end-user systems: (1) the system's structure, commands, and capabilities encourage browsing; (2) the browser cannot or has not defined the search objective; and (3) it takes less cognitive load to browse than it does to plan and conduct an analytical search. A few studies that compare subject–area experts and novice users of hypertext systems show that there are differences between their browsing strategies, indicating that a user's knowledge expertise influences browsing tactics (CARMEL ET AL.; MARCHIONINI ET AL.). Arguing that browsing is the most important form of searching for casual use, TUORI suggests that a system is more browsable if it does not create great demand on users with respect to intention (the degree to which the person begins with a well-defined goal or intention), structure (the real or apparent structure or search paths of the information space), language (the characteristics of the language by which a person communicates with a system), or modality of interaction (various forms of expression or channels of communication).

There are, of course, problems associated with browsing in traditional computerized systems: the systems require precise definitions or terms (thus reducing serendipity), and computer interactions often provide insufficient dialog, which reduces feedback and negotiation (AYRIS). Thus, several authors have suggested a wide-ranging list of new features and structures to facilitate online browsing—e.g., the availability of various types of information, interactive tables of contents, and displays of semantic networks (BATES, 1986b, 1989, 1990; BELKIN ET AL., 1993; ELLIS; HILDRETH, 1989; HUESTIS; LOSEE; MASSICOTTE). Some systems have been devised or suggested to remedy some of these problems and use some of these features (AGOSTI ET AL.; EGAN ET AL., 1989, 1991; ODDY & BALAKRISHNAN; STORY ET AL.; THOMPSON & CROFT).

Implications for browsing may vary across different kinds of systems, such as full-text systems, bibliographic information retrieval systems, and visual/graphics-based systems. Several studies that compare information-seeking behavior associated with printed and electronic versions of materials have implications for browsing. Users' experience with printed materials affects their initial information-seeking strategies when they use electronic versions (EGAN ET AL., 1989; JOSEPH ET AL.; MARCHIONINI & LIEBSCHER). Electronic newsreading has been difficult for "noninstrumental" or nontask-oriented viewers, given hierarchical menu-based database structures and the fact that browsing can be habitual for people using specific media or resources (DOZIER & RICE; ZERBINOS). Finally, users expect to be able to conduct such browsing activities as flipping pages, referencing back and forth, and scanning an entire table in a single display, activities not well supported by current online interfaces or systems (JOSEPH ET AL.).

AKEROYD analyzed three commercial OPAC system interfaces and indicates four reasons why people engage in browsing at OPACs: (1) to correct input errors (e.g., browsing backward to the correct position); (2) to establish the scope of the terminology (e.g., browsing in subject indexes); (3) to expand the scope of retrieved documents (e.g., browsing a hierarchical classified list); and (4) to specify a subset of a retrieved set in a Boolean set. He argues that in text-based bibliographic systems users cannot easily assess the overall size of the file because there are no physical indicators such as there are in a card catalog, for example.

Image- or graphics-based systems provide recognition-based strategies, reducing cognitive load and memory tasks (MARCHIONINI & LIEBSCHER). Pejtersen's Book House is an example that simulates browsing fiction shelves in a public library setting via an icon-based interface (PEJTERSEN). The visual system of BORGMAN ET AL. (1993) models a specific library's physical layout on the screen (including visual displays of book shelves, floor maps, and walking paths) to help children locate science books; interaction with the system is possible only via a mouse. Compared with a previously evaluated Boolean-based system, this browsing, direct-manipulation interface for children

was superior; it was more usable and more favored across the population and less sensitive to a child's computer experience. For the commercial Prodigy graphical videotex system (which models a shopping
mall environment) ANTONOFF reports that the small text window and
speed problems are major obstacles to browsing.

What are the consequences of browsing? Two positive results of browsing are finding what one wants and/or accidental learning (e.g., of the
contents or search path) (e.g., EGAN ET AL., 1989).

One drawback is disorientation, which arises from unfamiliarity
with the structure and conceptual organization of the document network due to the cognitive demands placed on the user (FOSS) or
elements of the interface design, such as the lack of contextual cues
(SODERSTON). Some ways to avoid these problems have been proposed (e.g., provide a history tree to keep track of the user's movement
through the system, or offer a layout display of the document network)
(AGOSTI ET AL.; FOSS; LELU; MCALEESE; THOMPSON & CROFT).

Browsing can also result in information overload. FOSS suggests that
overload stems from inexperience with learning by browsing, which
leads to difficulties in remembering, consolidating, and understanding
the semantic content. Others argue that information overload may arise
from the mode and amount of information presented (HILTZ & TUROFF;
MALONE ET AL.) or the complexity or relevance of the information
(ISELIN; LOSEE). Various techniques to deal with this problem have
been suggested, such as categorization and ranking of the electronic
messages (LOSEE) or a "summary box" for the user's annotations
during hypertext browsing (FOSS).

Concerned with computer-mediated communication systems in
which browsing as a screening strategy is often the only means to
identify relevant information from a huge amount of messages,
MALONE ET AL. propose three approaches to filtering messages to
reduce information overload as commonly experienced by users: (1)
cognitive filtering (characterizing the contents of a message and the
information needs of potential message recipients), (2) social filtering
(supporting the personal and organizational interrelationships of individuals in a community), and (3) economic filtering (cost-benefit assessments or explicit/implicit pricing mechanisms). Along with HILTZ &
TUROFF, these authors argue that users should be able to control these
retrieval and filtering capabilities directly because negative consequences
are essentially social issues that should not be programmed away and
opportunities for serendipity and exposure to diverse sources should
be maintained.

Browsing in computer systems is characterized by searching without
specifying; it is a recognition-based search strategy. The concept of
browsing has led to research on various display mechanisms to facili-

tate interactive exploration. The analysis of information-seeking behavior by using computer search logs with users' oral protocols has been fruitful for understanding the cognitive aspects of browsing (CARMEL ET AL.).

Consumer Behavior

Browsing is a recent concept in the marketing literature and has been investigated as a distinct consumer shopping behavior that is related to but not equated with buying behavior.

What is browsing?   BLOCH & RICHINS define browsing as "the in-store examination of a retailer's merchandise for informational and/or recreational purposes without an immediate intent to buy" (p. 389). Consumer browsing may be pleasurable in itself and can be done for various reasons. Because there is no "immediate intent to buy," browsing may be largely indeterminate and undirected (BLOCH & RICHINS; SALOMON & KOPPELMAN). Note that here browsing is considered purposeful but not necessarily goal directed or task oriented. Differences between browsing real objects (e.g., clothes) and representations (e.g., pictures and descriptions of clothes in mail-order catalogs) have been noted; real objects have more attributes than do representations (BUCKLEY & LONG; GROVER & SABHERWAL).

What influences browsing?   Browsing is positively associated with one's interest in the product, the propensity to engage in other forms of search behavior relating to the product, the knowledge of the product, and word-of-mouth activity (BLOCH & RICHINS). JEON reports that in-store browsing is directly influenced by the preshopping mood and affects both the psychological situation and consequent impulse buying which, in turn, influences post-shopping mood. Consumers browse primarily for information and/or recreation, but the receipt of such benefits is affected by the retail environment and by product involvement (BLOCH ET AL.).

Consumer research into browsing has direct implications for information system design, based on studies of new technologies, such as videotex marketing systems and home-shopping channels. For example, SHIM & MAHONEY find that most teleshoppers are motivated primarily by recreational interests and, counterintuitively, that teleshoppers are less concerned with convenience and time than are nonteleshoppers. BUCKLEY & LONG identify three variables that seem to have contributed to the failure of the Viewtron nationwide videotex system: (1) system variables (e.g., the jargon used or the extent of the description of goods); (2) knowledge variables (knowledge of brand names or knowledge of natural language and computer systems); and (3) goods variables (delivery delay or range of goods).

Methodologically, eye movement can be a useful indicator of browsing or scanning and has been used to test the effect of different print ads, catalogs, page layout, direct-mail material, packaging, and shelf-display design on browsers' attention (DRUCKER; VON KEITZ). HOWARD demonstrates how eye-movement research techniques could be usefully applied to IR studies of searchers' judgment of the relevance of retrieved citations.

What are the consequences of browsing? Possible results of in-store browsing include enjoyment, product knowledge, information gathering, opinion leadership, and impulse buying (BLOCH ET AL.; JEON).

The consumer literature emphasizes that browsing can be an "ongoing" information-acquisition activity apart from searching or a purchase plan (SALOMON & KOPPELMAN). As shown in the information science literature, the influence of subject expertise (in this case, product knowledge) on browsing is evident. Consistent with some of the other disciplines, five dimensions of browsing are implied by this literature: (1) behavior (examination or looking around), (2) cognition (without intent), (3) motivation (for fun, recreation, or to get information), (4) resource (merchandise), and (5) context (in-store, shopping mall, mail order). Unlike other fields, attempts have been made here to quantify browsing: consumers can be identified as browsers and nonbrowsers (BLOCH & RICHINS; JEON).

Mass Media Audiences

The notion of browsing is implicit in the media audience behavior known as television "zapping."

What is browsing? With so many television channels to choose from, thanks to cable and satellite TV, the use of a remote control to scan multiple programs (now called "zapping" or "grazing") is becoming more frequent (DORR & KUNKEL; HEETER & GREENBERG). Such interaction with television may indicate "a complex consciousness that derives satisfaction by sampling information in small, seemingly random chunks" (ARRINGTON). Zapping is thus a scanning process and involves both resource search paths (TV channels and schedules) and content (programs and commercials). HEETER & GREENBERG conclude that zapping is not an idiosyncratic behavior aimed solely to avoid TV commercials but one of several systematic approaches to watching television, used as an accompaniment to other activities in the household. Similarly, PERSE argues that zapping is a ritualistic pattern that is characterized by the viewer's high selectivity before and during television exposure and lesser involvement during exposure.

What influences browsing? HEETER & GREENBERG showed that zappers can be differentiated from nonzappers; they are more likely to have more remote-control channel selectors, do less planning of their TV viewing, watch programs that they do not watch regularly, change channels between and during shows and at commercials, be familiar with more different channels, and do more reevaluation during program viewing. Reasons for channel switching include: to see what else is on, to avoid commercials, to seek variety, to view multiple shows, and simple boredom.

Four theoretical approaches have been used in studying mass media audiences: (1) psychological, (2) social/structural, (3) cultural, and (4) phenomenological (MCGUIRE). From a psychological perspective, cognitive and affective motives are two underlying dimensions of all human motives, including reasons for browsing. The social/structural perspective emphasizes the impact of sociotechnical systems on human behavior (i.e., browsing can be influenced by system factors, including physical and social systems as well as computer systems). The phenomenological perspective focuses on the projected human action (i.e., considers browsing as a rational goal-oriented activity or utility-seeking behavior). Finally, the cultural perspective suggests that browsing can be a form of aesthetic satisfaction, which differs from fulfilling a utilitarian need. Indeed, the play theory of STEPHENSON suggests that much media use is best understood as primarily a pleasurable activity. He proposes that when people are doing things for entertainment, they tend to be less goal oriented and may develop ritualistic and habitual communication behaviors. Thus, as with TV use (both attending to a preselected program as well as zapping through channel offerings), browsing in other resources may be primarily a pleasurable, even ritualistic, process. Conceivably, some browsing activities may involve a combination of all these theoretical perspectives.

Organizational Communication

In the literature of organizational theory and communication, two phenomena may be considered browsing: (1) environmental scanning, and (2) informal communication or social browsing.

What is browsing?   The notion of browsing in environmental scanning implies a formal or systematic approach to obtaining information and tends to be goal directed, structured, and planned to identify organizationally relevant information. Scanning the environment assists top management in directing the organization's future course (AGUILAR; KATZER & FLETCHER). It is a process of systematic surveillance and interpretation designed to identify environmental events, elements, and conditions that can affect an organization (COATES). According to an investigation of executive scanning behavior (AUSTER

& CHOO), environmental scanning can be a result of either proactive behavior or a passive, situation-induced exposure behavior, which is often a personal, informal activity that is intrinsic to the managerial function.

SAUNDERS & JONES propose four types of environmental scanning: (1) undirected viewing (general scanning with no particular purpose); (2) conditioned viewing (searching an identified area); (3) informal searching (limited, unstructured effort to obtain particular information for a particular purpose); and (4) formal searching (deliberate, planned searching to obtain specific information for a particular purpose). Unlike undirected browsing in library and information science literature, undirected viewing, from an organizational point of view, implies the purpose of environmental surveillance or monitoring although specific goals for such scanning may not be present.

Serendipitous interactions, such as hallway chatting or after-meeting discussions (what ROOT calls "social browsing"), are a frequent, unplanned, and important component of knowledge-creation processes, especially in collaborative scientific work. They often lead to new ideas, socialization of organizational members, and better monitoring of project status (DOTY ET AL.; KRAUT ET AL.; POLAND). Typically, informal communication occurs through opportunities provided by physical proximity among members who are likely to bump into each other. A more intentional form of social browsing is "management by wandering around" (PETERS & WATERMAN), which emphasizes casual access and unpredictable exposure to social links and environmental information in an organization as a conscious aspect of effective management.

What influences browsing? Environmental scanning is influenced by such informational variables as perceived environmental uncertainty, perceived source accessibility and quality, and decision-makers' roles (AUSTER & CHOO; CHOO & AUSTER). Thus, the extent to which managers engage in environmental scanning is influenced by environmental characteristics and source characteristics as well as individual factors (for a detailed discussion, see the chapter by CHOO & AUSTER in this volume).

Based on the concept of physical "proximity" as defined by ALLEN, authors KRAUT & GALEGHER show how geographic separation may impair workers' ability to browse the social environment effectively, resulting in a reduction in the frequency of informal communication, which, in turn, degrades the intellectual teamwork. KRAUT ET AL. demonstrate how research on informal communication can be applied to the design of an audio and video communication medium to facilitate social browsing. However, the implied knowledge inherent in social interaction in a public space (i.e., whether the other party is receptive to a face-to-face conversation) cannot be easily transformed into electronic environments (FISH ET AL.).

The organizational communication literature demonstrates the utility of the two extremes of the concept of browsing: the ongoing information acquisition and monitoring activities, on the one hand, and the unplanned, unexpected encounter of the most dynamic resource—people—on the other. In contrast to MENZEL who sees informal communication as inefficient, some serious attempts have been made to encourage social browsing in the "electronic hallway."

Wayfinding and Environmental Design

Browsing is often implicitly assumed in discussions of perceptual experience in visual communication, which can be guided or confined by architectural and display design, and of wayfinding in a complex environment. In this context, browsing is fundamentally scanning and has been related to environmental perception and cognition (ARTHUR & PASSINI).

What is browsing?   As a goal-directed activity, wayfinding refers to the cognitive, perceptual, physical, and social process of moving through space, via various routes, to reach a destination in a familiar or unfamiliar environment. Wayfinding depends on how one understands the physical layout of the environment, how immediate and nearby locations are related, how different routes connect these locations, how decisions about directed movements affect reaching one's destination, and how one organizes his or her spatial behavior (DOWNS).

Two basic wayfinding learning processes operate simultaneously and give rise to two types of cognitive representations of environmental information: (1) "nondimensional learning," which generates sequential or route maps and suggests a linear design style for a wayfinding system; and (2) "dimensional learning," which produces a spatial or cognitive map and encourages a spatial design style (ARTHUR & PASSINI; DOWNS). Initial learning of a spatial environment necessarily involves nondimensional learning, but the two forms of representation are not mutually exclusive; they are stages in a learning process.

Keeping on the right track involves continued monitoring. For familiar routes monitoring may go on "outside" of normal consciousness. Sightseeing is an example of environmental browsing as a perceptual experience. People create an image of a city by scanning an environment that presents a large amount of information, but they do not completely absorb all the information. However, when they get lost, orientation can be a goal-directed activity and thus a conscious use of such perception.

Recognition of the objective is the final step in wayfinding, and it depends either on prior knowledge of what the destination looks like (finding some specific identifying sign) or on stimulation of associations between perceived and desired cues.

There are several implications of this literature for browsing. One type of browsing can be based primarily on perception with no specific goal or objective in mind when one processes external information, unless the perceptual experience itself is considered a goal. Another type of browsing can be goal directed, which may be stimulated either before or during perceptual scanning, with or without external demands.

What influences browsing? People's spatial behavior in an environment depends on environmental characteristics because these determine what browsers can be exposed to and have access to in a specific time and space (ARCHEA; DRUCKER & GUMPERT; WALSH & UNGSON). Environmental characteristics that influence people's spatial behavior can include size of the space, architectural design, symbolic aspects (e.g., woodwork and office size), physical audiovisual attributes, location, and layout (O'NEILL & JASPER). People's spatial behavior also depends on personal preferences for and knowledge about the spatial environment, which, in turn, depend on the individual's cognitive map of the environment.

Wayfinding, and thus browsing, can be facilitated or constrained by architectural and display design. For example, both physical and visual landmarks serve as anchor points, allowing people to retain and mentally structure environmental information. Other important spatial elements of wayfinding systems (entrances, exits, paths, and circulation system) can also contribute to the "legibility" of an environment. MICHEL reviews research on library design within the context of wayfinding, showing how physical structure and search aids heavily influence both general searching and browsing. He makes a strong case that library and information resource designs are sadly uninformed by what is known about how people find their way about the world. Conceptualizing wayfinding systems as essentially information systems, researchers in this area suggest that wayfinding systems should support both wayfinding and learning (ARTHUR & PASSINI; POLLET & HASKELL).

As more and more applications of information technology attempt to model physical environments (e.g., virtual reality, electronic libraries, and teleshopping malls), research on wayfinding and environmental design may contribute to a better understanding of browsing physical and electronic places, and to better system design. Interactive video wayfinding systems have indeed been implemented to address two common questions by first-time visitors in public settings: "How do I get where I want to go?" and "What is here that might interest me?" (ARTHUR & PASSINI, p. 203). BATES (1986b) points out that one of the most neglected areas in designing OPACs is the lack of "orientation" tools by which the user can get a feel of how the system works in order to move about easily and comfortably during later interaction with the system.

What are the consequences of browsing? DRUCKER & GUMPERT discuss differences between public and electronic space in terms of the degree of sensory and emotional involvement and the impact of such differences on unpredictable social interaction. Environmental design research suggests that environments can generate anger, fear, boredom, or pleasure. Further, architectural structure and layout influence personal access and exposure (ARCHEA). Therefore, Drucker and Gumpert assert that although computer-mediated interaction and face-to-face interaction are functionally equivalent, they are contextually and experientially dissimilar.

One reference to a very large and intriguing literature has been rarely considered in discussions of information searching. In looking at foraging/searching approximation mechanisms, BELL provides a remarkable summary of searching behavior in the animal world. Major consequences of scanning and wayfinding there, of course, include feeding, resting, nesting, finding mates, reproduction, depositing eggs or offspring, and survival. Since many disciplines, such as psychology and medicine, have progressed by drawing on animal research, our understanding of human searching behavior in general (and browsing in particular) may be also enhanced by learning from research on animals. For example, Bell describes animal searching behavior as a two-stage process. Before searching, there are movements concerning orientation, scanning, and assessment of resource units. During searching, there are movements concerning locating patches, restricting the search to a patch and foraging in the most profitable patches, and sampling among patches in learning to forage efficiently. In either stage, exploratory behavior may be demonstrated. Interesting questions can be asked: Are there similar behaviors to be found in human information searching behavior? Are some of these patterns of behavior associated with the notion of browsing? The model of ecology influencing animals' foraging/searching behavior may also provide some insights for the development of human information behavior theories.

A MULTIDIMENSIONAL TYPOLOGY

These reviews imply five general dimensions underlying the browsing phenomenon (CHANG). The context dimension indicates where browsing takes place, its associated constraints or features, how resources are organized and presented, the physical arrangement, the display or interface perceived by the user, and the access costs. The behavioral dimension concerns actions in which people engage, including physical movement and scanning. The motivational dimension is related to why people engage in browsing and what they intend to accomplish (e.g., to buy, borrow, or evaluate). The cognitive dimension is related to the mental state of the browser, including knowledge and experience. The resource dimension involves the relevant objects (physical items, representations, or informative symbols) and their local environment.

The important facets of these dimensions, as discussed below, can be used, first, to distinguish browsing from other types of information-seeking behavior and, second, to characterize different types of browsing. In the following sections, we first discuss the concept of each facet and then provide some examples to illustrate how these facets work.

Context Dimension

People construct meanings from a context. Four important aspects of context include: (1) organization (structure), (2) interface (display), (3) feedback, and (4) economics.

Organization (structure). Organization of resources occurs either in physical space or abstract (sometimes electronic) space (MICHEL). Information resources typically have an underlying abstract structure (e.g., the internal architecture for organizing relations among data, records, and files), which is usually invisible and may have no physical counterpart. The structuring of material resources typically is manifested in physical structure, although much of the crucial structuring (such as supports, wiring, and plumbing in a large office building) may also not be directly visible to the user. However, many information resources (such as books) may be visibly structured in visible physical structures (such as shelves in a library's stacks).

How resources are organized or structured influences the type and ease of browsing. For example, the display of journals alphabetically by title facilitates scanning, but journals that are next to each other physically are not necessarily related logically. Yet a structural approach, such as the Dewey decimal system, implies and requires relatedness among physically proximate items, making associative browsing easier.

The possibility of sampling at various depths of detail makes an important difference in terms of browsing objects vs. representations. In the latter, one often needs to take an extra step to locate the item physically in order to assess it fully. This extra step often leads to a different kind of browsing (e.g., orientation to find the location of an item) or to disappointing results that may not happen when scanning in a physical context (as, for instance, when the item identified through browsing an OPAC is not on the assigned shelf). However, although a person who is attempting to find a physical item may still find that it is not available, he or she can still see what else is available nearby.

Interface (display).   For both abstract and physical structuring, the interface or display is the user's view, what the user is exposed to or must use in order to obtain specific objects or representations in the resource environment. The interface affects scanning and movement to a great extent and is most often related to the layout of a spatial (perhaps audio) unit. "Interface" may include the design of window displays in a shopping mall, presentation of programs on television, status differences among offices and floors in corporate headquarters, and choice of signage in buildings. The major difference between scanning and movement in a library vs. a computer system is that browsers have to adjust their ideas from physical shelf arrangement to abstract computer procedures that are often not transparent (APTED; HANCOCK-BEAULIEU).

Scanning via the computer interface may not be the same as scanning via a physical interface; the former is mainly cognitive while the latter involves additional physical movement (walking, head rotation, touching). For example, in comparing various versions of an electronic library catalog system using the browsing metaphor, BORGMAN ET AL. (1993) report that adding the feature of "browsing physically adjacent items" seemed to confuse the children who were the test subjects. One explanation might be that movement in a physical setting also gives people a sense of place, multisensory stimulation, and social/recreational gratification, all of which may not be obtainable in electronic environments (SALOMON & KOPPELMAN). Although some evidence indicates that browsing experience in image-based electronic space can be effective for information seeking (PEJTERSEN), little is known about whether and how such spatial experience in electronic environments is different from that in a physical setting. Perhaps the growing research on virtual reality (VR) and information visualization will provide some insights into this question of electronic space and multimedia, multidimensional interfaces (MACKINLAY ET AL.; NEWBY; SPRING). Spring, for example, speculates on how a VR library interface might use different colors, shadings, or sounds to indicate various degrees of information relevance contained in the books or materials visible to the individual walking through the library stacks in the VR environment.

Feedback.   Browsing as an interactive, iterative process depends on the feedback available. A menu-based system that requires the user to specify each command for repeated searches makes the iterative process more time consuming, reducing feedback and choice of alternative routes, and thus makes the system difficult or ineffective to browse

(DOZIER & RICE). Two common forms of feedback in information systems (both physical or electronic systems) are relevance (content related) feedback and orientation (structure/path related) feedback.

Economic factors.   The least-effort principle suggests that people do not seek optimal results. Therefore, timing of feedback, accessibility of the system and its information, personal resources available (money, time, energy), and expected or required effort all influence browsing (JEON; MARCHIONINI & SHNEIDERMAN; MARCHIONINI ET AL., 1993). For example, the running cost of online charges during an online search or the length of one's lunch break for store shopping will influence the likelihood and extent of browsing and the criteria for successful outcomes in these contexts.

Behavioral Dimension

The behavioral aspect of browsing involves scanning and movement.

Scanning.   Browsing is characterized by scanning as an individual moves through an information or a physical environment. Scanning does not have to be visual and may involve more than one sense, so browsing systems may be differentiated on the basis of sensory involvement (OVERHAGE & HARMAN, p. 130). While scanning for orientation (e.g., identifying landmarks) is typically characterized by quick glances, exploratory scanning within new surroundings (e.g., identifying the potential of a resource environment) seems less hasty. Exploratory scanning may involve movement between resources (BATES, 1989; LANCASTER, 1968) or between "patches" and across "habitats" (BELL).

A consideration of scanning as sampling leads to two implications (O'CONNOR, 1993). Sampling implies an ongoing assessment before one decides whether to seek and/or then use a resource. Assessment depends on what is accessible, how the accessible resource is organized and displayed, how one exposes oneself to that accessible resource, and the extent to which one has the cognitive and practical skills to access and evaluate a resource. Sampling also implies control of exposure between the individual and the resource. Browsing is more possible in an information system in which the user has active and relatively rapid control of the items to be examined as well as initiative over and control of the scanning routes and depth of penetration (O'CONNOR, 1988; OVERHAGE & HARMAN).

Movement.   The most general form of browsing behavior is scanning a resource in a manner that allows continuous (random or structured) movement, leading to exposure to new information or objects and thus to learning and/or discovery (MICHEL). One extreme along this dimension is directed movement, which occurs when the person moves toward a specific destination, whether a place or object. The other extreme is undirected movement, when the person moves without a specific destination. In between is movement by interruption; this occurs when movement toward a specific destination is interrupted by unexpected information stimuli that might lead the browser to a new destination.

Because scanning and movement may not be easily observable (as when only eye movement, smelling, or hearing is involved), behavioral characteristics of browsing are necessary but not sufficient. Rather, people's motivations and cognition must be also understood to derive adequate descriptions of browsing.

Motivation Dimension

Motivational aspects of browsing include the overall purpose or motive for engaging in certain activities and the individual goal at the local activity level.

Purpose. Motivation as purpose may be extrinsic or intrinsic. Intrinsically motivated behaviors (such as curiosity-based behaviors and play) lack any apparent reward contingencies or lack expectations of extrinsic rewards (DECI & RYAN). Extrinsically motivated behaviors (such as browsing to find a needed book or to buy a gift) are instrumental in that a desired task, outcome, or reward is expected or has been identified. Purpose can also be driven by cognitive or affective motives (MCGUIRE). Information-related browsing behaviors tend to be motivated by cognitive processes. Affective motives tend to lead one to engage in browsing activities that are recreational. These two motives may occur simultaneously (BLOCH ET AL.; JEON).

Goal. The goal is what the person intends to accomplish during scanning. Scanning can be goal directed or nongoal directed.

Scanning activities may take place in three ways. In a goal-directed situation they may be used to support the overall purpose, or they may be incidental to the activities conducted toward the overall purpose. In either situation, the browser is aware of and is able to say what is intended for a given scanning activity. On the other hand, scanning may take place in its own right without an explicit goal to be accomplished, which is nongoal directed and usually manifested in externally driven activities such as window shopping on the way home. Further, a goal during scanning a resource can be content specific or noncontent specific, can be path specific or nonpath specific, or can be location specific or nonlocation specific, depending on the person's state of knowledge. When all three aspects of a goal (not of a resource) are known to be specific, the person's goal is well defined. If some of the aspects are nonspecific, the goal can be considered as semidefined. To the extent that during scanning neither the content nor path nor location is specific, the goal becomes ill defined. Because the layers of a goal are not explicit in the literature, it is important to note that a goal is well or ill defined depending on the anomalous state of knowledge about not only the content but also the structure or search path of a resource before the interaction with the resource.

At one extreme along this continuum of goal is the well-defined goal: knowing what one wants, how to find it, and where to get it. If one knows what to find and how to find it but does not know the exact location of the item, scanning may be observed while the item is being located. When the person's anomalous state of knowledge extends to the question of what paths to follow in order to find that specific item, scanning may be involved, perhaps to explore the possible search paths. On the other hand, one may scan familiar paths because one lacks a specific goal to begin with or does not know exactly what to look for until one sees something along the way, or one knows that there are usually some things of interest along these paths (such as scanning a familiar journal's table of contents) (BATES, 1989). Such scanning is often associated with serendipitous findings because one is exposed to other items near the targeted item and then to subsequent recognition of the value or relevance of those items. It may also become an ongoing, intrinsically motivated behavior that appears to be purposeless (e.g., looking through a newspaper or window shopping as one walks home) but is a form of preparatory information acquisition (BATES, 1986a). There is also a type of scanning that is nongoal directed but mainly externally induced. Cultural institutions, such as libraries, museums, and shopping malls, are more or less purposefully and more or less successfully designed to encourage such invitational browsing, perhaps through interrupting the browser, as noted above (CARR; FRIEDBERG).

Cognitive Dimension

Cognitive aspects of browsing include plan and knowledge/experience.

Plan. The task of accomplishing a goal can be planned or unplanned. People may accomplish some goals without a plan by taking advantage of a situation (CARR; O'CONNOR, 1988). Thus, browsing is often a situated action (SUCHMAN) or situated learning process (BROWN ET AL.). Indeed, JANES concludes that "a semiadaptive search plan (one which uses information gained during the process of searching) outperforms a nonadaptive plan" (p. 12).

Knowledge/experience. Browsing often takes place when users are in an anomalous state of knowledge, not knowing either the route (path to the desired items) or the destination (the target information) (MICHEL). Thus, necessary knowledge about a resource can be broadly categorized into content (expertise) knowledge and structure (search path) knowledge. Depending on the types of anomalous states of knowledge and goal, people may engage in different forms of browsing (O'CONNOR, 1993). Further, what a browser wants to find or find out should not be confused with what a browser actually finds or interacts with; for example, an understanding of structure (search path) may be gained while one is vainly seeking content. As a user's knowledge about content and search paths accumulates by using a resource over time, his or her expectations will also change. For example, BLOCH & RICHINS found that store browsing is positively related to the degree of self-perceived knowledge concerning the product class.

Related to path or structure knowledge is location knowledge, which can be the physical location of the item sought. Contexts that facilitate the scanning of neighborhoods along paths toward a location expose the searcher to other potential resources, which, in turn increases the chances for serendipity.

Resource Dimension

Form (objects and representations) and focus (content and path) of the resource may influence browsing.

Form: object or representation. An object in the material world occupies a single physical space and thus a single category in a classified arrangement. A representation is a surrogate or indicator for the object or its attributes. As a special case of the difference between an object and its representations, textual information can be considered both a representation of objects or knowledge and the object sought or browsed. Objects such as books offer more attributes and sensory experiences for browsers than do their representations (at least in traditional textual format). However, it is possible to arrange representations in, say, online catalogs in ways that are not possible in the material world, thus allowing for additional kinds of browsing (e.g., by classifications, title, subject headings). For online catalogs, it is desirable to have different levels of representation or exploratory power, such as citation, full MARC record, or abstract. Differences between objects vs. representations may have important implications for browsing in computer systems or virtual libraries because of the loss of attributes, physical movement, and authentic activity (BAILEY; BROWN ET AL.; STORY ET AL.).

Focus: content or path. One may scan a resource's content or path, depending on one's knowledge about the purpose, resource, and interface involved. While most systems emphasize content-based browsing, scanning for orientation focuses on a path. Television viewers usually "zap" through a linear path of channels (perhaps preprogrammed to expose only a selected subset of channels) for orientation and evaluation before selecting a particular program. Maps or relational graphics in wayfinding contexts help users to see the relationships among the current position, the neighborhood, and the path to the desired destination—a notable characteristic of a geographic information system (SHAFFER). However, little attention has been paid to a path focus in traditional IR systems (but see BATES (1986c) for a discussion of search paths in print sources and BELKIN ET AL. (1993)).

Summary

Each of these six disciplines looks at browsing from a different perspective. Nevertheless, some common dimensions emerge. For example, the concept of social browsing in organizations may seem at first to be quite different from browsing as a search strategy in a library. Nevertheless, one may begin to understand their similarity by comparing these two contexts in terms of the object of browsing (person vs. print) or means of interaction during browsing (visual and oral interaction vs. formal written communication).

The literature discussed above generally points to some salient characteristics of browsing, suggesting the multidimensional nature of browsing: (1) accessibility: the ability to expose oneself to and sample (not necessarily systematically) from many information stimuli that might be otherwise unknown or inaccessible; (2) flexibility: the ability to sample as easily as one wishes; (3) interactivity: the reduced burden with respect to cognitive load of specifying what is needed or intended because individuals may interact directly with informational stimuli that are potentially useful; (4) associativity: the linking of information stimuli (or making associations), which is manifested in or constrained by the underlying organizational structure (or paths) of the items browsed; and (5) multiplicity: the intrinsic and unplanned as well as extrinsic and expectational motivations for browsing.

TOWARD A CONCEPTUAL FRAMEWORK FOR BROWSING

Definition

Based on the above disciplinary and dimensional discussions, a more conceptual definition of browsing than the one that introduced this chapter and a general framework for understanding and studying browsing are proposed.

Browsing is the process of exposing oneself to a resource space by scanning its content (objects or representations) and/or structure, possibly resulting in awareness of unexpected or new content or paths in that resource space. Browsing may be planned or unplanned, habitual or situational, serving to identify (or select), familiarize (or learn), assess, and monitor resources in an environment. Browsing is influenced or constrained by various factors and can have both positive and negative consequences.

A general model for understanding browsing should include four major components—(1) context, (2) influences, (3) browsing process, and (4) consequences—with iterations over time. Figure 1 summarizes this model.

Contexts and Influences

Browsing behavior can be influenced by external factors, such as the way a context structures and displays a resource, and internal factors, such as the browser's motivation, goal, and knowledge about the object sought. Table 1 suggests some of the many different influences discussed in the various disciplines.

Context (organization, interface, feedback, economics)

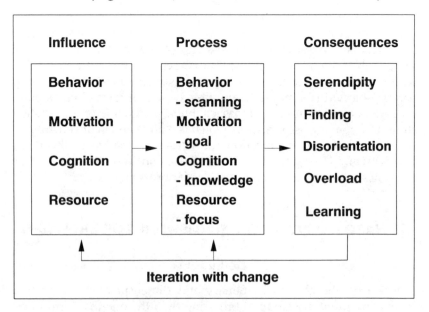

Figure 1. General model of browsing

Table 1
Factors Influencing Browsing in Each Discipline

Factors	Library	IR	Consumer	Media	Organization	Design
Individual Characteristics						
purpose/motive	-	-	xª	x	x	-
goal	x	x	-	-	x	x
plan	y	-	x	x	-	-
knowledge	x	x	-	y	-	-
experience	x	x	-	y	-	-
interest	-	-	x	-	x	-
mood/emotion	-	-	x	x	-	-
expectation	y	y	-	-	-	-
time/money	-	y	x	-	x	-
Contextual Factors						
Environment					ES^b	IC
atmosphere	-	-	x	-	x	-
uncertainty	y	-	-	-	x	y
Interface						
display	x	x	y	-	-	x
organizational structure	x	x	-	-	x	y
Computer-specific						
language	-	x	x	-	-	-
modality	-	x	x	-	-	-
screen size	-	x	x	x	-	-
speed	-	x	x	x	-	-
feedback	-	x	-	-	-	-
Objects/resources						
real things	x	-	x	-	-	-
representations	x	x	y	-	-	-
other attributes	x	y	x	x	x	x
					quality/accessibility	text/image

ªThe symbol "x" means that the dimensions are explicitly discussed; "y" means that the dimensions are implicitly assumed.
^bES = environmental scanning; IC = informal communication.

Process

Behaviorally speaking, browsing is characterized by iterative move-ment in a scanning and examining activity. Motivationally speaking, depending on whether browsers are aware of or expect a desired out-come, browsing can be extrinsically or intrinsically motivated. The browser may have but not necessarily express a goal, which can be well defined, ill defined, or not defined. From the cognitive perspective, both browsers' knowledge about the subject sought and experience with the information system in which they interact influence how and the extent to which people browse. The browsing object can be broadly categorized as content (referring to representations or real objects) or search path (such as meta-information or organizing structure).

Figure 2 suggests some important facets involved in differentiating browsing from other types of information-seeking behavior and in characterizing different types of browsing by applying several of the underlying dimensions discussed above. For example, browsing can be differentiated from direct searching such as keying in a title to find the

PURPOSE: [e.g., recreational or informational]	INTRINSIC	←——→	EXTRINSIC
GOAL: [e.g., learning or selecting]	NON-goal-DIRECTED	←——→	GOAL-DIRECTED
CONTENT KNOWLEDGE: [e.g., physical item or information]	NON-content-SPECIFIC	←——→	CONTENT-SPECIFIC
STRUCTURE KNOWLEDGE: [e.g., physical pathway or meta-information]	NON-path-SPECIFIC	←——→	PATH-SPECIFIC
LOCATION KNOWLEDGE: [e.g., position on a shelf or a list]	NON-location-SPECIFIC	←——→	LOCATION-SPECIFIC
RESOURCE FOCUS:	CONTENT	←——→	PATH

Figure 2. A dimensional typology of browsing

location of a specific item known to be needed by an experienced library user (i.e., knowing what to look for and how to look for the item); this is a goal-directed activity involving extrinsically motivated scanning of the shelves. The anomaly of the person's state of knowledge is location. If the needed item is not found, direct searching may turn into a browsing activity, which may involve scanning the small area near the known item to evaluate the potential relevant items or scanning the areas of interest to gain an overview of what is available. These two episodes characterize two types of browsing in which the goal is either to evaluate or to learn and what is sought is either relatively content specific or noncontent specific (i.e., an anomalous state of knowledge in terms of the content facet) and the resource focus during scanning is content oriented. In another situation, the person may scan the item to find out how its information is organized, which characterizes a type of browsing that focuses on path/structure of the resource. Thus, with more carefully defined operational definitions of each facet, it is possible to use these facets to analyze various information-seeking situations and derive a taxomony of browsing.

Outcomes

Possible consequences of browsing include satisfaction, serendipitous findings, modification of information requirements, finding the desired information, learning (e.g., about a research topic, product awareness, channel offerings, other R&D projects, route and neighborhood of destination), disorientation, information overload, search inefficiency, costs (time and money), enjoyment, general information gathering, opinion leadership, impulse buying, monitoring and surveillance, and socialization.

Iterations

Finally, the process and outcomes stages can influence change in the prior stages, both within specific browsing episodes as well as in longer-term social contexts. For instance, serendipitous findings can change a relatively ill-defined goal to a more well-defined one and may intensify one's underlying motivation. On the other hand, increased experience with and understanding of the paths provided in an information system may improve one's perception of the system's accessibility and thus increase the likelihood and ease of later use.

Even this brief typology can be used to describe various browsing situations generically. Take the goal aspect of the motivation dimension, for example. When people know what they are looking for but not how to look for it, they have a well-defined goal in terms of the content aspect but an ill-defined goal in terms of search path or structure. Thus,

Domain	Well-defined Goal	Semi-defined Goal	Ill-defined Goal
Library	Find a book by an author	Find books on a subject	Find whatever of interest
Shopping	Find an item of a brand of a category (e.g., Tide detergent)	Find an item in a category (e.g., any liquid detergent)	Find something for cleaning (e.g., soap)
TV	Choose specific channel and program	Choose a specific channel	Whatever catches the eye or ear
Communication	Talk to particular person at specific time (formal meeting)	Talk to someone sometime	Unexpected communication (informal conversation)

Figure 3. Example of using motivational dimension (goal) to analyze various browsing situations

their browsing behavior is more likely to focus on discovering how to find things; browsing through a menu system to find out or learn how to search is an example. For this type of user, a useful system design principle would be to make the search path or information structure explicit so that the user can easily browse and decide on the path. Figure 3 gives an example of using the goal aspect of the motivational dimension to help describe various situations in which browsing takes place.

CONCLUSION

This review of and framework for browsing addresses the four problems identified at the beginning of the chapter. First, browsing is not limited to information seeking at library shelves or information system retrieval but appears in a wide variety of human domains. It has been construed as a search strategy, a viewing pattern, a screening technique, and a recreational activity. While it is not yet well understood in any particular discipline, the contributions from each discipline do expand our ability to define, discuss, and analyze browsing. Second, there are many dimensions to browsing, so it is simplistic to dichotomize between, say, "intentional" search vs. "random" browsing. Rather, the degree of browsing differs, depending in part on the specificity of the goal and the types of anomalous states of knowledge. Although a clear taxonomy of browsing has yet to emerge, the inherent richness and complexity of browsing will require researchers to be more specific and explicit in their definitions, measurements, and evaluations of searching and browsing. Third, it should be evident that the traditional bias toward specific, direct searching is unwarranted. Researchers and practitioners should consider browsing as a rich and fundamental human information behavior. Without a better understanding of browsing, our concept of information-seeking behavior cannot be complete. Fourth, designers, evaluators, and users of new computer-based technologies and information resources should consider how these may better facilitate various types of browsing and may better avoid potentially negative outcomes associated with browsing. There are many conceptual and empirical resources concerning browsing from other disciplines that system designers and evaluators can take advantage of (e.g., involving multiple senses or wayfinding perspectives). An important step toward this end is to develop an appropriate conceptual framework for browsing and establish normative data within the browsing domain. We should note that a fundamentally difficult problem yet to be resolved is the operationalization of both the dimensional components proposed in our model as well as of the more fundamental process of browsing itself. While some of the studies referenced in this chapter have attempted to measure aspects of browsing, none is comprehensive, explicit, or consistent enough to use. Our own research is currently engaging this issue (CHANG).

Thus, the multidimensional framework proposed aims to provide a deeper and wider understanding of the concept and nature of browsing in various situations, to facilitate the development of propositions concerning browsing, and to stimulate designs for computer-based and library systems that facilitate successful and/or enjoyable browsing. Clearly this attempt is tentative; future research should elaborate and test the utility of the framework.

BIBLIOGRAPHY

AGOSTI, M.; GRADENIGO, G.; MARCHETTI, P.G. 1992. A Hypertext Environment for Interacting with Large Textual Databases. Information Processing and Management. 1992; 28(3): 371-387. ISSN: 0306-4573; CODEN: IPMADK.
AGUILAR, FRANCIS JOSEPH. 1967. Scanning the Business Environment. New York, NY: Macmillan; 1967. 239p. LC: 67-011688.
AKEROYD, JOHN. 1990. Information Seeking in Online Catalogs. Journal of Documentation. 1990 March; 46: 33-52. ISSN: 0022-0418.
ALLEN, THOMAS J. 1969. Information Needs and Uses. In: Cuadra, Carlos A., ed. Annual Review of Information Science and Technology: Volume 4. Chicago, IL: Encyclopaedia Britannica, Inc. for the American Society for Information Science; 1969. 1-29. ISSN: 0066-4200.
ALLINSON, LESLEY; HAMMOND, NICK. 1989. A Learning Support Environment: The Hitch-Hiker's Guide. In: McAleese, Ray, ed. Hypertext:

Theory into Practice. Norwood, NJ: Ablex Publishing; 1989. 62-74. ISBN: 0-89391-575-0.

ANTONOFF, MICHAEL. 1989. The PRODIGY Promise. Personal Computing. 1989 May; 13(5): 66-78. ISSN: 0192-5490.

APTED, S.M. 1971. General Purposive Browsing. Library Association Record. 1971; 73(12): 228-230. ISSN: 0024-2195.

ARCHEA, JOHN. 1977. The Place of Architectural Factors in Behavioral Theories of Privacy. Journal of Social Issues. 1977 Summer; 33(3): 116-137. ISSN: 0022-4537; CODEN: JSISAF.

ARRINGTON, CARL. 1992. The Zapper! All about the Remote Control. TV Guide. 1992 August 15; 8-13. ISSN: 0039-8543.

ARTHUR, PAUL; PASSINI, ROMEDI. 1992. Wayfinding: People, Signs and Architecture. New York, NY: McGraw Hill, Inc.; 1992. 238p. ISBN: 0-07-551016-2.

AUSTER, ETHEL; CHOO, CHUN WEI. 1991. Environmental Scanning: A Conceptual Framework for Studying the Information Seeking Behavior of Executives. In: Griffiths, José-Marie, ed. Proceedings of the American Society for Information Science (ASIS) 54th Annual Meeting: Volume 28; 1991 October 27-31; Washington, DC. Medford, NJ: Learned Information, Inc.; 1991. 3-8. ISSN: 0044-7870; ISBN: 0-938734-56-3; CODEN: PAISDQ.

AYRIS, PAUL. 1986. The Stimulation of Creativity: A Review of the Literature Concerning the Concept of Browsing, 1970-1985. Sheffield, England: Center for Research on User Studies (CRUS), University of Sheffield; 1986. 112p. (CRUS Working Paper no. 5). ISBN: 0-906088-27-5.

BAILEY, CHARLES W., JR. 1990. Intelligent Multimedia Computer Systems: Emerging Information Resources in the Network Environment. Library Hi Tech. 1990; 8(1): 29-41. ISSN: 0737-8831.

BAKER, SHARON L. 1986a. Overload, Browsers, and Selections. Library and Information Science Research. 1986; 8(4): 315-329. ISSN: 0740-8188.

BAKER, SHARON L. 1986b. The Display Phenomenon: An Exploration into Factors Causing the Increased Circulation of Displayed Books. Library Quarterly. 1986 July; 56(3): 237-257. ISSN: 0024-2519.

BAKER, SHARON L. 1988. Will Fiction Classification Schemes Increase Use? RQ. 1988 Spring; 27(3): 366-376. ISSN: 0033-7072.

BANKAPUR, M.B. 1988. On Browsing. Library Science with a Slant to Documentation. 1988 September; 25(3): 131-137. ISSN: 0024-2543; CODEN: LSSDA8.

BATES, MARCIA J. 1981. Search Techniques. In: Williams, Martha E., ed. Annual Review of Information Science and Technology: Volume 16. White Plains, NY: Knowledge Industry Publications, Inc. for the American Society for Information Science; 1981. 139-170. ISSN: 0066-4200.

BATES, MARCIA J. 1986a. An Exploratory Paradigm for Online Information Retrieval. In: Brookes, Bertram C., ed. Intelligent Information Systems for the Information Society. New York, NY: Elsevier Science Publishers; 1986. 91-99. ISBN: 0-444-70050-1.

BATES, MARCIA J. 1986b. Subject Access in Online Catalogs: A Design Model. Journal of the American Society for Information Science. 1986; 37(6): 357-376. ISSN: 0002-8231.

BATES, MARCIA J. 1986c. What Is a Reference Book? A Theoretical and Empirical Analysis. RQ. 1986 Fall; 26: 37-57. ISSN: 0033-7072.

BATES, MARCIA J. 1989. The Design of Browsing and Berrypicking Techniques for the Online Search Interface. Online Review. 1989; 13(5): 407-424. ISSN: 0309-314X.

BATES, MARCIA J. 1990. Where Should the Person Stop and the Information Search Interface Start? Information Processing and Management. 1990; 26(5): 575-591. ISSN: 0306-4573; CODEN: IPMADK.

BATLEY, SUSAN. 1988. Visual Information Retrieval: Browsing Strategies in Pictorial Databases. Aberdeen, Scotland: University of Aberdeen; 1988. (Ph.D. dissertation). Available from: the University.

BAWDEN, DAVID. 1986. Information Systems and the Stimulation of Creativity. Journal of Information Science (England). 1986; 12(5): 203-216. ISSN: 0165-5515.

BEHESHTI, JAMSHID. 1992. Browsing through Public Library Catalogs. Information Technology and Libraries. 1992 September; 11(3): 220-228. ISSN: 0730-9295; CODEN: ITLBDC.

BELKIN, NICHOLAS J.; CHANG, SHAN-JU; DOWNS, TRUDY; SARACEVIC, TEFKO; ZHAO, SHUYUAN. 1990. Taking Account of User Tasks, Goals and Behavior for the Design of Online Public Access Catalogs. In: Henderson, D., ed. Proceedings of the American Society for Information Science (ASIS) 53rd Annual Meeting: Volume 27; 1990 November 4-8; Toronto, Canada. Medford, NJ: Learned Information, Inc. for ASIS; 1990. 69-79. ISSN: 0044-7870.

BELKIN, NICHOLAS J.; CROFT, W. BRUCE. 1987. Retrieval Techniques. In: Williams, Martha E., ed. Annual Review of Information Science and Technology: Volume 22. White Plains, NY: Knowledge Industry Publications, Inc. for the American Society for Information Science; 1987. 109-145. ISSN: 0066-4200.

BELKIN, NICHOLAS J.; MARCHETTI, P.G.; COOL, COLLEEN. 1993. BRAQUE: Design of an Interface to Support User Interaction in Information Retrieval. Information Processing and Management. 1993; 29(3): 325-344. ISSN: 0306-4573; CODEN: IPMADK.

BELKIN, NICHOLAS J.; ODDY, ROBERT N.; BROOKS, HELEN M. 1982. ASK for Information Retrieval. Part I: Background and Theory. Journal of Documentation. 1982 June; 38(2): 61-71. ISSN: 0022-0418.

BELL, WILLIAM J. 1991. Searching Behaviour: The Behavioural Ecology of Finding Resources. New York, NY: Chapman and Hall; 1991. 358p. ISBN: 0-412-29210-6.

BLOCH, PETER H.; RICHINS, MARSHA L. 1983. Shopping without Purchase: An Investigation of Consumer Browsing Behavior. In: Bagozzi, Richard P.; Tybout, Alice M., eds. Advances in Consumer Research: Volume X. Proceedings of the Association for Consumer Research 13th Annual Conference; 1982 October 7-10; San Francisco, CA. Ann Arbor, MI: Association for Consumer Research; 1983. 389-393. ISSN: 0098-9258.

BLOCH, PETER H.; RIDGWAY, NANCY M.; SHERRELL, DANIEL L. 1989. Extending the Concept of Shopping: An Investigation of Browsing Activity. Journal of the Academy of Marketing Science. 1989 Winter; 17(1): 13-21. ISSN: 0092-0703.

BOLL, JOHN J. 1985. Shelf Browsing, Open Access and Storage Capacity in Research Libraries. Champaign, IL: University of Illinois, Graduate School of Library and Information Science; 1985. 34p. (Occasional Papers no. 169). 37p. ISSN: 0276-1769.

BORGMAN, CHRISTINE L. 1986. Why Are Online Catalogs Hard to Use? Lessons Learned from Information-Retrieval Studies. Journal of the American Society for Information Science. 1986; 37(6): 387-400. ISSN: 0002-8231.

BORGMAN, CHRISTINE L. 1989. All Users of Information Retrieval Systems Are Not Created Equal: An Exploration into Individual Differences. Information Processing and Management. 1989; 25(3): 237-251. ISSN: 0306-4573; CODEN: IPMADK.

BORGMAN, CHRISTINE L.; GALLAGHER, ANDREA L.; WALTER, VIRGINIA A. 1993. The Design and Evaluation of an Information Retrieval System Based on Children's Abilities: The Science Library Catalog. Information Processing and Management. (in press). ISSN: 0306-4573; CODEN: IPMADK.

BORGMAN CHRISTINE L.; WALTER, VIRGINIA A.; ROSENBERG, JASON. 1991. The Science Library Catalog Project: Comparison of Children's Searching Behavior in Hypertext and a Keyword Search System. In: Griffiths, José-Marie, ed. Proceedings of the American Society for Information Science (ASIS) 54th Annual Meeting: Volume 28; 1991 October 27-31; Washington, DC. Medford, NJ: Learned Information, Inc. for ASIS; 1991. 162-169. ISSN: 0044-7870; ISBN: 0-938734-56-3.

BROWN, JOHN SEELY; COLLINS, ALLAN; DUGUID, PAUL. 1989. Situated Cognition and the Culture of Learning. Champaign, IL: Center for the Study of Reading, University of Illinois at Urbana-Champaign; 1989 August. 25p. (Technical report no. 481). Available from: Center for the Study of Reading, 51 Gerty Drive, Champaign, IL 61820.

BUCKLAND, M. K. 1979. On Types of Search and the Allocation of Library Resources. Journal of the American Society for Information Science. 1979; 30: 143-147. ISSN: 0002-8231.

BUCKLEY, PAUL; LONG, JOHN. 1990. Using Videotex for Shopping: A Qualitative Analysis. Behaviour and Information Technology. 1990; 9(1): 47-61. ISSN: 0144-929X.

CANTER, DAVID; RIVERS, ROD; STORRS, GRAHAM. 1985. Characterizing User Navigation through Complex Data Structures. Behaviour and Information Technology. 1985; 4(2): 93-102. ISSN: 0144-929X.

CARMEL, ERRAN; CRAWFORD, STEPHEN; CHEN, HSINCHUN. 1992. Browsing in Hypertext: A Cognitive Study. IEEE Transactions on Systems, Man and Cybernetics. 1992 September/October; 22(5): 865-883. ISSN: 0018-9472.

CARR, DAVID. 1991. Minds in Museums and Libraries: The Cognitive Management of Cultural Institutions. Teachers College Record. 1991 Fall; 93(1): 6-27. ISSN: 0161-4681.

CELORIA, FRANCIS. 1968. The Archaeology of Serendip. Library Association Record. 1968 October; 70: 251-253. ISSN: 0024-2195.

CHANG, SHAN-JU L. 1993. Toward a Multi-Dimensional Framework for Understanding Browsing. New Brunswick, NJ: Rutgers University, School of Communication, Information and Library Studies; 1993. 120p. (Unpublished Ph.D. dissertation proposal). Available from: the author, School of Communication, Information and Library Studies, 4 Huntington Street, New Brunswick, NJ 08903.

CHOO, CHUN WEI; AUSTER, ETHEL. 1993. Environmental Scanning: Acquisition and Use of Information by Managers. In: Williams, Martha E., ed. Annual Review of Information Science and Technology: Volume 28. Medford, NJ: Learned Information, Inc. for the American Society for Information Science; 1993. 279-314. ISSN: 0066-4200.

COATES, JOSEPH F. 1986. Issues Management: How You Can Plan, Organize and Manage for the Future. Mt. Airy, MD: Lomond Publications; 1986. ISBN: 0-912338-55-5

CONKLIN, JEFF. 1987. Hypertext: An Introduction and Survey. Computer. 1987 September; 20(9): 17-41. ISSN: 0018-9162.

CONKLIN, JEFF; BEGEMAN, MICHAEL L. 1989. gIBIS: A Tool for All Reasons. Journal of the American Society for Information Science. 1989; 40(3): 200-213. ISSN: 0002-8231.

COVE, J.F.; WALSH, B.C. 1987. Browsing as a Means of Online Text Retrieval. Information Services and Use. 1987; 7(6): 183-188. ISSN: 0167-5265.

COVE, J.F.; WALSH, B.C. 1988. Online Text Retrieval via Browsing. Information Processing and Management. 1988; 24(1): 31-37. ISSN: 0306-4573; CODEN: IPMADK.

CUTTING, DOUGLASS R.; KARGER, DAVID R.; PEDERSEN, JAN O.; TUKEY, JOHN W. 1992. Scatter/Gather: A Cluster-based Approach to Browsing Large Document Collections. In: Belkin, Nicholas; Ingwersen, Peter; Pejtersen, Annelise Mark, eds. SIGIR '92: Proceedings of the Association for Computing Machinery Special Interest Group on Information Retrieval (ACMSIGIR) 15th Annual International Conference on Research and Development in Information Retrieval; 1992 June 21-24; Copenhagen, Denmark. New York, NY: ACM; 1992. 318-329. ISBN: 0-89791-523-2.

DAVIES, ROY. 1989. The Creation of New Knowledge by Information Retrieval and Classification. Journal of Documentation. 1989; 45(4): 273-301. ISSN: 0022-0418.

DECI, EDWARD L.; RYAN, RICHARD M. 1985. Intrinsic Motivation and Self-Determination in Human Behavior. New York, NY: Plenum Press; 1985. 371p. ISBN: 0-306-42022-8.

DERVIN, BRENDA; NILAN, MICHAEL. 1986. Information Needs and Uses. In: Williams, Martha E., ed. Annual Review of Information Science and Technology: Volume 21. White Plains, NY: Knowledge Industry Publications, Inc. for the American Society for Information Science; 1986. 3-33. ISSN: 0066-4200; ISBN: 0-86729-209-1.

DORR, AIMEE; KUNKEL, DALE. 1990. Children and the Media Environment: Change and Constancy amid Change. Communication Research. 1990 February; 17(1): 5-25. ISSN: 0093-6502.

DOTY, PHILIP; BISHOP, ANN P.; MCCLURE, CHARLES R. 1991. Scientific Norms and the Use of Electronic Research Networks. In: Griffiths, José-Marie, ed. Proceedings of the American Society for Information Science (ASIS) 54th Annual Meeting: Volume 28; 1991 October 27-31; Washington,

DC. Medford, NJ: Learned Information, Inc. for ASIS; 1991. 24-38. ISSN: 0044-7870; ISBN: 0-938734-56-3; CODEN: PAISDQ.

DOWNS, ROGER M. 1979. Mazes, Minds, and Maps. In: Pollet, Dorothy; Haskell, Peter C., eds. Sign Systems for Libraries: Solving the Wayfinding Problem. New York, NY: R.R. Bowker Co.; 1979. 17-32. ISBN: 0-8352-1149-5.

DOZIER, DAVID M.; RICE, RONALD E. 1984. Rival Theories of Electronic Newsreading. In: Rice, Ronald E., ed. The New Media. Newbury Park, CA: Sage; 1984. 103-127. ISBN: 0-8039-2272-8 (pbk).

DRABENSTOTT, KAREN MARKEY; DEMEYER, A.N.; GERCKENS, J.; POE, D.T. 1990. Analysis of a Bibliographic Database Enhanced with a Library Classification. Library Resources and Technical Services. 1990 April; 34(2): 179-198. ISSN: 0024-2527.

DRUCKER, MINDY. 1990. On Track with Eye-Trac Research. Target Marketing. 1990 September; 13(9): 57-58. ISSN: 0889-5333.

DRUCKER, SUSAN J.; GUMPERT, GARY. 1991. Public Space and Communication: The Zoning of Public Interaction. Communication Theory. 1991 November; 1(4): 294-310. ISSN: 1050-3293; CODEN: CNTHEV.

EGAN, DENNIS E.; LESK, MICHAEL E.; KETCHUM, R. DANIEL; LOCHBAUM, CAROL C.; REMDE, JOEL R.; LITTMAN, MICHAEL; LANDAUER, THOMAS K. 1991. Hypertext for the Electronic Library? CORE Sample Results. In: Hypertext '91: Proceedings of the Association for Computing Machinery (ACM) 3rd Conference on Hypertext; 1991 December 15-18; San Antonio, TX. New York, NY: Association for Computing Machinery; 1991. 299-312. ISBN: 0-89791-461-9.

EGAN, DENNIS E.; REMDE, JOEL R.; GOMEZ, LOUIS M.; LANDAUER, THOMAS K.; EBERHARDT, JENNIFER; LOCHBAUM, CAROL C. 1989. Formative Design-Evaluation of SuperBook. ACM Transactions on Information Systems. 1989 January; 7(1): 30-57. ISSN: 0734-2047.

ELLIS, DAVID. 1989. A Behavioural Approach to Information Retrieval System Design. Journal of Documentation. 1989 September; 45(3): 171-212. ISSN: 0022-0418.

FISH, ROBERT S.; KRAUT, ROBERT E.; ROOT, ROBERT W.; RICE, RONALD E. 1993. Video as a Technology for Informal Communication. Communications of the ACM. 1993 January; 36(1): 48-61. ISSN: 0001-0782.

FOSS, CAROLYN L. 1989. Tools for Reading and Browsing Hypertext. Information Processing and Management. 1989; 25(4): 407-418. ISSN: 0306-4573; CODEN: IPMADK.

FOX, M.S.; PALAY, A.J. 1979. The BROWSE System: An Introduction. In: Tally, Roy D.; Deultgen, Ronald R., eds. Proceedings of the American Society for Information Science (ASIS) 42nd Annual Meeting: Volume 16; 1979 October 14-18; Minneapolis, MN. White Plains, NY: Knowledge Industry Publications, Inc. for ASIS; 1979. 183-193. ISSN: 0044-7870; CODEN: PAISDQ.

FRIEDBERG, ANNE. 1991. Les Flaneurs du Mal(l): Cinema and the Postmodern Condition. PMLA: Publications of the Modern Language Association of America. 1991 May; 106(3): 419-431. ISSN: 0030-8129.

GECSEI, JAN; MARTIN, DANIEL. 1989. Browsing Access to Visual Information. Optical Information Systems. 1989 September/October; 9(5): 237-241. ISSN: 0886-5809.

GREENE, ROBERT J. 1977. The Effectiveness of Browsing. College and Research Libraries. 1977 July; 38(4): 313-316. ISSN: 0010-0870.

GROVER, VARUN; SABHERWAL, RAJIV. 1989. Poor Performance of Videotex Systems. Journal of Systems Management. 1989 June; 40(6): 31-37. ISSN: 0022-4839; CODEN: JSYMA9.

HANCOCK-BEAULIEU, MICHELINE. 1990. Evaluating the Impact of an Online Library Catalogue in Subject Searching Behavior at the Catalogue and at the Shelves. Journal of Documentation. 1990 December; 46(4): 318-338. ISSN: 0022-0418.

HEETER, CARRIE; GREENBERG, BRADLEY S. 1985. Profiling the Zappers. Journal of Advertising Research. 1985 April/May; 25(2): 15-19. ISSN: 0021-8499; CODEN: JADRAV.

HERNER, SAUL. 1970. Browsing. In: Kent, A.; Lancour, H., eds. Encyclopedia of Library and Information Science: Volume 3. New York, NY: Marcel Dekker; 1970. 408-415. LC: 68-31232.

HEWINS, ELIZABETH T. 1990. Information Need and Use Studies. In: Williams, Martha E., ed. Annual Review of Information Science and Technology: Volume 25. Amsterdam, The Netherlands: Elsevier Science Publishers for the American Society for Information Science; 1990. 145-172. ISSN: 0066-4200; ISBN: 0-444-88531-5.

HILDRETH, CHARLES R. 1982. The Concept and Mechanics of Browsing in an Online Library Catalog. In: Williams, Martha E.; Hogan, Thomas H., eds. Proceedings of the 3rd National Online Meeting; 1982 March 30-April 1; New York, NY. Medford, NJ: Learned Information, Inc.; 1982. 181-196. ISBN: 0-938734-04-0.

HILDRETH, CHARLES R., ed. 1989. The Online Catalogue: Development and Directions. London, England: Library Association; 1989. 212p. ISBN: 0-8536-5708-4.

HILTZ, STARR ROXANNE; TUROFF, MURRAY. 1985. Structuring Computer-mediated Communication Systems to Avoid Information Overload. Communications of the ACM. 1985 July; 28(7): 680-689. ISSN: 0001-0782.

HOWARD, DARA LEE. 1991. What the Eye Sees While Predicting a Document's Pertinence from Its Citation. In: Griffiths, José-Marie, ed. Proceedings of the American Society for Information Science (ASIS) 54th Annual Meeting: Volume 28; 1991 October 27-31; Washington, DC. Medford, NJ: Learned Information, Inc. for ASIS; 1991. 87-97. ISSN: 0044-7870; ISBN: 0-938734-56-3; CODEN: PAISDQ.

HUESTIS, JEFFREY C. 1988. Clustering LC Classification Numbers in an Online Catalog for Improved Browsability. Information Technology and Libraries. 1988 December; 7(4): 381-393. ISSN: 0730-9295; CODEN: ITLBDC.

HULLEY, ANGELA J. 1990. Navigation, Browsing and Understanding in an Anatomical "Hypermedia" Environment. Current Psychology: Research and Reviews. 1990 Summer; 9(2): 162-180. ISSN: 1046-1310.

HYMAN, RICHARD JOSEPH. 1971. Access to Library Collections: Summary of a Documentary and Opinion Survey on the Direct Shelf Approach and

Browsing. Library Resources and Technical Services. 1971 Fall; 15(4): 479-491. ISSN: 0024-2527; CODEN: LRTSAH.

HYMAN, RICHARD JOSEPH. 1972. Access to Library Collections: An Inquiry into the Validity of the Direct Shelf Approach, with Special Reference to Browsing. Metuchen, NJ: The Scarecrow Press; 1972. 452p. ISBN: 0-8108-0434-4.

ISELIN, ERROL. 1989. The Impact of Information Diversity on Information Overload Effects in Unstructured Managerial Decision Making. Journal of Information Science. 1989; 15: 163-173. ISSN: 0165-5515.

JANES, JOSEPH W. 1989. The Application of Search Theory to Information Science. In: Katzer, Jeffrey; Newby, Gregory B., eds. ASIS '89: Proceedings of the American Society for Information Science (ASIS) 52nd Annual Meeting: Volume 26; 1989 October 30-November 2; Washington, DC. Medford, NJ: Learned Information, Inc. for ASIS; 1989. 9-12. ISSN: 0044-7870; ISBN: 0-938734-40-7; CODEN: PAISDQ.

JARBOE, GLEN R.; MCDANIEL, CARL D. 1987. A Profile of Browsers in Regional Shopping Malls. Journal of the Academy of Marketing Science. 1987 Spring; 15(1): 45-52. ISSN: 0092-0703.

JEON, JUNG-OK. 1990. An Empirical Investigation of the Relationship between Affective States, In-Store Browsing and Impulse Buying. Tuscaloosa, AL: Graduate School of the University of Alabama; 1990. 177p. (Ph.D. dissertation). Available from: University Microfilms International, Ann Arbor, MI. (UMI order no. AAD 91-20303).

JOSEPH, BIJU; STEINBERG, ESTHER R.; JONES, A. RUSSELL. 1989. User Perceptions and Expectations of an Information Retrieval System. Behaviour and Information Technology. 1989; 8(2): 77-88. ISSN: 0144-929X.

KATZER, JEFFREY. 1987. User Studies, Information Science, and Communication. The Canadian Journal of Information Science. 1987; 12(3/4): 15-30. ISSN: 0380-9218.

KATZER, JEFFREY; FLETCHER, PATRICIA T. 1992. The Information Environment of Managers. In: Williams, Martha E., ed. Annual Review of Information Science and Technology: Volume 27. Medford, NJ: Learned Information, Inc. for the American Society for Information Science; 1992. 227-263. ISSN: 0066-4200; ISBN: 0-938734-66-0.

KRAUT, ROBERT E.; FISH, ROBERT S.; ROOT, ROBERT W.; CHALFONTE, BARBARA L. 1990. Informal Communications: Form, Function, and Technology. In: Oskamp, Stuart; Spacapan, Shirlynn, eds. People's Reactions to Technology in Factories, Offices, and Aerospace. Newbury Park, CA: Sage Publications; 1990. 145-199. ISBN: 0-8039-3852-7.

KRAUT, ROBERT E.; GALEGHER, JOLENE. 1990. Patterns of Contact and Communication in Scientific Research Collaboration. In: Galegher, Jolene; Kraut, Robert E.; Egido, Carmen, eds. Intellectual Teamwork: Social and Technological Foundations of Cooperative Work. Hillsdale, NJ: Lawrence Erlbaum Associates; 1990. 149-171. ISBN: 0-8058-0534-6 (pbk).

KUHLTHAU, CAROL COLLIER. 1991. Inside the Search Process: Information Seeking from the User's Perspective. Journal of the American Society for Information Science. 1991 June; 42(5): 361-371. ISSN: 0002-8231.

LANCASTER, FREDERICK WILFRID. 1968. Information Retrieval Systems: Characteristics, Testing, and Evaluation. New York, NY: John Wiley and Sons, Inc.; 1968. 222p. ISBN: 0-471-51240-0.

LANCASTER, FREDERICK WILFRID. 1978. Toward Paperless Information Systems. New York, NY: Academic Press; 1978. 179p. ISBN: 0-12-436050-5.

LARSEN, SVEND. 1988. The Idea of an Electronic Library: A Critical Essay. Libri. 1988; 38(3): 159-177. ISSN: 0024-2667.

LAWRENCE, GARY S.; OJA, ANNE R. 1980. The Use of General Collections at the University of California: A Study of Unrecorded Use, at-the-Shelf Discovery, and Immediacy of Need for Materials at the Davis and Santa Cruz Campus Libraries. Final Report. Berkeley, CA: University of California; 1980. 120p. (Research Report RR-80-1). ERIC: ED 191490.

LELU, ALAIN. 1991. From Data Analysis to Neural Networks: New Prospects for Efficient Browsing through Databases. Journal of Information Science. 1991; 17: 1-12. ISSN: 0165-5515.

LEVINE, MARILYN M. 1969. An Essay on Browsing. RQ. 1969 Fall; 9(1): 35-36, 93. ISSN: 0033-7072.

LICKLIDER, J.C.R. 1965. Appendix I: Proposed Experiments in Browsing. In: Overhage, Carl F.J.; Harman, R. Joyce, eds. INTREX: Report of a Planning Conference on Information Transfer Experiments; 1965 September 3; Cambridge, MA. Cambridge, MA: Massachusetts Institute of Technology (MIT) Press; 1965. 187-197. LC: 65-28409.

LIEBSCHER, PETER; MARCHIONINI, GARY. 1988. Browse and Analytical Search Strategies in a Full-Text CD-ROM Encyclopedia. School Library Media Quarterly. 1988; 16(4): 223-233. ISSN: 0278-4823.

LOSEE, ROBERT M., JR. 1992. A Gray Code Based Ordering for Documents on Shelves: Classification for Browsing and Retrieval. Journal of the American Society for Information Science. 1992 May; 43(4): 312-322. ISSN: 0002-8231.

MACKINLAY, JOCK D.; ROBERTSON, GEORGE G.; CARD, STUART K. 1991. The Perspective Wall: Detail and Context Smoothly Integrated. In: Robertson, Scott P.; Olson, Gary M.; Olson, Judith S., eds. CHI '91: Proceedings of the Association for Computing Machinery (ACM) Conference on Human Factors in Computing Systems: Reaching through Technology; 1991 April 27-May 2; New Orleans, LA. Reading, MA: Addison-Wesley Publishing; 1991. 173-179. ISSN: 0713-5424; ISBN: 0-89791-383-3.

MALONE, THOMAS W.; GRANT, KENNETH R.; TURBAK, FRANKLYN A.; BROBST, STEPHEN A.; COHEN, MICHAEL D. 1987. Intelligent Information-Sharing Systems. Communications of the ACM. 1987 May; 30(5): 390-402. ISSN: 0001-0782.

MARCHIONINI, GARY. 1987. An Invitation to Browse: Designing Full-Text Systems for Novice Users. The Canadian Journal of Information Science. 1987; 12(3/4): 69-79. ISSN: 0380-9218.

MARCHIONINI, GARY; DWIGGINS, SANDRA; KATZ, ANDREW; LIN, XIA. 1993. Information Seeking in Full-Text End-User-Oriented Search Systems: The Roles of Domain and Search Expertise. Library and Information Science Research. 1993; 15(1): 35-69. ISSN: 0740-8188.

MARCHIONINI, GARY; LIEBSCHER, PETER. 1991. Performance in Electronic Encyclopedias: Implications for Adaptive Systems. In: Griffiths, José-Marie, ed. Proceedings of the American Society for Information Science (ASIS) 54th Annual Meeting: Volume 28; 1991 October 27-31; Washington, DC. Medford, NJ: Learned Information, Inc. for ASIS; 1991. 39-48. ISSN: 0044-7870; ISBN: 0-938734-56-3; CODEN: PAISDQ.

MARCHIONINI, GARY; SHNEIDERMAN, BEN. 1988. Finding Facts vs. Browsing Knowledge in Hypertext Systems. Computer. 1988 January; 21: 70-80. ISSN: 0018-9162.

MARKEY, KAREN. 1987. Searching and Browsing the Dewey Decimal Classification in an Online Catalog. Cataloging and Classification Quarterly. 1987 Spring; 7(3): 37-68. ISSN: 0163-9374.

MARKEY, KAREN; ATHERTON, PAULINE. 1979. Part III: Online Searching Test. In: Online Searching of ERIC: Executive Summary of a Five Part Report with a Collection of Recommendations and Suggestions for Redesign of the ERIC Record and Online Data Base. Syracuse, NY: Syracuse University, ERIC Clearinghouse on Information Resources; 1979. 41p. ERIC: ED 180432.

MASSICOTTE, MIA. 1988. Improved Browsable Displays for Online Subject Access. Information Technology and Libraries. 1988 December; 7(4): 373-380. ISSN: 0730-9295.

MCALEESE, RAY. 1989. Navigation and Browsing in Hypertext. In: McAleese, Ray, ed. Hypertext: Theory into Practice. Norwood, NJ: Ablex Publishing; 1989. 6-44. ISBN: 0-89391-575-0.

MCGUIRE, WILLIAM J. 1974. Psychological Motives and Communication Gratification. In: Blumler, Jay G.; Katz, Elihu, eds. The Uses of Mass Communications: Current Perspectives on Gratifications Research. Beverly Hills, CA: Sage; 1974. 167-196. ISBN: 0-8039-0494-0.

MENZEL, HERBERT. 1966. Information Needs and Uses in Science and Technology. In: Cuadra, Carlos A., ed. Annual Review of Information Science and Technology: Volume 1. New York, NY: Interscience Publishers; 1966. 41-69. ISSN: 0066-4200; LC: 66-25096.

MERRIAM-WEBSTER, INCORPORATED. 1986. Webster's Third New International Dictionary of the English Language. Unbridged edition. Springfield, MA: Merriam-Webster, Inc.; 1986. p. 285. ISBN: 0-87779-206-2 (imperial buckram); ISBN: 0-87779-201-1 (blue sturdite).

MICHEL, DEE ANDY. 1992. A File Structure Model of Library Search Behavior. Los Angeles, CA: University of California, Graduate School of Library and Information Science; 1992. 441p. (Ph.D. dissertation). Available from: University Microfilms International, Ann Arbor, MI. (UMI order no. AAD93-01545).

MORSE, PHILIP M. 1970. Search Theory and Browsing. Library Quarterly. 1970 October; 40(4): 391-408. ISSN: 0024-2519.

MORSE, PHILIP M. 1973. Browsing and Search Theory. In: Rawski, C.H., ed. Toward a Theory of Librarianship: Papers in Honor of Jesse Hauk Shera. Metuchen, NJ: Scarecrow Press; 1973. 246-261. ISBN: 0-8108-0535-9.

NEISSER, ULRIC. 1967. Cognitive Psychology. New York, NY: Meredith Publishing Co.; 1967. 351p. ISBN: 0-390-66509-6; LC: 67-27727.

NEWBY, GREGORY B. 1993. Virtual Reality. In: Williams, Martha E., ed. Annual Review of Information Science and Technology: Volume 28. Medford, NJ: Learned Information, Inc. for the American Society for Information Science; 1993. 187-229. ISSN: 0066-4200.

NIELSEN, J. 1990. Miniatures versus Icons as a Visual Cache for Videotex Browsing. Behaviour and Information Technology. 1990; 9(6): 441-449. ISSN: 0144-929X.

NOERR, PETER L.; NOERR, KATHLEEN T. BIVINS. 1985. Browse and Navigate: An Advance in Database Access Methods. Information Processing and Management. 1985; 21(3): 205-213. ISSN: 0306-4573; CODEN: IPMADK.

O'CONNOR, BRIAN C. 1985. Access to Moving Image Documents: Background Concepts and Proposals for Surrogates for Film and Video Works. Journal of Documentation. 1985; 41(4): 209-220. ISSN: 0022-0418.

O'CONNOR, BRIAN C. 1988. Fostering Creativity: Enhancing the Browsing Environment. International Journal of Information Management. 1988; 8: 203-210. ISSN: 0268-4012.

O'CONNOR, BRIAN C. 1993. Productive Browsing: Concepts and Strategies for Document Searches outside the Formal Bibliographic Apparatus. Knowledge: Creation, Diffusion and Utilization. 1993; 15(1). (in press). ISSN: 0164-0259.

O'NEILL, MICHAEL J.; JASPER, CYNTHIA R. 1992. An Evaluation of Models of Consumer Spatial Behavior Using the Environment-Behavior Paradigm. Environment and Behavior. 1992 July; 24(4): 411-440. ISSN: 0013-9165.

ODDY, ROBERT N. 1977. Information Retrieval through Man-Machine Dialogue. Journal of Documentation. 1977; 33(3): 1-14. ISSN: 0022-0418.

ODDY, ROBERT N.; BALAKRISHNAN, BHASKARAN. 1991. PTHOMAS: An Adaptive Information Retrieval System on the Connection Machine. Information Processing and Management. 1991; 27(4): 317-335. ISSN: 0306-4573; CODEN: IPMADK.

OVERHAGE, CARL F.J.; HARMAN, R. JOYCE., eds. 1965. INTREX: Report of a Planning Conference on Information Transfer Experiments; 1965 September 3; Cambridge, MA. Cambridge, MA: Massachusetts Institute of Technology (MIT) Press; 1965. 276p. (p. 118-123, 130). LC: 65-28409.

PEJTERSEN, ANNELISE MARK. 1989. A Library System for Information Retrieval Based on a Cognitive Task Analysis and Supported by an Icon-Based Interface. In: Belkin, N.J.; van Rijsbergen, C.J., eds. SIGIR '89: Proceedings of the Association for Computing Machinery Special Interest Group on Information Retrieval (ACMSIGIR) 12th Annual International Conference on Research and Development in Information Retrieval; 1989 June 25-28; Cambridge, MA. New York, NY: ACM; 1989. 40-47. ISBN: 0-89791-321-3.

PERSE, ELIZABETH M. 1990. Audience Selectivity and Involvement in the Newer Media Environment. Communication Research. 1990 October; 17(5): 675-697. ISSN: 0093-6502.

PETERS, THOMAS J.; WATERMAN, ROBERT H., JR. 1982. In Search of Excellence: Lessons from America's Best-Run Companies. New York, NY: Harper and Row; 1982. 360p. ISBN: 0-06-015042-4.

POLAND, JEAN. 1991. Informal Communication among Scientists and Engineers: A Review of the Literature. Science and Technology Libraries. 1991 Spring; 11(3): 61-73. ISSN: 0194-262X; CODEN: STELDF.

POLLET, DOROTHY; HASKELL, PETER C., eds. 1979. Sign Systems for Libraries: Solving the Wayfinding Problem. New York, NY: R.R. Bowker Co.; 1979. 271p. ISBN: 0-8352-1149-5; LC: 79-11138.

RADA, R.; MURPHY, C. 1992. Searching versus Browsing in Hypertext. Hypermedia. 1992; 4(1): 1-30. ISSN: 0955-8543.

RICE, RONALD E. 1987. Computer-mediated Communication and Organizational Innovation. Journal of Communication. 1987; 37(4): 65-94. ISSN: 0021-9916.

ROBERTS, NORMAN. 1982. A Search for Information Man. Social Science Information Studies (England). 1982; 2: 93-104. ISSN: 0143-6236.

ROOT, ROBERT W. 1988. Design of a Multi-Media Vehicle for Social Browsing. In: Proceedings of the Conference on Computer-Supported Cooperative Work; 1988 September 26-28; Portland, OR. Baltimore, MD: Association for Computing Machinery, Inc.; 1988. 25-38. ISBN: 0-89791-282-9.

ROSS, JOHANNA. 1983. Observations of Browsing Behavior in an Academic Library. College and Research Libraries. 1983; 44(4): 269-276. ISSN: 0010-0870.

ROUGHTON, KAREN G.; TYCKOSON, DAVID A. 1985. Browsing with Sound: Sound-based Codes and Automated Authority Control. Information Technology and Libraries. 1985; 4(2): 130-136. ISSN: 0730-9295; CODEN: ITLBDC.

SALOMON, LIAN; KOPPELMAN, FRANK S. 1992. Teleshopping or Going Shopping? An Information Acquisition Perspective. Behaviour and Information Technology. 1992; 11(4): 189-198. ISSN: 0144-929X.

SAUNDERS, CAROL; JONES, JACK WILLIAM. 1990. Temporal Sequences in Information Acquisition for Decision Making: A Focus on Source and Medium. Academy of Management Review. 1990 January; 15(1): 29-46. ISSN: 0363-7425.

SAVOY, JACQUES. 1992. Bayesian Inference Networks and Spreading Activation in Hypertext Systems. Information Processing and Management. 1992; 28(3): 389-406. ISSN: 0306-4573; CODEN: IPMADK.

SHAFFER, CLIFFORD A. 1992. Data Representations for Geographic Information Systems. In: Williams, Martha E., ed. Annual Review of Information Science and Technology: Volume 27. Medford, NJ: Learned Information, Inc. for the American Society for Information Science; 1992. 135-172. ISSN: 0066-4200; ISBN: 0-938734-66-0.

SHARFMAN, MARK P.; DEAN, JAMES W., JR. 1991. Conceptualizing and Measuring the Organizational Environment: A Multidimensional Approach. Journal of Management. 1991; 17(4): 681-700. ISSN: 0149-2063.

SHIM, SOYEON; MAHONEY, MARIANNE Y. 1991. Electronic Shoppers and Nonshoppers among Videotex Users: Shopping Orientations, Videotex Usages, and Demographics. Journal of Direct Marketing. 1991 Summer; 5(3): 29-38. ISSN: 0892-0591.

SHNEIDERMAN, BEN; BRETHAUER, DOROTHY; PLAISANT, CATHERINE; POTTER, RICHARD. 1989. Evaluating Three Museum Installations of a

Hypertext System. Journal of the American Society for Information Science. 1989 April; 40(3): 172-182. ISSN: 0002-8231.

SODERSTON, CANDACE. 1986. A Study of Spatial Models and Human Navigation within Complex Computer Interfaces. Troy, NY: Rensselaer Polytechnic Institute; 1986 May. 285p. (Ph.D. dissertation). Available from: University Microfilms International (UMI), Ann Arbor, MI. (UMI order no. AAD86-19997).

SPRING, MICHAEL B. 1991. Informating with Virtual Reality. In: Helsel, Sandra K.; Roth, Judith Paris, eds. Virtual Reality: Theory, Practice, and Promise. Westport, CT: Meckler Publishing; 1991. 3-17. ISBN: 0-88736-728-3.

STEPHENSON, WILLIAM. 1986. Play Theory of Communication. Operant Subjectivity. 1986 July; 9(4): 109-122. (Originally presented at the Association for Education in Journalism, Syracuse, NY, 1965). ISSN: 0193-2713.

STONE, SUE. 1982. Humanities Scholars: Information Needs and Uses. Journal of Documentation. 1982; 38(4): 292-313. ISSN: 0022-0418.

STORY, GUY A.; O'GORMAN, LAWRENCE; FOX, DAVID; SCHAPER, LOUISE LEVY; JAGADISH, H.V. 1992. The RightPages Image-Based Electronic Library for Alerting and Browsing. Computer. 1992 September; 25(9): 17-26. ISSN: 0018-9162.

SUCHMAN, LUCY A. 1987. Plans and Situated Actions: The Problem of Human-Machine Communication. Cambridge. England: Cambridge University Press; 1987. 203p. ISBN: 0-521-33137-4; LC: 87-8013.

SWANSON, DON R. 1987. Two Medical Literatures That Are Logically But Not Bibliographically Connected. Journal of the American Society for Information Science. 1987 May; 38(4): 228-233. ISSN: 0002-8231.

SWANSON, DON R. 1989. Online Search for Logically-Related Noninteractive Medical Literatures: A Systematic Trial-and-Error Strategy. Journal of the American Society for Information Science. 1989 June; 40(5): 356-358. ISSN: 0002-8231.

TAYLOR, ROBERT S. 1968. Question Negotiation and Information Seeking in Libraries. College and Research Libraries. 1968; 29: 178-189. ISSN: 0010-0870.

THOMPSON, ROGER H.; CROFT, W. BRUCE. 1989. Support for Browsing in an Intelligent Text Retrieval System. International Journal of Man-Machine Studies. 1989; 30: 639-668. ISSN: 0020-7373.

TUORI, MARTIN IAN 1987. A Framework for Browsing in the Relational Data Model. Toronto, Canada: University of Toronto; 1987. 145p. (Ph.D. dissertation). Available from: University of Toronto, Department of Computer Science.

VON KEITZ, BEATE. 1988. Eye Movement Research: Do Consumers Use the Information They Are Offered? European Research. 1988 November; 16(4): 217-223. ISSN: 0304-4297; CODEN: ESOMAR.

WALKER, DONALD E., ed. 1971. Interactive Bibliographic Search: The User/Computer Interface: Proceedings of a Workshop on The User Interface for Interactive Search of Bibliographic Data Bases; 1971 January 14-15; Palo Alto, CA. Montvale, NJ: The American Federation of Information Processing Societies (AFIPS) Press; 1971. 311p. LC: 70-182192.

WALSH, JAMES P.; UNGSON, GERARDO RIVERA. 1991. Organizational
    Memory. Academy of Management Review. 1991; 16(1): 57-91 (p. 66).
    ISSN: 0363-7425.
ZERBINOS, EUGENIA. 1990. Information Seeking and Information Process-
    ing: Newspapers versus Videotext. Journalism Quarterly. 1990 Winter;
    67(4): 920-929. ISSN: 0196-3031.
ZOELLICK, BILL. 1987. Selecting an Approach to Document Retrieval. In:
    Ropiequet, Suzanne; Einberger, John; Zoellick, Bill, eds. CD ROM: Vol-
    ume 2. Optical Publishing: A Practical Approach to Developing CD ROM
    Applications. Redmond, WA: Microsoft Press; 1987. 63-82. ISBN: 1-
    55615-000-8.

III

Applications

Chun Wei Choo and Ethel Auster of the University of Toronto have provided the first *ARIST* chapter on environmental scanning. Their chapter, "Environmental Scanning: Acquisition and Use of Information by Managers," covers the nature of environmental scanning, organization theory as it relates to organizations and environments, and organizations as information-providing systems. Choo and Auster discuss information needs and uses within the contexts of the system-oriented research paradigm, the user-centered research paradigm, and information-use environments. They look at managers as users in terms of their managerial roles and in terms of their acquisition and use of information.

In environmental scanning, managers acquire and use information about the external environment to plan courses of action that shape their organizations' future. Choo and Auster review the relevant literature from organization theory, information needs and uses, and scanning studies from 1967 to 1992. Environmental scanning studies may be considered a subset of studies of managers as information users. Research has found that there is rising awareness of the value of scanning and that scanning increases with environmental uncertainty. Managers are most concerned with the market-related sectors of the environment. They use both internal and external sources in scanning, and personal sources are very important. Scanning methods vary from the informal to the formal and seem to depend on such factors as firm size, experience with planning and analysis, and perception of the environment. Choo and Auster underscore the need to recognize managers as an important but distinct group of information users, and they help us to expand our knowledge of managers as information users. Their review concludes that research on environmental scanning could productively combine perspectives from organization theory and information needs and uses studies. Organization theory views managers as decision makers and interpreters of environmental change. Information needs and uses studies approach managers as a special group of information users that has its own distinctive information needs, its own ways of defining and resolving problems, and its own information-use contexts. These perspectives complement each other and provide a richer framework for studying managers as information users.

7 Environmental Scanning: Acquisition and Use of Information by Managers

CHUN WEI CHOO and ETHEL AUSTER
University of Toronto

INTRODUCTION

Information is central to every facet of managerial work. A large part of the manager's information comes from or concerns the environment that is external to the organization. Managers use this information to respond to external change by planning and designing actions that shape the future of the organization. Environmental scanning is thus defined as the acquisition and use of information about events and trends in an organization's external environment, the knowledge of which would assist management in planning the organization's future courses of action.

As the first *ARIST* chapter on environmental scanning, this article is primarily a historical review that goes back to the earliest studies done in the 1960s. The review includes relevant literature from organization theory and information needs and uses studies in order to show the relationships between research on scanning and these broader disciplines. After an introduction on environmental scanning, we review organization theories that analyze organizations and their environments and that treat organizations as information-processing systems. Next we look at the research on information needs and uses. We follow this with a discussion of studies on managers as information users that

The invaluable help of Lydia Rett, research assistant, in scanning the literature, locating sources, and preparing the bibliography is gratefully acknowledged. This research is funded by the Social Sciences and Humanities Research Council of Canada, file no. 410-91-0065.

Annual Review of Information Science and Technology (ARIST), Volume 28, 1993
Martha E. Williams, Editor
Published for the American Society for Information Science (ASIS)
By Learned Information, Inc., Medford, N.J.

combine elements from organization theory and information needs and uses studies. This leads logically to research that investigates environmental scanning, and here we survey studies from 1967 to 1992. We conclude with a synthesis of the principal findings of the research done to date. The reader can preview the structure of this discussion by looking at the main headings in Figure 1 near the end of the chapter.

NATURE OF ENVIRONMENTAL SCANNING

The seminal study on environmental scanning was published by AGUILAR in 1967. Aguilar defines environmental scanning as "scanning for information about events and relationships in a company's outside environment, the knowledge of which would assist top management in its task of charting the company's future course of action" (AGUILAR, p. 1). Scanning then is the acquisition of information, and the importance of scanning stems directly from the importance of the decisions that result from it. Scanning spans a range of information activities. Aguilar usefully identifies four modes of scanning. In the first mode, undirected viewing, the manager is exposed to information with no specific purpose or informational need in mind. In fact, the manager is unaware of what issues might be raised. Undirected viewing takes place all the time and alerts the manager that "something" has happened and that there is more to be learned. Undirected viewing occurs, for example, when the manager converses with business associates during social gatherings. In the second mode, conditioned viewing, the manager is exposed to information about selected areas or certain types of information. Further, the manager is ready to assess the significance of such information as it is encountered. An example of conditioned viewing is the browsing of newspaper sections or periodicals that report regularly on certain topics. In the third mode, informal search, the manager actively looks for information to address a specific issue in a relatively limited and unstructured way. An example of informal search is the monitoring of the financial market to check the results of a new product pricing policy. Finally, in the fourth mode, formal search, the manager makes a deliberate or planned effort to obtain specific information or information about a specific issue—for example, the systematic gathering of information to evaluate a prospective corporate acquisition. Thus, environmental scanning includes both looking at information (viewing) and looking for information (searching). It ranges from a casual conversation at lunch or a chance observation of an angry customer to an extensive market research program to identify business opportunities.

Is environmental scanning different from information seeking? In a review of the literature of library science, management, psychology, and computer science, ROUSE & ROUSE define human information seeking as the process of identifying and choosing among alternative information sources. Information seeking is embedded in the larger processes of decision making, problem solving, and resource allocation that provide the context for establishing information needs. Information seeking is dynamic in that the methods and criteria for selecting or rejecting information vary over time and depend on intermediate results. At a conceptual level, then, environmental scanning may be seen as a special case of information seeking. Scanning is part of the process of strategic decision making, and a study of scanning as information acquisition should analyze the selection and use of alternative information sources. However, much of the field research, particularly in library and information science, deals with the information needs and uses of defined groups of users and with the search for and retrieval of information, often from documentary or bibliographic sources and online information systems. In most of these situations, a problem or information need is clarified, and information is then sought to address the specific question or need. This effort can be contrasted with scanning, which includes not only searching for particular information but also the simple exposure to information that could impact the firm. As explained earlier, scanning is often undirected viewing with no specific purpose or information need in mind and with no awareness of what future issues might be raised.

ORGANIZATION THEORY

The relationship between organizations and environments has been and continues to be a major area of study in organization theory. Indeed, the recent shift toward an "open systems" perspective of organizations has focused on the role of the environment as "the ultimate source of materials, energy, and information, all of which are vital to the continuation of the system" (SCOTT, p. 91).

Organizations and Environments

In organization theory, the external environment can be viewed as a source of information, a pool of resources, or a source of ecological variation (ALDRICH; ALDRICH & MINDLIN).

One of the first researchers to view the environment as a source of information was DILL (1958; 1962). He suggests that the best way to analyze the environment is not to try to understand it as a collection of other systems and organizations but rather to

treat the environment as information which becomes available to the organization or to which the organization, via search activity, may get access. It is not the supplier or the customer himself that counts, but the information that he makes accessible to the organization being studied about his goals, the conditions under which he will enter into a contract, or other aspects of his behavior (DILL, 1962, p. 96).

Changes, events, and trends in the environment continually send signals and messages, which organizations detect and use to adapt to new conditions. ARROW proposed a theory of control and information in large organizations in which managers receive signals from the environment and other managers. When decisions are based on these messages, further information is generated and transmitted, which in turn leads to new signals and decisions. The informational view of the organizational environment is implicit in the work of several other researchers, including BURNS & STALKER, CYERT & MARCH, GALBRAITH, LAWRENCE & LORSCH, THOMPSON, and WEICK (1979). The common perspective is that uncertainty is inherent in the environment, so that a basic task of management is to cope with this uncertainty by using information from the environment to maintain or change organizational structures and processes.

Another theoretical perspective views the environment primarily as a source of resources on which the organization depends. The degree of dependence varies according to three structural characteristics of the environment: (1) munificence (or perhaps scarcity) of resources; (2) concentration, the extent to which power in the environment is widely dispersed; and (3) interconnectedness, the number and pattern of links among organizations in the environment. Dependence would be high when resources are scarce and when entities in the environment are highly concentrated or interconnected. PFEFFER & SALANCIK assert that because external entities control the resources needed by the organization, they have power over the organization. An organization can manage resource dependence by setting up coordinating links among interdependent organizations in its environment.

In the third perspective, the environment is viewed as a source of ecological variation; that is, the environment differentially selects certain types of organizations for survival on the basis of the fit between organizational forms and environmental characteristics. The focus here is on the action of environmental selection in which the organizations are relatively passive and unable to determine their own fates. This ecological view of environmental selection is developed principally by HANNAN & FREEMAN (1977; 1989) and ALDRICH to explain why certain forms of organizations survive and thrive while others languish and perish.

Organizations as Information-Processing Systems

A number of important theories treat organizations as information-processing systems that perceive and interpret stimuli, store, retrieve, and transmit information, generate judgments, and solve problems (LARKEY & SPROULL). It is possible to identify two research orientations in the literature on organizational information processing (CHOO). The first views organizations as rational, decision-making systems. Unfortunately, the individual as decision maker is bounded by cognitive limitations. The task of organization design is thus to control the decision premises that guide decision-making behavior. The organization sets its goals first, then searches for alternatives and selects actions that lead to the goal. Information is processed to reduce or avoid uncertainty associated with decision making. This decision-making perspective was first developed by Herbert Simon, James March, and Richard Cyert (CYERT & MARCH; MARCH & SIMON; SIMON, 1957, 1976, 1977) and became very influential in organization theory. According to CYERT & MARCH, a theory of organizational decision-making processes must consist of a theory of search and a theory of choice. Decision makers are not automatically presented with problems to solve and alternative solutions. They must identify problems, search for solutions, and develop methods to generate and evaluate alternatives. In other words, decision makers must actively search for the information needed to make choices.

The second orientation sees organizations as social, loosely coupled systems in which individual actors enact or create the environment to which the organization then adapts (WEICK, 1977; 1979). Although organizations are still viewed as information-processing systems, the primary purpose of processing information is not decision making. Instead, it is to reduce the equivocality[1] of information about the organization's external environment. Managers as information processors receive information about the external environment and then enact the environment to which they will attend. The task of organizing is to develop a shared interpretation of the environment that provides a framework for action. Actions are often taken first and then interpreted retrospectively; in other words, action can precede goals. This enactment perspective was later extended into a model of organizations as

---

[1] The distinction between equivocality and uncertainty should be made clear. In uncertainty, managers can ask questions and obtain answers. Organizations respond to uncertainty by acquiring information and analyzing data. In contrast, equivocality means ambiguity, the existence of multiple and conflicting interpretations about the organizational situation. Managers are not certain what questions to ask, and if questions are asked, there may be no data to answer them.

interpretation systems (DAFT & WEICK; WEICK & DAFT). Organizations receive information about the environment that is ambiguous. Within the organization, various subunits adopt dissimilar frames of reference to view changes in the environment. As a result, the organization must interpret the external environment by collecting and exchanging information, and how the organization goes about its interpretation depends on how analyzable it perceives the environment to be and how actively it intrudes into the environment to understand it. The organizational learning process thus consists of scanning the environment, interpreting information about the environment, and learning from the consequences of taking action.

Summary

Organization theory conceptualizes the environment as a source of information, resources, and ecological variation. To study environmental scanning, the perspective of the organizational environment as source of information seems the most appropriate. Organizations process information to make decisions and to interpret changes in the external environment. Both the decision-making and interpretation perspectives are valuable for understanding environmental scanning. Rational, systematic decision making is probably better suited to solving problems where issues can be clearly identified. On the other hand, collective interpretation may be needed in dealing with problems when issues are unclear and information is ambiguous.

INFORMATION NEEDS AND USES

Because environmental scanning is essentially an information-seeking activity that is practiced by managers, a review of the research on information needs and uses could identify theoretical and empirical approaches that can be applied in studying managers as a distinct group of information users. Eleven *ARIST* chapters have reviewed information needs and uses studies, the most recent being those by DERVIN & NILAN and by HEWINS. TAYLOR (1990) also provides an analytical summary of the research on information-use environments. The tremendous diversity in context and scope of the needs and uses studies defies any attempt to generalize. Nevertheless, based on recent literature surveys, we can make three observations:

- Information needs and uses need to be examined within the work, organizational, and social settings of the user. Information needs vary according to users' membership in professional or social groups, their demographic back-

grounds, and the specific requirements of the task they are performing.
- Users obtain information from a wide range of formal and informal sources. Informal sources, including personal contacts, are frequently as important as and sometimes more important than formal information sources, such as libraries or online databases.
- Many criteria can affect the selection and use of information sources. Research has found that many groups of users prefer sources that are local or close at hand, which are not necessarily the best sources. For these users, the perceived accessibility of an information source is more important than its perceived quality.

A recent large-scale survey of U.S. aerospace engineers illustrates many of these observations. The study was conducted as part of the NASA/DoD-sponsored Aerospace Knowledge Diffusion Research Project (PINELLI; PINELLI ET AL., 1991a, 1991b). It found that U.S. aerospace engineers prefer informal sources of information, especially conversations with individuals within their organization, when solving technical problems. They seem predisposed to solve problems alone or with the help of colleagues rather than seek answers in the literature. They draw on past experience and consult reliable and efficient colleagues. The engineers' search for information seems to be driven more by a need to solve a specific problem than by a search for general opportunity. The engineers use the library without involving the librarian. When they need technical information, they use accessible sources such as colleagues, vendors, and internal reports (PINELLI, pp. 260-261).

System-Oriented Research Paradigm

DERVIN & NILAN identify several premises that define the attitude of "traditional" researchers in information needs and uses. Information is viewed as objective, something that has constant meaning. The user passively receives objective information, and the task of information delivery is to get the information into the user's hands. The research intent is to describe universal user information behaviors that apply across situations. Research concentrates on the intersection of users with information systems, leaving aside factors that lead to the encounter with the system or the consequences of such an encounter. Research also concentrates on external attributes, such as use of sources or systems as indicators of information needs rather than internal processes such as cognitive assessments. Finally, research looks for orderly patterns of behavior to guide system design, and there is concern that a focus on individual behavior would yield too much variation for systems to be able to integrate. As a result of this attitude, most information needs and uses studies observe users from the perspective of the information system. A typical systems-oriented study would thus examine the extent to which a user has used the information system, perceives barriers to the use of the system, and reports satisfaction with various features of the system. Differences in a user's information behavior are explained according to demography and the user's social group, life style, and task description. In her review of the literature, HEWINS also concludes that the large body of information needs and uses studies appears to share two themes: (1) it views the user as a member of a sociological group or (2) it examines the user's behavior in relation to an information system. A user's information needs are determined largely by the needs of the social or professional group to which he or she belongs. Group information needs are studied so that information systems can be designed to serve them better.

User-Centered Research Paradigm

In 1986 DERVIN & NILAN proposed that an alternative research paradigm in information needs and uses studies was needed—and was in fact emerging—to replace the traditional system-oriented paradigm. The new approach

> focuses on understanding information use in particular situations and is concerned with what leads up to and what follows intersections with systems. It focuses on the user. It examines the system only as seen by the user. It asks many "how questions"—e.g., how do people define needs in different situations, how do they present these needs to systems, and how do they make use of what systems offer them (DERVIN & NILAN, p. 16).

New research that illustrates this alternative paradigm includes the "value-added" approach (TAYLOR, 1986), the "sense-making" approach (DERVIN), and the "anomalous states of knowledge" (ASK) approach (BELKIN). For example, in the sense-making approach, the individual is a sense maker who is stopped in a situation because the individual's internal sense has "run out" and more information is needed to create new sense. Movement forward is prevented by a cognitive gap, which may require, for example, that certain questions be answered. The individual defines the gap and selects strategies to bridge it. Finally, the information obtained is put to use by the individual. According to

Dervin, the individual use of information and information systems depends on the individual's definition of the gap that is faced and on the strategies selected to bridge it. The methodology has developed a set of categories for defining and coding situations, gaps, and uses into what are assumed to be universally relevant dimensions of information needs and uses (DERVIN).

Four years after Dervin and Nilan's review chapter, HEWINS noted that the user-centered approach constituted the mainstream of research in information needs and uses. Studies that apply this approach start from the premise that user information needs occur cognitively as well as sociologically. Research thus examines cognitive characteristics that are unique to each user as well as cognitions that are common to most users. Hewins mentions several cognitive traits that are the subject of research, including categorization techniques, long- and short-term memory, learning styles, motivation, personality types, and semantic factors. A consequence of adopting the user-centered cognitive approach is that one must draw on multiple disciplines to analyze information needs and uses. The study of information-seeking and -retrieving behavior by Saracevic and colleagues (SARACEVIC & KANTOR; SARACEVIC ET AL.), which combines elements from several disciplines in a comprehensive framework to examine user and searcher characteristics, is perhaps a bellwether of the future of interdisciplinary research on information needs and uses.

Information-Use Environments

After surveying the user study literature, TAYLOR (1990) proposed that research on information needs and uses should encompass not only the user and the uses of information but also the contexts within which users decide which information is useful. These contexts are called information-use environments, and they comprise the factors that affect the flow and use of information and determine the criteria by which information is valued. Information-use environments can be divided into four components: (1) sets of people, (2) typical problems faced by those sets of people, (3) work settings, and (4) resolution of problems. Sets of people are defined in terms of their information behaviors, and Taylor identifies four classifications: (1) the professions, (2) the entrepreneur (including managers), (3) special interest groups, and (4) special socioeconomic groups. Each set of people has its own demographic (e.g., age, education) and nondemographic (e.g., media use, social networks, attitudes) characteristics that explain differences in information behavior. Each set of people is concerned with a distinct class of problems, created by the requirements of its profession, occupation, or life style. Problems change all the time as new information is obtained and as the user changes position and perception. Four attributes of the work setting influence information behavior: (1) attitude toward information, (2) task domain, (3) information access, and (4) past history and experience. Finally, each set of people has a different perception of what constitutes the resolution of a problem. Eight classes of information use are defined, along with several information traits that can be related to problem dimensions to determine information usefulness. Taylor believes that information-use environments "can become a generalizable model, a fruitful means for organizing, describing, and predicting the information behavior of any given population in a variety of contexts" (TAYLOR, 1990, p. 251).

Summary

After many decades of decrying the lack of a general theoretical framework for analyzing information needs and uses studies, we now appear closer to the development of models that give structure and order to a seemingly chaotic field. The work of DERVIN and of TAYLOR (1990) broaden the system orientation of traditional information needs and uses studies to include three additional elements: (1) the user as a sentient, cognitive person; (2) information seeking and use as processes extending over time and space; and (3) information-use contexts as crucial determinants of the usefulness of information. Their research suggests that while individual user behavior may exhibit infinite variety, order can be found by analyzing the user's sense-making processes and information-use contexts. Further, Taylor identifies managers as a distinct set of users who have their own information behaviors, types of problems to be handled, work settings, and ways of resolving problems. The orientation toward cognitive processes and information-use contexts provides a helpful focus for research on environmental scanning as an information activity of managers.

MANAGERS AS INFORMATION USERS

Traditionally, management research has always recognized the important role of information in managerial work. However, this recognition is expressed typically as research on the use of information in managerial decision making. As discussed in the final section of this chapter, the acquisition of information is assumed to be nonproblematic and is therefore seldom addressed. Although there is a very large literature on decision making, there are fewer studies on managers that elaborate on both the acquisition and the use of information. In a sense, these studies lie at the intersection of organizational research and information needs and uses studies in that they treat managers both as members of organizations and as information users. We highlight a selection of these studies in chronological sequence to give the reader a sense of the research questions pursued.

Managerial Roles

The conceptualization of managerial work by MINTZBERG clearly articulates how the acquisition, dissemination, and use of information lie at the heart of managerial work. Mintzberg divides the work of managers into three sets of interlocking roles: (1) interpersonal, (2) informational, and (3) decisional. By virtue of the formal authority vested in the position, the manager performs three interpersonal roles, as figurehead, leader, and liaison. These roles give the manager access to many internal and external sources of information and so enable three informational roles. As monitor, "the manager continually seeks and receives information from a variety of sources in order to develop a thorough understanding of the organization and its environment" (MINTZBERG, p. 97). As disseminator, the manager transmits special information to the organization. As spokesman, the manager dissemi-nates the organization's information into the environment. Unique ac-cess to information combined with authority empowers the manager to discharge four decisional roles. As entrepreneur, the manager initiates "improvement projects"; as disturbance handler, the manager deals with unexpected events; as resource allocator, the manager distributes organizational resources; and as negotiator, the manager engages in major negotiations with external organizations. Ultimately, "it is the [manager's] informational roles that tie all managerial work together—linking status and the interpersonal roles with the decisional roles" (MINTZBERG, p. 71).

Information Acquisition and Use by Managers

BLANDIN & BROWN examined the relationship between perceived environmental uncertainty and the information-search behavior of top-level managers in four electronics firms and four wood-products firms. They found significant positive correlations between the level of per-ceived uncertainty and: (1) their reliance on external information sources, (2) their use of informal sources of information, (3) their frequency of use of all information sources, and (4) the amount of time they allocate to environmentally-related information gathering. They suggested that the relationship between uncertainty and information search is one of interdependent cause and effect: an information search may be initiated to reduce uncertainties surrounding strategic choices, but as informa-tion is acquired, new uncertainties are revealed that require further investigation.

STABELL investigated the relationship between managers' perception of their information environment and their use of information sources. Perception was measured by the individual manager's integrative complexity. An integratively simple person who is choosing among information sources might use only a single rule, such as, "omit quantitative information." An integratively complex person recognizes several source attributes and gives added importance to some attributes in certain decision situations. Complexity theory predicts that the integratively complex person will sample more different sources and more information and will sample these sources more uniformly. By examining the actual investment decision making of 30 portfolio managers in a large U.S. bank, Stabell found significant support for the hypothesis for impersonal sources but weak support for personal sources.

O'REILLY looked at the impact of source accessibility and quality on the use of information sources by decision makers in four branch locations of a county welfare agency. Data collected in a survey of 163 respondents show that the reported frequency of use of the four major information sources is explained in three of the four cases by the accessibility of the source. The exception is the "group" source, consisting of sources within the work unit, including superiors and peers, which is highly accessible to all respondents. Although the rated importance of the sources was related to their perceived quality, the reported frequency of use was found to be mainly a function of perceived accessibility.

KOTTER (1982a; 1982b) studied the information behavior of 15 successful general managers of nine corporations in various industries in cities across the United States. Data were collected by interviews, observation, and questionnaires. He concluded that successful general managers are especially effective in "agenda setting" and "network building." In agenda setting, the managers develop loosely connected goals and plans that address their short- and long-term responsibilities. They construct their agendas incrementally over time by gathering information continuously. Successful general managers seek information aggressively, often by asking critical questions that provide useful answers for setting agendas. They rely more on information from discussions with individuals than on books, magazines, or reports.

In network building, the managers develop cooperative relationships among those people whom they believe are needed to implement their emerging agendas. They cultivate relationships with people and sources inside and outside the firm, mainly through face-to-face contact. The most successful managers create networks of talented people with strong ties. Kotter's study suggests that the performance of general managers is linked to an ability to seek information aggressively, to use this information in developing agendas, and to implement the agendas through information-sharing networks.

JONES & MCLEOD explored the use of information sources by senior managers in the four decisional roles proposed by Mintzberg. Data were collected by interviews, questionnaires, and the transaction logs of five senior executives over two weeks. Much of the executives' information came from people and organizational sources in the external environment. Information from subordinates was frequently obtained and valued highly. In the entrepreneur decisional role, executives preferred internal sources and verbal messages. In the resource allocator role, they preferred internal information but did not care if it was verbal or written. In the disturbance handler role, they preferred internal sources that used verbal media. Finally, in the negotiator role, they were indifferent about where information came from or how it was transmitted.

The Consultancy and Research Unit (CRUS) of the Department of Information Studies at the University of Sheffield did a number of studies in the 1980s that examined business information needs and uses (ROBERTS & WILSON). A 1984 study investigated the demand and supply of business information of manufacturing firms (ROBERTS & CLIFFORD). Data were collected by interviews with 60 firms in three selected geographical areas in the U.K. The study found that the main demand for external information concerned marketing, products, exporting, finance, and competitors. Information was demanded to respond to current events rather than longer-term issues. Information gathering was unsystematic, intermittent, and eclectic. The six main sources of external information were: (1) trade associations, (2) sales force, (3) customers, (4) suppliers, (5) chambers of commerce, and (6) public libraries. Fifty-four percent of the respondents, at some time or another, used pubic library services for business purposes.

In a pair of CRUS studies that shared the same research focus, WHITE and WHITE & WILSON examined the relationship between managers' functional roles and their information needs and uses. Data were collected by interviewing 82 managers of ten manufacturing firms in the South Yorkshire/Derbyshire region of Britain. The authors found no correlation between the managers' functional roles (production, sales, marketing, finance, or personnel) and their information needs. Significant numbers from all five functional areas ranked financial information as very important. Marketing and sales managers, who are typically considered to be externally oriented, were found to use large amounts of internally produced data. Conversely, managers who handle mostly internal data could encounter a problem that required outside information. Overall, the manager's major information resources are the personal contacts, who are seen as the best sources of intelligence on markets and competitors.

ACHLEITNER & GROVER investigated information-transfer patterns among managers and information workers in the finance department of a major defense/commercial contractor. All the managers identified people as their information sources. People were major sources of data, procedural information, interpretive information, source information (whom to see), current information, and some external information. Task-related information dominated daily activities—i.e., procedures, meeting objectives, and problem solving. The information workers requested data from trusted human sources in an informal network. Communication patterns generally followed the organization's hierarchy.

MCKINNON & BRUNS examined how middle and upper-level managers in Canadian and U.S. manufacturing firms obtain and use the information they need to control their daily operations. Data were collected by interviewing 73 managers (plant managers, sales directors, accountants, and other managers) in six U.S. and six Canadian manufacturing corporations. The authors found that managers' information needs are determined by operational tasks: production managers need information to order materials and manage production facilities; sales and marketing managers seek information about orders, prices, competitor actions, and customer needs. For them, "Yesterday's information is of little interest, and tomorrow's is hard to come by. It is today that must be managed, and only today's information will do" (MCKINNON & BRUNS, p. 19). The two most important sources of information that the managers valued and used were personal observation and management work itself. Other people were a third important source, especially when they proved to be reliable. Another frequently used source were reports, including informal as well as formal outputs of a management-accounting or management-information system.

Summary

From the relatively small number of studies on how managers acquire and use information, we can draw the following tentative generalizations:

- Managers indicate a substantial need for information about the external environment, which spreads over a number of environmental sectors;
- Managers' information needs are often task related and are typically driven by current, immediate problems;
- Managers prefer people sources and often have their own interpersonal networks of familiar, trusted sources; and
- Managers prefer verbal media and oral communication.

TAYLOR (1986) and KATZER & FLETCHER arrived at similar observations when they summarized the special information requirements of managers: (1) managers rely heavily on evaluated aggregated data; (2) they suffer from an abundance of irrelevant information; (3) they strongly favor verbal media; and (4) they have a critical need for external information.

RESEARCH ON ENVIRONMENTAL SCANNING

Research on environmental scanning forms a subset of the broader research on how managers acquire and use information. One of the earliest studies on how managers scan the business environment was the path-breaking research of AGUILAR, whose 1967 work continues to provide a reference point for current research. Most of the subsequent studies revolve around a handful of research themes: (1) the effect of perceived environmental uncertainty on scanning; (2) focus and scope of scanning; (3) information sources used in scanning; (4) scanning modes and methods; and (5) the influence of managerial job characteristics on scanning behavior.

Perceived Environmental Uncertainty

The concept of perceived environmental uncertainty is central to an understanding of how different levels of uncertainty affect scanning behavior (ACHROL; SHARFMAN & DEAN). DUNCAN identified dimensions of the environment that would determine its perceived uncertainty. He infers two dimensions from earlier theorists such as EMERY & TRIST, TERREBERRY, and THOMPSON: (1) the simple-complex dimension (the number of environmental factors considered in decision making) and (2) the static-dynamic dimension (the degree to which these factors change over time). Duncan found that decision makers in dynamic and complex environments experienced the greatest amount of perceived environmental uncertainty. This uncertainty itself is conceptualized as: (1) lack of information about environmental factors associated with a decision situation; (2) lack of knowledge about the outcome of a specific decision; and (3) inability to assign probabilities with confidence on how environmental factors affect success or failure.

Generally, research on scanning has found that managers who experience higher levels of perceived environmental uncertainty tend to do a greater amount of environmental scanning. KEFALAS & SCHODERBEK surveyed the scanning behavior of 40 executives from six companies in the farm-equipment and meat-packing industries. They found that executives in the dynamic environment (farm machinery) did more scanning than those in the stable environment (meat packing), although the difference was not statistically significant. NISHI ET AL. analyzed the scanning behavior of 250 executives in the Japanese computer industry and information-processing industry. Again, executives in the dynamic (computer) industry spent more time scanning than did those in the stable (information-processing) industry.

DAFT ET AL. studied scanning by the chief executive officers of small- to medium-sized manufacturing companies in Texas. They introduced the concept of perceived strategic uncertainty as a predictor of scanning activity. Perceived strategic uncertainty is a combination of the uncertainty of an environmental sector and the importance of events in that sector to the firm. Chief executives responded to greater perceived strategic uncertainty with higher scanning frequency of all available sources, implying that they use multiple, complementary sources to interpret an uncertain environment. Chief executives of successful firms did more frequent scanning through all media when strategic uncertainty was high, compared with low-performing less-successful firms. Moreover, their breadth of scanning was wider, and they tailored their scanning to the amount of perceived uncertainty in each sector.

BOYD studied the scanning behavior of executives in several industries.[2] He found a strong relationship between scanning of an environmental issue and the perceived importance of that issue, and he concluded that "perceived importance is itself the most important predictor of scanning activity" (BOYD, p. 95). This is true even when the issue being considered is changing only gradually or when the executive already has adequate information about that issue. Boyd's work confirms the finding of DAFT ET AL. that the perceived importance of environmental developments has a strong impact on scanning. Studies by AUSTER & CHOO (1991; 1992; 1993) of the environmental scanning behavior of chief executive officers in the Canadian publishing and telecommunications industries also found a substantial correlation between the executives' amount of scanning and their level of perceived environmental uncertainty.

Although HAMBRICK (1979; 1981; 1982) did not explicitly examine perceived environmental uncertainty, his study did analyze the effects of two sets of related environmental factors: (1) the strategy adopted by the organization vis-a-vis the external market and (2) the nature of the industry that the organization is part of. Based on a survey of executives from the top three levels of organizations in three industries (higher

---

[2]Most of the firms were in banking, health, insurance, and chemicals. Data were collected by mailing questionnaire surveys, which were completed verbally by telephone interviews.

education, health care, life insurance), he found that organizational strategy alone did not appear to affect the amount of scanning conducted but that the industry that the organization was part of strongly affected the content of what was scanned. Thus, hospitals stressed scanning of the engineering environment, insurance firms stressed the entrepreneurial environment, and colleges had mixed patterns of emphasis. Hambrick explains the lack of a connection between strategy and scanning as follows. Organizations that adopt different strategies have different propensities and capacities to act on environmental information; they may possess information that is generally the same, but they act on it in different ways to create their own competitive positions.

Focus of Environmental Scanning

The external environment of a business enterprise includes all outside factors that can affect the performance or survival of the organization. Although the factors are many, organizational research divides the external business environment into a few environmental sectors. For example, JAUCH & GLUECK identify six environmental sectors: (1) customers, (2) suppliers, (3) competitors, (4) socioeconomics, (5) technology, and (6) government. FAHEY & NARAYANAN distinguish between a macroenvironment, comprising social, economic, political, and technological sectors, and a task/industry environment, comprising mainly the customer and competitor sectors.

The research studies agree on those environmental sectors that form the primary focus of environmental scanning. The market-related sectors of the external environment, with information on customers, suppliers, and competitors, appear to be the most important. A 1967 scanning study involved interviews with managers in over 40 companies in the United States and Western Europe[3] (AGUILAR). It found that for these managers, the importance of information on "market tidings" was overwhelming—three times as important as the next area of concern ("technical tidings"). Similarly, NISHI ET AL. found that for both the Japanese computer industry and information-processing industry, the marketing sector was the major environmental sector, followed by the technology sector. JAIN studied scanning in Fortune 500 U.S. corporations through interviews and questionnaires. He found that scanning was directed at four areas: (1) economic, (2) technological, (3) political, and (4) social. Scanning of the economic area was the most significant, followed by the technological area. GHOSHAL & KIM surveyed the scanning practices of managers in the largest companies in the Republic

---

[3] The companies were mostly chemical manufacturing firms that supply industrial products.

of Korea (South Korea). The most important kinds of environmental information are those concerning the market, competition, technology, regulatory policies, resources, and broad issues. JOHNSON & KUEHN studied the scanning behaviors of managers and owners of small and large businesses in the U.S. southwest. Small-business respondents spend almost one-third of their information-seeking time looking for market-related information on sales, products, and customer problems. Next in importance is information about technology.

LESTER & WATERS investigated the environmental scanning activities of corporate planning departments in seven large U.K.-based companies. They found that the planners put the greatest effort into acquiring information on the competitor sector—i.e., information concerning competitive industries, companies, products and services, and markets. Relatively little attention was given to macroenvironmental influences such as economic, political, and sociocultural factors.

Information Sources

Almost every study on scanning seeks to identify those information sources that are used most frequently or are most important in environmental scanning. Because managers have access to many information sources, they are commonly classified as internal or external to the organization and personal or impersonal. Internal and external sources are self-explanatory. Personal sources communicate information personally to the manager, whereas impersonal sources are often defined as those that communicate information to broad audiences or through formalized, group communication (e.g., AGUILAR; KEEGAN, 1974). Thus, impersonal sources would include publications, conferences, the company library, and online databases. The pattern of source use in scanning that emerges from the literature is that while both internal and external sources are frequently used, personal sources, such as customers, associates, and staff, appear to be more important. Impersonal sources, such as the library and online databases, are not often used in scanning.

AGUILAR found that personal sources greatly exceeded impersonal sources in importance. The most important personal sources were subordinates and customers, and the most important impersonal source was publications. Managers of large companies tended to rely more on internal sources. Information from outside sources was mostly unsolicited, whereas information from inside sources was mostly solicited.

KEEGAN (1967; 1974) was one of the first to focus on the environmental scanning of multinational companies. He interviewed executives in 13 U.S. multinationals about recent instances of receiving external information. He found that external sources were more important than internal sources, the former accounting for 66% of information from all sources. Moreover, the flow of information within the company was strongly constrained by intraorganizational, departmental boundaries. O'CONNELL & ZIMMERMAN compared how policy-level executives and planning staff managers in 50 U.S. and 50 European multinational corporations scanned the international environment. Both groups identified their professional peers as their chief sources. The most important were those in the "home office top management" and "home office staff," both internal sources. KOBRIN ET AL. surveyed nearly 500 firms to see how large U.S. international firms assessed foreign social and political environments. The information sources considered important by most of the firms were internal: subsidiary and regional managers and headquarters personnel. Banks were clearly the most important external source. There was a preference for obtaining environmental assessments directly from people who were known and trusted. The firms relied on their subordinates, colleagues in other firms, banks, and personal observations during frequent trips to foreign countries. SMELTZER ET AL. analyzed the scanning practices of small business managers in the Phoenix and Kansas City metropolitan areas. Personal sources were significantly more important than impersonal ones. Family members and customers were the most prevalent personal sources, while magazines and journals were the most prevalent impersonal sources. In their study of large U.K. companies LESTER & WATERS found that traditional sources, such as libraries, were regarded as tedious and frustrating to use. Respondents were also skeptical about the value of information-brokering services, and they preferred raw rather than refined data. There was great interest in, and in some cases considerable use of, online information services. Generally, the use of formal, published resources was done in an ad hoc, informal, and low-key manner.

A few studies have attempted to examine some of the factors that might explain the selection and use of certain types of information sources in environmental scanning. For example, CULNAN looked at the scanning behavior of a few hundred professionals in a bank-holding company and in a diversified natural resources manufacturing firm. She looked at how perceived source accessibility and perceived task complexity affect the use of various information sources. Her study found that information acquisition was not entirely a function of perceived source accessibility; information needs associated with the complexity of the task to be performed were related to sources that were perceived as less accessible. The study of large South Korean firms by GHOSHAL & KIM concluded that information about the immediate business environment (competitors, existing technologies, and product markets), which is required daily for operational decisions, is usually obtained from business associates, such as customers, suppliers, trade associations, and bankers. On the other hand, printed sources in the public domain are more important for information about the broader environment (general social, economic, political, and technological changes); these sources include general and trade journals, special government publications, and reports from academic institutions, think tanks, and consulting organizations. AUSTER & CHOO (1992; 1993) showed that Canadian chief executives use multiple, complementary sources when scanning the environment. Personal sources (managers, staff, customers, associates) are among the most frequently used, while the company library and electronic information services are infrequently used. Perceived source quality is more important in explaining source use than either perceived accessibility or perceived environmental uncertainty. Auster and Choo's study suggests that the turbulence of the external environment, the strategic role of scanning, and the information-use contexts of managers all combine to explain why information quality is more important than source accessibility when managers scan the environment.

Scanning Methods

Several studies have attempted to classify different modes or methods of environmental scanning practiced by organizations. Scanning in business corporations can range from ad hoc and informal activities to highly systematic and formalized efforts. Field research seems to suggest that the size of the firm, its experience and proficiency with long-term planning and analysis techniques, and its perception of the external environment are some of the factors that influence the scanning choice.

Aguilar's case studies of small to large firms found that scanning in the small firms was done by top management as part of normal business operations and the information obtained tended to concern the immediate industrial milieu. In the medium-size firm, "a number of scanning systems were loosely linked at the top management level through internal communication characterized by an element of bargaining" (AGUILAR, p. 175). In the large firms, there was an increased amount and complexity of internal communications, a greater use of institutionalized scanning units, and an increased reliance by top management on staff assistants to filter information. In a study of multinational companies, KEEGAN (1974) found little evidence of any systematic method of information scanning; computer-based systems were not being used, and even manual systems did not play a significant role. THOMAS surveyed the scanning activities of nine very large corporations in the United States and Europe through published sources. He concluded that the practice of scanning for planning has taken firm root among these large firms. According to Thomas, the scanning process was characterized by its permanence (continuity over time), periodicity (linkage with planning), and pervasiveness (spread over multiple levels and units). Thus, some of the firms had operated scanning systems for several years, had integrated scanning into their corporate planning, and had involved many functional units at various organizational levels.

WILSON & MASSER explored the environmental monitoring activities of county planning authorities in England and Wales. They discerned two stereotypes: (1) those authorities who defined information as "hard data" and (2) those who defined it more widely as "qualitative data." The latter group was more likely to have a policy of comprehensive information acquisition and to regard information retrieval, processing, and evaluation as serious information management issues. However, information management is seen as a technical task undertaken by specialists and is to some extent divorced from organizational characteristics.

KLEIN & LINNEMAN conducted an extensive international survey of the environmental assessment practices of large corporations. Approximately half of the respondents had formalized environmental assessment as part of their planning. The increased importance of environmental assessment was attributed to greater environmental turbulence, longer planning time horizons, use of futures forecasting techniques, and greater experience with long-range planning. Extrapolation of trends was the most widely practiced form of forecasting, while scenario development was the most frequently used form for making judgments.

PREBLE ET AL. analyzed the scanning done by 95 multinational corporations based in the United States. Their key findings were:

- More than 53% of the firms were conducting continuous in-house international scanning;
- Nearly half of the executives reported some degree of computerization used in their scanning;
- Executives relied on internal sources of international environmental information much more than external sources; and
- Formal procedures were established in 51% of the firms in which executives were regularly involved in scanning publications.

Comparing these results with Keegan's study published 14 years earlier, it appears that at least among multinational companies there has been a shift toward more formalized scanning systems and more sophisticated scanning techniques.

A few researchers have attempted to cast a theoretical framework over the various modes of environmental scanning that they have observed in the field. Thus, FAHEY & KING suggested that corporate environmental scanning may be classified according to three distinct models: (1) the irregular, (2) the periodic, and (3) the continuous. In the irregular model, scanning is done on an ad hoc basis and is driven by some external occurrence or crisis. In the periodic model, scanning is done regularly and is directed at near-term decisions or issues. Finally, in the continuous model, scanning is structured and integrated with corporate planning and usually involves a central scanning unit. From their structured interviews with planning officers of 12 large corporations Fahey and King found that scanning in most of the firms was an ad hoc, event-driven activity. None of the firms had successfully integrated environmental scanning into its strategic planning. From his study of Fortune 500 U.S. corporations, JAIN proposed that organizational scanning systems go through four phases as they evolve: (1) primitive, (2) ad hoc, (3) reactive, and (4) proactive. As the firm progresses through the phases, its intensity of scanning increases, the time of the scanning lengthens, and the level of confidence in the scanned information rises. A scanning system needs time to evolve and adapt to the organizational culture and to gain the confidence of top management.

Managerial Job Characteristics

Another leitmotif in the research on environmental scanning is the effect of the manager's job-related characteristics on scanning activity. The expectation is that factors such as the manager's hierarchical level and functional specialization would affect the conduct of environmental scanning. Unfortunately, no coherent pattern emerges from the few studies that have examined job-related characteristics.

AGUILAR found that functionally specialized managers tended to use particular sources (e.g., production managers relied on suppliers), whereas top-level managers tended to rely on informal networks of contacts outside the company. Managers of large companies tended to rely more on internal sources. The study of KEFALAS & SCHODERBEK concluded that executives' hierarchical level was not related to the focus of scanning. Further, there was considerable scanning of the market sector by executives of all functional specialties. Similarly, HAMBRICK (1979) found that the scanning activities of executives did not appear to vary significantly with their hierarchical levels or with their functional specializations. The study of executives in the Japanese computer and information-processing industries by NISHI ET AL. concluded that upper-level executives spent more time on external scanning than lower-level executives did. In addition, all executives spent a

higher proportion of their time scanning the environmental sector closest to their functional specialties.

Among the five research themes that characterize the state of the
research on environmental scanning, the effect of managerial job characteristics on scanning is the least developed. A potentially useful
extension to the investigation of hierarchical level and functional specialization would be to relate scanning and the use of acquired information to the managerial decision-making roles suggested by organization
theory. For example, JONES & MCLEOD found that managers use
information sources according to the type of decision that they were
making. AUSTER & CHOO (1993) found that chief executives who scan
frequently tend to use environmental information more frequently when
making decisions in the entrepreneur role.

Because environmental scanning requires managers to make sense of
an uncertain environment, research on scanning should investigate the
cognitive processes by which managers assimilate and use environmental information. These processes go beyond job-related functions,
and raise research questions concerning how managers know what
information they need about the environment, how they deal with
multiple sources that provide information on the same topic, how they
interpret ambiguous messages about environmental change, and how
they detect, recognize, and frame problems using a stream of environmental information. Very few authors of past studies have addressed
such questions. An exception is STABELL, who found that how a
manager chooses between impersonal information sources is associated with the manager's cognitive ability to selectively apply multiple
source-selection rules (the manager's "integrative complexity"). More
recently, BOYD found tentative support for the hypothesis that managers with a high tolerance for ambiguity will engage in high levels of
scanning activity.

Summary

The following observations show what can be gleaned from the
research to date on environmental scanning:

- There is a growing awareness of the value of environmental scanning;
- Managers who experience high levels of perceived environmental uncertainty tend to do a great deal of environmental scanning;
- The market-related sectors of the external environment,
  with information on customers, suppliers, and competitors, appear to be the most important for environmental
  scanning;

- While managers use both internal and external sources
  frequently to scan the environment, personal sources
  such as customers, associates, and staff are more important. Libraries and online databases are not widely used
  in scanning;
- Scanning methods in business organizations can range
  from ad hoc, informal activities to highly systematic and
  formalized efforts. Scanning mode depends on firm size,
  experience with planning and analysis techniques, and
  perception of the external environment; and
- The job characteristics of managers (e.g., hierarchical
  level and functional specialty) do not have a clear effect
  on scanning behavior.

This is a parsimonious list; much more needs to be learned about
how organizations scan their external environments.

SYNTHESIS

Figure 1 shows the interrelationships among the sets of literature
that we have reviewed. It also summarizes the main findings and
principal variables that were investigated in those studies. Organization theory provides a useful perspective of the role of the external
environment as a source of information, continually creating signals to
which an organization attends. A lack of information about the environment is perceived as uncertainty. As decision-making and informa-
tion-interpretation systems, organizations need information to reduce
uncertainty and equivocality about environmental changes. On the
other side, the many field studies about information needs and uses
suggest that information needs must be considered in the context of the
user's work and organizational and social settings. Both formal and
informal information sources are important. For many, the use of a
source is strongly influenced by its perceived accessibility. Research is
shifting from a traditional system focus to a user focus that emphasizes
cognitive processes and information-use contexts. A few studies of
managers as information users combine elements from organization
theory and information needs and uses to investigate how managers
acquire and use information. These studies have found that managers
perceive a growing need for information about the external environment. At the same time, their information needs are mostly driven by
current, immediate problems. In acquiring information, managers prefer personal sources and verbal media. Generally, environmental scanning studies may be considered as a subset of studies of managers as
information users. Research has found that there is rising awareness of

ORGANIZATION THEORY	INFORMATION NEEDS & USES
• *Environment as source of information:* Lack of information about environment creates *Perceived Environmental Uncertainty.* • *Organizations as Decision Making and Interpretation systems:* Organizations need information to reduce uncertainty and equivocality.	• Information needs and uses depend on work and social *context.* • *Formal* and *informal* information sources are both important. • For many groups of users, source *accessibility* is more important than source quality.

MANAGERS AS INFORMATION USERS

• Managers perceive growing *need* for information about external environment.

• Information needs are determined by current, *immediate problems.*

• Managers prefer *people sources* and personal observation.

• Managers prefer *verbal media* and oral communication.

ENVIRONMENTAL SCANNING

• Scanning increases as *perceived environmental uncertainty* increases.

• Managers are most concerned with the *market-related* sectors of the environment.

• Managers use *internal* and *external sources* to scan. Personal sources are very important.

• The *method of scanning* depends on firm size, experience, and perception of the environment.

Figure 1. Overview of research literatures

the value of scanning and that scanning increases with environmental uncertainty. Managers are most concerned with the market-related sectors of the environment. They use both internal and external sources and find personal sources very important. Scanning methods vary from informal to formal and seem to depend on firm size, experience with planning and analysis, and perception of the environment.

Information Perspective in Organization Theory

There is a clear distinction between the information orientation of the research in organization theory and in information needs and uses studies. In organization theory, emphasis is on the utilization of information by managers in decision making and planning. The typical treatment of information excludes a substantive consideration of the problems associated with acquiring information in external environments. The assumption is that information will somehow "flow" into the organization so that its acquisition will not be a problem. Complex issues in the perception, evaluation, and selection of multiple sources from an expanding array of choices are not recognized. Relationships between managerial information roles and the selection and use of information sources are not explored. Information is regarded as a homogeneous commodity. However, information about the "real world" is far from homogeneous and has problems of accuracy, timeliness, relevance, trustworthiness, and so on. Managers do not regard all information alike and express distinct preferences for certain types and formats of information. Reliance on preferred channels would affect managers' information-seeking and decision-making behaviors. All these issues imply that information acquisition is the "missing link" in our efforts to understand the information-processing chain of the organization (ROBERTS & CLARKE, 1987; 1989).

Information Perspective in Information Needs and Uses Studies

The acquisition of information is one of the themes in information needs and uses studies. Most of the research concerns users' perceptions of sources, their methods of accessing and using sources, and their assessments of the value of the information. Research typically attempts to account for patterns of source or system use and satisfaction by analyzing users' demographic factors, their membership in social or professional groups, their life style, or their task requirements. Several reviewers of the literature on information needs and uses have pointed out limitations. There is overemphasis on a few specialized or professional populations, notably academics, engineers, and scientists. Too few studies have looked at the information behaviors of lay people, managers, or other professionals (BRITTAIN; CRAWFORD; KATZER). Traditionally, information needs and uses studies start with the information source or system and examine the user in relation to that system. Most of the studies are confined to formal information sources, such as documents and computer-based information systems, even though most information exchange is verbal and informal (ROBERTS & WILSON). Finally, traditional information needs and uses studies seldom relate information behaviors to the user's social or work settings (TAYLOR, 1990; WILSON). Partly in response to these criticisms, the research focus has broadened recently to examine cognitive processes of the information user and factors in the information-use setting that influence information usefulness (DERVIN; DERVIN & NILAN; HEWINS; TAYLOR, 1990).

CONCLUSION

This review underscores the need to recognize managers as a distinct and important group of information users and to expand our limited knowledge of managers as information users. A significant part of the information acquired and used by managers concerns the external environment. We believe that information science and the information profession have the tools and techniques to enhance the breadth and depth of environmental scanning by managers. At the same time we need to know more about how managers scan the environment. We need field studies to collect data and build theories about managers as information users and to guide the development of information systems and services. This review suggests that research on environmental scanning could fruitfully apply frameworks that integrate perspectives from both organization theory and information needs and uses studies. Organization theory views managers as decision makers and interpreters of environmental change. Information needs and uses studies approach managers as special information users with distinctive needs, ways of defining and resolving problems, and information-use contexts. The two perspectives complement each other and provide a brighter lens through which to scrutinize managers as information users.

BIBLIOGRAPHY

ACHLEITNER, HERBERT K.; GROVER, ROBERT. 1988. Managing in an Information-Rich Environment: Applying Information Transfer Theory to Information Systems Management. Special Libraries. 1988 Spring; 79(2): 92-100. ISSN: 0038-6723.

ACHROL, RAVI S. 1988. Measuring Uncertainty in Organizational Analysis. Social Science Research. 1988; 17(1): 66-91. ISSN: 0049-089X.

AGUILAR, FRANCIS JOSEPH. 1967. Scanning the Business Environment. New York, NY: Macmillan Co.; 1967. 239p. LC: 67-11688.

ALDRICH, HOWARD E. 1979. Organizations and Environments. Englewood Cliffs, NJ: Prentice-Hall; 1979. 384p. ISBN: 0-13-641431-1.

ALDRICH, HOWARD E.; MINDLIN, SERGIO. 1978. Uncertainty and Dependence: Two Perspectives on Environment. In: Karpik, Lucien, ed. Organization and Environment: Theories, Issues, and Reality. London, England: Sage Publications Inc.; 1978. 149-170. ISBN: 0-8039-9981-X; ISBN: 0-8039-9982-8 (pbk.).

ARCHIBALD, ROBERT WILLIAMS. 1976. Scanning the Canadian Business Environment: The Government Sector. Waterloo, Ontario, Canada: University of Waterloo; 1976. 260p. (Ph.D. dissertation). Available from: University of Waterloo, Waterloo, Ontario, Canada, N2L 3G1.

ARROW, KENNETH J. 1964. Control in Large Organizations. Management Science. 1964 April; 10(3): 397-408. ISSN: 0025-1909; LC: 56-21107.

AUSTER, ETHEL; CHOO, CHUN WEI. 1991. Environmental Scanning: A Conceptual Framework for Studying the Information Seeking Behavior of Executives. In: Griffiths, José-Marie, ed. Proceedings of the American Society for Information Science (ASIS) 54th Annual Meeting: Volume 28; 1991 October 27-31; Washington, DC. Medford, NJ: Learned Information, Inc. for ASIS; 1991. 3-8. ISSN: 0044-7870.

AUSTER, ETHEL; CHOO, CHUN WEI. 1992. Environmental Scanning: Preliminary Findings of a Survey of CEO Information Seeking Behavior in Two Canadian Industries. In: Shaw, Debora, ed. Proceedings of the American Society for Information Science (ASIS) 55th Annual Meeting: Volume 29; 1992 October 26-29; Pittsburgh, PA. Medford, NJ: Learned Information, Inc. for ASIS; 1992. 48-54. ISSN: 0044-7870.

AUSTER, ETHEL; CHOO, CHUN WEI. 1993. Environmental Scanning by CEOs in Two Canadian Industries. Journal of the American Society for Information Science. 1993 May; 44(4): 194-203. ISSN: 0002-8231.

BARTHA, PETER F. 1988. Managing Corporate External Issues: An Analytical Framework. Business Quarterly. 1988 Spring; 52(4): 81-90. ISSN: 0007-6996.

BELKIN, NICHOLAS J. 1982. Ask for Information Retrieval. Part 1: Background and Theory. Journal of Documentation. 1982 June; 38(2): 61-71. ISSN: 0022-0418.

BLANDIN, JAMES S.; BROWN, WARREN B. 1977. Uncertainty and Management's Search for Information. IEEE Transactions on Engineering Management. 1977 November; EM-24(4): 14-19. ISSN: 0018-9391.

BOURGEOIS, L.J., III. 1985. Strategic Goals, Perceived Uncertainty, and Economic Performance in Volatile Environments. Academy of Management Journal. 1985; 28(3): 548-573. ISSN: 0001-4273.

BOYD, BRIAN KENNETH. 1989. Perceived Uncertainty and Environmental Scanning: A Structural Model. Los Angeles, CA: University of Southern California; 1989. 129p. (Ph.D. dissertation). Available from: University of Southern California, University Park, Los Angeles, California, 90089.

BRITTAIN, MICHAEL. 1982. Pitfalls of User Research, and Some Neglected Areas. Social Science Information Studies. 1982; 2(3): 139-148. ISSN: 0143-6236.

BURNS, TOM; STALKER, G.M. 1961. The Management of Innovation. London, England: Tavistock; 1961. ISBN: 0-422-72050-X.

CHOO, CHUN WEI. 1991. Towards an Information Model of Organizations. The Canadian Journal of Information Science. 1991 September; 16(3): 32-62. ISSN: 0380-9218.

CONYERS, ANGELA D. 1989. The Use of External Information by Managers in Larger Industrial Companies with Special Reference to the Role of Electronic External Information Services. London, England: City University; 1989. 390p. (Ph.D. dissertation). Available from: City University, Northampton Square, London, UK, EC1V 0HB.

CRAWFORD, SUSAN. 1978. Information Needs and Uses. In: Williams, Martha E., ed. Annual Review of Information Science and Technology: Volume 13. White Plains, NY: Knowledge Industry Publications, Inc. for the American Society for Information Science; 1978. 61-81. ISSN: 0066-4200; ISBN: 0-914236-21-0.

CULNAN, MARY J. 1983. Environmental Scanning: The Effects of Task Complexity and Source Accessibility on Information Gathering Behavior. Decision Sciences. 1983 April; 14(2): 194-206. ISSN: 0011-7315.

CYERT, RICHARD MICHAEL; MARCH, JAMES G. 1963. A Behavioral Theory of the Firm. Englewood Cliffs, NJ: Prentice Hall; 1963. 332p. LC: 63-13294.

DAFT, RICHARD L.; SORMUNEN, JUHANI; PARKS, DON. 1988. Chief Executive Scanning, Environmental Characteristics, and Company Performance: An Empirical Study. Strategic Management Journal. 1988 March/April; 9(2): 123-139. ISSN: 0143-2095.

DAFT, RICHARD L.; WEICK, KARL E. 1984. Toward a Model of Organizations as Interpretation Systems. Academy of Management Review. 1984; 9(2): 284-295. ISSN: 0363-7425.

DERVIN, BRENDA. 1992. From the Mind's Eye of the "User": The Sense-Making Qualitative-Quantitative Methodology. In: Glazier, Jack D.; Powell, Ronald R., eds. Qualitative Research in Information Management. Englewood, CO: Libraries Unlimited; 1992. 61-84. ISBN: 0-87287-806-6; LC: 91-43579.

DERVIN, BRENDA; NILAN, MICHAEL. 1986. Information Needs and Uses. In: Williams, Martha E., ed. Annual Review of Information Science and Technology: Volume 21. White Plains, NY: Knowledge Industry Publications, Inc.; 1986. 3-33. ISSN: 0066-4200; ISBN: 0-86729-209-1.

DESS, GREGORY G.; KEATS, BARBARA W. 1987. Environmental Assessment and Organizational Performance: An Exploratory Field Study. In: Hoy, Frank, ed. Proceedings of the Academy of Management 47th Annual Meeting; 1987 August 9-12; New Orleans, LA. Washington, DC: Academy of Management; 1987. 21-25. ISSN: 0065-0668; ISBN: 0-915350-25-X.

DIFFENBACH, JOHN. 1983. Corporate Environmental Analysis in Large US Corporations. Long Range Planning. 1983 June; 16(3): 107-116. ISSN: 0024-6301.

DILL, WILLIAM R. 1958. Environment as an Influence on Managerial Autonomy. Administrative Science Quarterly. 1958 March; 2(1): 409-443. ISSN: 0001-8392.

DILL, WILLIAM R. 1962. The Impact of Environment on Organizational Development. In: Mailick, Sidney; Van Ness, Edward H., eds. Concepts and Issues in Administrative Behavior. Englewood Cliffs, NJ: Prentice-Hall Inc.; 1962. 94-109. LC: 62-12845.

DOWNEY, KIRK; SLOCUM, JOHN. 1982. Managerial Uncertainty and Performance. Social Science Quarterly. 1982 June; 63(2): 195-207. ISSN: 0038-4941.

DUNCAN, ROBERT B. 1972. Characteristics of Organizational Environments and Perceived Environmental Uncertainty. Administrative Science Quarterly. 1972 September; 17(3): 313-327. ISSN: 0001-8392.

DUTTON, JANE E. 1987. The Creation of Momentum for Change through the Process of Strategic Issue Diagnosis. Strategic Management Journal. 1987 May/June; 8(3): 279-295. ISSN: 0143-2095.

EL SAWY, OMAR A. 1985. Personal Information Systems for Strategic Scanning in Turbulent Environments: Can the CEO Go On-line? MIS Quarterly. 1985 March; 9(1): 53-60. ISSN: 0276-7783.

EMERY, FRED E.; TRIST, ERIC L. 1965. The Causal Texture of Organizational Environments. Human Relations. 1965; 18(1): 21-32. ISSN: 0018-7267.

FAHEY, LIAM; KING, WILLIAM R. 1977. Environmental Scanning for Corporate Planning. Business Horizons. 1977 February; 14(1): 61-71. ISSN: 0007-6813.

FAHEY, LIAM; NARAYANAN, VADAKEK K. 1986. Macroenvironmental Analysis for Strategic Management. St. Paul, MN: West Publishing; 1986. 200p. ISBN: 0-314-85233-6.

FLYNN, DAVID M. 1990. Intelligence for Strategic Decision Making in Multinational Corporations. In: Roukis, George S.; Charnov, Bruce H.; Conway, Hugh, eds. Global Corporate Intelligence: Opportunities, Technologies, and Threats in the 1990's. Westport, CT: Quorum Books; 1990. 93-108. ISBN: 0-89930-220-3.

GALBRAITH, JAY R. 1973. Designing Complex Organizations. Reading, MA: Addison-Wesley; 1973. ISBN: 0-201-02559-0.

GHOSHAL, SUMANTRA; KIM, SEOK KI. 1986. Building Effective Intelligence Systems for Competitive Advantage. Sloan Management Review. 1986 Fall; 28(1): 49-58. ISSN: 0019-848X.

GREENE, FRANCES H. 1988. Competitive Intelligence. Special Libraries. 1988 Fall; 79(4): 285-295. ISSN: 0038-6723.

GROSSER, KERRY. 1991. Human Networks in Organizational Information Processing. In: Williams, Martha E., ed. Annual Review of Information Science and Technology: Volume 26. Medford, NJ: Learned Information, Inc. for the American Society for Information Science; 1991. 349-402. ISSN: 0066-4200; ISBN: 0-938734-55-5.

HAMBRICK, DONALD CARROLL. 1979. Environmental Scanning, Organizational Strategy, and Executive Roles: A Study in Three Industries. University Park, PA: Pennsylvania State University; 1979. 321p. (Ph.D. dissertation). Available from: University Microfilms, Ann Arbor, MI. (UMI order no. 7922294).

HAMBRICK, DONALD CARROLL. 1981. Specialization of Environmental Scanning Activities among Upper Level Executives. Journal of Management Studies. 1981; 18(3): 300-319. ISSN: 0022-2380.

HAMBRICK, DONALD CARROLL. 1982. Environmental Scanning and Organizational Strategy. Strategic Management Journal. 1982 April/June; 3(2): 159-174. ISSN: 0143-2095.

HANNAN, MICHAEL T.; FREEMAN, JOHN. 1977. The Population Ecology of Organizations. American Journal of Sociology. 1977 March; 82(5): 929-964. ISSN: 0002-9602.

HANNAN, MICHAEL T.; FREEMAN, JOHN. 1989. Organizational Ecology. Cambridge, MA: Harvard University Press; 1989. 366p. ISBN: 0-674-64348-8.

HART, PAUL J.; RICE, RONALD E. 1991. Using Information from External Databases: Contextual Relationships of Use, Access Method, Task, Database Type, Organizational Differences and Outcomes. Information Processing and Management. 1991; 27(5): 461-479. ISSN: 0306-4573.

HEWINS, ELIZABETH T. 1990. Information Need and Use Studies. In: Williams, Martha E., ed. Annual Review of Information Science and Technology: Volume 25. Amsterdam, The Netherlands: Elsevier Science Publishers for the American Society for Information Science; 1990. 145-172. ISSN: 0066-4200; ISBN: 0-444-88531-5.

HUBER, GEORGE P.; O'CONNELL, MICHAEL J.; CUMMINGS, LARRY L. 1975. Perceived Environmental Uncertainty: Effects of Information and Structure. Academy of Management Journal. 1975; 18(4): 725-739. ISSN: 0001-4273.

JAIN, SUBHASH C. 1984. Environmental Scanning in US Corporations. Long Range Planning. 1984 April; 17(2): 117-128. ISSN: 0024-6301.

JAUCH, LAWRENCE R.; GLUECK, WILLIAM F. 1988. Business Policy and Strategic Management. 5th edition. New York, NY: McGraw-Hill; 1988. 940p. ISBN: 0-07-032347-X.

JOHNSON, LYNN; KUEHN, RALPH. 1987. The Small Business Owner/Manager's Search for External Information. Journal of Small Business Management. 1987 July; 25(3): 53-60. ISSN: 0047-2778.

JONES, JACK WILLIAM; MCLEOD, RAYMOND, JR. 1986. The Structure of Executive Information Systems: An Exploratory Analysis. Decision Sciences. 1986 Spring; 17(2): 220-249. ISSN: 0011-7315.

KASSEL, AMELIA S. 1989. Online Databases for Strategic Business Intelligence. In: Nixon, Carol; Padgett, Lauree, eds. Proceedings of the 10th National Online Meeting; 1989 May 9-11; New York, NY. Medford, NJ: Learned Information; 1989. 219-224. ISBN: 0-938734-34-2.

KATZER, JEFFREY. 1987. User Studies, Information Science, and Communication. Canadian Journal of Information Science. 1987; 12(3/4): 15-30. ISSN: 0380-9218.

KATZER, JEFFREY; FLETCHER, PATRICIA. 1992. The Information Environment of Managers. In: Williams, Martha E., ed. Annual Review of Information Science and Technology: Volume 27. Medford, NJ: Learned Information, Inc. for the American Society for Information Science; 1992. 227-263. ISSN: 0066-4200.

KEEGAN, WARREN J. 1967. Scanning the International Business Environment: A Study of the Information Acquisition Process. Cambridge, MA: Harvard University; 1967. 195p. (Ph.D. dissertation). Available from: Harvard University, Cambridge MA, 02138.

KEEGAN, WARREN J. 1974. Multinational Scanning: A Study of the Information Sources Utilized by Headquarters Executives in Multinational Companies. Administrative Science Quarterly. 1974 September; 19(3): 411-421. ISSN: 0001-8392.

KEFALAS, ASTERIOS; SCHODERBEK, PETER P. 1973. Scanning the Business Environment—Some Empirical Results. Decision Sciences. 1973 January; 4(1): 63-74. ISSN: 0011-7315.

KENNINGTON, DON. 1977. Scanning the Operational Environment: The Librarian's Role. Journal of Librarianship. 1977 October; 9(4): 261-269. ISSN: 0022-2232.

KIESLER, SARA; SPROULL, LEE. 1982. Managerial Response to Changing Environments: Perspectives on Problem Sensing from Social Cognition. Administrative Science Quarterly. 1982 December; 27(4): 548-570. ISSN: 0001-8392.

KLEIN, HAROLD E.; LINNEMAN, ROBERT E. 1984. Environmental Assessment: An International Study of Corporate Practice. Journal of Business Strategy. 1984; 5(1): 66-75. ISSN: 0275-6668.

KOBRIN, STEPHEN J.; BASEK, JOHN; BLANK, STEPHEN; LA PALOMBARA, JOSEPH. 1980. The Assessment of Noneconomic Environments by American Firms. Journal of International Business Studies. 1980 Spring/Summer; 11(1): 32-47. ISSN: 0047-2506.

KOENIG, MICHAEL E.D. 1992. Entering Stage III. The Convergence of the Stage Hypotheses. Journal of the American Society for Information Science. 1992 April; 43(3): 204-209. ISSN: 0002-8231.

KOTTER, JOHN P. 1982a. The General Managers. New York, NY: The Free Press; 1982. 221p. ISBN: 0-02-918000-7.

KOTTER, JOHN P. 1982b. What Effective General Managers Really Do. Harvard Business Review. 1982 November/December; 60(6): 156-167. ISSN: 0017-8012.

LARKEY, PATRICK D.; SPROULL, LEE S. 1984. Introduction. In: Larkey, Patrick D.; Sproull, Lee S., eds. Advances in Information Processing in Organizations: Volume 1. Greenwich, CT: JAI Press, Inc.; 1984. 1-8. ISBN: 0-89232-403-1.

LAWRENCE, PAUL R.; LORSCH, JAY W. 1967. Organization and Environment: Managing Differentiation and Integration. Boston, MA: Graduate School of Business Administration, Harvard University; 1967. 279p. LC: 67-30338.

LENZ, R.T.; ENGLEDOW, JACK L. 1986a. Environmental Analysis: The Applicability of Current Theory. Strategic Management Journal. 1986 July/August; 7(4): 329-346. ISSN: 0143-2095.

LENZ, R.T.; ENGLEDOW, JACK L. 1986b. Environmental Analysis Units and Strategic Decision-Making: A Field Study of Selected "Leading-Edge" Corporations. Strategic Management Journal. 1986 January/February; 7(1): 69-89. ISSN: 0143-2095.

LESTER, RAY; WATERS, JUDITH. 1989. Environmental Scanning and Business Strategy. London, England: British Library, Research and Development Department; 1989. 148p. (Library and Information Research Report 75). ISBN: 0-7123-3203-0.

LEWIS, MARY FRANCIS. 1982. Sources and Uses of External Information for Smaller Firms. Fayetteville, AK: University of Arkansas; 1982. 366p. (Ph.D. dissertation). Available from: University Microfilms, Ann Arbor, MI. (UMI order no. DA8305054).

MARCH, JAMES G.; SIMON, HERBERT A. 1958. Organizations. New York, NY: John Wiley; 1958. 262p. ISBN: 0-471-56793-0.

MCKINNON, SHARON M.; BRUNS, WILLIAM J., JR. 1992. The Information Mosaic: How Managers Get the Information They Really Need. Boston, MA: Harvard Business School Press; 1992. 265p. ISBN: 0-87584-317-4.

MILLIKEN, FRANCIS J. 1987. Three Types of Perceived Uncertainty about the Environment: State, Effect, and Response Uncertainty. Academy of Management Review. 1987; 12(1): 133-143. ISSN: 0363-7425.

MINTZBERG, HENRY. 1973. The Nature of Managerial Work. New York, NY: Harper & Row; 1973. 298p. ISBN: 0-06-044555-6.

NEWSOME, JAMES, ed. 1987/1988. Environmental Scanning in Libraries. Minnesota Libraries. 1987/1988 Winter; 28(12): 375-402. (Special issue). ISSN: 0026-5551.

NEWSOME, JAMES; MCINERNEY, CLAIRE. 1990. Environmental Scanning and the Information Manager. Special Libraries. 1990 Fall; 81(4): 285-293. ISSN: 0038-6723.

NISHI, KENYU; SCHODERBEK, CHARLES; SCHODERBEK, PETER P. 1982. Scanning the Organizational Environment: Some Empirical Results. Human Systems Management. 1982; 3(4): 233-245. ISSN: 0167-2533.

O'CONNELL, JEREMIAH J.; ZIMMERMAN, JOHN W. 1979. Scanning the International Environment. California Management Review. 1979 Winter; 22(2): 15-23. ISSN: 0008-1256.

O'REILLY, CHARLES A., III. 1982. Variation in Decision-Makers' Use of Information Sources: The Impact of Quality and Accessibility of Information. Academy of Management Journal. 1982; 25(4): 756-771. ISSN: 0001-4273.

PFEFFER, JEFFREY; SALANCIK, GERALD R. 1978. The External Control of Organizations: A Resource Dependence Perspective. New York, NY: Harper & Row; 1978. 300p. ISBN: 0-06-045193-9.

PINELLI, THOMAS E. 1991. The Relationship between the Use of U.S. Government Technical Reports by U.S. Aerospace Engineers and Scientists and Selected Institutional and Sociometric Variables. Washington, DC: National Aeronautics and Space Administration; 1991. 350p. NTIS: N9118898.

PINELLI, THOMAS E.; BARCLAY, REBECCA O.; KENNEDY, JOHN M.; GLASSMAN, NANCI; DEMERATH, LOREN. 1991a. The Relationship between Seven Variables and the Use of U.S. Government Technical Reports by U.S. Aerospace Engineers and Scientists. In: Griffiths, José-Marie, ed. Proceedings of the American Society for Information Science (ASIS) 54th Annual Meeting; 1991 October 27-31; Washington, DC. Medford, NJ: Learned Information, Inc. for ASIS; 1991. 313-321. ISSN: 0044-7870.

PINELLI, THOMAS E.; KENNEDY, JOHN M.; BARCLAY, REBECCA O. 1991b. The NASA/DoD Aerospace Knowledge Diffusion Research Project. Government Information Quarterly. 1991; 8(2): 219-233. ISSN: 0740-624X.

PORTER, MICHAEL E. 1980. Competitive Strategy: Techniques for Analyzing Industries and Competitors. New York, NY: The Free Press; 1980. 396p. ISBN: 0-02-925360-8.

PREBLE, JOHN F.; RAU, PRADEEP A.; REICHEL, ARIE. 1988. The Environmental Scanning Practices of US Multinationals in the Late 1980s. Management International Review. 1988; 28(4): 4-14. ISSN: 0025-181X.

PRESCOTT, JOHN E., ed. 1989. Advances in Competitive Intelligence. Vienna, VA: Society of Competitor Intelligence Professionals; 1989. 228p. ISBN: 0-9621241-0-9.

RENFRO, WILLIAM L.; MORRISON, JAMES L. 1984. Detecting the Signals of Change: The Environmental Scanning Process. The Futurist. 1984; 18(4): 49-53. ISSN: 0016-3317.

ROBERTS, NORMAN; CLARKE, D. 1987. The Treatment of Information Issues and Concepts in Management and Organizational Literatures. Sheffield, England: Consultancy and Research Unit, Department of Information Studies, University of Sheffield; 1987. 130p. ISBN: 0-906088-34-8.

ROBERTS, NORMAN; CLARKE, D. 1989. Organizational Information Concepts and Information Management. International Journal of Information Management. 1989 March; 9(1): 25-43. ISSN: 0268-4012.

ROBERTS, NORMAN; CLIFFORD, B. 1984. Regional Variations in the Demand and Supply of Business Information: A Study of Manufacturing Firms. Sheffield, England: Consultancy and Research Unit, Department of Information Studies, University of Sheffield; 1984. 111p. ISBN: 0-906088-26-7.

ROBERTS, NORMAN; WILSON, TOM D. 1988. The Development of User Studies at Sheffield University. Journal of Librarianship. 1988 October; 20(4): 270-290. ISSN: 0022-2232.

ROUSE, WILLIAM B.; ROUSE, SANDRA H. 1984. Human Information Seeking and Design of Information Systems. Information Processing and Management. 1984; 20(1): 129-138. ISSN: 0306-4573.

SAMMON, WILLIAM L.; KURLAND, MARK A.; SPITALNIC, ROBERT, eds. 1984. Business Competitor Intelligence: Methods for Collecting, Organizing and Using Information. New York, NY: John Wiley; 1984. 357p. ISBN: 0-471-87591-0.

SANDERSON, S.M.; LUFFMAN, G.A. 1988. Strategic Planning and Environmental Analysis. European Journal of Marketing. 1988; 22(2): 14-24. ISSN: 0309-0566.

SARACEVIC, TEFKO; KANTOR, PAUL. 1988. A Study of Information Seeking and Retrieving. Part II: Users, Questions, and Effectiveness. Journal of the American Society for Information Science. 1988 May; 39(3): 177-196. Part III: Searchers, Searches and Overlap. Journal of the American Society for Information Science. 1988 May; 39(3): 197-216. ISSN: 0002-8231.

SARACEVIC, TEFKO; KANTOR, PAUL; CHAMIS, ALICE Y.; TRIVISON, DONNA. 1988. A Study of Information Seeking and Retrieving. Part I: Background and Methodology. Journal of the American Society for Information Science. 1988; 39(3): 161-176. ISSN: 0002-8231.

SCOTT, W. RICHARD. 1987. Organizations: Rational, Natural, and Open Systems. 2nd edition. Englewood Cliffs, NJ: Prentice-Hall; 1987. 377p. ISBN: 0-13-641820-1.

SHARFMAN, MARK P.; DEAN, JAMES W., JR. 1991. Conceptualizing and Measuring the Organizational Environment: A Multidimensional Approach. Journal of Management. 1991 December; 17(4): 681-700. ISSN: 0149-2063.

SIMON, HERBERT A. 1957. Models of Man: Social and Rational. New York, NY: John Wiley; 1957. 287p. LC: 57-005933.

SIMON, HERBERT A. 1976. Administrative Behavior: A Study of Decision-Making Processes in Administrative Organization. 3rd edition. New York, NY: The Free Press; 1976. 364p. ISBN: 0-02-928971-8; ISBN: 0-02-929000-7 (pbk.).

SIMON, HERBERT. 1977. The New Science of Management Decision. Revised edition. Englewood Cliffs, NJ: Prentice-Hall, Inc.; 1977. 175p. ISBN: 0-13-616144-8.

SMELTZER, LARRY R.; FANN, GAIL L.; NIKOLAISEN, V. NEAL. 1988. Environmental Scanning Practices in Small Businesses. Journal of Small Business Management. 1988 July; 26(3): 55-62. ISSN: 0047-2778.

SNYDER, NEIL H. 1981. Environmental Volatility, Scanning Intensity and Organization Performance. Journal of Contemporary Business. 1981 August; 10(2): 5-17. ISSN: 0194-0430.

SPECHT, PAMELA HAMMERS. 1987. Information Sources Used for Strategic Planning Decisions in Small Firms. American Journal of Small Business. 1987 Spring; 11(4): 21-34. ISSN: 0363-9428.

STABELL, CHARLES. 1978. Integrative Complexity of Information Environment Perception and Information Use: An Empirical Investigation. Organizational Behavior and Human Performance. 1978 August; 22(1): 116-142. ISSN: 0030-5073.

STARBUCK, WILLIAM H.; MILLIKEN, FRANCES J. 1988. Executives' Perceptual Filters: What They Notice and How They Make Sense. In: Hambrick, Donald C., ed. The Executive Effect: Concepts and Methods for Studying Top Managers. Greenwich, CT: JAI Press; 1988. 35-65. ISBN: 0-89232-804-5.

STINCHCOMBE, ARTHUR L. 1990. Information and Organizations. Berkeley, CA: University of California Press; 1990. 391p. ISBN: 0-520-06781-9 (pbk.).

STUBBART, CHARLES. 1982. Are Environmental Scanning Units Effective? Long Range Planning. 1982 June; 15(3): 139-145. ISSN: 0024-6301.

TAYLOR, ROBERT S. 1986. Value-Added Processes in Information Systems. Norwood, NJ: Ablex Publishing Corp.; 1986. 257p. ISBN: 0-89391-273-5.

TAYLOR, ROBERT S. 1990. Information Use Environments. In: Dervin, Brenda; Voigt, Melvin J., eds. Progress in Communication Sciences: Volume 10. Norwood, NJ: Ablex Publishing Corp.; 1990. 217-254. ISSN: 0163-5689; ISBN: 0-89391-645-5.

TERREBERRY, SHIRLEY. 1968. The Evolution of Organizational Environments. Administrative Science Quarterly. 1968 March; 12(1): 590-613. ISSN: 0001-8392.

THOMAS, PHILIP S. 1980. Environmental Scanning: The State of the Art. Long Range Planning. 1980 February; 13(1): 20-25. ISSN: 0024-6301.

THOMPSON, JAMES D. 1967. Organizations in Action: Social Science Bases of Administrative Theory. New York, NY: McGraw-Hill; 1967. 192p. LC: 67-11564.

TUSHMAN, MICHAEL L.; NADLER, DAVID A. 1978. Information Processing as an Integrating Concept in Organizational Design. Academy of Management Review. 1978 July; 3(3): 613-624. ISSN: 0363-7425.

WEICK, KARL E. 1977. Enactment Processes in Organizations. In: Staw, B.M.; Salansik, Gerald R. New Directions in Organizational Behaviour. Chicago, IL: St. Clair; 1977. 267-300. ISBN: 0-914292-06-4.

WEICK, KARL E. 1979. The Social Psychology of Organizing. 2nd edition. New York, NY: Random House; 1979. 294p. ISBN: 0-394-34827-3.

WEICK, KARL E.; DAFT, RICHARD L. 1983. The Effectiveness of Interpretation Systems. In: Cameron, Kim S.; Whetten, David A., eds. Organizational Effectiveness: A Comparison of Multiple Models. New York, NY: Academic Press; 1983. 71-93. ISBN: 0-12-157180-7.

WHITE, DON A. 1986. Information Use and Needs in Manufacturing Organizations: Organizational Factors in Information Behaviour. International Journal of Information Management. 1986; 6(3): 157-170. ISSN: 0268-4012.

WHITE, DON A.; WILSON, TOM D. 1988. Information Needs in Industry: A Case Study Approach. Sheffield, England: Consultancy and Research Unit, Department of Information Studies, University of Sheffield; 1988. 142p. ISSN: 0140-3834; ISBN: 0-906088-37-2.

WILSON, TOM D. 1981. On User Studies and Information Needs. Journal of Documentation. 1981 March; 37(1): 3-15. ISSN: 0022-0418.

WILSON, TOM D.; MASSER, I.M. 1983. Environmental Monitoring and Information Management in County Planning Authorities. In: Dietschmann, H.J., ed. Representation of Knowledge as a Basis of Information Processes: Proceedings of the 5th International Research Forum in Information Science; 1983 September 5-7; Heidelberg, Germany. Amsterdam, The Netherlands: Elsevier Science Publishers; 1983. 271-284. ISBN: 0-444-87563-8.

IV
The Profession

Section IV includes two chapters. Maurice B. Line, Information & Library Consultant, and Margaret Kinnell of Loughborough University address the problem of "Human Resource Management in Library and Information Services." Jennifer MacDougall, Consultant, and J. Michael Brittain of the University of South Australia offer the first *ARIST* chapter on "Library and Information Science Education in the United Kingdom."

Line and Kinnell discuss a general shift in organizations from routine aspects of personnel management to human resource management (HRM), embracing a broader range of activities. They note that this shift is reflected in the library and information services (LIS) area, which is strongly affected by information technology (IT) as well as by pressures to improve efficiency and reduce staff; thus, it compels staff to make the most of its human resources. HRM needs to be integrated into strategic planning; aspects to be taken into account include staff allocation, equal opportunities, effective recruitment and appraisal, and counseling and grievance procedures. Much interest has been shown in ways of improving the quality of work life, principally by motivating staff and increasing job satisfaction. More delegation of responsibility is a main method for affecting job satisfaction. Participative management has become more common; teams, which have been used for some years, may now be self-managing. "Enabling" and "transformational" leadership styles are advocated. The level of "burnout" among LIS workers appears to be unexceptional; ways of tackling burnout and conflict (which is not always destructive) include greater involvement and participation. Matrix organization structures of various kinds appear to be not uncommon, and flatter structures are becoming the norm, but both may give way to networked structures. Training and staff development programs to meet new staffing needs (e.g., IT and communication skills) have received much special attention, although adequate resources have not always been made available. It is not clear how far the literature reflects practice.

MacDougall and Brittain examine the recent evolution of library and information science (LIS) education in the United Kingdom through a review of the literature over the past ten years. The historical context is briefly described with an outline of the manpower requirements of the emerging markets as well as the impact of the information, computer, and communications revolutions. The changes in LIS education over the past five years are examined, including the fundamental restructuring and reorganization of many departments of LIS and schools of library and information science (SLIS). The process of reevaluation and reassessment of the LIS curricula is described, with particular reference to IT, communication and interpersonal skills, information management, increased specialization, and distance education.

The impact of these changes on the current situation is discussed in relation to the new rationalization of higher education. Many SLIS are now developing modular courses similar to the American system of credit accumulation and transfer. Current concerns of LIS educators include customer care and client-centered services, the transfer of LIS skills, numbers of students, and the introduction of new subject areas into the curriculum.

The assessment of future trends describes the challenge of increasing recruitment with reduced resourcing which is facing SLIS in the United Kingdom. Despite such problems, there have not been any closures of library schools as experienced in the United States. Closer links with European LIS institutions are being developed, together with efforts to allow free movement of LIS professionals around Europe.

MacDougall and Brittain believe that the most important development in SLIS over the past ten years has been a recognition of the need to continually reassess and reevaluate the information requirements of an ever-changing society and to adapt courses and teaching methods accordingly.

8

Human Resource Management in Library and Information Services

MAURICE B. LINE
Information & Library Consultant

MARGARET KINNELL
Loughborough University

INTRODUCTION

This review covers human aspects of dealing with staff, focusing on the broad area that has come to be known as human resource management (HRM). It does not cover all human aspects of information management; in particular, it does not deal with users of information and library services.

While there is a very large general literature on HRM and a substantial one on the management of staff in libraries (mostly larger ones in the public sector), very little has been published on human aspects of management in small organizations or in private sector information services of any size. Necessarily, therefore, this review deals largely with human aspects of management in libraries in the public sector, and within that sector perforce on academic libraries, which accounts for most writings.

The review concentrates on the literature of the past ten or twelve years, although reference is made to some earlier key items. It is also necessary to warn that while most of the trends mentioned apply to the English-speaking world, it is known, for example, that management styles and practices in the U.K. differ substantially from those in some other countries in Europe.

GENERAL LITERATURE ON HUMAN RESOURCE MANAGEMENT

Human resource departments and functions in organizations have changed in recent years in response to the recognition that people are a

Annual Review of Information Science and Technology (ARIST), Volume 28, 1993
Martha E. Williams, Editor
Published for the American Society for Information Science (ASIS)
By Learned Information, Inc., Medford, N.J.

unique resource, and that this has implications for achieving corporate objectives. During the 1970s good practice in the management of people tended to be built around notions of standardization and good industrial relations, especially in countries like the United Kingdom, where trade unions were powerful and had a significant influence on organizational policy (STOREY, 1980). The 1980s saw a shift toward a more strategically focused approach, and the term "personnel administration" began to give way to "human resource management" in the early 1980s (GUEST, 1990). The influential paper by TICHY ET AL. was quickly followed by others. Although some authors argue that the change is largely cosmetic (e.g., ARMSTRONG, 1987), it was generally adopted to indicate a major shift of emphasis. "Personnel administration" had commonly covered mainly routine matters of personnel administration such as selection, appointment, sick leave and other absences, and trade union relations. Motivation, commitment, job satisfaction, team working, and the whole general area of getting the best out of human beings had certainly received attention, but often not systematically, and not usually as part of the job of the personnel department. This has now changed (STOREY, 1992).

A combination of external events and some influential writers led to the change. The external factors are well documented (e.g., HANDY; PETERS; SCHULER); they include increasing internationalization, indeed globalization of some industries, a greater need to be competitive, and dramatic developments in information technology (IT). These factors have made it vital for firms to be able to respond to changes rapidly, and to cut all unnecessary costs. Flexibility and "leanness" became key concepts. Innovation giving competitive advantage came to be more highly valued. IT furthered globalization by improving telecommunications; it also enabled organizations to downsize by shedding many manual and lower level clerical staff, and also led to an increased emphasis on highly skilled and highly trained staff, thus greatly altering the balance between upper and lower levels. Since staff were costly, and fewer in number, it was imperative to use them to the fullest extent possible. These effects, in turn, reduced the need for centralized control of firms, encouraged much greater delegation to units and to individuals, and made some layers of management redundant; flatter structures are rapidly becoming the norm, replacing the traditional pyramidal hierarchical structures. The recent worldwide recession has intensified these trends.

A strong contemporary trend (though it dates back some decades in Japan) has been Total Quality Management (TQM). Two essential features of TQM are the acceptance of responsibility by all workers for the quality of their own work, and team working. The simultaneous emphasis on individuals and teams is not inconsistent, since good teams encourage and support individual contributions while ensuring that they work for the organization as well as for their own goals. Several articles deal with the relationship of TQM to HRM (e.g., BOWEN & LAWLER; FERKETISH & HAYDEN).

The literature of HRM is largely descriptive or prescriptive (BOXALL). While there are several accounts of how certain practices have been introduced into individual firms with apparent success, or in the confident expectation of it, there has been little sound, objective research into the long- or even short-term effects of adopting the recommendations of the so-called Human Relations School (GUEST, 1991).

It is a matter of some debate whether HRM is a management style, a set of theories, an à la carte menu of techniques, or an integrated program. Moreover, there is as yet no accepted theory of HRM; while there are agreed goals—integration with the organization's strategy, employee commitment, flexibility and adaptability, and quality (GUEST, 1987)—the emphasis on each varies.

Within each organization, it is frequently stressed that there is a need to ensure (1) that there is an overall HRM policy, not a series of fragmented activities, (2) that the policy fits the organization's plans, and (3) that it is fully supported at the very top. Weaknesses in programs are often explained by the failure to see that these criteria are met (BAIRD & MESHOULAM). Strategic HRM is now a popular concept, although here again there are problems with its precise nature, and the strategy needs to be flexible (BOXALL; COOKE & ARMSTRONG). LEGGE provides a valuable critical review of the whole area of HRM.

It is also a matter of dispute whether HRM should be centralized in one department, or delegated to line managers, or something between the two. The trend seems to be for line managers to be responsible for HRM implementation (HOOGENDOORN & BREWSTER), leaving a small central department to coordinate HRM plans and activities throughout the organization.

An excellent, though highly selective, review of HRM literature up to highly 1987 by LENGNICK-HALL & LENGNICK-HALL concludes with an attempt to impose some structure on the topic.

Other trends are gradually becoming apparent as a result of the above factors, especially IT. Several authors, notably HANDY, foresee a division of workers into "core"—a limited number of more-or-less permanent employees—and "peripheral"—a floating pool (or rather sea, because their numbers will be much greater than the core) of workers who are called upon by different bodies at different times to serve particular needs. HANDY's observations can be supplemented by an interesting article by MOULT, which aims to explain some of the trends we are seeing and also looks further ahead. He sees "modernism" yielding to "post-modernism" as challenges to progress along present lines multiply. Corporate and cultural barriers are breaking down, boundaries are being blurred, IT has democratized us, and planning is giving way to strategy. Management appears to be becoming a "performance," and discussing management has become as much an "art form" as management itself.

GENERAL WORKS ON HUMAN FACTORS IN LIBRARIES

Most of the literature on human resources is concerned with industry, with its inevitable emphasis on the "bottom line." In the last decade public sector organizations have had to take much more interest in HRM as a result of the pressures they are facing. Since most of them deal in services rather than products, they tend to be labor-intensive and staff therefore account for a much higher proportion of expenditure than in much of the private sector. This certainly applies to libraries in the public sector, where typically staff account for over half (often two-thirds) of total expenditures; similar figures are probably true of the private information sector. The public sector has less freedom than the private sector to use staff to maximum effect. In particular, it cannot hire and fire staff nearly so easily. It cannot, therefore, take the easy step of getting rid of those who are no longer believed to be required and replacing them by better staff; usually it must use and develop its existing staff to the utmost.

The trends in management mentioned in the previous section therefore appear to be especially relevant to libraries. Increasing the effectiveness of human performance in libraries and other information services is now vital, for the above and other reasons. Managers need to cope with, or better anticipate, shortfalls in their budgets during recessions, in order to avoid involuntary redundancies. If and when resources become more plentiful, it will become equally important to ensure a sufficient supply of the right personnel. Also, high-level skills in the use of information technology have become important for the effective delivery of information. ROOKS (1989) reviews the evolution of personnel officers in academic libraries from narrow to broader functions, along the lines discussed above.

Nearly all books on library management contain sections on staffing, although these tend to be restricted to personnel administration in the older sense. The book by VEANER is unusual in discussing staffing issues in the wider context of where academic libraries are going and what they need to do. There are also several books devoted to personnel management, but these too mostly deal with the more routine aspects (e.g., CRETH & DUDA, RUBIN (1991b), VAN ZANT, and WHITE (1985)). EVANS covers the area better than most, and RUBIN (1991b) has a substantial chapter on human factors. Most of these books review

relevant general and library management literature, inevitably covering much of the same ground. The book by JONES is an altogether
different one, ranging widely in political and social issues. However, no
book appears to deal fully with the nonroutine aspects of human resource management.

Many writings discuss the various trends affecting libraries; one of
the best is the book by VEANER. MARTELL (1989) has a good concise
discussion of the whole range of critical human resource issues. He
simultaneously emphasizes the welfare of the human beings concerned
and the efficiency of the library; he reiterates the message of the human
relations school that only if human beings work in an appropriate
environment and are well motivated will they give their best.

One important paper that does not fit into the general framework of
this review is that by BURTON (1991). Apparently well-designed systems can fail because generally applicable patterns can be wrecked by
individuals. Information systems cannot but involve people, including
users. Systems thinking, derived from biology and other fields, offers a
solution because it forces examination of the whole system.

THE INFLUENCE OF INFORMATION TECHNOLOGY

Almost all kinds of organizations have been affected by information
technology to some extent. Information services were some of the first
to be affected because they need to keep large quantities of records. As
the article by MARCHANT & ENGLAND points out, they have been
even more intimately affected since the material with which they deal is
amenable to electronic storage, retrieval, and transmission. Since much
information will in the future, in theory at any rate, be accessible from
anywhere, doubts are being expressed about the future role, importance, and existence of libraries.

Automation, particularly since microcomputers have succeeded mainframes, has enabled libraries to reduce staff and improve services, has
deskilled some activities (such as local cataloging as a result of access to
external files), has created a need for higher level skills, and has given
more responsibility to lower-level staff. Users have also come to expect
more. Innovation, creativity, flexibility, and the ability to react quickly
have become crucial because of the pace of change and potential threats
from competitors. Competitive advantage, always a prime requirement
in the private sector, is rapidly becoming more important in information services.

IT can dehumanize organizations by making their procedures mechanical, or it can humanize them by distributing power and initiative.
As BURTON (1988) says, its effects can be controlled and directed. The
uncertainty that IT can lead to can be dealt with by ensuring fully

informed and involved staff, fear of the unknown can be reduced by training, and the benefits can be realized by participation.

The above points are among those made by DAKSHINAMURTI, MYERS (1986), MARCHANT & ENGLAND, and NORTON in general papers on the subject. BERGEN, largely on the basis of a thorough literature review and a study in four British libraries at various stages of automation, offers a wide-ranging analysis of human factors in the management of automation. MARTELL (1987a) looks at the problems created for middle managers, who can feel especially threatened, and SYKES urges the need to involve nonprofessional as well as professional staff. CARGILL (1990) outlines the steps staff will undergo in learning to cope with technology. FINE provides an historical overview of librarians' reactions to technological change. A useful bibliography is that by MYERS (1990), which appears in a special issue of the *Journal of Library Administration* devoted to "Personnel Administration in an Automated Environment," also available as a book (LEINBACH). Specific issues relating to IT are mentioned at appropriate places in the following text.

HUMAN RESOURCE ("MANPOWER") PLANNING
Strategic Planning

The need for libraries and information services to incorporate HRM into their overall policy making and strategic planning has become of greater concern in recent years. This is largely the result of libraries' recognizing the significance of the lessons they can learn from the business sector. The environment for information service managers mirrors that of business, and their structural and functional responses display similarities.

Strategic planning is the externally focused and long-term approach to ensuring that an organization's resource capability is matched to its objectives. In the hostile environment facing library and other information services, a more systematic approach to planning processes has become essential for developing a competitive advantage and ensuring that resources can be acquired and used effectively (J.M. BRYSON; VINCENT).

Much of the concern in strategic planning in libraries, as in the business sector, has been with the more effective use of the precious human resource asset. FORSMAN, for example, describes how the attitudes and beliefs of employees are important for their acceptance of and commitment to organizational goals. GOVAN considers staff participation in decision making in relation to the library's accountability. Identifying value systems should be the first step to engaging in strategic planning in libraries. WESTBERG, similarly, discusses how growing staff interest in the organization of the Chalmers University of Technology Library in Sweden led to the need to define new objectives before the planning process began. Staff involvement in strategic planning was a key to its success. For public libraries, too, the crafting of a strategic response to complex environmental pressures depends on attitudes and culture within the organization as a whole. The role of the chief librarian in shaping this culture is central to the process (KINNELL EVANS).

Human resource management is now being aligned more firmly with business strategy (LENGNICK-HALL & LENGNICK-HALL). The need to focus on the competitive environment facing business organizations (WALKER) strikes chords with library managers, whether in the profit or not-for-profit sector. RIGGS (1987) describes the "entrepreneurial spirit" in strategic planning for libraries. In examining the various stages of planning—the situation audit, definition of mission, goals and objectives, formulation of strategies and related factors—he assesses the human dimensions and discusses how strategy has to be "melded" with personnel. Again, the role of the director is crucial. Similar points are made in studies by GORMAN and PAO & WARNER. Direction and involvement are key concepts. People have to be involved in the preparation of strategic plans, and the planning of the human resource should be a central feature of both process and outcome.

Staff Allocation

There has been considerable emphasis on the issues raised for library and information managers when allocating staff to particular service points. These issues are generally concerned with the determination of tasks and responsibilities and the definition of structures. They differ from the much broader strategic approach, which has a longer planning time and includes a consideration of the long-term resource implications for the library. LORENZI describes the planning process for personnel at the University of Cincinnati and provides an early example of a more restricted view of human resource planning. A justification for additional staff is provided, but this appears less significant than the organizational structures and tasks allocated to staff. This was also the case in the standards of staffing provision developed from the work of the U.K.'s Local Authorities Management Services and Computer Committee (LAMSAC) in the mid-1970s (HARRISON). The approach continues to be seen in the various guidelines on staffing provision for specific sectors that professional bodies, such as the American Library Association (ALA) and the (U.K.) Library Association, provide for their members. The development of standards of provision has been a preoccupation, together with the need to consider how staff should be deployed according to their qualifications and skills. More broadly, and with fewer prescriptive recommendations, FRANK assesses the issues relevant to the deployment of staff in academic libraries, while MARCOTTE examines the value of operational audits in designing staffing deployment for the special library. There are obvious links to the concern for quality of working life (QWL) and customer focus in library services; MARTELL (1983) provides a useful synthesis of these concepts in his study of organizational modeling through a client-centered approach.

Equal Opportunities

A considerable impetus for change in thinking about how staff are recruited and allocated to undertake tasks at all levels in libraries and information services has arisen from concern to ensure equality of opportunity for women, ethnic minorities, and the physically disadvantaged. RADDON (p. 4) assesses the range of issues in the working environment, which relates to employment on equal terms for these groups:

> The implications in relation to libraries and information services cover many aspects of services, but include policies, planning, structures, resources, stock, recruitment and the implementation of an equal opportunities policy. In many cases such policies have been shown to be merely slogans, and are not supported by real practices.

A range of materials is available to managers who need guidance as they plan and implement equal opportunities policies. As with other areas of industrial relations practice, there are specific legislative considerations and there is a wide choice of advisory literature on the practical implications for recruitment practices, training, and so forth. The various national professional bodies have prepared guidelines for good management practice that are especially valuable for establishing and implementing policy on subjects such as AIDS (LIBRARY ASSOCIATION, 1989). However, as SQUIRE shows, there is a need for studies that focus on specific areas of concern to personnel from disadvantaged groups.

There has been particular concern about the paucity of senior women managers in the information profession, a situation familiar to other sectors as well, but particularly evident in a context where there is such a high overall proportion of women workers (RITCHIE, 1982). A recent study by COE of women in executive positions in all sectors notes that, since women will be making up 90% of the growth in the labor force over the next ten years, it is essential to increase the proportion of qualified women in top jobs. Women's career choices have been traditionally constrained by home and family ties. This is no longer acceptable to many women, and organizations of all kinds are recognizing the need to provide effective means of helping women break through "the glass ceiling."

Harmonizing the workforce is a related issue; developing common policies and practices that include all personnel, professional and non-professional, requires considerable negotiation before implementation. The attitudes of professional bodies, trade unions, and groups of employees have to be reconciled if an organization is to become "single-status," i.e., all employees are treated as having equal status although not equal rank. Bureaucratic procedures require scrutiny so that the organization can deal with the necessary changes. Conditions of service, salaries and wages, career opportunities, and training are some of the significant elements (CRETH & DUDA; INSTITUTE OF PERSONNEL MANAGEMENT; RADDON).

Recruitment, Selection, and Induction

Effectiveness in recruitment and selection in individual libraries and information services requires a human resource plan for the organization. As noted above, theorists agree that it should be closely related to the strategic planning processes for the organization as a whole. However, as TORRINGTON & HALL illustrate, this ideal relationship does not exist in many organizations. Library managers may have to prepare their plans without the benefit of a wider strategic view of where the organization is going in the long term. Human resource planning in this event can only be geared to maintaining present staffing levels or be tentatively based on trends in staffing. Analyzing existing staffing and wastage rates (loss through retirement, moves to other places, etc.), and from this assessment of the supply of staff moving on to analyzing staffing needs to maintain and improve existing services and develop new ones, forms the core of the plan. Balancing supply and demand is the aim of the exercise (CRETH & DUDA; JONES & JORDAN; RUBIN, 1991b).

Job description and personnel specification comprise the next stage in the recruitment of staff; in a period of retrenchment, this may mean restructuring and reallocating jobs rather than appointing new staff. Job analysis is a key component in organization design, and the methods of undertaking this can be controversial; in special libraries and public library services, job analysis may be a preliminary to job evaluation and may be carried out by a central work evaluation unit. There are considerable advantages to analyzing professional tasks in a systematic manner, as JO BRYSON illustrates in a general overview of the major issues in managing people in library and information services. An example in a specific sector is the evaluation of school library media center jobs in the United States in the early 1970s, which enabled better targeted advertising and recruitment (ROTHENBERG ET AL.). JONES & JORDAN and JO BRYSON provide further examples of descriptions for library jobs. TORRINGTON & HALL consider functional job analysis, a technique for analyzing information about jobs that was developed by the U.S. Training and Employment Service and that results in a narrative description for use in job advertisements.

The range of selection techniques available to library managers is considerable, and interest in this area of human resource management is increasing. A new journal, the *INTERNATIONAL JOURNAL OF SELECTION AND ASSESSMENT*, edited by Neil Anderson, has recently announced papers of direct relevance to library managers specializing in staff management. Integrity tests, selection methods used by executive search consultancies, and the validity of the employment interview will be included.

The induction of new staff requires care in planning. Often regarded as an adjunct to in-service training programs, it is more sensibly seen as part of the overall recruitment program in libraries. LUCCOCK provides a helpful guide to planning programs and offers guidance on techniques, including role playing, which is particularly good for instilling values and attitudes at the induction stage. CASTELEYN is also a valuable source. The need to provide suitable induction for managers is frequently overlooked in organizations and is given insufficient prominence in the literature; ERKKILA & MACKAY consider the problems faced by new supervisors and the kinds of guidance they should be offered in aspects of line management.

Appraisal Systems

Formal staff appraisal has become much more common in library and information services as part of the need to improve the performance of services and to be able to convince funders that every possible step is being taken to achieve this. Other important reasons for doing appraisals are to predict what an individual will be capable of doing in the future and to allocate and distribute rewards fairly (RANDELL ET AL.).

Because of the concern to increase effectiveness and efficiency, library managers are now attempting to measure organizational performance against predetermined sets of indicators, some of which may be laid down by governments or other funding bodies. The problem for managers is that this "supports the ethos of a market-driven economy, rather than that of employment (and education) as social processes fulfilling social needs" (RADDON, p. 16). Implementing concepts such as performance-related pay through appraisal systems can cause considerable difficulty for personnel, whose worth is regularly being measured in financial terms. Training, communication, and the involvement of all staff are therefore important, as is the acknowledgement that staff development should form part of the system. Peer review is one method of maximizing staff involvement, as practiced at Arizona State University; there the Librarians' Council has established two standing committees for personnel issues, including job performance and professional development (WURZBURGER). The culture of the library is a further important aspect of achieving high performance from individuals. Supportive organizations enhance the opportunities for individuals to develop and work in harmony and to achieve more for their library.

Counseling and Grievance Procedures

Achieving high performance from individuals also entails implementing effective industrial relations practice in libraries. While there has been considerable emphasis in the literature on human resource practices and planning, less has been written on the relationship between organizational structures and industrial relations in HR planning. This is an area of particular relevance for library managers who are restructuring their organization. A recent study of Canadian companies, for example, found that the specialization of HR and other functions was strongly correlated with less cooperation between management, staff and unions on a range of issues (DASTMALCHIAN & BLYTON). The formalization and centralization of organizational structure were also shown to have strong relationships with industry-wide bargaining structures; training was a further factor in enhancing good relations between management and workers.

The need for library managers to address counseling and grievance issues has become more pressing as the resource implications (the cost of hiring and firing) of staff invoking grievance procedures (and the problems for the organization if staff are wrongly dismissed) are considerable. An unhappy, disaffected staff cannot create an effective organization. Collective bargaining among the library, unions, and, where appropriate, the relevant professional bodies can be an important means of avoiding difficulties (DICKENS ET AL.; KARP; TODD).

The library manager should counsel staff as soon as disaffection becomes apparent, and whenever personnel require individual help. This is one of the more important management functions, requiring sensitivity and training in counseling techniques (ARMSTRONG, 1988; LUBANS; REDDY). In counseling there are inevitable problems of confidentiality, and managers must be aware of the ethical issues in balancing the competing demands of the organization and the individual (RUBIN, 1991a; ZIOLKOWSKI). However, library and information service providers also need the information gathered about their organization in sensitive interviews of staff. Exit interviews in particular can provide valuable insights into problems, and clarify reasons for staff turnover (JACOBS).

Many of the specific grievance procedures in individual information services will depend heavily on local bargaining cultures as well as on the legislative framework. Managers must distinguish between local, provincial, and national levels of negotiation and the appropriate response for particular issues. Dismissal of staff is never to be taken lightly and requires care in establishing the legal position and the impact on the organization's wider industrial relations policies and practices. RADDON discusses these in some depth and provides helpful sources.

As the literature demonstrates, managers are faced with a complex range of issues when developing a plan for human resource management. These issues interlock; the impact of IT, for example, pervades recruitment and selection and is an important aspect of induction training. A systematic and analytical approach to planning can, however, help to minimize the complexity and provide a way to control these variables.

QUALITY OF WORKING LIFE, MOTIVATION, AND JOB SATISFACTION

Although this section is divided into quality of working life, motivation, and job satisfaction, these areas tend to merge into one another; some writings (e.g., MARCHANT, 1982a) deal with more than one of these topics, and therefore relate to more than one section in this chapter. JONES & JORDAN offer a substantial discussion on the general theme of motivation and job satisfaction.

Quality of Working Life

"Quality of working life" (QWL) embraces various aspects of human resource management. MARTELL (1981), in the first of a series of articles on QWL, sets out his philosophy; in the last of these (MARTELL, 1985, p. 350) he offers a reappraisal of QWL, which he believes to be "necessary because operational practices in [American] academic libraries do not yet encourage changes in the design of jobs to accommodate the principles inherent in QWL." "To achieve an optimum QWL," he says, "six characteristics should be included in the employees' work:

Autonomy, Challenge, Expression of creativity, Opportunity for learning, Participation in decision making, Use of a variety of valued skills
and abilities" (p. 351). These are much the same as the characteristics
said to be required for job satisfaction and motivation.

There are various means of improving QWL. HACKMAN & SUTTLE,
in *Improving Life at Work*, cover a range of approaches. One means is job
redesign, which is discussed by MARTELL (1981) in general terms and
by MARTELL & UNTAWALE with a specific example. The introduction of automated systems at the University of California Library at
Berkeley enabled jobs to be both enlarged and enriched. Following
various studies and workflow analyses, several major changes were
made which increased job complexity, led to the reclassification of
some positions and to increased delegation of responsibility, and greatly
improved productivity.

Three interesting and related pieces, written from the viewpoints of
one administrator and two librarians (ALLEY; FINK; PRICE), deal with
what professional librarians expect from administrators. All deal in one
way or another with QWL factors. A short piece by LINE (1990) points
out that many if not most of the factors that lead to an enjoyable life
outside work can also be present at work, and that work can be regarded as an art form rather than a burden; in particular he stresses the
value of humor as giving perspective, generating creative ideas, relax-
ing tension, and creating bonds.

Motivation

A good deal of research addresses the factors that motivate people to
work. The key article by MASLOW (1943) on needs hierarchies was
followed after World War II by several major works: DRUCKER (1954);
HERZBERG (1966); HERZBERG ET AL., who separated "hygiene factors" such as salary and status, the absence of which leads to problems,
and "motivating factors" such as achievement and responsibility;
MCGREGOR, with his notion of theory X (top-down management) and
theory Y (participative management); ARGYRIS; and LIKERT. These
authors, who all emphasized job ownership, motivation, the need for
delegation, and so forth, transformed thinking about management.
MINTZBERG (1973; 1979) was a later but almost equally influential
writer. Later still, OUCHI, basing his thinking on a study of Japanese
management, introduced a "theory Z," an egalitarian model which
once again emphasizes the need for participation. DRUCKER (1974;
1990) has repeated his message in various ways over the years. Probably few organizations changed their style overnight, but few can have
been untouched by these philosophies. The classic article by HERZBERG
(1968; reprinted with additional material in 1987) titled "One More

Time: How Do You Motivate Employees?" provides evidence that the chief demotivators are overwhelmingly "hygiene" factors (or their neglect), while the chief motivators are equally overwhelmingly (in Herzberg's terms) "motivating" factors; "hygiene" factors like money do not motivate beyond the short term because people always want more of them.

Several LIS writers (BAKER & SANDORE; HANNABUSS; MARTELL, 1989) review the nonlibrary literature more or less briefly. ROOKS (1988) provides a more comprehensive review in a book specifically concerned with motivation. HANNABUSS comments that motivation and productivity are not automatically linked, and that ability/capacity is also necessary for productivity. Third world perspectives are offered from India (CHAMPAWAT) and Nigeria (HARRISON & HAVARD-WILLIAMS); the latter article points out that food, clothing, and shelter (basic hygiene needs) dominate in Africa, and that positive motivators cannot have much effect until these needs are met. Studies in organizations (including libraries) in western countries have shown that the less people have in the way of income, the more important such "hygiene" factors are to them.

Two papers are worth mentioning, if only because they do not deal with academic librarians. WASTAWY-ELBAZ surveyed the motivational needs of corporate librarians, coming to the predictably comfortable conclusion that "corporate librarians are motivated by achievement, concern for people and self-fulfillment." Librarians are evidently just like other human beings. KEMPSTER found that public library staff serving children and young people were most motivated by a liking for children and books, the influential nature of the work, and the responsibility for a specialist area. BANKS, who studied student assistants in academic libraries, drew few definite conclusions other than that pay affected their performance and that librarians paid little attention to their motivation.

The organizational environment is recognized to be an important factor in motivation. In a small study by SMITH & REINOW, female departmental supervisors in New Mexico expressed fairly strong commitment to their organization, with some reservations, but less certain views of the organizational climate, though they scored individual responsibility, warmth and support quite high.

"Plateaued" staff present special problems. As library staffs tend to shrink (especially at the more senior levels), and organizational structures flatten, opportunities for promotion are smaller. One of the few to address these issues is DELON, who stresses that a joint effort is required from management, the line supervisor, and the employee. Management and supervisors need to learn how to challenge and stimulate staff, to listen more, and to take measures such as lateral transfer, job rotation, and project work. Staff may, however, be not only plateaued but stuck because some jobs that have become more important (e.g., those involving IT or requiring entrepreneurial approaches, as in marketing) are beyond their aptitudes and skills.

One of the hardest problems, which appears to have received no attention at all, is that of the stagnated chief, a phenomenon that is not uncommon at a time of rapid change, new and difficult challenges, and increased pressure. There is usually nowhere else to put a chief in the organization, and often very limited scope for moving him/her out, particularly in most European countries.

Unfortunately there are more ways of demotivating than motivating staff, and they are much easier to adopt. Some of them are discussed by LINE (1992), with real examples. Demotivation is often carried out in unconscious and seemingly trivial ways, but the cumulative effect can be very damaging. BECHTEL draws on her experience of managing and being managed to make similar points.

Job Satisfaction

This section deals largely with studies of job satisfaction. Of the many studies, one of the largest and most influential is that of MARCHANT (1976), who studied 22 academic libraries, concluding that more participative management would lead to increased job satisfaction of both library workers and users. BENGSTON & SHIELDS used MARCHANT's methods at Brigham Young University and found that the results confirmed most of Marchant's. In particular, management style was found to be an especially strong predictor of job satisfaction.

LYNCH & VERDIN (1983) review other studies of job satisfaction and report one of their own, which was carried out in 1971-72 on all full-time employees in three university libraries. They found (as had previous investigators) a positive relationship between supervisory level and perceived job satisfaction. Professional librarians working in reference units reported the highest satisfaction levels, nonprofessional employees in circulation the lowest. Job satisfaction increased with length of service. A repeat of the study in 1986 (LYNCH & VERDIN, 1987) found no statistically significant differences.

SMITH & REINOW reported quite high job satisfaction and low job tension among female departmental supervisors in New Mexico, although some thought they had too much to do. ROCKMAN, studying faculty and professional librarians in the California State University system, found moderate positive relationships between job satisfaction and work autonomy and decision-making; unlike most previous researchers, however, she discovered a positive relationship between job satisfaction and gender (male), and no significant relationship with majority groups. SQUIRE suggests that ethnic minority librarians are likely to have lower job satisfaction, but presents no evidence.

Support staff in academic libraries have been the specific subject of two recent studies. In the study by FITCH in Alabama, relationships with job satisfaction were found for size of institution (negative), gender (female), and length of experience (negative). PARMER & EAST, who surveyed 12 academic libraries, confirmed previous findings that support staff in public areas were more satisfied than those in technical areas. However, general dissatisfaction was expressed with operational conditions, communication, contingent research rewards, and promotion. Surprisingly, part-time support staff were more satisfied than full-time. A study comparing professional and nonprofessional staff in the University of California Libraries (KREITZ & OGDEN), while finding generally very high levels of satisfaction, pointed to sharp differences to the disadvantage of nonprofessional staff, particularly with their level of work, opportunities for advancement, and salaries. A much more superficial study by ESTABROOK ET AL. did not reveal much difference; it also concluded that it was too early to say whether automation would improve job satisfaction, partly because the stage of early enthusiasm was not yet over.

As HERZBERG (1968) points out, job enrichment needs to be distinguished from job enlargement, which is almost bound to fail since it involves either taking on part of another person's job or adding unnecessary activities. Job enrichment implies job redesign.

What is striking about job satisfaction studies in libraries is not so much their general agreement with one another, although they differ in details, but the fact that they appear to be exclusively concerned with U.S. academic libraries. Is job satisfaction in public and special libraries, or in libraries of any kind in other countries, not a matter of concern, or are their librarians too busy to study it?

Observations

There is a general consensus that in libraries, as elsewhere, motivation and job satisfaction require a congenial environment, an appropriate organizational structure, extensive delegation of responsibility (not merely work), supportive, caring and listening management and supervision, jobs that are carefully designed to minimize boredom and give variety, good communication in all directions, participation at all levels (not only in deciding how processes are carried out but what the processes and indeed the policies should be), appropriate stimulus and challenge, and a development program to see that staff acquire desirable skills. The onus for motivation must be shared between management, which sets the tone, supervisors, who need to be alert to the behavior and feelings of all their staff, and every individual, who must accept some responsibility for his or her own development and job satisfaction. TQM (total quality management) techniques, which are increasingly coming into use in libraries, and which also emphasize individual responsibility and performance, can only reinforce these trends (MACKEY & MACKEY). Quality circles—self-selected groups of staff, usually at lower levels, studying particular issues in depth—were tried in some libraries before TQM as a whole way of life came to prominence; they are also a form of participation (MARTELL & TYSON; SEGAL & TREJO-MEEHAN).

MARCHANT (1982a, p. 268-269) concludes that "Much still remains to be learned about job satisfaction and motivation. No theory has emerged that lacks significant criticism...Still, important results [which he lists] have emerged from the research that can contribute to the improvement of the library as a place to work."

PARTICIPATIVE MANAGEMENT

A strong trend toward more participative management in libraries would be expected since involvement and participation are said to be crucial to meeting the needs of organizations for changed structures and styles in response to the IT revolution, to developing flexibility, to encouraging staff to generate ideas and to tapping their creative talents, to satisfying the increased expectation of individuals for self-realization, and to increasing productivity. There has undoubtedly been such a trend, but it is very difficult to quantify how widespread it is and how far it has gone. As in industry, much of what library directors say about their participative management may be self-deception or lip-service. Also, while it is clear that participation is more than occasional consultation, beyond that it can take a variety of forms, and it can be more full-blooded or less.

As with several aspects of human resource management, a good deal of the literature is of a missionary nature rather than being based on firm evidence. An example is the book by SAGER, which presents a case for participation that is highly plausible but is seemingly unsupported by practical experience. The work by MARCHANT (1976) was based on a careful study, although his earlier pioneering article (MARCHANT, 1971) provoked a strong response from LYNCH (1972b), which led to a further exchange (MARCHANT, 1972; LYNCH, 1972a). As LYNCH (1972b) pointed out, participation costs time; does it increase or reduce effectiveness? GOVAN expressed similar concerns. KAPLAN (1975; 1977) is another doubter, citing the danger of increased and unrealizable expectations, slow and frustrating decision making, alienation of staff whose opinions are not accepted, and conflict be-

MAURICE B. LINE AND MARGARET KINNELL

tween a cohesive staff and management. Also, some staff prefer not to have to make individual judgments.

Even where success has been claimed for participative management, it may be due to other factors: an inspirational leader, perhaps, or the very fact of change in itself (the well-known Hawthorne effect). In such cases the success may be short lived; the initial appreciation of staff for empowerment may give way to acceptance of involvement as a right, and enthusiasm to flatness. Likewise, where participation has not been successful the cause may be poor implementation. Introduction of participation is only the beginning.

In fact, as MARCHANT (1982b) himself points out, participation is merely one factor that contributes (if it does contribute) to library effectiveness. Staff must be competent as well as involved, and those who cannot discipline themselves should be removed. Clear goals are essential. Participative management is not an easy option; it requires more skilled and subtle leadership than top-down management at all levels if it is to work. Good leadership at the top is especially vital (see below) if the advantages of participation are to be realized and the disadvantages minimized.

In the past 10-12 years important changes have taken place as IT has penetrated libraries, barriers between departments have broken down, staff at all levels have had more responsibility thrust upon them, and structures have flattened, perhaps unobtrusively (a hierarchical organization chart does not necessarily mean that the library is run in a hierarchical manner). It is in any case doubtful if most staff would now accept the absence of participation; as BURCKEL says, "no one seriously questions that properly implemented and maintained, participatory management generally increases staff morale and job satisfaction" (p. 32). Nevertheless, MARTELL (1987b), in a wide-ranging discussion of authority and employee participation in academic library management, states that while "there has been steady progress in staff involvement in decision making over the past fifteen years, . . .a slowdown has occurred in the 1980s" (p. 119); he bases this conclusion on a comprehensive survey of relevant literature. There has certainly been a reduction in the literature of involvement after the excitement of the 1970s, but often the literature does not reflect the reality; it may precede or follow practice. It seems more likely that there has been some consolidation of previous efforts at staff involvement, with maybe a little backsliding where plans were overambitious or imperfectly conceived.

It would now be almost impossible to assess how successful participative management has been in terms of effectiveness. It has to be in place for some years before assessment can be useful, but there have been too many changes to make any comparison between the situation in a library ten years ago and today valid.

Team Management

Teams can exist with any type of management; BARLOW recounts how team management was implemented in three British public libraries in participative structures and how the teams were retained when the structures reverted to more hierarchical ones. However, teams are usually deemed essential in participative management. HAWKINS points to the contrast between Weberian mechanistic organizations and organic systems, where team members share responsibility and power, and the manager's role becomes one of facilitation rather than control. MIGNEAULT writes about "humanistic management by teamwork," which seems to be much the same thing as participative management. He goes on to claim that implementation of the "Zia model" (which is not explained) in the University of New Mexico General Library brought many benefits in a short time, including reduced administrative overheads, less bureaucracy, improved quality of decision making, and better accountability.

HACKMAN distinguishes between four types of performing unit— manager-led, self-managing, self-designing, and self-governing—each conferring progressively more power on the unit. Teams in some libraries may already have a high degree of self-management, assuming full responsibility for their performance; a few may go beyond this to govern themselves. Self-managing teams on Hackman's model are the subject of papers by LOWELL & SULLIVAN and BOHANNAN. Bohannan, in reviewing the literature and describing the concept of teams, emphasizes the importance of a team's "external leaders", who operate as facilitators and enablers along the lines of "superleaders" (MANZ & SIMS). Lowell and Sullivan claim swift increases in productivity from the introduction of self-managing teams in Yale University libraries.

LEADERSHIP

Leadership has been much discussed in the library and information science literature, as in the management literature in general. This is not surprising, since all the measures necessary to motivate and manage staff effectively are unlikely to succeed without good leadership. JUROW lists the factors that make good leadership more imperative than ever: an increasingly turbulent environment, an information-based, service-oriented society, a desire to maintain quality, expectations of shared responsibility, more complex organizations, different problem-solving requirements, and the need for a proactive approach (p. 60-63). She examines five basic competencies: vision, communication, trust, risk-taking, and empowerment. She also stresses that "leadership potential

is spread throughout our organizations from the top to the bottom and.
. .all we need to do is to identify it and develop it" (p. 71).

Empowerment is increasingly advocated as a leadership style. MANZ
& SIMS distinguish four types of leader: (1) the Strong Man, who
commands; (2) the Transactor, who rules by rewards; (3) the Visionary
Hero, who rules by inspiration; and (4) the Superleader, who leads by
leading others to lead themselves. They list seven steps to
superleadership, beginning with self-leadership. The theme is taken up
in the LIS field by SULLIVAN, who wants managers to act as coaches,
the essential features of coaching being partnership, commitment, compassion, communication, responsiveness, "honoring individuals," and
practice and preparation. Among other steps, problems should be seen
as learning opportunities, teams should be developed, jobs redesigned,
and achievement acknowledged. TOWNLEY sees the nurturing of personnel development—defined as "the process that creates the closest
possible match between personal interests of workers and organizational needs" (p. 16)—as a critical function of leadership.

ROBERTS appears at first sight to go contrary to this trend, believing
that the 19th century-style active and powerful leader should be synthesized with the 20th century bureaucratic manager, who tends to be a
passive respondent to the pressures that affect all organizations. She
wants to see firm leadership adapted to encourage delegation and
commitment and to use human resources to the full. Although RIGGS
(1988) discusses leadership at a level below the top (technical services),
his ideas are relevant at any level. He distinguishes between the transactional manager, who does things well, and the transformational leader,
who "possesses 'high-octane' energy" and "enjoys making things happen" (p. 29). He stresses the importance of power, without which
nothing important can be made to happen, but he also mentions the
need for compassion. The emphasis by Roberts and by Riggs on the
boss as boss, albeit an empowering one, is a useful corrective to a model
that might be seen as encouraging chiefs to opt out of responsibility.

The term transformational leadership is used also by CARVER in the
title of her "bibliographic essay." This is a useful selective review of the
relevant literature, which however casts some doubt on whether an
empowering leader can also be a transformational leader, since two of
the common (necessary?) characteristics of the latter seem to be cha-
risma and a degree of egotism; these belong to Manz and Sims's Visionary Hero, not to their Superleader.

EUSTER thinks that "the legitimate expectations of a highly
professionalized work force often run counter to organizational needs
to 'produce' and to keep all the parts of a very complex organization
functioning in reasonable synchronicity" (p. 41), and that leadership is

increasingly becoming a distributed function (p. 42). She calls for a revised concept of leadership in the knowledge-based library, with organizational data converted into meaningful information for decision making.

Whatever style of leadership is adopted—and it is accepted that there is no one right style that brings success—the leader's vision has to be communicated. This message is emphasized repeatedly by RIGGS (1991) in *Library Communication: The Language of Leadership*.

WOODSWORTH sheds a different light on library directors by suggesting that they are merely middle managers in their institutions, in dead-end jobs; and as such subject to the normal lot of middle managers, viz., being ignored, subject to pressure from above and below, having little scope for growth or advancement, and being lonely and isolated. Like their staffs, they need developing so that they are acceptable at higher levels. Is it really as bad as that? In the UK at least, several library directors have gone on to higher things.

The Leader and Manager as Mentor, Counselor, or Therapist

One way of empowering staff and developing them for the future is for the manager to serve as mentor. This is very common, and seemingly important, to judge by a 1980 survey conducted by the Association of Research Libraries to determine the extent to which library directors had experienced mentoring as both proteges and mentors (FERRIERO). Seventy-seven had been proteges at one time or another; one-fourth had had more than five mentors, and 84% rated the mentoring as significant (including one-third as very significant). Roles performed, whether by the directors' mentors or by themselves as mentors, included teacher or coach, role model, developer of talent, opener of doors, and sponsor. The nature, requirements, and benefits of mentorship are discussed by CARGILL (1989a), who also mentions the need for eventual weaning.

One possible expression of concern for the individual member of staff is acting as a kind of informal psychotherapist. BIRDSALL recounts the growth of the self-fulfillment movement, with its origins in MASLOW (1987). He believes "the management-staff relationship is increasingly analogous to a contractual arrangement between counselor and client, a relationship that is both impersonal and intimate" (p. 210). He points out that this can be as exploitative as authoritarian management, but it is more subtle—as he says, quoting Wright Mills, "less material and more psychological" (p. 211). He argues however that the effort to "combine rationally derived interpersonal management skills with genuine personal relationships" and to "promote both organizational goals and individual longings for self-fulfillment" can lead to heightened creativity (p. 212).

Counseling is usually regarded as distinct from both mentoring and therapy, and much of the article by LUBANS is concerned with what used to be known as the "problem staff member." There are nevertheless similarities between the three approaches or techniques. There is no reason why counseling should not be positive and constructive as well as remedial; and whether it is constructive or remedial, the identification and pursuit of clear goals that Lubans advocates can help.

STRESS AND CONFLICT

Burnout

"Burnout" (an inappropriate term for severe stress since it should surely mean *total* exhaustion) is given a section to itself because it has attracted an extensive literature (nearly 50 articles since 1979, when the first article on it in the library field appeared). Unusually, the literature covers every type of library. Fortunately, it is not necessary to read all of it; FISHER provides an admirable critical review, while BLAZEK & PARRISH analyze the articles for authorship, type of librarian, and content.

Fisher considers the early studies to be "essentially discursive documents, strong on opinion and supposition, weak on empirical investigation" (p. 218). The first study he views as worthy of the name (SMITH & NELSON) was based on a questionnaire to 75 U.S. universities and revealed a remarkable absence of stress among the respondents. HAACK ET AL., surveying academic librarians at a conference on reference services, concluded that 14% were "severely burned out" and 28% "showed ongoing signs of psychological stress." The sample was hardly random, and reference work is believed to be particularly stressful. A national survey of 548 U.S. public library reference librarians (BIRCH ET AL.) showed that the average respondent experienced medium levels of burnout, much the same level as teachers.

All of the above surveys, and others by SMITH & NIELSEN (of corporate librarians), NELSON (of law librarians), and NEWELL ET AL. (of Australian academic librarians), are based on questionnaires, which are not ideal instruments for studying burnout; they cannot, for example, explore causes. This may help to explain the contradictory findings. By contrast, BUNGE based his article on more probing studies of 850 librarians at workshops on stress management in 21 locations—again, hardly a random sample. He found that the main source of stress (reported by 41%) of public services librarians was patrons, followed at some distance by workload, which ranked highest (22% reporting) for technical services librarians. Supervisors and management (18%) and other staff members (13%) scored highest among support staff. There seem to be clear messages here for management, but they are familiar ones; and apart from patrons, who are an essential element in a public service, the situation does not appear to be especially worrying.

Blazek and Parrish's analysis of articles comes up with workload as the most commonly reported contributing factor, followed by a somewhat disparate cluster they call "lack of communication/role ambiguity/lack of support/intensity of task" and management style/organizational structure. The leading personal factors are unrealistic expectation and personality type.

Fisher's plea for much better research, and for research in different countries, must be endorsed; he points out that excellent studies have been carried out in other professions.

The most popular remedies for burnout are individual approaches (behavior modification easily leading the way), followed by organizational and managerial approaches. NAURATIL blames society for the alienation to which she attributes burnout (which society? She is a Canadian), and WHITE (1990) blames not only library managers but parent bodies who expect too much from resources that are too small.

Conflict

As most writers point out, conflict, like stress, is not always bad. Any organization in which there is no conflict is unlikely to challenge present assumptions or practices, generate creative ideas, or produce innovations. Problems arise not from conflicts of ideas but from conflicts between people, although the former can sometimes turn into the latter. A new idea, whether it comes from the top or a colleague at the same (or a lower) level, may well provoke hostile reactions and subsequent conflict. Likewise, competition for resources can become a personal matter. The way to deal with such situations is to accept that there are differences and focus the attention of staff on goals and objectives (DARLING & CLUFF). This should not only depersonalize the issues and reduce the risk of personal conflict, but expand the range of options available and thus help to develop staff. The recognition that conflict may be a sign of vitality has led to the replacement of the term "conflict resolution" by "conflict management" (p. 18).

Conflicts between people can be very harmful to the organization because energies that should go into work are absorbed by emotions. They can occur for various reasons, among them misunderstandings, incompatible personalities, rivalries, and competition for advancement. They can happen between staff at the same or similar levels, or between managers and the staff who report to them. Ways of handling personal conflicts include individual and group counseling; clumsiness or insensitivity in handling staff can be reduced by managerial training. HULBERT argues that both passive and aggressive techniques for handling conflict are likely to cause trouble and recommends assertive methods. Other reasons for conflict given by KATHMAN & KATHMAN include job ambiguity, failures of communication, and environmental stress. These can all be remedied by administrative action and seem to fall within the category of stress rather than conflict.

A more participative management style may actually increase conflict at first, because staff are called on to have more discussion and reach agreement on various issues. If participation is well handled, this should gradually give way to greater knowledge and understanding, and hence to less personal conflict and more creative conflict over issues. Whatever the management style, good communication at all levels is absolutely vital. KEMP provides a helpful table summarizing approaches to managing conflict and when (and when not) to use each of them (p. 25). Other useful papers are those by ALLRED and by PETTAS & GILLILAND.

ORGANIZATIONAL STRUCTURES

Participative management and teamwork are not easy to achieve without some organizational restructuring, as many of the writings cited above recognize. It is tempting for directors to play around with structures without bearing in mind the functions they need to serve: the attainment of the organization's objectives, effective decision making, decisive action, good communication, clear reporting lines, staff motivation, and efficient management. The book by SADLER is an excellent concise guide to designing organizations for control, motivation and commitment, and innovation and flexibility. Although it is based on experience in industry, most of it is equally applicable to libraries. He is clear that the organization of the future will have flatter structures, fewer levels of management, few direct workers and more "knowledge workers," built-in flexibility, fuzzy boundaries, complex structural networking, and autonomous work groups; networks will replace hierarchy, and influence will replace authority (p. 170).

There seems to be a general consensus in the LIS literature that IT has made changes in organizational structures inevitable (DE KLERK & EUSTER). Hierarchical structures can no longer perform the above functions adequately, for reasons explained by EUSTER and others. But no other structure has yet established itself as the norm. Euster believes that "Perhaps in the long run [hierarchy] will become irrelevant, and wither away, with more as yet undreamed of organizational structures replacing it" (p. 44). Networked structures may be the thing of the future, but they will probably evolve rather than be deliberately designed.

As noted above (see Team Management) team structures can exist in any type of structure. BARLOW shows how teams that were introduced in three libraries as part of participative structures in the 1970s were retained when all of the libraries reverted to more hierarchical structures as part of a general trend toward such structures in local government generally, and under new chief librarians.

Meanwhile alternative structures continue to be considered. Several writers report how they have restructured their libraries in whole or in part (e.g., HAWKINS; LOWELL & SULLIVAN; MARTELL & GORMAN; MARTELL & JOHNSON; MIGNEAULT). All of the reported restructurings seem to be in the firm direction of more participation and team working, perhaps because librarians who had retained or moved back to a hierarchy would be reluctant to publicize it. One who has no such inhibitions is ROYAN, who likes the clarity and authority of hierarchies.

Matrix management is a less popular topic in the literature than it was a decade or so ago. One of the few recent papers on it is that by EUSTER & HAIKALIS, who describe the implementation of a matrix structure in a division of San Francisco State University. This seeming neglect might mean that matrix management has fallen out of favor because of the problems of dual responsibility and reporting, or alternatively that it is now being increasingly implemented and is thus no longer a matter for discussion. The truth is probably somewhere in between, i.e., while there are few libraries structured entirely on matrix principles, many have elements of matrix management, with some staff having two quite different roles. There must be many "hidden matrices" lurking within apparently conventional structures. This is bound to happen in any but very large libraries as staff numbers no longer keep pace with the volume and range of activity and as certain kinds of knowledge and expertise are in short supply; for example, an academic library that wishes to offer a wide range of subject services as well as carrying out complex technical operations is unlikely to be able to afford full-time specialists for every operation and every group of subjects and languages. The somewhat slow but significant trend toward project management will lead in a similar direction. There is in any case a good theoretical case for such "doubling up" on the grounds of job variety.

P. JOHNSON revives the issue in an article arguing strongly for matrix management, although she appears to be concerned solely with an activity/project matrix. Various other matrices are of course possible, such as service/product, client group/activity, subject/function, and so on; three-way matrices are not impossible. The "parallel organization" recommended by FISHER & BRIN, following ZAND and others, differs from matrix management in placing alongside the bureaucratic hierarchy another organization structured to be more flexible, responsive, and participative. While matrices seem to be steps along the road to the evolving networked organization, parallel organizations may freeze present systems, albeit supplementing them.

Also related to matrix management are the ideas of LINE (1991), who wants libraries to be driven by objectives and services rather than by processes, and believes that this is more likely to be achieved if the top structure is organized by functions such as services, marketing, IT and so on rather than by operations such as collections and conservation; the latter should be at a subordinate level in the structure. The top staff would have no line management role, but would have to ensure that their objectives were fulfilled; this would require teams drawn from the staff "diagonally," that is, across divisions and down through grades. HOADLEY & CORBIN also argue for primacy to be given to service, but their proposed new structure does not depart far from conventional ones.

MARTELL (1983) certainly cannot be accused of forgetting objectives; his book on *The Client-Centered Academic Library* considers how to design libraries around clients, and provides a well-developed organizational model.

DE KLERK & EUSTER state that there is little evidence that organizational charts have changed much in the past decade or two, despite expectations of sweeping changes. This may be so, but, as suggested above, organizational charts do not necessarily show how organizations have changed. Participation can be increased with no change at all, and project management can also be introduced informally. Again, there may still be numerous grades of staff, but they may no longer equate closely with levels of responsibility, whatever charts say; unobtrusive flattening may have occurred. It is highly probable that some directors see the need for formal change but cannot decide exactly what change to make. Uncertainty will prevail for some years yet, and organizational structures will continue to attract interest.

STAFF DEVELOPMENT

Training and staff development are sometimes used synonymously. Here, we consider these two aspects of this vital organizational tool and assess developments that are relevant to library managers. Staff development is a much broader concept than "training," which is usually seen in terms of providing an individual with the necessary skills and knowledge to enable a task or set of tasks to be performed effectively. Developing an individual to his or her fullest potential, however, involves a much deeper concern for overall career and personal development. It encompasses training but seeks to provide added skills and knowledge which can carry the individual forward into a further grade or even beyond the organization into another job or career path.

Staff Development and Training Needs

Before embarking on the design of training programs, it is essential to identify the precise development and training needs of an organization. Although operating problems in a library may indicate the existence of a training need, other problems may require attention—e.g., the redesign of jobs or communication structures. CONROY, CASTELEYN and TAYLOR & LIPPITT offer guidance on the analysis of the training gap in libraries as well as on design and delivery of training. Training needs may be identified at various levels. At the organizational level, the human resource plan for the library will highlight skill deficits; at the department or functional level, information will be available by comparing absence or turnover levels and customer dissatisfaction; at the job level, similar analyses can be made to compare jobs or groups of jobs; and at the individual level, information from personnel appraisals and requests for further training provide useful data.

TORRINGTON & HALL also discuss the place of management development within organizations and provide a summary of significant theories on the subject. MINTZBERG (1973) has been one of the most influential writers on the nature of managerial work, with his analyses demonstrating the complexity of management tasks. Communication and interpersonal skills emerge as significant.

Managers are developed not only for jobs they are doing but for those they will be doing; hence the emphasis on future potential. "Management development is a vital aspect of career development, and from the organization's point of view both are methods of satisfying human resource needs while allowing individuals to achieve their career goals" (TORRINGTON & HALL, p. 389).

Staff Development Programs

Management development programs for staff with management potential or for those in middle-management positions with potential for the highest professional leadership posts have been of particular interest in recent years. A research review by I.M. JOHNSON of the management education being provided for librarians in Scotland focuses on middle and senior managers in mid-career. SHELDON and SUMMERS discuss the curriculum for the first two Snowbird Leadership Institutes, in 1990 and 1991. The need for training to be offered to middle and senior managers was a finding of the study of chief librarians' management strategies by KINNELL EVANS. At a time when U.K. public libraries are under particular strain, with senior managers facing local government restructuring, the contracting out of service elements and continuing budgetary constraints, the need to provide further training and development programs for senior staff has become more urgent. This has also been recognized by the Norwegian Directorate of Public and School Libraries, which has a program of management training and development designed specifically for chief municipal librarians (EIDET).

An education model of staff development is suggested by WEAVER-MEYERS, who surveyed staff developers in member libraries of the Association of Research Libraries (ARL) and found that most of the model describes practices appropriate to the academic/research library setting.

Less formal methods of developing managers include on-the-job development (mentoring, peer relationships, and self-development). SHELDON interviewed several prominent U.S. library professionals who described their experience of mentors who assisted their career development in this way. LINE & ROBERTSON advocate the use of consultants over an extended period to develop managerial skills (see also HUNT and NICHOLSON).

Training Systems

All staff, whether nonprofessional or professional, need adequate training to meet the requirements of the job at hand. BIRD and PARKER describe the uses of in-service training in U.K. public library authorities. Parker is particularly interesting on the relationship between library and education services, as she outlines how library professionals in the U.K. have become engaged in the training of teachers as well as school library personnel. CASTELEYN discusses more widely how training programs might be developed, with particular emphasis on methods. In a report to the British Library on the state of the art of training and management development in librarianship, RITCHIE (1988) identifies the realities of training provision and offers recommendations for meeting future needs, while PRYTHERCH has edited a volume on various kinds of training systems for use in different kinds of library service, with valuable personal accounts from practitioners.

Almost more than any other aspect of human resource management, training depends heavily on the specialist professional expertise of library managers skilled in training and on others from beyond the profession with relevant expertise. Cooperative efforts are therefore seen as especially worthwhile to ensure that trainers are used most cost-effectively and that library services can provide the best possible training for their staff. MACDOUGALL & PRYTHERCH indicate how cooperative training can be developed, particularly in academic and public libraries, and they describe successful programs.

The content of training programs has also been discussed at length, with initial professional education and continuing education/training particularly focusing on the acquisition of IT skills (MEADOWS). The emphasis has been on the process of skills and knowledge delivery and providing staff with current information on the selection and uses of various computer packages, CD-ROMs, and so forth. Library staff need to know how to operate various systems and to acquire a range of information-handling and information management skills, as CONNOR considers in an article on the implications of automation for staff training.

Increasingly, however, other communication skills are being stressed, partly as a result of the marketing approach to information services. Customer care policies are now regarded as equally important for delivering quality services, with considerable implications for personnel training. In their study of interpersonal skills training, LEVY & USHERWOOD identify this as a key area for development. One public librarian quoted in this work noted that this was "a cost effective means of enhancing services in straitened circumstances" (p. 47).

Policies and Resources

In all development programs, there needs to be the will within the library service to provide funding. In the current climate this is a particular problem. Training budgets are too often considered expendable. In drawing on experience at the British Library of Political and Economic Science, NICHOLSON demonstrates how a written policy and staff development plan are helpful, with one senior member of staff given the role of coordinator. Both time and money are required, and the culture of the organization must be receptive. SHAUGHNESSY also addresses the need for library managers to show the effectiveness of programs and offers some reasons for the failure of staff development in libraries.

Experience from industry suggests that HR budgets, including money for training, must show a return to the business in a time of recession. An HR mission statement that mirrors that of the organization as a whole might be a useful focus for setting goals, priorities, and strategies. Training then becomes such an important contribution to the enhancement of skills that recruiting new staff becomes less necessary: "As we improved the skills of our employees through training, we eventually dissolved the corporate recruitment function. The hope is that we can recruit from within" (HALCROW, p. 119). This approach can be particularly attractive for large library services which sustain a separate HR function but is less easy to apply in smaller libraries where training budgets jostle for priority with book funds and equipment bids.

Staff development has to be written into the objectives of the library service and to be seen as indispensable for achieving corporate objectives if training budgets are to be treated on a par with other budgetary categories. For example, if an equal opportunity policy is being defined and implemented, then a staff development program forms one part of the policy document, and resources are dedicated to training. Professional associations provide significant support to library services, partly through their training requirements for new professionals and also through the provision of training courses and materials. The (U.K.) LIBRARY ASSOCIATION (1987) has taken an increasing interest in the training needs of its members and has provided a statement of support for staff development and training. One of the most important functions of a professional association is its concern for the career aspirations of its members, and ensuring that training and management development programs are adequately funded is a major aim.

The literature confirms that staff development is a fundamental HR activity and one that requires adequate funding. Studies of practice show that it should be developed within the broad strategic plan for the library service and not as an additional program. The level of training in library services, as in other organizations, is frequently criticized as being inadequate but at present it is vital to protect training budgets.

ENVOI

In spite of reservations expressed by some authors, the literature on HRM in libraries and information services overwhelmingly stresses participation, supportive leadership, and enabling individual staff to reach their potential and thus to contribute more to organizations in the use of initiative and overall productivity. What is happening in practice is much harder to assess. There are a number of case studies, but these are almost invariably of organizations that have successfully applied recommended practices. Few studies have been reported of organizations that have not tried or that have tried and failed, and possibly reverted to old styles of management. Management styles are clearly changing under the numerous pressures, perhaps to an extent not fully recognized by the managers themselves. IT poses both threats, which need to be faced, and opportunities, which need to be grasped. Nevertheless, it still seems that few libraries and information services regard HRM planning as an essential and integral part of their overall planning; rather, they see it as a highly desirable supplementary process.

Among aspects of human resources that the literature does not cover well are: (1) the relationship of HRM planning in the library to that in the parent body; (2) middle managers and supervisors, with a few exceptions (BAILEY; ERKKILA & MACKAY); and (3) the difficulties created for both the organization and individuals by voluntary or involuntary redundancy. Perhaps the most important unaddressed issue that has been overlooked concerns the stability of staff and the prospect of permanent employment; these are goals of good management practice, but they can no longer be guaranteed at a time when more redundancies seem inevitable and more and more services of public sector libraries are likely to be contracted out to the private sector. Neither trend seems likely to be temporary.

BIBLIOGRAPHY

ALLEY, BRIAN. 1987. What Professional Librarians Expect from Administrators: An Administrator's Response. College and Research Libraries. 1987 September; 48(5): 418-421. ISSN: 0010-0870.

ALLRED, CAROL B. 1987. The Anatomy of Conflict: Some Thoughts on Managing Staff Conflict. Law Library Journal. 1987 Winter; 79(1): 7-32. ISSN: 0023-9283.

ARGYRIS, CHRIS. 1960. Understanding Organizational Behavior. Homewood, IL: Dorsey Press; 1960. 179p. LC: 60-10149.

ARMSTRONG, MICHAEL. 1987. Human Resource Management: A Case of the Emperor's New Clothes? Personnel Management. 1987 August; 19(8): 30-35. ISSN: 0031-5761.

ARMSTRONG, MICHAEL. 1988. Handbook of Personnel Management Practice. London, England: Kogan Page; 1988. 712p. ISBN: 1-85091-336-6.

BAILEY, MARTHA J. 1987. Middle Managers in Libraries/Information Services. Library Administration and Management. 1987 September; 1(4): 139-142. ISSN: 0888-4463.

BAIRD, LLOYD; MESHOULAM, ILAM. 1992. Getting Payoff from Investment in Human Resources Management. Business Horizons. 1992 January-February; 35(1): 68-75. ISSN: 0007-6813.

BAKER, BETSY; SANDORE, BETH. 1991. Motivation in Turbulent Times: In Search of the Epicurean Work Ethic. Journal of Library Administration. 1991; 14(4): 37-50. ISSN: 0193-0826.

BANKS, JULIE. 1991. Motivation and Effective Management of Student Assistants in Academic Libraries. Journal of Library Administration. 1991; 14(1): 133-154. ISSN: 0193-0826.

BARLOW, RICHARD. 1989. Team Librarianship. London, England: Clive Bingley; 1989. 175p. ISBN: 0-85157-450-5.

BECHTEL, JOAN M. 1993. Leadership Lessons Learned from Managing and Being Managed. Journal of Academic Librarianship. 1993 January; 18(6): 352-357. ISSN: 0099-1333.

BENGSTON, DALE SUSAN; SHIELDS, DOROTHY. 1985. A Test of Marchant's Predictive Formulas Involving Job Satisfaction. Journal of Academic Librarianship. 1985 May; 11(2): 88-92. ISSN: 0099-1333.

BERGEN, CERIS. 1988. Instruments to Plague Us? Human Factors in the Management of Library Automation. Bradford, England: MCB University Press; 1988. 55p. (Library Management, 1988; 9(6)). ISSN: 0143-5124; ISBN: 0-86176-019-6.

BIRCH, NANCY E.; MARCHANT, MAURICE P.; SMITH, NATHAN M. 1986. Perceived Role Conflict, Role Ambiguity, and Reference Librarian Burnout in Public Libraries. Library and Information Science Research. 1986 January; 8(1): 53-65. ISSN: 0740-8188.

BIRD, JEAN. 1986. In-Service Training in Public Library Authorities. London, England: Library Association; 1986. 151p. ISBN: 0-85365-826-7.

BIRDSALL, WILLIAM F. 1990. The Library Manager as Therapist. Journal of Academic Librarianship. 1990 September; 16(4): 209-212. ISSN: 0099-1333.

BLAZEK, RON; PARRISH, DARLENE ANN. 1992. Burnout and the Public Services: The Periodical Literature of Librarianship in the Eighties. RQ. 1992 Fall; 32(1): 48-59. ISSN: 0033-7072.

BOHANNAN, APRIL. 1993. Self-Managing Work Groups: The Role of the External Leader. Library Administration and Management. 1993 Winter; 7(1): 17-22. ISSN: 0088-4463.

BOWEN, DAVID E.; LAWLER, EDWARD E., III. 1992. Total Quality-Oriented Human Resources Management. Organizational Dynamics. 1992; 20(4): 29-41. ISSN: 0090-2616.

BOXALL, PETER F. 1992. Strategic Human Resource Management: Beginning of a New Theoretical Sophistication? Human Resource Management Journal. 1992; 2(3): 60-79. ISSN: 0954-5395.

BRYSON, JO. 1990. Effective Library and Information Centre Management. Aldershot, England: Gower; 1990. 409p. ISBN: 0-566-05637-2.

BRYSON, JOHN M. 1988. Strategic Planning for Public and Non-Profit Organizations: A Guide to Strengthening and Sustaining Organizational Achievement. London, England: Jossey-Bass; 1988. 311p. ISBN: 1-55542-087-7.

BUNGE, CHARLES. 1987. Stress in the Library. Library Journal. 1987 September 15; 112(15): 47-51. ISSN: 0363-0277.

BURCKEL, NICHOLAS C. 1984. Participatory Management in Academic Libraries: A Review. College and Research Libraries. 1984 January; 45(1): 25-33. ISSN: 0010-0870.

BURTON, PAUL F. 1988. Information Technology and Organisational Structure. Aslib Proceedings. 1988 March; 40(3): 57-68. ISSN: 0001-253X.

BURTON, PAUL F. 1991. Systems, People and Structures: Methodologies for Successful Systems Design. In: Cronin, Blaise, ed. Information Management: From Strategy to Action. London, England: Aslib; 1991. 67-83. ISBN: 0-85142-281-0.

CARGILL, JENNIFER. 1989a. Developing Library Leaders: The Role of Mentorship. Library Administration and Management. 1989 Fall; 3(1): 12-15. ISSN: 0888-4463.

CARGILL, JENNIFER. 1989b. Integrating Public and Technical Services Support Staffs to Implement the New Mission of Libraries. Journal of Library Administration. 1989; 10(4): 21-31. ISSN: 0193-0826.

CARGILL, JENNIFER. 1990. Personnel and Technology: An Opportunity for Innovation. Journal of Library Administration. 1990; 13(1/2): 31-46. ISSN: 0193-0826.

CARVER, DEBORAH A. 1989. Transformational Leadership: A Bibliographic Essay. Library Administration and Management. 1989 Fall; 3(1): 30-34. ISSN: 0888-4463.

CASTELEYN, MARY. 1981. Planning Library Training Programmes. London, England: Deutsch; 1981. 175p. ISBN: 0-233-97338-9.

CHAMPAWAT, C.S. 1981. Douglas McGregor Visits Jaipur Information Centre: More of "Y" and Less of "X" Is the Answer: A Case Study. Herald of Library Science. 1981 January-April; 20(1/2): 28-37. ISSN: 0018-0521.

COE, TRUDY. 1992. The Key to the Men's Club: Opening the Doors to Women in Management. Corby, England: Institute of Management; 1992. 38p. ISBN: 0-85946-224-2.

CONNOR, CLARE M. 1992. Staff Training in Libraries: The Implications of Automation. Library Management. 1992; 13(6): 15-24. ISSN: 0143-5124.

CONROY, BARBARA. 1978. Library Staff Development and Continuing Education: Principles and Practices. Littleton, CO: Libraries Unlimited; 1978. 269p. ISBN: 0-87287-177-0.

COOKE, ROGER; ARMSTRONG, MICHAEL. 1990. The Search for Strategic HRM. Personnel Management. 1990 December; 22(12): 30-33. ISSN: 0031-5761.

CRETH, SHEILA; DUDA, FREDERICK, eds. 1989. Personnel Administration in Libraries. 2nd edition. New York, NY: London, England: Neal-Schuman; 1989. 343p. ISBN: 1-55570-036-5.

DAKSHINAMURTI, GANGA. 1985. Automation's Effect on Library Personnel. Canadian Library Journal. 1985 December; 42(6): 343-351. ISSN: 0008-4352.

DARLING, JOHN R.; CLUFF, E. DALE. 1987. Managing Interpersonal Conflict in a University Library. Library Administration and Management. 1987 January; 1(1): 16-22. ISSN: 0888-4463.

DASTMALCHIAN, ALI; BLYTON, PAUL. 1992. Organizational Structure. Human Resources Practices and Industrial Relations. Personnel Review. 1992; 21(1): 58-67. ISSN: 0048-3486.

DE KLERK, ANN; EUSTER, JOANNE R. 1989. Technology and Organizational Metamorphoses. Library Trends. 1989 Spring; 37(4): 457-468. ISSN: 0024-2594.

DELON, BARBARA. 1993. Keeping Plateaued Performers Motivated. Library Administration and Management. 1993 Winter; 7(1): 13-16. ISSN: 0888-4463.

DICKENS, L.; TOWNSEND, B.; WINCHESTER, D. 1988. Tackling Sex Discrimination through Collective Bargaining. Manchester, England: Equal Opportunities Commission; 1988. 95p. ISBN: 0-11-701411-7.

DRUCKER, PETER F. 1954. The Practice of Management. New York, NY: Harper; 1954. 355p. LC: 54-8946.

DRUCKER, PETER F. 1974. Management: Tasks, Responsibilities, Practices. New York, NY: Harper & Row; 1974. 839p. ISBN: 0-06-011092-9.

DRUCKER, PETER F. 1990. Managing the Non-Profit Organization. New York, NY: Harper/Collins; 1990. 178p. ISBN: 0-06-016507-3.

EIDET, RANNVEIG. 1989. Better Management—Better Libraries. Scandinavian Public Library Quarterly. 1989; 22(4): 20-25. ISSN: 0036-5602.

ERKKILA, JOHN; MACKAY, PAMELA. 1990. Practical Supervision: The First Line of Management. Journal of Library Administration. 1990; 12(1): 103-115. ISSN: 0193-0826.

ESTABROOK, LEIGH; BIRD, CHLOE; GILMORE, FREDERICK L. 1990. Job Satisfaction: Does Automation Make a Difference? Journal of Library Administration. 1990; 13(1/2): 175-194. ISSN: 0193-0826.

EUSTER, JOANNE R. 1990. The New Hierarchy: Where's the Boss? Library Journal. 1990 May 1; 115(8): 40-44. ISSN: 0363-0277.

EUSTER, JOANNE R.; HAIKALIS, PETER D. 1984. A Matrix Model of Organization for a University Library Public Services Division. In: Dodson, Suzanne C.; Menges, Gary L., eds. Academic Libraries: Myths and Realities: Proceedings of the Association of College and Research Libraries (ACRL) 3rd National Conference; 1984 April 4-7; Seattle, WA. Chicago, IL: ACRL; 1984. 357-364. ISBN: 0-8389-6787-6.

EVANS, G. EDWARD. 1983. Management Techniques for Librarians. 2nd edition. New York, NY: Academic Press; 1983. 330p. ISBN: 0-12-243856-6.

FERKETISH, B. JEAN; HAYDEN, JOHN W. 1992. HRD & Quality: The Chicken or the Egg? Training and Development. 1992 January; 46(1): 38-42. ISSN: 1055-9760.

FERRIERO, DAVID S. 1982. ARL Directors as Proteges and Mentors. Journal of Academic Librarianship. 1982 January; 7(6): 358-365. ISSN: 0099-1333.

FINE, SARA F. 1986. Technological Innovation, Diffusion and Resistance: A Historical Perspective. Journal of Library Administration. 1986 Spring; 7(1): 83-108. ISSN: 0193-0826.

FINK, DEBORAH. 1987. What Professional Librarians Expect from Administrators: Another Librarian's View. College and Research Libraries. 1987 September; 48(5): 413-417. ISSN: 0010-0870.

FISHER, DAVID P. 1990. Are Librarians Burning Out? Journal of Librarianship. 1990 October; 22(4): 216-235. ISSN: 0022-2232.

FISHER, WILLIAM; BRIN, BETH L. 1991. Parallel Organization: A Structural Change Theory. Journal of Library Administration. 1991; 14(1): 51-66. ISSN: 0193-0826.

FITCH, DONNA. 1990. Job Satisfaction among Support Staff in Alabama Academic Libraries. College and Research Libraries. 1990 July; 51(4): 313-320. ISSN: 0010-0870.

FORSMAN, RICK B. 1990. Incorporating Organizational Values into the Strategic Planning Process. Journal of Academic Librarianship. 1990 July; 16(3): 150-153. ISSN: 0099-1333.

FRANK, DONALD G. 1989. Allocation of Staff in the Academic Library: Relevant Issues and Consideration of a Rationale. Journal of Library Administration. 1989; 10(4): 48-58. ISSN: 0193-0826.

GORMAN, MICHAEL. 1991. Strategic Planning: Implementation and First-Year Appraisal. Journal of Academic Librarianship. 1991 March; 17(1): 101-105. ISSN: 0099-1333.

GOVAN, JAMES F. 1977. The Better Mousetrap: External Accountability and Staff Participation. Library Trends. 1977 Fall; 26(2): 255-267. ISSN: 0024-2594.

GRUMLING, DENNIS K.; SHEEHY, CAROLYN A. 1993. Professional Development Program: Training for Success within Academic Librarianship. College and Research Libraries. 1993 January; 54(1): 17-24. ISSN: 0010-0870.

GUEST, DAVID E. 1987. Human Resource Management and Industrial Relations. Journal of Management Studies. 1987 September; 24(5): 503-522. ISSN: 0022-2380.

GUEST, DAVID E. 1990. Human Resource Management and the American Dream. Journal of Management Studies. 1990 July; 27(4): 377-397. ISSN: 0022-2380.

GUEST, DAVID E. 1991. Personnel Management: The End of Orthodoxy? British Journal of Industrial Relations. 1991 June; 29(2): 149-175. ISSN: 0007-1080.

HAACK, MARY; JONES, JOHN W.; ROOSE, TINA. 1984. Occupational Burnout among Librarians. Drexel Library Quarterly. 1984 Spring; 20(2): 46-72. ISSN: 0012-6160.

HACKMAN, J. RICHARD. 1986. The Psychology of Self-Management in Organizations. In: Pallak, Michael S.; Perloff, Robert O., eds. Psychology and Work: Productivity Change and Employment. Washington, DC: American Psychological Association; 1986. 85-136. ISBN: 0-912704-48-9.

HACKMAN, J. RICHARD; SUTTLE, J. LLOYD, eds. 1977. Improving Life at Work: Behavioral Science Approaches to Organizational Change. Santa Monica, CA: Goodyear; 1977. 494p. ISBN: 0-87620-411-6.

HALCROW, ALLAN. 1992. The HR Budget Squeeze. Personnel Journal. 1992 June; 71: 114-128. ISSN: 0031-5745.

HANDY, CHARLES. 1991. The Age of Unreason. 2nd edition. London, England: Business Books Limited; 1991. 217p. ISBN: 0-7126-4931-X.

HANNABUSS, STUART. 1983. Motivational Theories and Managerial Questions. Information and Library Manager. 1983; 2(4): 98-101. ISSN: 0260-6879.

HARRISON, D.J. 1979. The Staffing of Public Libraries: An Appraisal of the 1976 LAMSAC Report. Journal of Librarianship. 1979 July; 11(3): 183-196. ISSN: 0022-2232.

HARRISON, KALU U.; HAVARD-WILLIAMS, P. 1987. Motivation in a Third World Library System. International Library Review. 1987 July; 19(3): 249-260. ISSN: 0020-7837.

HAWKINS, KATHERINE W. 1989. Implementing Team Management in the Modern Library. Library Administration and Management. 1989 Winter; 4(1): 11-15. ISSN: 0888-4463.

HERZBERG, FREDERICK. 1966. Work and the Nature of Man. Cleveland, OH: London, England: World Publishing Co.; Staples Press; 1966. 203p. ISBN: 0-258-97011-1.

HERZBERG, FREDERICK. 1968. One More Time: How Do You Motivate Employees? Harvard Business Review. 1968 January/February; 46(1): 53-62. Reprinted with comments in: Harvard Business Review. 1987 September/October; 65(5): 109-120. ISSN: 0017-8012.

HERZBERG, FREDERICK; MAUSNER, BERNARD; BLOCH, BARBARA SNYDERMAN. 1992. The Motivation to Work. With a New Introduction by Frederick Herzberg. New Brunswick, NJ: Transaction Publishers; 1992. (First published 1959). 157p. ISBN: 1-56000-634-X.

HOADLEY, IRENE B.; CORBIN, JOHN. 1990. Up the Beanstalk: An Evolutionary Organizational Structure for Libraries. American Libraries. 1990 July/August; 21(7): 676-678. ISSN: 0002-9769.

HOOGENDOORN, JACOB; BREWSTER, CHRIS. 1992. Human Resource Aspects: Decentralization and Devolution. Personnel Review. 1992; 21(1): 4-11. ISSN: 0048-3486.

HULBERT, DORIS. 1990. Assertive Management in Libraries. Journal of Academic Librarianship. 1990 July; 16(3): 158-162. ISSN: 0099-1333.

HUNT, CHRISTOPHER J. 1991. Library Staff Development Consultancy: A Means to Achieve a Better Library. INSPEL. 1991; 25(1): 17-23. ISSN: 0019-0217.

INSTITUTE OF PERSONNEL MANAGEMENT. 1977. Staff Status for All. London, England: Institute of Personnel Management; 1977. 70p. ISBN: 0-85292-150-0.

INTERNATIONAL JOURNAL OF SELECTION AND ASSESSMENT. 1993-. Anderson, Neil, ed. Oxford, England: Blackwell. ISSN: 0965-075X.

JACOBS, CAROL. 1991. The Use of the Exit Interview as a Personnel Tool and Its Applicability to Libraries. Journal of Library Administration. 1991; 14(4): 69-86. ISSN: 0193-0826.

JOHNSON, IAN M. 1992. Management Education and Training for Librarians in Scotland. Scottish Libraries. 1992 January/February; 31: 11-13. ISSN: 0950-0189.

JOHNSON, PEGGY. 1990. Matrix Management: An Organizational Alternative for Libraries. Journal of Academic Librarianship. 1990 September; 16(4): 222-229. ISSN: 0099-1333.

JONES, KEN. 1984. Conflict and Change in Library Organizations: People. Power and Service. London, England: Clive Bingley; 1984. 274p. ISBN: 0-85157-367-3.

JONES, NORAH; JORDAN, PETER. 1987. Staff Management in Library and Information Work. 2nd edition. Aldershot, England: Gower; 1987. 315p. ISBN: 0-566-03563-4.

JUROW, SUSAN. 1990. Preparing for Library Leadership. Journal of Library Administration. 1990; 12(2): 57-73. ISSN: 0193-0826.

KAPLAN, LOUIS. 1975. The Literature of Participation: From Optimism to Realism. College and Research Libraries. 1975 November; 36(6): 473-479. ISSN: 0010-0870.

KAPLAN, LOUIS. 1977. On Decision Sharing in Libraries: How Much Do We Know? College and Research Libraries. 1977 January; 38(1): 26-31. ISSN: 0010-0870.

KARP, RASHELLE SCHLESSINGER. 1988. Public Library Unions: Some Questions. Public Library Quarterly. 1988; 8(3/4): 73-80. ISSN: 0161-6846.

KATHMAN, JANE MCGURN; KATHMAN, MICHAEL D. 1990. Conflict Management in the Academic Library. Journal of Academic Librarianship. 1990 July; 16(3): 145-149. ISSN: 0099-1333.

KEMP, JANICE C. 1989. A Primer on Conflict Management. Library Management Quarterly. 1989 Fall; 12(4): 20-25. ISSN: 0271-3306.

KEMPSTER, GRACE. 1988. Motivating Staff in Public Library Services to Children and Young People. International Review of Children's Literature and Librarianship. 1988 Summer; 3(2): 98-125. ISSN: 0269-0500.

KINNELL EVANS, MARGARET. 1991. All Change? Public Library Management Strategies for the 1990s. London, England: Taylor Graham; 1991. 174p. ISBN: 0-947568-50-6.

KREITZ, PATRICIA A.; OGDEN, ANNEGRET. 1990. Job Responsibilities and Job Satisfaction at the University of California Libraries. College and Research Libraries. 1990 July; 51(3): 297-312. ISSN: 0010-0870.

LEGGE, KAREN. 1989. Human Resource Management: A Critical Analysis. In: Storey, John, ed. New Perspectives on Human Resource Management. London, England: Routledge; 1989. 19-40. ISBN: 0-415-01040-3.

LEINBACH, PHILIP E., ed. 1990. Personnel Administration in an Automated Environment. New York, NY: Haworth Press; 1990. 214p. ISBN: 1-56024-032-6. Also published as Journal of Library Administration. 1990; 13(1/2): 1-214. ISSN: 0193-0826.

LENGNICK-HALL, CYNTHIA A.; LENGNICK-HALL, MARK L. 1988. Strategic Human Resources Management: A Review of the Literature and a Proposed Typology. Academy of Management Review. 1988; 13(3): 454-470. ISSN: 0363-7425.

LEVY, PHILIPPA.; USHERWOOD, BOB. 1992. People Skills: Interpersonal Skills Training for Library and Information Work. London, England: British Library Research & Development Department; 1992. (Library and Information Research Report 88). ISBN: 0-7133-3266-9.

LIBRARY ASSOCIATION. 1987. Support for Staff Development and Training. London, England: Library Association; 1987. 2p. Available from: the Library Association, 7 Ridgmount St., London WC1E 7AE, England.

LIBRARY ASSOCIATION. 1989. Equal Opportunities Information Pack. London, England: Library Association; 1989. (multiple parts). Available from: the Library Association, 7 Ridgmount St., London WC1E 7AE, England.

LIKERT, RENSIS. 1961. New Patterns of Management. New York, NY: McGraw-Hill; 1961. 279p. LC: 61-13167.

LINE, MAURICE B. 1990. Why Isn't Work Fun? Library Management. 1990; 11(5): 15-17. ISSN: 0143-5124.

LINE, MAURICE B. 1991. Library Management Styles and Structures: A Need to Rethink? Journal of Librarianship and Information Science. 1991 June; 23(2): 37-44. ISSN: 0961-0006.

LINE, MAURICE B. 1992. How to Demotivate Staff: A Brief Guide. Library Management. 1992; 13(1): 4-7. ISSN: 0143-5124.

LINE, MAURICE B.; ROBERTSON, KEITH. 1989. Staff Development in Libraries. British Journal of Academic Librarianship. 1989; 4(3): 161-175. ISSN: 0269-0497.

LORENZI, NANCY M. 1976. The Art of Planning for Library Personnel. Bulletin of the Medical Library Association. 1976 April; 64(2): 212-218. ISSN: 0025-7338.

LOWELL, GERALD R.; SULLIVAN, MAUREEN. 1989. Self-Management in Technical Services: The Yale Experience. Library Administration and Management. 1989 Winter; 4(1): 20-23. ISSN: 0888-4463.

LUBANS, JOHN, JR. 1988. The Manager as Counselor: How Goals Help. Library Administration and Management. 1988 January; 2(1): 28-30. ISSN: 0888-4463.

LUCCOCK, GRAHAM. 1986. Induction Training. In: Prytherch, Ray, ed. Handbook of Library Training Practice. Aldershot, England: Gower; 1986. 3-36. ISBN: 0-566-03543-X.

LYNCH, BEVERLY P. 1972a. Organizational Structure and the Academic Library. Illinois Libraries. 1972 March; 56(3): 201-206. ISSN: 0019-2104.

LYNCH, BEVERLY P. 1972b. Participative Management in Relation to Library Effectiveness. College and Research Libraries. 1972 September; 33(5): 382-390. ISSN: 0010-0870.

LYNCH, BEVERLY P.; VERDIN, JO ANN. 1983. Job Satisfaction in Libraries: Relationships of the Work Itself, Age, Sex, Occupational Group, Tenure, Supervisory Level, Career Commitment, and Library Department. Library Quarterly. 1983 October; 53(4): 434-447. ISSN: 0024-2519.

LYNCH, BEVERLY P.; VERDIN, JO ANN. 1987. Job Satisfaction in Libraries: A Replication. Library Quarterly. 1987 April; 57(2): 190-202. ISSN: 0024-2519.

MACDOUGALL, ALAN F.; PRYTHERCH, RAY. 1989. Co-operative Training in Libraries. Aldershot, England: Gower; 1989. 289p. ISBN: 0-566-05709-3.

MACKEY, TERRY; MACKEY, KITTY. 1992. Think Quality! The Deming Approach Does Work in Libraries. Library Journal. 1992 May 12; 117(9): 57-61. ISSN: 0363-0277.

MALLEY, IAN. 1992. Cash Is the Key for Management Training: Paying the Piper and Calling the Tune in Skill Training. Library Association Record. 1992 December; 94(12): 792-793. ISSN: 0024-2195.

MANZ, CHARLES C.; SIMS, HENRY P., JR. 1991. Superleadership: Beyond the Myth of Heroic Leadership. Organizational Dynamics. 1991 Spring; 19(4): 18-35. ISSN: 0090-2616.

MARCHANT, MAURICE P. 1971. Participative Management as Related to Personnel Development. Library Trends. 1971 July; 20(1): 48-59. ISSN: 0024-2594.

MARCHANT, MAURICE P. 1972. And a Response [to Lynch 1972b]. College and Research Libraries. 1972 September; 33(5): 391-397. ISSN: 0010-0870.

MARCHANT, MAURICE P. 1976. Participative Management in Academic Libraries. Westport, CT: Greenwood Press; 1976. 260p. ISBN: 0-8371-8935-7.

MARCHANT, MAURICE P. 1982a. Managing Motivation and Job Satisfaction. In: McClure, Charles R.; Samuels, Alan R., eds. Strategies for Library Administration: Concepts and Approaches. Littleton, CO: Libraries Unlimited; 1982. 261-273. ISBN: 0-87287-265-3.

MARCHANT, MAURICE P. 1982b. Participative Management, Job Satisfaction, and Service. Library Journal. 1982 April 15; 107(8): 782-784. ISSN: 0363-0277.

MARCHANT, MAURICE P.; ENGLAND, MARK M. 1989. Changing Management Techniques as Libraries Automate. Library Trends. 1989 Spring; 37(2): 469-483. ISSN: 0024-2594.

MARCOTTE, FREDERICK A. 1982. Operational Audit and Library Staffing. Special Libraries. 1982 January; 73(1): 39-45. ISSN: 0038-6723.

MARTELL, CHARLES R., JR. 1981. Improving the Effectiveness of Libraries through Improvements in the Quality of Working Life. College and Research Libraries. 1981 September; 42(1): 25-31. ISSN: 0010-0870.

MARTELL, CHARLES R., JR. 1983. The Client-Centered Academic Library: An Organizational Model. Westport, CT: London, England: Greenwood Press; 1983. 136p. (Contributions in Librarianship and Information Science, no. 42). ISSN: 0084-9243; ISBN: 0-313-23213-X.

MARTELL, CHARLES R., JR. 1985. QWL Strategies: People Are the Castle, People Are the Walls, People Are the Moat. Journal of Academic Librarianship. 1985 January; 10(6): 350-354. ISSN: 0099-1333.

MARTELL, CHARLES R., JR. 1987a. Automation, Quality of Work Life, and Middle Managers. Library Administration and Management. 1987 September; 1(4): 134-138. ISSN: 0888-4463.

MARTELL, CHARLES R., JR. 1987b. The Nature of Authority and Employee Participation in the Management of Academic Libraries. College and Research Libraries. 1987 March; 48(2): 110-122. ISSN: 0010-0870.

MARTELL, CHARLES R., JR. 1989. Achieving High Performance in Library Work. Library Trends. 1989 Summer; 38(1): 73-91. ISSN: 0024-2594.

MARTELL, CHARLES R., JR.; GORMAN, MICHAEL. 1983. QWL Strategies: Reorganization. Journal of Academic Librarianship. 1983 September; 9(4): 223-225. ISSN: 0099-1333.

MARTELL, CHARLES R., JR.; JOHNSON, HERBERT J. 1983. QWL Strategies: Investing in People. A Case Study: Restructuring Technical Services at Emory. Journal of Academic Librarianship. 1983 March; 9(1): 33-35. ISSN: 0099-1333.

MARTELL, CHARLES R., JR.; TYSON, JOHN. 1983. QWL Strategies: Quality Circles. Journal of Academic Librarianship. 1983 November; 8(5): 285-287. ISSN: 0099-1333.

MARTELL, CHARLES R., JR.; UNTAWALE, MERCEDES. 1983. Work Enrichment for Academic Libraries. Journal of Academic Librarianship. 1983 January; 8(6): 339-343. ISSN: 0099-1333.

MASLOW, ABRAHAM H. 1943. A Theory of Human Motivation. Psychological Review. 1943 July; 50(4): 370-396. ISSN: 0033-295X.

MASLOW, ABRAHAM H. 1987. Motivation and Personality. 3rd edition. New York, NY: Harper & Row; 1987. xli, 293p. ISBN: 0-06-041987-3.

MCGREGOR, DOUGLAS. 1960. The Human Side of Enterprise. New York, NY: McGraw-Hill; 1960. 246p. LC: 60-10608.

MEADOWS, JACK. 1989. Educating the Information Professional. In: Oppenheim, Charles; Citroen, Charles L.; Griffiths, José-Marie, eds. Perspectives in Information Management: Volume 1. London, England: Butterworths; 1989. 169-186. ISBN: 0-408-03401-7.

MIGNEAULT, ROBERT LALIBERTE. 1988. Humanistic Management by Teamwork in Academic Libraries. Library Administration and Management. 1988 Fall; 2(3): 132-136. ISSN: 0888-4463.

MINTZBERG, HENRY. 1973. The Nature of Managerial Work. New York, NY: Harper and Row; 1973. 298p. ISBN: 0-06-044555-6.

MINTZBERG, HENRY. 1979. The Structuring of Organizations: A Synthesis of the Research. New York, NY: Prentice-Hall; 1979. 512p. ISBN: 0-13-855270-3.

MOULT, GERRY. 1990. Under New Management: The Practice of Management in a World without Certainties. Management Education and Development. 1990 August; 21(3): 171-182. ISSN: 0047-5688.

MYERS, MARGARET. 1986. Personnel Considerations in Library Automation. In: Shaw, Debora, ed. Human Aspects of Library Automation: Helping Staff and Patrons Cope. [Papers Presented at the 22nd Annual Clinic on Library Applications of Data Processing; 14-16 April 1985; Urbana, IL]. Urbana-Champaign, IL: University of Illinois Graduate School of Library and Information Science; 1986. 30-45. ISSN: 0069-4789; ISBN: 0-87845-072-6.

MYERS, MARGARET. 1990. Library Automation and Personnel Issues: A Selected Bibliography. Journal of Library Administration. 1990; 13(1/2): 205-214. ISSN: 0193-0826.

NAURATIL, MARCIA J. 1987. Librarian Burnout and Alienation. Canadian Library Journal. 1987 December; 44(6): 385-389. ISSN: 0008-4352.

NELSON, VENEESE C. 1987. Burnout: A Reality for Law Librarians? Law Library Journal. 1987 Spring; 79(2): 267-275. ISSN: 0023-9283.

NEWELL, GRAEME; STEVENSON, AILEEN; REDGROVE, ERIKA. 1988. Stress Levels among University and College Librarians. Australasian College Libraries. 1988 June/September; 6(2/3): 51-58. ISSN: 0811-112X.

NICHOLSON, HOWARD. 1991. Staff Development: Getting It Done. Personnel Training and Education. 1991; 8(3): 65-68. ISSN: 0960-1619.

NORTON, BOB. 1992. Human Resource Implications of Adopting IT. Aslib Proceedings. 1992 September; 44(9): 299-303. ISSN: 0001-253X.

OUCHI, WILLIAM G. 1981. Theory Z: How American Business Can Meet the Japanese Challenge. Reading, MA: Addison-Wesley; 1981. 283p. ISBN: 0-201-05524-4.

PAO, MIRANDA LEE; WARNER, ROBERT M. 1989. Strategic Planning for the 1990s: A Challenge for Change. Education for Information. 1989 September; 7(3): 263-271. ISSN: 0167-8329.

PARKER, ANN. 1986. New Skills, New Opportunities: The Role of In-Service Training. International Review of Children's Literature and Librarianship. 1986; 1(1): 1-21. ISSN: 0269-0500.

PARMER, COLLEN; EAST, DENNIS. 1993. Job Satisfaction among Support Staff in Twelve Ohio Academic Libraries. College and Research Libraries. 1993 January; 54(1): 43-57. ISSN: 0010-0870.

PETERS, TOM. 1987. Thriving on Chaos. New York, NY: Alfred A. Knopf; 1987; London, England: Macmillan; 1988. 563p. ISBN: 0-330-30591-3.

PETTAS, WILLIAM; GILLILAND, STEVEN L. 1992. Conflict in the Large Academic Library: Friend or Foe? Journal of Academic Librarianship. 1992 March; 18(1): 24-29. ISSN: 0099-1333.

PRICE, CHERYL A. 1987. What Professional Librarians Expect from Administrators: One Librarian's View. College and Research Libraries. 1987 September; 48(5): 408-412. ISSN: 0010-0870.

PRYTHERCH, RAY, ed. 1986. Handbook of Library Training Practice. Aldershot, England: Gower; 1986. 444p. ISBN: 0-566-03453-X.

RADDON, ROSEMARY. 1991. People and Work: Human and Industrial Relations in Library and Information Work. London, England: Library Association; 1991. 171p. ISBN: 0-85157-431-9.

RANDELL, GERRY; PACKARD, PETER; SLATER, JOHN. 1984. Staff Appraisal: A First Step to Effective Leadership. 3rd edition. London, England: Institute of Personnel Management; 1984. 112p. ISBN: 0-85292-333-3.

REDDY, MICHAEL. 1987. The Manager's Guide to Counselling at Work. London, England: Methuen; 1987. 120p. ISBN: 0-901715-70-0.

RIGGS, DONALD E. 1987. Entrepreneurial Spirit in Strategic Planning. Journal of Library Administration. 1987 Spring; 8(1): 41-52. ISSN: 0193-0826.

RIGGS, DONALD E. 1988. Leadership versus Management in Technical Services. Journal of Library Administration. 1988; 9(1): 27-39. ISSN: 0193-0826.

RIGGS, DONALD E., ed. 1991. Library Communication: The Language of Leadership. Chicago, IL: American Library Association; 1991. 188p. ISBN: 0-8389-0581-1.

RITCHIE, SHEILA. 1982. Women in Library Management. In: Vaughan. Anthony, ed. Studies in Library Management: Volume 7. London, England: Clive Bingley; 1982. 13-36. ISBN: 0-85157-322-3.

RITCHIE, SHEILA. 1988. Training and Management Development in Librarianship. London, England: British Library; 1988. 88p. (Library and Information Research Report 34). ISBN: 0-7123-3049-6.

ROBERTS, ANNE F. 1985. The Academic Librarian as Leader or Manager. Journal of Academic Librarianship. 1985 March; 11(1): 14-18. ISSN: 0099-1333.

ROCKMAN, F. 1984. Job Satisfaction among Faculty and Librarians: A Study of Gender, Autonomy and Decision Making Opportunities. Journal of Library Administration. 1984; 5(1): 43-56. ISSN: 0193-0826.

ROOKS, DANA C. 1988. Motivating Today's Library Staff: A Management Guide. Phoenix, AZ: Oryx Press; 1988. 160p. ISBN: 0-89774-269-9.

ROOKS, DANA C. 1989. The Technicolor Coat of the Academic Library Personnel Officer: The Evolution from Paper-Pusher to Policy-Maker. Journal of Library Administration. 1989; 10(4): 99-113. ISSN: 0193-0826.

ROTHENBERG, LESLIE BETH; LUCIANOVIC, JUDITH; KRONICK, DAVID A.; REES, ALAN M. 1971. A Job-Task Index for Evaluating Professional Staff Utilization in Libraries: Theory and Practice. Library Quarterly. 1971 October; 41(4): 320-328. ISSN: 0024-2519.

ROYAN, BRUCE. 1990. Staff Structures for Today's Information Services. British Journal of Academic Librarianship. 1990; 5(3): 165-169. ISSN: 0269-0497.

RUBIN, RICHARD E. 1991a. Ethical Issues in Library Personnel Management. Journal of Library Administration. 1991; 14(4): 1-16. ISSN: 0193-0826.

RUBIN, RICHARD E. 1991b. Human Resource Management in Libraries: Theory and Practice. New York, NY: London, England: Neal-Schuman; 1991. 430p. ISBN: 1-55570-087-X.

358   MAURICE B. LINE AND MARGARET KINNELL

SADLER, PHILIP. 1991. Designing Organizations: The Foundation for Excellence. London, England: Mercury; 1991. 190p. ISSN: 1-85251-088-9.
SAGER, DONALD J. 1982. Participatory Management in Libraries. Metuchen, NJ: Scarecrow Press; 1982. 196p. ISBN: 0-8108-1530-3.
SCHULER, RANDALL S. 1990. Repositioning the Human Resource Function: Transformation or Demise? Academy of Management Executives. 1990; 4(3): 49-60. ISSN: 0896-3789.
SEGAL, JOAN S.; TREJO-MEEHAN, TAMIYO. 1989. Quality Circles: Some Theory and Two Experiences. Library Administration and Management. 1989 Winter; 4(1): 16-19. ISSN: 0888-4463.
SHAUGHNESSY, THOMAS W. 1988. Staff Development in Libraries: Why It Frequently Doesn't Take. Journal of Library Administration. 1988; 9(2): 5-12. ISSN: 0193-0826.
SHELDON, BROOKE E. 1991. Leaders in Libraries: Styles and Strategies for Success. Chicago, IL: American Library Association; 1991. 93p. ISBN: 0-8389-0563-3.
SMITH, HOWARD L.; REINOW, FRANK. 1984. Librarians' Quality of Working Life: An Exploration. Journal of Library Administration. 1984 Spring; 5(1): 63-76. ISSN: 0193-0826.
SMITH, NATHAN M.; NELSON, VENEESE C. 1983. Burnout: A Survey of Academic Reference Librarians. College and Research Libraries. 1983 May; 44(3): 245-250. ISSN: 0010-0870.
SMITH, NATHAN M.; NIELSEN, LAURA F. 1984. Burnout: A Study of Corporate Librarians. Special Libraries. 1984 July; 75(3): 221-227. ISSN: 0038-6723.
SQUIRE, JAN S. 1991. Job Satisfaction and the Ethnic Minority Librarian. Library Administration and Management. 1991 Fall; 5(4): 194-203. ISSN: 0888-4463.
STOREY, JOHN. 1980. The Challenge to Management Control. London, England: Kogan Page; 1980. 182p. ISBN: 0-85038-187-8.
STOREY, JOHN. 1992. Developments in the Management of Human Resources. Oxford, England: Basil Blackwell; 1992. 272p. ISBN: 0-631-18397-3.
SULLIVAN, MAUREEN. 1991. A New Leadership Paradigm: Empowering Library Staff and Improving Performance. Journal of Library Administration. 1991; 14(2): 73-85. ISSN: 0193-0826.
SUMMERS, F. WILLIAM. 1991. Library Leadership 2000 and Beyond: Snowbird Leadership Institute. Wilson Library Bulletin. 1991 December; 66(4): 38-41. ISSN: 0043-5651.
SYKES, PHIL. 1991. Automation and Non-Professional Staff: The Neglected Majority. Serials. 1991 November; 4(3): 33-43. ISSN: 0953-0460.
TAYLOR, BERNARD; LIPPITT, GORDON, eds. 1983. Management Development and Training Handbook. 2nd edition. New York, NY: London, England: McGraw-Hill; 1983. 506p. ISBN: 0-07-084598-0.
TICHY, NOEL M.; FOMBRUN, CHARLES J.; DEVANNA, MARY ANN. 1982. Strategic Human Resource Management. Sloan Management Review. 1982 Winter; 23(2): 47-62. ISSN: 0019-848X.
TODD, KATHERINE. 1985. Collective Bargaining and Professional Associations in the Library Field. Library Quarterly. 1985 July; 55(3): 284-299. ISSN: 0024-2519.

TORRINGTON, DEREK; HALL, LAURA. 1987. Personnel Management: A New Approach. Englewood Cliffs, NJ: London, England: Prentice Hall; 1987. 580p. ISBN: 0-13-658501-9.

TOWNLEY, CHARLES T. 1989. Nurturing Library Effectiveness: Leadership for Personnel Development. Library Administration and Management. 1989 Fall; 3(1): 16-20. ISSN: 0888-4463.

VAN ZANT, NANCY PATTON, ed. 1980. Personnel Policies in Libraries. New York, NY: Neal-Schuman; 1980. 334p. ISBN: 0-918212-26-X.

VEANER, ALLEN B. 1990. Academic Librarianship in a Transformational Age: Programs, Politics, and Personnel. Boston, MA: G.K. Hall & Co.; 1990. 520p. ISBN: 0-8161-1866-3.

VINCENT, IDA. 1988. Strategic Planning: Does the Model Fit? Journal of Library Administration. 1988; 9(3): 35-47. ISSN: 0193-0826.

WALKER, JAMES W. 1992. Human Resource Strategy. 2nd edition. London, England: McGraw-Hill; 1992. 378p. ISBN: 0-07-067846-4.

WASTAWY-ELBAZ, SOHAIR. 1991. Investigation of the Motivational Needs of Corporate Librarians: A Framework. In: McCabe, Gerard B.; Kreissman, Bernard, eds. Advances in Library Administration and Organization: Volume 9. Greenwich, CT: London, England: JAI Press; 1991. 105-139. ISSN: 0732-0671; ISBN: 1-55938-066-7.

WEAVER-MEYERS, PAT. 1990. ARL Libraries and Staff Development: A Suggested Model for Success. College and Research Libraries. 1990 May; 51(3): 251-265. ISSN: 0010-0870.

WESTBERG, SVEN. 1990. Objectives, Organization and Decision-Making in Chalmers University of Technology. IATUL Quarterly. 1990 December; 4(4): 250-256. ISSN: 0950-4117.

WHITE, HERBERT S. 1985. Library Personnel Management. White Plains, NY: London, England: Knowledge Industry Publications; 1985. 214p. ISBN: 0-86729-136-2.

WHITE, HERBERT S. 1990. Librarian Burnout. Library Journal. 1990 March 15; 115(5): 64-65. ISSN: 0363-0277.

WOODSWORTH, ANNE. 1989. Library Directors as Middle Managers: A Neglected Resource. Library Administration and Management. 1989 Fall; 3(1): 24-27. ISSN: 0888-4463.

WURZBURGER, MARILYN. 1990. Peer Review Committees for Personnel Action. College and Research Libraries. 1990 April; 51(4): 305-306. ISSN: 0010-0870.

ZAND, DALE E. 1974. Collateral Operation: A New Change Strategy. Journal of Applied Behavioral Science. 1974 January/February/March; 10(1): 63-89. ISSN: 0021-8863.

ZIOLKOWSKI, DARLENE M. 1993. Common Sense, Integrity, and Expectations of Excellence: Practical Advice on Dealing with Employee Problems. Library Administration and Management. 1993 Winter; 7(1): 24-29. ISSN: 0888-4463.

9

Library and Information Science Education in the United Kingdom

JENNIFER MACDOUGALL
Consultant

J. MICHAEL BRITTAIN
University of South Australia

INTRODUCTION

Library and information science (LIS) education in the United Kingdom (U.K.), as in the United States, has been undergoing a period of fundamental change and reorganization. This chapter examines these recent developments in the U.K. by looking at the literature over the past five years. Following an outline of the historical context, the chapter examines the changes during the past five years and their impact on the current situation, with an assessment of future trends.

THE HISTORICAL PERSPECTIVE

Formalized education for librarianship (followed a decade later by information science) developed rapidly in the U.K. after 1947. As MOORE (1990) describes in a useful overview, until the late 1960s LIS education, which evolved as a result of local rather than national initiative, was encouraged and coordinated by the U.K. Library Association, whose national syllabus and examinations provided overall consistency. The Library Association was influential in setting up some new schools of librarianship—e.g., at Sheffield University in 1964 by SAUNDERS. Since the late 1960s individual educational institutions have been responsible for their own curricula and educational structures. The Library Association and the Institute of Information Scientists approve courses but do not control the curriculum or the syllabus.

In contrast to the United States, where LIS education has taken place largely at the postgraduate level, the predominant emphasis in the U.K.

Annual Review of Information Science and Technology (ARIST), Volume 28, 1993
Martha E. Williams, Editor
Published for the American Society for Information Science (ASIS)
By Learned Information, Inc., Medford, N.J.

has been on awarding diplomas and then on undergraduate teaching, although in recent years many postgraduate diplomas and degrees have been developed. In the past five years in particular, the number of diploma courses that have been upgraded to postgraduate-degree status has increased.

Post-World War II development of LIS education occurred mainly in colleges of higher education and in technical colleges. When polytechnics were established in the 1960s, there was a great expansion in the number of new departments and schools of LIS. All 16 LIS departments and schools in the U.K. are now based in universities because polytechnics were redesignated as universities in 1992.

Tertiary education in the United Kingdom (that is, education for post high school students) developed in the 20th century along two main lines—further and higher education. Until the 1960s higher education was dominated by the university system, and further education consisted of a multiplicity of colleges, variously financed, that offered mainly nondegree courses, but nevertheless included nationally (and sometimes internationally) recognized qualifications. In the 1960s higher education expanded rapidly in two ways. The number of universities increased over a period of ten years, and new institutions of higher education (designated polytechnics) were established. These were under the control of local authorities, as opposed to universities which continued to receive funding from the national government.

The original intention of the polytechnics was to concentrate more upon teaching (particularly vocationally oriented courses) and less on research; the universities continued their traditional role of research and teaching, increasingly paying particular attention to the acquisition of research funds from outside the university system. During the 1960s and 70s there was a great growth in the number of library schools; with few exceptions the new ones were established in the polytechnics. It could be argued that degrees in librarianship and information science were seen to be more appropriate in the vocationally oriented polytechnics rather than in the traditional universities. The exceptions were at Loughborough and Strathclyde Universities, which joined the only other university based library school at University College, University of London.

However, the polytechnics did not develop as originally envisaged: increasingly, they became involved in research. Universities became more vocationally oriented and established links with business and industry, and government departments; polytechnic degrees were not as vocationally oriented as had been planned.

As a result of an act of the U.K. Parliament, all the polytechnics were allowed to apply for university status in 1992; most did and were successful. Therefore, LIS education is now in the universities, although some LIS departments have not maintained their separate identity. For example, some have become subdivisions of business schools, departments or schools of communication and information, and other combinations but surprisingly, the majority still have a separate and clearly defined identity. The diversity of qualifications available remains. Students at undergraduate level can obtain a B.A. or a B.Sc., depending on the orientation of the course and the subjects they select. Traditionally, in British universities, B.A.'s are given to students with an arts orientation in terms of course content and B.Sc.'s. to science and technology oriented courses. Much the same applies at the postgraduate level— students obtain an M.A., an M.Sc., or (what is usually regarded as a slightly higher degree) an M.Phil., depending upon whether their thesis and selected courses are science, or arts and humanities, based. Diplomas are still offered in some library schools. A diploma is regarded as a lower qualification than a Bachelor's or Master's degree. Diplomas are sometimes given, according to well-defined regulations, to students who have undertaken part of a Master's course.

The number of students proceeding to doctoral study in LIS is small. No exact figures are available, but perhaps less than 5% of students graduating in LIS (at any level of Bachelor's or Master's degree) go on to a Ph.D. For LIS graduates working as lecturers in universities there is now great pressure to obtain a doctorate; many do this by registering as members of staff, and therefore may take many years to complete their doctorates.

There is no discernible correlation between the type or level of degree, and the positions filled by graduates. Past experience, preferences, and personality appear to be a much greater determinant of type of job, rather than academic qualifications. For example, there are many senior librarians and information scientists with only a first bachelor's degree; similarly, many graduates are employed in junior posts who have higher degrees.

In the 1970s and 1980s the largest library school in the U.K. (although no longer so) was the College of Librarianship, Wales, which was supported by the local authority. It maintained its independent status until 1989, when it was incorporated into the University of Wales as the Department of Information and Library Studies. ROBERTS & HYWEL give an account of the merger.

The polytechnics and the universities each had a wide catchment area and, because of the paucity of LIS education in Scotland, many students traveled to the English library schools. Even in England students often traveled long distances to study. For example, those living in the south west of England originally had to travel as far as Birmingham or London and later to Brighton for their nearest LIS school or department.

The early years saw a great emphasis on the recruitment of under-graduate students with library experience and on gaining experience during the first two years of degree study. Many staff in library schools demanded that these 18-year-old students demonstrate a strong com-mitment to librarianship and information work. Until the middle 1980s female library students outnumbered male students in most library schools by as much as ten to one.

Most graduates went to work in public libraries, and a substantial number went to academic and special libraries. Until the late 1970s it was rare for graduates to enter information jobs outside the traditional library structure. Most graduates became chartered through the Library Association in the U.K. by completing a year's probation with suitable supervision.

Viability

The wholesale closure of Schools of Library and Information Science (SLIS) in the U.K. is not envisaged in the foreseeable future, unlike the situation in the United States, where many library schools have been closed since 1978 (HYMAN). Although it is often claimed that develop-ments in LIS in the U.K. follow those of the United States, it seems that U.K. SLIS have on this occasion learned from their American colleagues. U.S. library schools have suffered similar upheavals as their U.K. coun-terparts in terms of name changes, restructuring and reorganization, mergers with other academic departments, and a crisis in recruitment. PARIS diagnoses the problems as a combination of the inability of the American LIS educators to define their discipline adequately along with social and academic isolation. This lack of communication with other academic colleagues and departments and with university librar-ies has apparently led to deep hostilities towards SLIS staff. Paris believes that the lack of definition of librarianship is a result of too much emphasis on technological developments and a loss of the sense of service as the cornerstone of the profession.

In the U.K., contacts between LIS departments and other academic departments have been stronger. Recent restructuring has led, in some cases, to departments merging with others as a result of economic pressures. Good relations with academic colleagues in other depart-ments has meant a successful outcome as described by MARTIN (1991). Most SLIS, however, have maintained their individual identities while developing strong mutual links with other departments. These links typically involve teaching modules in other departments, students from other departments taking modules in LIS, university committee work, and joint research projects. At Loughborough University, for example, staff in the information and library studies department teach knowledge-based systems in the computer studies department and modules in other departments such as the social sciences.

Staff in the U.K. SLIS are well aware of the dangers of concentrating too hard on the technological changes at the expense of other aspects of the LIS curriculum, particularly the newer disciplines of communication and marketing skills. As DAY (1989, p. 33) comments, "Technology is not an end in itself." The importance of customer care and the concept of service is recognized and is an integral part of most LIS courses.

Manpower Requirements and the Emerging Markets

As MOORE (1987, p. 16) reports in a major study of the emerging markets for new types of information professionals: "The end of the 1970s and early 1980s saw a period of stagnation in the traditional markets for librarians and information workers." This report details how a steady growth in the output of library and information professionals led to a rapid rise in graduates' unemployment, from 4.4% in 1972 to 15.4% in 1981 (MOORE, 1987 p. 18). As a result LIS departments scaled back enrollment by approximately 30% between 1976/1977 and 1983/1984. This was accompanied by a period of severe financial restraint. The competition for jobs in all markets was fierce, and LIS graduates who sought alternative careers generally fared badly. However, there was no unanimous agreement that the widening of job opportunities for LIS graduates was a long-term solution to the short-term problem of overproduction. SLATER (p. 285) suggested that the emerging markets could be only a short-term solution: "As a topic of continuing concern the alternative careers option is a nonsensical preoccupation. It implies an illogical and wasteful state of perpetual overproduction. Such a situation would surely be more easily and rationally tackled at source by regulating production."

During the 1980s a number of studies were undertaken to review the manpower, education, and training requirements of the LIS profession. A working party of the Library and Information Services Council (LISC) was given the task of identifying these requirements and providing guidance on actions to be taken, with particular attention to the impact of technological, economic, social, and other changes (LIBRARY AND INFORMATION SERVICES COUNCIL). Their report was followed by a study commissioned by the University Grants Committee and the National Advisory Body for Public Sector Higher Education. The Transbinary Group (as it became known) studied the teaching of librarianship and information studies in universities, polytechnic schools, and colleges (TRANSBINARY GROUP). Some LIS schools had already embarked on reform. However, the Transbinary Group recommended that schools look carefully at some of the new courses being offered by other institutions that were new to the field. A new approach and the development of further expertise were required if LIS schools were to fill the ever-widening gap in the market (MARTIN, 1987). As MUDDIMAN ET AL. (p. 43) noted, the traditional markets were regarded as "but one part of a large heterogeneous employment sector in which a wide variety of skills may be practised in a wide variety of contexts."

Moore's important study of the emerging markets in information-related disciplines and occupations highlighted the fact that employers' requirements were often not met by LIS graduates, particularly in areas of computing, statistics, journalism, and public relations: "Even where employers specified that library and information work qualifications were essential, more than half the jobs were taken by people who did not possess these qualifications" (MOORE, 1987, p. 143).

In their paper on demand and supply in information work, DAVENPORT & CRONIN stated that schools/departments of LIS (SLIS) must address "this mismatch of demand and supply." These authors suggested various strategies, including a shift of emphasis to employer-oriented training. The issue of transfer of LIS skills is discussed in the sections on curriculum and current concerns later in this chapter.

A report financed by the British Library Research and Development Department, edited by BRITTAIN (1989) elicited the views of a wide range of information professionals on the emerging market for graduates in LIS. Contributions include papers on academic libraries, marketing, online business databases, information work in broadcasting, the National Health Service, the psychology of personal information management, and expert systems. Some of these papers are referred to individually in this chapter. The contributors agreed on the importance of the emerging market, its rapid growth, and the need for SLIS to educate new graduates for new employment opportunities. There was less agreement on the content and orientation of LIS courses.

The Information, Computer, and Communications Revolutions

As CORBIN (p. 77) identified in his lucid exposition of LIS education in the age of information technology, the years since World War II were witness to three concurrent revolutions "which are fueling each other," and which, "when combined are as sweeping and traumatic as was the Industrial Revolution in the nineteenth century." These revolutions were those of information, computers, and communications. Rapid developments in the computer industry and the increasing dependence of society on information of all types led to a world that was reliant on an information-driven computerized infrastructure. These advances led inevitably to the communications revolution so that instant transmission of voice, text, and graphics is now possible anywhere in the world. As Corbin described, these three revolutions have fundamentally altered the structure and organization of society and altered the lives of all citizens.

Such dramatic developments over only 30 years inevitably imply a need for equally dramatic changes in library and information science education. In his chapter on the information society, MOORE (1987) shows how the traditional manufacturing sector is being replaced by the new information sector in the economy, with the resulting increase in importance of information handling to all organizations. Information is now recognized as a vital asset and valued resource. This change is also emphasized by DAY (1989, p. 26), who notes that information technology (IT) has transformed the storage and communication of information and that "librarians are now part of this marketplace and already have the basic skills required but need to develop and enhance them to operate effectively in the changing world."

To better reflect the new information society the term "librarianship" was expanded to include information studies during the 1970s. MARTIN (1987) provides an insightful discussion of the terminology used, including library studies, library science, documentation, information studies, and information science. As MCGARRY (1987a, p. 89) remarks: "Information is a chameleon-like term changing its semantic colours according to the refracted light of a particular context, or the epistemological stance taken by the use of the term." Martin argues the need for qualitative change in the theory and practice of LIS education, resulting in improved educational opportunities.

RECENT CHANGES IN LIS EDUCATION

Since the mid-1980s many LIS schools and departments have been involved in a fundamental review and revision of both their recruitment policies and curricula, including an examination of the skills and expertise required by employers in the emerging markets. At the same time, many schools and departments have undergone major reorganization and restructuring. New staff have been recruited, with a wider range of skills and knowledge, and existing staff have been encouraged to enlarge and update their skills and knowledge.

Reorganization

Restructuring and reorganization in LIS education have involved mergers with other schools or departments. For example, the former Department of Information Studies at Queen's University of Belfast

gave up its separate status and joined the Department of Accounting to
form the new School of Finance and Information. This is described by
MARTIN (1991) and is discussed later in this chapter.

In some cases more than one reorganization within an institution has
taken place. The Department of Information and Library Studies at
Liverpool Polytechnic moved into the School of Information Science
and Technology in 1988. In 1991 a further reorganization placed the
School in the Department of Computing, Information and Mathemati-
cal Sciences. In 1992 the move was made into the Liverpool Business
School. Also during 1992, Liverpool Polytechnic became Liverpool John
Moores University. Another department that became part of a business
school was the Information Science Department at the University of
Strathclyde.

The hitherto independent College of Librarianship, Wales, as al-
ready mentioned, has now become the Department of Information and
Library Studies within the University College of Wales, Aberystwyth
(ROBERTS & HYWEL). The Department of Library and Information
Studies at Leeds Polytechnic has been dissolved and now functions as the
Information Services Group, providing teaching on a modular basis.

Despite these far-reaching changes for the minority, most LIS departments have maintained their separate identity and have not been assimilated into other schools or departments as has happened to many in
the United States. Several departments have changed their name to
reflect the shift in perception and practice toward the information
industry as a whole. However, many schools have maintained the term
"library." For example, the Department of Librarianship and Information Studies at Newcastle upon Tyne Polytechnic is now the Department of Information and Library Management, University of
Northumbria at Newcastle. At Loughborough University, the Department of Library and Information Studies merely altered the order to
Department of Information and Library Studies. Others have dropped
the term "library" altogether; the Department of Librarianship and
Information Studies at Birmingham Polytechnic, for example, is now
the School of Information Studies at the University of Central England
in Birmingham.

Recruitment

The number of students in U.K. universities has increased in recent
years along with generally more flexible recruitment policies and attitudes toward admission qualifications and experience. This is reflected
in the wider age profile of undergraduate students in particular. There
are many women returning for study and many mature students who
bring a wide range of work experience, much of it outside the tradi-

tional library environment. Entry qualifications vary from one institution to another and are now more flexible than a decade ago. The male/female ratio is becoming more balanced, and the new courses are attracting more men and a higher percentage of ethnic minorities and overseas students. ROBERTSON & YATES-MERCER found that the new M.Sc. degree in Information Systems and Technology at City University attracted students from a wide range of backgrounds: teachers, computer experts, and other subject specialists as well as systems librarians, information officers, management services personnel, and systems analysts and programmers who wanted to broaden their subject base.

The recruitment of the right kind of undergraduates, however, can be problematic. As DAY (1989) notes, in a general review of recent developments in LIS courses, many applications are still received from "shy and retiring" persons who are fond of reading and have therefore been recommended by their counselors for a career in librarianship. However much the changing nature of courses is publicized, it is the practicing professionals who project the public image and provide role models "and it will take a major, long-term public relations campaign by the profession at large to change the stereotype" (DAY, 1989, p. 29).

The Curriculum

As MCGARRY (1987a) explains, in his exposition on curriculum theory and LIS, traditional library education has been based on bibliography, cataloging, classification, and administration, and many schools still regard these as the core curriculum. "The radical change came when information began to be seen as a political and economic entity" (MCGARRY, p. 141). The advent of computer and communications technologies has necessitated a complete reevaluation of the needs of the profession and the content of LIS syllabi.

Information technology.   The greatest impact on the curricula in LIS educational institutions in recent years has been the introduction of IT. In many cases a "bolt-on approach" was used to revamp existing information science courses and include aspects of IT. Justifiably, this practice was criticized (DAVINSON & ROBERTS). However, LIS schools lacked revenue, equipment, and particularly staff expertise. Thus, there was a wide variety in the extent and quality of IT teaching among the different schools.

In 1985 the Transbinary Working Group on Library and Information Studies (so called because it looked at both universities and polytechnic schools) was set up to advise on LIS courses in the U.K., with particular reference to the changing nature of the profession. The group's report (unpublished but available and widely quoted) had an important impact on the development of IT teaching in the U.K. (TRANSBINARY GROUP). Librarianship was classified as an arts-based subject until the past few years and received a correspondingly low allocation of institutional resources compared with science and technology subjects.

The Transbinary Group viewed IT as an essential element of the curricula in SLIS and identified four stages of development in IT teaching:

- Initial experiments in information retrieval, computerized cataloging, and so forth, leading to permanent features of courses;
- "Bolted on" units giving a broad introduction to IT in general, and computing in particular;
- Permeation of IT into the whole course, with IT and non-IT aspects of a topic taken together; and
- New IT-oriented courses in information systems or information management.

In 1985, when the Transbinary Group compiled their data, most of the 16 SLIS were at the second stage and moving toward the third stage. A few SLIS had reached the fourth stage, which demands a radical reassessment and new approaches to IT teaching. By 1989 DAY (1989) felt that most SLIS had reached the third stage, the most popular areas of development being design and development of expert systems, desktop publishing, and CD-ROM technologies. As Day explains, the challenges that faced the SLIS in their increasing commitment to IT were intensified by the speed of change demanded by external and internal pressures. Resourcing is always a problem, although it is now tempered by some support from the IT industry. Lack of adequate technician support has led to much staff time being applied inappropriately, at a period of academic staff cuts. Staff development in IT skills is an ongoing requirement, and new staff with existing skills are being sought to support and enhance courses.

A crucial recommendation in the report of the TRANSBINARY GROUP (p. 103) was that LIS departments be funded for computing equipment on the same basis as computer studies departments rather than as social studies or arts and humanities departments (as had been the case). This has led to greatly increased funding of microcomputer laboratories, local area networks (LANs), and associated software in LIS departments generally, as ROWLAND & TSENG (p. 50) report in their review of computer methods in the teaching of LIS.

Recruitment of the right caliber of student is another challenge. The review of the course at the University of Northumbria at Newcastle, described by DAY (1989), emphasizes a more integrated approach to the teaching of IT and teaching with IT as well as more attention to communication skills and marketing principles. The need for increased flexibility has led to modular courses. The impact of modularization is looked at in more detail later.

As part of a National Advisory Body IT Initiative, the Department of Library and Information Studies at Manchester Polytechnic (now the Manchester Metropolitan University) recruited an additional cohort of students to its B.A. (Honours) Library and Information Studies degree in 1984. This group studied IT intensively, including an elective in systems analysis and design. The overall success of this initiative, described by ROWLEY, showed that this approach benefits all students (not just those in the IT cohort) with improved awareness and skills as well as increased hardware and software resources. The application of IT to the teaching of management and business studies has also been developed, as described by STEPHEN, and facilities have been significantly improved with the establishment of an Information Technology Unit (ROWLEY ET AL., 1990).

Communication and interpersonal skills.   Running concurrently with the highly publicized emergence of IT as a major constituent of the LIS curriculum was the generally less well-recognized need for communication and interpersonal skills (B. MORRIS). Employers in the newly emerging markets specified that these skills were, in fact, more important than computing skills (ANGELL). BEDNAR notes that some professional backroom staff were being replaced by IT systems and moving into closer contact with the public. As more advanced information services were developed (e.g., online searching) the traditional library sector needed to extend and improve client-centered services. More focused in-house training could help, but, as BURTON (1990) argues, interpersonal and communication skills need to be fostered by the SLIS.

During the past five years there has been a much greater emphasis in SLIS on these transferable personal skills. As WATSON (p. 37) comments, "the information professional needs to be an effective communicator and therefore needs to understand the theory of communication, ranging from interpersonal communication to mass communication, before being able to interpret it into the information environment." This view is also supported by BLACKIE (1988, p. 62) in describing the course at Newcastle. She states that the student should learn "to communicate orally, visually, technologically and graphically in an effective way." Interpersonal skills should be developed by students working in pairs or groups.

COLLIER argues in a thought-provoking paper that there is a strong correlation between professional flexibility and interpersonal skills. It is important that concern for the development of IT does not override what is considered more important by employers. DAY (1989, p. 33) also believes that "equal importance must be given to developing other 'new' skills like marketing, communication and problem solving." She is concerned that the technology is not seen as an end in itself but rather as an "enabling mechanism" to provide improved information services. Having at last recognized the importance of the user, it would be a disaster if attention were diverted toward the technology and away from the client.

Information management.   Information management (IM) has developed over the past decade as a new subject in the LIS curriculum. As WILSON (1989) explains, the term originated in a move by the U.S. government to control the amount of federal paperwork. The real costs of handling large amounts of information were being realized just when IT was beginning to influence the methods used by organizations to manage it. In his discussion of the definition of IM, MCKEE (p. 31) states that "the focus of IM is overall corporate strategy rather than individual operational activity."

As KIRKHAM (p. 9) notes in her account of the course at the University of Central England in Birmingham, it was recognized that "information management was gaining a stronger profile in organizations of all kinds and that an increasing number of career opportunities existed in this area." WILSON (1989) describes how the SLIS were eager to take up the challenge that this new discipline offered but that different departments (not only of LIS) interpreted IM in various different ways. Wilson provides a picture of the relationships among IM, librarianship, and information science and discusses the emerging content of IM as a separate field. This rough classification includes:

- Areas of application (e.g., banking, health services) artificial intelligence (AI);
- Economics of information;
- Education for information management;
- Information management (including computer-based records, corporate information, information mapping, manpower, online systems, and strategic monitoring);
- Information policy;
- Information systems and systems theory;
- Information technology; and
- Information use and users.

At Sheffield University School of Management and Economic Studies, the M.B.A. program contains an option in IM provided by the Department of Information Studies. The relevance of some courses in the M.B.A. to students in the M.Sc. in Information Management program and vice versa provides opportunities for further collaboration (WILSON, 1989, p. 207).

The former Department of Information Studies at Queen's University, Belfast, decided to drop librarianship entirely in favor of IM as a result of overriding considerations of financial and educational viability as well as strategic changes within the department. As MARTIN (1991) explains in a frank and reasoned account, increased resources resulted in the formation of a successful IM division within the new School of Finance and Information. The courses are modular and emphasize their practical and applied elements as well as the academic content: "a particular effort has been made to make the courses as relevant as possible to the needs of industry and commerce" (MARTIN, 1991, p. 26).

Increased specialization. The influence of fundamental changes in the marketplace and the pressures of recent social, economic, and political policies have resulted in increased specialization, which encourages a more focused approach to career paths. This trend has also been influenced by the general reduction in staff in LIS departments, which narrows the choice of optional subjects available. At the same time, employers are demanding more specialization, but as MOORE (1990, p. 154) suggests, "As our subject becomes more technical and complex, it is difficult to fit everything into the syllabus and still provide the degree of depth required."

The debate over breadth vs. depth, and theory vs. practice continues in staff rooms and the professional press. COLLIER (p. 14) argues that theory should not be used simply "to prop up an ailing academic course" and should not "lurch from the academic to the practical, but present a continuum which allows the students to develop and demonstrate their academic and practical talents simultaneously."

MCLAIN ET AL. state that there is a real need for IT to be taught in order to meet the obvious needs of the modern library but that the curriculum should emphasize both the traditional theory of librarianship and the "operational elements of automation." ROBERTSON & YATES-MERCER believe that some courses are necessarily broad in scope. The M.Sc. in Information Systems and Technology at City University, for example, aims to provide students with a knowledge of computer science, business systems analysis, information science, and the general implications of IT in order to produce generalists who understand the whole field. Whereas there are specialists in many organizations, there are far fewer, they claim, with the knowledge to understand the relationships among the constituent elements.

Some SLIS have openly sought to concentrate on courses to suit a particular aspect of the professional market. At the University of Strathclyde, for instance, the Department of Information Science has developed a curriculum that emphasizes the importance of advanced technology information services in the private business sector. The increasing importance of business information skills has been recognized in other SLIS as, for example, at Sheffield, where it has been a major part of the curriculum for some years. In their paper on business information courses, ROBERTS ET AL. discuss the attitudes and practices currently evident in the SLIS in the United Kingdom.

In contrast, at University College London, the School of Library, Archive and Information Studies maintains a strong reputation for its courses in archives studies. At other SLIS, new courses to meet the demands of the emerging markets are currently being developed (e.g., in health care information, which are discussed in the next section).

THE CURRENT SITUATION

Since 1992 all schools and departments of LIS have university status. This rationalization of higher education in the U.K. is not extended to curriculum content as advocated by COLLIER (p. 14). However, as ROWLAND & TSENG have reported there is now considerable variety in the courses provided by the SLIS of the U.K. This reflects the various faculty structures in which they are now situated. At the University of Strathclyde the Department of Information Science, based in the Business School, emphasizes business information needs and specializes in high-technology information services. The courses at the University of Brighton Department of Library and Information Studies overlap pure computing courses because the department is part of the computing faculty; community information services are prominent at the University of North London where the department is in the faculty of Social Sciences. This point is also reiterated by WHITBECK (1990) in his brief review of developments in five U.K. SLIS.

Modularization and Subject Combinations

Most LIS departments already offer or are currently developing courses on a modular basis. This enables students to "mix and match" their own subjects according to individual interests, aspirations, and abilities. Modularization moves the British universities much closer to the American system of credit accumulation and transfer, allowing students to move easily from one course to another and from one institution to another. Some institutions are already operating under this scheme—e.g., the Liverpool John Moores University where Information and Library Studies is part of the Business School.

Modularization also allows new subjects to be introduced into the curriculum more easily. In addition, local professionals can attend relevant modules to update their knowledge (DAY, 1989). IT modules are particularly attractive, and demand is growing for this type of continuing education.

Another advantage of modularization is the increased link it affords between departments and subjects, making the possibilities of choice and combination of subjects much wider. Nine of the sixteen SLIS in the United Kingdom offer joint degrees or modules from other departments. At Queen's University, for example, joint degrees are offered in Information Management with Computer Science, French, German, Spanish, or Italian and a combined degree with French and Manufacturing Engineering. The modular degree structure facilitates links with all other faculties in the university. The Department of Information and Library Studies at Aberystwyth is able to offer joint honors degrees with 22 other departments in the University of Wales.

The B.A. (Honours) in Information and Library Studies at the School of Information Studies, University of Central England in Birmingham, offers a choice of four study pathways according to the interests and career ambitions of its students: (1) business information, (2) information management, (3) public libraries, and (4) libraries in education. These are introduced by means of foundation units, and it is possible to specialize in one of these areas or choose a more general selection of modules as required. Up to nine months are spent working in a library and information unit that reflects the chosen area of study.

At the Department of Information and Library Studies, Loughborough University, all undergraduate degrees have a minimum input of 40% from other departments in the university. For example, the B.Sc. in Information and Computing comprises 40% from Information and Library Studies, 40% from Computer Science, and 20% from Human Sciences. Sheffield's Department of Information Studies has developed links with the departments of archaeology and prehistory, town and regional planning, and medical microbiology as well as computer science.

There are also courses in other institutions that overlap considerably with the SLIS curricula (ROWLAND & TSENG). These include: publishing courses at Oxford Brookes University and Napier University, Edinburgh; communications and information courses at, for example, Queen Margaret College, Edinburgh; courses for teacher-librarians at the University of the West of England, Bristol, and Anglia College of Higher Education; and many related courses in computing and information technology (ROWLAND & TSENG, p. 50).

Growth and Expansion

Since 1991 the quotas that each university allows for undergraduate programs have increased rapidly, and the previous emphasis on postgraduate courses is being played down. Even universities that have lacked undergraduate programs are now looking into introducing them. The market for information professionals is again expanding, and SLIS are expected to increase their output (MOORE, 1990).

Resources for SLIS, however, as MOORE (1990) writes, have not increased to match this new demand; rather the government has made it clear that more students must be recruited at a lower unit cost. Staff–student ratios have deteriorated dramatically in the past few years, and now over half the SLIS have a ratio of between 1:15 and 1:23. The strain on teaching staff will affect the quality and standard of education. New teaching methods already being developed (e.g., video courses) will need to be improved and expanded if student numbers continue to increase.

There has been a general increase in the number of foreign students to universities in the U.K. particularly in the sciences, medicine, technology, and LIS. Except for Canada, the United States, Russia, and the former Soviet Union countries, students come from all over the world. The numbers from Africa, Malaysia, and Southeast Asia tend to fluctuate according to local policies and financial arrangements for student study abroad. The numbers from the European Community (EC) have increased dramatically in the past three years due to the development of closer links between LIS institutions in Europe through organizations like ERASMUS (European Community Action Scheme for the Mobility of University Students). The implications for the future of closer ties with Europe are discussed in more detail later. A few students come from South America, particularly Brazil, and from Australasia.

Current Concerns

Customer care.   An issue of current concern to practicing professionals and SLIS staff, BURTON (1992) defines customer care as a set of linked service features:

- Access (effective access to all types of information in various formats);
- Quality (efficient provision of reliable, accurate, and relevant information); and
- Proactivity (knowledge of users, which aspects of the service they require, and how to help them to the best effect).

Burton argues that what is missing in information services is a "service strategy" designed with an understanding that users' needs are paramount.

SLIS are now incorporating more emphasis on interpersonal and communication skills in their courses, but more attention needs to be given to client-centered services that are provided on a proactive basis (BURTON, 1990). Recruitment policies for LIS courses also play a significant role in providing information professionals who can implement the new service strategies and meet the demands of the changing profession.

The transfer of LIS skills. As previously mentioned, the provision of a LIS trained staff for nontraditional professions and information work and the need for transferable skills are now receiving more attention. SLIS are gradually adapting curricula to meet these needs, particularly in the area of communication and interpersonal skills and IT. In many areas LIS knowledge and skills form a strong basis on which to build, as MOORE (1987) demonstrates.

One of the main shortages of information-handling skills currently in the United Kingdom is in the National Health Service (NHS). The past five years have seen a massive outlay of money to develop existing information systems and to procure new ones for all health authorities. This has given rise to a huge requirement for information management skills and knowledge. BRITTAIN (1992) estimates conservatively that there are currently about 5,700 NHS information jobs in England and Wales. This figure does not include additional jobs in health promotion and consumer health information services, which are also increasing rapidly.

The growth in consumer health information follows the U.K. government's publication of the Patient's Charter in 1991, which requires health authorities to provide information services for patients, care givers, and the public. An overview of all aspects concerning the use of health information, including staffing and training issues, is given in a recent report to the British Library Research and Development Department by MACDOUGALL & BRITTAIN.

Many of the skills required of NHS information workers are familiar to LIS graduates, and system-specific skills and knowledge could readily be acquired through in-service training (BRITTAIN, 1992). There are no undergraduate courses in health care information management at present in the United Kingdom, but a few diplomas and higher degrees are available. These include an M.Sc. in Health Information Management at Aberystwyth, where the Department of Information and Library Studies collaborates with the Institute of Health Informatics (HEPWORTH, 1991). Courses in informatics tend to concentrate more on the technology, as at Glasgow University, where computer programming, applications in clinical care, nursing informatics, software engineering, and networking are emphasized. New courses, such as those being developed at the University of Manchester Health Services Management Unit and at Loughborough University Department of Information and Library Studies, will help to fill the current skills gap for health care information specialists (BRITTAIN & MACDOUGALL).

New areas of the LIS curriculum. One of the fastest growing areas of IT
in recent years has been knowledge-based and expert systems, although they have made slower progress into general library and information work. Knowledge-based systems have much to offer, particularly in the business and industrial sectors, where there is much interest
in expert systems for specific tasks. A. MORRIS (1989, p. 144-145) notes
the obvious skills and knowledge required by students in this area:

- A knowledge and understanding of the basic principles
  of knowledge-based systems;
- A knowledge of how, where, and when knowledge-
  based systems are being used in industry, research, and
  information science;
- Practical hands-on experience in using knowledge-based
  systems;
- Ability to evaluate knowledge-based systems;
- Techniques of maintaining and updating simple expert
  systems; and
- A detailed understanding of knowledge-acquisition techniques.

In the late 1980s LIS educators were asking whether knowledge-based
systems were a serious long-term development or a passing trend. Did
these systems demand a radically new approach to the syllabus, or
could teaching methodology be adapted and modified to accommodate
them? A recent survey by A. MORRIS (1993) found that knowledge-
based systems were being taught as a core subject in seven out of the ten
undergraduate courses in SLIS and as options in another two; similar
figures were recorded for postgraduate courses. New technologies are
continually evolving—e.g., hypertext and virtual reality—and these
must also be accommodated in the already crowded IT curriculum.

Human factors and the psychology of users of information is another
area of growing importance in LIS curriculum. An understanding of
how people perceive, interpret, use, and store information is vital for
the development of any information service. Identifying and responding accurately to their needs as well as involving them in the development of the service are methods of empowering customers to achieve
the kind of service they require. LANSDALE explores the psychological
theory of information management. The human factors involved are of
special importance in the design and development of information systems, and human factors studies have been a feature of the M.Sc. at
Loughborough University Department of Information and Library Studies for some years.

The current concentration on the teaching of IT and more general
subject areas as well as the government policy of larger classes has led

to some concern that certain specialty areas are being neglected. TURBET writes that it is difficult to generate the necessary research in subject librarianship if the practicing subject librarians are overworked due to the lack of subject teaching at the SLIS. Music librarianship, for example, is not currently taught at any SLIS, although it is one of the most popular services provided by public and academic libraries. Here the argument for a coordination of SLIS curricula is strengthened; perhaps one school could offer a music option, and others could offer alternative specialties. Distance-learning modules and credit transfer will ensure that students can still be based at one university.

Distance education.   Opportunities for continuing professional development and distance learning in LIS have not, with one or two exceptions, been well developed in SLIS in the UnitedKingdom. As JOHNSON (1990) explains, even those SLIS strongly committed to continuing education have been constrained by a lack of key skills, reduced staff, and severe financial pressure over the past decade. Schools are also under pressure to increase their income or at least break even on courses (MEADOWS). As a result SLIS are reluctant to offer courses without a guaranteed return on investment. There are many competitors in the short-course market, and government policy encourages a more businesslike approach. Some SLIS, like the School of Information Studies at the University of Central England in Birmingham, have set up continuing education units to meet the need for short courses and in-house training. SLIS must operate in the marketplace and employ more sophisticated marketing techniques for their continuing education programs.

In their survey, *Distance Education in Library and Information Studies,* HAYTHORNTHWAITE & WHITE (1989) found much resistance to distance education in some quarters and much anxiety about the market for, and viability of such an enterprise. The report provides an annotated list of distance education packages in LIS available at that time, which covered all the developed English-speaking countries. The most interesting course offered was the master's degree in Management of Library and Information Services from the College of Librarianship Wales (now the Department of Information and Library Studies, University College of Wales, Aberystwyth). This was the first LIS master's degree to be available in the distance-learning mode, and Aberystwyth has continued to develop and increase its role in this important area (EDWARDS ET AL.). Since 1990 the department has also offered a master's course in School and Young People's Librarianship, and an M.Sc. in Information Systems and Services for Health Care (HEPWORTH, 1991).

Another interesting development has been the establishment of a collaborative, distance-learning master's program by the Department of Information Studies, University of Sheffield, with the Centre for Technical Information for Industry in Portugal (CORREIA & WILSON). The students are registered for the M.Sc. degree in Information Management at the University of Sheffield, but the course, which is in a modular form, takes place in Lisbon. Staff in Sheffield prepare distance-learning units, approve teachers from local Portuguese universities, and make regular visits to lecture and give tutorials.

Outside the confines of the LIS are a number of distance-education courses for the professional seeking to be updated. Newcastle offers a useful short course on statistics for librarians (BLACKIE, 1985), and other U.K. institutions provide courses on modern library technology, educational technology, indexing, marketing, and management. These are described by HAYTHORNTHWAITE (p. 33-35) in her article on distance education and the information scientist.

THE FUTURE

Information UK 2000, a think-tank report commissioned by the British Library Research and Development Department, was published in 1990 (MARTYN ET AL.). It sought to stimulate debate in the profession by forecasting technological, communication, demographic, social, and economic advances, and by emphasizing the need for LIS workers to take a wider view and a more proactive stance in a changing environment. The report emphasizes the need for more transferable skills, information management and language teaching, attention to technological developments and information transfer, and well-educated, flexible recruits. In response, ELKIN comments that the report underestimates the fundamental changes already taking place in LIS education and reveals a lack of communication between practitioners and educators: "To what extent will the LIS community redefine its roles, responsibilities and tasks in informing educators, to make this a much more positive relationship for the future?" (ELKIN, p. 23).

Recruitment and Resourcing

The greatest challenge facing LIS education in the U.K. is the requirement to increase output at a time of reduced resources. The demand for more information specialists, particularly in the emerging markets and also in school libraries and information management, requires constant attention to ensure a relevant curriculum. Courses must be continually developed and updated.

Modularization is part of the changing face of LIS education in the United Kingdom. The aim in many programs now is for total flexibility after the first year, with a basic core of information studies plus other subjects as required. In many schools the number of students taking only information and library studies will continue to decrease as other combinations of subjects, such as information and computing, become a popular way to meet the changing needs of the employment market.

The increasing emphasis on continuing education and personal development will continue as individual performance review and work-based assessment schemes become more prevalent. As WOOD & ELKIN demonstrate, modular course structures will enable the LIS professional to gain additional expertise and to accumulate credits for further qualifications either through part-time study or distance-education courses.

The increase in numbers of students is expected to continue over the next two years but then to stabilize or even decrease. A severe impact on recruitment is the reduction in numbers of the 16–19 year-old population between 1988 and 1995 by about 40%. This, as MOORE (1990) argues, combined with fewer applicants overall for undergraduate degrees in LIS, means that SLIS will have to attract students from different backgrounds, particularly mature students. Many SLIS have already had much success with this strategy, but competition will become more fierce. Postgraduate students, while not lacking in numbers, are severely restricted by a lack of funds, which are controlled by central government. Successful marketing of courses by SLIS is becoming increasingly significant but requires adequate funding.

Europe

The year 1992 and the creation of a single European market within the EC provided a focus for the development of growing links between SLIS in all European countries. The impact on the information world has been dramatic, and the implications for LIS training and education are no less far reaching. Links with European institutions have been given a high priority in SLIS for several years. The importance of languages as part of students' qualifications is stressed at many schools where language options are popular. In addition, many European students now come to the U.K. In 1992-1993 the Department of Information and Library Studies at Loughborough was teaching approximately 22 students from France alone.

The harmonizing of professional qualifications to allow the eventual acceptability of qualifications and free movement of professionals in Europe is one of the most important developments affecting SLIS. There are many practical difficulties in implementing this directive, as DAVIES (1990a) points out, particularly in reconciling the different requirements and types of qualifications of member countries of the European Community. A mutually beneficial dialog between many

European schools and departments of LIS has been developing. These dialogs (in the past, mainly informal) are now gaining impetus from new initiatives, including financial incentives from European Community (EC) programs.

The European Community has been running a number of education and training programs, such as ERASMUS (European Community Action Scheme for the Mobility of University Students), DAAD (Deutscher Akademischer Austausch Dieust), COMETT (Community Action Programme for Education and Training for Technology) and TEMPUS (Trans European Mobility Scheme for University Studies, Central and Eastern Europe), to facilitate the mobility of students among European countries. ERASMUS, in particular, offers scope for curriculum development studies and a range of individual study programs (WILSON, 1992).

The most important recent development has been the establishment of EUCLID (European Association for Library and Information Education and Research). This organization was set up in 1991 (WILSON, 1992) for tertiary-level educational institutions offering courses in librarianship, information science, or information management, represented by their heads or deputies. The main areas of activity for future development and expansion include:

- Facilitating easier participation in EC programs, such as ERASMUS, and other informal staff and student exchanges and collaborative research projects;
- Acting as a lobby and pressure group in members' interests in relation to the European Commission and other international organizations such as Unesco;
- Collecting information on the member institutions (e.g., courses, staff, research) to help identify partners for collaboration and produce directories of this information; and
- Disseminating this information by electronic and other means and producing a newsletter.

As the general trend in Europe is toward working more closely together, EUCLID will fill a gap in the LIS field by facilitating collaborative research projects and an increased exchange of views and personnel. The benefits, as Wilson describes, are considerable. An increase in the number of exchanges of students and staff will produce a broadened perspective and international awareness of LIS, which could be a vital stimulus to curriculum design and development. Participating SLIS will attract a wider range of students due to their heightened international image. It is hoped that EUCLID will play a major role in the development of more links with European institutions involved in the rapidly changing world of library and information science and information management.

The Pluralistic Society

We live in a pluralistic society, in which members of various minority groups seek to maintain their independent cultural or social traditions while integrating with society as a whole. The implications for information professionals are fundamental, yet little attention is paid to the different needs of minority groups by SLIS. As Sever eloquently writes, we accept that different types of libraries restrict access and provide a differential service to special groups (e.g., academic, industrial, government libraries): "Are educators of library science as prepared to endorse the idea of differential service to social groups existing within a pluralistic society?" (SEVER, p. 66–67). Sever argues that educators need to determine the needs for information among different groups of users and to integrate this knowledge into curricula. He contends that differences in educational, economic, religious, language, ethnic, and cultural backgrounds may require the development of special library services. This is a different angle on the argument for a more user-centered approach to LIS education and training as advocated by DAY (1989), BURTON (1990), and others, and which has tended to be neglected in many LIS curricula.

CONCLUSION

This chapter has described how the traditional librarianship curriculum (in the form of diploma studies) has evolved into a graduate profession in information, of which librarianship is one part. As recent thinking on information provision and management and IT has developed, so have the teaching and research developments, which are established to educate and train students for the information professions.

The past decade has been one of fundamental change, both in institutional structures and in the organization of courses, curricula, and student recruitment. The impact of the emerging markets has meant an injection of new concepts and new methods into the traditional subject areas of librarianship. The influx of new staff and students with innovative ideas and different skills, often not from traditional library backgrounds, has led to a rejuvenation of the old-style library schools.

The results of these changes are the more remarkable since the whole process has been conducted in a largely creative, proactive spirit and despite wholesale cuts in higher education in the late 1980s; this situation has now been reversed as many U.K. universities expanded by about 25% between 1990 and 1993. SLIS are now well established in universities; they are increasingly research based; and although postgraduate courses continue to flourish, their future is less certain than undergraduate courses that continue to expand and attract students with increasing breadth of backgrounds and aspirations.

BIBLIOGRAPHY

ANGELL, CAROLYN. 1987. Information, New Technology and Manpower: The Impact of New Technology on Demand for Information Specialists. London, England: British Library Board; 1987. 105p. (Library and Information Research Report 52). ISSN: 0263-1709; ISBN: 0-7123-3083-6.

AULD, L.W.S. 1990. Seven Imperatives for Library Education. Library Journal. 1990; 115(8): 55-59. ISSN: 0363-0277.

BEARMAN, TONI CARBO, ed. 1987. Educating the Future Information Professional. Library Hi Tech. 1987 (Issue 18); 5(2): 27-40. ISSN: 0737-8831.

BEDNAR, M. 1988. Automation of Cataloging: Effects on Use of Staff, Efficiency and Service to Patrons. Journal of Academic Librarianship. 1988; 14(3): 145-149. ISSN: 0099-1333.

BIGGS, MARY. 1991. A Perspective on Library Science Doctoral Programs. Journal of Education for Library and Information Science. 1991; 32(3/4): 188-193. ISSN: 0748-5786.

BIGGS, MARY; BOOKSTEIN, ABRAHAM. 1988. What Constitutes a High-Quality M.L.S. Program? Forty-Five Faculty Members' Views. Journal of Education for Library and Information Science. 1988 Summer; 29(1): 28-46. ISSN: 0748-5786.

BLACKIE, EDNA. 1985. Statistics for Librarians: A Distance Learning Package: A Summary. London, England: Further Education Unit; 1985. 14p. ERIC: ED 278395.

BLACKIE, EDNA. 1988. On Designing an Honours Degree in Information and Library Studies. Training and Education (England). 1988; 5(3): 57-63. ISSN: 0264-8466.

BOYCE, BERT R.; HEIM, KATHLEEN M. 1988. The Education of Library Systems Analysts for the Nineties. Journal of Library Administration. 1988; 9(4): 69-76. ISSN: 0193-0826.

BRADLEY, SUSAN J.; WILLETT, PETER; WOOD, FRANCES E. 1992. A Publication and Citation Analysis of the Department of Information Studies, University of Sheffield, 1980-1990. Journal of Information Science. 1992; 18: 225-232. ISSN: 0165-5515.

BRITTAIN, J. MICHAEL, ed. 1989. Curriculum Development in Information Science to Meet the Needs of the Information Industries in the 1990s. London, England: British Library Board; 1989. 220p. (Library and Information Research Report 70). ISSN: 0263-1709; ISBN: 0-7123-3170-0.

BRITTAIN, J. MICHAEL. 1992. The Emerging Market for Information Professionals in the U.K. National Health Service. International Journal of Information Management. 1992; 12(4): 261-271. ISSN: 0268-4012.

BRITTAIN, J. MICHAEL; MACDOUGALL, J.   1993.   New Opportunities for National Health Service Librarians and Information Scientists.   Health Libraries Review (England). 1993; 10. (In press). ISSN: 0265-6647.

BROADBENT, MARIANNE. 1990. Information Management Education: Alliances and Alignments. Education for Information. 1990; 8(1): 3-13. ISSN: 0167-8329.

BURTON, PAUL F.   1990.   Accuracy of Information Provision: The Need for Client-centred Service.   Journal of Librarianship.   1990; 22(4): 201-215. ISSN: 0022-2232.

BURTON, PAUL F. 1992. Customer Care in Information Services: A Conflict of Perceptions? In: Trott, Fiona, ed. Customer Care in Information Services: Proceedings of a Seminar; 1991 November 6; Ipswich, England. Ipswich, England: Library Association Information Services Group, East Anglian Section; 1992. Available from: Library Association, 7 Ridgmount St., London WCIE 7AE England.

BUSCHMAN, JOHN; CARBONE, MICHAEL.   1990.   A Critical Inquiry into Librarianship: Applications of the "New Sociology of Education". Library Quarterly. 1990; 61(1): 15-40. ISSN: 0024-2519.

CLUFF, E. DALE, ed.   1990.   Library Education and Employer Expectations. Binghamton, NY: Haworth; 1990. 246p. ISBN: 0-86656-896-4.

COLLIER, M.W.   1989.   The Role of Information Technology in the Management of Academic Libraries and Information Services.   In: Brittain, J. Michael, ed. Curriculum Development in Information Science to Meet the Needs of the Information Industries in the 1990s. London, England: British Library Board; 1989. 4-15. ISSN: 0263-1709; ISBN: 0-7123-3170-0.

CORBIN, JOHN.   1988.   The Education of Librarians in an Age of Information Technology. Journal of Library Administration. 1988; 9(4): 77-87.   ISSN: 0193-0826.

CORNES, PHIL. 1991. Computer Based Training: At What Cost?   The Computer Bulletin. 1991 May; 3(4): 8-10. ISSN: 0010-4531.

CORREIA, ANA MARIA RAMALHO; WILSON, TOM D. 1992. The MSc in Information Management of the University of Sheffield Taught in Portugal: An Example of Knowledge Transfer in Education. Journal of Information Science. 1992; 18: 77-82. ISSN: 0165-5515.

CRONIN, BLAISE.   1991.   Library Orthodoxies: A Decade of Change. London, England: Taylor Graham; 1991. 248p. ISBN: 0-947568-46-8.

DAVENPORT, LIZZIE; CRONIN, BLAISE.   1988.   Demand and Supply in Information Work. Education for Information. 1988; 6(1): 61-70.   ISSN: 0167-8329.

DAVIES, J. ERIC. 1987/88. The Importance of Spreading the Word: The Data Protection Act and Staff Training.   Training and Education (England). 1987/88; 5(1): 3-22. ISSN: 0264-8466.

DAVIES, J. ERIC. 1990a.   Information Scientists and 1992: A Personal View from a British Perspective. Journal of Information Science. 1990; 16: 327-335. ISSN: 0165-5515.

DAVIES, J. ERIC. 1990b.   Professional Development and the Institute of Information Scientists. Journal of Information Science. 1990; 16: 369-379. ISSN: 0165-5515.

DAVINSON, D.E.; ROBERTS, N. 1985. Curricula in Schools of Librarianship and Information Studies: An Investigation of Constraints and Possibilities. Journal of Documentation. 1985; 41(3): 156-164. ISSN: 0022-0418.

DAY, JOAN M. 1988. CD-ROM: An Online Training Tool? Education for Information. 1988; 6(4): 403-410. ISSN: 0167-8329.

DAY, JOAN M. 1989. Are They Switched On? IT and the Education of Librarians. Education Libraries Journal. 1989 Autumn; 32(3): 25-34. ISSN: 0957-9575.

DAY, JOAN M.; O'DONOVAN, K. 1988. Online Education and Marketing: A Joint Approach. Education for Information. 1988 September; 6(3): 315-322. ISSN: 0167-8329.

DYER, HILARY. 1988. Teaching Library Automation. Aslib Information (England). 1988; 16(9): 230. ISSN: 0305-0033.

EDWARDS, R.J.; ROBERTS, D.; HYWEL, E.; TUNLEY, M.F. 1990. Aberystwyth: At a Distance. Education for Information. 1990; 8(4): 341-348. ISSN: 0167-8329.

ELKIN, JUDITH. 1992. Information UK 2000: Response on Behalf of the Education Committee of the Library Association. Personnel Training and Education (England). 1992; 9(1): 18-24. ISSN: 0264-8466.

FORGIONNE, GUISSEPPI A. 1991a. The College of Information Science: A Mechanism to Consolidate Information Science Education. Education for Information. 1991; 9: 285-304. ISSN: 0167-8329.

FORGIONNE, GUISSEPPI A. 1991b. Providing Complete and Integrated Information Science Education. Information Processing and Management. 1991; 27(5): 575-590. ISSN: 0306-4573.

GARLAND, KATHLEEN. 1990. Gender Differences in Scholarly Publication among Faculty in ALA Accredited Library Schools. Library and Information Science Research. 1990; 12: 155-166. ISSN: 0740-8188.

GARLAND, KATHLEEN. 1991a. The Nature of Publications Authored by Library and Information Science Faculty. Library and Information Science Research. 1991; 13: 49-60. ISSN: 0740-8188.

GARLAND, KATHLEEN. 1991b. The Relationship of Faculty Size to Scholarly Productivity and Quality Ranking: Implications for Education for Librarianship. Journal of Education for Library and Information Science. 1991 Fall/Winter; 32(3/4): 250-253. ISSN: 0748-5786.

HALL, TRACEY. 1991. Hybrid Courses in Action. The Computer Bulletin. 1991 May; 3(4): 14. ISSN: 0010-4531.

HAVARD-WILLIAMS, PETER. 1987. Looking towards the Future: An Overview. Education for Information. 1987; 5(2): 91-104. ISSN: 0167-8329.

HAYTHORNTHWAITE, J.A. 1990. Distance Education and the Information Scientist. Aslib Proceedings. 1990; 42(1): 31-39. ISSN: 0001-253X.

HAYTHORNTHWAITE, J.A.; WHITE, FRANCIS C.P. 1989. Distance Education in Library and Information Studies: A Survey. London, England: British Library Board; 1989. 119p. (British Library Research Paper 50). ISBN: 0-7123-3176-X.

HAYTHORNTHWAITE, J.A.; WHITE, FRANCIS C.P. 1991. The Role of Distance Education in Library and Information Studies Education. Education for Information. 1991; 9: 305-316. ISSN: 0167-8329.

HEALY, JAMES S. 1988. The Electronic Library School: An Alternative Approach in Library Education. Technical Services Quarterly. 1988; 6(2): 17-26. ISSN: 0731-7131.

HEPWORTH, JOHN B. 1988. Database Teaching in the Information Storage and Retrieval Syllabus. Education for Information. 1988; 6(7): 3-25. ISSN: 0167-8329.

HEPWORTH, JOHN B. 1991. Through the Training Maze. Health Service Journal (England). 1991 December 12; 101: 33-34. ISSN: 0952-2271.

HYMAN, RICHARD. 1991. Library Schools in Crisis: Stemming the Tide. Wilson Library Bulletin. 1991; 65(5): 46-49. ISSN: 0043-5651.

JOHNSON, IAN. 1990. Schools of Librarianship and Continuing Education in Britain. Journal of Education for Library and Information Science. 1990 Winter; 30(3): 232-237. ISSN: 0748-5786.

JOHNSON, IAN. 1992. Library Education Update. Focus on International and Comparative Librarianship (England). 1992; 23(1): 10-12. ISSN: 0305-8468.

KIRKHAM, SANDI. 1991. Customizing Graduate Education for Information Management. Journal of Education for Library and Information Science. 1991; 32(1/2): 8-12. ISSN: 0748-5786.

KOCHTANEK, THOMAS R. 1987. Procedural Logic versus Object-Oriented Logic in Library Automation Instruction. Journal of Education for Library and Information Science. 1987 Summer; 28(1): 55-57. ISSN: 0748-5786.

KOENIG, MICHAEL E.D. 1991. The Transfer of Library Skills to Non-Library Contexts. Advances in Librarianship. 1991; 15: 1-27. ISSN: 0065-2830.

LANSDALE, MARK. 1989. On the Psychology of Personal Information Management. In: Brittain, J. Michael, ed. Curriculum Development in Information Science to Meet the Needs of the Information Industries in the 1990s. London, England: British Library Board; 1989. 82-112. ISSN: 0263-1709; ISBN: 0-7123-3170-0.

LARGE, ANDREW. 1991. Curriculum Development: Some Reflections on UNESCO's Role. Journal of Education for Library and Information Science. 1991; 32(1/2): 77-83. ISSN: 0748-5786.

LESTER, J. 1990. Education for Librarianship: A Report Card. American Libraries. 1990; 21(6): 580-586. ISSN: 0002-9769.

LIBRARY AND INFORMATION SERVICES COUNCIL. 1986. Professional Education and Training for Library and Information Work. London, England: Library Association; 1986. 177p. ISBN: 0-85365-707-6.

MACDOUGALL, J.; BRITTAIN, J. MICHAEL. 1992. The Use of Information in the National Health Service. London, England: British Library Board; 1992. 63p. ISBN: 0-7123-3275-8.

MALLEY, IAN. 1992. Cash Is the Key for Management Training. Library Association Record. 1992; 94(12): 792-793. ISSN: 0024-2195.

MARTIN, WILLIAM J. 1987. From Library Studies to Information Science. Education for Information. 1987; 5: 123-131. ISSN: 0167-8329.

MARTIN, WILLIAM J. 1991. Education for Information Management: Restructuring and Reform. Education for Information. 1991; 9: 21-28. ISSN: 0167-8329.

MARTYN, JOHN; VICKERS, PETER; FEENEY, MARY, eds. 1990. Information UK 2000. London, England: Bowker-Saur; 1990. 293p. ISBN: 0-86291-620-8.

MCCROSSAN, JOHN A. 1989. Schools of Library and Information Science in the United States and the United Kingdom: A Comparison. Journal of Educational Media and Library Sciences. 1989; 26(4): 316-324. ISSN: 1013-090X.

MCGARRY, KEVIN J. 1987a. Curriculum Theory and Library and Information Science. Education for Information. 1987; 5: 139-156. ISSN: 0167-8329.

MCGARRY, KEVIN J. 1987b. Editorial. Education for Information. 1987; 5(2): 87-90. ISSN: 0167-8329.

MCKEE, BOB. 1988. Information Management and Library/Information Studies: Diffusion, Confusion? Training and Education (England). 1988; 5(2): 31-38. ISSN: 0264-8466.

MCLAIN, JOHN P.; WALLACE, DANNY P.; HEIM, KATHLEEN M. 1990. Educating for Automation: Can the Library Schools Do the Job? In: Leinbach, P.E., ed. Personnel Administration in an Automated Environment. Binghamton, NY: Haworth; 1990. 7-20. ISBN: 1-56024-032-6.

MEADOWS, A.J. 1987. Course Angling. Aslib Information (England). 1987; 15: 207. ISSN: 0305-0033.

MILLER, WILLIAM. 1989. Developing Managerial Competence for Library Automation. Library Hi Tech. 1989; 7(2): 103-112. ISSN: 0737-8831.

MOORE, NICK. 1987. The Emerging Markets for Librarians and Information Workers. London, England: British Library Board; 1987. 158p. (Library and Information Research Report 56). ISSN: 0263-1709; ISBN: 0-7123-3090-9.

MOORE, NICK. 1989. Developing the Use of a Neglected Resource: The Growth of Information Management. Journal of Information Science. 1989; 15: 67-70. ISSN: 0165-5515.

MOORE, NICK. 1990. Library and Information Education in Britain: The Scope and European Cooperation. Libri. 1990; 40(2): 153-157. ISSN: 0024-2667.

MORAN, BARBARA B. 1991. Evaluation of Faculty in Schools of Library and Information Science: An Element in Educational Excellence. Journal of Education for Library and Information Science. 1991; 32(3/4): 207-215. ISSN: 0748-5786.

MORRIS, ANNE. 1989. Expert Systems and Their Implications for Information Science. In: Brittain, J. Michael, ed. Curriculum Development in Information Science to Meet the Needs of the Information Industries in the 1990s. London, England: British Library Board; 1989. 125-152. ISSN: 0263-1709; ISBN: 0-7123-3170-0.

MORRIS, ANNE. 1993. The Teaching of IT in Departments of Information and Library Studies in the UK. Journal of information Science. 1993; 19: 211-224. ISSN: 0165-5515.

MORRIS, BERYL. 1992. Predicting the Skills of Tomorrow. Library Association Record (England). 1992; 94(10): 662-663. ISSN: 0023-2195.

MUDDIMAN, D.; MURPHY, M.; ROBINSON, L. 1990. Information Studies: Developing the Pluralist Curriculum. Personnel Training and Education (England). 1990; 7(3): 43-53. ISSN: 0264-8466.

NANKIVELL, CLARE. 1991. The Class of '88: National Cohort Study of Librarians and Information Workers: Interim Report. Birmingham, England: Birmingham Polytechnic, Faculty of Computing and Information

Studies; 1991 May. Available from: The Faculty of Computing and Information Studies, University of Central England in Birmingham, Perry Barr, Birmingham B42 2SU, England.

PARIS, MARION. 1990. Why Library Schools Fail. Library Journal. 1990 October 1; 115(16): 38-42. ISSN: 0363-0277.

ROBERTS, D.; HYWEL, E. 1989. The University College of Wales Department of Information and Library Studies. Focus on International and Comparative Librarianship (England). 1989; 20(2): 22-24. ISSN: 0305-8468.

ROBERTS, N.; WILSON, TOM D.; ELLIS, DAVID. 1988. Business Information Courses: A Consideration of Requirements. Education for Information. 1988; 6(1): 27-37. ISSN: 0167-8329.

ROBERTS, STEPHEN A. 1987. Education and Training in the Information Fields: The Curriculum and Research. Education for Information. 1987; 5(2/3): 157-168. ISSN: 0167-8329.

ROBERTSON, S.E.; YATES-MERCER, P.A. 1988. Information Technology, Systems and Management: Education and Training. International Journal of Information Management. 1988; 8(1): 55-60. ISSN: 0268-4012.

ROWLAND, FYTTON; TSENG, GWYNETH M. 1991. Computer Methods in the Teaching of Library and Information Studies. Education for Information. 1991; 9: 47-54. ISSN: 0167-8329.

ROWLEY, J.E. 1987. Teaching Information Systems Analysis and Design. Library Association Record (England). 1987; 89(10): 528-529. ISSN: 0024-2195.

ROWLEY, J.E.; FARROW, J.F.; OULTON, A.J.; WOOD, A.J. 1988. The Use of INFO, a Database Management System, in Teaching Library and Information Studies at Manchester Polytechnic. Education for Information. 1988; 6(1): 71-82. ISSN: 0167-8329.

ROWLEY, J.E.; KAYE, D.; FARROW, J.F.; WHITTAKER, K.A. 1990. Education for Library and Information Studies at Manchester Polytechnic 1979-1990. Library Review. 1990; 39(6): 10-15. ISSN: 0041-9788.

SAUNDERS, W.L. 1989. The University of Sheffield Department of Information Studies, 1964-89. Journal of Information Science. 1989; 15: 193-202. ISSN: 0165-5515.

SCHWARTZ, C. 1990. Teaching Database Management. Database. 1990; 13(1): 91-93. ISSN: 0162-4105.

SEVER, SHMUEL. 1992. Library Education in a Pluralistic Society. Journal of Education for Library and Information Science. 1992; 33(1): 66-71. ISSN: 0748-5786.

SLACK, FRANCES; LETT, BRENDA. 1992. Developing Skills to Supervise Research. Library Association Record (England). 1992; 94(10): 659. ISSN: 0024-2195.

SLATER, MARGARET. 1984. Alternative Careers for Library-Information Workers. Aslib Proceedings (England). 1984; 36(6): 277-286. ISSN: 0001-253X.

STEPHEN, PETER. 1987. More Information Technology at Manchester Polytechnic Library School. Information and Library Manager. 1987; 7(3): 76-77. ISSN: 0260-6879.

THURSTON, ANNE. 1990. Archival Training in Europe: Dilemmas. Education for Information. 1990; 8(2): 149-150. ISSN: 0167-8329.

TRANSBINARY GROUP. 1986. Education for Librarianship and Information Science: Report of the Transbinary Group on Librarianship and Information Studies. 1986 June. Available from: British Library Research and Development Department, 2 Sheraton Street, London, England W1V 4BH.

TURBET, RICHARD. 1992. Information Fascism Militates against Music Specialism. Library Association Record (England). 1992; 94(6): 376. (Letter). ISSN: 0024-2195.

WATSON, MARGARET. 1990. Communication across the Curriculum. Personnel Training and Education (England). 1990; 7(2): 37-40. ISSN: 0264-8466.

WEDGEWORTH, ROBERT. 1991. Some Thoughts on the Perils of Library Education: Real and Perceived. Wilson Library Bulletin. 1991; 65(5): 46-48. ISSN: 0043-5651.

WEINGAND, DARLENE E. 1988. Continuing Education in Information Technology. INSPEL (Germany). 1988; 22(3): 226-229. ISSN: 0019-0217.

WHITBECK, GEORGE W. 1990. Recent Developments in Library and Information Science Education in the United Kingdom. Journal of Education for Library and Information Science. 1990; 30(3): 238-241. ISSN: 0748-5786.

WHITBECK, GEORGE W. 1991. Doctoral Programs in Library and Information Science. Journal of Education for Library and Information Science. 1991; 32(3/4): 178-187. ISSN: 0748-5786.

WILSON, TOM D. 1989. Towards an Information Management Curriculum. Journal of Information Science. 1989; 15: 203-209. ISSN: 0165-5515.

WILSON, TOM D. 1992. Enter EUCLID: A New Forum for Library and Information Studies Educators. British Book News. 1992 August; 526-527. ISSN: 0007-0343.

WOOD, FRANCES E.; ELLIS, DAVID. 1988. Employment Patterns and Curriculum Development. Information and Library Manager. 1988; 7(5): 120-127. ISSN: 0260-6879.

WOOD, KATE; ELKIN, JUDITH. 1993. They Are the Very Module. . . Library Association Record (England). 1993; 95(1): 29. ISSN: 0024-2195.

Introduction to the Index

Index entries have been made for names of individuals, corporate bodies, subjects, geographic locations, and author names included in the text pages and for author and conference names from the bibliography pages. The page numbers referring to the bibliography pages are set in italics, and are listed after the page numbers relating to the text pages. This format allows one to distinguish references to bibliographic materials from references to text.

Acronyms are listed either under the acronym or under the fully spelled-out form, depending on which form is more commonly used and known. In either case a cross reference from the alternate form is provided. Postings associated with PRECIS, for example, would be listed under PRECIS as readers are generally less familiar with the full name "Preserved Context Index System." In a few cases, such as names of programs, systems, and programming languages, there is no spelled-out form either because there is none or because the meaning has been changed or is no longer used.

The index is arranged on a word-by-word basis. The sort sequence places special characters first, followed by alpha characters, then numbers. Thus, O'Neill would precede Oakman and 3M Company would file after the "Z"s. Government organizations are generally listed under country name, with *see* references provided from names of departments, agencies, and other subdivisions. While index entries do correspond precisely in spelling and format, they do not follow the typographical conventions used in the text. Author names, which are all upper case in the text, and both programming languages and software packages (such as expert system shells), which are in small caps in the text, are in upper and lower case or normal upper case in the index.

Subject indexing is by concepts rather than by words. When authors have used different words or different forms of the same word to express the same or overlapping concepts, the terminology has been standardized. An effort was made to use the form of index entries for concepts that had previously appeared in *ARIST* indexes and in the May 1993 draft *ASIS Thesaurus of Information Science*. Cross references have been used freely to provide access to subject concepts. *See also* references are used for overlapping or related (but not synonymous) concepts; *see* references are used to send the reader to the accepted form of a term used in the index.

The index was prepared by Debora Shaw, using the MACREX Plus Indexing Program, version 5.10 developed by Hilary and Drusilla Calvert and distributed in the U.S. by Bayside Indexing. The overall direction and coordination of the index were provided by Martha E. Williams. Comments and suggestions should be addressed to the Editor.

Index*

---

*Italicized page numbers refer to bibliography pages.

ASIS (American Society for Information Science)
Annual Meeting
1979, *268*
1982, *178*
1986, 42
1989, *95*, 270
1990, 265
1991, *264, 266, 268, 269, 272, 306, 312*
1992, *41, 43, 225, 306*
electronic government information, 58
ASK (anomalous states of knowledge), 122, 124, 286
browsing, 233, 236, 255-256, 262
ASM (Acquisition of speech by machines), *see* Speech recognition
Assessment, browsing, 253
Association for Consumer Research, Annual Conference, 1982, *265*
Association for Education in Journalism, Annual Meeting, 1973, *143*
Association for Education in Journalism and Mass Communication, Annual Meeting, 1988, *145*
Association for Information Management, London, 9
Association of American Publishers (AAP), 64
Association of College and Research Libraries (ACRL), National Conference, 1984, *350*
Association of Research Libraries (ARL), 74, 337, 344, *95*
Associativity, browsing, 257
AT&T
competitor intelligence, 24
computer speech recognition, 168
Atherton, Pauline, 124, 128, 210, 239, *140, 224, 272*
Attitudes, information users, 288
Attorneys, government information policy, 76
Atwood, Rita, *138*
Audio interfaces, virtual reality, 197
Audio-visual Experience Automatic Virtual Environment, *see* CAVE

Auditors, government information policy, 76
Auld, Lawrence W.S., *384*
Auster, Ethel, 246, 294, 298, 301, *264, 267, 306*
Australasian students, library and information science education, U.K., 376
Australia, telephones, 17
Authors, gatekeepers, 114
Automation, libraries, *see* Library automation
Automobiles, simulation, 191
Autonomy, library employees, 329
Aviation, computer speech recognition, 167-168
Aviation Week & Space Technology, 193, *219*
AWACS (Airborne Warning and Control Systems), computer speech recognition, 168
Axelrod, Morris, 125, *138*
Ayris, Paul, 232, 233, 235, 236, 238, 242, *264*

Babchuk, Nicholas, *150*
Babcock, Wally, 45
Baber, C., 163, *176*
Bailey, Charles W., Jr., 212, 256, *219, 264*
Bailey, Martha J., 347, *347*
Bailly, G., 157, 162, *176*
Baird, Lloyd, 319, *347*
Baird, Patricia M., 19, *28, 32*
Baker, Betsy, 330, *347*
Baker, Janet M., 166, *176*
Baker, Sharon L., 235, *264*
Balajthy, Ernest, 165, *176*
Balakrishnan, Bhaskaran, 232, 239, 242, *273*
Balch, Philip, *148*
Ball State University, online catalog interface, 171
Ballard, Steve, 82, *95*
Banister, Michael, *141*
Bank of America, 22
Bankapur, M.B., 234, 235, *264*

Europe, library and information
science education, 381-382
European Association of Information
Services, *see* EUSIDIC
European Community
library and information science
education, 381-382
U.K., 376
European Community Action
Scheme for the Mobility of
University Students, *see*
ERASMUS
European Conference of Library and
Information Science Deans,
Directors, and Deputies, *see*
EUCLID
European Conference on Speech
Communication and Technology,
1989, *176*
European Speech Communication
Association, 157
Eurospeech, *see* European Confer-
ence on Speech Communication
and Technology
EUSIDIC (European Association of
Information Services), 24
Euster, Joanne R., 336, 340, 341, 342,
349, *350*
Evans, G. Edward, 320, *350*
Exit interviews, library employees,
328
Exosomatic memory, 214
Expansion, browsing, 236
Experience, information users, 288
Expert systems
information professionals, 366
library and information science
education, 370, 378
Exports, information needs, 291
Extrapolation, environmental
scanning, 299
Eye movements
browsing, 245
computer input, 196
EyePhone head-mounted display,
193, 203

Facsimile transmission
gatekeepers, 132
government documents, 51

Fagan, Lawrence M., *184*
Fahey, Liam, 295, 300, *308*
Fairchild, Kim M., 211, *222*
Fallside, Frank, 161, *178*
Familiarization, browsing, 237
Family Educational Rights and
Privacy Act, 60
Fann, Gail L., *313*
Farid, Mona, *141*
Farkas, George, 114, *142*
Farm equipment industry, environ-
mental scanning, 293-294
Farmers
gatekeepers, 128
opinion leaders, 115
Farrow, J.F., *389*
Fax, *see* Facsimile transmission
Federal Advisory Committee Act, 60
Federal Computer Week, 48
Federal High Performance Comput-
ing Program, 17
Federal Information Exchange, Inc.,
87, 97
Federal Information Locator System
(FILS), 75
Federal information policy, *see*
Information policy
Federal Information Processing
Standards (FIPS), 70-72
Federal Maritime Commission, 78
Federal Records Act, 68
Federal Register, 27, 55, 56, 65, 33
FEDIX, *see* Federal Information
Exchange, Inc.
FEDLINE online information product
catalog, 54
FedWorld bulletin board, 55
Feedback
browsing, 241, 242, 252-253, 259
computer speech processing, 162,
163
human-computer interaction, 196
information retrieval, 210, 239
telerobotics, 205
virtual reality, 201, 217
Feeney, Mary, *387*
Feminists, gatekeepers, 114
Ferketish, B. Jean, 319, *350*
Ferriero, David S., 337, *350*
Fetzer, Mary, 50, *101*

Introduction to the Keyword and Author Index

The following section is an author and keyword index to *ARIST* chapters for Volumes 1 through 28. It has been produced to assist users in locating specific topics, chapters, and author names for all *ARIST* volumes to date. The index terms are sorted alphabetically and include all author names and content words from titles (a stop-word list of articles, conjunctions, and other non-content words was used). Multiple forms of the same word have been combined. The sort word is followed by the author(s) name(s) and the *ARIST* citation.

Keyword and Author Index
of *ARIST* Titles
for Volumes 1-28

Abstracting
    Keenan, Stella, **4**, p273
Access
    Fox, Edward A. **23**, p85; Hildreth, Charles R. **20**, p233; Lynch, Clifford and Preston, Cecilia **25**, p263
Acquisition
    Choo, Chun Wei and Auster, Ethel. **28,** p279
Activities
    Adams, Scott and Werdel, Judith A. **10**, p303
Adams, Peter D.
    Lerner, Rita G., Metaxas, Ted, Scott, John T., Adams, Peter D., and Judd, Peggy. Primary Publication Systems and Scientific Text Processing. **18**, p127
Adams, Scott
    Adams, Scott and Werdel, Judith A. Cooperation in Information Activities through International Organizations. **10**, p303
ADI
    Cuadra, Carlos A. **1**, p1
Adkinson, Burton W.
    Berninger, Douglas E. and Adkinson, Burton W. Interaction between the Public and Private Sectors in National Information Programs. **13**, p3
Agricultural
    Frank, Robyn C. **22,** p293
Aids
    Caruso, Elaine, **16**, p317
Aines, Andrew A.
    Aines, Andrew A. and Day, Melvin S. National Planning of Information Services. **10**, p3
Allen, Bryce L.
    Allen Bryce L. Cognitive Research in Information Science: Implications for Design. **26**, p3
    Kinnucan, Mark T., Nelson, Michael J., and Allen, Bryce J. Statistical Methods in Information Science Research. **22**, p147
Allen, Thomas J.
    Allen, Thomas J. Information Needs and Uses. **4**, p3
Alper, Bruce H.
    Alper, Bruce H. Library Automation. **10**, p199

About the Editor . . .

Professor Martha E. Williams assumed the Editorship of the *ANNUAL REVIEW OF INFORMATION SCIENCE AND TECHNOLOGY* with Volume 11 and has produced a series of books that provide unparalleled insights into, and overviews of, the multifaceted discipline of information science.

Professor Williams holds the positions of Director of the Information Retrieval Research Laboratory and Professor of Information Science in the Coordinated Science Laboratory (CSL) as well as Professor of Information Science in the Graduate School of Library and Information Science and affiliate of the Computer Science Department at the University of Illinois, Urbana-Champaign, Illinois. As a chemist and information scientist Professor Williams has brought to the Editorship a breadth of knowledge and experience in information science and technology.

She has served as a Director and Chairman of the Board of Engineering Information, Inc.; she is founding editor of *Computer-Readable Databases: A Directory and Data Sourcebook;* Editor of *Online & CDROM Review* (Learned Information, Ltd., Oxford, England); and Program Chairman for the National Online Meetings, which are sponsored by *Online & CDROM Review.* She was appointed by the Secretary of Health, Education and Welfare, Joseph Califano, to be a member of the Board of Regents of the National Library of Medicine (NLM) in 1978 and has served as Chairman of the Board. She has been a member of the Numerical Data Advisory Board of the National Research Council (NRC), National Academy of Sciences (NAS). She was a member of the Science Information Activities task force of the National Science Foundation (NSF), was chairman of the Large Database subcommittee of the NAS/NRC Committee on Chemical Information, and was chairman of the Gordon Research Conference on Scientific Information Problems in Research in 1980.

Professor Williams is a Fellow of the American Association for the Advancement of Science, Honorary Fellow of the Institute of Information Scientists in England, and recipient of the 1984 Award of Merit of the American Society for Information Science. She is a member of, has held offices in, and/or is actively involved in various committees of the American Association for the Advancement of Science (AAAS), the American Chemical Society (ACS), the Association for Computing Machinery (ACM), and the American Society for Information Science (ASIS). She has published numerous books and papers and serves on the editorial boards of several journals. She is the founder and President of Information Market Indicators, Inc., and consults for many governmental and commercial organizations.

ASIS and Its Members

For over 50 years the leading professional society for information professionals, the American Society for Information Science is an association whose diverse membership continues to reflect the frontiers and horizons of the dynamic field of information science and technology. ASIS owes its stature to the cumulative contributions of its members, past and present.

ASIS counts among its membership some 4,000 information specialists from such fields as computer science, management, engineering, librarianship, chemistry, linguistics, and education. As was true when the Society was founded, ASIS membership continues to lead the information profession in the search for new and better theories, techniques, and technologies to improve access to information through storage and retrieval advances. And now, as then, ASIS and its members are called upon to help determine new directions and standards for the development of information policies and practices.

Individual Membership Application

New Member
Renewal

asis *AMERICAN SOCIETY FOR INFORMATION SCIENCE*

Please print or type in black ink.

Name (Last, First, Middle)————————— Day Phone ( )——————————Ext.——

Title ———

Organization —————————————————————————————————————

Mailing Address ————————————————————————————————————

City —————————————State ——————— Zipcode——————— Plus 4: —————

Province (Outside U.S.) ————————— Country ——————— Mail Code ——————————

   Check One—The Above Address is My ☐Work ☐Home

Please select category of membership:

☐ Regular $95 $————————————

☐ Student $25 $————————————

   I am a full-time student at ————————————

   Faculty advisor's signature————————————

Special Interest Group (SIG) Dues

☐ Check here if one free SIG selected.

Additional SIGs ————— x $6 each $ ————

Total Membership and SIG Dues $————

Contribution to ASIS Scholarship Fund $————

Contribution to ASIS Development Fund $————

Total Payment Enclosed $————(US)

Chapter Membership: You will automatically become a member of the chapter serving your geographic area (if one exists). Information about your chapter and additional chapters you may want to join will be sent to you upon receipt of your membership application.

Check or money order enclosed (Payable to ASIS)
or charge my   ☐ VISA   ☐ Mastercard

Account #————————————————————

Expiration Date————————————————

Signature————————————————

Because your ASIS membership is individual rather than organizational, your membership goes with you if you make a career move. All membership fees and contributions are tax-deductible to the full extent of the law in the United States. You will receive notification of your active membership when your application form is processed. Please allow 4-6 weeks for delivery. For new members, membership is for one year from the month in which dues are received. Membership fees are non-refundable.

Of the annual membership dues, $11 is payment for the *Bulletin*, $19 is payment for the *Journal*.

All ASIS members may select one SIG at no charge. You may join additional SIGs at $6 each. Please note *all* selections here. Enclose payment of $6 for the second and succeeding selections.

☐ **Arts and Humanities** (AH)
☐ **Automated Language Processing** (ALP)
☐ **Biological and Chemical Information Systems**(BC)
☐ **Behavioral and Social Sciences** (BSS)
☐ **Classification Research** (CR)
☐ **Computerized Retrieval Services** (CRS)
☐ **Education for Information Science** (ED)
☐ **Foundations of Information Science** (FIS)
☐ **Human-Computer Interaction** (HCI)
☐ **Information Analysis and Evaluation** (IAE)
☐ **International Information Issues** (III)
☐ **Library Automation and Networks** (LAN)
☐ **Management** (MGT)
☐ **Medical Information Systems** (MED)
☐ **Numeric Data Bases** (NDB)
☐ **Office Information Systems** (OIS)
☐ **Personal Computers** (PC)
☐ **Information Generation and Publishing** (PUB)
☐ **Storage and Retrieval Technology** (SRT)
☐ **Technology, Information and Society** (TIS)

Please mail this form with your payment to
American Society for Information Science
Ben Franklin Station
P.O. Box 554
Washington, DC 20044-0554

All other correspondence to ASIS Headquarters.

8720 Georgia Avenue, Suite 501, Silver Spring, MD 20910
Tel.: 301-495-0900 FAX 301-495-0810